STALIN'S AMERICAN SPY

TONY SHARP

Stalin's American Spy

*Noel Field, Allen Dulles and the
East European Show Trials*

HURST & COMPANY, LONDON

First published in the United Kingdom in 2014 by
C. Hurst & Co. (Publishers) Ltd.,
41 Great Russell Street, London, WC1B 3PL
© Tony Sharp, 2014
All rights reserved.
Printed in the USA

Distributed in the United States, Canada and Latin America by
Oxford University Press, 198 Madison Avenue, New York, NY 10016,
United States of America

The right of Tony Sharp to be identified as the author of
this publication is asserted by him in accordance with the
Copyright, Designs and Patents Act, 1988.

A Cataloguing-in-Publication data record for this book
is available from the British Library.

ISBN: 978-1-84904-344-1

www.hurstpublishers.com

This book is printed on paper from registered sustainable
and managed sources.

For
Fran
Natalie
Trisha
David and Helen
Ian and Chrissie

CONTENTS

Acknowledgements ix

List of Abbreviations xi

Introduction 1

'THE STRONG SENSE OF "OTHERNESS"', 1904–1934

1. 'An outsider from the beginning': Swiss Childhood,
   1904–22 11
2. New World: Harvard, Social Work and Pacifism, 1922–26 17
3. 'Perfect bureaucrat': State Department Years, 1926–34 23

SERVING THE CAUSE, 1934–1941

4. I Spy: The Massings and the Fields, 1934–36 33
5. 'Working for the same boss': Hiss, Hede and Noel,
   1935–36 43
6. Murder and Defection: The Fields, Reiss and Krivitsky,
   1936–37 51
7. Promised Lands: Pilgrimage to Moscow; Mission in Spain,
   1937–39 61
8. 'At the risk of death': Hermann Field, 1939–40 71
9. Family Breakdown: Noel, Herta and Erica, 1939–41 81

'CROWNING ACHIEVEMENT', 1941–1949

10. Cadres and Camps: The USC and the KPD Foreign
    Secretariat 89

CONTENTS

11. 'Saving our Cadres': Marseille and Geneva, 1941–44   99
12. Dangerous Liaisons: Noel, Dulles and the OSS, 1942–45   107
13. Teetering Edifice: USC Europe, 1945–47   117
14. The Searchers: Noel and Herta, 1947–49   125

THE MARCH OF EVENTS

15. Past Becomes Present: Hede's Friends, Old and New   137
16. 'Decisive measures on our part': Stalin's Role   147
17. Heresy: Tito versus Stalin   159

STAGING THE RAJK TRIAL, 1949

18. Less Than Rhapsodic: Rákosi's Hungary   175
19. Fateful Contact: Noel and the 'Szőnyi Group'   187
20. The Spider and the Spy: Netting the Fields   197
21. 'Whatever you want me to say': Torture and Truth   209
22. 'The enemy's man': László Rajk   219
23. Jigsaw Justice: Aspects of the Rajk Trial   233

TIME OF TRIALS, 1949–1953

24. The Urge to Purge: Trial and Terror, 1948–53   245
25. The Evaded Show Trial: Sacrificing the Polish 'Fieldists'   253
26. 'Former German political émigrés': Witch-hunt in the GDR   263
27. The Laggards of Prague: The Fields and the Slánský trial   275
28. 'Terrorist activities': Stalin's Last Killings   285

THE GHOSTS RETURN

29. Belated Tears for Stalin: Prison, Release and Asylum   299
30. Fade-out: Bystander, Apologist, Nobody   309

Notes   321
Bibliography   395
Index   403

ACKNOWLEDGEMENTS

Now a Canadian citizen, my good friend and former student Trisha Danyluk (now Doyle) assiduously perused the entire book in draft. Deftly blending support and criticism, she rescued me from a number of careless errors and waged a just war upon some stylistic excesses. Dr Michael Kubina in Berlin generously provided me with material upon the careers and fates of the German 'Fieldists'. My brother-in-law, Peter Bull, skilfully accessed some vital material on Noel Field and his family, Hede Massing and her husbands, and Lisa Zarubina. Werner Schweizer, the Swiss director of the film, *Noel Field: der erfundene Spion*, provided certain details about the Field and Glaser families, and generously permitted the use of a photograph from the Field estate. This photograph of Noel Field was taken in the Budapest headquarters of the Hungarian secret police on 12 May 1949, shortly after Noel had been kidnapped in Prague. Reproduced by my close friend and neighbour, the graphic artist Kay Ryder, it features on this book's jacket.

LIST OF ABBREVIATIONS

ÁVO/ÁVH	Hungarian security service
BCP	Bulgarian Communist Party
BCRC	British Committee for Refugees from Czechoslovakia
CALPO	French-based Free German Committee for the West
CIA	US Central Intelligence Agency
Cominform	Communist Information Bureau, 1947–56
Comintern	Communist International, 1919–43
CPGB	Communist Party of Great Britain
CPSU	Communist Party of the Soviet Union*
CPUSA	Communist Party of the United States of America
CPY	Communist Party of Yugoslavia
CRTF	British-based Czech Refugee Trust Fund
CzCP	Czechoslovak Communist Party
ECCI	Executive Committee of the Comintern
FO	British Foreign Office
FBI	US Federal Bureau of Investigation
G2	US Army intelligence
GDR	German Democratic Republic/East Germany
GRU	Soviet military intelligence agency
GUGB	Soviet security service within the NKVD, 1934–43
HCP	Hungarian Communist Party*
HUAC	US House Committee on Un-American Activities
ILO	Geneva-based International Labour Organisation
INO	Soviet Foreign Intelligence Department 1920–41
INS	US Immigration and Naturalization Service

INU	Soviet Foreign Intelligence Directorate 1941–54
IUEIC	Investigative Unit for Especially Important Cases of the MGB
JAC	Soviet Jewish Antifascist Committee
JAFRC/JARC	American Joint Anti-Fascist Refugee Committee
KATPOL	Hungarian military intelligence
KPD	German Communist Party
KZ	Nazi concentration camp
MBP	Polish Ministry of Public Security
MfS	GDR Ministry for State Security
MGB	Soviet Ministry of State Security, 1946–53
MNFF	Swiss-based Hungarian National Independence Front
MVD	Soviet Ministry of Internal Affairs, 1946–90
NKFD	KPD-dominated National Committee for Free Germany
NKGB	Soviet People's Commissariat of State Security, 1943–46
NKVD	Soviet People's Commissariat of Internal Affairs, 1934–46
NPP	Hungarian National Peasant Party
OGPU	Soviet security service, 1923–34
OMGUS	Office of Military Government of the United States in Germany
OSE	French-based Organisation to aid Jewish children
OSS	United States Office of Strategic Services
OZNA	Yugoslav security service
PCE	Spanish Communist Party
PCF	French Communist Party
PCP	Polish Communist Party*
RFE	Munich-based, US-controlled Radio Free Europe
RSFSR	Russian Soviet Federative Socialist Republic
SDP	Hungarian Social Democratic Party
SED	East German Socialist Unity Party
SHP	Hungarian Smallholders Party
SIM	Spanish Republican security service
SKOJ	CPY Youth Organisation
SMERSH	Red Army Counter-Intelligence 1943–46
SOZ	Soviet Occupation Zone of Germany 1945–49

LIST OF ABBREVIATIONS

SPD	German Social Democratic Party
StB	Czechoslovak security service
SwCP	Swiss Communist Party
Stasi	GDR security service
UB	Polish security service
UDB	Yugoslav security service
USC	Unitarian Service Committee
YPA	Yugoslav People's Army
ZPKK	Central Party Control Commission of the SED

* For ease of reference I have used CPSU throughout this book, even though the Soviet communist party did not adopt this title until the Nineteenth Party Congress in October 1952. Similarly I have used HCP and PCP throughout to describe the Hungarian and Polish communist parties, even though both bodies went through several changes of name.

INTRODUCTION

In this book I have endeavoured to do two things. Firstly, I have sought to present as accurate a picture as possible of Noel Field's often secretive life, particularly his role as a communist and a Soviet agent. Secondly, I have attempted to gauge how his tangled past was utilised in the years 1949 to 1953 as a crucial element in the production of the Rajk and Slánský show trials, as well as in the less publicised persecutions in East Germany and Poland.

Noel Field was both a factual and a fictional spy. He became an agent of Soviet intelligence in the 1930s for his own reasons. In the next decade, and for very different reasons, Stalin and the Hungarian communist dictator Rákosi transformed him into a major 'American spy'.

The personal trials that Field underwent in the years 1949 to 1954 were kidnap in Prague, followed by torture, degradation and solitary confinement in Budapest. He was never put on trial in person; he only appeared off-stage in the trials of others.

His name and alleged activities as an 'American spy' were first aired through forced confessions in the show trial of László Rajk and his so-called 'accomplices'. From then on the 'evidence' regurgitated in a Budapest courtroom in September 1949 set the tone for Field's spectral presence in further frame-ups.

Once the Rajk trial 'proved' that Noel was a leading American spy, the trials and tribulations of others began in an atmosphere of terror. The many communists who had experienced direct or even indirect contact with Field knew that they were now 'infected', as if by some bacillus. The 'cure' for such could only be investigation by party and security authorities, followed by a range of sanctions: censure, dismissal from office, expulsion from the Party, arrest, torture, secret trial, imprisonment, or even a death sentence.

Born in London in 1904, but raised and schooled in Switzerland, Noel was strongly influenced by the example of his American Quaker father. Herbert Field was a noted scientist and an ardent pacifist, who died in 1921. The following year, Noel, his siblings and his widowed mother moved to Massachusetts. Having shone at Harvard University, and briefly indulged in social work, Field entered the State Department in 1926.

Noel's leftward drift began about this time. He was never a member of the American Communist Party (CPUSA), although he believed that he had been registered as an underground member in 1938. However, throughout the Second World War he behaved as a convinced communist, and was treated as one by those he helped in Vichy France and Switzerland. But in the post-war years his ambiguous party status, and Field's continuous efforts to resolve it, would augment Moscow's suspicions about him. For concerns had already arisen during his brief espionage career.

That Noel was a Soviet spy in the State Department is no longer in doubt; Field admitted it in statements written in his prison cell in Budapest. However, he did not operate as a spy for long, perhaps for one year from spring 1935. There is no clarity about the time-scale, nor about the quantity or quality of the material that he passed to Moscow.

In late 1935 Field resigned from the State Department in order to take up a position in the secretariat of the League of Nations in Geneva. Noel's main reason for seeking the new post was that he could not cope with the divided life that he led in Washington as a spy. Despite a number of specious excuses he knew that he was indulging in treason. However, as an international civil servant at the League his loyalty would not be tested. Yet, by his own admission, in Geneva he learned nothing worthwhile to pass to his handlers in any case.

Despite this the Soviet Foreign Intelligence Department (INO), which was part of the Soviet People's Commissariat of Internal Affairs (NKVD), persevered with him. However, two leading operatives of INO, who were in contact with Field, defected in rapid succession in 1937 at the height of the purges in the USSR. Later his two original controllers also crossed to the anti-Soviet side in the Cold War. Unsurprisingly such factors exacerbated Moscow's suspicions about Noel.

Other doubts arose when Field operated from 1941 to 1947 as the head of an American relief agency, the Unitarian Service Committee (USC), first in Vichy France, then in Switzerland, and finally in parts of Eastern Europe. In this capacity Noel provided aid in the form of food, clothing, money and medical care to hundreds, if not thousands, of the antifascists that were trapped in Europe by war and its aftermath.

Field's principal aid was directed towards other communists, and particularly towards party cadres, the tested, long-serving officials of various European parties. These men and women were either interned in Vichy France and Switzerland, or living illegally in those countries.

They comprised principally members of the disbanded International Brigades, who had fought in the Spanish Civil War, plus former officials of the Foreign Secretariat of the German Communist Party (KPD). Shielded by an American passport, Noel also acted as a courier between Marseille and Switzerland for the KPD, and assisted certain of his flock to escape from Europe to Mexico, and from France to Switzerland.

However, in the spring of 1943 Field was deemed to have refused an INO order to leave his USC work and revert to an espionage role for Moscow. Moreover, he did not disguise the fact that he was in contact with America's wartime intelligence organisation, the United States Office of Strategic Services (OSS), and particularly with its Swiss-based mission-chief Allen Dulles. This relationship involved Noel peripherally in an OSS operation to return the so-called 'Szőnyi group' of Hungarian communists to their homeland in early 1945.

Field's connection with both the OSS and the 'Szőnyi group' would eventually become the catalyst for the actions taken by Stalin and Rákosi, which led to the Rajk trial. However, they acted in the wider context that also impacted upon the East European show trials.

First, there was the ideological conflict between the Soviet-dominated 'east' and the American-led 'west'. This contest, dubbed 'the Cold War', was just about entering the political equivalent of the ice-age when the show trials began. Yet the cowing of dissent on both sides of the 'Iron Curtain', in order to promote ideologically divided minds, merely overlaid existing east-west divisions in the political, economic and military spheres.

This is not to make an exact comparison between the conformity of thought induced by Stalin's show trials on the one hand, and the investigation into private beliefs, both past and current, by the House Committee on Un-American Activities in the USA. HUAC's investigations, and later the smears of Senator McCarthy, resulted in some Americans losing their jobs and reputations. Few lost their liberty as well, and only the Rosenbergs lost their lives.

In the American context I have given some consideration to that *cause célèbre*, the Hiss-Chambers case, solely because Alger Hiss was a close friend of Noel Field, and each knew that the other was both a communist and a Soviet agent.

The arraignment of Hiss in December 1948 deterred Noel from returning to the USA, or even remaining in Western Europe, where he feared he could be kidnapped and forced to testify at Hiss's trial. As a result he decided to settle in Eastern Europe–despite the very real, and ultimately fulfilled, risk of kidnap. East of the Iron Curtain he was still obliged to 'name names', but under conditions of arbitrary imprisonment and torture, and without the recourse to legal norms that he would have had on the Western side.

A second factor influencing the show trials was Stalin's campaign against 'Titoism'. Following the breach between Yugoslavia and the USSR in June 1948, certain senior communists in all of the Soviet satellite states came under pressure. While domestic factors and leadership struggles were involved, there was also a drive to label these men, like Tito, as so-called 'national communists'.

Those betraying such tendencies were not necessarily in some way less Stalinist than their accusers; Tito was a ruthless Stalinist too, which helped him to survive the breach with Moscow. The factor marking certain communists for the fall was that they were primarily 'home communists' because they had undergone the war years outside of the USSR, either in their own country or as *émigrés* in Western European states.

Otherwise the pattern was broadly the same. The returning 'Muscovites' were always in a stronger position in the East European people's democracies. They were known to and favoured by the Kremlin. They were close-knit from experience. They were Russian-speaking, and often Soviet citizens. They had built up patronage and/or 'security' relationships with individuals or institutions in the Soviet hierarchy. They were far more attuned to the party line and could realign themselves swiftly when it changed. The exception was the Slánský trial, where the Jewish origins of certain defendants trumped any 'Muscovite' solidarity.

The third contextual factor to the trials, and probably the dominant leitmotif, was Stalin's anti-Semitism. It coincided with the fact that many of the communists who were closely connected with Field were Jews. Therefore I have given some consideration to the attraction that the Bolshevik revolution exerted upon a section of the Jewish community as well as their prominence in party and security bodies in certain states at certain times. To ignore this would be as dishonest as accepting the hoary myth of 'Judeo-communism'.

Stalin's deep-seated anti-Semitism was not evident for many years, but it was revealed blatantly by the January 1948 murder of Solomon Mikhoels, the head of the Jewish Antifascist Committee (JAC). Later other JAC leaders were arrested and tortured. Their judicial murder, following a secret trial, occurred in August 1952.

Stalin was also preparing the so-called 'Doctors' Plot' in this period. This undertaking quite possibly presaged Stalin's own version of the 'Final Solution' to the 'Jewish Question', a mere handful of years after the Holocaust. Stalin's death in March 1953 at least removed the possibility of mass pogroms and deportations from the Soviet agenda.

The anti-Semitism that became central to the policy of Stalin's last years spilled over into Eastern Europe. The overtly anti-Semitic Slánský show trial in Prague in November 1952 is rightly cited as the preeminent example, but it would be wrong to ignore the influence of this anti-Semitism in the Rajk trial. The communist party leadership in Poland evaded the sacrifice of one of their own. Instead they offered up a dozen minor Jewish communists, all of whom had known Field. In East Germany it was no accident that the senior figure to fall was the gentile Paul Merker, who argued that the Jews were a special case among Hitler's victims, and were deserving of special treatment.

None of the senior communists who fell had any direct connection with Field, save for the KPD Politburo member Paul Merker. The majority of the *émigrés* with whom Noel had extensive contacts were second-rank cadres, as were those aided by Noel's younger brother Hermann in Poland in 1939.

Those assisted to safety in Britain by Hermann, as well as those aided by Noel in France and Switzerland, became by definition 'Westerners'. Some of them were also 'Spaniards', men and women who had served in Spain. Many were Jews as well. Quite a number belonged in all three categories. By the time that the show trials began, 'Westerners', 'Spaniards', and 'rootless cosmopolitans' were all highly suspect categories in Moscow.

It was these lesser cadres who bore the brunt of the persecution. If I treat them with sympathy, this is not through empathy with their motives. However, I see no reason to overlook the sacrifices that these individuals made for a cause in which they believed, and for which they sacrificed family, relationships, homes, creature comforts, often their liberty, and in some cases their lives. So, where I can, I give them human identity and recognise their courage and dedication, in the clear awareness that this does not represent a blanket endorsement of their activities.

Moreover, if this book concentrates upon the persecution of communists by other communists, this is because such is its subject matter. I am perfectly aware that far more numerous crimes were perpetrated against non-communists both in the Soviet Union and Eastern Europe. Likewise, if I focus upon the suffering in the concentration camps of Vichy France and Nazi Germany, this does not entail ignorance of the slave camps established under the rule of Lenin and Stalin.

I have also tried to give a human face to the INO operatives with whom Field worked. In the case of Hede Massing I have both endorsed and discredited the account of her relationship with Field and Alger Hiss, which she provides in her very readable memoirs. Yet for far too long she has been uncritically accepted as a credible witness to her own and others' activities, which she most certainly was not.

Members of Noel's family also feature in my account of his life. Field and his German-born wife, Herta, shared most of their lives together from 1913, when both were nine years old, until Noel died of cancer in 1970. Some observers believe that Herta was the stronger character and more committed communist. Whether or not this was true, she certainly played a major role in their activities and shared his captivity.

Noel's brother, Hermann, was never a party member, although at certain points in his life he might just as well have been. His first wife was in the Party and his second wife may have been, while Noel's foster-daughter, Erica Glaser, was a member of the KPD for a few years. Like Noel and Herta, both Hermann and Erica were imprisoned for several years behind the 'Iron Curtain'. How and why this happened is detailed in the account which follows.

While this study owes much to the works of many authors, who are acknowledged in the end-notes and bibliography, I must single out one source for tribute. This is the magisterial two-volume German-language work of Dr Bernd-Rainer Barth on the Noel Field affair. Much of the factual kernel of my book comes from this collection of documents and essays, although the interpretation of these and other facts is, of course, my responsibility alone.

'THE STRONG SENSE OF "OTHERNESS"', 1904–1934

1

'AN OUTSIDER FROM THE BEGINNING'

SWISS CHILDHOOD, 1904–22[1]

Fields and Eschweges

On Saturday 23 January 1904, almost nine months to the day after his parents' marriage, Noel Haviland Field was born in the London home of his maternal grandparents. His American Quaker father, Dr Herbert Haviland Field, registered the birth on 17 February. Identifying himself as a 'director of a public scientific institution', Herbert gave as his address his father-in-law's residence.

Hermann Eschwege's house was at 20 Mayow Road in Forest Hill, south-east London. A large detached dwelling, called 'Sunnyside', he had purchased the property in the 1870s.[2]

Born in Hanau in western Germany in 1831, Hermann came to Britain in 1853, but did not become a British citizen until 1889. He died on 11 July 1918, aged eighty-seven, shortly before his homeland was defeated in the First World War. In his last will, which he signed on 6 June 1918, he left nearly £68,000 net (£79,000 gross), which would make him a multi-millionaire in today's money.

In the decennial censuses between 1871 and 1901 Hermann gave as his profession either 'naphtha manufacturer' or 'merchant'. As administrator of his wife's will he specified 'coffee manufacturer'. Noel simply wrote that he was engaged in colonial trade.[3] Whatever the exact nature of his business, Hermann was well able to afford his spacious house and employ several servants to tend his growing family.

When he was thirty-five Hermann married Elizabeth Letitia Foot, the twenty-two-year-old daughter of an Ulster snuff merchant.[4] The wedding took place in a City of London church on 19 April 1866. Their first three children, Kathleen Lilian, Sydney Hermann and Ida Eugenie were born between 1867 and 1869. On 24 October 1874 Noel's mother, Nina Sefton Eschwege, came into the world. A last child, Fritz Salo, was born in 1882.[5]

Nina Eschwege met her future husband while holidaying in the Grindelwald in Switzerland in 1901. They married in St Paul's Church, Forest Hill on Saturday 25 April 1903, and honeymooned in England before returning to Switzerland.[6] As the law then stood, after her marriage Nina automatically became a United States citizen.

Herbert Haviland Field was nearly six feet tall, burly, blue-eyed and bearded.[7] He descended from a long line of Quakers, who had left England in the early seventeenth century to escape persecution. His father, Aaron Field (1829–97), co-founded an auctioneering business in New York City in 1868. It would seem to have been profitable. In his final years Aaron lived at the desirable Brooklyn address of 106 Columbia Heights, facing across the East River towards Manhattan.

Aaron's first wife, Charlotte Cromwell (1831–62), bore him a daughter Fanny in 1856 and two sons, Henry in 1858 and Edward in 1862. Following Charlotte's death, quite probably in childbirth, Aaron married Lydia Seaman Haviland (1838–1918) in December 1865. Herbert Haviland, their oldest child, was born on 25 April 1868. Their second son Hamilton Easter (1873–1922) would become a well-known painter and a leading figure in the American modernist movement. A daughter, Hannah, was born in 1876.

Herbert grew up and was educated in Brooklyn. In 1888 he enrolled in Harvard University, gaining both his first degree and doctorate from that university. Later he studied in Freiburg (Switzerland), Leipzig and Paris.

In 1895 Herbert became director of the Concilium Bibliographicum in Zurich, 'which I have made my life's work', he wrote in 1909. Founded by the International Congress of Zoology, with the support of Swiss, American and French institutions and private donors, the

Concilium's work consisted of 'collecting the bibliographic notices from all current publications in zoology, palaeontology, microscopy, anatomy and physiology, and of printing and distributing them in card form'.

To aid this arduous process, Herbert became 'a land-owner in Zurich', and 'built a dwelling for myself on the hill back of the town, and a building for the Concilium in the town itself'.[8] The former building, a huge four-storied villa, was at 9 Köllikerstraße. The latter was situated nearby at 49 Hofstraße.

Shortly after his birth Noel left with his parents for Zurich. Over the next decade Nina gave birth there to three more children; Elsie in July 1906, Hermann Haviland in April 1910, and Letitia in September 1914. Like Noel, all automatically became American citizens, and all of them grew up in a Quaker environment.

Even before he went to school, Noel had travelled to his distant 'homeland'. In summer 1907 Herbert visited the USA as a delegate of the Swiss government to attend an international zoological conference, returning in November. Nina, Elsie and Noel accompanied him. On this journey Noel travelled on his father's passport. However, for his next trip he required a document of his own.

Noel's first passport was issued in November 1907. Describing himself as a 'student', the three-year-old applicant stated that he wanted to travel to Italy and France to study, as well as to visit relatives in England.[9]

'An extremely dreamy, girlish child'

In his role as an 'old-fashioned *Pater familias*'[10] Herbert influenced his entire family, particularly his first-born. Noel described his father as an unambitious yet idealistic intellectual and pacifist, whose indifference towards money often drove the family into financial difficulties.

As a pacifist on both religious and humane grounds, Herbert abhorred violence and bloodshed. As a young man he gave up his ambition to be a doctor, because he couldn't watch operations. Noel too couldn't stand the sight of blood.[11] As a child, the virtues of pacifism were so self-evident to Noel, that he couldn't understand how anybody could think differently.

The pacifism extended to the animal world too, inasmuch as the smallest creatures could not be killed. Instead, Noel and his siblings grew up surrounded by pet animals. Yet, while their villa overlooking

Lake Zurich may have resembled a menagerie, it was also a source of learning, inasmuch as it unlocked Noel's talent for languages.

At home the family spoke English, while from his nursemaids Noel learned to speak *Hochdeutsch*. Then, following a year at Kindergarten, the six-year-old Noel began full-time education. From February 1910 he attended the local *Volksschule* for four years, where he had to learn *Schweizerdeutsch*.

Shy and sensitive, with an intense need for privacy, Noel described himself as 'an extremely dreamy, girlish child'.[12] He had no male friends. He hated boys' brawling ways and had a preference for female friendships. Living in his own world, he avoided contact with his peers, save for his future wife, Herta, who was his school-fellow from the age of nine.

Even as a child Noel had a pathological fear of death. This led to sleeplessness and tormented him most of his life. Only in his prison cell in Hungary did he claim to have finally rid himself of it, as well as his physical—as opposed to moral—cowardice. Quite unashamedly he described himself as neurotic and later others would also assess him as such.

He viewed himself as 'an outsider from the beginning'.[13] Before going to school Noel claimed that he had never felt like a foreigner; now he did. Not only was he American, but he was also bourgeois. His part of Zurich was then like a village, and middle-class children were a distinct minority when set alongside the poor peasant kids who comprised most of his schoolmates. Not surprisingly, Noel conceded that there were also elements of snobbishness and arrogance in his make-up.

To add to his woes he encountered a sadistic, drunken and chauvinistic teacher who made his life a misery throughout his first three years at *Volksschule*. He tormented Field constantly and encouraged Noel's schoolmates to do the same. The situation became so dire that Field refused to go to school. So he was sent to a children's home in the mountain village of Engadin, east of St Moritz, joining his consumptive sister Letty, who was seeking relief in the Alpine air.

With the outbreak of the First World War in August 1914 the whole family, with the exception of Herbert, moved to Lugano for two years, because of financial problems.[14] There Noel had to learn Italian when he attended a private girl's school for one year. This was followed by a year in a so-called 'German school'.

In autumn 1916 the family rented a home in a village near Zurich and Noel spent six months in the local school.[15] He also received intensive private tuition, because the move to Lugano had put his education back by one year. The result of such diligent study was his admission to the second class of the local *Gymnasium* in the spring of 1917, which he attended until matriculating in summer 1922. By completing his course in five years instead of the normal six and a half, Noel set a precedent for his Harvard education.

At the *Gymnasium* he was again bullied, but he astonished both himself and the school when he beat up one particular thug. During this period the family moved back to Zurich, first to the Concilium building and then to the Köllikerstraße villa, where they remained until leaving for the USA in 1922.

The Fields were a musical family. Both parents and the two daughters were pianists, while Noel and Letty learned the cello, and Hermann the violin. Later Noel was a member of the student orchestra at Harvard, while 'playing' symphonies in his head in his Budapest cell helped to preserve his sanity. During his high school years he also became an accomplished stenographer; a talent which would later aid his career as both diplomat and spy.

There was also a short period during his middle years at the *Gymnasium* when Noel claims to have fallen into 'bad company'. His school-reports deteriorated so badly that he was nearly excluded. Not for the only time, Herta took him in hand and helped return him to the status of star-pupil.

It was at this time too that he began to stretch himself well beyond the school curriculum, although in a rather indiscriminate fashion. He read Roman classics in Latin, and worked his way through both New and Old Testaments. He consumed Kant's *Critique of Pure Reason* and other philosophical works, along with books on astronomy and anatomy, as well as a range of highbrow literature. He also began to compose a five act drama in verse. As he wrote later, throughout his life, he had striven 'to know as much as possible about as many things as possible'.[16]

'A pathological state of mourning'

During the war Nina frequently took Noel to the station, where they observed trainloads of seriously wounded combatants in transit through neutral Switzerland. This made a deep impression on him which was augmented by a 1920 tour of French battlefields around Verdun taken with his father.[17]

The war and its immediate aftermath had placed a great strain upon Herbert Field. Not only were there problems with the Concilium because of lack of funds, but his overall work-load increased.

He sailed to the USA to urge increased wheat exports to Switzerland. Later Field worked closely with his fellow-Quaker Herbert Hoover, organising post-war relief in Europe. Field was also acquainted with President Wilson, who sent him to report upon conditions in Bavaria in early 1919, during the short-lived Soviet republic there.[18] In addition he was a member of the American delegation to the Versailles Conference. He was also co-trustee of Hermann Eschwege's estate.[19]

On the morning of 5 April 1921 he died of a heart-attack. It seems that he had suffered one earlier when Noel tried to hasten his tardy father to the theatre.[20] If this was true, then it accounts in part for Noel's traumatic reaction to his father's early death, twenty days short of his fifty-third birthday.

Noel described his loss as 'perhaps the most decisive event in my life'. He made his dead father into an idol and worshipped him like a god. For years he was in 'a pathological state of mourning'.[21] He claimed that his loss brought to the fore another fatal characteristic; a tendency to indulge in exaggerated, self-tormenting (selbstquälerisch) self-criticism.

Noel convinced himself that he was to blame for his father's death and he had to atone by becoming a 'saint' (Heiliger), who would dedicate his life to the service of mankind

The first practical act of 'Saint' Noel was to found the Youth World Peace League (der Weltfriedenbund der Jugend), whose initial meeting took place in the Fields' villa in 1921, with Noel as self-appointed president. There the twenty-odd young people present drew up a programme and statutes for the entire world. Over the winter of 1921–22 the movement had some small success both in Zurich and other Swiss cities. But after moving to the USA Noel lost interest in his creation.

Following Herbert's death and Noel's matriculation Nina kept two promises to her late husband: first to have the children raised as Americans; and second for Noel to fulfil Herbert's profound desire that his son too would study at Harvard.

In the summer of 1922 Nina and her four children left Switzerland. In Liverpool they boarded the American liner *Pittsburgh*. On 15 August they disembarked in Boston and travelled to their temporary home at 16 Berkeley Street in Cambridge, Massachusetts. Here they settled in with Herbert's step-brother Henry C. Field.[22]

2

NEW WORLD

HARVARD, SOCIAL WORK AND PACIFISM, 1922–26[1]

'Brilliant in the classroom'

In the fall of 1922 the eighteen-year-old Noel entered Harvard. He probably looked much like his self-assessment when applying for a passport in January 1921; six foot tall, rather gangly, hair brown and wavy, his green eyes and straight nose surmounting a broad chin. At some time during his Harvard years he grew a moustache, which made him look older. It was to make occasional reappearances in later life.

Noel's ultimate objective was to emulate his father by obtaining a doctorate from this august university. However, he scuppered his chances through academic burn-out. He chose to take his BA in two years rather than the usual four, and this required him to take twice as many courses as normal.

In the two semesters of his first year he studied English literature, History of Philosophy, Administration, Political Science, International Law, Colonial History, History of Capitalism, and Musical Theory amongst other courses. In his second and final year he concentrated upon Political Science, Political Economy, and above all Social Ethics. He also pursued two International Law courses. One of these allowed him to write what was effectively a doctoral dissertation on 'The League of Nations and Disarmament', for which he obtained a distinction. He passed his BA *cum laude* in summer 1924.

In Cambridge the Fields had moved a few doors along Berkeley Street to number 21 and Noel lived at home rather than in college. 'The result', suggests Flora Lewis, 'was brilliant in the classroom, sad in solitude'.[2] Noel recognised this too, noting that his intensive studies and leaps between years had left him no time to make friends. The 'college atmosphere', he wrote in his cell, passed him by completely. Again he was a stranger, this time a cultivated European in the USA. It is doubtful that his 'strong sense of "otherness" ("*Anders-sein*")' had diminished.[3]

Although Nina was prepared to finance his education further so long as he remained at home, Noel declined. He wanted to marry Herta and to earn his own income.[4] However, this did not prevent him from first availing himself of what was probably a treat by Nina for her clever son. In summer 1924 Noel returned alone to Europe. He wandered through Holland, Germany, France and Switzerland, and then returned home from Le Havre aboard *La Savoie*, docking in New York on 12 October.

Shortly after stepping onto dry land Noel began classes at the Boston School for Social Work, an affiliate of Smith College, one of the most prestigious women's universities. That semester the institution experimented with the admission of men for the first time. In fact Noel was the only male in his class, which must have suited him. The course involved three days per week of study and three of practical social work, both paid and unpaid. The class in psychiatry particularly interested the neurotic Noel.

The practical work involved prison reform. The Massachusetts Department of Mental Diseases was conducting an inquiry into the matter, with the spadework performed by a team of psychiatrists, assisted by a staff of 'psychiatric social workers'. As one of the latter, earning $75 per month, Noel visited prisons throughout the state, interviewing inmates and obtaining their life-stories. Later, banged up in a Budapest cell, Noel probably appreciated the irony of writing about his period of visiting such places voluntarily.

After talking to the prisoners Field had to conduct interviews with their friends, relatives and former teachers, before writing up a 'social analysis' on each jailbird. This journey into the underworld made the sensitive and rather snobbish Noel quite ill; he had no idea how the 'lower' classes lived. Even their speech was alien to him, and he found it difficult to win their trust. He could only conclude that an unbridgeable chasm divided him from the world of the proletariat.

A married man

Born on 25 February 1904 in Karlsruhe in Baden, Herta Katherina Vieser was little more than a month younger than Noel. Her mother, Katherina Mönch, born in 1881 in Owen in Teck, came from a farming family. Herta's father, Karl Johann Ludwig Vieser, was a German civil servant. Pensioned-off early, he had moved his family to Switzerland in 1913.

From the age of nine, Herta had shared some, if not all, of Noel's schooldays. Later Herta qualified as a social worker. She was employed as a carer in Germany before she joined Noel in the USA. It is not clear whether this was her own spontaneous act, or the result of a long-planned decision by the two. However, initially she either decided not to distract the zealous undergraduate by her proximity, or was not allowed to do so.

Her father was dead when Herta, not yet nineteen and travelling alone, left Karlsruhe and boarded the *President Fillmore* in Bremen. She arrived in New York on 29 October 1922 and gave her destination as Elmhurst, New York state. She was registered as having no occupation.

She worked for a year as a nursemaid and later as a designer in a textile factory.[5] Later she joined the Field household. It may be true that Nina treated her simply as a mother's helper. Possibly she thought Herta unsuitable for her son. If she did, she lost out. Noel and Herta, both barely twenty-one, were married in Cambridge on 4 May 1925.

It was a small, family affair. More precisely, the Field family were present at the wedding while Herta's kin were on the high seas. Her widowed mother and seventeen-year-old sister, Gertrude (called Traudy), had left Bremen on 2 May. They arrived in New York ten days after the marriage. The coincidence of the two events is suggestive. Had they been trying to attend the ceremony? Had the Fields simply gone ahead without them?

Whatever the case, the Viesers also intended to stay in the USA. The final destination given by both Katherina and Traudy was Chicago. However, it seems that they both stayed nearer to Herta, who wrote that her mother obtained a domestic post in Mount Vernon, while Traudy was employed as a nursemaid by a Washington family.

Herta now became a housewife. It is unclear whether or not the newly-weds lived in Nina's house or had their own place.[6] Equally uncertain is how they managed for money, although Noel might still have been working for the Department of Mental Diseases. Otherwise, very little cash was coming in. Herta had no private means, and although Noel, once he was twenty-one, enjoyed a small legacy from his father's estate, it provided only a few hundred dollars per annum as income, and then virtually disappeared after the 1929 Wall Street crash.

However, Noel, encouraged by his Boston uncle and perhaps his wife as well, had made a career decision; now that he was old enough, he would apply to join the State Department.[7]

Pacifism and exams

Around this time Noel wrote that he had always had 'a firm intention of entering the Foreign Service'. He felt that it was 'by far the most practical field in which an individual can do his bit towards international understanding'.[8] This sounds like a rather pompous way of interpreting his vocation to be a 'saint' and to serve mankind.

By now he had resumed his pacifist activities. In 1924 he joined the Fellowship of Youth for Peace, the newly-formed youth section of the Quaker-influenced Fellowship of Reconciliation. The latter body had been established in 1914 in Britain, and Noel had joined it in Boston. The youth section appeared to be slightly more radical in membership and activity than its parent body. In his prison writings Noel emphasised the contacts he made at this time with leftists of varying hues.

In the spring and summer of 1926 Noel held a research post with another Quaker body, the National Council for the Prevention of War. There he wrote a monograph entitled 'Banishing War Through Arbitration—A Brief Sketch of Post-War Arbitration Treaties', which was published in Washington DC that year. Recalling events in his cell, Noel noted that it was the only thing written by him that had been published under his name. He was pleased to discover later that it was utilised in the international law course at Geneva University.

Before writing about arbitration Noel had to undertake the written State Department exams in January 1926. He learned to his horror that his Harvard studies would be of little help, since the most important subjects were Commercial Law, Finance, Economic Geography and

American History. However, in Washington there were private schools that prepared applicants. Noel couldn't afford such luxury, nor did he want to defer his application. Typically, he simply bought the relevant books and crammed new knowledge into his head.

It worked. The minimum score for success was 80 per cent correct answers. Noel achieved 82 per cent. Next he had to face the greater ordeal of the oral exams in spring. He had no information regarding the questions to be asked. In his view the obvious purpose of the orals was to eliminate 'undesirable' (*mißliebig*) candidates, like Jews and women, by posing them impossible questions.[9]

Noel had a relatively easy ride. To him this demonstrated that he was not an 'undesirable'. It meant that the authorities either did not know, or did not care about his pacifist activities.

In this he was somewhat mistaken as he was later to recognise. Word had come down about his pinkish past and present. On the other hand, he had received fine recommendations from his Harvard professors, who saw him as a 'student of high distinction' and a 'reliable and proper person of excellent standing'. He was also a gifted linguist.

Yet his timidity and callowness, his complex personality, his idealism, his 'otherness' must all have counted against him in the hard-headed estimation of the examiners. They noted that although 'lacking in social experience, he has good breeding and is distinctly a gentleman'.[10]

In May, Noel was informed that he was one of the eighteen candidates out of 300, who had been accepted by the State Department. On 1 September 1926 he presented himself for duty in Washington.

3

'PERFECT BUREAUCRAT'

STATE DEPARTMENT YEARS, 1926–34[1]

'A pretty good club'

In 1924 a new law merged the former US diplomatic and consular services into a Foreign Service. It was not something that the elite of the former favoured. One senior diplomat felt that 'they belonged to a pretty good club' and that their *esprit de corps* would be ended by the adoption of a joint promotion list.[2]

Although losing out on the merger, the 'club' suffered little from the influx of middle-class and mid-west recruits that ensued. These mainly aped the ways of the east coast aristocrats, once they had cleared the bar of the recently introduced formal examinations.

Every new entrant now had to start as a vice-consul, and on 1 September 1926 Noel was appointed a Foreign Service officer with this rank, at a salary of $2,000 per annum. As a preliminary to practical work, he and the seventeen other successful applicants attended a compulsory six month course in the Foreign Service school, in order to prepare them for work in the State Department.[3]

In the mornings they heard lectures by various experts, including diplomats sojourning in Washington from foreign postings. In addition they were addressed by representatives of other government agencies concerned with the outside world, above all the Department of Commerce.

In the afternoons the novices were apprenticed to various divisions. This was to familiarise them with State's administrative methods, the consular service's work, and methods of correspondence, including the preparation of coded telegrams. Each new entrant also received a thick volume of consular regulations on which they sat oral and written tests.

When the course ended in early 1927 most of the new entrants were appointed to foreign postings. However, Noel Haviland Field was sent to the State Department library.

He was left in no doubt as to the reason for this. His course leader told Noel that they had received certain information about his 'radical' past. Obviously such things were simply youthful errors, but he was advised to break off all compromising contacts. It was made clear that he would be kept in Washington until he had clearly proved his 'loyalty'. Noel promised to conform and resigned by letter from the Fellowship of Youth for Peace, although he apparently remained a member.

For the present Noel was put at the service of the lady heading the library. For some six months he read literary reviews, made book recommendations, and often found himself engrossed in the volumes that he had ordered.

This relative idleness lasted until the end of summer 1927 when he had a conversation with the deputy-chief of the West European Division. Asked about his interests, Noel made reference to his Harvard thesis on the League of Nations and disarmament. His superior asked to read it. A few days later Noel found himself allocated to the Swiss 'desk', where League affairs were furtively handled.

Not only did the United States not join the League, but in the early 1920s it treated that body as non-existent and never replied to its communications. Since the League was in Geneva, it was the Swiss 'desk' which had the responsibility for ignoring it. Given that Swiss affairs required minimal attention and the League virtually none, the incumbent of this 'desk' spent half the day reading novels.

However, by the time of Noel's appointment, the American attitude had gradually changed, and the USA began to participate tentatively in League affairs. The usual form was through 'observer' status, and the primary interest was in economic matters. Then in mid-summer 1927 a naval conference was held in Geneva with American participation, and reports from its delegates overwhelmed the Swiss 'desk'. Not only did the incumbent have to lay aside his novels, but he asked for assistance; hence Noel's transfer.

So while the 'deskman' dealt with the conference, Noel attended to lesser affairs, which chiefly involved the study of League documents and their distribution to interested departments and agencies. Once the conference ended Noel's superior returned to his books. However, his zealous assistant, who was generally viewed as 'a bear for work',[4] gradually became recognised as the expert on League affairs. His workload so increased, particularly after the advent of the Roosevelt administration in March 1933, that in time Noel himself needed to have one or two assistants.

For three years Field was nominally a Foreign Service officer with the rank of vice-consul. However, under the terms of an August 1930 law, no official could hold this rank for longer than three years whilst remaining in Washington. So in late summer 1930 Noel resigned from the Foreign Service and became an ordinary State Department official, with the title 'Drafting Officer'. This was a broad middle category of officials perching between the lower-ranked employees, the clerks, and the top men, the chiefs of divisions.

Conference seasons

From his position as the drafting officer in charge of the Swiss 'desk', and unofficially the man to see about League affairs, Noel now moved into the sphere of disarmament when the USA began to take an increased interest in this issue.

In 1922 the Treaty of Washington had set agreed limits on the size and composition of the American, British and Japanese navies. Efforts to revise and extend the terms of this agreement had failed at Geneva in 1927. Another attempt was made at the London naval conference which ran from 21 January to 22 April 1930.

By then Noel had gained plaudits for his painstaking papers upon disarmament questions. In recognition of his expertise he was made one of several assistant secretaries to the American delegation, and his annual salary increased from $2,750 to $3,000 that April.[5]

Noel and Herta, who had naturalised in 1927, sailed out with the delegation on 9 January 1930. While Noel advised, Herta, who was visiting London for the first time, took in the sights and haunted the art galleries. Then she made a trip to the Continent.

Her mother had returned to Germany in 1929 to visit relatives and was unaware that the Fields were in Europe. Herta wanted to surprise her on her birthday. So, following a stay with friends in Brussels and a brief visit to Cologne cathedral, she proceeded to Ludwigsburg, near Stuttgart, where her mother was staying with her sister. Then together they travelled to Owen to see Herta's grandmother, before setting off to her birthplace in Karlsruhe.

Herta stayed several weeks in Germany before rejoining Noel in London. Once the conference had concluded the Fields travelled around France, Italy and Switzerland, seemingly for nearly two months, before sailing home. They arrived in New York on 9 June 1930, the day after Katherina Vieser's own arrival there from Bremen.

In Washington Noel functioned as the link-man (*Bindeglied*) between higher authorities there and American representatives in Geneva. He worked on the latter's reports, sent them on to the relevant bodies, and dealt with their replies. With his shorthand talents, he sometimes acted as the secretary at inter-departmental discussions, on occasion even in the White House.[6]

Noel was also involved in President Hoover's 1931 proposal for a moratorium on Germany's reparations payments. In addition he drafted speeches on pacific themes for President Roosevelt, Secretary of State Cordell Hull, and sometimes members of Congress.

'Mr. Field was one of the most brilliant men we have ever had in this Division', wrote one of his superiors in 1940. 'He was so skilled in drafting that we pressed him into service on questions outside his assignment'.[7] Another colleague simply dubbed him 'PB' for 'perfect bureaucrat'.[8] On the other hand, Noel was still assessed in reports as 'a thinker rather than a doer', who still did 'not face up to the larger practical problems'.[9]

In the summer of 1934 Noel took part in a pre-conference (*Vorkonferenz*) in London relating to the extension of the 1930 agreement.[10] He also participated in another full naval conference there, which ran from 28 October to 19 December 1934.

Shortly after the Fields arrived Herta headed off to Karlsruhe to visit her mother and sister, who had both left again for Germany.[11] She returned to London when Norman Davis, the leader of the American delegation, decided to withdraw from the conference and return home at once. But the return was delayed and this allowed Herta to make a surprise visit to Karlsruhe at Christmas. Finally leaving Le Havre on 29 December, the Fields sailed on the *Washington* and arrived in New York on 6 January 1935.

Noel would also attend the final rites of these naval conferences at the end of 1935. But on this occasion the 'perfect bureaucrat' would be behaving somewhat differently.

'I remained an "outsider"'

'Just as at school, I remained an "outsider" in the State Department', wrote Noel in his cell.[12] From the outset of their stay in Washington the Fields went out of their way to spurn the diplomatic social life. Herta went without make-up and wore home-made clothes, while Noel, crumpled and rumpled at the best of times, dressed ever more sloppily.

They lived at 419, 4th Street N.W. 'in a greasy apartment house in downtown Washington', a contemporary recalled, with a kitchen full of cats. 'The place smelled dreadfully'.[13] Noel emphasised that they had no car or maid. Herta did everything on the rare occasions when colleagues were invited to dine.

They realised at an early stage that there would be no 'brilliant career' for Noel. This bothered them little, since, like his father, Noel was unambitious and showed little interest in material wealth.

Both he and Herta were members of several book clubs. They read widely and were avid theatre-goers. Classical music was rarely absent from the gramophone. They had a houseboat on the Potomac which they converted into a motor-boat of sorts. They indulged in camping and naturism. As an 'eternal student' Noel added typing to his short-hand talents, and became interested in meteorology.

Whether or not this was all inverted snobbery, the net effect was probably what they wanted. They were struck off the social lists by Noel's colleagues, and they in turn were left to live their own lives and see whom they chose to see. Noel's best friend was Laurence Duggan, who from 1930 was a colleague in the State Department and later a fellow-spy. Following Duggan's marriage he and his wife Helen moved into the apartment beneath the Fields and remained there from 1933 to 1935.

Politically Noel lived a muddled life. Around 1927 he was involved in organising an 'International Friendship Club' which seemed to cater mostly for foreign students. Although originally established upon paci-fist lines it rapidly became involved in the race question. Noel con-tended exaggeratedly that the idea of complete social equality was self-evident for a European; while at the same time he 'gave orders to, and was served by, the deferential Negro messengers' at work, whom he derisively termed 'the dray horses' of the State Department.[14]

Yet, given the virtual apartheid that existed at that time his attitude, for all its limitations, was commendable. Blacks in Washington were excluded from 'white' restaurants, hotels and theatres. But Noel and Herta went with their black friends to the theatre and, however furtively, invited them to their home. Later he took the view that the race question could only be solved by a social revolution, and after a few years Noel ceased attending the club.

The cause of Nicola Sacco and Bartolomeo Vanzetti engaged him too. These two Italian anarchists were convicted in Boston of murder in July 1921 and sentenced to death. The verdict, which many held to be a condemnation of innocent men upon other than legal grounds, polarised the nation.

Noel was involved in the demonstrations calling for their release. When the 'poor shoemaker and fish-peddler' were executed on 23 August 1927 Noel wept openly. He never forgot the night that they were electrocuted, even observing the anniversary of their deaths when he was himself a prisoner in Hungary, and he contended later that their executions drove him to the left.[15]

In October 1929 the last toots of the Jazz Age were silenced by Wall Street's collapse, which led to the traumatic miseries of 'the Great Depression' for millions of Americans. Noel doesn't provide any portrait of how he was affected by the experience. He was not cast out of work himself and simply wrote that 'the Great Depression stimulated further searching'.[16]

He claims to have participated in demonstrations by the unemployed, strikes and hunger marches. But the high point of his radical activity was to rush from his desk and throw sticks and stones at the police and soldiers, who were clearing the so-called 'Bonus Army' of impoverished veterans from the streets of Washington in June 1932.

One witness would claim before the Dies Committee in 1938 that Field was already a communist in 1928. However, he was most certainly not a member of the Party at this juncture.[17] Even his overall outlook could hardly be termed Marxist, except perhaps of the armchair variety. He was a radical 'outsider' who hated war, violence, racism, mass unemployment and poverty. But he had little clear idea how to 'cure' these social ills. Like millions of others he stood on the fringes of political commitment, confused, looking for answers. The label that Noel gave himself at the time was 'pacifist idealist'.[18] Earl Browder, leader of the CPUSA since 1930, preferred to dub him 'a stupid child in the woods'.[19]

Noel's diaries were filled with his indecision.[20] The chief factor inhibiting any move towards communism was a profound pacifism, which was reinforced by his work on disarmament. Even during his interrogations in Hungary he confessed that he was unable personally and without scruples to condone the application of force, although he accepted that it was necessary for the triumph of his new ideal.

He also felt restrained by such 'petty-bourgeois' concepts as loyalty and honour, which made it hard for Noel to bite the hand that fed him. Then there was his 'objective' outlook which permitted him to see both sides of an argument. Yet the 'eternal student' was prepared to make the effort and he began to read Marxist literature and attend study groups.

Noel taught himself Russian, after buying some *Linguaphone* records from a colleague and purchasing a grammar and dictionary from a journalist who had been in Moscow. Not only did he like the sound (*Klang*) of the language, but he wanted to study Lenin and Stalin in the original. He read Russian-language newspapers and books. By the time he went to Moscow in 1938 he could understand the language well, although he spoke it badly.

Stoically he waded through the first volume of *Das Kapital*, Stalin's *Problems of Leninism*, *My Life* by Trotsky and John Reed's *Ten Days that Shook the World*. He read the CPUSA 'theoretical' journal *New Masses* and the Comintern's *Inprecor*. Via an accommodation address he received the CPUSA's paper the *Daily Worker*.

The transition had begun. However, it seems doubtful that left to himself he would have crossed into the committed world of communism. For that to happen Field needed a little help from some friends.

SERVING THE CAUSE, 1934–1941

4

I SPY

THE MASSINGS AND THE FIELDS, 1934–36

Spies and lies[1]

From March 1947 American FBI agent Robert Lamphere conducted several long interviews with 'a tall, middle-aged, carefully dressed woman'. Although 'no longer the striking beauty she had obviously been in her youth', she was still attractive and vivacious, and 'her coquettishness and wit were much in evidence during our sessions. It was easy to see why many men had desired her'.[2]

How many men had realised their desires with this *femme fatale* is neither known nor particularly relevant to our tale. However, we do know that Hedwig Tune married three times, each time to committed communists. Yet it is as Hede Massing, a one-time recruiter and courier for Soviet intelligence, that she is best known to history.

The problem is that Hede's history was written and often invented by Hede herself, and dissecting the scattered and often contradictory evidence in order to arrive at an approximation of the truth is no easy task. Of necessity spies are intrinsically linked with lies and Hede was a spy and a liar. But so were those who sought to rebut her evidence: namely, her first husband Gerhard Eisler; the Soviet spy Alger Hiss, whom she helped send to jail in 1950; and the former Soviet spies rotting in the bowels of a Hungarian prison, Noel and Herta Field.

With this array of flawed witnesses to the 'truth', it becomes a question of whose accounts appear more credible. Moreover, the FBI's role in the whole affair was hardly above criticism, nor particularly efficient.

Hede comes across as a charming and devious lady, but that was her job. It is hard not to believe that she knew exactly what she was doing when she entitled her very readable, highly unreliable, and ultimately deceitful autobiography as *This Deception* in English, before upgrading it to *The Great Deception* (*Die Grosse Täuschung*) in German. Her memoirs are clearly self-serving, although one must question whether there is in fact any other variety.

As Jeff Kisselhoff reveals, the original work was already co-written in outline in 1949, when Hede was still being interviewed by the FBI. Her marriage to Paul Massing had by then ended in separation, she was now fifty,[3] and a great deal of money was on offer for her story. She also had the opportunity through her book to ingratiate herself not only with the FBI, but also with the American public. After all, in 1947 she had been under threat of denaturalisation and deportation, if not imprisonment, for her own documented perjuries.

But she glimpsed the light, and to save her skin she became an informant. Hede also submitted the manuscript of her book to the FBI before publication, and allowed them to rewrite certain sections. This was in order to remove potentially embarrassing details regarding her relationship to some of its agents. The FBI noted too that there were a number of discrepancies between what she had written and what she had told them in her interviews. Hede cheerfully admitted that she had altered certain facts to 'improve' her tale.

The imprisoned Fields were hardly in a position to contest Hede's 'facts' when her selective memoirs were published early in 1951. Yet their statements and interrogations in Budapest, when both were totally ignorant of outside events, shine a very different light on some of Hede's activities.

'The upper crust'

Hede is usually referred to as Viennese. She may well have been born in Vienna, although she never claims that city as her birthplace in her autobiography.[4] Yet it is quite possible that Hede was born in less cosmopolitan circumstances, as were her parents.

Hede's mother, Rosa, was born about 1875.[5] She was the daughter of a well-off and respected rabbi in the East Galician *shtetl* of Jezierna.[6] When she was seven Rosa's parents died and she moved to Vienna to be with her much older brother, Max, a prosperous businessman.

Seventeen years later Rosa and Max returned to Jezierna to visit their parents' graves, and it was here that Rosa was seemingly bowled over by a farmhand and circus rider named Philip Tune, whom she very soon married, much to her brother's disapproval.[7]

Their first child, Hedwig (Hede), was born on 6 January 1900. Nearly five years later, in the company of her mother, Hede made the first of her transatlantic voyages in order to join her father, who was living on East Houston Street in Manhattan. Sailing from Hamburg on the *Graf Waldersee*, they arrived in New York on 25 November 1904.

They stayed in New York and Massachusetts for three to four years; probably three, since Hede describes certain events in Vienna when she was seven. In the Habsburg capital she attended a Catholic school and even recited a poem before Emperor Franz Josef. She left school at fourteen and worked in a millinery shop. Soon after, mature for her age, 'a tall, slim young woman with reddish-blond hair',[8] she won an acting scholarship, and later became a professional actress.

Hede 'fell into the Bohemian life of the Vienna cafés with great ease', and it was in the *Café Herrenhof* that she met Gerhart Eisler early in 1919. Eisler was 'small, squat and had a slight lisp', which he compensated for with 'very beautiful eyes'.[9]

Born in February 1897 in Leipzig, Eisler too had 'interesting' parents. His father Rudolf (1873–1926) came from a religious and middle-class Czech-Jewish family. Rudolf, an atheist, spent most of his adult life as a philosopher, specialising in Kant. Gerhart's mother, Ida Fischer, was the daughter of a butcher.

Gerhart was an enthusiastic footballer, mountaineer and cook. He wrote poetry and theatrical pieces, but never became the playwright of his mother's dreams. Already a radical at school, he received his *Abitur* in spring 1915. From October 1915 until November 1918, Eisler fought as a much-decorated junior officer on the bloody and mountainous Isonzo front against the Italians. On his return to post-war Vienna, like his sister, Ruth Fischer, Gerhart joined the fledgling Austrian Communist Party.

Hede married Eisler in Vienna in a civil ceremony on 27 June 1921, shortly before they left for Berlin.[10] There Gerhart joined the German

Communist Party, the KPD, and edited the Party's theoretical journal *Die Internationale*. Later he was also editor of *Rote Fahne* (Red Flag), the KPD daily paper. While Eisler wrote, Hede spent a year playing Gwendolen in Oscar Wilde's *The Importance of being Earnest* at the Tribune theatre.

After joining the KPD herself in 1922, Hede split from Eisler the following year. However, Hede never provided a convincing answer about when they divorced, offering four different years. When taxed about her faulty memory in 1949, she replied, 'I wanted to forget this marriage. It's not a marriage I am very happy about'.[11]

Eisler went further and denied that they were ever married at all. When questioned in East Germany in July 1951 about how long they had been married, Gerhart replied that 'I was never married to her. We lived together from 1921 to 1922 and then we split'.[12]

Why should he say this? Certainly, both he and Hede treated their marriage as a formality. However, by 1951 Hede had publicly joined the 'other side', so Eisler had every reason to distance himself from her.

In 1923 Hede met Julian Gumperz. Like her and Gerhart he was Jewish. Born May 1898 in the USA, the son of a German father who had made his fortune there and then returned to Germany, Julian was a well-off left-wing publisher and intellectual. Hede gave up acting and lived with Julian in a house that his mother bought for them.

On 26 August 1926 they arrived in New York aboard *The Leviathan*. Whether they were already married, or whether the wedding took place in the USA, is not clear. However, Hede obtained US citizenship in January 1927, and her American passport the following December. In the process she perjured herself, by swearing under oath that she was not a communist party member.[13]

Julian returned alone to Germany to finish his doctorate at Frankfurt University. Hede followed him there in January 1928. And it was in Frankfurt that she met the man who was to be her third husband, Paul Wilhelm Massing. Separating from Julian, Hede moved to Berlin and from winter 1928 she lived with Massing.

Six foot tall, with brown hair and eyes, Paul was born in Grumbach in rural *Rheinprovinz* in August 1902. He had studied in Frankfurt, Paris and Cologne, and was awarded his doctorate in 1928. Like Hede he was a KPD member, and even in the 1920s he was connected to Soviet intelligence. In 1929 he moved to Moscow to work in the International Agrarian Institute.

Hede remained in Berlin where she came into contact with Richard Sorge, the first of the so-called 'great illegals' she would come to know. He introduced her to another in late 1929, whom Hede claims to have known only as 'Ludwig'. This was Ignace Reiss, who will be discussed further in Chapter 6. Hede's induction into an *apparat* of Soviet intelligence now began.

In 1930 Hede joined Paul in Moscow, where both saw Reiss quite frequently. In spring 1931 they returned to Berlin. While Paul taught at MASCH, the Marxist workers' school, Reiss ordered Hede to drop out of open party work. It was no hardship; as Hede conceded, she 'never faced the reality of everyday work within the movement', since she operated 'only among the upper crust of the Communists'.[14] Now began Hede's covert training as a recruiter. She also worked as a translator for the Münzenberg outfit.[15]

When Hitler was appointed German Chancellor in January 1933, Hede, using her American passport, began escorting Jewish children, and later KPD members, to Czechoslovakia. Meanwhile Paul moved to an 'underground' apartment in the Pankow district of Berlin. In August 1933 Hede was ordered to Moscow. From there she travelled to Paris with funds for the French party.

In Paris she learned of Paul's arrest. Imprisoned and tortured by the Nazis in the notorious Columbia House, a former military prison near to Tempelhof airport, he was then interned in the Nazi concentration camp (KZ) Oranienburg, near Berlin.[16] Hede travelled to Berlin and a young woman comrade conducted her to the camp. She saw a limping Paul among the marching prisoners. 'Nothing but his eyes and his nose were the same', she lamented. 'His mouth was a line, thin and narrow, in his pitiful shorn head'.[17]

She returned to Oranienburg on several occasions, but did not risk direct contact. Having collected Paul's secreted passport from the Pankow apartment, Hede travelled to Saarbrücken and left it with Paul's non-communist brother.[18] Then she returned to Paris in September 1933 and rejoined Reiss, who informed her that she was being sent to the USA.

For the next few evenings she was entertained by another of the 'great illegals', the Hungarian, Teodor Mally, whom Hede knew only as *der Lange*, 'the Long Man'. Mally, who would later oversee the early espionage careers of some of the 'Cambridge Five' in Britain, thought he was being posted to the USA as Hede's superior.[19]

Soon after, Hede sailed aboard the *Deutschland* to the USA, to act as a courier and recruiter for Soviet intelligence. She arrived in New York on 20 October 1933, with the cover of a correspondent for the liberal German paper *Weltbühne*. It proved to be 'the most plausible and easiest cover operation' for her, allowing her to be accepted for years by the 'innocents' among the antifascist literati.[20]

Hede moved in with Helen Black, the Soviet Photo Agency representative; they had met on her last visit to the USA.[21] There she awaited contact. The apparatus that Hede joined was the illegal Soviet *rezidentura* in New York, headed since 1932 by Valentin Markin, whom Hede knew as 'Walter'. When she finally met him, Hede 'disliked him on sight'.[22]

Paul was released by the Nazis on Christmas Day 1933 and Markin allowed Hede to meet him. Naturally, she was required to carry microfilm to Paris as well.[23] She sailed on the *Mauretania* in late December 1933, met Paul in Paris, and returned with him from Le Havre on the *Ile de France*. Paul travelled on a visitor's visa, giving his occupation as 'teacher'. They arrived in New York on Tuesday 30 January 1934. Very soon they would meet the Fields.

'Noel was my main assignment'[24]

In 1933 Noel became friendly with two Washington correspondents of the *Daily Worker*, Marguerite Young and her husband Seymour Waldman. Young was a friend of the CPUSA leader, Earl Browder, and brought the Fields into contact with many like-minded people.

Noel began to pass information to the two journalists, and later he even wrote unsigned articles for their paper. Moreover, with their help, he began to sound out the possibility of illegal membership of the American Communist Party.

It was through Marguerite that Hede met the Fields. She told Hede that extracts from Paul's pending book *Fatherland* had been published in the CPUSA journal *New Masses*, and 'had made a terrific impression on all "good" people in Washington'. The journalist had 'indicated to some of them that she knew the author's wife', and she was able to tell Hede that among those keen to meet her were the Fields.[25]

So Hede went to their home in Washington for this express purpose, since Noel 'was important enough to warrant such a trip'. Their first meeting took place some time in 1934, probably spring. 'We hit it off extremely well', Hede recalled. From the start it was 'an intensive relationship' that became 'so intimate and genuine on both sides, that I did not always know where "business" ended and friendship began'.[26]

Noel and Herta also conceded that the acquaintanceship rapidly developed into a deep friendship.[27] Soon Hede would stay at their flat during her visits to Washington, while from time to time the Fields visited Hede and Paul in New York.

From the outset Hede felt at home in the Field apartment, 'with an atmosphere of home-cooking' about it. She compared it to that of 'a European intellectual'. On the other hand, she was not too struck by the *kleinbürgerlich* (petty-bourgeois) slipcovers, which were 'pale and timid', or the bland style and arrangement of the furniture. Nor was the Wagner emanating from Noel's gramophone to her taste.[28]

However, she had been instructed by Markin to 'develop' Noel, and it was clear that 'Noel was my main assignment'.[29] And only Hede was involved in the initial meetings, for after a few months stay in New York, Paul had left to teach in an Arkansas college, and to finish his book.[30] Noel only met Paul later, and his assessment was that, of the pair, Hede was older in both age and political experience.

From her perspective Hede saw before her two hypochondriacs, 'given to talking a great deal about their physical ills'. Yet they were also a couple who were deeply concerned about Nazi Germany, and generally very well-informed about all important political issues.

Hede discerned that Noel 'had come from a better station in life' than Herta, 'with more money, more tradition, more culture'.[31] Yet he was a 'restless, hypersensitive, fundamentally insecure man'; a full-blown 'neurotic', who was 'worried by politics, by his sex life, by preoccupation with his destiny'. Moreover, 'he shrank from decisions' and had an 'extremely unrealistic' attitude towards life.[32]

She described Field as 'tall, long-limbed, lanky', with 'a mane of soft, slightly wavy brown hair', and–inevitably–'wide, beautiful and intelligent eyes'. Herta was an attractive 'Nordic-looking woman', with a 'full-busted, average figure' and 'goldenspun hair' worn in a low bun. Bright blue and 'enthusiastic' eyes and a fine nose topped a wide mouth with protruding teeth. In conversation, conducted in fluent English 'with just a seasoning of German accent', Herta was prone to utilise 'her charming, slender hands' for emphasis.[33]

At the outset of their relationship the Fields knew the Massings solely as German communists, who played an important role in firming up their woolly convictions. Only in the autumn of 1934 did the Massings disclose that they were Soviet agents, and that for Noel, as a State Department official, there was only one way to serve the USSR. Unsurprisingly, their proposal that Field should spy for that country stimulated the usual inner conflict.

Although as an American he was prepared to do secret work for the CPUSA, Noel had reservations about working for a foreign state, even if it was the Soviet Union. Both he and Herta realised that they were not sufficiently advanced in their convictions to undertake this leap at once. It was only after much discussion between themselves, all the while prodded by the Massings working in tandem, that they conceded.[34]

So around the beginning of 1935 Noel and Herta finally agreed to 'work' for Moscow.[35] Noel now perceived it as 'an honourable duty' (*ein ehrenvoller Auftrag*),[36] which, in the great ideological scheme of things, entailed no treason against his compatriots.[37]

However, one of the first instructions the Fields received was a severe blow to Noel, at least. The Massings told them that there could be no question of their joining the CPUSA. Instead, Field had to break off all party contacts, particularly those with Marguerite Young, and give the impression that he had defected from the cause.[38]

Besides working on the Fields and making fresh contacts, Hede continued to function as an NKVD courier to Europe.[39] She also appears to have married Paul at some point in 1934.[40]

That September Hede was in Paris, enjoying the attention of Reiss and Mally, when she learned that Markin had been killed in New York in suspicious circumstances.[41] She hoped that Mally would replace him. Instead, at the end of 1934 she got Iskhak Abdulovich Akhmerov, whom she knew as 'Bill'. Once more Hede poured out her scorn upon the intellect, looks and abilities of her new chief, yet her assessment of his talents as an operative would seem to be wide of the mark.[42]

'I gave him lots'[43]

Although Hede implies that Noel only made verbal reports to her and Paul, this is blatantly untrue. Noel admitted that not only did he supply verbal and written information to the Massings, but he sometimes passed over copies of documents as well.[44]

In statements made while imprisoned in Budapest, Herta specified that Noel systematically provided the Massings with any information that he judged to be of interest to the USSR. His sources were his own work, plus reports and documents which crossed his desk, such as those circulating in the West European division. In addition he could also borrow from the registry documents which had no direct bearing on his own work. Further sources were conversations he held with officials of both his own and other governmental departments.

Noel's method was to prepare shorthand notes of conversations, and to copy in whole or in part reports and documents. These he read to Paul when they met. Sometimes Herta got this job, operating under Field's instructions. Noel used the German *Stolze-Schrey* shorthand system which he had adapted to English. Different systems were used in the USA and so Herta contended that even a trained stenographer would be unable to read these notes.

Field was known for his assiduity at work. He invariably kept on going long after office hours had ended. By staying once others had left, he had the opportunity to copy what interested him in peace. In his time at the State Department, Noel recalled, there was an incredible carelessness in handling state secrets.[45]

Herta could not recollect any particular document which Noel had passed to Paul. However, in Geneva in December 1948, she read about the extensive hoard that Whittaker Chambers alleged that he had received from Alger Hiss, the so-called 'Pumpkin Papers'. She asked her husband then if he had passed a similar amount to Paul. Field replied, 'I gave him lots' (*Ich habe ihm eine Menge gegeben*).[46]

The difficulty with this account is that, according to Hede, Paul Massing left the USA for Europe 'to fight fascism' in March 1935.[47] There he joined the *apparat* that Reiss ran in Paris.

This leaves a gap from March 1935 until late November, when Noel sailed to Britain, when the two men were not in contact. Moreover, Hede too was not in the USA from July to October 1935. Therefore, for several months Noel was not passing any information at all, since he only dealt with the Massings. Of course this does not preclude the possibility that he was storing up material to be handed over later.

However, when it came to working abroad the picture is somewhat clearer. Noel, but not Herta, attended the final London naval conference, which ran from 9 December 1935 until 25 March 1936. During its sessions Paul came over to London from Paris several times to collect reports and documents. In addition Noel spent Christmas 1935 with

Paul in the Swiss ski-resort Arosa, where he wrote a detailed report on the conference for Massing.

Field had already resigned from the State Department when this conference took place. However, the US delegation leader, Norman Davis, wanted Noel in London.

Noel claimed that quitting his job was something that he had been thinking of doing since 1934. But when he was offered a post in the disarmament section of the League of Nations secretariat in 1935, typically he prevaricated for several months.

He discussed the matter with his colleagues and head of division. The latter made it clear that if Noel transferred to the sinking ship at Geneva, there was no way back for him into the State Department.[48] He was even offered a rise, if he stayed, from the $4,600 he had been earning for the last three years to $5,600. However, the suggestion that he was offered the German 'desk' to keep him in Washington seems unlikely.[49]

Late in 1935 Noel decided to take up the League post. He listed several reasons for leaving the State Department. He claimed that he had never intended a permanent career there, while both he and Herta hated the social obligations in Washington. In addition, he was ill from overwork and losing interest in the job. On the other hand, the new post was enticing in material terms and it would allow him to return to his first home.

Yet Noel had to admit that the main reason for his decision was the double life that he now led. It tore him apart and made him deeply unhappy.[50] Feeling compelled to seek another position in which the concept of loyalty mattered less, he plumped for the League secretariat, since he could not muster the slightest degree of loyalty to that body.

He had spoken with the Massings about leaving the State Department. Initially they pressed him to stay, although they had not irrevocably countered his decision.[51] After the incidents described in the next chapter though, Soviet intelligence was happy to see Noel depart for Europe.

Sailing from Southampton on the *Manhattan*, Noel arrived back in New York from the London naval conference on Thursday 19 March 1936. His contract with the State Department ended in April and he was expected to start work in Geneva on 1 May. However, there was still time for him to rock the boat before he left.

5

'WORKING FOR THE SAME BOSS'

HISS, HEDE AND NOEL, 1935–36

INO and GRU[1]

The first Soviet state security agency, known as the Cheka, was established on 20 December 1917, a few weeks after the Bolsheviks seized power in the October Revolution. In 1922–23 it was renamed the GPU, and then the OGPU.[2] From July 1934 until April 1943 (save for a few months in 1941) these secret police functions were reincorporated in the NKVD (People's Commissariat for Internal Affairs) as the GUGB (Main Administration for State Security). From 1920 until 1941 all of these agencies were served in the field of foreign intelligence by a single body, INO (the Foreign Department).[3]

Individuals mentioned in the previous chapter, the Massings, Reiss, Markin, Akhmerov, Mally, all worked as 'illegals' for INO. However, Richard Sorge was an agent of the Fourth Directorate of the Red Army general staff. Later the Fourth Directorate became the GRU (Chief Intelligence Directorate).[4] This body collected its own foreign intelligence, although for the brief period running from April 1937 to November 1938 military intelligence was subordinated to the NKVD.

Both INO and the GRU operated 'legally' and 'illegally', and often at both levels in the same country. The legal *rezidentura* (residency) was usually established in Soviet embassies, consulates or trade bodies, and had the advantages for its personnel of regular communications and diplomatic immunity. The 'illegals' could face prison or expulsion, but they had fewer problems with visibility; they could travel and integrate behind false passports and assumed identities.

Until the mid-thirties the majority of intelligence professionals and illegal operatives were non-Russian. They included a high proportion of what I shall call 'internationalist' (non-religious) Jews, as well as Poles and Balts, all of whom offered levels of culture and linguistic ability lacking in the proletariat and peasantry of the USSR. In many cases these individuals also maintained a more intense and longer-held belief in the mission to build a better world, which had first impelled them into the communist movement.

Some of these factors feature in the lives of the five communist agents (the Massings, Reiss, Krivitsky and Hiss), who had a crucial impact on Noel Field's career as communist and spy.

The remainder of this chapter introduces Alger Hiss, who was an agent of the GRU, and discusses the contest between him and Hede Massing to obtain the allegiance of Noel to their respective illegal *apparats*.

'The epitome of success'[5]

The fourth of five children, Alger Hiss was born in Baltimore, Maryland on 11 November 1904. His family suffered several tragedies. In 1907 his father committed suicide. In later years a sister would take her own life too, while Alger's elder brother effectively killed himself through a hedonistic lifestyle.

One of his contemporaries depicted Hiss as 'the child of shabby gentility'.[6] Growing up in straitened circumstances, he was obedient to a domineering mother and her strict moral code. He attended the Episcopalian church and Sunday school, and was a Boy Scout.

Hiss progressed through the Baltimore state school system, and entered Johns Hopkins University in 1922, the same year that Noel began at Harvard. Like Noel, during his university years Hiss lived at home for financial reasons. Unlike Field, Hiss was gregarious. At university he was editor of the college newspaper, president of the student council, and a member of the Reserve Officers Training Corps. Intelligent, popular, handsome, the college yearbook exalted him as 'the epitome of success'.[7]

Hiss graduated in 1926 and entered Harvard Law School where he was prominent both socially and academically. A friend recalled that he 'gave you a sense of absolute command and absolute grace'.[8] During these years, Hiss, like Noel, was involved in the campaign to save Sacco and Vanzetti. Unlike Noel, he never revealed its impact upon his thinking. Therefore it is only conjecture that this was a factor in his radicalisation.

After completing his Harvard studies in June 1929, he travelled with his younger brother Donald to France. Donald became ill, so they abandoned any thoughts of a 'grand tour' and relocated to Giverney in Normandy. There, in the village containing Claude Monet's house and famous garden, Hiss wrote that they settled into 'a charming but plumbingless little inn […] and swam and tennissed and read prodigiously'.[9]

In October 1929 Hiss became law clerk to Supreme Court Justice Oliver Wendell Holmes. Born in 1841 and wounded three times in the American Civil War, Holmes retained both a zest for life and great intellectual vitality. Hiss's legal duties were not overly arduous, but he was also expected to play the role of intellectual 'companion' to the judge.

Hiss fulfilled this function excellently. However, he had another relationship to consider too. For in December 1929, much against his mother's wishes, he married Priscilla Fansler, the divorced daughter of a Philadelphia insurance executive. A year older than him, educated and independent, she had first met Alger in 1924 but had spurned his interest in her then. She married instead a wealthy Yale graduate called Thayer Hobson in 1925. Soon after the birth of their son Timothy the Hobsons separated, and they divorced in January 1929. By then Priscilla was working at the new weekly magazine *Time* in New York, and had also completed a postgraduate degree in literature at Columbia University. When she and Hiss met again in 1929, Priscilla was involved with a married man by whom she became pregnant. She had an abortion after he returned to his wife.

Hiss was a decent catch. He had a prestigious job, grossing $3,600 a year, which paid for a Washington apartment. Unlike Noel, he could employ a cook and a maid. His year with Holmes only improved his marketability. He was tall, slim and very good-looking. He was also sexually inexperienced, possibly still a virgin. 'Promiscuity has always seemed to me a sign of confusion' he would later tell his son Tony.[10]

After marrying Priscilla, at her behest Hiss abandoned his plans to return to Baltimore and practice law. Instead, from October 1930 until spring 1932 he worked for a Boston law firm, until Priscilla had him moving again to New York.

Priscilla joined the Socialist Party in 1930, and her views, combined with the breadlines and soup-kitchens of Depression-hit New York, probably catalysed Hiss's radicalisation. Like many of his contemporaries, he discovered that his 'social and political values were tested and altered by the Great Depression'. Its 'vast misery' forced 'my sense of social responsibility to become more concrete'.[11]

With the inauguration of President Franklin Roosevelt in March 1933 and the onset of what came to be known as the New Deal, Hiss moved to Washington that same month. He joined the Agricultural Adjustment Administration (AAA), a new body established within the Department of Agriculture.

Within the AAA the so-called 'Ware Group' formed, consisting mainly of underground CPUSA members. Hiss was a member of the group and a dues-paying member of the Party. But in the summer of 1934 Hiss was separated from the group to become the charter-member of a new illegal *apparat* of Soviet military intelligence, whose courier was Whittaker Chambers, Alger's future nemesis.

In July 1934 Hiss was 'lent' by the AAA to the Nye Committee, a congressional committee investigating profiteering by the munitions industry during the First World War. This body could summon documents from government departments, all of which would pass through the hands of the committee's chief counsel, the Soviet spy, Alger Hiss.

'The unforgivable indiscretion'[12]

Introduced by a mutual acquaintance, Noel first met Hiss in early 1934 when Hiss was working for the 'Triple A'. Their shared left-wing views and educational background soon forged a close friendship, which Herta Field and Priscilla Hiss came to share. Through their conversations it became clear to Hiss and Noel that they were both communists.[13]

At least twice Hiss made determined approaches to Noel regarding espionage. There may have been other occasions.[14] The first approach probably occurred in November 1935 and the second in April 1936. To my mind the imbroglio between Noel, Hiss and Hede can only be understood if we accept that there were two known occasions when Hiss pressurised Field, and not by trying to fit the evidence into a solitary event.[15]

Paul Massing left the USA for Europe in March 1935. Late in July, carrying microfilm and cash, Hede followed. She holidayed in Montreux with Paul and Reiss,[16] and returned to New York from Boulogne on 13 October 1935.

On her return, Field informed Hede that he was being pressurised by a government colleague and friend to join another intelligence organisation. She asked for the name of the interloper. When Noel told her, Hede said she wanted to meet Hiss. Some days later Noel notified her that she could meet Hiss at the Fields' apartment for dinner.

Hede took the idea to her new boss, Boris Bazarov, who had assumed control from Akhmerov in May 1935, and would prove to be the only Soviet official whom Hede would rate as other than a cold *apparatchik*.[17] After some hesitation, since he was reluctant to become involved in a likely jurisdictional squabble, Bazarov assented.[18]

'A week or so later I did meet Hiss', related Hede. 'It was in the fall of 1935'. In fact, it had to be in the period late October to late November; that is, from some time after Hede's return from Europe to Noel leaving for the last London naval conference. Following dinner, 'standing by a window in the Field apartment, Hiss and I had the brief but decisive talk that later figured in the (second) trial' of Hiss in 1949:

I understand that you are trying to get Noel Field away from my organization into yours.' Alger grinned and countered with, 'So you are this famous girl who is trying to get Noel Field away from me.' And I said: 'Yes.' And he said, as far as I remember: 'Well, we will see who is going to win.' To which I replied: 'You realize that you are competing with a woman, and women generally win in such situations.' At which either he or I said—the gist of the sentence was—'Whoever is going to win, we are working for the same boss.[19]

When she reported this meeting to Bazarov he ordered her to provide a full account in writing that same day.[20] This went to Moscow Centre, which issued a directive that Hiss was 'the neighbor's (i.e. the GRU's) man and that it is necessary to stay away from him'.[21] Some time later Bazarov instructed Hede to completely forget about Hiss. 'Don't mention him ever! Don't speak about him to Noel or to Herta or to Paul. Never see him again'.[22]

Hede understood that there had been a reprimand and some emphatic orders. She had met a member of another *apparat*, and had disclosed that she was in a parallel body.[23] However, neither she nor any of her colleagues met with Hiss again.

As Akhmerov informed Moscow on 18 May 1936, Hede met Hiss 'on only one occasion during the entire time of her stay in this country, in the winter'. And after being told that Hiss was with the GRU 'we did not meet with him'. In this letter Akhmerov specifies that the Hede-Hiss meeting took place at Noel's apartment.[24] Conversely, both Field and Hiss always denied that a meeting of Hiss and Hede ever took place, let alone in Noel's flat.

However, Hiss did impact upon Hede's activities once more, after she came back from another trip to Europe on 18 February 1936. Following Noel's own return from London on 19 March, Hiss contacted Field. Noel informed Hede about this. So she in turn was obliged to report upon these events, which she did in a note that was appended to a communication sent to Moscow on 26 April 1936. In it Hede used Alger Hiss's full name, because she did not know his GRU code-name.[25]

Hede informed her superiors that on the day before he sailed to Europe to take up his League post, Noel told her about the second incident involving Hiss, which had occurred about a week previously.

'Alger let him know that he was a Communist, that he has ties with an organization working for the Soviet Union'. He knew that Noel had 'ties as well', but he feared that they were insufficiently robust, and that 'his knowledge was probably being misused'.

Hiss 'bluntly proposed' that Noel should give him an account of the London conference. Because they were 'close friends', Field did not refuse to discuss the topic, but he told Hiss that he had already delivered his report.[26] When Hiss insisted upon receiving a report himself, Noel replied that he 'would have to contact his "connections" and ask their advice'.

However, within a day Hiss dropped this request, but asked Noel to put him in contact with the Duggans, which Noel did, much to the dismay of the vacillating Larry Duggan. In the process, of course, Noel revealed to the Duggans that both he and Hiss were Soviet agents.[27]

When Hede pointed out to Noel 'what a terrible lack of discipline he had shown', and the way he had endangered the whole enterprise by linking himself, Hiss and Duggan, 'he acted as if he did not understand'. He thought that because Hiss 'had been the first to show his cards' he had no reason 'to keep everything secret'. And why not put Duggan and Hiss in contact? Since Hiss lived in Washington, he could meet with Duggan more frequently than the New York-based Hede, who was in any case soon off to Europe for a while.

Noel's version is that he had thoughtlessly committed 'the unforgive-able indiscretion' of revealing to Hiss that he already worked for Soviet intelligence. At least he did not mention his connection with the Massings.[28] Noel immediately reported the approach to Hede, who gave him a severe dressing-down, saying that she had no idea what her superiors would say. Some time later (possibly in Europe), she informed Noel that he had caused serious problems and had made it necessary to reorganise the entire illegal *apparat*.[29]

Although Noel dates his account as summer or autumn 1935 and not 1936,[30] the dressing-down that he admits he received would seem to confirm Hede's reaction in 1936. The 1936 date is also implicit in the subject of the demand from Hiss: a report on the London conference which had only ended in March 1936. It is confirmed too by Hiss specifically asking Noel who would be his successor.

Neither Hede in her autobiography, nor Noel in his prison statements refers explicitly to the April 1936 encounter; our knowledge of it comes from Vassiliev's notebooks. Noel's account, written in prison, may have conflated the two incidents with Hiss into one simply from confusion. Or should we see calculation by both Hede and Field? Perhaps they both exhibited perfectly sound and selfish reasons for ignoring the events of April 1936.

Hede withheld or distorted details of her espionage career when inter-viewed by the FBI in 1947–49. Giving them the meeting with Hiss in Noel's flat was crucial to her. It corroborated the charges made by Whit-taker Chambers against Hiss, which the Justice Department required. Producing this evidence was enough to save Hede from any charges against herself. So why provide further detail that might be investigated and challenged? She was having enough trouble wriggling around questions about her marriages.

As for Noel, he could provide information to his Hungarian inter-rogators on his relationship with Hiss. Alger had already been charged with perjury in December 1948, before Field's own kidnapping and incarceration in May 1949. What he may have been reluctant to expose was the fact that he had revealed his agent status to his closest friend Larry Duggan in April 1936.

Duggan plunged to his death from the sixteenth storey of his Manhattan office on 20 December 1948, shortly after being interviewed by the FBI in the preparatory phase of the Hiss-Chambers affair. To this day it remains a moot question whether he jumped or was pushed. And as we shall see, Noel had direct experience of the NKVD assassination of Reiss. Conceivably, Noel believed that the Soviets had murdered Duggan, a man who might reveal secrets about Soviet intelligence in the USA.

In the circumstances Noel may have thought it prudent to distance himself from Duggan, whom he describes as too underdeveloped ideologically to have become a communist or a spy.[31] On the other hand, the illegal New York *rezidentura* believed that Noel was unaware that Duggan did 'steady work for us'.[32]

Hede's note also contains the elliptical line that Hiss asked Noel 'to help him in getting into the State Department', which Field 'apparently did'.[33] However, it remains impossible to do more than speculate about how Noel achieved this, if in fact he did.

Since August 1935 Alger had worked in the solicitor general's office. Yet in September 1936 he joined the State Department, where he was employed in the office of assistant secretary of state, Francis B. Sayre. Sayre had taught Hiss at Harvard, and Noel as another Harvard man may have intimated Alger's interest in joining State. Hiss received confirmation of his appointment to the State Department from Sayre in May 1936.

Hiss didn't seek a job at the State Department for financial reasons, since he saw his annual salary drop from $7,500 to $5,600 with the transfer;[34] however, this new posting profited him as a spy.

It was probably with a sense of relief that Moscow noted on 3 May 1936 that Noel had departed for Switzerland, since 'this isolates him to a certain extent', and Hiss 'will gradually forget about him'. The exodus was completed when that 'impetuous' lady, 'Redhead [Hede's codename], who is ill-suited to handle either an agent or even herself',[35] left for Europe at the end of June.

However, Noel's unfortunate experiences in the world of espionage were by no means at an end once he moved to Switzerland. After a tranquil beginning his career as a spy would be marked not by mere bumbling, but by the twin disasters of death and defection.

6

MURDER AND DEFECTION

THE FIELDS, REISS AND KRIVITSKY, 1936–37

'An absolute solution'[1]

Initially at least, the communist movements of Russia and parts of Eastern Europe contained a highly visible Jewish presence, although these Jewish communists never represented more than a minority of local Jews. Their presence was in part a consequence of the treatment of Jews in the areas where they had been most numerous, namely the Russian and Habsburg empires. In the late eighteenth century, these two entities–along with Prussia–had partitioned the Polish-Lithuanian state, and together absorbed most of its substantial Jewish population.

The Polish Jews annexed by the Habsburg wing of the Austro-Hungarian Empire were concentrated in the province of Galicia (now southern Poland and Western Ukraine). However, unlike the Jews in the Tsarist 'Pale of Settlement',[2] these Austrian subjects had at least enjoyed full civil rights since 1867, and had been spared the pogrom for the most part.[3]

Poverty, not the pogrom, encouraged emigration. Some 350,000 Jews left Galicia in the years 1881–1914. Yet, despite this and the even greater exodus from 'the Pale', in 1914 there were still 5.5 million Jews in Russia and 2.5 million in the Habsburg Empire. In effect their natural population increase had merely been transferred elsewhere, with over 2 million immigrating into the USA and creating there a mass urban Jewry.[4]

Of those remaining behind in Europe, significant minorities channelled their political frustrations into various strands of Zionism, the Bund, the Social Revolutionaries, and the Menshevik and Bolshevik wings of the Russian Social Democratic and Labour Party.

While racially Jewish, those joining revolutionary organisations were not religious Jews. They had consciously abandoned the world of the *shtetl* and the side-lock for the creed of 'internationalism', in the belief that this would liberate them from the prejudices that had determined and limited their lives.

Thus, for Walter Krivitsky the October revolution offered 'an absolute solution to all problems of poverty, inequality and justice', and he joined the Bolsheviks with his 'whole soul'. Marxism-Leninism was for him 'a weapon with which to assault the wrongs against which I had instinctively rebelled'.[5]

Krivitsky was born Samuel Gersevich Ginsberg on 1 January 1899, the very same day as his lifelong friend and comrade, Nathan Markovich Poretsky, who would enter history as Ignace Reiss.[6] The two men would later count among the 'great illegals' of Soviet intelligence.

Both were born in the small town and customs post of Podwołoczyska, which lay on the western bank of the River Zbruch, the frontier between Galicia and Tsarist Russia.[7] At that time the population of Podwołoczyska was less than three thousand, of whom over half were Jews.

Krivitsky and Reiss were both sons of minor merchants. Both were brought up by widowed mothers. Both were in the same socialist youth group in Vienna during the First World War. Both were well-educated and multilingual.[8] Both began their clandestine careers in the Comintern, operating in post-war Austria, and later (on the Soviet side) as saboteurs in Poland during the Russo-Polish war.[9] Both became Soviet citizens.

Once their operations were taken over by military intelligence, Reiss and Krivitsky became officers of the GRU. In 1931 they were transferred to INO, although Krivitsky, following his defection in 1937, would falsely claim to have resisted transfer and still be working for the GRU rather than the NKVD.

Between them Reiss and Krivitsky undertook or headed illegal operations in Germany, France, the Netherlands, Austria, Czechoslovakia and Switzerland. They also underwent periods of desk-work in an increasingly oppressive Moscow. By the time that Noel and Herta were recruited in early 1935, Krivitsky was in Moscow, following a spell of imprisonment in Austria, while Reiss was the illegal *rezident* in Switzerland, although he maintained a base of operations in Paris.

A chain-smoking teetotaller, Krivitsky was slight of build and about five-foot-five-inches tall. Pale-faced and red-haired, his deep blue eyes were crowned by bushy brows, giving him 'a stern look which contrasted sharply with his childish smile'. The dark-haired Reiss was also small, but stout, with shrewd azure eyes and 'an infectious smile'.[10]

It is unlikely that either man was smiling overmuch in the summer of 1936, shortly before they met the Fields. Both were disturbed by events in the USSR, where the purges which would lead to the blood-letting of 'the Great Terror' had begun, with Poles and Jews being especially targeted.[11]

Reiss and his wife were on a short holiday in Czechoslovakia with their 'close friend of long standing', Paul Massing, when the Zinoviev show trial opened on 19 August 1936.[12] Eleven of the sixteen defendants were Jewish, and five of these were INO operatives. When the trial ended on 24 August all sixteen were sentenced to death and shot.

Reiss contacted Krivitsky and the two men met in Paris. Reiss wanted to break with Stalin in protest against the execution of the 'old Bolsheviks'. Krivitsky countered that 'a victorious revolution in Spain', where the Civil War had just begun, 'would save the remnants of the October revolution in Russia and would sweep Stalin away'. In any case, he argued, where could they defect; neither Western intelligence nor Trotsky were options.[13]

Family affairs[14]

In Geneva the newly-arrived Fields had no such cares. 'From a bourgeois standpoint', recalled Noel in his proletarian cell in Budapest, 'it was the most agreeable time of our lives'.[15]

Noel had begun work in the Disarmament Section of the League of Nations Secretariat on 4 May 1936.[16] He had a contract for five years and the title 'member of section', which he deemed roughly equivalent to that of 'drafting officer'. The annual remuneration of 24,000 Swiss francs was about what he would have earned had he remained in the State Department at the enhanced salary offered him. It was considerably more than what he had been earning though, and it went further because of the lower cost of living.

His income allowed him to rent a spacious chalet named *La Chotte* in the village of Vandoeuvres, which lay a few kilometres outside of Geneva. The Fields could afford two cars and, for the first time, a maid. They travelled extensively, especially Herta, who paid several visits both to her mother in Karlsruhe and to Stuttgart, a city she liked very much. In their spare time the Fields became engrossed in their vegetable garden. They read extensively, attended lectures, and listened to music.

Politically, Noel's work was of little interest either to himself or Moscow. In any case, as members of the League the Soviets had their own resources in Geneva. Moreover, a feeling of decline permeated the entire organisation following events in Manchuria, the Rhineland and Abyssinia, and any work conducted was of a *pro forma* nature.

Noel was involved with the Montreux Conference of June–July 1936, which amended the 1923 convention on the Turkish straits. Loaned to the Mandates Commission, he worked on the Palestine issue. He also dealt with the arms trade and, although hopes for disarmament were long-dead, the League still concentrated on it.

Noel also saw something of his mother, his brother Hermann and his sister-in-law Jean, and, through Paul Massing, he began to involve them in 'fighting for the cause'.

In Hermann's view, it was not until the death of her husband in 1921 that Nina Field became 'a person in her own right'. She adhered to Herbert's Quaker tradition of social concern, albeit with a tendency 'to respond straight from the heart'. Later, Hermann reflected that perhaps her activism was partially inspired 'by a deep inner need to share in her children's aspirations' for the 'better world' that their father had fought for.[17]

In Massachusetts Nina worked on behalf of the underprivileged. She involved herself with striking workers, risking the Field home as surety to bail those arrested on the picket-lines. She was also an activist for the rights of women and blacks and she joined in the protests against the executions of Sacco and Vanzetti.

Whereas Hermann proceeded through the state school system in Cambridge, his younger sister and confidante, Letty, enjoyed a 'progressive' private education at Shady Hill School. Later she attended Cambridge High and Latin School. And it was during her senior year, while Hermann was at Harvard, that Letty became critically ill and died from a botched operation at the age of seventeen.[18]

It was through Letty that Hermann met his first wife Jean Ainslee Clark. Born in 1912, Jean was the daughter of a Boston newspaperman, whose children attended the same school as Letty. Later she studied at the leading women's institution, Vassar College in Poughkeepsie, New York. She and Hermann married in 1932 when both were still students.

Artistically inclined like his late uncle, Hamilton Easter Field, Hermann graduated in architectural studies from Harvard in 1933. The following year he and Jean travelled on separate postgraduate scholarships to Zurich; Hermann to study architecture at the polytechnic and Jean to pursue a doctorate in philology at the university.

On their way there, they sailed to Leningrad in summer 1934 and attended a seminar on city planning at Moscow University. Following this they worked as agricultural labourers on a *Sovkhoz* (state farm) near Saratov in the Volga German republic. They were in the USSR for about three months.

At Noel's suggestion they were contacted in Zurich by Paul Massing, following his return to Europe in March 1935. As a result Jean came to London as a courier on Paul's behalf, in order to collect reports from Noel during the 1935–36 naval conference. Paul stayed in contact with Jean in particular, and used her as a courier on at least four occasions, once sending her to a Soviet source in Berlin.

Nina also acted for Massing as a courier to Nazi Germany. Hede Massing met her in 1935. She described Nina as 'a lean, tall, dignified, gray-haired Quaker lady', who was very well-off. When Hede spoke about the rise of Nazism and Paul's experiences, she responded immediately with an offer to help in any way she could, which Paul took up.[19]

Nina had originally come to visit Hermann in 1935 or early 1936, before sailing back to the USA from Hamburg with Herta's four-year-old niece, Ancy. They arrived in Baltimore on 2 April 1936, about a fortnight after Noel had returned from the last London naval conference.[20]

However, Nina must have left for Europe again, probably soon after delivering Ancy. There is a very clear picture in Hede's autobiography of the Fields, the Massings and Nina driving on a long trip through France and Switzerland.[21] No date is given for this event, but it can only have been between July and late October 1936, the period when Hede was in Europe.[22] Moreover, Noel suggests that his mother served Paul Massing as a courier only after he and Herta had moved to Geneva in May 1936.[23] It seems that Nina stayed on in Europe and visited the USSR in 1937 before returning to the USA.[24]

Did all this mean that the entire Field family were communists? Noel, the trail-blazer (*Bahnbrecher*) liked to think so, but most of the connections were tenuous. Hermann was never a party member, although at this juncture he might as well have been. Nina returned from her trip to the USSR as a communist, according to Noel. However, it is hard to envisage her hewing constantly to any party line. Jean was probably a member of the Swiss party, like her second husband Sali Liebermann. According to Noel, his sister Elsie, who also knew the Massings in the States, was in the CPUSA, but she let her membership lapse during the war.[25]

'Der Dicke'[26]

Before Noel left the USA in April 1936, Hede had told him that he would be contacted either by herself or Paul in Switzerland. But initially he saw nothing of the Massings. Noel thought wrongly that Paul had gone back to the USA and had then travelled with Hede to Europe. However, Paul had remained with Reiss's *apparat* in Paris, while Hede travelled to Europe in July 1936 for her three month vacation.

Hede stated that Paul had met the Fields a few times in Geneva. 'I, too, went to visit them on one of my many trips abroad. I really had no business dealings with them any more. They were incorporated in the European apparatus'; as of course was Hede. 'I never asked Paul for whom they worked', then again she hardly needed to.[27]

According to Noel, the Massings suddenly appeared in autumn 1936 and remained in contact with Noel and Herta, as well as Hermann and Jean, for several months. Noel wrote later that in his view Paul and Hede showed no political weaknesses at this time, for 'given our close friendship I would certainly have noticed'.[28]

This friendship meant that the Fields had no problem in working with them again. And although little of political interest emanated from the League, Noel made reports about colleagues working there, as well as about the staff of the American consulate in Geneva. Beyond this we encounter contradictory accounts of who met whom and when.

Noel places all of his meetings with Reiss and Krivitsky in 1937. But if the Massings were present, then at least the initial meetings must have occurred in 1936, because Hede arrived back in New York on 2 November 1936 and Paul on 5 January 1937. Moreover, Herta, who seems much more reliable on certain details than Noel, thought that the first meeting with Reiss took place in 1936.

Hede had met with Reiss as soon as she arrived in Paris. But it was only after the carefree car journey to France that Reiss asked to be introduced to the Fields. Noel says that he came into contact with Reiss through Paul, although Hede's account suggests that she was also present when Reiss met the Fields. Moreover, Reiss's wife Elsa was there too, although neither the Fields nor Hede mention her presence, nor that they all went to the cinema that day.[29]

Noel recalled that the Massings said that this unnamed visitor was their boss, and that they were handing the Fields over to his jurisdiction, because they were being recalled to Moscow. They did not identify Reiss to the Fields, not even as 'Ludwig'. So Noel christened him 'Fatty' ('*der Dicke*') on account of his corpulence. Noel thought that this meeting was very short, and he could not remember what they spoke about.

However, there were certainly impressions on both sides. 'The meeting of these three people fell flat completely', recalled Hede. Reiss viewed the Fields as 'neurotic weaklings', and they thought him 'a Philistine'. Paul reported that Noel 'did not take a personal liking' to Reiss.[30]

Hede claims not to know if they ever met again, although she made arrangements for Reiss to contact the Fields if he needed to. However, Reiss did meet with Noel on at least one more occasion after the Massings' departure.

Noel could not date this encounter, but he said that it had no official character, and they did not talk about important matters. Reiss was simply passing through Geneva, and he left the next day. His interrogator inquired archly and pertinently whether it was normal for a case officer to spend the night with a contact. Herta claimed to have no knowledge of this second meeting, although one wonders how she could have missed his presence if Reiss stayed overnight.

In her memoirs Hede wrote that she 'assumed' that Reiss suggested the Fields as co-workers for Krivitsky.[31] However, this was Hede covering her tracks, since it was the Massings who brought Krivitsky to the Fields' chalet and introduced them. They explained again that since they were going to Moscow, Krivitsky would be Noel's chief contact from now on. And before the meeting the Massings gave Noel a brief description of

Krivitsky's status: that he was a Soviet citizen, who had fought as a partisan in the Russian civil war, and that he held the rank of general.[32]

Yet again Noel could not remember in detail what he and Krivitsky spoke about, other than arranging procedures for future contact. In fact, there would be only one more meeting between them. But this was seismic.

'Reiss has been liquidated'[33]

Reiss broke openly with Stalin on 17 July 1937 in the letter he addressed to the Central Committee of the CPSU. 'I intend to devote my feeble forces to the cause of Lenin', he proclaimed. 'I want to continue the fight, for only our victory–that of the proletarian revolution–will free humanity of capitalism and the USSR of Stalinism'.[34]

Such conduct at the height of the Stalinist purges was courageous. However, Reiss's plans were executed in a careless or perhaps fatalistic fashion. He was already under suspicion, and the NKVD's mobile-squads of killers were gathering in Paris to deal with Stalin's enemies on both the right and the left. On 18 July, under his cover-name of Hans Eberhard, a Czech businessman, Reiss left the French capital for Switzerland.

In New York, Akhmerov called on the Massings constantly, in case they had received letters from Reiss. At the end of July they did, in the form of a copy of his missive to Moscow, plus a personal letter warning his friends that they might thereby become involved in the 'Reiss affair'.

Hede claims to have sympathised with Reiss's deed. However, it seems equally clear that both she and Paul helped Akhmerov, who by now had superseded Bazarov in New York.[35] His natural concern was that Reiss might betray the illegal *apparat* in the USA.[36]

There was also anxiety about what would happen if Reiss turned to Noel. Paul's view was that if Reiss tried to recruit him again, Noel 'would fear for his fate and would prefer to sever ties' with both the Massings and Reiss.

Akhmerov therefore suggested to Moscow on 15 August that it would be 'exceedingly valuable if you renewed your connection' with Field, and 'worked him over both politically and professionally'. In this way it might be possible both to retain Noel as an agent, and also establish a connection between him and Reiss, should the latter turn to Field.[37]

It would appear that this advice was heeded. One day, possibly in late August, the Fields were at home with guests when Noel was summoned by telephone to a *Treff*. The caller was Krivitsky, who had travelled from Paris to Geneva.[38] Krivitsky told Noel that they had to drive to Paris that night. Herta recalled how disagreeable it was, having to explain Noel's sudden departure to her visitors.

What was so important? According to Noel, Krivitsky told him that Reiss had turned traitor and, given his importance in the NKVD, they would have to take preventive measures. On reaching Paris they called into a café, where Krivitsky introduced him to a man whom Noel and Herta only ever knew as 'the man with the Order of Lenin'. Krivitsky then disappeared, and the stranger told Noel that he must have nothing further to do with him.

The man facing Noel was Sergei Mikhailovich Shpigelglas.[39] Born Solomon Moseiovich Shpigelglas in today's Belarus in 1897, he was deputy director of INO, and had arrived in Paris in June 1937 to oversee the investigation of Reiss. He was now arranging his murder. He told Noel that the Reiss defection was the worst case of treachery in the history of the USSR, since Reiss could jeopardise dozens of agents. Therefore the duty of every comrade was to help liquidate him.

Noel agreed. He knew that Reiss was important, although he had no knowledge of his exact role. Nor did he have any idea then of the reasons for Reiss's 'treachery'. He simply assented to Stalinist orders.

Shpigelglas instructed Field to return to Switzerland in the company of 'a very sympathetic young Russian',[40] whom Noel knew only as 'Max'. Since it was known that Reiss was in Switzerland, he would probably try to make contact with the Fields there. If he did, they were to receive him in friendly fashion and immediately inform Max.

Directly after the meeting Noel drove back to Geneva with his young Soviet comrade. As instructed, he introduced him to Herta and explained the situation. Over the next few days Noel and Herta met Max daily, but there was nothing to report.

Herta recalled that on 4 September they drove with Max into a nearby mountain range. Unused to the heights and the sharp bends, their guest grew giddy. On the way home they dined *al fresco* in the French village of Machilly. That same night Reiss was gunned down on the road from Lausanne to Geneva by an NKVD hit-squad.

It was on a small beach next to Lake Geneva that the Fields read of the murder. From the reports and photos in the press they finally learned 'Fatty's' true identity.

'Raymond (Reiss) has been liquidated', Moscow informed Akhmerov a week after the event. 'His wife so far has not'. The same communication noted that Noel was 'well-mannered and impressed a comrade with whom he is connected as a sincere man, willing to report back about Reiss as soon as the latter turns to him'.[41] Presumably the impressed comrade was Shpigelglas.

Meanwhile, 'Max' turned up for the last time and asked Noel if he had seen the papers. If Noel took this as a warning about his own future conduct, he does not mention it. He was more concerned about two other matters: first that his contact with Soviet intelligence had been broken; and second that the police might have learned about his own connection with Reiss.

Since reports about the murder filled the Swiss press for several weeks, he was worried that their maid might remember Reiss staying with him. Moreover, they had eaten together in the local hostelry. However, nothing happened.

In the meantime Krivitsky, always more clinical than Reiss, was planning his own defection, and left Paris for a hide-out on the Mediterranean coast on 6 October.[42] Taking note of his disappearance, on 23 October Moscow complained to Akhmerov that the connection with Field 'has been disrupted again'.[43]

That same day the Massings left New York on a Swedish ship bound for Gothenburg. Their escort was one of the most intriguing female agents in the NKVD.

7

PROMISED LANDS

PILGRIMAGE TO MOSCOW; MISSION IN SPAIN, 1937–39

'Purge de luxe'[1]

In the first week of August 1937 Iskhak Akhmerov escorted an important comrade to the Massings' West 22nd Street apartment in Manhattan. Introducing herself as 'Helen', the newcomer was to feature constantly in the Massings' lives that month.

'Helen' was just one of many cover-names adopted by the woman born Lisa Rozenzweig on 1 January 1900 in the *shtetl* of Rzhaventsy. Now in Western Ukraine, it was then in Tsarist-ruled Bessarabia, and lay very close to the frontier with the Habsburg province of Bukovina.

Lisa came from a revolutionary family related to that of a founder of the Romanian Communist Party, Ana Pauker, and joined the youth wing of the Communist Party of Bessarabia at an early age. Later she combined party and intelligence work with further education.

In 1920 she studied history and philology at the University of Czernowitz (Cernăuți), which was then in Romania.[2] From September 1921 until August 1922 she was at the Sorbonne in Paris. Two months later she enrolled in the University of Vienna to read languages, and remained there until graduating in June 1924. Besides Russian and Yiddish, Lisa spoke excellent English, German, French and Romanian.

In 1924, while in Vienna, she joined the Austrian party, and also served with the Soviet embassy and trade delegation there. Taking Soviet citizenship in 1925, from March of that year until May 1927 she worked for INO as a member of the Vienna *rezidentura*. Lisa was in Moscow in early 1928, where, following formal recruitment into INO, she Russified her surname to Gorskaya.

In 1929 occurred the incident for which she became notorious. Yet there are so many variants of this tale that it is difficult to relate it with any real confidence, once we have left its initial event. This was the assassination in July 1918 of the German ambassador in Moscow by the Left Social Revolutionary and Chekist, Yakov Blumkin.

Trotsky's protection allowed the twenty-year-old Blumkin to escape punishment. He later joined the Bolsheviks and became the *rezident* in Istanbul. In summer 1929 he visited the Turkish island of Prinkipo, where Trotsky lived in exile after Stalin banished him from the USSR that year. At their meeting Blumkin either handed over OGPU funds to Stalin's mortal enemy, or undertook to carry letters to his supporters in the Soviet Union.

Blumkin was enticed back to Moscow by Lisa playing one of the following roles: she was his long-term lover; his former wife; an outraged colleague; or a seductress operating a honey-trap. Later that year Blumkin was executed for treason, becoming the first 'Trotskyist' and senior security officer to suffer this fate.

At some time in 1929 Lisa married Vassili Mikhailovich Zarubin. Born in Moscow in 1894, the son of a railwayman, Zarubin was badly wounded while serving in the Tsarist army against the Germans. Despite this he fought in the Red Army during the Civil War. He joined the Cheka in 1920 and INO in 1925. That same year he split from his first wife.[3]

In 1926–29 Zarubin was the illegal *rezident* in Finland and Denmark, and Lisa joined him as an agent in Copenhagen. From 1930 to 1933 he and Elizaveta Yulievna Zarubina, as Lisa now styled herself, operated illegally in Paris. In 1931 their son Peter was born.

In 1934–39 the Zarubins, either singly or together, operated illegally both in Nazi Germany and the United States, their missions interspersed with spells at Moscow Centre. They carried doctored US passports in the names of Edward and Sara Herbert. Vassili's cover in Berlin was as a representative of Hollywood's Paramount studios, where one of his American agents worked.

Reiss's wife viewed the blond and blue-eyed Russian Zarubin as 'a pudgy, jolly, rather likeable man'. However, she, Reiss and their circle avoided Lisa 'like the plague' on account of her role in the Blumkin affair.[4]

Others admired her. 'Slim, with dark eyes, she had a classic Semitic beauty that attracted men', recalled a colleague. 'Usually she looked like a sophisticated, upper-class European, but she had the ability to change her appearance like a chameleon'.[5]

Unsurprisingly, Hede Massing noted Lisa's 'strange, beautiful eyes– large, and dark, heavy-browed, with long, curled eyelashes. They shone from a face of small, delicate features, dark-skinned, and narrow of mouth'. She had a 'warm and engaging smile' which 'exposed large, beautiful teeth'. After that it was all downhill, as Hede itemised Lisa's small, frail body, poor posture, big feet and ugly hands.[6]

Hede contended that Lisa's function was to discuss with the disillusioned Hede her wish to resign from the NKVD, and then to escort the Massings to Moscow. Yet two points in her account undermine this claim. First, Hede claims that she raised the issue of resignation with her first boss, Valentin Markin, as early as 1934.[7] Despite this, the NKVD apparently let her continue as a recruiter and courier for another three years. Second, Hede writes that the matter of travelling to Moscow was raised by Lisa. Yet Noel was under the clear impression that this had already been arranged, when the Massings were in Switzerland in late 1936.[8]

According to Hede, she only agreed to leave for Moscow after Paul announced that he intended to go. However, she took a number of precautions. She rejected the use of false papers in favour of her American passport. Hede chose the ship on which they sailed, and she purchased *Intourist* vouchers to enable them to live like average American tourists. Hede also suggested to some communist friends that they write to her in Moscow. For his part Paul left a deposition with a lawyer, which was to be opened if he did not return within a year.

Escorted by Lisa, the Massings arrived in Moscow on 5 November 1937 and ensconced themselves in the *Hotel Metropole*. Thus began what Hede termed sardonically their 'purge de luxe'.[9]

The initial interrogations of the Massings were conducted by Lisa and Vassili Zarubin, posing as 'Helen' and 'Peter'. Hede described Vassili as 'a stocky, blond man, with broad Russian features and watery blue eyes', who 'spoke English fairly well'.[10] The main topic was their relationship with Reiss.

In January 1938 a 'small, stout, blond man with bulging eyes' joined them;[11] Shpigelglas introduced himself by name. At that juncture neither Hede nor Paul knew of his role in the murder of Reiss, and they both warmed to him. 'He seemed as European as Peter was Russian', noted Hede, 'cultured, civilized, pleasant', speaking German 'almost fluently'.[12] Once he had tied up a few loose ends, the Massings were free to party with the NKVD.

The first event was *chez* Madame Slutski. She was the widow of the recently deceased head of INO, Abram Slutski, who had expired in his office on 17 February 1938, either from a heart-attack or cyanide poisoning.[13] A lighter note was struck at the Zarubins. 'Peter' strummed his balalaika and sang in the strong voice that he had honed in a church choir. The vodka flowed and the need for escapism was understandable; tomorrow 'the Great Terror' might consume any one of them.

The next sybaritic experience was at an NKVD rest home in the Caucasus, where the radio regaled them with the proceedings of the third great Moscow show trial staged in March 1938, and featuring Bukharin, Rykov and Yagoda amongst the defendants. Returning to Moscow, the interrogations and outings resumed, until one day at the beginning of June the Massings confronted the Fields.

'Hop through the looking-glass'[14]

Noel maintained that he and Herta had planned to visit the Soviet Union even before the Massings left Switzerland in 1936. After the death and disappearance of Reiss and Krivitsky, they had the added incentive of needing to re-establish contact with Soviet intelligence. Moreover, they also wanted to overturn the Massings' ban on their joining the Party.

In autumn 1937 Field tried unsuccessfully to get an entry visa through the Geneva branch of Thomas Cook, which represented the Soviet state travel agency *Intourist*. He even sent a telegram to the foreign ministry in Moscow, which he later conceded was 'an act of extreme stupidity'.[15]

Later that autumn Noel received a telegram from his sister, telling him that Nina had cancer. Elsie advised him to travel to the USA immediately if he wanted to see his mother alive again, since the doctors were of the view that she had at most two years to live.[16]

So Noel and Herta decided to spend that year's vacation in the USA. They sailed from Cherbourg on the *Queen Mary*, with both travelling on the same passport, and cavalierly giving their address as the Department of State. They arrived in New York on 29 November 1937.

During the voyage Herta was thrown off her feet and suffered severe bruising. Once on land she spent several weeks in hospital, and Noel divided his time between sick wife and sick mother. However, he did manage to visit Washington and probably met both Hiss and Duggan.[17] He also called on his sister-in-law Traudy Bakonyi, who was back in the USA.

Returning to Europe in January 1938, the Fields redoubled their efforts to get to the USSR. They had no success until they drove to Paris in May and besieged the *Intourist* office there.[18]

Within a week they obtained their entry permits and immediately set off for Dresden, driving overnight and throughout the next day. In Dresden they left their car and boarded the overnight train to Warsaw. From the Polish capital they caught the weekly train to Moscow and arrived at their destination on the morning of 29 May.[19]

For the first two or three days they saw the Potemkin sights with *Intourist*. They did not look up the Massings, because they wanted to bask in their new world without getting involved straightaway in problems. It was the Massings who discovered that the Fields were in Moscow. Hede and Paul waited for them in the foyer of their hotel and 'made a terrible scene' about the Fields not informing them of their arrival. Noel recalled that it was the very first time that they had fallen out.[20]

In Hede's memoirs there is no 'scene'. She simply conflates her extensive contacts with the Fields in Moscow into a single meeting, involving a lengthy heart-to-heart between the two couples in the Massings' hotel-room. It is well-written, dramatic, and mostly false. The *denouément* she provides in fact relates to another meeting entirely.

The one part that may be true is her description of the Fields' reaction to Paul's account of the murder of Reiss. 'They were unmoved', fumed Hede, 'totally, completely unmoved. Not a sign of disapproval! Not a word of regret!'[21] As the Fields had willingly played their roles as accessories in the liquidation of a 'traitor' this does not seem surprising.

After this first meeting the Massings introduced the Fields to 'Peter', whom Noel dubbed their 'Mentor'. He and Herta visited the Zarubins both in town and at their dacha. Peter strummed and sang again and Noel got to join in some Russian songs. For her own meetings with the Fields Lisa Zarubina morphed from 'Helen' into 'Natasha'. Naturally, there were discussions about the Fields' earlier 'work' for the USSR.

That Noel was squired by ranking Soviet intelligence officers is not mentioned in Hede's account. Nor is there a word about the Massings joining the Fields and 'Peter' on various 'outings', to which both Herta and Noel independently attested in their prison statements.[22]

Again, Hede, the repentant Soviet spy, cosying up to her American readers when writing in 1950, would not want to draw attention to these jaunts with both the Fields and the NKVD. Instead she concentrated on another activity, and left Noel's part in it out of her account. Hede attempted to discover how many of her German comrades, who had fled to Moscow after 1933, had survived Stalin's purge. She does not mention Noel's involvement in this process, or the fact that she prevailed upon him to provide money for the families of some of those arrested.[23]

The last meeting between the two couples took place shortly before the Fields left for Leningrad on 8 June. It was here that Hede's *denouement* actually occurred. She picked up the phone, rang the unfortunate Boris Bazarov, and threatened to go to the American embassy with the Fields as witnesses, to complain about the delay in issuing her with an exit visa.[24]

The Massings got their papers while the Fields were in Leningrad. Hede writes that 'we did not see them until many years later'.[25] In Gothenburg on 17 June 1938 they boarded the *Kungsholm*, the same Swedish liner on which they had arrived. They were diverted from New York and docked at Philadelphia eleven days later.[26]

Meanwhile, after visiting Leningrad the Fields travelled to Stalingrad. From there they toured among other places, Saratov, Rostov, Baku, Tiflis, Sochi, Yalta and Kiev. Sometimes they were accompanied by their new NKVD friends, who facilitated their visits to factories and collective and state farms. They even got to see Soviet justice at work, when they were taken to a minor political trial in Moscow.

'These were perhaps the most beautiful days of our lives', Noel wrote in his cell, and after their five week tour they returned to Moscow on 13 July 'full of inspiration'.[27]

The Fields had already put in applications to be admitted to the Party. On their return, 'Peter' and 'the man with the Order of Lenin'

(Shpigelglas), offered them the choice of joining the Soviet or American Party. After talking it over, and doubtless considering the small matter of treason, the Fields plumped for the CPUSA and wrote their applications in English.

'Peter' explained that their application would be sent on to the American section of the Comintern in Moscow, and that they would be registered there as secret members of the CPUSA. On account of the nature of their work, the party in America would not be informed. But given the services that they had already performed, their membership would be backdated by two years to 1936.

Noel was told to wait several months after returning to Geneva, and then to travel to a Paris address that 'Peter' gave him, and to introduce himself by the password 'Brook'. There, Noel would receive instructions about his future intelligence work, as well as formal confirmation of his party membership. It was even possible, said 'Peter', that 'Natasha' (Lisa) would be Noel's contact there.

'Everything appeared to be settled', recalled Noel. 'Full of hope', the Fields left the Soviet Union on 15 July. Back in Geneva Noel gushed to his family in the USA about the wonders of 'our hop through the looking glass'.[28]

Perhaps Vassili Zarubin's smile was rivalling that of the Cheshire Cat, because when Noel visited the address in Paris he found solely a deserted and dilapidated house. As far as Soviet intelligence was concerned, there were doubts about the links of the Fields to Reiss and Krivitsky, and indeed to the Massings.

In the jargon of Soviet espionage they had been 'conserved' as agents,[29] or put on ice, and it would be almost five years before they were briefly defrosted. Nor had Noel got his party card, and his inability to prove that he was a covert member of the CPUSA, if indeed he was so registered, would later inspire suspicion about his precise status.

Last rites in Spain[30]

Travelling via Poland and Germany, Noel and Herta reached Geneva on 19 July 1938. By then the Spanish Civil War had raged for two years, and Franco's Nationalists, aided by Mussolini's divisions and Hitler's 'Condor Legion', were in the ascendant.

Franco's rebellion against the legally elected Popular Front government had occurred shortly before the August 1936 show trial of

Zinoviev and Kamenev. This ensured that Stalin's policy in Spain would be coterminous with 'the Great Terror' inflicted upon his own country.

He supplied the Republican side with tanks, planes, munitions, and, initially, Soviet pilots and tank-crews. In return he plundered Spain's gold reserves, and imposed upon the Republican parties and military forces the dubious blessings of Soviet 'advisers', most noticeably in the field of security. These shadowy forces were also to be found liquidating 'opposition' elements within the International Brigades.

The Brigades were composed of both communist and non-communist volunteers, who converged on Spain in rehearsal for the greater war to come. Some 35,000 antifascists from over sixty countries joined these formations, while another 5,000 volunteers fought in separate units. In addition there were some 10,000 doctors, nurses and engineers from foreign lands.[31] Perhaps a quarter of the combatants died. Jews formed a significant proportion of both fighters and medics.

It was in order to oversee the withdrawal and repatriation of these foreign fighters that Field was sent to Spain. He was secretary to a League of Nations multinational commission of military officers, which was in Spain from October 1938 until February 1939.[32] As Noel wrote later, the lack of any official party contacts at this time proved very inconvenient for him.

Field was in Madrid, Barcelona and Valencia. He visited the front, Brigade hospitals and bases, and the French frontier. As was agreed with the Spanish government the commission registered the volunteers by name, and Noel kept a list of his own. Later he toured the French internment camps, and on his own initiative sent a confidential report on them to the American ambassador in Paris. He also assisted in drawing up the commission's final report.

The remaining volunteers in Spain paraded in Barcelona for their farewell on 15 November 1938. By mid-January 1939 over 4,600 men from twenty-nine nations had returned home. But still there were some 6,000 who could not go back to Germany, Austria, Czechoslovakia, Hungary and Yugoslavia.[33] Instead, they would be caught up in the collapse in Catalonia and then find themselves herded into grim camps in France. Many of these would come to know Noel and be sustained by him. Tainted by such association, they would suffer in the terror permeating Stalin's last years.

Upon returning to Geneva, Noel was tasked with acting as a League representative at the New York World Fair.[34] He arrived in that city from

Cherbourg aboard the *Queen Mary* on 8 May 1939. He stayed several weeks in order to assist in the arrangement of the League Pavilion. Most of his spare time was spent with his sick mother.

On occasion Noel also saw the Massings who had moved to 106th Street. Hede 'could not remember a thing as to the state of his mind', but she and Paul saw him off on his return, and 'we embraced each other as good friends'.[35]

Noel's retrospective view was different. He conceded that outwardly they parted good friends, but he now felt uneasy in the Massings' company, and considered that the old friendship was over. He thought that since their meeting in Moscow, Hede in particular had slid further down the path towards 'treachery', even though she maintained that she was still a communist. He didn't know whether they were both still connected with Soviet intelligence, but he could scarcely believe it possible that they were. As we shall see, his judgement was wrong.

In fact both Noel and the Massings were the subject of Moscow's interest at that time. Walter Krivitsky had arrived in the USA in November 1938, and the press articles which were to form the basis of his book began appearing in April 1939.

'We will have to assume', Moscow Centre informed New York on 7 July 1939, that 'Enemy (Krivitsky) betrayed Peter and his wife (the Massings), as well as the agent Ernst (Noel), who was recruited by the latter two and who works in Europe, but is at pres(ent) in the USA'.[36]

Why should Soviet intelligence be aware of Noel's presence in the USA? One possibility is that the Massings informed the New York *rezidentura*. Another is that the information came from Hiss and was passed by the GRU to the NKVD. Noel certainly saw both Duggan and Hiss when he visited Washington and he unburdened himself to the latter.

From press reports Noel knew that Krivitsky was in the USA and he was concerned that Walter might betray him. As Hiss already knew about Field's links to Soviet intelligence, Noel 'could inform him without any further breach of discipline', of this possibility. Therefore the two men agreed that if Hiss learned anything he would issue a warning to Noel, using a code-name.[37]

There was another matter from his past that Noel had to deal with while he was in the USA. In November 1938 one Joseph B. Matthews had testified before the Dies Committee, the predecessor of HUAC. Matthews, who had known Noel in the 'International Friendship Club', had denounced him as a communist as long ago as 1928.[38]

In a notarised letter to the Dies Committee dated 6 June 1939, Noel emphatically denied that he had ever been a communist or even a radical. The wording seems a shadowy precursor of the formulaic denials uttered by those summoned before HUAC after the war.[39] He sent a copy to the State Department.

It is not clear precisely when Noel sailed back to a Europe teetering on the brink of war. He may have visited the Polish pavilion at the World Fair beforehand where visitors were invited to enter the essay contest: 'I would like to visit Poland because...'. The first prize was a vacation in Warsaw.[40] That city, like the rest of Poland and its people, would soon endure an unparalleled ordeal, and Noel's younger brother would be caught up in those initial days of terror and suffering.

8

'AT THE RISK OF DEATH'

HERMANN FIELD 1939–40

Changing partners[1]

By 1939 the marriage of Hermann Haviland Field and Jean Ainslee Clark was over, and they would divorce that year. In 1938 Jean had met Sali (Salomon) Liebermann, who worked as an upholsterer and decorator in the Zurich theatre. Born the son of a Russian Jew in 1912, Sali was both a Swiss citizen and a member of the Swiss Communist Party (SwCP).[2] Jean would marry Sali in 1940, the same year as the SwCP was made illegal.

It seems likely that the Fields' marriage was affected by career choices and separation. While Jean remained in Zurich, working on her doctorate, from early 1937 to March 1939 Hermann was in Britain, supervising the building of a factory in Welwyn Garden City. Moreover, in summer 1938 he too had met someone else.[3]

Kate Margaret Thornycroft was born in 1912 in Hampstead, the eldest child of five of a successful engineer, Oliver Thornycroft, and Dorothy Rose, a Labour Party activist and councillor. Kate attended Bedales, an experimental and co-educational public school. Then, like her mother, she read economics and politics at Cambridge. Despite graduating with an honours economics degree in 1934, the only job offered to Kate was as a bank teller.

So she accepted a one-year fellowship at Smith College in Massachu-setts. Her experience in Depression-hit America made Kate's 'thinking more radical' and she 'made some attempts at reading Marx', while concluding that 'by temperament I was not a revolutionary'.[4]

On her return to Britain she became a schoolteacher and joined the Labour Party. She and Dorothy cared for Basque children in Worthing, and Kate accompanied them to Hendaye, when they were repatriated to Spain following Franco's victory there in 1939.

Kate and Hermann found that they held shared views 'against the rise of dictatorships, against the brutality of anti-Semitism, and against the aggressive nationalism of Mussolini and Hitler'.[5] But such a statement cloaked a more pro-communist stance which both adopted at the time.

Noel contended at one point that Kate was a member of the CPGB. He later retracted such certainty, while Hermann specifically denied that Kate had ever been a member. However, Kate must have been close to the Party. Her younger sister Priscilla was a member and married to the refugee German communist Hans Siebert. Moreover, her brother Christopher was a member of the CPGB Central Committee in the 1950s.[6]

Hermann was never a party member, preferring to distance himself from the 'unquestioning discipline' required. But at the time of his missions to Prague and Krakow in 1939, Hermann felt 'nearer to the communists […] than at any time before or after in my life'. He was deeply impressed by 'their unremitting and courageous resistance against the Nazis, when acquiescence was the easy way out'.[7]

Prague and Poland[8]

On 30 September 1938 the British and French prime ministers signed the Munich agreement with Hitler and Mussolini. This consigned to Nazi Germany the Sudetenland, the main defensive area on the fringes of the Czech lands. In anticipation of its transfer, Jews, as well as Sudeten German and Czech antifascists living in the territory to be ceded, flooded into the residue of Czechoslovakia. There they joined the numerous refugees from Germany and Austria already there.

The plight of these unfortunate people stirred certain sections of opinion in Britain, and appeal funds were launched by the Lord Mayor of London and the liberal *News Chronicle* and *Manchester Guardian* newspapers, as well as some trade union and refugee organisations.

In October 1938 the British Committee for Refugees from Czechoslovakia (BCRC) was formed to administer these funds. It would also organise transport to Britain and provide temporary maintenance for those refugees deemed to be in the greatest peril. Between October 1938 and March 1939 the BCRC brought 2,500 Sudeten Germans and 1,000 *Reich* Germans and Austrians to Britain.

But on 15 March 1939 the threat to the remaining refugees increased when Hitler's armies marched into Bohemia and Moravia and reduced these Czech lands to a German 'protectorate'. At the same time Slovakia declared itself an independent state. Now many Czechs, Slovaks, and Hungarians (from Slovakia) were also in grave danger.

In March 1939, on completion of his architectural work in Britain, Hermann returned briefly to Switzerland. He stayed with Noel and Herta for two days, before travelling to London with a view to returning to the USA. It was at this juncture that Kate Thornycroft, who had worked for the BCRC from its inception, helped conscript Hermann for an unofficial mission to Prague.

As Hermann recalled, this mission had its origins 'in that twilight world of political struggle against Hitler'. He was approached by certain refugee leaders who had already been granted asylum, and who now wanted him 'to help rescue some highly endangered German and Austrian Communists' trapped in Prague by the Nazi occupation.[9]

Aided by his American passport and fluent German, and using funds provided by the BCRC, Hermann went to Prague in April 1939 for about one week. The alleged purpose of his visit was to retrieve a Czech film for International Pictures.

His actual task was to hand over a slush-fund. This was to be used to bribe officials, and thereby facilitate the emigration of refugees to Katowice in Polish Silesia. There the British vice-consul was issuing visas for travel to Britain. It was at this time that Hermann clashed with the enigmatic Leo Bauer.

Bauer was born in October 1912 into an Orthodox Jewish family, the eldest son of a watchmaker. With the onset of the First World War Bauer's family moved from his birthplace, the East Galician *shtetl* of Skałat, to Chemnitz in Saxony.

Although he learned Hebrew from the age of five, Leo also learned French and Latin at school. When he joined the youth wing of the German Social Democratic Party (SPD) his political activities led to conflict with his religious father, so Bauer moved to Berlin. In 1932 he completed his *Abitur* there, entered university, and joined the KPD.

When Hitler came to power in 1933, Leo was permanently thrown out of university on racial grounds, and briefly detained in a concentration camp on political grounds. Upon regaining his freedom he resumed underground work for the Party. At the end of 1933 the KPD ordered him to leave Germany, first for Prague and then for Paris, where the exiled KPD leadership was located.[10]

In Paris, Bauer's main field of activity was refugee work. In June 1936 a conference in the French capital founded an organisation to represent exiled Germans, and Bauer became its secretary. In this capacity he participated in international conferences in Geneva and London that same year, and became deputy secretary to the League of Nations High Commissioner for Refugees.

It was with this authority that Bauer came to Prague in October 1938 under the cover-name Rudolf Katz. His function was to arrange the evacuation of antifascists from Czechoslovakia, and in particular to ensure that communists got their 'fair' share of visas to Britain, France and Scandinavia.[11]

By the time that Hermann arrived in Prague in April 1939 Bauer was no longer there,[12] so Hermann left his funds with another German communist. Then he set off to Poland, first to Katowice and then to Krakow, where a large number of refugees had gathered.[13]

Hermann was now working officially for the BCRC and later for the British-based Czech Refugee Trust Fund (CRTF), which superseded the BCRC in July 1939. The new body disposed of British government funds and was subject to Home Office control.

There were never enough visas, and confronted with round-ups of the refugees by the Polish police, Hermann was obliged to vouch for some, while the remainder would be shuttled back across the border into the clutches of the Gestapo. This was the 'most heartbreaking misfortune I had to endure in all those heartbreaking months of 1939', Hermann lamented.[14]

Bauer had turned up in Krakow after the Germans had allowed him to leave Prague by night train on 1 April.[15] Apparently he criticised the way the refugees were being brought illegally from the 'Protectorate' to Poland. In turn Hermann objected to Bauer's negative attitude regarding the provision of visas for ex-communists and left-wing socialists. The clash of personalities between them was exacerbated by the considerable pressure of the life-or-death situation they were in.[16]

Hermann reported his views to London, and from there the matter went to the KPD leaders in Paris, who sided with Hermann. Bauer was banned from further activity, and presumably recalled to Paris.

However heartbreaking Hermann found his situation, he carried out his instructions 'to save the most endangered people', which 'certainly included the communists, not one of whom had been shipped back to the border'.[17] This was hardly surprising; one of his Czechoslovak Communist Party (CzCP) assistants recalled that Hermann 'was very active in helping those of the refugees who were Communists, indeed he gave them preference'.[18]

All three of his chief assistants, Evžen Loebl, Dr Karel Markus and Vilém Nový were CzCP members, and they probably cursed the names of the Field brothers when they were all arrested in 1949. However, in 1939 they were deeply grateful for Hermann's courage and dedication, which probably saved their lives. Later they transferred this gratitude to Noel and sought to help him.

Loebl was born in 1907 in Holič, a village of some 5,000 inhabitants in western Slovakia.[19] One of three children, he came from a Jewish merchant family and later studied at the High School for World Trade in Vienna. He joined the CzCP in 1934 'because of an inner need, a commitment to the cause of the workers', although this link 'was not conceived spontaneously, but only intellectually'.[20]

Loebl had wanted to go to the Soviet Union, but in 1938 the CzCP ordered him to leave for Poland. In Krakow he assisted Hermann in his work on a daily basis. As a reward for his efforts Hermann arranged for Loebl to travel to Britain in August 1939. His passage from Warsaw to London was paid for by the BCRC, and when he arrived in Britain he worked for the CRTF until 1941.[21]

Karel Markus was born in 1903. According to Noel he was Hermann's closest friend among the Czechoslovak communists, and they corresponded with each other after the war. Other than that he was a party official, we know very little else about him.[22]

Vilém Nový was born in the Moravian town of Jihlava in 1904. Of authentic proletarian stock, he joined the CzCP on its foundation in May 1921. The Party sent him to Moscow in 1929. Returning in 1931, he operated primarily in Moravia, combining the roles of party official, journalist, speaker and propagandist.

After Munich the new collaborationist Czech government banned the CzCP, and Nový slipped into the world of illegality until the Party ordered him to emigrate in June 1939. Following a series of hair-raising adventures Nový arrived in Krakow. He was there, confined to bed with a fever, when a dreaded but long-expected event occurred.[23]

'A column of fire and iron'[24]

At 4.45 a.m. on Friday 1 September 1939 Germany launched its murderous invasion of Poland. Leading the assault was the cream of the *Luftwaffe*, dive-bombing airfields, railway junctions, communications centres, munition dumps, and every sinew of war upon which the Polish high command depended.

A 'noise like doors banging' woke the young journalist Clare Hollingworth in Katowice around five a.m. 'Running to the window I could pick out the planes, riding high, with guns blowing smoke rings below them'.[25] Beneath the escaping German bombers, much of the small and largely obsolete Polish air force was destroyed where it stood; 'crippled machines [...] pinned to the ground by bombs, like butterflies in the collection of a clumsy-fingered entomologist'.[26]

Exploiting the breaches punched into the Polish lines by the 'air artillery', tanks, self-propelled guns and motorised infantry poured into Poland from East Prussia, Pomerania, Silesia and Slovakia. An Irishwoman married to a Pole recalled how 'the Germans came into Poland in a column of fire and iron [...] rolling like the cars of Juggernaut over those terrible dry roads, where they would have been bogged for weeks if the heavens had only sent us a little rain'.[27]

But the usual rains had not fallen. Even the weather conspired against Poland that summer. 'Translucent mornings after dewless evenings', recalled a renowned Polish author, with 'sunsets entangled in scarves of carmined clouds, succeeded by windless days'. Instead of the traditional downpours, 'only storms brief and stimulating; nights as spacious as cathedrals', and the 'vault of heaven sprinkled with stars, stars and stars'.[28]

In less elegiac terms the drought had transformed Poland's plains into a *Panzer* playground of hard dry soil, while her rivers were no longer wide and deep static lines of defence, but shallow and fordable.

The German attack cut through the Polish Corridor, depriving Poland of her narrow seaboard and ports, and swung out two arms of an inner pincer movement from East Prussia and Silesia. Meeting at Warsaw on 8 September, the pincers closed around the shattered Polish armies west of the Vistula. The German high command then directed an outer pincer movement towards the river Bug and captured Brest-Litovsk on 14 September. It was a totally one-sided war, effectively won by the Germans in a fortnight.

Poland presaged the great migrations of Belgium and France. Streams of human misery, for whom 'suit-cases became the centre of all things', passed through towns 'as through a sieve'.[29] Roads were jammed with refugees, soldiers searching for their commands, and others just drifting with the tide. Laden peasant wagons trundled alongside municipal buses and the swanky cars of the elite.

From above came wanton German air-attacks, cold-bloodedly sowing confusion and death; bullets all that rained from cloudless skies. Children scattering like sparrows, peasants hurling themselves from their wagons, 'a confusion of running figures, of flying skirts, overturned carts and prams and baggage. Flat in the fields, they covered their heads in a fold of coat or sacking, with the ostrich-impulse of terror'.[30] With more nobodies notched on their cannons, the killers winged away.

Amongst the refugees heading east were the Polish government and high command, plus the foreign diplomatic corps and sundry overseas journalists. Soon they all began to concentrate in south-east Poland, near to the then Hungarian and Romanian frontiers.

On 17 September the Red Army invaded eastern Poland. Stalin, at Hitler's behest, was grabbing the first tranche of his allotted booty under the Nazi-Soviet Pact.

Caught between two fires, the stream of refugees which had flowed east now turned back towards the west. There was nowhere left to hide within Poland. On the night of the Soviet invasion, the discredited government and military chiefs crossed into Romania.

Thousands of disorganised soldiers followed them there or trudged across the Hungarian and Lithuanian borders. Besides some isolated units which fought on with blind courage until October, all that remained of the republic's authority in Poland was the besieged capital.

After continuous air raids and artillery bombardments on 25 and 26 September, Warsaw surrendered the following afternoon. That evening the Nazi foreign minister, Ribbentrop, arrived in Moscow to re-consecrate Germany's unholy alliance with Stalin. Having plunged his knife into the smitten republic's back Stalin would now wield it for a new carve-up: a fourth partition of Poland.[31]

Flight and return[32]

The travails of Hermann and the refugees he endeavoured to lead to safety mirrored the terrifying chaos sketched above. Unsurprisingly, the whole affair is clouded by the fog of war. We do not really know how many refugees were involved in events. According to one source, some 1,600 refugees from Czechoslovakia were still in Poland when Hitler launched his attack,[33] while Herta Field claimed that Hermann headed a party of 600.[34]

On the night of 1 September Hermann and Karel Markus bundled the ailing Vilém Nový into a car, but they were unable to leave Krakow until 3 September. On the second day of the invasion the other refugee group in Katowice travelled by rail and reached Kielce on 4 September.

On 6/7 September German tanks scythed through Hermann's party and scattered them; only Hermann in his car and a few refugees reached Sandomierz, where they crossed the Vistula. The next day he met up with the Katowice group who had walked from Kielce. On 9 September Hermann and Nový reached Lublin, which was full of Polish troops and heavily bombarded.

Five days later they reached Łuck in the Volhynia region of Poland. There Hermann sought the protection of a convoy guarding the Polish gold reserves, and he and Nový travelled further south through Eastern Galicia. On 17 September they crossed the river Dniester at Zaleszczyki into Romania. After walking to nearby Cernăuți (Czernowitz), where the young Lisa Zarubina had studied, they caught a bus to Bucharest.

Perhaps fifty other refugees from Czechoslovakia finally reached Romania and one hundred Lithuania. An unknown number found refuge with the advancing Red Army. Some three hundred perished.[35]

The rescue work of the BCRC/CRTF was thus forcibly ended. However, owing to the courageous and committed work of those such as Hermann, acting 'at the risk of death, to protect human rights that were being violated',[36] between seven and eight thousand refugees from Czechoslovakia found sanctuary in Britain.[37]

Nový was not yet among the saved. He carried a Czechoslovak passport and a so-called 'landing-card', which could be exchanged for a visa at any British consulate. He also had instructions from the CzCP to travel to London after his work in Poland was completed. In Bucharest he telegraphed London for further instructions, and obtained a transit visa for France and an entry visa into Britain.

He also visited the Soviet embassy and asked to be put in contact with the CzCP leadership in Moscow. This was refused. Then he asked to be allowed into that part of Poland now occupied by the Red Army. This too was denied him. They did permit him to write a report to Gottwald in Moscow.

His visit drew the interest of the Romanian secret police, who gave him three days to quit the country. The problem was that there were no direct flights from Romania to France. He would have to land in Belgrade, Zagreb, Venice and Milan, but neither Yugoslavia nor Italy would provide visas to holders of passports issued by the pre-Munich Czechoslovak state. However, Nový had to chance it, and with good fortune he got to Milan.

From the French frontier Nový travelled by train to Paris. It took two nights and a day, since his train had to wait for hours at main stations, ceding priority to military transports. He stayed in Paris for one day and then journeyed with Hermann to Calais. Once across the Channel, they travelled to London.

This was Novy's account of his journey and throughout he uses the plural form 'we' (*wir*), implying that he had company from Romania to London. However, he only specifies Hermann's presence once they left Paris for Calais.

In the 1952 Slánský show trial, by which time the Field brothers had been transformed into Anglo-American spies, it was claimed that Hermann was received by leading 'reactionary' Romanian politicians in Bucharest. Moreover, Hermann's importance as an alleged intelligence agent was further demonstrated by the alacrity with which the authorities provided a plane to fly him and Nový back to Britain.[38] However, Novy's detailed account makes it quite clear that Field and Nový did not fly directly from Bucharest to London.

What seems to have happened is that they split up in Milan. From there Hermann travelled to Geneva and then to Zurich.[39] Possibly this trip was primarily intended to sort out the question of his divorce from Jean. We know that Hermann visited the Liebermann household because a visitor, Bruno Goldhammer—of whom more in the next chapter—wrote about meeting him there. Many years later Goldham-mer recalled that he was impressed by Hermann's assured but by no means arrogant demeanour. He seemed 'like the hero in a Western', bronzed and marked by recent hardship. Fascinated, Bruno listened as Hermann related the adventures that he and Nový had undergone.[40]

Presumably, Hermann then travelled to Paris and rejoined Nový. After returning to Britain in early October 1939, Hermann gave a radio talk and wrote at least three articles about his experiences. He and Kate continued to work for the CRTF until May 1940. During this time Hermann established and directed a home for Czechoslovak refugees in the countryside.

On 14 June Hermann and Kate married in Worthing registry office.[41] On 7 July they caught the last American evacuation ship sailing from Galway in Ireland and arrived in New York six days later. They would return to Poland in 1947, and Hermann would visit that country again in 1949, with tragic consequences.

9

FAMILY BREAKDOWN

NOEL, HERTA AND ERICA, 1939–41

Erica[1]

Erica Margarete Therese Glaser was born on 19 February 1922 in Schlawe, a small town in Pomerania in north-eastern Germany (now Sławno in Poland). Her parents were then in their mid-thirties. Dr Wilhelm (Willy) Glaser had studied medicine in Berlin and qualified in 1914. In the First World War he served as a doctor in the German navy on the *Dresden*. It is not known when Willy married Erica's mother, Maria Therese Fittiger.[2]

Willy was Jewish, Therese may have been, while Erica's older brother Kurt Joachim made no bones about his sense of identity. Born on 3 September 1919 in Africa, Kurt died in April 1945 leading a Jewish and German-speaking British commando unit against his former countrymen.[3]

A member of the German Democratic Party, Willy was a staunch anti-fascist. So was his wife, who made a point of buying only in Jewish stores after the Nazis came to power. Quite well-off, and determined that his children would not be polluted by what now passed for education in Germany, Willy enrolled Kurt in a British public school.

The solution for Erica was more drastic. Willy sent Therese to Spain, where they had both lived before, to scout out prospects. Then in December 1935 Willy left behind his large house and its entire contents, and took Erica to Hamburg. From there they sailed to La Coruña. In Spain the family opened a *pension* in Madrid, but it provided little income.

When the civil war broke out in July 1936 Dr Glaser offered his services to the Republican army. Transferred later to the International Brigades, he clashed several times with the communists. Therese and Erica both took nursing courses and the teenage Erica worked in hospital operating theatres. Kurt was in Spain too in the International Brigades, but whether he served in a military or medical capacity is not clear.[4]

Noel's League commission had the right to inspect Brigade hospitals, and it was in the hospital at Vich, some fifty miles north of Barcelona, that he first met Willy. Later the Glasers visited the Fields in their Barcelona hotel. They were now stateless, they had lost their home and possessions once again, and they were worried about Erica's future. The Fields offered to help.

Early in 1939 Noel's commission withdrew to Perpignan to write its report. At the same time, on the other side of the Pyrenees, the Republican front around Barcelona collapsed. Thousands of refugees, the Glasers among them, poured into France after the frontier was opened on 28 January. Unprepared and unwelcoming, the French authorities penned these hapless people into open-air camps surrounded by barbed wire.

Once the commission finished its official work, the Fields stayed on to help in the camps. Alerted by Therese, Herta and a woman friend smuggled Therese and Erica from Le Boulou in their car. Later they picked up Willy from the beach at Argelès. With the Glasers reunited in Perpignan, the two families came to an agreement.

Written in Spanish, by the terms of this accommodation the Fields undertook to care for Erica as their foster-daughter, and to provide her with a home and allowances in Switzerland. The time-span for this arrangement was to be dictated by the course of future events.[5]

Soon afterwards Willy got a job driving a truck to Paris. He hid his wife in the vehicle, while Herta followed in her car with Erica. Noel travelled to Paris later. Without papers, Erica's parents were once more interned following a police round-up but Noel managed to get them freed. Later in 1939 the Quakers' German Emergency Committee helped them get to Britain, where they joined their son. They then worked for the CRTF, where they met both Hermann and Kate.[6]

In March 1939 Erica moved into the Fields' chalet in Vandoeuvres. She soon met Jean and Sali Liebermann in Zurich. And it was at the

Liebermanns' house in autumn 1939 that Noel made his first contact with the KPD, in the person of Bruno Goldhammer.

Born in February 1905 into a middle-class Jewish family in Dresden, Goldhammer joined the KPD in 1922. He served the Party as both a journalist and functionary, before fleeing to Czechoslovakia in February 1933, and then emigrating to Zurich in October 1936. Here he worked illegally for the Party's *Abschnittsleitung Süd* (Southern sector leadership). He met the Liebermanns in 1937 and Noel, Herta and Erica in autumn 1939.

Noel and Erica told Goldhammer about their experiences in Spain. Later, whenever he was in Zurich, Noel attended meetings of the illegal Marxist circle which the German conducted. However, these gatherings would end in July 1940 when Goldhammer was interned. Bruno would enjoy the dubious distinction of being the first European communist to get to know both Field brothers, and later he would pay dearly for it.

Goldhammer was also privy to the real reason why Erica left the Fields' chalet in March 1940 and moved in with the Liebermanns in Zurich. Ostensibly it was because she found attending school in Geneva problematic, because she then knew little French. However, the chalet was the source of far greater problems, and these emanated from the Fields' ambivalent sex-life.

'He was spooky about sex'[7]

In Budapest in the early 1960s Noel spoke about his imprisonment to the American *émigré* writer, Edith Anderson. His worst ordeal, he joshed, was having to invent an elaborate history of his sex-life, which his interrogator still dismissed as totally inadequate.[8]

However, inadequacy and inexperience would appear to be the hallmark of this aspect of Noel and Herta's life together. Although they were probably both virgins when they wed, one would like to think that the marriage was consummated. Yet even this is uncertain, given some of Noel's prison statements.

Both in Washington and Geneva Noel tried to imply that he and Herta enjoyed an 'open' marriage. However, most men 'got the impression that Noel was talking a game, not playing it', and it is difficult to disagree with this assessment. 'He was spooky about sex', was another man's judgement.[9]

That the Fields were childless is not, of itself, proof of sexual absti-
nence. Herta may well have wanted children. Although she claimed to
a friend that she was glad that they had none, since 'they might come
between Noel and me',[10] her words appear to echo a decision made by
her husband.

In a prison statement Field asked himself and answered the question
of why they had no children.[11] According to Noel there were various
reasons. At the beginning of their marriage they had the usual aspirations of young people, who just wanted to enjoy life unburdened by
offspring. Later there was a fear of unemployment, both because of the
Depression and because of his possible dismissal on political grounds.

However, the chief reason was that the Fields had seen how other
comrades became more cautious in their activities, and sometimes
ceased party work entirely after having children. According to Noel, the
Fields wanted to avoid this. Instead of having children, they dreamed of
participating side by side in the struggle for a new world order. Their
wartime work for the USC seemed to justify this reasoning as children
would have made such activities impossible.

In other statements Field dealt with the question of fidelity. From the
age of nine, contended Noel, he had loved only one woman. At first he
and Herta had been playmates, and later they were like brother and
sister. After this came close personal friendship and political camarade-
rie. The only thing lacking in their relationship was passion (*Leiden-
schaft*). Despite this, prior to Christmas 1939 he had never looked at
another woman.

But at this point he had an experience 'that shattered my former way
of life and threw me out of kilter for years'.[12] For, given the inexperience
of each of the trio involved, within weeks a tragedy of love, hate and
jealousy developed, which Erica resolved by running away. So what had
happened?

Erica gave an account to Bruno Goldhammer. She told him that she
could not stay with the Fields, because both Noel and Herta had had sex
with her.[13] She asked his advice, and Goldhammer suggested that she
move to Zurich and stay with the Liebermanns, on condition that Noel
was prepared at least to pay for her studies and provide her with an
allowance.

Erica heeded this counsel and moved to Zurich in March 1940,
where she stayed and studied for nearly two years, later moving into her

own flat. Following her departure, Noel related that he and Herta descended into the darkest period of their lives, from which they only emerged some eighteen months later, their marriage truly happy and committed, because it had been so sorely tested.

Later he re-established his relationship with Erica upon a new basis. In early 1942, while heading the USC in Marseille, Noel was making one of his visits to Switzerland as a courier for the KPD. He looked up Erica in Zurich and offered her his friendship. Erica accepted, on condition that he never again attempted to touch her. Noel complied fully, not even shaking her hand in greeting thereafter.

Out of work

To add to the Fields' earlier woes Noel lost his job. Despite having a contract which ran to the end of April 1941, Noel was dismissed on 30 June 1940, although his salary was paid to the end of that year. Nina sent him small sums of money, but his financial problems mounted, for not only did the Fields retain their chalet until March 1941, but Noel also had to support Erica. She, being stateless, was not permitted to work in Switzerland.

His linguistic talents provided him with some work. He translated a book on disarmament from French into English, and some German-language articles for an American journalist. Field also tried to get a job as a radio reporter, but he was told that his voice was unsuitable.

Noel was convinced that the State Department had played a role in his dismissal from the League, although this seems by no means certain. However, the State Department does appear to have pulled the rug on him when he sought to take up three job offers.

The first came from John Winant, an American politician who served as director of the Geneva-based International Labour Organisation (ILO) in 1939–41, and then became American ambassador in London. This offer was withdrawn, because the State Department informed the US Department of Labor that Field was a communist.

The second offer involved Noel's friend and fellow-spy, Alger Hiss, who had joined the State Department in September 1936. Until September 1939 Hiss was employed in the office of assistant secretary of state, Francis B. Sayre. When Sayre was appointed high commissioner in the Philippines, Hiss became an assistant to the political adviser of the State Department's Far Eastern Division.

At Sayre's request, Hiss recommended two people who might be considered for the post of his political adviser in the Philippines. One of them was Noel, who had no experience of the Far East. The only reason Hiss gave for recommending Noel was that he 'is an expert draftsman and has a brilliant and flexible mind'.[14] In Geneva, Field received a telegram offering him the job, which he accepted. But because Noel's name had been mentioned before the Dies Committee in 1938, there was sufficient opposition within State to his appointment for the offer to be withdrawn.

The third offer came from Field's old boss at the London naval conferences. Currently president of the Red Cross, Norman Davis offered Noel the job of American Red Cross representative in Greece. Again Noel accepted and again there was silence thereafter. Later he learned that certain circles in the State Department had scotched the prospect.

Following these failures Noel applied to the YMCA, whose International headquarters were in Geneva. He had heard that they were involved in aiding refugees. Although they currently had nothing to offer, the YMCA promised to keep him in mind.

By now the Fields' finances were even more straitened, and they had just enough cash to pay for the voyage home. Noel had even reserved berths on a ship. It was then that he received a telegram 'that completely changed my life'.[15]

'CROWNING ACHIEVEMENT' 1941–1949

10

CADRES AND CAMPS

THE USC AND THE KPD FOREIGN SECRETARIAT

'So, go help the refugees'[1]

The telegram that completely changed Noel's life came from Marseille. It was sent in early March 1941 by Dr Charles Joy, the fifty-five-year-old, Lisbon-based director of the Unitarian Service Committee's operations in Europe.[2]

With headquarters in Beacon Street, Boston, the USC was founded by the Association of Unitarian Churches of America in May 1940. The initiative came from a number of senior Unitarians who had witnessed Hitler's takeover of Czechoslovakia in 1938–39. Chief among these were the Canadian-born Dr Robert Dexter, his wife Dr Elisabeth Dexter, and a younger couple, then in their thirties, the Reverend Waitstill Sharp and Martha Sharp.[3]

The Dexters visited Czechoslovakia in 1937–38 and reported on the plight of Sudeten refugees. The Sharps arrived in Prague in February 1939, shortly before Hitler's forces invaded Bohemia and Moravia. Their relief and rescue mission overlapped with that of the CRTF. Martha remained in the Czech capital until August, under increasing threat of arrest, before she and Waitstill returned to the USA in September 1939.

When the USC was formally established Dexter became its executive director, and it was decided to set up an office in Europe to aid refugees in flight from Czechoslovakia. Soon afterwards the Sharps left on a second mission to Europe. On 20 June 1940, shortly before the French surrender, their *Pan-Am* 'Clipper' landed in Lisbon. After making certain arrangements there, they moved on to Marseille to confront a refugee crisis of now quite different dimensions.

Operating both independently and in tandem with Varian Fry, the representative of the New York-based Emergency Rescue Committee (ERC), the Sharps assisted in relief and rescue work for endangered refugees in Vichy France. Waitstill left Marseille for Lisbon at the end of September 1940 and Martha finally followed in late November.

Joy, who had his own following amongst the Unitarians, arrived in Lisbon by 'Clipper' on 17 September. There he met both Fry and Martha. The latter eventually returned to the USA with some refugee Jewish children in December 1940. However, Joy had a different slant on how to proceed, arguing 'that it is better to keep 6000 children alive in France than to take a hundred or so to America'.[4]

Joy also intended to expand USC work in the French internment camps, and Boston agreed to let him hire his own director for France in place of Martha's nominee. Learning from a Geneva source that Noel was looking for a position, Joy offered him the post of USC director in Marseille, which effectively meant director for all of Vichy France. Field immediately travelled to Marseille, and Joy hired him on the spot.

Without counting them, Joy passed to Noel a wad of French francs. 'So, go help the refugees', he exhorted. 'How, is your problem. Send us reports as often as you can. We'll send you as much money as possible. I can't promise how much. That depends on the results of our collections in the States'.[5] Joy left next day for Lisbon.

In addition to the money, Field inherited a dark, unheated office in a ship's chandler's store in rue Fortune in Marseille harbour. For themselves, he and Herta had 'a dirty and bug-ridden room'[6] in rue Rouvière, plus an undetermined joint income. Their only employee was a young Greek who spoke little English.

Noel later contended that his immediate thought was to use the USC as a front (*Aushängeschild*) for a sort of 'Red Aid' (*Rote Hilfe*).[7] According to Field the antifascist orientation of the USC favoured his doing this. So for the first time he could combine his regular and party activities. He could also work with Herta, as his 'closest colleague and most trusted comrade'.[8] In fact, given Noel's frequent absences, the bulk of the organisational work would fall upon her shoulders.[9]

Noel pushed the antifascist policy of the USC in a pro-communist direction, by defining aid to antifascist refugees to include communists. These, he claimed with some justification, were getting no help from any other charitable organisation.

He was helped in this 'reorientation' by the fact that Boston's control over his operations was virtually non-existent. Postal traffic in wartime conditions became ever more difficult, and after the German occupation of Vichy France in November 1942 it ceased completely, until the liberation of most of France in 1944. As for censored *en clair* telegraphic traffic, this could be used solely for technical matters.

'During the war', Noel recalled smugly in his cell, 'I was in the fortunate position of receiving ever larger sums of money, while having to give ever fewer accounts of how it was spent'.[10]

With these funds he provided extensive material and financial aid to communists interned in the camps of south-west France, as well as to those who were living illegally in Vichy and Switzerland. He directed this aid primarily and deliberately towards saving cadres, the long-serving and committed core of functionaries around whom the various communist parties were built.

His main aid was to the largest and best organised party groups, the German KPD and the Spanish Communist Party (PCE). Virtually all those KPD cadres with whom he came into contact would later suffer dismissal from their posts, expulsion from the Party, and sometimes imprisonment.

Party in exile[11]

'The whole period of Comintern history from its creation down to the advent of Hitler can be described [...] as the German period of the Comintern. All experiments, all changes of tactics and methods of organization, started in Germany'.[12] Amongst these features were disastrous armed uprisings by the KPD, its intense factionalism, and its thoroughgoing Stalinisation.

Stalin's hegemony ensured KPD acceptance of the Comintern's 'Third Period' of 1928–34, which proclaimed the policy of opposition to the 'Social Fascism' of the Social Democrats. This unprincipled concept meant treating the German Social Democrats (SPD) as the fascist 'main enemy', while cooperating with the Nazis against them. The policy was primarily determined by Stalin's foreign policy aims of keeping France and Weimar Germany apart. However, within the KPD there was enough animosity towards the SPD for this policy to have a 'German' element too.

The tragic outcome is well-known. Hitler became chancellor in January 1933 and blamed the burning of the *Reichstag* in February on the KPD. The Party was banned, and Hitler's private army of SA thugs arrested, tortured and imprisoned KPD members. Soon they were herded into the newly-established Dachau and Oranienberg concentration camps, precursors of an even more inhuman regime that would scar Europe in the wartime years. Thousands of KPD members were incarcerated and hundreds executed or simply murdered.[13] The Gestapo infiltrated and destroyed most of the Party's clandestine organisation in Germany.

Shattered leadership bodies operated abroad in Prague, Paris and Moscow. Yet the Soviet capital was hardly a haven, for Stalin's purges of 'Trotskyites' and 'traitors' in the late thirties engulfed the foreign parties too. The NKVD executed some 60 per cent of the German communists who had sought sanctuary in the USSR. Stalin liquidated more members of the KPD Central Committee and Politburo than did Hitler.[14] Other German communists, women in particular, were swallowed up by a system of slave-labour camps which predated those of the Nazis.

Hitler's absorption of the Saarland in 1935, followed by Austria, the Sudetenland, and the Czech provinces in 1938–39, reduced still further the physical security of KPD members, as well as the Party's operational bases. Then in August–September 1939 the Nazi-Soviet Pact was followed swiftly by the outbreak of the Second World War.

The alliance between Stalin and Hitler ensured that the KPD leadership in Paris, the *Auslandssekretariat* (Foreign Secretariat), was destroyed by this latest twist in Soviet policy.[15] By endorsing the pact with Hitler, the KPD leadership converted obedient communists into enemies of 'imperialist' Britain and France. The antifascists of the 'Popular Front' period now arrayed themselves alongside their Nazi persecutors, and played into the hands of French officialdom.

The Daladier government ordained that all male foreign refugees register with the French authorities; non-registration would result in expulsion. So in contravention of Comintern instructions that they leave France rather than suffer internment, the members of the Foreign Secretariat tamely registered in September 1939 in the Colombes sports stadium in Paris. Both the leaders and led of Hitler's new KPD allies were held and then transferred to concentration camps in south-western France.

Stalin closed down the Paris Secretariat; in future the KPD leadership would operate exclusively in Moscow. In August 1940 those members of the KPD Central Committee who were still alive in the USSR declared that 'the Foreign Secretariat made up of comrades Dahlem, Merker and Bertz had liquidated itself'.[16] All three men cited would later play roles in the Field affair. But at this juncture none of them had heard of Noel. Their immediate priority was to survive the grim conditions of Le Vernet concentration camp.

Situated near to the town of Pamiers in Ariège department, the camp was built in 1918 to house French colonial troops. Between the wars it was a military depot. Thereafter it was a prison for defeated Spanish Republican troops, foreign antifascists, and 'non-returnable' members of the International Brigades. Later it would be a holding-camp for Jews, prior to their transport to yet more horrendous and lethal destinations.

Le Vernet was 'a collection of ramshackle wood huts at the foot of the Pyrenees, without beds, without light and without heating'.[17] Barbed wire 'ran all around the camp in a three-fold fence and across it in various directions, with trenches running parallel'.[18] Within its verminous confines shaven-headed, ragged, undernourished prisoners slept on foul straw on planks. Crowded huts each held two hundred men.

There were no stoves, blankets, soap or cutlery. Epidemics were rife, but there was no infirmary. There were four roll-calls a day, each lasting up to an hour in the bitter climate. Beatings by the *gardes mobiles*, 'the most reactionary and brutal force in France',[19] were the standard response for the slightest offence. Deaths from privation and suicide were commonplace.

Then a new threat to the senior KPD prisoners emerged, following the defeat of France and signature of the Franco-German armistice on 22 June 1940. Article 19 of this agreement required the Vichy government 'to deliver on demand all German nationals designated by the *Reich* government who are located in France, as well as in French possessions, colonies, protected and mandated territories'.[20]

Although a few prisoners were released by the French bureaucracy, and some others escaped into illegality, the only remaining way out of the camps was through emigration. The procedure for this was both

Kafkaesque and Byzantine, and often had to be repeated if visas expired or ships were not available.

In order to leave France the putative emigrant required a certificate of release from his camp, valid identity papers, and an exit visa from Vichy. The latter was not forthcoming to persons on Gestapo extradition lists, of course. In addition the refugee required an entry visa into a host country, funds for a ticket, and most of all a ship; this last being ever less certain as the war intensified.

The main destinations sought were the USA and Mexico. American entry and transit visas were difficult to acquire, and almost impossible for those defined as communists under the 1940 Smith Act. However, Mexican visas could be obtained relatively easily, thanks to the enlightened attitude of President Cárdenas and Gilberto Bosques, the like-minded colleague whom Cárdenas appointed as consul in Marseille.

According to Bosques, in the years 1939–42 the Mexican consulate helped six thousand refugees to get to Mexico from France, while another four thousand with Mexican visas remained in the USA or other places. Bosques also distributed funds to the camps, and provided papers for other inmates who simply joined the resistance on their release.[21] However, not all internees could be helped.

The fate of cadres

The leading KPD cadres interned in Le Vernet were Politburo members Paul Merker and Franz Dahlem, as well as Central Committee member Paul Bertz. Politburo candidate member Anton Ackermann had joined the others in registering with the French authorities, but was released on health grounds. However, he was well enough to make his way to Moscow and add his voice to the usual KPD intrigues against absent comrades.

Also interned in Le Vernet were several other senior officials of the Paris Secretariat, such as Hede Massing's former husband Gerhart Eisler, the commander of the Eleventh International Brigade Heinrich Rau, former *Reichstag* deputy Siegfried Rädel, and the journalist Lex Ende, who had also sat in the *Reichstag*. Whether Leo Bauer was originally in Le Vernet is unclear, but by the time of the French defeat he was in a small camp in Nîmes, from where he escaped to Marseille.

Dahlem, Rau and Rädel left Le Vernet in November 1941, but only for the prison in Castres, from where they were to be deported to Germany. Acting under KPD orders, Noel visited the US embassy in Vichy in a vain attempt to get the American government to intercede for them.[22] It appears that Field also tried to bribe certain French authorities to obtain the trio's release.

However, the plan fell through and the three men were deported to Germany on 4 August 1942. Dahlem and Rau were sent to KZ Mauthausen in Austria, while Rädel was condemned to death for high treason and beheaded in Brandenburg prison on 10 May 1943.[23]

Others such as Lex Ende were more fortunate. Born in the Bavarian spa town of Bad Kissingen in April 1899, the son of a Jewish art dealer, he originally bore the first name Adolf. With remarkable prescience he changed it to Lex in 1920. Having escaped with false identity papers in August 1940, he could not therefore emigrate himself.[24] Instead, using the alias Philippe Gautier, he operated illegally in Marseille as the representative of a new KPD leadership in Toulouse, assisting others to leave France.

Eisler was one of those who got out, eventually reaching the USA. Another who escaped across the Atlantic was Paul Merker, the most senior KPD figure to be purged because of his relationship with Field.

Like many KPD leaders Merker's proletarian background was impeccable. He was born into a Protestant working-class family in Saxony in February 1894, and after completing basic education he became a waiter and hotel-worker. Following service in the First World War, he joined the USPD (Independent Social Democratic Party) in 1918 and the KPD in 1920.

Thereafter he combined trade union work with party officialdom. He also served from 1924 to 1932 as a deputy in the Prussian parliament (*Landtag*). From 1926 he was a member of the KPD Central Committee and from 1927 of its Politburo. From 1931 to 1933, accompanied by Grete Menzel, later his second wife, Merker acted as a Comintern adviser in the USA, living there illegally under the pseudonym Max Fischer.[25] From 1933 until 1937 he served in Moscow and clandestinely in Germany. In February 1937 he joined the Foreign Secretariat in Paris.

Merker had been an enthusiastic supporter of the 'Social Fascism' policy, and was later a fan of the Popular Front. Indeed, there was little to mark him out as anything other than a loyal party hack until the Nazi-Soviet Pact was signed. At this point, according to Ackermann's report to officials in Moscow, he angrily denounced it. It was 'always the same story', he fumed. 'What the foreign communists build up is again destroyed by the Soviet Union's foreign policy'.[26] Merker always denied Ackermann's charge and none of the others present–Dahlem, Bertz, Eisler–confirmed it. Yet it stayed in his file.

Interned in Le Vernet in October 1939, Merker received a Mexican visa from Bosques in February 1941, and was then transferred to the camp at Les Milles, some ten kilometres from Aix-en-Provence.[27] Here the internees could leave camp on daily passes between 6 a.m. and 10 p.m., meaning they could travel to Marseille to make arrangements for their emigration.

The two hour tram-ride to the port also allowed Merker to make contact with Grete and other KPD members. This regime continued until a few days after Hitler's attack upon the USSR. Then on Tuesday 1 July 1941, a newspaper headline caught the vigilant eyes of Merker and his three companions; Vichy had broken off diplomatic relation with Moscow.

As they returned to Les Milles that evening, they learned that the commandant had ordered an indefinite ban on departures from the camp. Fearing that this would lead to their transfer to Le Vernet and extradition to Germany, the four men decided to return to Marseille. And since their camp passes, their sole identity papers, were only valid for that day, they now entered the world of illegality.

Lex Ende found them hiding places. Merker's was in a farmhouse some two hours from Marseille. He was hiding there when he came into contact with Noel Field.

Paul Bertz too was living in deep illegality when he met Noel, but in somewhat less threatening circumstances. As the oldest member of the Foreign Secretariat, Bertz was known as 'the Old Man' (*der Alte*) amongst other names. He was also a fractious man, and from experience not too trusting of others. 'Mistrust was his very essence' (*Mißtrauen war sein ganzes Wesen*), recalled one subordinate.[28]

Born in August 1886 in Mühlhausen in Thuringia, the son of a cobbler, Bertz trained as a toolmaker (*Werkzeugschlosser*), and joined the SPD in 1910. He spent the years of the First World War as a toolmaker in Kiel, and was a founder member of the KPD. During the Weimar Republic Bertz performed various party and trade union functions, and was a *Reichstag* deputy from 1924 to 1930. He was dropped from the parliamentary list in 1930 because of his links with the KPD 'Left Opposition', and was only a candidate member of the Central Committee in the 1920s.

When Hitler took power Bertz operated illegally in Germany until October 1934, when he left for France. Two months later he was in the USSR. From June 1935 to February 1936 he headed the KPD's southern sector leadership (*Abschnittsleitung Süd*) based in Switzerland, and then the *Abschnittsleitung West* operating in the Netherlands.[29]

In August 1935 Bertz was finally made a member of the KPD Central Committee and in May 1937 he joined the Paris Secretariat. He was made responsible for all *Abschnittsleitungen* in Europe, for cadre selection, and the security of KPD couriers and liaison men.

Bertz, who had opposed the Nazi-Soviet pact, was interned in Orléans and then in Le Vernet, but was in a labour camp in Nîmes when France surrendered. Then, on party orders, and accompanied by the French-speaking Bauer, he entered Switzerland on the night of 20/21 July 1940. Submerging himself with his usual skill, Bertz lived illegally in Basel as the KPD chief in Switzerland until May 1945.

Willi Kreikemeyer was not among the KPD elite. One metre eighty centimetres tall, powerfully built, and balding, he seemed content to execute orders doggedly and bravely. Born in Magdeburg in January 1894 into a working-class and socialist family, he trained as a lathe operator (*Dreher*). From 1913 to 1918 he served on a German torpedo boat in the eastern Mediterranean, and was decorated by both his own country and Turkey.

He joined the USPD in 1918 and the KPD in 1920. Following employment in Magdeburg's railway repair works, Kreikemeyer became a full-time KPD official in 1924 and operated in several parts of Germany. From 1928 he worked for Münzenberg's publishing enterprises in Germany and abroad.

In 1936 Kreikemeyer was an officer and commissar in the Eleventh International Brigade. Severely wounded near Madrid in summer 1937, he was later withdrawn from active duty to perform cadre work in the Brigades' headquarters base in Albacete. It was here that he had a fateful meeting, which will be discussed in Chapter 26.

Returning from Spain in May 1938, Kreikemeyer undertook 'border work' (*Grenzarbeit*) for *Abschnittsleitung Südwest* based in Brussels. Operating in Luxemburg he was in contact with illegal KPD groups from the Ruhr and Rhineland. In April 1939 he married Marthe Fels, who was fourteen years his junior. The daughter of a socialist mechanic, born in Alsace and bilingual in French and German, Marthe had first met Kreikemeyer in 1935 while working for Münzenberg in Paris.

When the couple returned to France in September 1939 Kreikemeyer was interned near Verdun, while his French wife was released. He was then recruited into a labour unit of the French army. In May 1940 he was in a barracks near Bordeaux. As the French front collapsed, his commander released him and his comrades from the unit. Eventually Willi made it to Toulouse, where the city's population was swollen with refugees and policing had virtually collapsed.

An August 1940 decree by the Vichy regime excluded from fresh internment all Germans married to French citizens. Aided by the Quakers, from September 1940 until May 1941 the Kreikemeyers lived in a village southwest of Toulouse. Then they moved to Marseille to help Lex Ende in his task of assisting endangered refugees.

11

'SAVING OUR CADRES'

MARSEILLE AND GENEVA 1941–44

Making contact[1]

It was one thing for Noel to conceive the idea of 'Red Aid', as a means of saving the cadres of the KPD and other parties in France and Switzerland. It was quite another to deliver the goods to the internees rotting in the camps, not to mention frightened and hunted fugitives, often living clandestine lives.

Noel's solution was to approach the leadership of the Swiss party, of which he was then a candidate member. The SwCP had been declared illegal in November 1940 and activities on its behalf were punishable by imprisonment. But in April 1941, a few weeks after taking up his post in Marseille, Noel travelled to Geneva and informed the illegal party leadership of his ideas for future work.

They referred him to Hans von Fischer, the head of the *Centrale Sanitaire Suisse* (CSS), a left-wing medical organisation set up by the Swiss party in 1937 to aid the Republicans in Spain. Fischer provided Field with a list of needy (*hilfsbedürftig*) comrades in the camps in southern France. He also gave Noel the names of Maria Weiterer and Hilda Maddalena, whom Noel first met in May or June 1941.

Born in Essen in February 1899, Maria Weiterer joined the KPD in 1921. She held various party offices, mainly in women's, social and trade union affairs. Arrested by the Nazis in September 1933, she was held in KZ Moringen for six months and then fled to Prague. In 1934–35 she was in Moscow and from January 1936 in Switzerland. Here she was engaged in 'border work' with the KPD's *Abschnittsleitung Süd*, which was then headed by Siegfried Rädel, her partner since 1928.

Both were arrested by the Swiss and expelled to France in October 1936. In Paris Maria held various posts in the Foreign Secretariat. Arrested again in January 1940, she was interned in the Rieucros women's camp in Lozère department. Later, because she held a valid visa for emigration to Mexico, she was moved to Bompard camp in Marseille.[2]

Hilda was nine years younger than Maria. She was the wife of the trade unionist and one-time KPD *Reichstag* deputy Max Maddalena, who was arrested in Berlin in March 1935 and sentenced to life-imprisonment in 1937. He would die in prison of stomach cancer in 1943, while Hilda emigrated to Mexico in early 1942.

Once the Swiss party guaranteed Noel's reliability, both women worked with him in the distribution of relief supplies. Maria (they called her Mia) became a firm friend of the Fields and Noel's closest adviser. He referred to her as his 'Political Commissar'. Unlike Grete Menzel, and even though she had valid papers, Mia refused to leave for Mexico without her man, the ill-fated Rädel. But later she discovered that she too was on the Gestapo's extradition list, and Noel helped organise her illegal flight to Switzerland in June 1942.

Maria also brought Field into contact with Paul Merker, then living illegally in a farmhouse in Gémenos. Their first meeting took place in November 1941. Both men thought they had met before at Marguerite Young's, when Merker (as Max Fischer) and Earl Browder visited the journalist's home in New York. Thereafter Noel met Merker along with Maria on a monthly basis, until Merker escaped to Mexico on 4 May 1942 under the name Siegmund Ascher.[3]

Merker later recalled his impression of Field, contending that in the USA he had met many Americans like Noel. 'He was the sort of uncomplicated, middle-class American, who from a religiously motivated outlook and morality [...] took the side of the weak and needy in society'. For Merker, 'Field was an idealist in the best sense of the word, free from any fixed doctrine'. However, he could never envisage Noel as a party functionary, since he would be unable to cope with the strict discipline required. Despite this, in the period of their cooperation he viewed Noel as utterly reliable and trustworthy.[4]

To keep Noel's activities secure, it was agreed that all of his contacts with other foreign party groups should take place under the aegis of the KPD. His KPD link was originally Henny Stibi. When she emigrated to Mexico Kreikemeyer took over the role in October 1941. He was then living legally in Vichy France by dint of his marriage to a French woman. Noel met with Henny, and later Kreikemeyer on a daily basis and consulted them on all aid questions.

Under Noel and Herta the USC helped create facilities which all refugees could enjoy, such as the sophisticated medical and dental clinic established in rue Fortia in Marseille in July 1941, and a well-stocked dispensary in rue d'Italie. There was a kindergarten at the Rivesaltes internment camp, and a small hospital in Toulouse.[5] They also provided medical and dental services for those in the camps, and food packages and financial support to both internees and illegals.

Noel's funds and supplies came from several sources. Initially USC church and public collections predominated. There were also contributions from the CSS and the Red Cross. The most remarkable source was the New York-based and CPUSA-controlled Joint Anti-Fascist Refugee Committee. This body funnelled several million dollars to Field as a 'trustee', which he distributed to Spanish refugees and interned former Interbrigadists.[6]

At an early stage Noel hit upon the idea of having his dollars sent to Switzerland and not to France. By converting dollars into Swiss francs and these into French francs, he got twice as many in exchange as he would have done by directly changing dollars into French currency in Marseille. He used this 'surplus' to finance further 'unaccounted' (to Boston) aid to the various communist parties.

Kreikemeyer later recalled receiving his first seriously large sum of money when Field handed over 100,000 French francs in late 1941 or early 1942. Even more remarkable for the German was that Noel required no detailed information about how the money was spent.[7]

On his trips from Marseille to Geneva, which he undertook about every two months, Noel also acted as a courier between the ranking German communists in France and Switzerland. In this way Merker in Marseille and Bertz in Basel kept in contact. Field performed the same function for the Spanish party. On each occasion he was strip-searched at the frontier by French gendarmes acting under Gestapo supervision. To circumvent these searches, Noel's usual method was to write down his instructions in his esoteric shorthand, commit these to memory as he approached the frontier, and then destroy his notes. Once across the border he would immediately rewrite his instructions in shorthand. On one occasion he transported a PCE 'archive', written on tissue-paper and sewn into the lining of his suit. However, the KPD put a stop to such practices by the Spanish party.

Field's first meeting with Paul Bertz took place in early October 1941, and following Merker's departure for Mexico, Noel always treated him as his chief. In theory Bertz was not only the official KPD leader in Switzerland, he was also the unofficial leader of the German communists in France.

Noel knew 'the Old Man' first as 'Johann' and then as 'Helm', and didn't learn his real name until summer 1944. The mistrustful widower Bertz took to Noel. He 'loved me like a son', Field recalled,[8] and the affection and respect between the two men was mutual. Yet their relationship was also rather formal. Bertz addressed Noel as *Herr Field* and used the *Sie* form of address, rather than the usual comradely *Du*.[9]

Return to Geneva[10]

When Vichy France was occupied by the Germans on the night of 10/11 November 1942, Noel and Herta narrowly escaped capture. Assisted by the Kreikemeyers, the Fields hastily packed their few belongings and caught the last train from Marseille to Geneva. Although held for twelve hours at the frontier, they eventually crossed into Switzerland with the help of the French resistance.

The Fields had to start their USC work all over again in Geneva. Now entitled the USC Directorate for France and Switzerland, they set up headquarters at 37 Quai Wilson on the western shore of Lake Geneva. For themselves they rented a small room in the cheapest pension in Geneva. Located at 12 rue de Vieux Collège, it was run by the Swiss section of the Women's International League for Peace and Freedom.

It suited Noel. 'Of course it's not quite the thing', he wrote flippantly to his mother on 2 December, 'me male alone among a batch of females, from sweet 17 up. But then, my hair is grey, my wife is with me, and Erica is our daughter, even if only foster'. The events that had driven Erica away must have been in his deluded mind, when he added that 'at long last and most unexpectedly, we're again reunited with our beloved child–and all three of us are very happy about it'.[11]

It is impossible to say how happy Erica was about rejoining the Fields. She had enrolled at the University of Geneva in spring 1942, where she was studying to be an interpreter. Moving into the Fields' apartment might have been a financial choice as much as an emotional one. She had received a little money from her parents, since her father was now practising as a doctor in Surrey. However, this dried up with the German occupation of Vichy.

Then again, her motive might have been 'political', in the sense of choosing to be where the action was. Still only twenty and of proven courage, Erica had already undergone considerable hardship and danger. Moreover, by race and experience she was an instinctive antifascist. So it was hardly surprising that soon she would combine her studies with 'border work'. She was arrested three times by the Swiss authorities, only for Noel to negotiate her release. She was also involved in 'the Bauer affair' which will be discussed in the next chapter.

Noel was criticised both by Boston and by many refugees for living little better than those of them who were at liberty. It was not that he had a predilection for dwelling in bug-ridden rooms and cramped pensions, instead of paying for a comfortable berth in a hotel. Rather, it was Noel's view that every unnecessary dollar that he spent on himself was in effect theft from the refugees.

Until their journey to the USA in 1945–46 the Fields received no actual salary. In Geneva Noel budgeted 1500 Swiss francs per month to keep himself, Herta and Erica. He admitted later that he was often hungry. He also worked tirelessly in Marseille and Geneva, Sundays and Bank Holidays included. He 'worked with amazing speed and efficiency', observed one visitor. 'He had no fixed hours. He worked all the time'.[12]

Inevitably there was a toll on his health. Field was in an eye hospital in Basel from October 1943 to May 1944.[13] In early 1946 Herta described to Hede Massing 'in great and harassing detail an eye disease and operation that Noel had undergone'.[14]

Although contact with Kreikemeyer was re-established early in 1943, Noel's funds in Geneva were initially limited, since the Swiss government placed restrictions upon the aid work of American charities. Like other neutrals they bowed yet further to the hegemony of the Axis powers, particularly since Germany and Italy now surrounded them on all sides. This situation changed again following the Soviet triumphs at Stalingrad and Kursk in 1943, when it became clear that it was a question of when, not if, Hitler would be defeated.

From January 1944 there was a considerable increase in the funds that Field could disburse. At this time Noel began a policy of 'Aid to National Groups' (*Nationale Gruppenhilfe*), whereby he dealt with a trusted representative of each communist group, and supplied them with monthly funds in proportion to their numerical strength. In line with this policy most overall help was given to the German, Spanish, Italian and Yugoslav groups, and less to the Hungarian, Polish, Czechoslovak and French.

To cover his aid to the various groups, Noel indulged in a complex system of double book-keeping. He produced one set of accounts for USC Boston, while retaining the real receipts under lock and key in his private office. After his dismissal in 1947 he stored most of these in a loft he rented from a blind woman in Vandoeuvres. The most compromising receipts of all, those signed by well-known communists, he held in a bank vault.

He kept these in the hope that they would aid his hoped-for confirmation as a party member. For once again his status as a communist had become ambivalent.

'Brook'[15]

At the time he joined the USC Noel was a candidate member of the illegal Swiss party. He and Herta were enrolled under the names Richard and Senta Wolf. On account of the SwCP's illegal status they had no party cards, but they paid their monthly dues of $5 to Sali Liebermann.

They had been admitted in 1940 by the SwCP's veteran leader Jules Humbert-Droz, after he had made further inquiries to the Comintern. But when he was replaced as party chairman in 1942, the new leadership refused to recognise the Fields' membership; it was deemed invalid because it had not been approved by the central committee. However, they did treat the Fields as sympathisers.

The vagaries of Noel's life as a cardless communist and one-time spy were soon known to Merker, Bertz and Maria Weiterer. According to Noel, Bertz even considered convoking a hearing on whether to allow Noel to join the KPD on a temporary basis, although this seems unlikely.

Then, quite unexpectedly, in late February or early March 1943 Noel received a telephone call from a man who introduced himself with the password 'Brook', which Field had been given in Moscow in 1938. They arranged to meet that afternoon at Noel's office.

Noel adjudged 'Brook' to be a Soviet citizen. He had been searching for a 'Noel Haviland' for over a year,[16] and it was only after consulting Jean Liebermann in Zurich that he was eventually directed to the correct name and address.

He told Noel and Herta that they had both been admitted into the Party. When Noel confirmed that he was prepared to work for the Soviet Union, 'Brook' quizzed them about their lives, work and relationships. He instructed Noel to break off all party contacts, resume his previous lifestyle and live as an apolitical person. He was to build up relationships both with employees of the US consulate in Geneva and with other Americans. Funds would be supplied for his new persona.

Noel explained that he was helping communist and antifascist refugees, and that this was impossible without extensive party contacts. He could not give an immediate answer concerning these new instructions. He wanted to consult his political leader (Bertz) first. They arranged that 'Brook' would return in a week and Noel would give him a concrete answer then.

On the advice of Bertz, Noel wrote a letter to the Executive Committee of the Comintern which Maria Weiterer encoded for him. In this missive Noel described his USC work and the considerable difficulties involved in changing political direction. He asked for a formal Comintern decision about how his talents could best be used. Noel took the letter with him to the projected *Treff*, but the Soviet agent did not turn up.[17]

A later Soviet report on Field provided a radically different version of the meeting with 'Brook'. This contended that once Moscow learned in 1942 that Noel was working in Geneva as the director of USC, he was contacted in spring 1943. But after a long talk with the NKVD agent, Noel and Herta announced that in their view the password was now obsolete and insufficiently credible. In the five years during which there had been no contact with them, they had taken on new commitments and entered into another line of work. Asked what these commitments were and with whom, Field refused to say. After that, all contact with him was broken off.[18]

How should one account for the considerable differences between the two accounts? It is impossible to say in which language the interview took place or whether 'Brook' was linguistically-challenged. It is quite possible that 'Brook's' original report was altered to conform to subsequent events in the Field affair. However, the bottom line was that 'Brook's' account represented another black mark for Noel.

Yet in the final analysis Noel versus 'Brook' was a sideshow in the Field affair. In the greater scheme of things, it was Noel's relationship with the OSS and Allen Dulles that would prove to be central.

12

DANGEROUS LIAISONS

NOEL, DULLES AND THE OSS 1942–45

Dulles and Field[1]

In his prison statements Noel endeavoured to clarify his relationship with US intelligence. He freely admitted that from 1942 to 1945 he had sporadic contacts with the Office of Strategic Services. Moreover, on a number of occasions he had personally met with Allen Dulles, the head of the OSS mission in the Swiss capital Bern.

Noel made no secret of this relationship, because it had nothing to do with espionage and he was never an agent of the OSS. After all, Dulles had far better sources of information than him. Dulles gave him no orders, and after their first meeting he never requested intelligence material from Field. Save for their first encounter in December 1942, all of their meetings had taken place at Field's initiative. Once Dulles left Switzerland for Wiesbaden in July 1945 there were no further meetings between the two men.[2] 'I gave Dulles no information', asserted Noel, 'either orally or in writing'.[3]

Was Noel being evasive? The interrogations he underwent in 1954 ultimately produced more meetings between him and Dulles than he initially owned up to. Moreover, the Hungarians found it hard to understand the casual first-name relationship existing between the two Americans, which allowed Noel simply to 'drop in' on Dulles when he needed to.[4] Aside from American informality, the reason for this was that Noel and Dulles knew each other beforehand.

Allen Welsh Dulles was born in New York State in April 1893, the son of a Presbyterian minister. His grandfather and uncle were American secretaries of state, and his older brother John Foster would serve in that position during the Eisenhower administration, with Allen joining him as the first civilian director of the US Central Intelligence Agency (CIA).

After graduating from Princeton, Allen entered the diplomatic service in 1916. That year he was posted to Vienna and in 1917 he moved to Bern. It was there that he began his involvement in intelligence. He also got to know Noel's father, Herbert Field, and it is possible that he met Noel too.

According to one author, Herbert Field shopped the American consul in Zurich, because the latter maintained wartime contact with his German son-in-law. This seems odd, given Noel's observations that his father too kept up contacts with the German 'enemy'. This account also has Herbert declining to work for US intelligence, which mirrors Noel's response to Dulles in the Second World War. Then there is the picture of Dulles asking the fourteen-year-old Noel what he wanted to do with his life, and eliciting the solemn reply, 'bring peace to the world'.[5]

Despite extensive questioning about their relationship, Noel never mentioned this encounter with Dulles to his Hungarian interrogators. He may have forgotten the occasion. He may have dismissed the event as inconsequential. Conversely, he may have deliberately withheld knowledge of this meeting. This would have been understandable; a relationship, however tenuous, stretching back over thirty years might simply have stored up even more trouble for him. Then again, the event may never have happened.[6]

After serving at the Versailles conference in 1919, and then in Berlin and Istanbul, Dulles headed the State Department's Near East Division. Noel heard him lecture in that capacity when he was in the Foreign Service school. He also met Allen on the odd occasion at Washington cocktail parties, but they had no working relationship.

Dulles resigned from the State Department in September 1926, shortly after Noel's entry. He joined John Foster's law firm Sullivan and Cromwell, and his career there involved him in many foreign undertakings. On occasion he also acted as a legal adviser to the State Department. He served in this capacity with the US delegation at the Geneva disarmament conference in 1932–33, and Noel thought he might have met him before he left. Their next encounter occurred a decade later.

Dulles arrived in Switzerland on 9 November 1942 only hours before the German occupation of Vichy France began.[7] He proceeded to establish his OSS residency in the American embassy in Bern. But by then Noel had already come into contact with the OSS.

Wartime contacts[8]

Dr Robert Dexter, the then USC director in Lisbon, visited the Fields' Marseille headquarters in September 1942. He informed Noel that he was in contact with the OSS, and proposed that Field too should work with them, particularly by handing over information of a military nature.[9]

Noel discussed the issue with Kreikemeyer, his party liaison, who suggested that, while making no commitments, Noel should not fully decline the offer either, since it was their duty to support the war against fascism. Moreover, in an emergency, in exchange for such information they could get assistance from the OSS.

Dexter also met Kreikemeyer in Marseille. Noel, who translated their conversation, thought that Dexter was unimpressed by the German. Later Dexter travelled to Geneva for a few days in the company of Noel, who was making one of his courier trips for the KPD.[10]

When the two Americans returned to Marseille Noel accompanied Dexter to the US consulate, where Field met an unidentified OSS agent. Noel contended that on conscientious grounds he could not directly or indirectly collaborate with the OSS. However, from the perspective of his duty as an American citizen he might possibly pass on military information, should such come to his attention. Although he tried to get a firmer commitment, the official seemed content with this. Noel never saw the man again.

In December 1942 after the Fields had escaped from the German occupation of Vichy France, Noel took a call from the US consulate in Geneva, asking him to drop by. He complied and found Dulles awaiting him there. Until then Noel hadn't known he was in Switzerland. Dulles made the same proposal as had the OSS official in Marseille, and Field gave him the same answer. This committed Noel to nothing. Dulles made no attempt to influence his decision.

The second meeting between Dulles and Field took place sometime in the first half of 1943. It concerned the imprisoned Leo Bauer.

Noel knew about the conflict between his brother Hermann and Bauer in Krakow in 1939. However, he only met the German for the first time in early October 1941. Noel, on Merker's orders, was then endeavouring to organise contact between Marseille and the submerged Paul Bertz in Bern. Having checked Field out, Bertz instructed Bauer to meet the American in Geneva, and so the link was set up.

One year later Noel introduced the visiting Robert Dexter to Bauer in Geneva, at the latter's request. Leo's previous work with refugees impressed the Unitarian minister. Field was present during these talks.

However, unknown to him, Dexter and an OSS official met Bauer on a later occasion. Bauer emphasised that he was prepared to cooperate, but he would not participate in military espionage, since the KPD considered that this posed too great a risk to its refugee status in Switzerland. However, he accepted an English-language OSS questionnaire.

Some days later, on 27 October 1942, Bauer was arrested by Swiss security police at the Geneva house where he lived illegally under the name Paul-Eric Perret, a bank employee. The police discovered much compromising material, including a set of Noel's handwritten reports for Bertz. Fortunately for Field these were signed only with his party name 'Hauser'. The police also found Erica Glaser's address, several thousand Swiss francs belonging to KPD funds, and the OSS questionnaire.

Bauer was told to keep his mouth shut and to expect no help from the OSS. He underwent investigative detention for nearly a year in Geneva's St Antoine prison. On 21 October 1943 he was sentenced on various charges to thirty months in jail and a fifteen year banning order from Switzerland. His case was reviewed in March 1944. Certain charges were dropped and his jail-term was reduced to two years, less time spent in custody. Bauer was in fact released on 27 May 1944, whereupon he entered a sanatorium to treat his stomach problems, with his stay funded by the USC.

During the initial investigation Erica, acting under KPD orders, posed as his distraught fiancée, who understood nothing about politics, and a sympathetic warder allowed her constant visits, even at night.[11] As a result the KPD got to know the content of Bauer's interrogations within a few hours, and could take counter-measures. Conversely, Erica informed Bauer of developments outside. Noel managed to liberate the seized party funds, by getting Bauer to sign a false receipt stating that he had received the money for refugee work in France.

Leo had several letters smuggled out of jail, and in one of them he asked Noel to contact various people who might intercede on his behalf with the Swiss authorities. Dulles was one of those he named.

Field sought Allen out in his office in the US embassy in the first half of 1943. Dulles stated flatly that he couldn't get involved, since he would be unable to explain to the Swiss just what sort of interest he had in the matter.

It was after the KPD-dominated National Committee for Free Germany (NKFD) was set up near Moscow in July 1943 that Noel's third and fourth meetings with Dulles occurred. Both were prompted by Kreikemeyer's dire need of funds to succour his comrades, and they came at a time when the Swiss government was placing restrictions on the finances of American aid organisations.

First in Marseille and then in Paris, Kreikemeyer was responsible for providing all forms of aid to the KPD throughout France, and as far as Noel knew he was Kreikemeyer's sole source of revenue. Kreikemeyer also distributed the funds which Noel received from the American Joint Anti-Fascist Refugee Committee to former members of the International Brigades.

Kreikemeyer suggested that Noel should tap his American contacts, and this was what happened. With Bertz's agreement, it was decided to provide Dulles with some material produced by CALPO (*Comité Allemagne Libre pour l'Ouest*/ the Free German Committee for the West). Aping the NKFD, this body was set up by the KPD leadership in France in September 1943. The conditions Bertz imposed for the meeting with Dulles were that Noel didn't reveal his source, and that he undertook no commitments in return for any funds provided.

So in late 1943 Noel made an appointment with Allen, and when they met for the third time he handed over the CALPO material. Dulles read this through, but made no particular comment. He asked if 1,000 American dollars (about 4,000 Swiss francs) would be a sufficient contribution. Noel assented and Dulles went to his safe for the money. He got no receipt. As Noel observed, this sum was only a fraction (*Bruchteil*) of the SF80–100,000 that Field had given Kreikemeyer in those difficult days. However, Field had not asked for more, since he had no wish to be obligated.

This scenario repeated itself in the first half of 1944 when Kreike-meyer, now based in Paris, again urgently requested funds. He sent fresh material to prove that CALPO was still in business. At this fourth meeting Dulles asked if a sum like the last would suffice, and so Noel obtained another 4,000 Swiss francs. There was possibly a third contribution of 2,000 Swiss francs on a separate occasion.[12]

At one of his meetings with Dulles, Noel made two other requests. In the years of German triumph, the Swiss National Bank imposed various restrictions on the transfer of funds. This forced Noel to exchange his dollars illegally, whereby he got only SF3 to SF3.5 to the dollar, when the official exchange-rate was around SF4.5. So Noel asked Dulles for the OSS to act as a sort of bank for the USC, sending funds from Boston through official channels in the same way as the embassy's money was handled. Noel also wanted confidential USC telegrams to be sent encoded through embassy or OSS channels.[13] Dulles refused both requests.

The fifth meeting between the two men concerned the so-called Szőnyi group of Hungarian communists. Since this was an integral feature of the Rajk show trial, it will be discussed later in Chapter 19.

A sixth meeting at the end of 1944 also concerned Hungary, when the leaders of the OSE (*Oeuvre de secours aux enfants*), a French-based Organisation to aid Jewish children, handed Noel a memo for Dulles. This requested that the Americans should bomb the routes whereby the murderous Arrow Cross regime was deporting Hungary's Jews. Dulles offered no opinion on the document.

OSS Paris and CALPO[14]

The seventh meeting with Dulles took place at the end of 1944. It concerned Noel's need to reach Paris in order to make arrangements to deceive a pending USC Boston inspection. Field turned to Dulles since the US consulate in Geneva refused him a travel permit, because Noel had left Switzerland illegally.[15]

Initially Dulles was unwilling to help, although later he decided to inform OSS Paris that Field would be arriving there, and that possibly they could use his expertise on German antifascist refugees. However, he gave Noel no instructions, other than to report his presence to the OSS in Paris.

In a telegram to OSS Paris on 30 November Dulles referred to Noel's contacts with CALPO, and thought it possible that 'that group contains valuable personnel for German penetration'. He considered it 'urgent that Field discuss whole problem with you and put you in touch with certain of their leaders who are now in Paris and whom he knows personally'.[16]

On 20 January 1945 Dulles informed them that Field was travelling to Paris in the coming week, and suggested that Noel, 'after preliminary talk with you, (should) see his CALPO friends (in Paris) and advise you of his impressions'. Dulles thought Field 'might be useful in certain respects for liaison'.[17]

Dulles supplied Noel with the necessary travel papers, which he presented to the OSS representative in Annemasse on the Franco-Swiss frontier. This official arranged for Field to drive to Lyon with the regular OSS courier. In Lyon Noel contacted the US military authorities and obtained a train ticket to Paris.

Once in Paris Noel concerned himself with USC business for about one week. He wanted everything in order, because he thought that he might be entrusted with work by the OSS. He also made contact with the KPD leadership in Paris concerning his relationship with the OSS, and requested instructions on the matter. He met with Kreikemeyer and Maria Weiterer, who had slipped back across the border in December 1944. He also consulted Otto Niebergall, the KPD leader of CALPO.

Then he presented himself at the Paris headquarters of OSS. There he received an army ration card, which entitled him to eat in a canteen, and he was given a room in a requisitioned hotel.

He also ended up with an OSS major to whose terms of reference CALPO belonged. This officer was Arthur Schlesinger Jr, later a noted historian.[18] They talked for half an hour, and Noel gained the impression that he knew little about either Field or CALPO. However, Schlesinger asked Noel to write a memo on CALPO. It would be discussed at a meeting in a few days time, and he invited Noel to attend.[19]

Niebergall viewed Field's position with regard to the OSS as correct, and considered that he could be very helpful for future CALPO activities. He instructed Noel to compose the requested memo and to attend the meeting where it would be discussed.

What CALPO particularly sought was United States recognition of it as the official representative of all German antifascist refugees in France.

Such strengthened prestige would broaden its support. The CALPO leadership hoped to participate in the military struggle too, especially behind enemy lines, and even to set up their organisation in Germany itself. This was something that was impossible without American permission and assistance.

Field told Niebergall that he wouldn't be much use regarding the recognition question, save in emphasising the allegedly non-communist character of CALPO. As USC director he would have to concentrate above all on familiar subjects, such as the emergency situation of anti-fascist refugees and the supply of material aid.

With the German's help Noel produced a long memo, composing it solely from CALPO's own publications with no confidential material included. Field's memo was essentially a description of CALPO's achievements, and he also emphasised that it was a broad-based non-communist movement.

He then visited a former State Department colleague who had an office in the American embassy. In return for a copy of the document, the diplomat provided a stenographer, and Field dictated the entire document of about twenty typed pages in the embassy. This was done on the day of the projected meeting and Noel handed Schlesinger a copy beforehand.

There were about fifteen participants at the OSS meeting on CALPO, all in uniform, save Noel and Dulles, who turned up later.[20] Not only was Dulles in attendance for only part of the meeting, but he contented himself with the role of observer. Noel had no idea why or when Dulles had arrived in Paris. He presumed that he had other business there. The meeting lasted about two hours. Noel spoke briefly, but only about supplying refugees.

The meeting resolved that the recognition of CALPO could only be decided at a higher level. More attention was given to the possibility of by-passing the CALPO leadership and recruiting its militarily-trained members for operations behind German lines. It was finally decided to send two or three OSS groups throughout liberated France to look for suitable refugees, whether or not they belonged to CALPO.

It is hard to see that Noel deceived anybody with his memorandum on CALPO, and certainly not Dulles. As Field said later, there couldn't have been any doubt about his sympathy for CALPO, since his memo was little more than a propaganda brochure. Nor did he influence OSS policy. If the OSS was cooperating with CALPO, then those decisions had already been taken.

Following the meeting, he reported to Maria Weiterer and later to Niebergall that same day. Noel wanted to present a typed report. Mia was aghast, fearing somewhat exaggeratedly that this could earn Noel a court martial for treason and the firing-squad. However, it was in keeping with this brave and decent woman's concerns for him. She further forbade Field to speak about the meeting with anyone other than Niebergall, and even with him he was only to mention the matter of recruiting CALPO members, not the question of recognition.

Having performed his comradely duty, Noel left Paris a few days later to visit USC affiliates in southern France. He then returned to Paris. On the day before his departure to Geneva he reported to the OSS and received fresh documentation, with which he travelled by train to Dole. There his contact with the OSS ended.

An army truck took him to the Swiss frontier at Basel. He crossed the frontier on foot and was detained for several hours at the border, because of inadequate documentation. After he was allowed to contact the consulate in Basel, he was released and travelled directly to Geneva.

Thereafter Noel made no use of the OSS for future journeys, since the consulate in Geneva now issued him with permits. However, as we shall see, he did look up Dulles once more for help in a matter that concerned Erica. However, she was not the only woman involved in Noel's activities.

13

TEETERING EDIFICE

USC EUROPE 1945–47

USC France, Jo and Ilona[1]

Following the liberation of most of France in 1944, Noel established USC branches (*Filialen*) in Paris, Toulouse, Marseille and Lyon. Once the war in Europe ended in May 1945 he extended his little empire further, setting up USC offices in Austria, Poland, Czechoslovakia and Hungary. In each instance primary support was given to communist groups. 'The bulk of material aid was used to support party members', asserted Field, 'and above all the cadres'.[2]

In 1946 Noel had a budget of several hundred thousand dollars but there was a sharp reduction in funding when, in his view, 'reaction' set in with the onset of the Cold War. His funding was not divided evenly: USC France received 60 per cent of all funds, since in Noel's view USC Europe stood or fell with the Paris office; Geneva and Lisbon were allocated 10 per cent each; Poland and Czechoslovakia both got 5 per cent; Germany and Italy combined received 5 per cent; and a similar amount went to Austria and Hungary.

In 1945–46 USC Europe had about one hundred employees, of whom some 50 per cent worked in France. At least half of the employees were communists, as were three-quarters of leading personnel. This situation gradually changed. Although the wartime staff were Europeans and mostly communists, by the time that Noel was dismissed in September 1947 most branches of USC Europe operated under American and non-communist leadership.

Amongst those communists working for Field were several remarkable women, of whom two can be singled out for their dedication, courage, and versatility. They were both important in Noel's life, as women often had been. He wrote to an unidentified correspondent that 'I have a tendency to idolize and to let my whole inner life center around a small number of revered women of the most varying ages, while there are virtually no men to whom I feel a very close kinship'.[3]

One of those he revered was Jo Tempi, whom Noel described as an 'extraordinarily beautiful woman'.[4] Trilingual like the Fields, she had certainly led a colourful life. She was born Herta Sommerfeld in Berlin in August 1907, the daughter of Jewish working-class parents. She married Werner Jurr, a KPD youth functionary, and served both the Comintern and Soviet intelligence in a number of capacities and countries.

After Hitler came to power, Jo operated secretly for the KPD in Germany. Her husband was less fortunate, being imprisoned by the Nazis from 1934 to 1945.[5] In 1934 Jo was in Britain, and from October 1935 in France where she worked for Münzenberg's organisation. When Münzenberg was expelled from the KPD in May 1938, Jo's own party status was thrown into doubt for some time, even though she denounced her former boss.

In 1938 she contracted a presumably bigamous 'passport-marriage' with a French communist called Raoul Tempi, and thereby obtained French citizenship. Following the French collapse in June 1940, like thousands of others she fled to the south of the country. By autumn 1940 Jo was in Geneva, where she first met the Fields. They even went skiing.[6]

Jo worked for Noel in Marseille and Toulouse, and also acted as a courier for both the French resistance and the KPD. In 1941–43 she headed a Swiss organisation in Toulouse which helped refugee children, and she played a pivotal role in saving many Jewish orphans. On at least four occasions she risked her life to lead parties of children through mountains controlled by Germans and collaborationist French police, bringing them illegally into Switzerland.

Early in 1944 Jo was ordered to Paris, where she led a USC centre which was in constant contact with the resistance, the French Communist Party and the KPD. Some months before the liberation of Paris in August 1944, at the urging of the KPD leadership there, Noel appointed Jo as director of USC France. This was done without the knowledge of Boston but Jo's charms would later ensure the ratification of this *fait accompli*.

In January 1945 when Noel arrived in Paris with OSS help, he had several aims in mind other than aiding CALPO. He wanted to organise assistance for the various national groups that he funded and begin the process of establishing USC branches in other parts of France. Furthermore, he planned to set up hospitals under communist leadership, and to ensure that they were available to party members in the first instance.

He also needed to show Jo how to disguise these communist institutions as 'bourgeois' assistance, and how to adapt the accounting system in order to deceive (*verschleiern*) Boston regarding the actual use of its funds. The matter was urgent, because the USC's new executive director Charles Joy, who was currently on an inspection tour in Italy, was planning to visit France too.[7]

It was not a good time for the general population of Paris. The winter of 1944–45 was bitter. Communications, power and food supplies were all disrupted. Noel slept first at Jo's and then on the freezing floor of her prospective in-laws.[8] Maria Weiterer was living with Jo too, as well as working with her at USC Paris at 61 rue Jouffroy.

After attending the OSS conference on CALPO, Noel drove with Jo to Lyon and then to the south of France. In Marseille, by a fateful coincidence, they met up with the 'Szőnyi group' (p. 191). Then they drove to Toulouse, where it was agreed to set up a hospital for the Spanish comrades, as well as a convalescent home for PCE cadres near Pau.

At the end of the tour, which had lasted about six weeks, Noel returned to Geneva. About two months later he again travelled to Paris, this time without OSS assistance. He then journeyed again with Jo to Marseille to meet the Reverend Joy in May or June 1945.[9]

The three of them travelled to south-west France that summer. The trip included a one week stay in Biarritz. Influenced by Jo's charms, Joy sent a cable to Boston demanding recognition of her as director of USC France, instead of the person Boston had selected for the post.

Joy remained in Europe for over six months, and according to Field he returned to Boston as a 'sympathiser'. There he ensured that Noel was formally elevated to the title of USC director for Europe, while bestowing upon Jo the post of deputy director for Europe in addition to that of director for France.

Also working briefly for USC France in summer 1945 was Ilona Kojsza, who later headed USC Hungary. Herta was certainly a fan of Ilona and liked and admired her very much. She described the Hungarian as a warm and vivacious woman who was never downhearted. Tireless, resourceful, and utterly fearless, Ilona always stuck vigorously to her own opinions.

Ilona was born in Budapest in September 1904, the thirteenth child of a poor Catholic family. After her first marriage ended in 1927, she joined the illegal Hungarian Communist Party (HCP) the following year. In 1932 she was in Vienna and a member of the Austrian party. She married an Austrian comrade that same year, and operated as a courier between the Hungarian and Austrian parties.

In 1936 she moved to Paris, split from her second husband, and operated as a fund-raiser for the International Brigades. Returning to Vienna, Ilona was imprisoned without trial in 1937–38. Amnestied, she returned to Paris in 1938. Arrested by the French in 1941, she was interned until September 1943.[10]

On her release Ilona operated under the alias Liliane Prevost Simone, and acted as a courier for the KPD and HCP groups in southern France. From September 1944 to April 1945 she built up an organisation on the Franco-Swiss frontier at Annemasse, a half-hour tram-ride from Geneva. It was there in December 1944 that she first met Noel. He recruited her as a courier on the recommendations of both Maria Weiterer and Ferenc Vági.

Known as 'the angel of Annemasse', Ilona led those illegally leaving Switzerland to resistance groups operating in France, northern Italy and Yugoslavia. She also assisted anti-fascist Germans in France to enter Switzerland before their return to Germany.[11]

In July 1945 Ilona travelled to Paris, hoping to get back to Hungary from the French capital. She worked with USC Paris, and Noel met her there in late August while on his way to the USA. There he offered her the post of head of USC Hungary. In early October 1945 Ilona made her way back to Hungary via Yugoslavia.

Travelling man[12]

Leaving their Geneva office under the control of Elsie Haus, a Swiss communist who would later head the USC branch in Vienna, Noel and Herta travelled to the USA in September 1945.

On arrival at the USC's Boston headquarters the Fields were initially feted as heroes, for having created such an influential organisation from such modest beginnings. They spoke on the radio and were interviewed by the press. Despite his shyness, Noel also addressed public meetings of people who had contributed to and collected the funds which he had spent.

However, later there were problems. Tales about the pro-communist orientation of USC Europe were already reaching Boston.[13] Naturally, Noel ascribed these reports to 'Trotskyites' and 'reactionaries'. He also spent much time in Boston fighting about senior personnel. During his time there he was obliged to sack the communist head of USC Czechoslovakia, with consequences that would later haunt him.

At least the Fields finally received a proper salary. Until then a nominal fifty dollars per month had been put by for them in Boston. Now they were awarded a joint annual salary of $4,000, which later rose to $6,000.[14] Only some of this money was sent to Geneva. The rest was retained in Boston, and Noel received the balance when he was fired.

Noel and Herta also spent some time in New York, staying in Brooklyn with Hermann and Kate Field and their two sons.[15] Presumably they saw Nina too, although there is no mention of this.

In December 1945 Noel and Herta, along with the Spanish-speaking American communist Persis Miller, visited Mexico for about two weeks. In Mexico City Noel renewed his acquaintance with Paul Merker. Among others he met the so-called 'raging reporter' Egon Erwin Kisch and his wife Gisela, as well as the KPD member and novelist Anna Seghers.[16]

Back in New York the Fields had their last meetings with the Massings (Chapter 15). They returned to Europe in late February 1946, worked with USC Paris for a month, and reached Geneva at the end of March.

Noel departed for Germany in May. From then until November he represented the USC on CRALOG (Council of Relief Agencies Licensed for Operation in Germany), an umbrella organisation for the aid agencies operating in the US occupation zone of Germany.[17]

In May 1946 Noel was in Berlin. There he managed a secret meeting with Franz Dahlem. He also saw Mia, Kreikemeyer, Bertz, and Werner

Jurr. From 16 August to 15 October he travelled throughout the US zone, making a series of reports and recommendations for CRALOG which later became that body's 'Bible'. In November he returned to Geneva, where Herta had held the fort for six months.

Noel was on the move again in 1947 although there is no clear chronology of his travels. It is unclear where Noel was when his mother died in New York on 31 July, nor do we have any idea of his reaction to her death.[18] The sources show that in the early summer of 1947 Noel was in Poland and Czechoslovakia.[19] In Katowice in Polish Silesia his hostess was Tonia Lechtman.

Born Antonina Bialer in Łódź in 1918, Tonia's family migrated from Poland to the British mandate of Palestine in 1935. Two years later she married the Austrian communist Sioma Lechtman. The British expelled the couple on account of their political activities, and they settled in France.

Although now a stateless person, Sioma fought in the Austrian battalion in Spain. Following Franco's victory he was interned in Gurs and Le Vernet. Later he was deported to Auschwitz. In January 1945 when that camp was evacuated, he escaped from a 'death march' but was apparently killed by some Poles.

Tonia was also interned in France, but friends helped her to escape. Entering Switzerland illegally with her two children, she was initially interned. Later she worked for the USC, and in 1946–49 she was involved with the USC hospital for miners established near Katowice. Tonia was another who would suffer from knowing Field.

That same summer Noel made another trip to Germany to visit a USC orphanage in the British zone. He also travelled to Berlin for three or four days in July accompanied by Erica. There he met Bertz, Kreikemeyer and others from his Geneva days. Through Mia he tried to contact Paul Merker, but the latter claimed to be too busy to see him.

At some point that summer Hermann Field met briefly with Noel. Accompanied by Kate, Hermann was leading a delegation of American architects on a six-week tour of Britain, France, Switzerland, Poland, Czechoslovakia and Sweden.

Noel was 'depressed', recalled Hermann. 'I gathered that the controversy about his political bias' in directing USC Europe 'was likely to cause his forced departure from the work he had given so much of himself to during the war years'.[20]

In late summer 1947 Noel was in Vienna. This was a farewell visit, for, by then, he had been sacked.

Finale[21]

While Noel was in Germany in 1946 Jo Tempi was in the USA. In Noel's view 'the old grandfather', the Reverend Joy, had completely lost his head over her, and had arranged a triumphal visit to Boston for Jo that summer. Against Noel's advice she made the voyage to the USA.

According to Noel she was followed everywhere by the FBI. Despite conducting herself politically in a reserved manner, Jo failed to understand the difference between Paris and Boston. She and the married Joy were caught *in flagrante* on an overnight train journey to New York, and they apparently also registered as man and wife in a New York hotel.

The USC gave Joy the choice of resignation or dismissal, and he chose the former. Jo refused to resign and simply left the USA.[22] She was soon followed to Paris by a USC commission of inquiry, and Noel left Germany to attend a meeting in Paris on 10 September 1946. Despite the rumours, the sympathetic commission members, who were given the full itinerary, gave the 'red' USC a clean bill of health.

However, the story would not die, and Noel was summoned to Boston for more discussion about Jo Tempi's activities. On 6 January 1947 Noel flew by *Pan-Am* 'Clipper' from Lisbon to New York to defend himself and Jo against the 'reactionary' attacks on the 'orientation' of USC Europe. On his flight registration he somewhat quixotically gave as his job description, 'Worker'.[23]

He refused to sack Jo either then or when the new USC executive director visited Europe in May 1947. Ultimately a letter sent from Boston in June dismissed Jo from her post, effective 1 July. Noel too wanted to resign but the Party dissuaded him, and he doused his ire by sending a 'stinging' (*geharnisch*) letter of protest to Boston.

Noel and Jo proceeded to transfer the remaining budget of USC France to Geneva, where it was soon spent. Rather than letting them resign in sympathy, Jo fired her Paris staff, thereby obliging the USC to pay each of them three months salary. Thereafter she went through the files, rendering them useless, and wrecked the office car. In August Noel and Herta too were sacked, effective as of 30 September 1947.

Noel would extol his time with the USC as 'the crowning achievement of my entire life'. It was the time when 'I lived and worked more and more completely as a communist, without inner doubts. And the harder the work, the happier I was. I was conscious that I was making a valuable contribution to the antifascist struggle and saving our cadres'. He felt that judged by this measure, 'my life's work stands or falls'.[24]

14

THE SEARCHERS

NOEL AND HERTA 1947–49

Creating a new life [1]

On 1 October 1947 both Noel and Herta were out of a job. To them it was worse than mere unemployment. Noel viewed their recent downfall as 'practically the end of our lives'. [2]

Given the intense level of commitment that he had invested in the USC, and the sense of achievement he derived from his work, it is hardly surprising that neurotic Noel suffered a physical and mental collapse, when he was finally ousted from his post as European director.

For six months he was plagued with a recurrence of stomach ulcers and the serious eye infection he had contracted in 1943. He had to lie in bed for half the day, although most afternoons he would voluntarily traipse down to the USC Geneva office at 37 Quai Wilson to help his successor, Hélène Matthey. The Fields had moved home too. From September 1947 to January 1949 they lived in a flat at 21 rue de Contamines.

Despite having no income from employment, the Fields were hardly destitute. For six months they lived on redundancy money paid to them by Boston. Noel also had about $15,000 in savings in the USA. Moreover, his mother had left him securities worth $40–50,000, although the income from these remained uncertain. The trustees were still reinvesting them, but Noel hoped they would pay him $1,500–2,000 per annum.

He also caught up on his reading, since he had had no time for such diversion while running the USC. Among other classics he read Homer, Shakespeare, Voltaire, Goethe, Tolstoy and Chekhov. Later he began to study Polish in preparation for his coming travels, and soon he could read the newspapers.

As he slowly recovered Noel decided to create a new life for himself as an expert on Eastern Europe. He hoped that his knowledge of the area might get him a job as a reporter for the newly-formed Progressive Party. Led by one of Roosevelt's former vice-presidents, Henry Wallace, and supported by the CPUSA, it planned to contest the 1948 presidential election. Field also decided to write 'from a progressive standpoint, a long scientific work about the People's Democracies',[3] which he hoped might be published in Britain or France, even if it was rejected in the USA.

In April 1948, two months after the communist takeover in Czechoslovakia, two government officials currently in Geneva invited the Fields to Prague.[4] Both Oskar Kosta and Evžen Klinger had lived in London during the war. Whether they were amongst those whom Hermann Field had helped to reach Britain is unclear, although both would later be arrested in the early stages of what became the Slánský affair.

It seems unlikely that they acted on their own initiative. Yet it is impossible to say whether this was a significant step in setting-up Noel, if it was one at all.[5]

At the beginning of May 1948 Field travelled to London for about one week. He visited the offices of the left-wing weekly the *New Statesman* as well as two publishers. His talks about possible publications produced no tangible results, although the *Statesman* invited him to submit articles 'on spec'. On 6 May Field met with a former colleague from the League of Nations, Konni Zilliacus, who was now a Labour MP. He also saw Erica.

Poor man's Svengali[6]

Noel considered himself to be an expert about his foster-daughter. 'I know what I'm talking about', he asserted in his cell, 'for other than my wife, there's nobody I know so well as Erica Glaser'.[7]

Such statements by men about women are rash at the best of times, and in the case of the inexperienced Noel they verged on the ludicrous. He 'knew' only the aims that he had in mind for Erica. He wanted her to fit his idealised notion of a party cadre.

Although at first Erica allowed herself to be swayed by him, later she would come to want things she had never had since she was thirteen, such as a home, a family, some belongings. In the final analysis she ensured that her own ambitions for her future trumped his.

In 1942 Erica commenced her studies at the University of Geneva's school for interpreters. She received her diploma (in English, French and German) in summer 1944.

In March 1945 Erica formally joined the KPD, whose leadership in Switzerland decided to infiltrate her into the OSS. They ordered Noel to try to execute their plan, and he managed it without difficulty. Field simply called on Dulles, who sent Noel to a young colleague. The latter gave Noel a long application form for Erica to fill in and send off. According to one source Dulles even signed her character reference.[8]

In May Erica became a member of the OSS. She worked first as a translator in Bern, and from July as secretary to the head of the Labor Desk in OSS headquarters in Wiesbaden in Hesse. She was also in Berlin for a while, and for some of the time she apparently interrogated German scientists, officials and POWs.

Also in Hesse was Leo Bauer, who had left Switzerland illegally in June 1945. Now he conducted various activities for the KPD *Land* organisation, as both an editor and a functionary.

Erica passed all the information she obtained from her OSS post to Bauer, from where it went to Franz Dahlem. Recently released from KZ Mauthausen, Dahlem was now the number three man–after Ulbricht and Pieck–in the KPD hierarchy in East Berlin. Responsible not only for the Party's cadres, Dahlem also oversaw its underground activities in the western occupation zones of Germany.

President Truman closed down the OSS in September 1945, but a rump organisation remained, dispersed among other US agencies. The question arose as to whether Erica should join a new civilian espionage organisation. Dahlem ruled that she should not do so under any circumstances.[9]

Erica spent Christmas 1945 with her parents in the Surrey town of Epsom, where they lived at 'Woodcote House' in Woodcote Green Road. Registered as a medical practitioner on 11 August 1941, Willy Glaser had his surgery in Epsom too, at 57 Church Street.

Their reunion must have been an emotional occasion for all three. It was the first time they had been together for over five years. However,

Kurt was not there to join them, for Erica's older brother had been killed in the war, aged just twenty-six.[10]

After Dahlem ordered her to leave the OSS, Erica resigned in January 1946, resumed her German citizenship, and came out openly as a communist. She worked with Bauer in Wiesbaden, and edited a KPD journal in Frankfurt. She also studied law there.

From summer 1946, if not earlier, Erica was in a relationship with US Army Captain Robert Wallach. Wallach was not a member of the OSS, but served in Wiesbaden as an administrative officer in the US military government of Hesse.

In spring 1948 Erica became pregnant. At about the same time she learned that her father was dying of lung cancer. So with the KPD's permission she travelled to Britain. Not that her journey was that simple. When the Office of Military Government of the United States in Germany (OMGUS) refused her permission to leave the US occupation zone, Erica resolved the problem by flying illegally from the British occupation zone to the UK. There she was arrested, but later released on compassionate grounds.

In March 1948 Wallach was in the USA, having travelled there in order to demobilise himself from the army, while Erica was with her dying father. It was then that Noel visited Epsom and endeavoured unsuccessfully not only to prevent her forthcoming marriage, but also to win her back to the Party.

Of course Noel 'knew' that Erica was only getting married because she was pregnant.[11] He claimed that Erica told him she was prepared to carry on working for the KPD, if Wallach could find a job in Europe. If they left for the USA, she would join the American Party. She may well have said these things, if only to get Field off her back.

Convinced that Erica was not yet 'lost', Noel left for Paris, where he called on Jo Tempi and met with Artur London, whose vital role in Field's fate is discussed in Chapter 20. Then he headed home to prepare for his trip to Czechoslovakia and Poland.

On Tuesday 8 June 1948 the twenty-six-year-old Erica married the thirty-two-year-old Robert Robbins Wallach in Epsom registry office. The copy of their marriage certificate shows that the groom bore the same name as his father, a colonel in the US army. Therese Glaser was present at the ceremony, but not Willy. No signatures are recorded on this typed-up copy. Possibly the original was lifted by British or American spooks after Erica was arrested in East Berlin in 1950.

Twelve days later, at the age of sixty-two, Willy Glaser died at his home of 'carcinoma of the lung' in the presence of his wife and daughter. Soon after his death the Wallachs moved to Paris, where their daughter Madeline was born on 4 November 1948. According to Noel it was a difficult birth. At about the same time Erica apparently wrote a letter of resignation from the KPD.

Problems in Poland[12]

In mid-May 1948 the Fields set out on their study trip. They drove to Germany in a car that had once belonged to USC Geneva and was now allocated to USC Poland. There they stayed with Herta's mother in Karlsruhe for three days.

Next they made for Prague, again staying three days. Then they travelled to the USC hospital in Silesia, which was administered by Tonia Lechtman. They stayed there for ten days. Most of the summer they spent in Warsaw, and they remained in Poland until 15 September.

In Poland Noel pursued his objective of studying the current situation from 'a progressive standpoint'. He interviewed a number of personalities in the political and economic spheres, and visited various industrial and agricultural concerns. He and Herta also undertook several trips, mainly in the so-called 'Recovered Territories' east of the Oder-Neisse Line.[13]

In Warsaw—at the recommendation of Hiss—Noel received an offer to write a series of articles for the *National Guardian*, the newly-founded weekly newspaper of Wallace's Progressive Party. Naturally, he accepted, but he only produced one article, which he didn't submit because Herta deemed it not up to scratch.

As he assiduously followed the Hiss-Chambers case in the American press, Noel feared that he too would be drawn into the affair. So he temporarily backed out of his agreement with the *National Guardian*, citing health grounds. Later, while in Prague, when his 'naming' by the HUAC actually occurred, he formally withdrew from the project because he didn't want to cause problems for the Progressive Party.

There is considerable irony here. On the one hand, Noel dreaded being named in America for what he was, a communist and a Soviet spy. On the other hand, in Eastern Europe he wished to have precisely such laurels bestowed upon him. For, as he wrote later, besides visiting old friends and researching his project, Noel's chief reason for visiting Poland was 'finally, finally to clarify my party status'.[14]

Whereas previously this issue was not so pressing, now growing mistrust surrounded him. Without a party card Noel could offer no proof about his earlier role and activities as a communist. Nor did his professional status appear convincing, since Field was commencing a journalistic career at the age of forty-four. People were entitled to wonder 'who was I exactly, and what was the purpose of my work?'[15]

In a desperate effort to promote a new channel to Moscow, Noel approached Anna Duracz, a young Polish communist and former resistance fighter, whom he had met at a USC convalescent home in France. Anna was now secretary to Jakub Berman, the Politburo member overseeing the Soviet-controlled Polish secret police.

Doubtless aware of Moscow's increasing suspicions of Noel, Berman naturally had 'no time' to meet Field personally. Therefore on 9 September, shortly before he left Poland, Noel wrote a letter to Berman in French. He gave this to Anna, along with a 'short party history' of himself written in German. Anna told Field later that Berman had read his letter and would see what he could do, while making no promises.

The letter was plaintive. It spoke of the Fields' 'unusually difficult situation', the solution to which was 'literally a matter of life or death' to them. For 'outside of the Party, without party work, our existence is meaningless'. He begged Berman to read his 'short party history', which noticeably made no reference to Dulles, and then advise Noel what course he should follow in order to clarify his party status.[16]

Panic in Prague[17]

Noel and Herta returned to Prague on 16 September 1948. Throughout their stay they were under observation by the Czechoslovak secret police, the *Státni Bezpečnost* (StB).

As in Poland Noel conducted interviews, gathered material, and took trips outside of Prague with Herta. He also met several of the people that Hermann had helped in 1939, such as Karel Markus, Vilém Nový, and Evžen Loebl, now a deputy-minister of Foreign Trade.

The Fields were in contact with Leo Bauer too. He was convalescing in the Tatra Mountains following a serious automobile accident. From mid-September Bauer was in Prague and the Fields met with him several times. Bauer reported on the efforts of Paul Merker to bring Field to East Berlin, and there grant him a hearing in order to finally resolve his party status.

This matter became even more pressing when Noel learned that the Massings had been summoned before HUAC on 21 September. He was worried that they had mentioned his name to the committee. His fears increased when testimony by Whittaker Chambers, given before a closed session of HUAC, was released to the press: for the first time Noel was named publicly as both a communist and a Soviet agent.

On 16 October 1948 the Paris edition of the *New York Herald Tribune* reported that Chambers had spoken of two pre-war communist underground networks operating in the State Department, one headed by Alger Hiss and the other by Noel Field.[18]

Field read this article in the Czechoslovak foreign ministry on 18 October, less than two days before his planned departure for Switzerland, and three days before the expiry date of his passport. Noel feared that if he returned to Switzerland to renew it, it would either be confiscated or made out as valid solely for travel to the USA. Once there he would be summoned before HUAC, and would inevitably perjure himself and be sent to prison.

With his plans thrown into disarray, Field was in a panic. After consulting various comrades, it was decided that Herta, whose passport was valid until June 1949, should leave alone for Switzerland on 21 October. Noel would simply lie low and let the storm pass.

To do that he needed to obtain a residence permit to stay in Czechoslovakia, and that required the permission of the 'grey eminence' of the CzCP, Bedřich Geminder. So he wrote to Bauer on 20 October asking him to get Merker to contact Geminder.

Four days later he wrote directly to Merker, and his letter was carried by Gisl Kisch to Berlin. As a result, on 8 November 1948 Merker and Dahlem wrote to Geminder, and Gisl delivered their letter to him in Prague on the thirteenth. The two German Politburo members vouched for Field, and asked Geminder to get the Prague government to grant him residence, until he could be brought to Berlin to have his case examined and settled.[19]

This letter would help to put a noose around Geminder's neck in that lethal farce, the Slánský trial. It would feature too in Merker's fall.

Although a number of Czechoslovak communists supported Field's request for a residence permit, the StB remained suspicious. On 19 November they interrogated Noel. They learned of his earlier work for Soviet intelligence and listened to, but declined to act upon, his request to be put in touch with Moscow again. After the interrogation the Czechoslovak authorities approved his residence permit, valid until 15 May 1949, on the grounds that Field was 'of the socialist persuasion'.[20]

In the meantime Noel had renewed his passport without difficulty at the US embassy in Prague on 29 October. It was valid for two years. After all the earlier fuss Field had made, this only helped fuel suspicions about him. The StB were also of the opinion that no such newspaper as the *National Guardian* existed, since those journalists they questioned had never heard of it.

On 21 November Noel left Prague for Paris.[21] He stayed for a fortnight. He visited Jo Tempi, her husband and their new baby, as well as Erica, Robert and their child. He also met with Artur London, who would be deeply involved in the 'Field affair', and who was then readying himself to take up a diplomatic post.[22] Noel asked him to fix up a contact with Soviet intelligence so that he might clarify past misunderstandings.[23]

In early December Noel rejoined Herta in Geneva. That winter he devoted himself to reading the voluminous records of the HUAC hearings, which a sympathiser working in the ILO sent to him. Fearing that HUAC might serve him with a subpoena, they arranged that only Herta would answer the door and the telephone.

Field was determined not to settle in any West European country, from where he could be forced to go back to the USA. He feared that if he did return there, he would either be interrogated by HUAC, or called as a witness in the forthcoming trial of Alger Hiss, or both. In either eventuality the likeliest result for Noel would be a five-year jail sentence following his inevitable perjury.

So Noel's plan was to return to Prague and stay there with Herta for an indeterminate period, while he awaited the call from Berlin. But he had come to no final decision about where he would ultimately settle. He had thoughts of teaching at Leipzig University. He also considered registering in a university in one of the people's democracies, in order to write the PhD which had eluded him at Harvard.

In the meantime Noel went skiing. He also worked on the shorthand notes he had made about his time in Poland and Czechoslovakia. The Fields closed down their flat in January and moved into a *pension*.[24] Noel 'purged' his personal and USC archives and rented a room in the country to store them, along with their furniture and belongings.

It was at this moment in January 1949 that Stalin gave the order to arrest Field. It was no instantaneous decision. Noel's file had been 'current' since at least early 1948. But the ageing tyrant in the Kremlin had been developing other schemes as well. Noel's fate was just part of a multi-layered plot forming in that eternally suspicious mind. Events had created the opportunity for Stalin to strike in several directions at once, events that were to snare Noel Field.

Among these events was the imbroglio involving the Massings and Hiss.

THE MARCH OF EVENTS

15

PAST BECOMES PRESENT

HEDE'S FRIENDS, OLD AND NEW

'The good life'[1]

In our last sight of the Massings they were embracing Noel before he sailed back to Europe in 1939. That November Moscow Centre informed the head of the illegal NKVD *apparat* in New York that 'we are sending in this mailing a letter to Peter (Paul Massing), in which we propose that his wife (Hede) should take steps to renew ties with "19" (Duggan)'.[2]

There is no way of knowing from available sources whether the 'proposal' reached the Massings, or, if it did, whether they acted upon it. However, it would seem that Moscow still considered them to be deactivated agents, and possibly held this view of them until 1948 when they were officially classified as 'traitors'.[3]

Yet if we refer to Hede's account of these years we get a very different picture of the Massings' lives. The disillusioned couple moved out of New York to bucolic bliss in rural Pennsylvania. Their lives were filled with satisfying hard graft as they restored buildings and tilled the soil. When war came Hede patriotically served in a shipyard in New Jersey, first as a carpenter and then as a supervisor.

Her only elements of concern were a number of encounters with 'Helen' (Lisa Zarubina), whose ideological temptations were easily

137

spurned by Hede, now a born-again non-communist. Eventually the FBI called by, but only because they wanted her help regarding her first husband, Gerhart Eisler. This led the guilt-ridden Hede to confess her sins to the 'Feds' little by little, until finally she felt able to produce the testimony that helped imprison the Soviet spy, Alger Hiss.

Following that coup Hede and her ghost-writer produced a series of extremely well-paid press articles on her life, which soon led to the publication of her well-crafted autobiography. These memoirs fitted seamlessly into the mores of Cold War America, where Reds were not only under beds, but had burrowed deep into government, education, Hollywood, unions, indeed the whole fabric of society.

There were spies everywhere, it seemed, and where there happened to be none there was still suspicion. The 'Hissteria' that surrounded Alger's trial was simply the culmination of a series of genuine espionage cases that involved Canada, Britain and the USA. All of them compromised American security, particularly by betraying the 'secret' of the atomic bomb to Moscow, and thereby ending the US monopoly of that awesome weapon. After Igor Gouzenko came Elizabeth Bentley. After her came Whittaker Chambers and Klaus Fuchs. After Hiss came the Rosenbergs.

Beyond the spies there were the clear-cut Reds of the CPUSA. At Stalin's behest the Party had dumped its leader, Earl Browder, in March 1945, after he had appeared too conciliatory towards capitalism. Then there were the Pinks who condoned and often followed the Party line. HUAC called on these fellow-travelling sinners to repent by 'naming names'. Later Senator Joe McCarthy 'investigated' the 'loyalty' of federal employees, usually by plucking numbers of the alleged 'disloyal' out of thin air.

It was the time of taking the Fifth Amendment to avoid self-incrimination. It was the era of the 'blacklist'. Why go out on a limb? To get along, you had to go along. There was suburbia, there was TV, there was consumerism. A generation buttoned down their thoughts and opinions as conveniently as their shirt-collars.

Yet Hede's elevation to celebrity status in this conformist world rested upon a rewrite of her life that was just as perjured as Hiss's defence. She and Paul had only come clean about their pasts to avoid deportation or prison. Even then they distorted what they admitted. According to Hede, this period of her life was 'for the most part, very vague in my memory'.[4] Indeed it was.

She didn't remember exactly how she got the money to buy the farm. Somehow she also overlooked the fact that both she and Paul appeared before the US Immigration and Naturalization Service (INS) and per-jured themselves. She forgot to inform the authorities about the Zaru-bins. Nor does she recall telling the Fields that she had no intention of shopping them to the FBI. And as for the dinner-party with Hiss and the Fields in 1935, she only managed to recollect that event after being interviewed by the FBI for twenty-one months.

The period of selective amnesia began in 1939 when Hede met Nina Field–'Fieldy' as she called her–on Hermann's farm in Shirley, Massa-chusetts. When Nina learned that the Massings were themselves going to buy a farm, Hede recalled that 'she wanted to join us'. 'Fieldy' was alone; both Noel and Hermann were then in Europe, while Elsie was in the mid-West.[5] A farm close enough to New York's attractions 'would be a wonderful solution for her old age'. Nina 'would put a mortgage into it, we would share living expenses, and lead "the good life."' Hede wrote to Noel and Hermann about the plan and they seemed pleased, since 'this arrangement relieved their feelings of anxiety' about their mother.[6]

In October 1939 Paul bought the farm. By spring 1940 the Massings had finished remodelling it. However, Nina had a serious operation in early summer, which required radiotherapy twice a week thereafter. Round trips from farm to hospital were impractical, so 'Fieldy' had to be 'released from her farm commitments'.[7] The Massings sold up and bought another smaller farm nine miles from Quakertown.

The Field brothers saw it differently. Noel spoke of the 'disgraceful way' the Massings had used an old lady, by inducing his mother to lend them money to buy a farm. Once he returned to the USA in 1940 Hermann got them to pay it back by threatening a law-suit. He also accused them of 'political treachery', so that what began as a personal quarrel with the Massings became bitter hatred.[8]

Then there is Hede's account of her relationship with Vassili and Lisa Zarubin. The first contact occurred when Lisa summoned Hede to New York in summer 1940. The next meeting was in the winter of 1942–43, and there were two visits in 1943. The Massings concluded that the Zarubins were simply conducting 'a routine check-up to ascertain whether we would be any danger to them', should they suddenly learn of the Zarubins' presence in the USA.[9]

Clearly the Massings presented no danger, since they had no inten-tion of denouncing the Zarubins as Soviet spies. There are other points too that do not gel with this cosy portrait of the relationship between the two couples.

First is the dating of the initial meeting between Hede and Lisa as summer 1940. For this to be true, then Lisa was making one of her illegal entries into the USA. She was certainly available for such a task. Lisa had been discharged from INO in March 1939, but reactivated in April 1940. Yet passenger travel by sea at this time was problematic, so while a meeting in 1940 cannot be ruled out, the only known date for arrival of the Zarubins in the USA was much later, and probably involved travelling through Asia.

On Christmas day 1941 they arrived in San Francisco from Manila. They were no longer the Zarubins, but the Zubilins. Their passports, issued in Moscow on 5 September 1941, described Vassili Zubilin as a forty-one-year-old government executive, born in Moscow.[10] Vassili had six years knocked off his age, but Elisabeth (Lisa) Zubilin, aged forty in her passport, lost only one year. She too was recorded as born in Moscow, which was another lie. That this NKVD captain was described as 'a housewife' certainly adds a whole new dimension to that calling.

With them was their nine-year-old son, Peter, travelling on his mother's passport. The fact that they were able to bring him with them, rather than leaving him in the USSR as hostage to their conduct, indicated that they were highly-trusted operatives.

Vassili was ostensibly a third secretary in the Soviet diplomatic service, assigned to the New York consulate. In June 1943 he transferred to the embassy in Washington, serving there until his recall in August 1944. In both posts he headed the legal INU *rezidentura* in the USA.[11] Assisted by Lisa, when she could tear herself away from housework,[12] he ran several networks of agents. These were mainly CPUSA members and sympathisers, and they provided the Soviets with an impressive array of intelligence and industrial secrets. Iskhak Akhmerov, who had arrived in the USA in September 1941, was also back at work as head of the illegal *rezidentura*, operating from New York.

Another question raised by Hede's account is whether the Massings were in fact reactivated by the Soviets. The answer is that they were, and although only one episode has come to light there are likely to have been others. Moreover, this single incident suggests that while Paul was involved in providing intelligence to Lisa, Hede may not have done. Yet even if this was the case, she must have known about her husband's activities.

In early 1942 Franz Neumann, a former member of the Frankfurt Institute of Social Research, was working in the Research and Analysis

Branch of the OSS in New York. He was contacted by 'Mary' (Paul Massing). Neumann certainly passed over classified information to both Paul and to Lisa, which ended up in Moscow.[13] Given this fact, the tale that Hede spins about the Massings' innocent wartime relationship with the Zarubins is entirely worthless.[14] So is most of her account of their last meetings with Noel and Herta.

Farewell to the Fields[15]

In late 1945 the Massings had learned from the press that the Fields were in the States. However, the Fields had tried to avoid any contact with the Massings. According to Hede, when Paul phoned him, 'Noel was embarrassed and contradictory in his explanations of why he had not looked them up'. He said that he could not arrange a meeting just now, 'because he was on his way to Canada or somewhere else'.[16]

While in Mexico Field informed Merker of his earlier relationship with the Massings and asked his advice. Merker told him not to contact them without party permission, and if they did meet they should avoid any discussion of political questions.

In January or early February 1946, after the Fields returned from Mexico, Paul Massing telephoned and said he must see them. As agreed between the Fields, Herta went alone to the Massings' apartment, where she and Hede conducted a 'non-political' chinwag.

Hede's account is very different. She says that they had forgotten all about the Fields, when one night around ten o'clock Herta paid a surreptitious surprise visit to the Massings' 82nd Street apartment. Paul was out and so the two women had a long chat, catching up with events from the intervening years.

Paul came back about midnight. They arranged a luncheon date for the two couples, and about half-past midnight Paul left to escort Herta to the subway. He did not return until four in the morning, having walked Herta to the Fields' hotel on East 33rd Street. During this time, according to Hede, he told Herta where he and his wife now stood politically, and he accused his former agents of still working for the Soviets. He told Herta that he did not want to see the Fields again, and he cancelled the luncheon.

Herta's account differs considerably. She claims that Massing expressed his indignation that the Fields had made no attempt to contact him and Hede. He said that a high-ranking State Department official had sworn to 'fix' Noel sooner or later. Paul told her his name, but refused to say where he had obtained this information.[17] He added that neither he nor Hede would make any incriminating (*belastend*) statements about the Fields. However, he managed to find out from Herta that Jean Liebermann was in the USA.[18]

Hede wanted to see Noel, so she telephoned Herta. Lunch was arranged (or rearranged). When Noel arrived for the meal, Hede saw 'a gaunt torn man', his hair 'almost completely white', looking 'harder and more manly'. He was still having trouble with his sight, for 'the weak eye was very noticeable'.[19]

According to Noel, Hede said that she had no objection to the Fields informing others of her anti-Soviet standpoint. Noel denied her accusation that he was still working for Soviet intelligence (and, of course, he wasn't). Hede said that although she and Paul no longer worked for INU, they had not contacted the US authorities. Nor would she inform on the Fields, unless she learned that they were participating in some hostile action against her.

Hede says that they left together and walked to the end of the block. 'Noel and I parted with an almost formal good-bye, Herta gave me a quick hug and went on behind Noel as he crossed the avenue'.[20]

Herta does not concur with this dramatic farewell. She recalled that Hede invited her into her office, introduced her to her colleagues, and got Herta to write down her Geneva address in their presence. The detail is virtually irrelevant, but it is the sort of trivia that rings true, and leads me to give greater weight to the account by her and Noel than to that of Hede.

One thing is clear from the above; the Massings did not shop the Fields at this juncture. Herta thought that Hede's concern for her own reputation and security was the chief reason that she had said nothing about them. Nor would she want to be involved in all the publicity that would attend a trial. Moreover, if the full story came out, there was the matter of potential consequences for the Massings on the issue of naturalisation.[21]

'Political prisoner'[22]

'Paul encountered difficulties as he had not yet naturalized', wrote Hede.[23] So in October 1941 Massing filed an application for naturalisation with the INS. This body interviewed him three times in 1942, and Hede once on 6 December 1941. All sessions were conducted under oath.

Hede swore that neither she nor Paul had been communists, and that the purpose of their 1937 trip to Moscow was to arrange for Paul to edit an agricultural magazine. Paul too denied being a KPD member, and said that the purpose of his trip to Europe in 1937 was to deal with his finances, visit his family (in Nazi Germany!), and check out an offer of work from the International Agrarian Institute in Moscow.

The INS found that both had perjured themselves regarding their communist party membership, as well as concealing the real purpose of their trip to the USSR. It seems too that the FBI kept tabs on them during the war, but came up with nothing. However, in March 1947 FBI agents sought the Massings' cooperation regarding the prosecution of Hede's first husband Gerhart Eisler.[24]

One has to wonder if they really needed such help. Eisler had managed to create much of the US government's case against himself through his lies and duplicity.[25]

Leaving his wife and child in Moscow, from July 1933 until June 1935 Eisler was illegally in the USA. Living under the name 'Edwards', he was there as the official Comintern representative. During his stay he applied for an American passport under a false identity and used it on his travels.

He left for Moscow to attend the Seventh Comintern Congress (July–August 1935), and the so-called 'Brussels' congress of the KPD (3–15 October). He returned to the States in late October 1935. Recalled to Europe in April 1936, Eisler was briefly in Prague, and then in Spain. After that he served in the Foreign Secretariat in Paris and was interned in Le Vernet.

Gerhart was amongst those who got out of Vichy France. With documents issued in Marseille on 15 April 1941, he left that port on 6 May. He arrived in New York via Trinidad on 13 June. There his details were registered. Aged forty-four, of Hebrew race, he was stateless, a reporter by occupation, and in transit to his destination in Mexico. He was also with the woman who would become his third wife, Hilde Rothstein.[26]

Refused the right to continue their journey to Mexico, Eisler and Hilde were held on Ellis Island.[27] At an INS hearing Eisler lied repeatedly: he had never been in the USA; he had never been a communist; he had never even been married!

143

Eventually he and Hilde gained permission to live and work in New York on short-term permits. So during the war, while Hilde tackled various jobs, Eisler received a monthly stipend from the Joint Anti-Fascist Refugee Committee and wrote articles under a pseudonym. They rented a modest apartment in Queens. On several occasions Eisler sought permission for them to travel to Mexico, but without success.

During this stay in America Eisler had neither the authority nor the inclination to involve himself in the affairs of the CPUSA. So it was somewhat ironic that he was denounced by a former communist as a Kremlin agent, directing all communist activities in the USA. It fitted his earlier role in the Thirties, but now even his nemesis in the FBI saw only 'a small, balding, bespectacled man' who 'looked like a bookkeeper'.[28]

Eisler was arrested by the INS and brought before HUAC on 6 February 1947. There he added to his problems by demanding to make a statement before he was sworn in. He claimed too that he was a political prisoner. Eventually he was cited for contempt of Congress.[29]

Tried on this count in New York in March–April 1947, Eisler was found guilty, but bailed. On 27 June he was sentenced to one year in prison. He remained free, but only until his second trial in Washington took place in July. Accused of plotting against the government and passport fraud, he was found guilty and sentenced to three years in prison. Bailed once more, Eisler remained free until February 1948 when he was arrested again by the INS and returned to Ellis Island.

Freed again, but now threatened with an additional charge of tax evasion, Eisler solved his problems by stowing away on the Polish liner *Batory* on 6 May 1949. He was rearrested in Southampton eight days later and imprisoned, until a British court held that there were no grounds for extraditing Eisler to the USA. Released once more, he was put on a plane to Prague. From there he made a 'triumphant' entry into Leipzig at the end of May.[30]

The experienced old cadre immediately assumed some senior posts. However, an ominous cloud rapidly appeared on his bright horizon. Soon after Eisler's return to the GDR, Noel Field was named as an American spy in the Rajk trial indictment, and Eisler had briefly met with Field in the USA in 1946.[31]

'How was I going to speak about Eisler without involving myself?' wondered Hede. There was no alternative for either her or Paul. 'We decided to tell our story'.[33]

Of course there was a sub-text to their collaboration. If Paul wanted US citizenship he needed to cooperate with the FBI. If Hede didn't want to lose hers then she too must follow that path. Unless both welcomed deportation or jail, the message was the same. So from March 1947 to December 1948 both were interviewed more than a dozen times each. According to Jeff Kisselhoff they gave the FBI scores of names, although in his account not a single one is mentioned.

After nine months of naming names, Paul decided to resubmit his application to the INS. On 30 December 1947 an FBI agent telephoned the INS to inform them that Paul had been very cooperative. Six days later they learned that the INS still opposed his naturalisation on the grounds that his evidence in 1942 was patently false. The FBI feared 'the termination of the very valuable service of both Paul and Hedwig Massing as informants'.[34]

The Massings appeared before HUAC on 21 September 1948. Although both were sworn in most of the questions were directed at Paul. Questioned about Field, he characterised Noel not as a party member (which he wasn't), but as a 'critical Trotskyite' (whatever that was). Noel refused to be an agent out of loyalty to the United States, said Paul, and he never discussed espionage with Field. Hede merely observed that, as with sex and money, one never discussed espionage in polite company.

According to the FBI files Hede said nothing about Hiss until 7 December 1948. Then she informed the agency of her meeting with Alger and their alleged conversation at the Fields' flat in 1935 (Chapter 5). The Justice Department despatched her to New York the next day to testify before the Grand Jury investigating Whittaker Chambers' allegations against Hiss. The actress repeated her lines. The Grand Jury indicted Hiss on 15 December 1948.

In early 1949 the INS was still reluctant to naturalise Paul. The FBI stepped up their interviews with Hede. Now she was called in twice a week, with each session lasting three hours. The results were written up in a report of 8 July 1949. On 27 July Hede told the FBI that she had been offered the then exorbitant sum of $50,000 for a series of articles. Obviously, she had to remain free to spend it.

By October 1949, if not earlier, Hede and Paul had separated. Many of her friends had abandoned her. She attributed the disappearance of the Fields that summer to her impending testimony. Not unreasonably, she feared a Soviet attempt upon her life.

The first Hiss perjury trial ran from 31 May to 7 July 1949 and resulted in a hung jury. The judge agreed with the defence that Hede's testimony as 'rebuttal on a collateral material' would be mostly 'inflammatory and prejudicial' and did not allow it. And it is difficult to see how Hede's evidence was germane to the two charges against Hiss: that he lied when he denied seeing Chambers after 1 January 1937; and that he lied when he denied handing government documents to Chambers.

But at the second trial, which began on 17 November 1949, a new judge allowed her testimony. Hede was sworn in on 9 December as a prosecution witness. Once more she told her story of the dinner party at the Fields' apartment. Hiss was convicted on 21 January 1950. Four days later he was sentenced to a five-year stretch.[35]

The following day Hede's syndicator delivered eighteen press articles to the FBI. Soon afterwards they received an advance copy of her book. The assistant director of the FBI reported to J. Edgar Hoover that it was 'most favorable' to the agency and was 'factual for the most part with the exception of a few phases of her work'.[36]

16

'DECISIVE MEASURES ON OUR PART'

STALIN'S ROLE

The Boss

In May 1949 Noel Field was abducted on Stalin's orders, and thereafter converted into an 'American master-spy' at the tyrant's behest. That Stalin was directly involved goes without saying, since neither the kidnap of Noel nor the staging of the Rajk trial could have happened without his consent.

If there are documents showing his involvement in Field's fate, then they are probably stashed in a closed archive in Russia. More than likely they have been destroyed.[1] Therefore some of this chapter is only plausible speculation grounded upon known events and procedures.

As we shall see, the order to arrest Noel was given in January 1949, but it is impossible to specify at which point Stalin first actively involved himself in Field's fate. Noel's abduction was part of a convoluted plot by Stalin, designed to resolve various issues related to Soviet foreign and domestic policy, the question of succession, and control over his East European empire.

Whether or not he was mentally deranged, Joseph Stalin was an inordinately suspicious and vindictive man. The Boss (*Khoziain*) was also a patient and cunning operator. The *mafioso* dictum that *la vendetta è un piatto che va mangiato freddo* was his trademark too. He once described his version of revenge being a dish best eaten cold as follows: 'To choose one's victims, to prepare one's plans minutely, to slake an implacable vengeance, and then go to bed…there is nothing sweeter in the world'.[2]

In the post-war years the Boss had considerable opportunity for plotting 'implacable vengeance'. In the period 1945–51 Stalin spent from two to four months each year on vacation at various Black Sea resorts. His need for rest was hardly surprising. Through sheer will-power he had led the USSR throughout four titanic years of war. He had suffered a heart-attack in October 1945, and two months later he celebrated his sixty-sixth official birthday, although he was in fact a year older.[3] Despite the air-brushed photos, he looked his age.

During his vacations Stalin received regular deliveries of state papers. However, on a daily basis he also received two files which were essential reading for him. These were the reports from his secret police and translations of the foreign press.[4]

His remote control of Soviet policy was conducted primarily by telegram and telephone, although when necessary he could summon his minions to join him. However, to execute his complex plot Stalin relied on his secret police.

This organisation had undergone various structural changes since the murderous rampage of 'the Great Terror'. On 25 November 1938 the head of the NKVD, the drunken bisexual Russian Nikolai Yezhov, was replaced by the Georgian vegetarian rapist Lavrenti Beria.[5] From February to July 1941, and again from April 1943, the security element of the NKVD, the GUGB, was made into a separate commissariat, the People's Commissariat of State Security (NKGB), headed by Vsevolod Merkulov, a Beria satrap.

In March 1946, when the people's commissariats were rechristened ministries, the NKGB and the NKVD became respectively the Ministry of State Security (MGB) and the Ministry of Internal Affairs (MVD). However, more than bureaucratic name-changes were involved, since personnel and their powers were affected too.

Sergei Kruglov had already replaced Beria as head of the NKVD on 15 January 1946. Then on 4 May Viktor Semyonovich Abakumov took over the MGB from Merkulov, and would hold this post until July 1951.[6] It was Abakumov, not Beria, who implemented Stalin's orders in the Field affair and Rajk trial, and, initially at least, in all of the persecutions of this period.[7]

The file

So what did Stalin and the MGB know about Field? The answer to this question is that they knew a great deal and that by late 1948 Noel's file was probably bulging. By then he was already a target under observation by agents of Soviet, Czechoslovak and Hungarian security.[8] Given such interest, Noel's file would have been 'live', and Stalin would have known about any fresh developments since Abakumov reported directly to him.

Being omniscient, Stalin did not require too much data in order to believe something, or to act upon such 'knowledge'. As he told Khruschev in 1937, 'Ten per cent of the truth is already the truth, it already demands decisive measures on our part, and we will pay if we do not act accordingly'.[9] Yet, after poring over Field's dossier, even someone less cavalier about 'truth' and less congenitally suspicious than Stalin might have wondered about Noel's status.

Files on Noel and Herta Field existed in Moscow Centre years before the pair were employed by the USC in 1941. These would have recorded the recruitment of the Fields by the Massings, their relationship with the illegal New York *rezidentura*, and the incidents with Hiss in 1935–36.[10]

Noel's meetings with Reiss, Krivitsky and Shpigelglas in Geneva and Paris in 1936–37 may have been on file. Certainly the product of weeks of subtle debriefing in Moscow by the Zarubins and Shpigelglas would have been recorded, as well as the doubts about Field which led INO to 'conserve' Noel as an agent in 1938, rather than use him further.

The NKVD was aware of Noel's membership of the Swiss party in 1942 and of his work for the USC. They would also have filed some record of the meeting between the Fields and 'Brook' in early 1943, after which Moscow had terminated all contact with them.

Once the war in Europe ended, *émigré* communists were required to report to their home parties about their activities during their years of exile. It is possible that party members returning from France and Switzerland mentioned their relationship with Noel and that this information was passed to Moscow.

Field's visits to Berlin in 1946 and 1947 were probably reported upon by those he met. The same applies to his travels in Poland and Czechoslovakia in 1947 and 1948. The discussions which he had with Artur London in 1947 and 1948 must also have found their way to Moscow since, as we shall see, London was working for both Czechoslovak and Soviet intelligence.

Noel had sought clarification of his status from senior communists in the USA in early 1946 and Poland in 1948. It seems likely that his letter to Berman was added to his file. Records of his panic in Prague, and the StB interview with him there in autumn 1948 were probably part of his Moscow dossier too.

Taken as a whole, the above offered potent grounds for Soviet mistrust, which even Noel conceded in his letter to the CPSU Central Committee in March 1954. Then he outlined some superficially suspicious facets of his past.[11] I have suggested some others.

Field was a middle-class American who had spent ten years in the US State Department. America was now the 'main enemy' of the USSR. He had headed an American philanthropic organisation for six years, working much of the time in Geneva, a well known centre of espionage according to Noel. Moreover, he had been in contact with Dulles and the OSS there.

All of Field's controllers had become 'traitors'. He was 'conserved' in 1938 because there were doubts about him. He had then refused to obey orders when offered a second chance by 'Brook' in 1943.

Field knew the 'Szőnyi group',[12] as well as dozens of party cadres who had operated outside of Moscow's control for several years. From this suspect milieu, numerous Jews, 'Spaniards' and 'Westerners' had returned to their homelands, and were now serving as second-rank officials in the People's Democracies of Eastern Europe.

Field had claimed to be an American communist, but he couldn't produce a party card. Ostensibly under suspicion in the USA, he was never interviewed by the authorities there. In fact they granted him a new passport. Therefore the so-called 'accusations' against him by Chambers and HUAC must be part of the 'cover' for his activities.

Noel now claimed to be a journalist for an unknown newspaper, yet he only took up this a profession in his forties. He collected 'confidential' material in Poland and Czechoslovakia, but never used it. Recently he had sought to be put in touch with Soviet intelligence again. Now he wanted to live in Czechoslovakia or the Soviet Occupation Zone of Germany.[13]

When Stalin closed this file, he would have had considerably more than 'ten per cent of the truth' to hand. And he would certainly have to take 'decisive measures', because Noel Field looked like an 'Identikit' American spy. So how could Field best be used, given that Stalin had other problems too, both at home and abroad? One of these was Tito's Yugoslavia. Another derived from Stalin's now paranoid anti-Semitism. This would feature in the trial of members of the JAC (Jewish Anti-fascist Committee) and in the so-called 'Doctors' Plot'. It was present too in the most prominent show trials in Eastern Europe.

The anti-Semitic component of the September 1949 Rajk trial was almost subliminal, pushed into the background by the focus upon the renegade Tito. But the Slánský trial in November 1952 reversed these priorities. A band of 'Zionist' plotters, allegedly spying on behalf of the 'main enemy', the United States, would crowd the dock in Prague.

This paranoid anti-Semitism was a feature of Stalin's last years. Earlier in the 1940s Stalin's bigotry had been muted as he wooed America's Jews through the JAC, and later hoped that the new state of Israel would swing into his orbit. Both proved to be brief and unsuccessful affairs, following which a rebuffed and vengeful Stalin turned overtly and murderously against Jews in the years 1949–53.

A coy anti-Semite

'He never liked Jews', wrote Stalin's daughter, Svetlana, of her father, although only after the war was he 'blatant about expressing his hatred for them'.[14]

It seems likely that his anti-Semitism developed in the early twentieth century, when he dropped all of his other pseudonyms for that of Stalin, and converted himself from a Georgian into a Great Russian.[15] As Lenin observed, 'Foreigners who become Russified always overdo it in terms of the real Russian mood'.[16] And there was little doubt about the 'mood' of the Russians, and indeed of all the peoples in the west of the Tsarist Empire, when it came to Jews.

The two Russian revolutions of 1917 removed the legal restrictions upon Jewish citizens.[17] However, the Bolshevik seizure of power and the subsequent civil war proved a mixed blessing for the Jews of the Russian Empire, and for those of Central and Eastern Europe as a whole.

Lenin's revolution burdened Jews with one more collective stereotype. Already tagged variously as Christ-killers, usurers, capitalist exploiters, and vilified by the blood-libel, Jews were now pilloried as the 'chosen people of the Bolsheviks'.[18]

This concept of 'Judeo-Bolshevism' or 'Judeo-Communism' posited the idea that a Jewish-dominated international communist movement planned to destroy the Christian world and replace it with one under Jewish control. Contemporary forgeries, such as *The Protocols of the Elders of Zion*, fanned such fears.

The First World War had broken down the Pale of Settlement and dispersed Russia's Jews. For the first time they appeared in large numbers in Russia's northern cities. Equally novel was their entry into official and government posts under Lenin's regime, as well as their prominence in leading positions in the Red Army and the secret police.[19]

Yet the fact remained that few Russian Jews were Bolsheviks. Those who were, the non-religious 'internationalist' Jews, did not consider themselves to be Jews, save by the accident of racial origin. When asked his religion, Trotsky replied, 'Social Democrat'. During the civil war a delegation of Jews appealed to him to do nothing which might provoke the 'Whites' into further pogroms against them. Trotsky told them, 'Go home to your Jews and tell them I'm not a Jew and don't care about the Jews or what happens to them'.[20]

Perhaps as many as 150,000 Jews would be slaughtered in the civil war, primarily at the hands of the 'White' anti-Bolshevik forces and mostly in Ukraine.[21] Many of these, mostly peaceful and religious *shtetl*-dwellers, would die precisely because of this identification of Jews as 'Reds'. After the German invasion of the Soviet Union in 1941 many more would suffer the same fate, particularly in the lands acquired by Stalin in 1939–40. However, Stalin's primary concern with Jews was not with such nonentities.

During his struggle for power in the 1920s Stalin's chief rivals were the Jewish Bolshevik leaders Trotsky, Zinoviev and Kamenev, and the CPSU members who supported them. Even after Stalin's triumph Jews remained 'over-represented' in the government, party, army, the foreign commissariat, and the police. The NKVD head, Genrikh Yagoda, was Jewish, while several of Stalin's closest collaborators, such as Molotov, Kirov, Voroshilov, Andreyev, and Poskrebyshev, had Jewish wives.

'I trust that we shall never seek to settle our inner-party differences in a Jacobin manner', opined Lenin in 1918.[22] Put another way, repression, camps and death sentences were not for Bolsheviks, but applied only to such trash as 'former people'(*byvshie liudi*), *kulaks*, 'Whites', and non-communist 'oppositionists'.[23]

Of course Stalin did believe in the Jacobin solution to inner-party differences, with a bullet in the back of the head replacing the guillotine.

Moreover, dead men not only told no tales, they also created vacancies. And Stalin was the focus of loyalty for the many thousands of young, ill-educated, semi-proletarian Russians who had entered the Party since the civil war. They would be only too happy to displace the 'Old Bolsheviks' and render thanks and homage to the *Vozhd* (leader).

Initially the pruning of the over-represented Jews, Poles and Balts from positions of authority had to be selective, in case the regime collapsed entirely. However, 'the Great Terror' of 1937–38 savaged the minority 'suspect nations' of the USSR out of all proportion to their numbers both in the NKVD and the USSR as a whole.[24]

In the case of the Jews the process had to be conducted with some subtlety, or else people might think Stalin was indeed an anti-Semite. So shortly before the Zinoviev-Kamenev show trial in August 1936, in which eleven of the sixteen in the dock were Jewish, Stalin staged another trial to dispel such unsavoury impressions.

In late May 1936 two Russians were charged with the murder of a Jewish doctor. It was a run-of-the-mill murder case, yet the trial was conducted in public in a major Moscow location, and heard by the Supreme Court of the RFSR. Moreover, it was not prosecuted by the procurator of a mere constituent republic, but by Andrei Vyshinsky, chief procurator of the USSR. The defendants were even allowed to deny their guilt.

Trying his first murder case, Vyshinsky would have none of it. The accused had dared 'to directly violate the marvellous instructions of our leader and teacher on the inviolable friendship of the peoples of our country'. It was Vyshinsky's job 'to lance this shameful anti-Semitic boil'. Yet the defendants were sentenced to death neither for anti-Semitism nor for murder, but for banditry.[25] Still, it was job done.

Having established his leader's anti-anti-Semitic credentials, Vyshinsky next addressed himself to some real criminals; the sixteen 'Trotskyites' and 'Zinovievites' who featured in the first of the three Moscow show trials.[26] There was no allusion to the racial origin of Zinoviev, Kamenev and the other Jewish defendants, and behind the scenes all sixteen were promised their lives. All were shot.

For those who still doubted the Boss's credentials, a statement made by Stalin in January 1931 to the Jewish Telegraph Agency of the United States was wheeled out. 'Anti-Semitism is an extreme expression of racial chauvinism and as such is the most dangerous survival of cannibalism'.

Strangely, it was not prominently cited in the Soviet press until November 1936, when Molotov mentioned it in a speech.[27]

Having now proved that he was not a cannibal, Stalin devoured a few more enemies in the second great show trial in January 1937. Eight of the seventeen defendants were Jewish. There were thirteen death sentences, but the two chief Jewish defendants, Karl Radek and Grigori Sokolnikov, escaped with ten-year jail terms. They were later murdered in prison.

The twenty-one defendants in the Bukharin-Rykov trial in March 1938 were a very mixed bag. At least five were Jews, including Yagoda; there were perhaps more. Only three of the accused were spared the death penalty, and naturally they were liquidated later. This trial introduced the concept of medical murder into the proceedings, which was something that the Boss would keep very much in mind.

Stalin and the JAC

Solomon Mikhoels was a renowned Yiddish actor and the director of Moscow's State Jewish Theatre. Born Solomon Vovsi in Dvinsk (now Daugavpils in Latvia) in 1890, he received a traditional and religious education, after which he trained as a lawyer. He only took up acting in 1919, which was when he adopted Mikhoels as his stage-name. The state richly rewarded his talents, and Mikhoels even received the Order of Lenin, although he was not a party member.

It was because he was a non-communist that Mikhoels was selected to head the JAC. This body, which included a number of noted Yiddish writers, poets, and other cultural luminaries, was established in April 1942. Antifascist committees for science, women, youth, and Slavs were formed at the same time. All five committees were designed to garner differing elements of foreign support for the Soviet war against Hitler. In the case of the JAC it was Jewish-American money, both for war purposes and peacetime reconstruction.

These five committees were supervised by Solomon Abramovich Lozovsky. Born in Ukraine in 1878, he changed his surname from Dridzot to Lozovsky in 1905, four years after joining the Bolshevik underground. Exiled to Siberia, he escaped to France, where he both picked grapes and studied at the Sorbonne. Besides Russian, French and Hebrew, he spoke German and English.

For seventeen years Lozovsky was secretary-general of *Profintern*, the Moscow-controlled international trade union movement. For twenty years he was also a member of the ECCI. In 1939 Molotov chose him as one of three deputy commissars for foreign affairs. In addition, in June 1941 Lozovsky was appointed vice-chairman of *Sovinformburo* which dealt with the foreign press. It was in this capacity that he supervised the antifascist committees.

From May 1943 Mikhoels and the poet Itzik Fefer toured North America and Britain for seven months as representatives of the JAC. On their return they considered the possible resettlement of displaced Jews in the Crimea. There had been a long history of Jewish settlement in the north of the peninsula. The Nazis had massacred these Jews, while in spring 1944 the NKVD had deported the Tatar population of southern Crimea as collaborators.

Mikhoels, Fefer and the journalist Shakhno Epshteyn met with Molotov. When they proposed a Jewish republic in the Crimea, Molotov said 'write a letter and we'll look into it'.[28] On 21 February 1944 the trio sent a letter to Molotov, which had been reviewed by Lozovsky beforehand. In it they proposed the creation of a Jewish Soviet republic in the Crimea.[29] The sole Jew in the Politburo, Lazar Kaganovich, commented acidly that 'only actors and poets could come up with such an idea'.[30]

There appears to be no evidence of serious governmental support for a Jewish Crimea. Molotov's tepid encouragement may simply have been a deliberate provocation by Stalin. The wartime reality for Soviet Jews was the continuation of purges and slights.[31]

The Nazi extermination of the Jews led the JAC to seek to broaden its functions. 'As much as we would like to keep within narrow bounds, we are unable to do so', asserted Mikhoels in October 1944. 'Life is persistently knocking at our door…. We cannot escape the multitude of Jewish problems'.[32] Within the JAC there was some explicit endorsement of Zionism too, as well as talk of converting the JAC into a commissariat for Jewish affairs.

In August 1946 supervision of the JAC was transferred from Lozovsky to Mikhail Suslov of the Foreign Relations Department of the CPSU Central Committee. Both he and Abakumov addressed memoranda to Stalin proposing the committee's liquidation.

Suslov pointed out the JAC's 'increasingly nationalistic, Zionist character', which was 'strengthening the Jewish reactionary bourgeois-nationalistic movement abroad'. Abakumov noted that the JAC had replaced 'the class approach' with 'an approach on national principles'. It acted as an 'intermediary' between the Jewish population and 'the Party-Soviet organs'.[33] But Stalin was not yet ready to liquidate the JAC. He still had hopes that his support of the Palestine Jews might pay dividends.

Reinvigorated by a four month sojourn in the sun, he returned to wintry Moscow on 21 November 1947. In pursuit of one strand of Stalin's policy towards Jews, the Soviet delegation at the United Nations voted for the partition of Palestine on 29 November. Then in late December the Boss ordered Abakumov to murder Mikhoels. Whether this act was prompted by Stalin's obsession with personal secrecy, or was intended simply to behead the JAC is a moot point.

On 10 December 1947 the MGB had arrested Yevgenia Alliluyeva, Stalin's sister-in-law from his second marriage. She was accused of convening 'anti-Soviet meetings' at her home, where 'she disseminated foul slander regarding the head of the Soviet government'.[34] Other members of his late wife's family and their circle followed her into custody.

Abakumov had learned that an acquaintance of Mikhoels knew the family, and that through them and Svetlana, the actor was seeking to approach the *Vozhd*. Stalin's fear was that his in-laws were supplying Mikhoels with personal information about himself, which would find its way to Jews in the USA. After all, no deity could survive gossip and scribbling in the capitalist press.

'They talked a lot', he snarled to Svetlana when she queried him about her aunts. 'They knew too much and they talked too much. And it helped our enemies'.[35]

The enemy Mikhoels was despatched to Minsk by the Stalin Prize Committee, ostensibly to review a new play. Along with his companion (an MGB agent), he was lured to the dacha of Lavrenti Tsanava, the Georgian head of the Belorussian MGB. Both men were murdered late on the night of 12/13 January 1948. Their bodies were dumped in a snow-covered road and reportedly run over by a truck, to simulate a road accident.

The corpses were brought back to Moscow, where Mikhoels was granted a state funeral. On 27 January Tsanava received without fanfare the Order of Lenin. It was awarded 'for exemplary execution of a special assignment from the government'.[36] The following day *Pravda* denounced Dimitrov's grandiose plans for an East European federation, and the

Boss began the process which would lead to the excommunication of Tito from the true Church of Stalinism.

Abakumov churned out more memoranda on 'bourgeois nationalism' and even 'espionage' by JAC members, but it remained too soon for Stalin to act. The Palestine question was still on his agenda. He recognised the new state of Israel immediately after its formation on 14 May 1948. During the subsequent Arab-Israeli war, Stalin supplied Israel with arms and advisers, mainly through Czechoslovakia.[37]

In May too Stalin began the process of demoting his ostensible heir-apparent, Zhdanov. A sickly alcoholic at the best of times, Zhdanov was ordered into hospital. He died there on 31 August in circumstances which Stalin would resurrect and utilise several years later.[38]

Having beheaded the JAC, isolated Tito, and reopened the succession question, Stalin dutifully participated in Zhdanov's funeral, and then headed south on 8 September 1948. When he returned three months later his long-standing anti-Semitism would be a dominant feature of his policies.

On 3 September Golda Meir arrived in Moscow as head of the Israeli legation. On 16 October, when she attended Yom Kippur services in Moscow's central synagogue, tens of thousands of worshippers packed the building and the streets outside. Moreover, despite Stalin's aid to Israel, the pro-American sympathies of its government and people were obvious even before the first election there in January 1949.

To Stalin all this meant that in the final analysis Soviet Jews too were pro-American, and were potential spies for the 'main enemy'. Stalin had had enough. He issued his commands while still on vacation in the south.

On 20 November 1948 the CPSU Politburo ordered the immediate dissolution of the JAC, 'since, as the facts show, this committee is a centre of anti-Soviet propaganda and regularly submits anti-Soviet information to organs of foreign intelligence'.[39] The MGB obliged the following day, a Sunday, closing down the JAC's headquarters and its Yiddish-language journal *Eynikayt* (Unity).

Stalin returned to Moscow on 2 December, and the arrests of JAC members began on 24 December. Eleven of the fifteen Jews who would be defendants in the JAC trial were arrested between 24 and 28 January 1949, the precise period when the CPSU leadership prepared its onslaught upon 'cosmopolitanism'.[40]

The MGB now linked Lozovsky with the JAC. On 13 January 1949 he was questioned about the Crimea letter of February 1944.[41] Expelled from the Central Committee and the Party on 18 January, he was arrested eight days later. He seemed fated to be the chief accused in a trial of the JAC.

Another possibility briefly emerged when in late December Molotov's wife, Polina Zhemchuzhina (*née* Perl Karpovskaya), was accused of contacts with 'enemies of the people' and expelled from the CPSU. Stalin forced Molotov to divorce her. She was arrested on 21 January and imprisoned in relative comfort. Although her relationship with Mikhoels was investigated, she was ultimately separated from the pending JAC trial and sentenced to five years of exile in Kazakhstan.

On 24 January 1949 Malenkov chaired a meeting which took the decision to launch a campaign against 'rootless cosmopolitans' in the ideological sphere; their 'rootlessness' implied their Jewishness. As arranged, on 28 January *Pravda* published an editorial 'On an Unpatriotic Group of Theatre Critics'. Seven named critics were accused of 'having lost a sense of responsibility towards the people, of having become bearers of a stateless cosmopolitanism detestable and hostile to Soviet man'.[42]

This was January 1949. Stalin's war upon the Jews was now overt. That same month he sanctioned the arrest of Noel Field, while in Hungary Rajk was put under investigation (p. 225). Early in February Tibor Szőnyi was placed under strict surveillance by the Hungarian secret police (p. 194), and Stalin sowed the seeds of the 'Leningrad Affair' (Chapter 24).[43]

This cluster of events could suggest that either the Boss was lashing out wildly, or he was drawing together various threads of his plot, even if it was not yet fully-formed. However, he would have known his initial target. It was seven months since Stalin had ordained the expulsion of the Communist Party of Yugoslavia (CPY) from the Cominform, and Tito had still not been ousted.

17

HERESY

TITO VERSUS STALIN

'Hero Tito'

It was in January 1949 too that the Slovene-born American writer, Louis Adamic, flew into Belgrade. He listed some of the slogans to be found on walls and buildings: *'People, Party, Tito: We Are One... Tito Is All Of Us... The More They Slander Tito, the More We Love Him... Long Live Tito!... Hero Tito... Tito Is Everything...*or, as on the wing of the plane, just *Tito'*.[1]

That a considerable 'cult of personality' surrounded both Marshal Tito and Generalissimo Stalin was never in doubt.[2] Ostensibly the rift which became public in June 1948 was between the Communist Party of Yugoslavia (CPY) and the Communist Party of the Soviet Union (CPSU), or between the Yugoslav and Soviet states. However, the driving force behind it was the clash of two unbending human wills.

Both Stalin and Tito headed their parties, their governments, and their armed forces. Both had made themselves undisputed dictators of their states by their control of the secret police. Both had emerged from the war with the aura of victors. Both men were very aware of their historical role. Both looked to and guarded their legacy.

Although 'ideological' labels such as 'Titoism' and 'national communism' would be affixed to the Yugoslav stand, in the final analysis the conflict had a far simpler cause. As CPSU Politburo member Nikolai Voznesensky put it in 1948, 'Every Communist Party must obey the Communist Party of the Soviet Union unconditionally'.[3] As a senior Yugoslav communist expressed it, the basic issue was simply 'whether or not Belgrade had to dot every Russian "i" and cross every Russian "t" on command'.[4]

When the rift became public in late June 1948 it came as a great surprise to virtually the whole world.[5] The Stalinist nature of Tito's regime, the speed and ruthlessness of its revolutionary measures, and its incessant eulogy of the Soviet prototype had together earned Yugoslavia the dubious accolade of 'Satellite number one'. How could there possibly be differences between master and apprentice?

But Tito saw himself as a master too, a master in his own house. It was over the issue of who called the shots in Yugoslavia that his conflict with Stalin would erupt, but it had simmered for some years.

In 1937 the apprentice dictator took the name Tito. He had begun life as Josip Broz, born on 7 May 1892 to a Slovene mother and Croatian father.[6] Leaving school at twelve, he trained as a locksmith. On his youthful travels as a locksmith and engineer Tito became fluent in Czech and German. He added Russian when he was wounded and captured on the Eastern Front in March 1915 while serving as an NCO in the Habsburg army.

Not until November 1920 did Tito return from Russia to the new Kingdom of the Serbs, Croats and Slovenes (renamed the Kingdom of Yugoslavia in 1929). There he joined the recently-formed CPY, whose activities were made completely illegal in August 1921.

After working as an engineer, and operating illegally as a trade union activist and party member, Tito became a full-time CPY official in February 1928. He was imprisoned from 1928 until 1934. In summer 1937 he was appointed acting head of his party. On 5 January 1939 the Bulgarian leader of the Comintern, Georgi Dimitrov, informed Tito that he had been appointed secretary-general of the CPY.

Now indisputably in charge of his faction-ridden party, Tito pushed through his organisational reforms: the Central Committee and Politburo were now based in Yugoslavia not abroad; the CPY was financed by its own members and not by the Comintern; each Yugoslav nationality or region now had it own party organisation. Overall membership soon increased.[7]

On 17 September 1941 Tito left Belgrade for the mountains. He was responding not to the Axis attack on Yugoslavia in April, but to Hitler's invasion of the USSR on 22 June. 'I felt myself to be an independent leader from the very beginning in 1941', Tito claimed later, since 'we saw that nobody would help us and we were on our own'.[8]

Tito's Partisans were harried in the war years by combinations of German, Italian and Bulgarian forces, aided by Croat *Ustaša* and Serbian Chetnik units. They lacked weapons, ammunition, footwear and uniforms. They endured long marches, hunger, cold, epidemics, and primitive medical facilities. They came through seven enemy 'offensives' in the mountains of Serbia, Bosnia-Hercegovina, and Montenegro. Their courage, stoicism, and fanatical determination to create a new Yugoslavia were never in doubt.

Tito's primary aim was to expand and preserve his forces in order to eliminate his internal enemies, particularly the Serbian royalist Chetniks. Tito had also to deal with the issue of the Red Army advancing from Bulgaria and Romania, which had met up with units of the National Liberation Army, as the Partisans were now styled, on 6 September 1944.

Leaving the Adriatic island of Vis in a Soviet plane, Tito flew to Romania, before going to Moscow, where he met Stalin for the first time. Lacking both tanks and artillery in eastern Yugoslavia, Tito asked for the Red Army 'to help our units liberate Serbia and Belgrade'.[9] Stalin agreed to provide a tank corps. The two marshals also came to an understanding about where and for how long the Red Army should operate in Yugoslavia.

The six-day Battle of Belgrade ensued, with heavy casualties on all sides, until the Yugoslav capital was finally liberated on 20 October. In July 1948 Tito would only concede that the 'heroic Red Army helped us liberate Belgrade, Eastern Serbia and Vojvodina'.[10] The Soviets saw the Yugoslav contribution somewhat differently.

As the Red Army pushed on into Hungary and Austria, the Yugoslav People's Army (YPA), as the National Liberation Army was rechristened in March 1945, was left with the task of fighting the German forces retreating from Greece and Macedonia. It was to prove a costly exercise in terms of casualties, particularly after a general offensive was ordered on 20 March. The YPA entered Trieste on 1 May, and also penetrated into southern Austria. The Germans resisted in Yugoslavia until 15 May, before surrendering.

It was victory, but at an enormous cost, and the bloodletting was not finished. The ruthlessness which the CPY had shown in war would be carried over into the revolution they forced on their devastated and exhausted land.

'Titolitarianism'

Like the other warring factions, both foreign and domestic, the Partisans had contributed to the horrendous death-toll of the wartime years.[11] Moreover, Tito's regime stands accused of killing an estimated 250,000 Yugoslavs in mass shootings, forced death marches, and concentration camps in 1945–46.[12]

The murderous aspect of their policy was hardly surprising. Tito's professed aim was always 'to prepare to seize power and to seize it in such a way that the bourgeoisie would never regain it'.[13] And in emulation of the Soviet (and Nazi) prototype, seizing and holding power required the establishment of a secret police force.

The Yugoslav security service OZNA (*Odsek za zaštitu naroda/* Department for the Protection of the People) was set up in May 1944 and headed by Aleksandar Ranković. Senior OZNA officers were exclusively members of the CPY and the CPY's Youth Organisation (SKOJ). Like their counterparts in the YPA, they were sent to the USSR for training immediately after the war. There were also Soviet advisers attached to OZNA units in Yugoslavia.

'There are those who say that the war is over, that the Army should be disbanded and OZNA dissolved', declared Tito in July 1945. 'I, too, once wished the [royalist] gendarmerie to be abolished. But let us away with such illusions…. We shall never disband OZNA or listen to such advice'.[14] Its function was, in Tito's words, 'to strike terror into the bones of those who do not like this kind of Yugoslavia'.[15]

Currency speculators, black marketers, those spreading 'racial' hatred, all faced the death penalty, as did others deemed to be members of such elastic categories as 'fascists' and 'collaborators'.[16]

OZNA was also responsible for issuing the *Karakteristika*, a sealed document which was 'a sort of certificate of political reliability or unreliability'.[17] Without a favourable variant it was impossible to obtain a domicile, job, university education, identity papers, food coupons, pension, or the right to vote.

Adding to the monopoly of force which the CPY controlled was the YPA. Perhaps 800,000 strong in a population of about fourteen million, in 1948 94 per cent of its officers were members of the CPY. In all 85,000 party members were in the YPA, together with an unknown number of members of SKOJ.[18] Before the rift Soviet officers were attached to virtually every command.

The CPY itself was much-changed in composition. By early 1942 one quarter of the Party's pre-war membership of 12,000 were dead, as were 7,000–10,000 of the 30,000 young communists then in SKOJ. By the end of the war only three thousand of the CPY's 1941 membership were left alive. In all the CPY lost 50,000 members in the war for national liberation, including ten Central Committee members.[19]

But it was now a mass party, recording a membership of about half a million in 1948. Most of its new entrants were wartime recruits from the peasantry and youth of the various nationalities of Yugoslavia. Their overall level of education, both academic and political, was low. Their loyalty was primarily to Tito as their wartime commander and party leader. Their primary functions were to act as so-called 'Tito-tooters', and unquestioning executors of the party line as ordained by its close-knit coterie of leaders.

Despite its size the CPY disguised its existence behind a People's Front. The Party was not even registered at the Ministry of Interior as the law required. Its leadership structure was not publicised. 'The Communist Party is not illegal', explained Tito, 'but its members have merged with other progressive elements in the People's Front with the aim of reconstructing the country as, during the war, they united in the struggle against the aggressor'.[20]

However, it was not invisible. CPY headquarters were to be found at the five-storeyed Madera Palace, a pre-war nightclub. Hammer and sickle signs were conspicuous in the building, while above the main entrance, emblazoned in gold letters, was written 'Central Committee of the Communist Party of Yugoslavia'.

However, the CPY Central Committee had not met since 1940. Besides Tito and his deputy, Eduard Kardelj, the CPY Politburo contained only two other members. These were Ranković, the Interior Minister and boss of OZNA, and Milovan Djilas who headed the CPY's *Agitprop* section. Most decisions were made by this close-knit quartet. Sometimes other CPY leaders were invited to attend an 'expanded Politburo' meeting.

It was this shy party, backed by its secret police and army, which would transform the political, economic and social structure of Yugoslavia with a speed and zeal that was the envy of every communist leader in the Soviet bloc. It began with the removal of the opposition.

New laws enfranchised women. The voting age was fixed at eighteen. The ballot was also given to children aged from ten to fifteen who were accepted as 'fighters against the enemy'. Conversely, 'collaborators' and 'war profiteers' were disfranchised, as were their relatives.

It was virtually impossible for the non-communist parties to get across their message. The CPY controlled the distribution of newsprint and printing equipment, and could always order 'spontaneous' strikes by print unions. Opposition papers could be banned for spreading 'false and alarming news contrary to the national interest'.[21] The three that were published printed only a few issues before being suppressed.

Eventually all the opposition parties boycotted the election campaign. This lasted for two months and took the form of a plebiscite. The population was exhorted to 'confirm our victory!' and to 'show our joy to our beloved Tito, who leads us to prosperity'.[22]

A blind box was provided at polling stations into which votes for the non-existent opposition could be dropped. The number of such votes was never revealed. Unsurprisingly, the unopposed People's Front won the elections for the Constituent Assembly on 11 November 1945, obtaining a modest 96 per cent of the vote according to official figures.

The formal abolition of the monarchy took place when the Federal People's Republic of Yugoslavia was established on 29 November. A new constitution, modelled on the 1936 constitution of the USSR, was adopted in January 1946. The Constituent Assembly morphed into the People's Assembly. On 13 March OZNA became the UDB (*Uprava Džavne Bezbednosti* or State Security Administration).[23]

'Satellite number one'

Tito's revolution was introduced into a poor, underdeveloped, and war-torn land. Vast material losses, particularly in communications and housing, had been inflicted upon a mountainous country whose economy and society were dominated by its peasantry. The bulk of Yugoslav exports were agricultural. She also produced bauxite, lead, chromium, copper, zinc, and molybdenum. Stalin was happy to leave her in this condition. Tito was determined to industrialise and electrify his backward state.

An initial land reform divided the estates and set a maximum ownership of land. Some 160,000 acres of church land were redistributed to the peasantry. A nationalisation law put over 80 per cent of Yugoslav industry under state control. This drastic legislation was passed by parliament's unanimous vote in a single day in December 1946.

A Five Year Plan was presented to parliament in April 1947. Moscow saw no need for it. 'What do you want with a heavy industry?' queried a Soviet negotiator. 'We have everything you need in the Urals'.[24]

What was needed in Yugoslavia, in Moscow's view, were joint-stock companies run by Soviet directors, in which the Yugoslavs supplied most of the investment, while the USSR creamed off most of the profits. Exempt from Yugoslav taxation and jurisdiction, these would give the Soviets control over important sectors of the Yugoslav economy, and allow an almost colonial exploitation of her raw materials.

However, the Yugoslavs haggled and by February 1947 only two joint-stock companies had been created. When Kardelj visited Moscow in March, Stalin brazenly conceded that such companies 'are only suitable for satellite countries'.[25] He offered instead a credit agreement of 135 million American dollars, of which the Yugoslavs only ever saw 800,000. Belgrade also griped about the Soviet use of world market prices in their trade agreements, which, given Yugoslavia's high production costs, caused them staggering financial losses.

Of course none of these measures took any account of consumers. The privations of the ragged and undernourished citizenry continued.

Despite the April 1945 Soviet-Yugoslav treaty of alliance, Stalin had serious political problems with Tito. He ordered Tito to withdraw his forces from the Slovene-populated fringes of Austria, and afforded him little support over his claim to Trieste. At this time Stalin's great power relations with the USA and Britain predominated over the concerns of his feisty satrap.

Tito angrily condemned these priorities in a speech in Ljubljana on 27 May 1945. 'We demand that everyone should be master in his own house. We do not wish to pay other people's debts, or to serve as small change in bargains between them; we will not be mixed up in the politics of spheres of interest'.[26]

Somewhat disingenuously Tito maintained that this was a reference solely to the Western powers. Yet the Yugoslavs had some inkling of what Stalin had been up to. In October 1944 he and Molotov had agreed 'percentages' of influence in the Balkans with Churchill and Eden. Initially Churchill had suggested that London and Moscow would go fifty-fifty in Yugoslavia in terms of influence.[27] Yet during the haggling over various 'percentages' Molotov had even hinted at the division of Yugoslavia's territory between the two powers.[28]

Stalin reacted furiously to Tito's speech, instructing his envoy in Belgrade to tell the Yugoslavs that he regarded it 'as an unfriendly attack on the Soviet Union'. If Tito transgressed again 'we shall be forced to reply with open criticism in the press and disavow him'.[29]

Tito also had problems with the Soviet civilian and military advisers that he had requested. Not only did they cost the earth in salaries, but they ignored the Partisan experience entirely. In Moscow's view, the role of the YPA was simply to be an adjunct of the Red Army in a Soviet strategic plan. 'We wanted advisers, not commanders', Tito grumbled.[30]

These 'advisers' also tended to try and recruit Yugoslav citizens into the NKGB/MGB and GRU. Tito knew this because of complaints by loyal CPY members and because Ranković's OZNA/UDB spied upon the spies.

Tito and the CPY did prove useful when Stalin set up the Cominform (Communist Information Bureau) in September 1947. The meeting was held in a secret police rest-home in Poland's 'recovered territories'.

Invited to attend were representatives of the CPSU, the CPY, and the Hungarian, Polish, Bulgarian, Czechoslovak, Romanian, French and Italian parties. Djilas and Kardelj were given the task of belittling the policies of the two last. This they did with all the relish and arrogance of chosen ones, deluding themselves that the CPY was now the second most important party in the communist world.

The attendant parties were informed that the world had split into 'two camps', one led by the USA and the other led by the Soviet Union. They were in the latter. The Boss spoke to them through Zhdanov, who gave the main report, and demanded that the constituent parties of the Cominform conform to Stalin's will.[31]

When the CPY balked at this, Stalin decided to reduce 'Hero Tito' to zero. The occasion rather than the cause of their showdown emerged from the complexities of a projected Balkan federation.

HERESY: TITO VERSUS STALIN

Balkan tours

One of the main aims of Tito's foreign policy was the creation of a South Slav state combining Yugoslavia and Bulgaria. Negotiations about an initial federation began as early as November 1944.

The problem was its form. The Yugoslavs wanted Bulgaria first to cede Pirin Macedonia to the Yugoslav unit (Vardar Macedonia). After that a truncated Bulgaria would enter the federation on 'equal' terms with the six Yugoslav 'republics' of Serbia, Croatia, Slovenia, Macedonia, Bosnia-Hercegovina, and Montenegro. Such blatant Yugoslav hegemony held few attractions for the Bulgarian communists, who preferred a one-to-one federation of Bulgaria with Yugoslavia in its entirety.

On 25 November 1947 Tito was in Sofia where he addressed a crowd of 300,000.[32] 'We shall establish co-operation so general and so close', he proclaimed, 'that the question of federation will be a mere formality'.[33] Dimitrov, now boss of Bulgaria, and Tito then retreated to Varna, and on the afternoon of 27 November they signed their treaty of friendship and mutual assistance. The Yugoslav delegation left Bulgaria the next day since Tito was busy. He had treaty-signing trips to Hungary (6–8 December) and Romania (17–19 December) on his agenda.

On 23 December Stalin sent a cable summoning a Yugoslav delegation to discuss the situation in Albania, whose semi-colonial status under Belgrade's authority rivalled that of the Soviet-Yugoslav nexus.

Djilas arrived in Moscow on 17 January 1948 and was summoned by Stalin immediately. 'We have no special interest in Albania', declared the Boss. 'We agree that Yugoslavia swallow Albania', and 'the sooner the better'.[34] Then everything went quiet. 'Complications have arisen', Djilas was told.[35]

The main complication was an interview given by Dimitrov on 17 January. Asked about East European federations, he replied, 'The question of a federation or confederation is premature for us. It [...] has not been a subject of discussion at our conferences'. But when that question was ripe for decision, then 'the nations of people's democracy, Roumania, Bulgaria, Jugoslavia, Albania, Czechoslovakia, Poland, Hungary, and Greece–mind you, and Greece!–will settle it'.[36]

Stalin was livid. It was time to end the red carpet treatment that the Yugoslavs and Bulgarians had enjoyed of late, in favour of a red carpeting. On 28 January *Pravda* announced that the countries of Eastern

Europe 'require no questionable and fabricated federation or confederation, or customs union'.[37]

Stalin summoned Tito and Dimitrov to Moscow. Tito decided that he was unwell and sent Kardelj in his stead. Kardelj arrived in Moscow on 8 February. Two days later, together with Djilas and the Bulgarian delegation, he was seated before the Boss and selected henchmen.[38]

Stalin taunted Dimitrov mercilessly. The latter promised to learn from his mistakes. 'Mistakes are not the issue', Stalin retorted harshly, 'the issue is conceptions different from our own'.[39] At another point he roared angrily, 'When I say "no" it means NO'.[40]

Having told his Balkan satraps what was not permitted, he allowed that there might be federations between Poland and Czechoslovakia, and between Hungary and Romania. As for Yugoslavia and Bulgaria, the federation between them 'should be proclaimed immediately, the sooner the better'. After they had united 'they should annex Albania'.[41]

Throughout the meeting Stalin complained that the two Balkan states had not consulted him. The following day Kardelj was forced to sign a humiliating 'agreement' to consult in matters of foreign policy. On 12 February it was reported that portraits of Tito were being taken down in Bucharest. At the end of February Moscow broke off negotiations for a new trade treaty with Belgrade.

On 1 March 1948 Tito held an 'expanded Politburo' meeting. The participants criticised every aspect of Soviet-Yugoslav relations. On the question of federation with Bulgaria, Tito had cooled. 'They differ from us ideologically. There would be a Trojan horse within our Party'.[42]

A Trojan horse was the least of their worries, since they were already infiltrated by a 'mole'. Finance minister Sreten Žujović said nothing at the meeting, but scribbled copious notes. He later reported on proceedings to the Soviet ambassador, as he had done for some time.

Red letter days

On 18 March the Soviets informed Tito that they were withdrawing their military advisers. The following day he learned that the civilian advisers were being pulled out too.

On 20 March Tito wrote to Molotov that he and his comrades could not understand and were 'deeply hurt' by Moscow's decisions. He wanted the USSR to 'openly inform us what the trouble is'.[43] But Tito was not that naive. He knew perfectly well what the trouble was. In Stalin's view he no longer reigned; he was to be reined in.

This was confirmed by a letter from Stalin and Molotov.[44] It was dated 27 March 1948, which was the seventh anniversary of the overthrow of Regent Paul's government. Then a previous attempt to disobey the dictator of another great power, Nazi Germany, and assert Belgrade's independence, resulted in the invasion, dismemberment, and brutal occupation of Yugoslavia.

The eight page letter was typed in Russian, and marked at the top in (imperial?) purple ink with the word 'Confidential'. Later the CPY learned that this 'confidential' letter was sent to the other Cominform parties, who were invited to declare their positions on the issue.

Stalin's reply was deliberately insulting, as were his other letters.[45] Yugoslavia's 'socialist achievements' were denigrated. The CPY leadership contained 'questionable Marxists' and 'English spies'. Stalin reminded them of Trotsky's 'instructive' career.[46] The CPY was undemocratic, 'semi-legal', and controlled by the minister of state security, and could not be considered Marxist-Leninist.

It took the crisis in Tito's relations with Stalin for him finally to call a plenum of the CPY Central Committee on Monday 12 April 1948.[47] Its twenty-six members discussed and slightly amended Tito's draft reply. Following further talks the next day they sent their response.

The letter signed by Tito and Kardelj took up Stalin's points firmly but politely. It deemed 'it as improper for the agents of the Soviet Intelligence Service to recruit' in Yugoslavia, and stated that the Soviet ambassador had 'no right to ask any one for information about the work' of the CPY. It contained the oft-quoted line: 'No matter how much each of us loves the land of Socialism, the USSR, he can, in no case, love his country less, which also is developing socialism'.

Stalin was unimpressed by this prickly proletarian patriotism. He didn't want to be loved, he wanted to be obeyed.

He informed the CPY leadership that it was the USSR 'which liberated Yugoslavia from the German occupation'. He referred to the 'anti-Soviet attitude of Comrade Tito' and 'the unbounded arrogance of the Yugoslav leaders'. The absence of collectivisation in Yugoslavia disturbed his Marxist-Leninist soul. He harked back to Tito's Ljubljana speech and Djilas's earlier 'insult' about the Red Army liberators.[48] As 'the question of Soviet-Yugoslav differences has already become the property' of all

Cominform parties, Stalin proposed that the question be discussed at the Cominform's next session.

Feeling 'so unequal', the CPY stated that they couldn't agree 'to have this matter decided now by the Cominform'. Stalin mocked them. Djilas and Kardelj could dish out criticism of the French and Italian parties, but the CPY couldn't take the same treatment. He didn't believe their assurances that 'they will remain true to the Soviet Union'.

Refusing to appear before the Cominform meant that the CPY had 'taken the path of cutting itself off from the united socialist people's front of people's democracies headed by the Soviet Union'. Whether or not the CPY attended the next Cominform session in June, the CPSU would still insist upon discussing there 'the situation in the CPY'.

In late April the CPY introduced a new nationalisation law to meet some of the Soviet criticisms. Later a rash collectivisation programme was undertaken. Tito's main counter-move was to convene a Fifth Party Congress on 21 July, which would finally bring the CPY fully into the open.[49] By the time the congress met though, the Yugoslav party had been expelled from the Cominform. A satellite was now in outer darkness.

Vidovdan

The second Cominform meeting in Bucharest lasted from 19 to 23 June. Zhdanov again made the keynote speech, while servile leading figures of the other parties parroted the requisite denunciations of Tito. However, the communiqué of this meeting was not published until 28 June, when it appeared in *Rudé Právo*, the daily of the Czechoslovak party. Stalin was celebrating another anniversary, for 28 June was St Vitus's Day; and *Vidovdan* was the most significant day in the history of the most numerous Yugoslav nation, the Serbs.[50]

On 29 June the CPY Central Committee decided to publish both the communiqué and their reply to it, and both documents appeared next day in the party daily *Borba* (Struggle). Neither said much that was new.[51]

The communiqué stated that the CPY had placed itself 'outside the ranks' of the Cominform. However, the latter was certain that there were 'sufficient healthy elements' in the CPY 'to compel their present leaders' to rectify their errors. If these leaders remained intractable, then the 'job' of the 'healthy elements' was 'to replace them'.

Stalin didn't expect Tito to be ousted at once. 'I feel from your report that you're counting on the defeat of Tito and his group at the Yugoslav CP Congress', he wrote to Czechoslovakia's President Klement Gottwald on 14 July. Stalin demurred. 'I have to say that we Muscovites have not been and are not counting on so early a defeat of Tito's group. Our objective in the first stage was to isolate it in the eyes of other Communist parties, and to reveal its shady machinations. We have attained this objective'.

The second stage of his plan involved 'gradually detaching Communist-Marxist groups' within the CPY from Tito. 'This takes time and we have to be good at waiting'. He advised Gottwald 'to arm yourself with patience', since there could be no doubt that 'Marxism-Leninism will in time prevail in Yugoslavia'.[52]

The CPY didn't expect armed intervention by the USSR and its Cominform neighbours. But just to be on the safe side they surrounded the meeting-place for their Fifth Congress with anti-aircraft and machine guns. The congress ran from 21 to 29 July 1948.

Its main feature was an eight-hour speech by Tito. He lauded the CPY's socialist achievements. Only at the end did he refute the Cominform charges, without attacking Stalin personally. Tito went out of his way to answer three accusations: that the CPY had 'turned our backs' on the USSR and the people's democracies; that 'we are nationalists and not internationalists'; and that they had 'renounced the science of Marxism-Leninism'.[53]

Away from the Congress, Ranković and his UDB neutralised pro-Stalin elements of the CPY. Žujović was imprisoned in May and thousands of Yugoslav 'Cominformists' were interned in horrendous conditions on Goli Otok (Bare Island) in the northern Adriatic.

The war of nerves between Tito and the Cominform would involve partial severance of diplomatic relations, and a drastic reduction in trade which struck at Yugoslavia's Five Year Plan. There were countless frontier incidents, real and rumoured movements of military forces, and a continuous propaganda barrage by Cominform radio stations. The theme of the latter was that those who turned their back on the peace-loving Soviet camp were bound to end up in that of the American 'war-mongers'.

Stalin's deliberate heavy-handedness had aggravated minor disputes into a major challenge. The problem was no longer solely Tito's insubordination, but both a fear and an expectation that the 'Titoist' contagion had spread to other communist parties.

For satellite leaders the scenario was fairly straightforward. The mightiest communist leader next to Stalin had been condemned for heresy, and heretics were not only excommunicated, they also went to the stake. But if Stalin could not reach Tito, surrogates would have to suffice. Therefore the best way to propitiate the god in Moscow was to offer him a human sacrifice, before he chose his own.

As Stalin's plot unfolded, he enjoyed the willing collaboration of one vassal, who would play the most active supporting role in the looming terror. This was the ugly, intelligent and ruthless Jew who ruled Hungary: Mátyás Rákosi.

STAGING THE RAJK TRIAL, 1949

18

LESS THAN RHAPSODIC

RÁKOSI'S HUNGARY

The disciple

During his tyrannical reign as Hungary's dictator, Mátyás Rákosi was wont to style himself as 'Comrade Stalin's best Hungarian disciple'. His suffering subjects used earthier terms to portray their unprepossessing ruler, such as 'Arsehead', 'the bald murderer', or 'the Toad'.

One of his victims described Rákosi as 'an ugly little man, much too fat, with no neck at all, his chin almost between his shoulders, a completely bald head and an utterly commonplace face'.[1]

The playwright Gyula Háy recalled the disciple's 'short, squat body, as if the creator had been unable to finish his work for abhorrence'. An extremely large head was 'topped by an enormous bald dome and fronted by a pallid, bloated face with a sweet-and-sour smile frozen onto it'.[2]

The fourth of twelve children, Rákosi was born on 9 March 1892 in the southern Hungarian town of Ada.[3] His father was a Jewish merchant who Magyarised the family name from Rosenfeld to Rákosi in 1904.[4]

In 1898 the family moved to Sopron on the border with Austria. They returned to the Bácska in 1906, and settled in Szabadka (now Subotica), although Mátyás was schooled in Szeged, some fifty kilometres to the northeast. Intelligent, with a considerable talent for languages, Rákosi studied from 1910 to 1912 at the 'Oriental Academy' in Budapest. He had by then joined the Hungarian Social Democratic Party (SDP). Rákosi's further training was sponsored by an import-export firm, and his work for them took him to Hamburg and then London. Here he worked as a clerk and joined the Labour Party.

He returned to Szabadka in 1914. Conscripted into the Austro-Hungarian army, Rákosi was captured by the Russians in July 1915. As a POW he learned Russian, and became so fluent that he could later attend meetings with Stalin without the encumbrance of an interpreter. After the Bolshevik revolution, he escaped from his camp and made the long and perilous journey to Petrograd. He returned to Szabadka in May 1918.

Six months later Rákosi was a founding member of the Hungarian Communist Party (HCP). When the short-lived Hungarian Soviet Republic led by Béla Kun was proclaimed on 21 March 1919 Rákosi acted briefly as commissar for Socialist Production. From mid-April to early July he was at the front as political commissar to the Second Division of the Hungarian 'Red Army', which was resisting the French-sponsored invasions by Czech and Romanian forces. Later he was commander of the Red Militia.

By the standards of Bolshevism the 'Red Terror' of Kun's regime was relatively merciful, with some five hundred victims executed for so-called 'crimes against the revolution'. The killers were the 'Lenin boys', criss-crossing the country in 'the train of death'.

When Kun's forces were finally overwhelmed by the Romanian army, Rákosi, along with other HCP leaders, fled to Vienna on 1 August, where they were interned. The Romanians duly entered Budapest three days later, and to the victors went the spoils, in considerable quantities. Under Allied pressure the laden Romanians finally withdrew on 15 November 1919.

The following morning the man who was to be Hungary's erratic ruler for over twenty years entered Budapest. Mounted on a white Arab charger, Admiral Miklós Horthy rode at the head of the so-called Hungarian National Army.

Within its ranks were sadists and fanatics who would launch the 'White Terror' from 1919 to 1921. Their victims were not only real and perceived communists, but recalcitrant peasants, liberal intellectuals, and, above all, Jews. The number of victims of the 'Whites' would greatly exceed the body-count of the 'Lenin boys'. Thousands were murdered or interned. Some 100,000 Hungarians went into exile.[5]

To complete Hungary's woes she was forced to sign the Treaty of Trianon on 4 June 1920, and surrender lands to Romania, Czechoslovakia, Yugoslavia and Austria. Excluding semi-autonomous Croatia-Slavonia from the calculations, historic Hungary lost some two-thirds of its territory and nearly 60 per cent of its population. The bulk of the departing people were Romanians, Slovaks, Serbs, and Croats. However, 3.2 million Magyars were now placed under foreign rule, even though half of these lived in communities contiguous to truncated Hungary.

In 1918–20 some 400,000 Magyars fled or left the lost territories. Given this influx and the departure of the national minorities, 'Trianon Hungary' was the most ethnically homogeneous state in Eastern Europe.[6]

The new 'minority' was Hungary's largely assimilated Jewish population, since 'Judeo-Bolshevism' was now an established concept in Hungary. Although they had comprised only a tiny fraction of Hungary's Jewish population, the commissars and hangmen of Kun's regime had been overwhelmingly Jewish by race. Of course these individuals viewed themselves as 'internationalists' and rejected their Jewish identity.

Ignoring such subtleties, the Horthy regime introduced Europe's first post-war anti-Semitic legislation. The 1920 *numerus clausus* law limited Jewish enrolment in higher education to 5 per cent of total enrolments; the proportion that Jews were deemed to be of Hungary's population. The law was routinely circumvented and ultimately repealed, yet it gave notice of the dreadful shape of things to come.

Horthy's regime banned the HCP, but allowed the SDP to function, although only in urban areas. Operating or agitating on behalf of the HCP now constituted sedition and could be tried before a military court. This body could pass only two sentences, discharge or death with the latter punishment to be meted out within two hours of judgement. This was the fate potentially awaiting Rákosi if he returned to Hungary.

Freed from internment in April 1920, Rákosi was then expelled from Austria. He journeyed to Moscow in May where he became active in the ECCI, dealing in particular with the Italian Communist Party.[7]

He also made several clandestine incursions into Hungary, commuting between Vienna and Budapest. Yet despite such accoutrements as a broad-brimmed hat, horn-rimmed spectacles, and a bushy moustache, on 22 September 1925 he was arrested in Közraktár utca in Budapest, during an extensive round-up by Horthy's secret police.

Under interrogation Rákosi named names. This fact was established by the Comintern in 1926. Rákosi's explanation both then and later was that he had merely confirmed what the police already knew.[8]

Rákosi and his fellow-accused appeared first before a military court in November 1925. Aided by international protests organised by the Comintern, they won their first victory. Their case was referred to the criminal court and they thereby escaped the death penalty.

On 5 August 1926 Rákosi was sentenced to eight and a half years imprisonment. Jailed first in Budapest, and then in Vác, he was finally transferred to Csillag Prison in Szeged.[9] As Rákosi's stretch neared its end, the regime decided to try him afresh, this time for his role in the events of 1919. Despite renewed clamour Rákosi was sentenced to life imprisonment in February 1935.

Yet whatever the democratic limitations of Horthy's Hungary, Rákosi and his fellow-accused enjoyed rights that the disciple never granted to his opponents once he took power. They employed their own defence lawyer, who was a party member. They could retract their confessions and harangue the court.[10] In prison Rákosi wrote and received letters from his family, had a radio in his cell, and was allowed to read newspapers.

There had been earlier prisoner-exchanges between Hungary and the Soviet Union. In the case of Rákosi it was a matter of standards, and possibly money too. In October 1940 Hungary reclaimed some banners captured by the Russians in 1849, while Rákosi left prison and arrived in Moscow in early November.[11]

There, much of Rákosi's contact was with Dimitrov. In their meetings in December 1941 and January 1942, Rákosi proposed that he should travel to the USA to work among the Hungarians there. 'Not feasible!' noted the Bulgarian in his diary,[12] for by now the world was at war.

War and 'liberation'

By dint of Hitler's awards and conquests, in the years 1938–40 Hungary 'regained' southern Slovakia, sub-Carpathian Ruthenia, northern Transylvania, Baranya, the Bácska, and chunks of Croatia.[13] Now it was payback time. On 27 June 1941 Hungary declared war on the USSR, and joined the advance of the *Wehrmacht* and Hitler's assorted allies.

The ill-equipped Hungarian Second Army was destroyed at Voronezh in January 1943. Its remnants were withdrawn to the rear. The advancing Red Army penetrated 'Trianon Hungary' from east and south. The country became a brutal war-zone from September 1944 until early April 1945.

Having blundered into war, the Horthy regime botched their attempts to extricate Hungary from its throes. Seeking to forestall occupation by Germany or the USSR, they brought both upon themselves.

The Germans occupied Hungary in March 1944, but allowed Horthy to remain as regent. He did little to prevent the destruction of Hungary's Jews, who had been stripped of their civil rights and economic role by ever more drastic Hungarian legislation in the years 1938–41. Aided by the Hungarian gendarmerie and anti-Semitic officials, the mass-murderer Adolf Eichmann and his SS *Sonderkommando* organised their annihilation.

Between 15 May and 8 July 1944 about 440,000 provincial Hungarian Jews were transported to Auschwitz. Most who arrived there alive died in the gas-chambers of that infernal camp. Some 502,000 Hungarian Jews lost their lives during the German occupation.[14]

Although the Jews of Budapest remained relatively unscathed, their nightmare began when Horthy was overthrown by the Germans on 15 October 1944. He was replaced by Ferenc Szálasi, the mystic, near-certifiable leader of Hungary's racist Arrow Cross Party (*Nyilaskeresztes Párt*).[15]

The Arrow Cross men (*nyilasok*) began their own pogrom. This merged with the siege of Budapest. From 24 December until 13 February 1945 there was savage fighting in the city. Soviet and Romanian troops, plus those Hungarian forces which had heeded Horthy's call to change sides, battled with the city's German and Hungarian defenders.

The capital's civilian population fared terribly. In addition to mortal danger, cold, and hunger, they were plundered by the 'liberating' Red Army, and women faced the horror of gang rapes. 'The seven weeks of the siege were child's play', wrote one in her diary, 'compared with the three weeks of torture we have endured since'.[16] The HCP was blamed for the Red Army's crimes, and Rákosi was fully aware of them.[17]

Soviet troops 'went quite gaga over the gadgetry of Western civilization', recorded Hal Lehrman. In Budapest he watched 'three delighted infantrymen push round and round in a revolving door, then unscrew it, carry it half-way down the street, and wonder why it wouldn't work when they set it up in the road'.[18] Bicycles were another wonder, but top of the list were watches, unknown down on the *kolkhoz*.

These were worn in great numbers by Soviet soldiers and arrayed the length of both arms. The usual method of liberating them was to poke a tommy-gun in the stomach of the local liberatee, and grunt the words '*Davai chasi!*' No one was exempt, man or woman, soldier or civilian, democrat or communist.[19]

The Soviet tommy-gun liberating all manner of private property taught the word *davai* (give, cough up, hand over) to the whole Soviet sphere, and was nicknamed the *davai-guitar* by its victims. In consequence the Man-God Stalin earned himself another title–that of the *Davai Llama*. Local war memorials to the heroism and sacrifice of the Red Army dead lost any sanctity for the indigenous population because of the behaviour of their living comrades, and were irreverently dubbed 'Tomb of the Unknown Watch-Stealer'.[20]

'We don't want another war', one Hungarian later told a British journalist, 'but if we must have one, then we don't want it to be followed by another liberation'.[21]

The USSR set the Hungarian reparations bill at \$300 million, of which it was to take two-thirds. However, by utilising various exploitative devices Moscow probably extracted over one billion dollars from the Hungarian post-war economy.[22]

The Potsdam declaration of August 1945 entitled the USSR to seize all German assets in Hungary as reparation. The Soviets also dismantled Hungarian productive capacity. They priced reparations deliveries from Hungarian current production at 1938 world prices, so that many items were shipped at prices well below the cost of production. As they had in Yugoslavia, the Soviets instituted joint-stock companies. The Hungarians had to pay shipping costs and late shipment penalties.

'They ate us at the start like wild beasts', complained one Hungarian, 'now they use knives and forks'.[23]

Adding to Hungary's economic burdens was the Soviet demand that she supply the occupying Red Army with food, animal fodder and coal. Much of this Moscow simply exported to the West.

Desperately short of tax receipts, the government added to the pressure of already high inflation by printing money. Before the war the pengő was valued at five to the dollar. On the last day of July 1946, just before the new forint was introduced, the dollar fetched 4,600,000 quadrillion pengős.[24] The hyperinflation of 1945–46—the worst the world had ever seen—totally ruined Hungary's middle classes.

'Salami tactics'

Behind the battling armies the HCP set up a provisional government and assembly in Debrecen in December 1944. This government contained as many former Horthyite generals as overt communists. Other participating parties were the SDP, the Smallholders Party (SHP), and the National Peasant Party (NPP).

The HCP line was to direct this 'antifascist coalition', remove the remnants of the old order from power, introduce land reform,[25] and augment its own numbers and influence. The 'transition to socialism' was definitely not on the agenda at this time.[26]

An armistice between Hungary and the three allied powers was eventually signed in Moscow on 20 January 1945. Under its terms Hungary was placed under a tripartite Allied Control Commission (ACC), chaired by Marshal Voroshilov. The US and British elements of the ACC would be doing a lot of protesting, once Moscow permitted their arrival. In the meantime the Red Army was in complete control.

Rákosi arrived back in Hungary on 1 February 1945 and was in Budapest later that month. With the unification of the 'Muscovite' and 'home' wings of the HCP on 23 February, he was elected general secretary of the Party. The Politburo and a twenty-five strong Central Committee contained both 'home' and 'Muscovite' elements.

Party membership, which was perhaps 2,500 at the beginning of 1945, rose to 30,000 in February, to 150,000 in May, to 220,000 in July, and was about 500,000 in October.[27] Besides the opportunist and careerist entrants, Jews showed their support for the one party that might defend them in the future.[28] A party card also helped avoid deportation to work in the USSR.

Encouraged by Rákosi, the working-class, rank-and-file 'little fascists' (*kisnyilasok*), also joined the HCP in significant numbers. Rákosi was of the opinion that it was easier to make good communists out of them than Jewish intellectuals.[29]

The provisional government moved to Budapest on 12 April 1945. Universal suffrage was introduced for the forthcoming elections, with the voting age fixed at twenty. 'War criminals' and members of twenty-five 'right-wing' bodies were disfranchised.

On Sunday 7 October 1945 municipal elections took place in Budapest. Running on a joint list with the SDP, Rákosi anticipated winning 70 per cent of the vote. He was hopelessly over-optimistic. Women, who were 60 per cent of the electorate, largely practising Catholics, and frequently rape victims, helped provide a decisive victory for the SHP. They gained nearly 51 per cent of the vote, while the HCP-SDP list received less than 43 per cent.

In the national elections held on Sunday 4 November communist weakness was even more evident. On this occasion the SDP rejected a joint list. With a massive 92 per cent turnout, the Hungarian electorate gave the SHP 57 per cent of its vote, through which it obtained 245 of the 409 seats in the new parliament. The HCP with 17 per cent of the votes won seventy seats. The SDP had just over 17 per cent of the votes cast and was awarded sixty-nine seats. Polling only 7 per cent of the votes, the NPP obtained twenty-three seats. How Rákosi must have envied Tito his 'unopposed' victory one week later.

Although the SHP had benefited from the ban on right-wing parties, its heterogeneous composition and support sowed the seeds of its destruction. There was no other party for the authentic 'reactionary' to join or vote for. There was no other 'Christian' party. There was no other party for the genuine smallholder and peasant to turn to. Another 'attraction' was that the SHP, unlike the HCP and SDP, was not 'controlled' by Jews.[30]

The first Smallholder premier was Zoltán Tildy, 'a chain-smoking Protestant clergyman, with a face like Pinocchio's'.[31] His father-in-law had been murdered in the 'White Terror', and, like his friend and successor Ferenc Nagy, Tildy stood on the left of the SHP. Rákosi's view was that Tildy was 'someone we could do business with', since he had 'a realistic sense of politics and did not forget about the Soviet Union'.[32] As if he could!

Despite the SHP victory the four-party coalition continued. Such an arrangement, agreed between the SHP and Viceroy Voroshilov before the election, was realistic; there was no way that the Soviets would have allowed the HCP to be excluded from government.

More important was the equal division of portfolios, nine to the SHP and nine to the three leftist parties. Hal Lehrman carped about 'winner takes half'.[33] The main fight for posts was over the Interior Ministry, which was previously held by a crypto-communist member of the NPP. The SHP wanted it for their strongman, Béla Kovács. The HCP refused to agree to this, and finally the post went to the 'moderate' Muscovite, Imre Nagy.[34] Within three months hard-man Rajk replaced him.

Hungary was proclaimed a republic on 1 February 1946. Tildy became president and Ferenc Nagy replaced him as premier. Yet the SHP's parliamentary majority meant nothing. As the fellow-travelling SDP leader, Árpád Szakasits, phrased it, 'Electoral arithmetic cannot form the basis of our political life!'[35]

Like Szakasits, Rákosi became a deputy premier in the new government. With no departmental responsibilities, he was free to scheme, and to remember. One revolutionary failure had cost him fifteen years of freedom. There would be no 'errors' this time. A teetotaller, faithful to the Soviet wife he had married in 1942, the disciple had other vices; he was a power-junkie who desired to serve Stalin. The end willed the means, however amoral and ruthless they would be. As he told the court in 1926, 'revolutions are not made with rosewater'.[36]

It was at this point that Rákosi's so-called 'salami tactics' came into play. The HCP would carve up all opposition to it slice by slice, until the whole adversarial 'sausage' was whittled away and devoured.

Ignoring 'electoral arithmetic', a 'left-wing bloc' comprising the HCP, SDP, NPP, and the trade unions was established on 5 March 1946. Two days later it drew 300,000 demonstrators onto the streets of Budapest. They mustered under the slogan, 'Out with the people's enemies from the coalition'.[37] The SHP leadership caved in and expelled twenty-two 'reactionary' deputies.

The greatest HCP coup came in December, when its police uncovered an alleged plot by the 'Hungarian Community' (*Magyar Közösség*) to overthrow the government and restore the Horthy regime. The 'Hungarian Community' was a secret organisation of 'pure' Magyars with semi-Masonic rites and totally moronic aims. It was linked with other groups and certain SHP deputies. As a result more of the latter were expelled and some had their parliamentary immunity lifted and were brought to trial.

There was plenty of suspicious material surrounding the 'plot' for the HCP to misuse, but there were no armed groups, nor any concerted plan of action, while the alleged plotters' ineptitude in matters of basic security was staggering. Torture by both Hungarian and Soviet police was used on some defendants. Eventually several show trials were conducted in 1947–48. Most of the sentences were relatively light.[38]

The SHP leadership refused to lift the immunity of Béla Kovács, the party's secretary-general, so the Soviets simply arrested him in February 1947. The following May Ferenc Nagy himself was linked to the 'plot' which was ostensibly directed against his own government. At the time he was vacationing in Switzerland. Invited to face trial when he returned, he took Rákosi's other option; his small son was delivered to him and he resigned the premiership and went into exile in the USA.

His post went to a compliant Smallholder, Lajos Dinnyés, who was instructed to call for new elections two years before they were due. The electorate was rejigged. Members of some thirty pre-war political organisations were disqualified from voting. So were those who had lost their jobs after 1945 for political reasons. Such suspect categories as women who were 'overzealously religious' were also disfranchised.[39]

Perhaps 500,000 voters, 10 per cent of the electorate, were struck from the rolls.[40] Interior Minister Rajk introduced the 'blue ballot', which permitted 'non-resident' voters to cast their vote outside their own constituency; no frequency was specified. The HCP encouraged the creation of new 'bourgeois' parties, which formed from opposition groups within the fragmenting SHP, as well as those already expelled from it. In such manner more slices were hacked from the diminishing 'salami'.

In the elections held on 31 August 1947 over three-quarters of the electorate voted against the HCP, which only received 22 per cent of the vote. It had, however, obtained the largest share of the poll, and together with its three coalition partners, including the 'rump' SHP, it garnered 61 per cent of the vote.

The six 'bourgeois' opposition parties, which together had taken 39 per cent of the vote, had served their purpose. After the election they were dissolved by Rajk's ministry on various spurious grounds, and their dismissed deputies were either arrested or fled the country.

Although Dinnyés remained premier and the four-party coalition continued, such forms were now of little relevance. The main ministries were in the hands of the HCP or its stooges, and the opposition cowed and neutered. The 'transition to socialism' could begin.

In August 1947 a Three Year Plan was introduced. In March 1948 the nationalisation of all companies with over one hundred employees was decreed from above, followed later that year by state ownership of most light industry.

On 12–13 June 1948 a unification congress between a heavily purged SDP and the HCP took place. Following the merger, the new party was purged afresh of former SDP members and the now redundant *kisnyila-sok* entrants.

LESS THAN RHAPSODIC: RÁKOSI'S HUNGARY

In July Rákosi forced President Tildy to resign and he was placed under house-arrest. It would last eight years. His replacement was Szakasits, who would later be imprisoned. In December István Dobi, 'a hard-drinking, crafty old man',[41] replaced Dinnyés as premier.

Rákosi had orchestrated the nature and pace of these domestic changes in line with Stalin's will. He behaved in the same fashion during the Soviet-Yugoslav rift, when he led the satellites' attack upon Tito. However, in this enterprise Rákosi had to stuff many past words and deeds down the Orwellian 'memory hole'.

Rákosi versus Tito

A speech by Rákosi on 10 September 1946 had oozed with praise for the Yugoslav cause: 'During this great world war we saw with tremendous enthusiasm that there were two peoples who justified the hopes of mankind–the Soviet people and the Yugoslav people'.[42]

The HCP daily *Szabad Nép* (Free People) of 4 January 1947 gushed in similar fashion: 'Apart from the Soviet Union, no other country has shown us so much friendship as Yugoslavia'. That country 'did not wish to take revenge upon a democratic Hungary for the crimes committed by the Horthyists'.[43] In an unpublished article on Yugoslavia, Rákosi referred to 'the magnanimous policy of her great leader Tito'.[44]

In April 1947 Molotov asked the visiting Rákosi if Yugoslavia was popular in Hungary. 'Even more popular than the Soviet Union', replied the disciple. 'The Hungarian people are not afraid of the Yugoslavs, but the traditional fear of the Russians still lingers on'.[45]

Moreover, Tito had opposed the expulsion of Hungarians from Slovakia; an issue which had strained relations between Budapest and Prague. On the other hand, all the CPY heard when Rákosi and other HCP leaders visited Belgrade were complaints about Soviet plundering and anti-Semitism. Regarding these and other matters they sought Yugoslav support and advice.[46]

From 6–8 December 1947 Tito was in Budapest, signing a treaty with the Hungarian government. Reportedly, hundreds of thousands turned out to see him. The extravagant security precautions taken by the Hungarians at Yugoslav insistence were to feature in the Rajk trial.[47]

During this visit, Tito supposedly said to some HCP leaders that 'Comrade Stalin was too cautious after the war. He should have let the

French and Italian comrades seize power the way we did–and he didn't like what we were doing either'.[48] A few months later Stalin was making it crystal-clear that he didn't like Tito's behaviour, and on 16 April 1948 Tito received from Rákosi a letter in which he sided with Stalin on every point.

Later, Rákosi had the temerity to disparage the CPY's wartime role. He was also present at the Cominform conference in June 1948, actively demanding the CPY's expulsion. A few days later he forecast the pending collapse of the Tito regime.[49]

Rákosi was the most zealous 'anti-Titoist' among the satellite leaders, and no less could be expected of 'Stalin's best Hungarian disciple'. Moreover, in helping to bring about Tito's fall he might have been able to promote Hungary into the now vacant slot of 'Satellite Number One'.

Nor was this nexus totally one-sided. Rákosi had something to offer which Stalin could use in his developing plot. He had the 'Szőnyi group' which had been in contact with Field, Dulles, the OSS and Tito's OZNA. In addition to their involvement with American and Yugoslav intelligence, the group's members were all Jewish, and this would prove to be a godsend for Stalin.

19

FATEFUL CONTACT

NOEL AND THE 'SZŐNYI GROUP'

The Szőnyi group[1]

In wartime Switzerland Noel came into contact with a small Hungarian communist group which had coalesced around Dr Tibor Szőnyi.[2]

Born in Budapest in 1903, Szőnyi and his bourgeois family fled to Vienna when the Kun regime fell in August 1919. From 1922 to 1928 he studied medicine and neurology at Vienna University. There he made contact with the illegal HCP and in 1930 he joined the Party. Returning to Hungary, he acted as a courier and was arrested. Following his release Szőnyi left for Vienna in 1931, where he worked as a psychiatrist until 1936. At the same time he acted as the liaison man (*Verbindungsmann*) between the external and internal bodies of the HCP.

When the *Anschluß* between Germany and Austria took place in March 1938 the HCP ordered Szőnyi to Prague. He was not there long. Following the Munich settlement Szőnyi fled to Switzerland in October. There he worked for a year as a doctor in a refugee camp and then in the psychiatric clinic of Zurich University. In 1941 he married a fellow-doctor, Anna Abonyi (*née* Bernstein), a Soviet citizen born in Romania.

Until 1942 Szőnyi worked illegally for the Austrian communist group in Zurich. But in the years 1943–45 he became leader of both the *émigré* group of the HCP in Switzerland and of the MNFF (Swiss Organisation of the Hungarian Independence Front). Neither were large organisations and membership was virtually coterminous.

Like their leader the members of the Szőnyi group were Jewish. Unlike him they were young, mostly in their twenties. The majority had gone to Switzerland to further their education, because the anti-Semitic laws enacted in Hungary in 1938–41 restricted advanced study in their homeland.

These young men and women were mostly from middle-class backgrounds, with little or no connection to working-class movements. Idealism and antifascism propelled them into the HCP, and such backgrounds would render them suspect to its Stalinist leadership.

'The group consisted of students, intellectuals, and politically vacillating elements', strongly influenced by 'the theory of Browder', recited Szőnyi at the Rajk trial. Another member of the group, posing as a 'witness', referred to them as 'Hungarian refugees with rather confused political attitudes'.[3]

The five members of the group who would return to Hungary with Szőnyi in March 1945 were Ferenc Vági, György Demeter, Dr Gyula Kuti, János Dobó and Dr András Kálmán. Iván Földi would be left in charge of the members remaining in Switzerland. György Hódos would be one of those staying behind.[4]

Kálmán, like Kuti, a qualified doctor, was a veteran of the Spanish Civil War who had escaped to Switzerland from internment in France early in 1940. Demeter had lived and studied in Palestine and Italy, and was a mechanical engineer. Hódos began as an engineer, switched studies to history, and ended up as a journalist.

Földi was an electrical engineer, who from 1943–44 worked on high frequency research at Zurich Polytechnic. Dobó was a chemist. Like Kálmán and Földi, he had a Swiss wife, and she would die of neglect in a Hungarian prison. Vági too studied chemistry, but his political activism and frequent arrests brought an end to his student days, and propelled him into the number two spot in the group.

Planning their return[5]

Noel dated his first contact with the group to a visit from Vági some time in the first half of 1944. The Hungarian brought with him a long memorandum on the activities of the MNFF in Switzerland, and asked Field to hand it to Dulles, along with a request that he receive a representative of their group.[6] Noel recalled that the document included quixotic plans to parachute group members into Hungary to form partisan units. The MNFF also hoped to get material support from Dulles.

Treating Vági's request as a party order, Field contacted Dulles, who told Noel that he would first have to assure himself about the reliability of the Hungarians. Noel informed Vági of this, and with that his role in the matter was finished. Or so he thought. As Vági did not contact him again on the matter, this suggested to Field that a meeting with Dulles had taken place. However, Noel emphasised that he had no definite knowledge about this.

Noel provided financial help to some members of the Szőnyi group on an individual basis and he supplied the MNFF with four to five thousand Swiss francs for the production of propaganda material. Field also introduced the Hungarians to leaders of the relatively wealthy OSE (*Oeuvre de Secours aux Enfants*), a Zionist organisation seeking to save Jewish children. Noel suggested that the group might get finance from them, in exchange for a promise to organise the flight of Hungarian Jewish children to the Yugoslav Partisans.

Vági was also in contact with Miša Lompar, who was the leader of the Yugoslav communists in Switzerland as well as being consul-general in Zurich. He too seems to have suggested that Vági approach the OSE.

The Hungarians wanted to go home so Lompar had the idea of disguising them as a Yugoslav medical mission. He offered to supply them with the requisite false papers, for as citizens of an enemy state the Hungarians would receive no help from the Anglo-American authorities. The plan was that the Hungarians would travel on a ship leaving Marseille which was transporting repatriated POWs to Yugoslavia.

In late summer 1944 negotiations took place between Demeter and Kuti, as representatives of the Szőnyi group, and the leader of the OSE, Dr Joseph Weill, and his deputy. According to another account, not only were Lompar and a second Yugoslav, Lazar Latinović, also present, but so was Noel Field.[7]

Weill agreed to get the Hungarians out of Switzerland illegally. In addition he supplied them with 5,000 Swiss francs and medical equipment in exchange for a report on the situation of Hungary's Jews, which either Szőnyi or Vági prepared for him.

On Lompar's orders, fake identification papers were provided by the Yugoslav consul in Geneva, which Kálmán collected from the consul's flat. These disguised the Hungarians as officers in the Yugoslav army, travelling to Yugoslavia on a relief mission. All were given birthplaces in the Vojvodina, that part of Yugoslavia with a sizeable Hungarian minority. Lompar asked them to destroy their false papers when they arrived in Hungary, in case they fell into the hands of 'unauthorised' persons.

Lompar also supplied them later with two letters of introduction: one to Latinović, now Yugoslav consul-general in Marseille; the other to the Belgrade headquarters of OZNA, the CPY's secret police.

The precise nature and extent of the collaboration between Szőnyi and Dulles is impossible to assess without access to the relevant OSS and Dulles papers. However, as Field suspected, it seems that there was some contact between them.

At the Rajk trial Szőnyi stated that his 'first personal meeting' with Dulles took place in Bern at the end of September 1944. Thereafter 'I met Dulles regularly until my return home in January 1945'. At a meeting at the end of November 1944 Dulles said 'that he himself would organise the transference of the group to Hungary'. This encounter and another meeting in December 1944 represented their 'last two talks'.[8]

What Dulles would be getting from the deal is unclear. Presumably he hoped to obtain intelligence from Hungary. Naturally, at the Rajk trial it was asserted that the function of the Szőnyi group was espionage and 'wrecking activities' on behalf of American intelligence.

Another question is whether, as the Hungarian secret police contended, Szőnyi really travelled with a letter from Dulles to OSS Marseille. He probably did, if we are to explain why there was such extensive OSS and US military help to this small group. Moreover, members of the group told Noel in Marseille that they were enjoying OSS technical assistance, as well as the support of OSE finance.[9]

Return to Hungary

On 5 January 1945 the six prospective HCP returnees gathered at Földi's house in Geneva. At ten that night they met Weill and another person in the back room of an inn. The latter guided them illegally across the border into France, using a route that Weill had established in order to bring Jewish refugees into Switzerland. They spent the night in a farmhouse. The next day Ilona Kojsza drove them to Grenoble and then to Marseille.

In Marseille they reported to Latinović. The ship with returning POWs had already left, and no future sailings were foreseen. As a result the group would have to fly, and for this they needed the permission of G2 (US Army intelligence). Latinović provided them with credentials to introduce them to the US military and the local French command. The former they needed in order to apply for transport home, and the latter for accommodation and canteen facilities. Latinović probably gave Szőnyi letters to both the Yugoslav military mission in Bari and OZNA in Belgrade.

A fateful encounter took place in early February 1945. During their 'inspection tour' in the south of France, Noel and Jo Tempi were walking along a street in Marseille when they bumped into Vági and Demeter quite by chance. The two Hungarians invited Field and Jo to their quarters in the so-called 'Yugoslav chateau', where they introduced Noel to Szőnyi.[10]

Field saw Szőnyi again in a bar next day, and asked him in what form USC post-war aid in Hungary could best be organised. He suggested that Szőnyi send him a report about whether aid activities were possible or necessary in Hungary. Noel also gave the group several thousand French francs, and provided them with further material through Ilona Kojsza. When Szőnyi asked Noel to supply them with 'certificates' describing them as USC representatives, Field complied.

Latinović's efforts to put the Hungarians in contact with G2 paid off at the beginning of March, when G2 put a plane at their disposal. They flew from Marseille to Naples and there they were put up in a hotel as Allied officers for two or three days. A US transport aircraft then flew them on to Bari and from there to Belgrade, where they arrived on 12 March. Kálmán and Vági reported to OZNA, which sent a car to fetch the others from the aerodrome to OZNA headquarters. There Szőnyi handed over the letters from Lompar and Latinović.

In Belgrade they were accommodated in a hotel and ate in the canteen for OZNA officers. Since their stay and crossing into Hungary was an OZNA responsibility, they were instructed to keep secret their identities, particularly the fact that they were Hungarians. This was hardly onerous and they spent their days in Belgrade seeing the sights and going to the cinema.

Their chief contact was an OZNA major whom Kálmán knew from Spain. He organised the group's journey by truck via Novi Sad to Subotica. From there they travelled in two cars to Szeged in south-east Hungary, where OZNA delivered them to the local committee of the HCP on 16 March 1945.

Having reported for duty, Szőnyi ordered the group to destroy their forged Yugoslav IDs, as requested by Lompar. While still in Szeged he wrote a short report on the activities of his group for the HCP. Although this referred to the help provided by Noel and OZNA, it is unclear whether it mentioned the role of Dulles and the OSS.[11]

Most of the other members of the Swiss group filtered into Hungary in 1945 and 1946. However, Földi did not finally leave Switzerland for Hungary until February 1947, although he travelled back and forth between the two countries before that.

Vági was in Switzerland on official missions in August 1945 and April 1946. During the latter visit he saw Field on a few occasions. He asked Noel to arrange a meeting with a Hungarian-speaking member of the US consulate in Geneva. Later they had a wide-ranging talk in Arosa, discussing Soviet 'excesses' and the November 1945 election.

Whether or not Noel ever received written reports from Szőnyi was an important point in the Rajk trial, when it was portrayed as espionage material. Originally Noel replied that he didn't know, adding that in any case such was not correspondence between two secret agents. Later he conceded that he received a report that must have been sent either by Vági or Szőnyi. Its content was probably that alluded to in the trial; straightforward news material about plans to stop inflation and items concerning the strength of the HCP.[12]

None of the group, except Szőnyi, attained high-ranking posts in post-war Hungary. They held middle-ranking administrative and management positions where, according to the format of the Rajk trial, they could conduct 'espionage and wrecking activities'.

Szőnyi became head of the HCP's cadres section in September 1947, and a Central Committee member in June 1948. He was also elected to the Hungarian legislature in both the August 1947 and May 1949 elections. In the Rajk trial, it was naturally alleged that he used his position in cadres to place the group members in 'sensitive' posts. Yet the whole group may have been an object of suspicion to the Hungarian secret police from as early as 1945.

State security[13]

Pedestrians crossed the road when passing 60 Andrássy út, 'the most terrifying address in Hungary'.[14] This building was the headquarters of Hungary's post-war secret police, the ÁVH (*Államvédelmi Hatóság* or State Security Authority).[15]

Number 60's chequered history reflected much of Hungary's own. Originally a high-class building for well-off Jewish families, it was leased to the Arrow Cross Party as its headquarters. Later the *nyilasok* simply expropriated it from its Jewish owners. During their brief but murderous rule the *nyilasok* turned the building into their prison.

So when the ÁVH took over 60 Andrássy út everything was already to hand. The facilities included cells, subterranean dungeons, instruments of torture and execution chambers. The HCP's consciously-delivered 'message' was the continuity of terror for the regime's opponents.[16]

Moreover, certain denizens of 60 Andrássy út had only to move out briefly, since the ÁVH's recruitment policies mirrored those of the HCP. Thus 'its complement was a politically bizarre mixture that included former Horthyite experts and Arrow Cross thugs as well as many Jewish survivors of concentration camps disposed to seek revenge'.[17]

Of the first 113 recruits, eighty-three were communists and twenty-three came from the SDP. There were no members of the SHP. Seventy were 'workers' and twenty-one were 'intellectuals'. Twenty-eight of the 113 were Jews. By April 1945 the ÁVH had over 400 employees. By the end of that month it had arrested 12,000 'war criminals' and by July almost double that number.[18]

The head of PRO/ÁVO/ÁVH was Lieutenant General Gábor Péter. He was born Benjamin Eisenberger in May 1906 in a small town in the northeast of today's Hungary. Péter had little schooling and was a tubercular tailor in his pre-war days. He joined the HCP in 1931. Arrested several times by Horthy's police, he was badly mistreated by them when in custody.[19] He remained in Hungary throughout the war.

The HCP appointed Péter as head of the political police in January 1945 when the war still raged in Budapest. Although he was not a 'Muscovite' he remained in this post for eight years.[20]

'He was a short man with rodent eyes and a Hitler moustache', recalled one of his victims.[21] Another Hungarian described Péter as 'a small, thin, slightly stooping man, as tailors often are, speaking in a kind of piercing whisper and walking with an irregular gait'.[22]

Giving Péter's character a different slant, a former SHP minister saw 'a shy, sweet-smiling, effeminate little ladies' tailor with a small Hitler mustache'. He 'flutters, minces, lisps, his wrists are limp, his hands never still'.[23]

Presumably the 'coded' implication from this book (published in the USA in 1952) was that Péter was gay, although other accounts talk of him having several mistresses. Similar stories surround his wife, Jolán Simon, who was Rákosi's secretary. She is credited with having a three-way affair with a professor's wife and a noted Budapest actress.[24]

One story that is credible is Péter's love of flowers. There are numerous descriptions of the geranium-filled window-boxes adorning the exterior of the hell-hole that was 60 Andrássy út. More geraniums bloomed in the windows of neighbouring buildings, which this voracious monster swallowed up to house its growing complement of staff and inmates. Nor was the interior neglected. 'Peter's trim, sunny little office is like Titania's bower. Geraniums are everywhere'.[25]

It is not known whether Colonel Ernő Szűcs, Péter's deputy since 1947, was a fan of flowers. An obese, medal-wearing man, with 'tiny, hardly discoverable eyes in his beefy red face',[26] he was born Ernő Szűsz in Györ in 1908. As a textile-worker he joined first the SDP and then the HCP. He served two stretches amounting to seven years in Horthy's prisons.

Following his release in 1940 he travelled to Moscow. There he married a Russian. As one of the tasks he performed in the USSR, Szűcs reported upon Rákosi and the exiled HCP leadership to the NKVD.

He returned to Hungary in August 1945 and joined the Interior Ministry in September. On orders from the then deputy head of the ÁVH, Szűcs opened dossiers on various people. Amongst those on file were Noel Field, Ilona Kojsza, and László Rajk and his wife.

Szűcs also had his suspicions about the Szőnyi group. As early as 1945 they were put under observation by the security police and their mail was intercepted. Apparently the ÁVH knew about the contact between Field and Szőnyi, and that the group had returned to Hungary with the help of the Americans and OZNA. What they had not worked out was the purpose of Noel's contact with Szőnyi.[27] Let us concede that the super-efficient ÁVH had indeed gathered all this information. Presumably they had simply read the report written by Szőnyi and Vági in Szeged in March 1945.

It is unclear whether or not they passed their findings to Rákosi. If they did, then it certainly begs the question why Szőnyi was appointed as head of cadres, effectively the HCP's personnel officer, if he was under any sort of a cloud. Such a senior appointment must have been sanctioned, if not made, by Rákosi.

Perhaps Rákosi did not know of the ÁVH suspicions. Perhaps he did know and dismissed them as unfounded. Perhaps he saw in Szőnyi simply a loyal and efficient *apparatchik*. After all, he was trusted to bring 'fraternal greetings' from the HCP to the First Conference of the Socialist Unity Party (SED) in East Berlin which ran from 25–28 January 1949.

However, by the time that Szőnyi made his prepared speech to the SED Noel Field's arrest had been ordered, and Szőnyi would certainly have been under suspicion.

In February 1949, on Rákosi's instruction, Gábor Péter put Szőnyi and his deputy, András Szalai, under strict surveillance. From April their telephones were tapped, but this produced nothing of an incriminating nature.[28]

However, there were other ways to confirm the assumption of Stalin and Rákosi that the 'Szőnyi group' were agents of 'imperialist espionage organisations'. The ÁVH would have to beat the 'proofs' out of them. Moreover, there was someone who could tell them the whole story: Noel Haviland Field.

20

THE SPIDER AND THE SPY

NETTING THE FIELDS

Tarnished halo[1]

Max Horngacher worked at an international student aid body based at 13 rue Calvin in Geneva. Noel had·spoken with him on the phone several times before meeting him in person in 1944. Like many other people Max knew that Noel was in contact with Dulles, since Noel made no secret of this relationship.

On 13 April 1945 Noel wrote a brief covering letter in French to the twenty-five-year-old Horngacher on USC headed notepaper, and sent it to Max's office. It read as follows:

Dear Sir,
I enclose the letter to Mr Dulles which I promised you earlier today.
Yours sincerely,
Noel H. Field.

Enclosed with this covering letter was another in English addressed to Dulles. It asked him to render 'any advice and aid you can appropriately give to M. Horngacher', who had been 'delegated by his organization to visit Yugoslavia with a view to studying problems of aid' to students there.[2] Whether this led to any contact between Dulles and Horngacher is unknown.

In the entire Field affair this is the only letter from Noel to Dulles whose contents can actually be proven to exist. Others are referred to in various accounts, and will be noted. And to be clear on this matter, Noel did write other letters to Dulles besides the one cited above.[3]

Obviously this signed covering letter by Noel could be used to refer to other, possibly forged, letters. Moreover, both this and the letter to Allen demonstrated unambiguously that Noel was in contact with the 'master-spy' Dulles. In such manner, given the fervid atmosphere of the late 1940s, Noel could be portrayed as a spy himself.

Besides his day-job, Horngacher was a member of the illegal Swiss Communist Party (SwCP), and by 1948 he was working for the Hungarian and Czechoslovak security services, and possibly other organisations. His Czechoslovak contact, Artur London, took him on in 1947 and ran him during his stays in Switzerland in 1947–48. Throughout this period London was an agent of the StB, and was probably working with the MGB too. Moreover, as Karel Bartosek's researches in the Prague archives demonstrate beyond question, London played a major role in promoting Noel as an alleged American agent.[4]

'London knows very little about me', claimed Noel in 1954. 'I had only been accidentally involved 'in' the Field business' contended London in 1968.[5] Neither statement is true and the relationship between the two men was to have catastrophic results for both.

Artur London was born into a working-class Jewish family in the Moravian town of Ostrava in February 1915. As a young communist he, like Noel, had marched in protest against the execution of Sacco and Vanzetti in 1927. He joined the communist youth at the age of fourteen, and later the CzCP. He was arrested several times before the Party sent him to Moscow in 1934, where he was presumably trained by Soviet state security.

Sent to Spain in March 1937, London was never at the front during the civil war, but worked exclusively in the security services, purging 'Trotskyites' and other 'traitors'. He ended up as deputy head of the Spanish Republican security service, SIM (*Servicio de investigación militar*). As his combatant comrade, Otto Hromadko, caustically phrased it, SIM was simply 'a branch (*filiale*) of the NKVD'.[6]

Early in 1939 London left Spain for Paris. Later he operated as one of the leaders of the Czechoslovak groups in the French resistance. In August 1942 he and his French wife, Lise Ricol, were arrested by the Gestapo.

Lise was sent to KZ Ravensbrück and London to KZ Mauthausen, where he was a member of the illegal camp committee. Beyond such personal ordeal, he also lost virtually his entire family in the Holocaust. On liberation from Mauthausen he returned to Paris and became head of the Czechoslovak information office there. In April 1947, armed with a letter of introduction from Jo Tempi, London turned up at USC Geneva. He sought and obtained USC finance to cover a three-month stay in a Swiss sanatorium to cure the TB he had contracted in Mauthausen. After that he recuperated with his family in a small hotel on Lake Geneva. In 1948 he had further treatment in Switzerland.

During his stays in Switzerland London helped set up a Czech intelligence network. In the summer of 1948 he recruited Max Horngacher as an agent for the StB. Learning of Noel's letter of recommendation to Dulles, he got Horngacher to photocopy it, and sent this to Prague.

Around November 1948 London passed to the StB what was apparently another letter from Noel to Dulles, which detailed resistance strength and political conditions in Nazi-occupied countries. However, this letter, if it ever existed, does not reappear in later events.

Field claimed to have met London on only three occasions. Their first meeting was in July 1947, when Noel was considering his own resignation after Jo Tempi was fired from the USC. London talked him out of it. In August or September 1947 Noel discussed USC affairs with him again.

Their third meeting was in Paris in May 1948. They spoke about Noel's planned study-trip to Czechoslovakia and London gave him addresses of Prague friends, most of which Noel already had. However, as we have seen (p. 132), the two men met in Paris in November 1948. Noticeably, Noel did not mention this fourth meeting to his interrogators.

The Hungarian connection[7]

Dr Edmond Ferenczi was born in Vienna in 1920 into a well-off Hungarian-Jewish family. In 1921 they moved to Geneva, where Edmond's father worked for the ILO. Educated in Switzerland, the left-leaning Ferenczi never joined the SwCP, although he did become a member of Szőnyi's MNFF. In August 1947, after the HCP had effectively taken control of Hungary, Ferenczi was appointed their representative to the Paris-based United Nations body UNESCO.

In September 1947 he was recruited as an agent by KATPOL (*Kantonapolitikai Osztály*), the Military-Political Department of

Hungary's armed forces, formed in April 1945. He reported to Colonel Zoltán Gát, who was one of the few intelligence officers of the Horthy era retained in key positions by the Hungarian communists, specifically on Soviet orders.

In February 1948 Ferenczi informed Gát that Horngacher was in contact with Field. According to this report, Noel had told Horngacher that he had been linked with the Szőnyi group during the war. Not only had Noel supported them, he had supplied them with IDs and an American aircraft for their return! Later Ferenczi supplied Gát with a photocopy of a pass, which allegedly proved that Field was in contact with the US Army's CIC (Counter-Intelligence Corps) in Munich.

Gát was concerned that he might have stumbled upon a communist network, and that if he probed too deeply he might blow its cover. So, with his superior's consent, he consulted Soviet military intelligence in Hungary. The GRU advised him to take up the matter with the ruling HCP 'troika' composed of Rákosi, Mihály Farkas and Ernő Gerő (p. 223). No answer came from them for months, and nor do we know what it was.

However, the GRU did ask for a photocopy of the pass 'proving' that Noel was in contact with the CIC, although thereafter nothing more is heard of this mysterious matter. Nor do we know any details about five further 'cases', presumably bearing upon Field and/or Szőnyi, which Gát accumulated.[8] All of these had to be discussed by the 'troika', and since he heard nothing from them, Gát didn't follow up these leads.

What he did do, with some rather woolly support from his KATPOL superiors, was to interview Szőnyi. It is not clear exactly when this event occurred, other than it was some time in late summer 1948, and Gát had nothing to do with Szőnyi's later fate. Its only relevance is to indicate that Szőnyi had intimations of what was coming before the axe actually fell.

Since Szőnyi was head of the Party's cadres department, Gát visited HCP headquarters where Szőnyi worked in the next room to Rákosi. He talked around the subject for a while and then asked Szőnyi his opinion of Field. Szőnyi responded that Noel, whom he described as a Unitarian minister, was a 'decent fellow' who had helped the Hungarian *émigrés* in Switzerland. When Gát said that they had information that Field was in contact with the Americans, and was possibly an 'enemy', Szőnyi replied brusquely that he knew nothing about that.

Gát reported that Szőnyi spoke throughout in an officious and cool tone, and gave abrupt and evasive answers.[9] Gát didn't attribute Szőnyi's icy and laconic responses to the fact that he had posed ticklish questions about his relationship with Field. Rather he thought it was because he had been an officer under the Horthy regime. Afterwards Gát decided that Field couldn't be a part of a communist network because Szőnyi would have said so if he was. Therefore he instructed Ferenczi to send all he knew about Field and his activities. He received two more reports. He couldn't remember their contents, other than that Horngacher told Ferenczi that Field was planning to travel to Czechoslovakia.[10]

Gát's involvement became largely irrelevant when his superior, Lieutenant General Révész, got his hands on Ferenczi's dossier. This contained a copy of Field's letter of recommendation to Dulles, and a record of Noel's acquaintanceship with Szőnyi. Révész showed the dossier to Farkas in January 1949. A couple of weeks later he was instructed to send to Farkas a photocopy of Noel's letter, and later to pass the entire dossier to the heads of the ÁVH, Gábor Péter and Ernő Szűcs.

One wonders what the 'troika' had been doing with Gát's earlier information. It seems likely that Rákosi had been sitting on it while he awaited a decision by Stalin, who may only have given him the green light in January 1949.

On 23 January Colonel Szűcs appeared in Prague with a request that the StB should arrest Field as 'a collaborator of A. Dulles'. The ÁVH wanted the StB to lure Noel to Prague, arrest him, and hand him over to them. Szűcs had not only the letter that Field had written to Dulles regarding Horngacher, but another one, which allegedly requested that Dulles grant permission to Szőnyi to organise a committee of Hungarian anti-fascists.[11] If such a letter existed, it too makes no further appearance in the accounts we have.

On 7 February 1949 Szűcs reported on his visit to Prague. He and his Czechoslovak comrades had agreed that the StB, through its agents in Switzerland, would establish Field's exact whereabouts. The StB would also organise a meeting of so-called progressive journalists, to which Noel would be invited. Once he set foot in Czechoslovakia, they would secretly arrest him and hand him over to the ÁVH.[12]

'Detain Field'[13]

In early February 1949 Noel received letters from his brother Hermann, and from Hermann's first wife Jean Liebermann, who was now in California. He learned that both had been questioned by FBI agents about their pre-war activities in Switzerland. Jean denied being a communist party member or participating in espionage. 'She further denied', according to the agent's report, 'having any knowledge regarding possible connections with the CP, Soviet Government, or any underground intelligence activities on the part of Noel Field'.[14]

Unable to transport the mass of material he had collected in Poland and Czechoslovakia, Noel took only a small selection from it to Switzerland. In Prague he had applied for an export licence and arranged with a transport firm to bring the remainder to Geneva, but it never arrived.

The same happened with his Polish material; seemingly there were complications with the necessary export permit. So he asked Tonia Lechtman to fix things. He received no reply to his letter, but he learned from others that Tonia would have nothing to do with it, because Noel was now under suspicion as a spy. This information merely made Field all the more determined to travel to Prague and Berlin to clarify his status.

Since he had a six-month residence permit for Czechoslovakia, he applied for an entry visa. He was told in Prague that he would not have problems in obtaining it, yet in December 1948 and again in March 1949 the Czechoslovak embassy in Bern made difficulties about issuing it.

It was in March too that MGB Lieutenant General Mikhail Ilyich Bielkin made his move. Born Moisei Yelnovich Bielkin in 1901, the son of a Jewish trader in Roslavl (south-east of Smolensk), Bielkin was already a Chekist as a teenager. There followed a long career in counter-espionage in OGPU, the NKVD and Red Army Counter-Intelligence (SMERSH). In June 1947 Abakumov appointed Bielkin chief of MGB counter-espionage for the central group of Soviet forces, as well as head of intelligence in south-east Europe.

Bielkin was now the man on the ground, charged with executing the instructions of Stalin and Abakumov. From his headquarters in Baden bei Wien in the Soviet occupation zone of Austria, Bielkin instructed the StB chief Jindřich Veselý to invite Field to Prague.[15]

It is possible that the StB developed a plan to lure Noel back to Czechoslovakia. The pretext apparently was to promise him to expect an interview with Artur London, now back in Prague, in order to clarify his status with Moscow. If this was the bait, then Noel took it. Yet it is equally possible that Noel, having mapped out his future, made his own arrangements to get to Prague.

Both Noel and Herta travelled to Paris on 14 April. Noel hoped to participate in the first World Congress of the 'Partisans for Peace', which met there from 20–25 April 1949. However, the French government refused visas to a number of delegates on political grounds. Therefore certain sessions of the Congress were to be held in Prague and all delegates automatically received a visa to travel there.

Noel was not a delegate, nor had he received an invitation to attend the Congress. However, through wartime connections he was invited by the French delegation to be their guest, and in this fashion he was able to obtain the required entry visa for Czechoslovakia from the Paris embassy. He immediately sent a telegram to Artur London telling him that he would get in touch when he got to Prague.[16]

The day before he left, Noel made another unsuccessful attempt to 'save' Erica for the Party. She was working unpaid as an interpreter at the Congress. During its proceedings she handed the leader of the SED delegation an unsigned scrap of paper to be given to Leo Bauer. On this Noel had written in German, 'I'm still waiting for news'.[17] Such an ambiguous message did little to dampen suspicions regarding Noel, and later it created problems for Bauer.

On Thursday 5 May 1949 Herta flew back to Geneva. That same day Noel caught the first available *Air France* flight to Prague.

The StB informed the ÁVH of his arrival. As a result Colonel Szűcs immediately journeyed to Prague to request Noel's arrest. Veselý refused to act because of lack of grounds, so matters went to higher levels.

'Please comply with our request and detain Field, who has just arrived in Prague', wrote Rákosi to President Gottwald on 9 May, and Bielkin made the same demand. Gottwald knew who stood behind Bielkin, and there was no way that he would defy Stalin. 'If even General Bielkin has looked into this and supports it', Gottwald instructed Veselý, 'let them have their way'.[18]

In the meantime Noel registered at the Palace Hotel, daily awaiting a summons to Berlin in order to clarify his party status and deal with the increasing suspicions about him. He telephoned Artur London several times but was unable to reach him. He wanted London to help expedite Herta's visa; at least that was the reason Field later gave.

Noel soon noticed that certain friends and acquaintances in Prague could no longer be reached. He wrote to other friends about the improved supply situation there, albeit accompanied by a rise in food prices. He began to look for cheaper accommodation, because the costs of staying in the Palace Hotel were too expensive for a long stay.

Noel's last letter to Herta was dated Monday 9 May. He had a short telephone conversation with her the next day. He also wrote a letter to his sister Elsie. That evening he joined Gisl Kisch and Anna Seghers for a meal. On Wednesday 11 May he sent Herta a telegram.

That afternoon he was given the address of a warehouse, where his trunk of undelivered material was supposedly stored. He took a taxi to a dilapidated area on the outskirts of Prague.

Field was hunting for the right address when a car drew up. A youngish man alighted and asked him if he was Noel Field. When Noel assented, he was arrested by the StB, hustled into the car and chloroformed. He was handed over there and then to Szűcs, whose driver immediately headed for the Hungarian frontier.

When Noel awoke he was handcuffed, blindfolded, and his head was covered by a sack. In the early hours of 12 May 1949 Field arrived in Hungary. His captors then drove him to 60 Andrássy út.

Disappearing tricks[19]

Since receiving Noel's telegram of 11 May Herta had sent four letters and two telegrams to him, without receiving any response. Now anxious, Herta made a telephone call to the Palace Hotel on 18 May. She was told that her husband had departed without leaving a forwarding address. For a while she thought that Noel's planned secret journey to see Bauer and Merker in East Berlin had actually come off.

On 22 May she wrote, 'It's a long time since I had news from thee, dearest'.[20] When she received no reply to either this or a subsequent letter, she began to fear that Noel had been kidnapped by the Americans, in order to make him testify against Alger Hiss.[21]

In July she wrote to Artur London. She informed him that she was certain that Noel had fallen into 'a trap set by agents of the American government, either on the 11th May or on the evening of the 12th'.[22] London did not reply. In desperation Herta sent out a call for help to Hermann Field through his wife Kate, who was then in London.

It was not as if the two brothers were in constant contact. Their last meeting was in Paris in the summer of 1947, when Hermann was leading a party of architects touring European cities (p. 122).

On his return to the USA, Hermann, Kate and their children had moved to Ohio when Hermann got the job of planning new buildings at Western Reserve University in Cleveland. In summer 1949 he was expecting to take up the post of dean of the university's architecture faculty, while Kate had embarked on a new career as lecturer in economics at Cleveland College.[23]

Hermann had planned to lead another delegation to Eastern Europe in 1949, and had acquired the requisite Czechoslovak visa. However, there was insufficient interest in the trip. So at his own expense he arranged to travel to Bergamo in July to attend a leftist architects' meeting, entitled *Congresso internazionale d'architetura moderna*.

On 6 June 1949 Hermann and Kate held a birthday party for their younger son who would be four the following day. That evening Hermann drove Kate and his boys to the railway station. The next morning the latter were in New York, boarding the Polish liner *Batory*, on which Gerhart Eisler had stowed away when it last left the USA. Eight days later they were met in Southampton by Kate's mother, who was living in Hampstead again, at 82 Corringham Road. Hermann, who could not get such a lengthy vacation, planned to fly to Britain in July.

In Hampstead Kate received a letter and telegram from Herta, begging Hermann to travel to Geneva at once. In response to this 'mysterious cry for help'[24] Kate booked her husband a flight to Geneva for 20 July, the day after his delayed arrival from Ohio.

In Geneva Hermann learned the reason for Herta's *cri de coeur*, when she told him in a hushed voice that Noel had disappeared in Prague in May. Herta wanted Hermann to help her locate Noel without any fanfare. He was to make no reference to Noel's disappearance in his correspondence. Other than to Kate he was simply to say that his brother was ill.

Hermann promised to accompany Herta to Prague after attending the Bergamo congress. Since he had helped the current Czechoslovak interior minister, Vaclav Nosek, to escape to Britain in 1939, he hoped to approach the Prague authorities privately through friends in order to help locate his brother.

Returning from Italy on 31 July Hermann met Herta in Geneva. She had decided to travel to Prague, but was still waiting for a visa. Since

Hermann had already obtained his in the USA, he flew direct to Prague on 1 August.

Herta, having finally obtained her visa, flew to Prague on 3 or 4 August.[25] The following day she and Hermann went to the Interior Ministry, where officials promised to conduct an inquiry into Noel's disappearance. They were told to come back in a week.

Both were under constant observation by the StB from the moment they entered Czechoslovakia. The ÁVH had asked Czechoslovak security to arrest and hand over Herta, but Hermann's appearance on the scene had complicated matters.

Hermann had met the Polish architects Szymon and Helena Syrkus on his previous visit to Warsaw in 1947.[26] They were involved in planning the reconstruction of the Polish capital, and at Bergamo they had invited Hermann to make another visit. From Prague Hermann telephoned Helena and another acquaintance, Mela Granowska, in Warsaw, asking for help in getting a visa.

Both women reported these calls to the Polish Ministry of Public Security (MBP). This body was aware of the preparations for the Rajk trial, and the pressure then coming from Rákosi in Hungary to act against Noel's Polish 'collaborators'.[27] Therefore the MBP authorised Hermann's visa, with the intention of arresting him in Poland.

Hermann flew to Warsaw on 15 August, telling Herta that he would be back in one week. In the meantime Herta finally met with Artur London. He and Karel Markus came to her bugged hotel room. Both men knew that Noel had been arrested, and both were instructed by the StB on how to conduct the conversation.

'She wept' recalled London, 'as she told me about her husband's life and the sacrifices he had made for the communist cause, but there was nothing I could do'.[28] Herta repeated her belief that Noel had been kidnapped by the Americans, and contended that she and Hermann were prepared to start a political campaign on the issue. London and Markus advised her to turn to the StB for help.

On Monday 22 August Hermann was dropped off at Warsaw airport by the Syrkus couple and Mela Granowska. Having waved farewell to his hosts, Hermann proceeded through customs and followed his porter into the departure room. An official ordered him into another room. Awaiting him was Józef Światło, a deputy head of Department Ten of the MBP (p. 258). Hermann's flight to Prague left without him.

After initial interrogations at police headquarters, Hermann was taken to a villa maintained by Department Ten at Miedzeszyn on the east bank of the Vistula. Incarcerated in a dank underground cell, this was to be his grim habitat for almost five years.

In London on 26 August Kate read a letter from Herta which informed her of Hermann's non-arrival in Prague. Taking her father's advice, she rang the American embassy in London to report Hermann's disappearance. For the first time at least part of the 'Field affair' was known to American officialdom.

Another letter from Herta, dated 25 August, arrived from Prague. It gave Herta's address at the Hotel Paris, and suggested that Helena Syrkus could clear matters up. Kate wired back on 29 August that she had asked the embassy to make inquiries.

Herta never received this telegram. On 26 August Gottwald sanctioned Herta's arrest. The StB informed her that Noel had been wounded in an American 'provocation' and was hospitalised in Bratislava.

Generous to a fault, the StB drove Herta to the Slovak capital on 28 August. There she was handed over to the attendant ÁVH, brought to the villa in Eötvös út and interrogated that same day.

Herta's interrogation lasted until the end of October. She was probably not physically tortured, although other women involved in the case were, even when pregnant. As Dr Barth suggests, since the format of the Rajk trial was by then settled, information from Herta was no longer particularly relevant, except as a 'control' on the earlier evidence obtained from Noel.

21

'WHATEVER YOU WANT ME TO SAY'

TORTURE AND TRUTH

'A tiny piece of truth'[1]

The false confessions of Noel and other victims involved in the preliminaries to the Rajk trial were coerced through a mixture of physiological, physical and psychological torture. These methods, applied primarily by the ÁVH, combined 'traditional' Hungarian police practices with 'sophisticated' innovations introduced by Soviet 'advisers' from the MGB, who became involved in the interrogations once they came on the scene.

Soviet methods were developed in the USSR under Lenin and Stalin. They reached their 'zenith' at the time of the Moscow show trials and 'the Great Terror' of 1937–38.

The most potent Soviet innovation was the 'conveyor', whereby the victim was interrogated for hours–sometimes days–on end by relays of investigators. This procedure was routinely applied by the ÁVH, along with other forms of sleep deprivation.

Prisoners lay on their backs in discomfort on boards, with few if any covers, and usually in damp, cold cells illuminated by constant electric light. In order to prevent suicide attempts they were forced to expose wrists and throat to warders peering through the spy-holes. Those periods of sleep permitted them were broken by constant interruptions by warders, or the exhausted prisoner might simply be summoned to a fresh interrogation.

Prisoners were fed irregularly with gruel or left without food altogether. Some were made to lap up large quantities of salt. It was standard practice for prisoners to be left to wear the clothes in which they were arrested, although such items as belts, ties, braces, shoe-laces, stockings and suspenders were taken away. Those arrested in summer clothes suffered dreadfully in the winter.

Physical tortures involved beatings with fists and rubber truncheons on the face, body, and genitalia. The crippling bastinado, or 'soling', whereby the truncheon was applied to the soles and heels of the victim's feet, was not a Soviet import, although it was used in the USSR too.[2] Needles pierced flesh, cigarettes were extinguished on bodies, prisoners stood touching a wall for hours on end. They were interrogated standing and kneeling, with devastating consequences to their limbs. Their hands and feet might be manacled day and night.

For those whose resistance was strongest there were threats to imprison and torture loved ones and relatives, and to place children in state orphanages. There were comradely appeals for victims to sacrifice themselves to serve the Party's 'historical' needs. There were promises that imposed death-sentences would not be carried out, while long prison sentences would in fact be minimal, and simply precede transfer to the sunshine of the Crimea under fresh identities.

Noel was certainly beaten, 'soled', starved and fettered. Later he wrote sardonically about 'means used to refresh my memory'.[3] And he reacted in the same way as did almost all of these broken beings:

What does a man, or rather a coward, say when he's just been tortured and is now frightened to death he'll be killed? He says: 'No, no, please don't torture me, I'll tell you the truth…' In reality he means: 'I'll say whatever you want me to say, I'll say whatever *you* consider to be the truth. I won't say what *I* consider to be the truth, because I'd only be tortured again.'

Recalling one false confession, he stated that he had written 'it in the belief that he could not survive the next bout of torture'. Although most of what he had written was true, he included just enough fabrication to prevent further torment, just enough concessions and compromises 'to stay alive at least, and to gain time'.[4]

The interrogators had different objectives. In the first place anyone arrested by the ÁVH was *ipso facto* guilty. As Colonel Szűcs put it, he could not 'be anything but an enemy', since the ÁVH didn't arrest innocent people. Given that those detained were enemies, Szűcs ordered his interrogators not to let themselves be influenced by facts.

Later he amended this slightly to allow for facts that supported an initial 'assumption'. In that case he ordered 'the interrogators to shape the interrogation reports according to the assumption'. Yet the 'shaped' reports deriving from the 'assumption' still had to 'be based on just a tiny piece of truth' around which 'the story could be built, and that made the reports one hundred per cent acceptable'.[5]

Thus it was that in the Rajk trial and other show trials, there were instances of tiny bits of truth drowning in a sea of lies. Before the People's Court Rajk gave a largely accurate account of events which occurred in his life as a dedicated communist. Yet the import of each event was turned into its opposite by the treasonable interpretation placed upon it, and to which he 'confessed' in his 'own' words.

Moreover, the prisoners themselves supplied the initial material for their 'confessions' by writing their 'autobiographies'. Subsequently they were questioned upon details therein, as their interrogators sought to 'shape' their reports according to the assumption that the victim was by definition an 'enemy'.

Initially there was chaos, as different interrogators, working on different 'assumptions', produced nothing but reams of conflicting evidence. More names were named, more arrests were made, more assumptions were introduced, and more contradictions were generated.

It was only with the arrival of Lieutenant General Bielkin and his troop of MGB 'advisers' that the Stalin-Rákosi co-production took final shape. The 'Field-Szőnyi espionage plot' was merged with the 'Tito-Rajk conspiracy' to form the didactic 'testimony' of the Rajk trial, with its 'lessons' for all communists.

By this juncture Noel was consigned to a Banquo-like 'ghost at the feast' role as far as the trial was concerned. For it is unlikely that Stalin and Rákosi ever considered putting him on trial publicly.

However, in the initial stages of his ordeal, at least up to the end of June 1949, he was a central character in the shaping of the forthcoming trial in Hungary. He was also an important influence upon pending productions in Poland, Czechoslovakia and the GDR.

Ordeal by stages[6]

Once they reached Budapest on the morning of 12 May, Szűcs and his driver took Noel directly to ÁVH headquarters at 60 Andrássy út. There, Noel was immediately interrogated in German by a young officer who was not in the loop. Noel protested that there had been a misunderstanding; he was not an American spy, but a Soviet agent. He listed his contacts in Washington, Switzerland and Moscow, and even specified his password 'Brook'. The astounded officer reported this, and the next day he was taken off the case.

To preserve the secrecy of the entire operation, and particularly Field's presence, after one or two days in the bowels of Andrássy út Noel was transferred to an ÁVH villa at 41 Eötvös út in the *Svábhegy* (Swabian hills) in Buda. The 'villa period', as Noel termed it, lasted from mid-May until mid-June 1949.

Although Field offers no detailed description of the villa, it could not have been too unlike the picture presented by Béla Szász, who was arrested on 24 May and taken to the villa that same day.

Behind a steel door concrete steps descended to the coal cellar, which had been sub-divided into several minute dungeons. From the ground floor a wooden staircase led up to the first floor. Here the windows 'were hung with black curtains shutting out daylight and the outside world. Above a double door, coloured bulbs glowed'.

This door led into an enormous room with two long refectory tables pushed into the shape of a capital T. A curtained semi-circular window behind the horizontal line of the T 'created a theatrical effect and optically lengthened the stem of the T extending towards the entrance'. The prisoner stood at the foot of the stem, while his interrogators sat behind the horizontal.

Above this room was the villa's second storey, and from there a narrowing staircase, again with black-curtained windows, led into a hexagonal room. This was the villa's tower, with five of the six walls dominated by huge oblong windows, again 'blind and dead-black'. There was an armchair in it and a carpet. Otherwise there was plenty of space for several men to 'work' on a prisoner.[7]

Noel's first interrogators in the villa were Szűcs, speaking in Russian, and Péter, speaking through an interpreter.[8] Later, Defence Minister Mihály Farkas interrogated Field in German. To all of them Noel maintained his story that he was not an American spy, but a communist who had worked for Soviet intelligence. He admitted that he had contacts with the Szőnyi group, but denied that these had anything to do with espionage. Rather they were of a humanitarian and antifascist nature. One of the few extant protocols from this period is dated 14 May 1949. In it Noel conceded that in November 1944 he had organised a meeting between Dulles, Szőnyi and Vági, and recommended the Hungarians to Dulles as men who could provide him with political information. The Hungarians were 'fully aware that Dulles was the head of an intelligence service', and before organising the meeting, Noel told Vági that 'they would have to provide Dulles with information about Hungary and their own activities in Switzerland'.[9]

The following day Noel stated that although he knew Szőnyi's name from hearsay beforehand, he had only met him in person in Marseille, and couldn't remember what they had spoken about. Since then he had 'never seen him again or been in contact with him either directly or indirectly'.[10]

Late on the night of Monday 16 May Szőnyi and his deputy András Szalai were arrested,[11] although Szalai had nothing to do with the Swiss Group or Field. From 16–18 May the ÁVH also picked up Vági, Földi, György Demeter and his wife Róza, and János Dobó and his Swiss wife. Ilona Kojsza was arrested too, although she was not a member of the Szőnyi Group.[12]

Under interrogation Szőnyi denied that he had conducted hostile activity, so Péter ordered the use of physical force.[13] As soon as the physical violence began Szőnyi 'confessed' that not only he, but others too, had engaged in 'espionage' with Field. He also admitted that he had conducted 'wrecking activities' in the cadres department. A few more beatings helped firm up his confession.

One of the interrogators later recalled that once he had been worked over, Szőnyi seemed to adopt an 'it's all the same to me' attitude. Another complained that once Szőnyi had confessed his own guilt, his only interest lay in avoiding further beatings. The poor man never knew when Szőnyi was lying or telling the truth, because, without turning a hair, Szőnyi cynically invented stories when he realised that this was expected of him.

Once Szőnyi 'cynically' told his interrogators that a great many of the wartime émigrés to the West were spies, and that he had placed them in various important posts, they too were arrested. The new prisoners 'lied' in confrontations too, even when Szőnyi called them spies to their face. So they too had to be beaten until they 'confessed'.

However, Vági held out for weeks, even though he was tortured mercilessly and forced not only to lick salt from the floor, but from a toilet-bowl too. It was probably on account of such stubborn resistance that he was given the sole death sentence when the 'Swiss group' were tried. Ilona Kojsza also didn't break until the beginning of 1950.

Noel confesses[14]

It would seem that initially Noel did not suffer physical torture. When this began we do not know. Apparently the worst came around the end of May. Under this level of pressure Noel drifted further and further from the truth, until he finally suffered 'a complete moral breakdown', during which he could 'no longer differentiate between truth and lies'. Not only did he speak and write 'the most terrible untruths', but sometimes he 'even believed them too'.[15]

Földi saw both Szőnyi and Field at this time. Szőnyi was unrecognisable from the beatings he had taken. His face was small and crumpled up, and Noel looked the same. These battered beings would have seen each other too, when there was a confrontation between them in the second half of May.[16]

Noel made his statement on Szőnyi sometime between 24 and 28 May 1949. On 28 May he made a written statement about the Slovak communist Pavlík (Chapter 27). Later he provided false statements about Rajk.

Noel was interrogated for weeks about Szőnyi in 1949, so that 'actual memory and fantasy became entangled [*verknäulte*]'.[17] In June 1954 he tried to recall what was certain and what was doubtful in what he had said and written five years before.

He was certain that, although he had heard the name Hoffmann (Szőnyi's name in Switzerland) in 1943 or 1944, he had first heard the name Szőnyi only in his interrogations in 1949. He was equally definite that other than their confrontation in the villa, he had only met Szőnyi once and that was in Marseille in early February 1945.[18]

In 1949 he had said that Szőnyi came to the USC office expressly to thank Field for interceding with Dulles. In 1954 Noel sought to explain that as follows:

They told me that Szőnyi had said he'd met me several times in Switzerland, and that I'd even accompanied him to a meeting with Dulles. I persuaded myself that Szőnyi was speaking the truth and was probably trying to remind me of the facts. So I concluded that all this was quite possible, and in my statement the possibility became actuality.[19]

Noel also made a similar 'confession' about Rajk. He told his interrogators that he had primarily supported the internees in Le Vernet through a scheme of general assistance, which Willi Kreikemeyer administered. He only helped individuals when the KPD ordered it for particularly sick or endangered comrades.

However, when he was working in Marseille, Noel was occasionally asked by Boston to provide information on refugees who had relatives or friends in the USA. Such a request came from a former German SPD parliamentarian who worked for the JARC in New York. He asked Field to look out for a certain László, since the German was ready to pick up the costs of this man's emigration to America. Noel could only remember the name László.

During a visit to Le Vernet in summer 1941 Noel asked the camp commandant if he could speak to him. When László was called in, Noel relayed the offer in the presence of the commandant, but László said nothing. However, later on he approached Field surreptitiously and informed him that he couldn't consider leaving for safety. His place was with his comrades. Noel never saw him again.

He was first questioned about Rajk in June 1949. Noel knew Rajk's name from the press and had seen photos of him. His interrogator told Field that his László was László Rajk, an 'American agent', and that Rajk had made a similar statement to Field's regarding the Le Vernet meeting. He showed Noel a photo in which about fifteen uniformed men could be seen. One face was known to Field, although he couldn't say from where.[20]

His interrogator told him that he had recognised László Rajk, and thereafter he treated Noel in an exceptionally friendly manner. He instructed Field to formulate a statement contending that he had visited Le Vernet to contact 'László Firtos'. In order not to lose such transient goodwill, and because he had convinced himself that Firtos-Rajk was in fact the person he had met, Noel signed this protocol.[21]

All interrogations ceased on 21 June 1949 for about ten days, when Bielkin and his MGB 'specialists' arrived in Budapest at Rákosi's request, and sought to impose order upon the chaotic investigation.[22] For the last ten days of June, Field was held in MGB headquarters at 32 Gorki fasor (now Városligeti fasor), an elegant street running parallel to Andrássy út.[23] During this period he was not tortured.

On the last day of the Soviet interrogations, Noel was hauled up for questioning late at night and told that he was going to be returned to the Hungarians, where his fate would be decided. Noel began to cry like a child and begged the MGB to keep him for a few more days.

He was given a pencil and told that this was his last chance to save himself. So he wrote a document that in the main corresponded to the factual truth, but in which he placed false interpretations on the facts, and included one conscious lie.

His lie was to say that he had accompanied Szőnyi to the meeting with the OSE, but in truth Szőnyi had not attended this meeting, although other members of the group, as well as Noel, were there (p. 189).[24] He introduced this lie, because it seemed to him to be the minimum which might save him. It didn't. That same night he was returned to the Hungarians.

Noel was probably moved back to 60 Andrássy út, because in early July there was a stool-pigeon in his cell,[25] and it was not the only time that the mercurial Sándor Cseresnyés performed this function.

Sidelined[26]

For several weeks in 1949–50 an imprisoned American engineer, Robert Vogeler, shared a cell with Cseresnyés in 60 Andrássy út.[27] He described Sándor as 'a dark, heavy man, dressed in filthy grey flannels, a ragged sweater, and a British sports jacket that was out at the elbows. His laceless shoes were badly worn around the outer edges and he walked with a painful limp'.[28]

Cseresnyés was born in September 1909 into a working-class family in Temesvár (now Timişoara) in the Bánát, which became part of Romania after the First World War. He may have been Jewish, and his real name was probably Alexander Kirschner, which he Magyarised to Cseresnyés. After graduating from a Romanian *lycée* in Arad, he worked in a bank, served in the Romanian army, and then became a journalist for Hungarian-language newspapers in Brassó (now Brasov) and Bucharest.

Sympathetic to the communists, although he only joined the Party in 1940, Cseresnyés travelled to Spain in March 1937. In September he got to know Rajk and other Hungarian volunteers in the International Brigades. Like them he was later interned in France. In March 1941 he was transferred to a camp in Algeria, where he worked on the Trans-Sahara railway. He was liberated following the Anglo-American landings in North Africa in November 1942.

Cseresnyés joined the British army. He worked as a radio monitor for its Psychological Warfare Branch, and came into contact with Tito's military mission in Bari. Until he was demobilised in Austria he was in contact with OZNA, the Yugoslav intelligence service.

Returning to Hungary in November 1946, Cseresnyés began working as a journalist again. On 13 January 1947, at Rajk's recommendation, he was appointed head of the Interior Ministry's press department. At the same time, and with the knowledge of the ÁVH, he maintained his contacts with Yugoslav intelligence and made several trips to Yugoslavia with ÁVH delegations. Cseresnyés apparently also worked for a special Soviet section that kept tabs on both the HCP leadership and the returning *émigrés* from Switzerland.[29]

Despite, or because of such qualifications, on the night of 23 May 1949 he was arrested by the ÁVH. Brought to 60 Andrássy út, he was bastinadoed for a week,[30] and forced to confess that he was the liaison man between British and Yugoslav intelligence and Rajk's clique. Later he would serve as a 'witness' at the Rajk trial.[31]

Noel recalled that on 6 July 1949, during 'my deepest moral confusion', Cseresnyés persuaded him to write a note to the American minister in Budapest, which a friendly warder would smuggle out and deliver.[32]

Noel wrote this clandestine message the following day. In it he explained how he had been kidnapped in Prague, and was now being kept prisoner on the 'laughable' grounds that he was America's chief agent against the East. He noted that he was being put through 'the third degree' and asked for the legation's 'urgent but discreet intervention' on his behalf. He named Allen Dulles as a reference.[33]

The result was predictable. The letter was intercepted and used by Péter as further evidence of Field's links with Dulles.

By now though Noel was no longer centre-stage. The MGB and ÁVH producers of Rajk's show trial would simply place snatches of Field's distorted biography in the mouths of others during the main performance. Yet these snippets would constitute fearful warnings to certain 'brands' of communists in Hungary, Poland, Czechoslovakia and the GDR.

Noel was no longer tortured and he was interrogated only sporadically. Recovering his mental stability, Field sought to retract certain confessions. Possibly from July and certainly from August Noel withdrew the false statements he had made, and despite sustained pressure he maintained his position for the remainder of his incarceration.[34] Despite his efforts by August 1949 it was too late; since Szőnyi and Rajk had made their own decisions. In any case, the ÁVH simply refused to accept Field's retractions, being content with his original confessions.

Some three weeks later Noel and Herta were interrogated separately in their cells in Andrássy út by Polish state security.[35] Lieutenant Colonel Józef Światło and General Roman Romkowski sought information about Polish 'Fieldists'.[36] Światło later reported that Noel had lost a good deal of weight and looked wan, although there were no marks from beatings on his face. Herta 'looked tragic, like a half-skeleton'.[37]

On 11 October Noel was transferred to Conti utca prison in Pest. This, next to the prison at Vác, was the chief ÁVH prison in Hungary and Herta was already there. The Fields were registered under the names Földes János and Földes Jánosné (Mr and Mrs John Field). They were to fester in this gaol until May 1954.

László Rajk was also in the Conti utca prison when Noel arrived there. However, he was under sentence of death.

22

'THE ENEMY'S MAN'

LÁSZLÓ RAJK[1]

'One solution: Lenin'

Since virtually every event in the short, fraught existence of László Rajk would be twisted into its opposite at his show trial, I shall try to provide as much accurate detail as possible about his life. This is no easy task, given Rajk's often clandestine activities and the secrecy and hearsay which surround them.

Rajk was born on 8 March 1909 in the Transylvanian market-town of Székelyudvarhely (now Odorheiu Secuiesc in Romania), which lay some 200 km south-east of the provincial capital Kolozsvár (now Cluj). He was the ninth of eleven children born to his boot-maker father, József Reich, whose family origins were Saxon.[2]

The Reichs were Szeklers and Calvinist by religion. Following his marriage in 1890, József Magyarised his surname, which he thought sounded too Jewish, to its nearest Hungarian equivalent, Rájk. After the First World War some of his offspring dropped the accent from its spelling to produce the Magyar-sounding name Rajk (pronounced 'Royk').[3]

László's early education was in his home-town, but at the age of fifteen he moved to Budapest and then to Nyíregyháza in the north-east of 'Trianon Hungary', where he joined his elder brother Endre. It was there that he completed his secondary education.

In 1927 he entered university in Budapest to study Hungarian and French. He spent most of 1929 in Besançon. In France he 'became acquainted with progressive ideas and began to learn about Marxism'. On his return to Hungary in 1930 Rajk sought out 'people of Marxist ideas'.[4] Around this time László told his friend and fellow-student, Béla Szász, that there was 'only one solution: Lenin'.[5] In March 1931 Rajk joined KIMSZ, the communist youth movement,[6] and shortly afterwards the HCP.

In autumn 1931 Rajk was arrested for communist activities among students. On hearing of this, László's brother Gyula went into action. Holding a senior position in an Anglo-Hungarian bank in Budapest, Gyula Rajk, a lifelong bachelor, was the *paterfamilias* of those brothers who had moved from Transylvania (now part of Romania) to 'Trianon Hungary'. He contacted police-captain Lajos Bokor, a lawyer in the Budapest police and the brother-in-law of Lajos Rajk.[7] Bokor immediately contacted the chief of the security police, and László was released.

He was arrested again in June 1932. This time Gyula did not intervene and László spent several months in custody. In February 1933 he was arrested once more, but was acquitted at his trial. However, on release he was expelled from university.[8]

Unemployed, living with fellow-communist Ilona Schillinger, Rajk made a little money as a French teacher. He was arrested again in spring 1935. After that the Party found him a job as a building worker, and László was one of the leaders of the major strike of Budapest construction workers in July–August 1935.

Since he still carried a Romanian passport the Hungarian authorities endeavoured to expel Rajk as a Romanian citizen. At the end of September the Party directed him to operate clandestinely, and later decided that he should quit Hungary altogether. On 1 July 1936, carrying the papers of one János Bertak, Rajk left for Prague, where the communist party was legal. Later he operated in Bratislava.

In October 1937, as László Firtos, he travelled from Paris to Spain. With the rank of sergeant he became the political commissar/party secretary of the Hungarian 'Rákosi battalion' serving in the Thirteenth International Brigade. There proceedings were initiated against Rajk as a 'Trotskyite', which the Comintern later quashed as groundless.

In summer 1938 Rajk was wounded in the battle of the Ebro, his arm fractured by a shell fragment.[9] He was hospitalised in Catalonia, but was back in action in January 1939, covering the retreat of Republican forces and civilians into France. After crossing the Pyrenees in early February, Rajk was interned in the camps of St Cyprien and Gurs, and from September 1939 in Le Vernet.

On 29 August 1940 Germany and Italy satisfied some of Hungary's revisionist aims, by granting her Northern Transylvania under the Second Vienna Award. Székelyudvarhely and all the Szekler lands came once more under Hungarian rule. Two days later Rajk wrote to the Hungarian legation at Vichy. Without mentioning his activities in Spain, he provided a bland CV, and requested help in obtaining recognition of his Hungarian nationality. He also asked the legation to facilitate his release from Le Vernet and repatriation to Hungary.

The legation was not taken in. When Gyula Rajk added his support, they replied that they had spoken to the Mexican embassy about whether László could emigrate there, given its policy of accepting former Republican fighters. László then tried to win their support for his transfer to the less severe conditions in Les Milles camp, but the legation and the Le Vernet camp authorities continued to hamper any progress.

However, help was at hand in the grim form of the SS, which regularly recruited labour from Vichy's camps to work in German mines and factories. On 2 June 1941 Rajk informed the legation in Vichy that he had accepted a job offer in Germany, and hoped to return to Hungary once his contract expired.

From July Rajk worked as a builder near Leipzig. In August, with the aid of the illegal KPD, he escaped to Austria. Then, helped by Austrian comrades, he secretly crossed into Hungary on 25 August.

In October 1941 Rajk was arrested in Budapest. He was interned in various camps in Hungary until 9 September 1944 when the HCP, using faked release papers, sprang him from Budapest's Margit körút prison. From there he went to the flat of his future wife Júlia Földi.[10]

Using false papers in the name of András Barna, Rajk resumed illegal work and became secretary of the HCP. He negotiated with the SDP to form a Hungarian Front, and endeavoured to infuse the pitifully weak Hungarian resistance movement with greater purpose.

On 15 October 1944 Horthy was ousted by the Germans and replaced by the inept but murderous Arrow Cross 'government'. On 11 December their police arrested Rajk and Júlia Földi. The usual brutal tortures ensued. 'We could barely stand on our feet', Júlia recalled.[11]

Since the Red Army was already fighting in the Budapest suburbs, on 13 December Rajk, Júlia, and other prisoners were transported to Sopronkőhida in western Hungary, to where the 'government' had already decamped. There they escaped execution through the intervention of Rajk's brother, Endre, an official in the Szálasi regime.[12] On 23 March 1945 Endre appeared in full Arrow Cross uniform before a military tribunal and testified to the virtues of his wayward sibling. After that their cases were transferred to a civil court.

The Red Army was closing in once more. So on 29 March 1945 the 'government' again upped sticks and fled towards Bavaria, while their prisoners were marched towards KZ Mauthausen, some 300 kilometres away. Exhausted and undernourished, they were forced to trek thirty kilometres a day. Eventually Rajk and his companions found themselves in Bavaria where on 17 April, their guards having fled, they were released.

Almost immediately Rajk and Júlia made their way towards Hungary. By dint of walking, a train journey, hitching lifts on American jeeps, and rowing down the Danube, they reached Vienna on 11 May.

Rowing on, now with Red Army permits, they abandoned their boat when the first signs in Hungarian appeared. They trudged to the frontier town of Hegyeshalom from where they caught a rare train, which deposited them in Budapest's southern suburbs. Plodding through the ruins of the capital, they reported to party headquarters on 13 May. Two days later the HCP daily *Szabad Nép* (Free People) announced Rajk's return.[13]

'Forged like steel'

László was immediately made a member of the HCP's Politburo and secretariat, and appointed to the provisional National Assembly. He was also named secretary of the important Budapest party organisation. It was the future Hungarian dictator, János Kádár, who had to give up this post to Rajk, and he didn't surrender it gladly.[14]

In June Rajk accompanied Rákosi on visits to Belgrade and Prague.[15] According to Júlia, Rajk was the only person who used the familiar second person singular with Rákosi. In his turn Rákosi, who wanted to shed any idea that the HCP tolerated 'loose morals', insisted that Rajk wed Júlia, and they married on 1 July 1945.

Initially they lived at 31 Thököly út in Pest. After Rajk became interior minister they moved to a villa at 27b Vérhalom Tér in Buda, and were joined there by Júlia's mother, László's nephews, and an Airedale terrier called Pájtas.[16]

Rajk took care of his family in other ways too. He got his younger brother Béla back from Siberia. He convinced a parliamentary commission to remove the name of Endre Rajk from a list of war criminals to be repatriated to Hungary for trial. He ensured that the medical practice of his compromised brother Lajos was well away from Budapest.[17]

Rajk was a slender, good-looking man, nearly two metres tall. 'Away from the field of battle he had calm and charming manners', recalled an opponent.[18] He was intelligent, charismatic, and a good speaker who could deliver a long speech without notes.[19]

He is generally credited with a degree of popularity amongst the younger HCP members, the intelligentsia, and the veterans of Spain. He was chief patron of NÉKOSZ, the People's Colleges which educated the poorer children of the peasantry. As an 'honorary building worker' he was used to break strikes. He was also president of the Hungarian-Yugoslav society.

The chief factors in Rajk's relative popularity were that he was not a 'Muscovite' and he was not Jewish, unlike the dominant HCP quartet of Rákosi, Ernő Gerő,[20] Mihály Farkas[21] and József Révai.[22] Pre-PC wags said that Rajk was only in the Politburo because somebody had to be available to sign decrees on Saturdays.[23]

Some people thought that Rajk was an anti-Semite like his older brothers.[24] Yet, his pre-war girl-friend Ilona Schillinger was Jewish. Moreover, the Rajks were initially good friends with Gábor Péter and his wife, and they regularly vacationed with the Révais and looked after their child.[25]

Rajk had spent some six years of his life imprisoned and interned by reactionaries and fascists in Hungary and France. Like Rákosi he was determined to destroy the old order and ensure that it never reclaimed power, and he fully endorsed Rákosi's salami tactics.[26] Whenever he had doubts, Rajk would refrain, 'One must have a compass, and my compass is the Soviet Union'.[27]

Rajk was Hungary's minister of the interior from 20 March 1946 to 5 August 1948. He replaced Imre Nagy in the post, allegedly because of the latter's ill-health.[28] Other sources suggest that Nagy was not ruthless enough for Rákosi's tastes.

In July 1946 Rajk ordered the disbandment of over two hundred 'right-wing' organisations, including the Boy Scouts. He assisted in the purge of 60–100,000 persons from the state bureaucracy in autumn 1946.[29] In 1946–47 Rajk played a leading role in exposing the 'plot' by the 'Hungarian Community'.

Speaking on 18 January 1947, Rákosi chose to say 'a few words of appreciation of the activities of Comrade László Rajk, Minister of the Interior'. In Rajk the 'conspirators' had met their match, he opined, for here was 'a man who had come from the Hungarian working people', and had been 'a courageous and intrepid fighter in the Hungarian workers' movement'. He had fought in Spain, suffered with 'death-defying courage' at Sopronkőhida, and was 'forged like steel' in the battle against Horthyite reaction.[30]

Later Rajk controlled the printing and distribution of the 'blue tickets' which allowed multiple voting in the August 1947 election. When the SDP minister of justice ordered the arrest of plural voters, Rajk simply countermanded the order, arguing that he must authorise each arrest individually.[31]

At the end of 1947 Rajk came into conflict with Gábor Péter and Farkas. They wanted an independent ÁVH reporting directly to Rákosi, while Farkas had the extra incentive of wishing to eliminate a man he saw as a rival for the succession to Rákosi's position. In December Péter accused Rajk of 'anti-Party and anti-regime behaviour', while Farkas charged that the Interior Ministry 'was not in the Party's hands'. In January 1948 he even called Rajk an 'enemy'.[32]

Rákosi sent both Rajk and Kádár to Moscow and 'not for a summer holiday'.[33] The two men visited the Soviet capital for a month in May 1948. This would be Rajk's one and only visit to the USSR. We know nothing about his impressions, or the impression that he made upon the Soviet comrades.

Following 'unification' of the communists and socialists in June 1948, Rajk became a member of the new party's Politburo, secretariat and Orgburo. However, there were renewed attacks upon his conduct as interior minister. Farkas accused Rajk of having dissolved the party organisation in the ministry, and Rajk was forced to restore it. Then in July Gerő queried why Rajk had organised a special well-equipped police unit, answerable only to himself.[34]

Rajk probably clashed with the disciple over the Cominform resolution of June 1948. 'I have a different opinion than Rákosi on some issues', he told a fellow-prisoner after his arrest. 'I never believed that

Tito was a traitor. I always believed that this accusation would cause fateful disunity of the socialist camp'.[35]

In limbo

Such a radical difference led to Rákosi's decision on 5 August to demote Rajk to foreign minister and replace him at Interior by János Kádár. As he put it in a speech on 30 September 1949, it was 'not by chance that we removed Rajk from the Ministry of the Interior five weeks after the Cominform declaration'.[36]

In November 1948 the Czechoslovak ambassador observed that 'Rajk no longer plays the decisive role he used to and is no longer well-informed about what's happening in the party. The orientation headed by Rákosi and backed by the Cominform has strengthened'. Rajk's 'orientation' was rumoured to be 'to the right wing of the party which shows a nationalist deviation from the Marxist-Leninist line'.[37]

The British legation reported similarly in January 1949 that Rajk, 'though still nominally high in the party hierarchy has been without important influence' since his removal from Interior.[38]

At least Rajk's personal life provided some joy when, after two miscarriages, Júlia gave birth to a son on 26 January. Perhaps this brought them closer together. Both were workaholics, with Júlia heading the Hungarian women's organisation MNDSZ. They slept in separate rooms. Rajk may have had a mistress. Yet there is no doubting the delight of both parents in the birth of László Jr.[39] Kádár became his 'godfather' in a secular name-giving ceremony.

However, behind the scenes Rajk was under threat. When he visited Prague on 23 January 1949 to request Field's arrest, Colonel Szűcs told the Czechs that Rajk was being secretly investigated.[40] So perhaps January 1949 was the point when Rajk was cast as the leading-man in his own show trial. However, this is conjecture, since there are no known documents that record such a decision.

In February 1949 Rajk was elected general-secretary of the newly-formed Hungarian People's Independence Front. Its function was to absorb the remnants of the other parties and to represent HCP-controlled mass organisations, such as those for women and youth.

On 26 April the new British minister to Budapest met with Rajk, 'whose French is adequate but spoken in a surprisingly small voice'.

Their conversation touched upon a number of controversial issues, but he 'found Mr Rajk to have a far more agreeable personality than I had anticipated'.[41]

At the May Day celebrations in Budapest portraits of Rákosi, 'generally flanked by those of Stalin and Lenin, glared down from almost every edifice'. Others were less prominent, although 'portraits of Szakasits, Gerő, Rajk and Révai were also in evidence'.[42] At the time of the 15 May 1949 elections, Rajk's name was fourth on the HCP list and his portrait was occasionally seen in Budapest streets along with those of Rákosi, Farkas and Gerő.[43]

On 16 May Rajk addressed a rally celebrating the 'landslide victory' of the Hungarian Independence Front in the elections. In his speech he attacked the 'traitor' Tito and praised the leadership of Stalin and Rákosi.[44]

Szőnyi was arrested that night. Later he was asked with whom he most sympathised in the HCP leadership. When he named Rajk, Szőnyi was interrogated about him, but he originally answered in a straightforward manner that did not implicate Rajk. Yet step by step–and blow by blow–he 'confessed' that they had conducted hostile activities together.

Rajk's name first surfaced in an interrogation protocol on 23 May, in which Szőnyi 'confessed' that Rajk had been recruited by the Americans as an agent. Twice Szőnyi had received written instructions to contact Rajk. The Americans also ordered Szőnyi to form a faction in the HCP in which Rajk would assume a leading role. The faction was to be grounded upon the 'well-known' opposing views of Rajk and Rákosi.[45] That same day Farkas and Péter put a tap on Rajk's phone,[46] while the ÁVH began to arrest certain of Rajk's closest colleagues.[47]

Farkas was also head of the HCP delegation attending the Ninth Congress of the CzCP in Prague which met from 24 to 29 May, while Lieutenant General Bielkin was part of the Soviet delegation.[48] In Prague Farkas sought permission to cast Rajk as the chief defendant in a forthcoming trial. After consulting with Moscow, Bielkin consented.[49]

On 28 May Rajk promised a written reply to a protest note that the Yugoslav minister in Budapest had presented to him that day.[50] The following day the Rajks lunched with Rákosi.

In a statement on 30 May Szőnyi 'confessed' that he had informed Rajk of the instructions from US intelligence to contact him. Thereafter he and Rajk met regularly. Rajk contended that they must 'form a new party leadership which, in the manner of Tito, would fashion an independent policy for Hungary'. In late summer 1949 Rajk intended to summon leaders of his faction for discussions, at which they would prepare an overall plan.[51]

Monday 30 May was also the date of Rajk's arrest. The decision was taken that morning by Rákosi, Farkas, Gerő and Kádár. Apparently Kádár diverted Rajk that evening with one of their frequent games of chess, so that Rajk arrived home late enough for the ÁVH to arrest him under cover of darkness. Late that night an ÁVH 'commando' arrived at Rajk's villa. Júlia watched her resisting husband being pushed feet first into a black car.[52]

The arrest was not publicised.[53] On 1 June *Szabad Nép* announced that Rajk would attend the opening ceremony of Book Week in a Budapest suburb. Three days later it reported that the Council of Ministers had considered a suggestion by him.

'Brutally mistreated'

On the night of 30 May Rajk's emotions may have mirrored those of another Hungarian communist, when he realised that it was the Party which had ordered his arrest: 'I felt like someone who is kicked in the stomach by his mother'.[54]

It seems probable that Rajk was taken directly to the villa in Eötvös út, since Béla Szász had a confrontation with him there on 2 June. This account also suggests that Rajk had not yet been physically tortured in methodical fashion. But he may have been 'roughed up' to bring home to him his changed status from party and government bigwig to 'traitor', and it was highly likely that he had been on the 'conveyor'.

Brought into the room with the T-shaped table, Szász found Péter and his cohorts seated and Rajk standing. Without jacket or tie, shirt crumpled, his beltless trousers had slipped below his waist. 'His usually rugged but now ashen face' was turned towards Szász, 'but his eyes, gazing at me, were sightless'. Lines in his forehead 'had deepened into hard hollows and three straight parallel furrows marred his exhausted face, as if drawn with a ruler'.[55]

The next sighting of Rajk was on 7 June, again at the villa. Confronted with the forced confessions of two broken men, Szőnyi and Cseresnyés, Rajk retorted, 'It's all slander with no basis in fact'. He told Szőnyi, 'Look me in the eye when you say that!'[56]

Late that night Rajk was brutally interrogated by Farkas and Kadar.[57] Rajk protested that he had made 'no contact of any kind with any foreign power'. Nor could he see that it was in the Party's interest 'for a man to accept martyrdom for the sake of a bunch of lies'.

Of course the Party's interest was precisely that. 'You're not our man', rasped Kádár, 'you're the enemy's man. And don't you forget it'. Nor should Rajk have any illusions that the ÁVH was exceeding its authority, because the 'Party leadership is in full agreement about this thing'.

Rajk conceded that he had made mistakes, but his interrogators insisted that there were no such things as 'honest' mistakes; Rajk had either been recruited at a young age by the enemy, so that the 'police and later the Americans got you tighter and tighter by the throat', or 'you were a deliberate enemy from the word go'.

Rajk promised not to 'act in a manner detrimental to the Party, or show a damaging attitude either in court or anywhere else'. He realised too that 'there's no other alternative for me but the ending of my life'. However, he asked for forty-eight hours to write the 'facts'.

Left in the hands of Gábor Péter, Rajk was warned that he would undergo 'the worst night of your life unless you write what I tell you.... We don't need you writing for two days. I will be satisfied with certain sentences. I am guilty of this and that.... Half an hour is plenty to make such a list'. By doing this 'you'll save yourself a lot of grief. If not, your wife will be in here, too, this very night'.

When Rajk wouldn't or couldn't comply, Péter responded menacingly, 'The game is over! Take him away!' Rajk was then presumably seized by some ÁVH thugs. 'They're going to beat you', Péter enlightened his victim, 'until what's inside you comes out'.[58]

On 8 June the newly-elected parliament met. Of course Rajk wasn't there, nor was his name read out. The British minister in Budapest informed the Foreign Office that he had hesitated before reporting 'the more than usually active crop of rumours' about the arrest of Rajk and some of his entourage on charges of nationalism.[59] Western journalists were told that Rajk was 'out of town', that he was on a 'mission'. On 10 June a new government was announced with a new foreign minister in Rajk's stead.[60]

On 16 June *Szabad Nép* reported a resolution of the HCP Central Committee, which announced the expulsion from the Party of Rajk and Szőnyi 'as spies of foreign imperialist powers and Trotskyite agents'.[61]

'THE ENEMY'S MAN': LÁSZLÓ RAJK

The British legation reported a 'most insistent rumour' that Rajk had been taken to Moscow.[62]

On 19 June the Interior Ministry reported that the ÁVH had arrested Rajk, Szőnyi and Pál Justus, along with seventeen accomplices, 'for espionage activities in the service of foreign powers'.[63] That same day *Szabad Nép* declared that the 'familiar surroundings and ideological morass out of which grew Rajk and his accomplices consisted of Trotskyism, Fascism, Zionism and anti-Semitism'.[64]

This veritable morass didn't exclude much, although it didn't specifically identify any links to 'Titoism'. That was to come after the trial's producers had worked on both the problem and their victims a little longer.

During these days Rajk was on the 'conveyor' day and night, these sessions interspersed with physical torture. 'Rajk stubbornly denied everything', recalled one interrogator, 'although he was brutally mistreated'.[65] After a week, recollected another, 'we were more tired than he was'.[66]

The central issue in these savage interrogations, explained one participant later, was that Rajk had been recruited by Horthy's police. 'This was what they desperately wanted him to confess'.[67] Indeed all else flowed from this. However, it seems that Rajk resisted 'confessing' this vital detail until after the arrival of Bielkin and his band of Soviet 'advisers' in Budapest on 21 June.[68]

Bielkin, 'a squat man with curly grey hair', was referred to as 'the Governor' by his minions.[69] In his retinue the Jewish Bielkin had two of the MGB's vilest anti-Semites and most sadistic torturers.

The Ukrainian Colonel Vladimir Komarov had 'the face of a simple peasant, kind and jolly'. Colonel Mikhail Likhachev was Russian, fortyish, balding, and spoke in a 'cold, expressionless, nasal voice'.[70] Both were deputy directors of the MGB's Investigative Unit for Especially Important Cases. Both would also be involved in the initial stages of the Slánský trial, the 'Leningrad affair', and the JAC frame-up.

One wonders what indignities this pair inflicted upon the relatively high number of Jewish communists under arrest in Hungary, although this treatment would come later. For now the MGB had other problems. Bielkin stopped the arrests and the tortures for ten days, while his team sought to bring order to the mass of conflicting 'evidence' garnered from the forced confessions.

The arrival of Bielkin's team was probably the catalyst for extending the initial Hungarian 'confessions' into an anti-Tito trial, as Stalin wished. This was a development that Rákosi was perfectly happy to embrace.

If Rajk's 'compass' was indeed the Soviet Union, then it is probable that it was Bielkin who navigated Rajk's course to final degradation in the Party's interest. Clearly Rajk had accepted his role as a 'Horthyite police spy' when Bielkin arranged a confrontation between him and Dr Lajos Bokor.

Bokor was arrested by the ÁVH in June. They wanted him to testify that Rajk was only freed so rapidly in 1931, because he had signed a declaration that he would serve as a police spy.[71] Bokor was taken to the villa, interrogated by Bielkin and tortured by the MGB. Bokor finally agreed 'to say anything against Rajk, provided Rajk said it first in his presence'. At their confrontation, which probably occurred in July, Rajk 'recited the whole "script" in a monotonous voice'.[72]

The last recorded sighting of Rajk before his appearance at his trial is at another confrontation between him and Szász in Andrássy út. It appears to have taken place in August. Rajk was thinner and paler than on 3 June, 'but the ghastly network of wrinkles had disappeared from his face'. From his friend's expressions and actions Szász concluded 'that Rajk had no illusions left, that he realized that he had come to the end of the road'.[73]

Meanwhile *Szabad Nép* featured a range of 'spontaneous' demands that no mercy be shown to 'the traitor Rajk and his gang'.[74]

In mid-August 1949 Rákosi met with the public prosecutor, Dr Gyula Alapi, and Dr Péter Jankó, who would be presiding at the Rajk trial. He laid down in the minutest detail how the trial should be conducted, as well as how the indictment, which Rákosi had himself drawn up, should be handled.[75] Rákosi was pleased with his handiwork. He told Gábor Péter that 'every attorney would be proud, if they were able to come up with something like this'.[76]

In Moscow on the evening of 20 August Rákosi discussed the trial and indictment with Stalin for over two hours. Certain of Stalin's coterie were there, including Abakumov for some of the time. Stalin went through the indictment page by page and made observations, and Rákosi inserted the proposed changes into the Hungarian text.

Since all eight of the accused were by definition guilty, Stalin asked if the Hungarians had decided on their sentences. It was of course standard procedure in Stalinist justice to sentence the accused before trying them. Rákosi replied that from discussions he had held it didn't seem necessary to impose any death sentences.

The Boss was initially non-committal regarding such leniency, but soon added that this would depend upon the effect of the trial upon the 'working masses' (who had already spoken with one spontaneous voice in favour of the harshest penalties). Stalin proposed that the matter be discussed again between the conclusion of the court proceedings and the verdict.

The following day Rákosi returned to Budapest and handed the amended indictment to Gábor Péter. 'Don't even change a comma!' he ordered. 'Publish it exactly as it is!'[77]

Rajk's trial was announced on 10 September and the indictment was published the next day. Signed by Alapi, it concluded with the words: 'The indictment is proved by the confession of the accused' and 'there is no reason preventing their punishment'.[78]

On 14 September Rákosi wrote to Stalin that the trial of Rajk and his accomplices would begin in two days time, and that the verdicts would probably be announced on Saturday 24 September. The presiding judge Jankó had already submitted his view on the sentences. He thought that save for the 'spy Ognjenovich' the death penalty should be imposed upon all the accused.

'In our opinion, seven death sentences would be too many', opined Rákosi mercifully. He outlined his own view on the sentences. Stalin telegraphed Rákosi on 22 September that he had no objection to these proposals,[79] and amazingly it came to pass that the verdicts were exactly as the two tyrants agreed.

23

JIGSAW JUSTICE

ASPECTS OF THE RAJK TRIAL

Supporting cast

Besides Rajk, arrested on 30 May 1949, seven other men were indicted as his 'accomplices'. For the purposes of the trial they all represented particular categories of 'conspirators', 'traitors' and 'spies'. All, save Ognjenovich, were accused of being leaders of an organisation 'aiming at the overthrow of the democratic state order', and all, except Korondy, were accused of espionage and sedition. Some other 'crimes' were tagged on for particular defendants.

The seven men, in the order that they were listed in the indictment, were György Pálffy (arrested 5 July), Lazar Brankov (19 July), Szőnyi (16 May), András Szalai (16 May), Milan Ognjenovich (5 July), Béla Korondy (6 June) and Pál Justus (18 June). All were married, save Brankov, and he was also the only one who was not a Hungarian citizen.[1]

György Pálffy was born in Temesvár (now Timişoara) on 16 September 1909. Until 1934 his surname was Österreicher.[2] At the time of his arrest he was a lieutenant general, deputy defence minister, and inspector-general of the Hungarian People's Army. Earlier he had headed KATPOL and Hungary's border guards.

He had trained at the Ludovica military academy, but had resigned from the army in 1939 because his prospective wife was Jewish, and as a professional officer he couldn't marry her. He joined the HCP in 1943 and was active in the military arm of the Hungarian wartime resistance, such as it was.

Born in July 1912 in what is now the Serbian province of Vojvodina, Lazar Brankov joined the CPY in 1931.[3] From the summer of 1941 he fought with Tito's Partisans and by 1944 he was both a CPY and Partisan leader in the Vojvodina. He was the UDB *rezident* in Budapest from 1947 onwards, heading the extensive Yugoslav espionage networks in Hungary.

Brankov was also counsellor at the Yugoslav embassy and was in close contact with Rákosi, Rajk and Gábor Péter. Following the June 1948 Cominform resolution, Interior Minister Ranković ordered Brankov to claim political asylum in Hungary and infiltrate the 'enemy'. Enticed to Moscow by a subterfuge, Brankov was arrested there in May 1949. Following torture and interrogation in the Lubianka, he was moved to Hungary on 19 July to play his role in the Rajk trial.

András Szalai was Szőnyi's deputy in the cadres section and was arrested at the same time as his boss. He was born Ervin Ländler in the southern Hungarian city of Pécs in February 1917. He joined the communist youth in 1932 and was arrested that year. According to one source, Szalai was beaten half to death by the Horthyite police, but never betrayed the Party.[4] He served in a Jewish labour battalion in the war and was imprisoned again in 1943–44.

Milan Ognjenovich was born in 1916 in Sárok, which lies virtually on today's frontier between Hungary and Croatia. He fought with Tito's Partisans. Later he was secretary of the Democratic Federation of the South Slavs of Hungary, a cultural organisation that endeavoured to take a neutral stance in the conflict between Stalin and Tito.

Béla Korondy was born Béla Dergán in the Transylvanian town of Erzsébetváros (now Dumbrăveni) in August 1914. He changed his surname to Korondy in 1937.[5] He came from an army family, had attended the Ludovica military academy, and married into an army family. In 1939 he was assigned as a lieutenant to the provincial gendarmerie, but was brought back to Budapest in 1942.

In 1945 he fought against the Germans during the siege of Budapest. As a reward for his services, he was appointed a major in KATPOL, and later in the frontier guard which was then the main element of the new Hungarian army. In November 1946 he was transferred to the police as a colonel in order to organise their armed units.[6]

Pál Justus was born in Pécs in April 1905. Slender, good-looking, Jewish, multilingual, Justus was a poet as well as a politician. A left-wing member of the SDP, from 1932 to 1936 he lived abroad, mainly in France. He organised protests against the Moscow trials and denounced the Nazi-Soviet Pact. In the war he was conscripted into a labour battalion. Following the 'unification' of the communists and socialists in June 1948, Justus was made a Central Committee member. At the time of his arrest he was also an MP and vice-chairman of Hungarian radio.[7]

'Some other person'

All of the accused, with the possible exception of Ognjenovich, were men who knew too much and had made enemies. Yet their former lives and positions largely defined their roles in the trial, once these were remoulded to meet the requirements of co-producers Stalin and Rákosi.

The 'Horthyite police-spy' Rajk was cast as a constant traitor and provocateur.[8] He disrupted the 'Rákosi battalion' in Spain. He passed information to the Hungarian and Vichy secret police, the Gestapo, American intelligence, and Ranković and the 'Tito clique'. Finally he planned a *coup d'état* in Hungary on behalf of Tito and the USA.

Pálffy and Korondy, both middle-class military officers of the Horthy era, would assume their alleged pre-communist identities. Daubed now in 'fascist' hues, they would provide the military and police muscle required to overthrow the benevolent rule of the 'troika', prior to liquidating this trio of beloved leaders.[9]

Brankov, a genuine UDB officer and double-agent, was Tito's linkman. He collected 'intelligence' from this band of Hungarian traitors who were now on trial[10] and from others as well.[11] He also brought constant 'instructions' from Ranković to the vacillating Rajk about how and when to mount the coup.

Szőnyi and the 'witnesses' Földi and Kálmán had the function of implicating Field and Dulles, and establishing the espionage connection with the US and Yugoslavia. Rajk too was meant to promote a link with Noel, but his testimony was totally unconvincing.

Ognjenovich was on trial to indicate that there could be no 'neutrality' in the struggle between Stalin and 'Titoism'. Justus, the left-wing socialist, was there as a combination 'Trotskyite' and police spy.[12] He had also had the temerity to denounce the Moscow trials and the Nazi-

Soviet Pact. Szalai, as Szőnyi's deputy, knew too much about cadres and Szőnyi's role. Like Justus, he was also Jewish.

The purpose of the trial was to 'try' Tito through the person of Rajk, with additional finger-pointing by the supporting cast.[13] They were to condemn 'Tito and his clique' as 'Trotskyite traitors' who now served the USA. These renegades had left the camp of socialism in order to return their country to capitalism, if not outright fascism.

Tito sought not only to return Yugoslavia to this enslaved status. Through the federations he had proposed forming he had obviously intended to extend the horrors of the imperialist yoke to the other people's democracies, and thereby surround the peace-loving USSR with American-dominated anti-Soviet regimes.

On Friday 16 September the trial opened in the headquarters of the iron and steel workers' union on Magdolna utca in Pest. Packed into the vast auditorium were several hundred po-faced ÁVH employees representing the 'outraged' Hungarian public, plus a number of journalists, mostly writing for the communist press in both Western and Eastern Europe.[14] The trial proceedings, which ran from 16 to 24 September 1949, were broadcast on Hungarian radio twice a day.[15]

The trial was presided over by Jankó, flanked by a panel of four lay judges. These comprised the journalist Sándor Barcs, together with a peasant and two workers. This quartet was purely decorative.[16]

Once the indictment and personal details of the accused were dealt with, Rajk gave his scripted answers to Jankó's scripted questions for four hours. He spoke 'clearly and mechanically without emotion'. Later the British legation recorded that alone of the defendants Rajk 'was never servile or abject'. His self-accusation was spoken 'as if he were recounting a story about some other person',[17] which of course he was.

However, what the British did not know was that Rajk had also indicated that his testimony was a pack of lies.

In the indictment and at the end of his testimony Rajk's date of birth is given correctly as 8 March 1909. Yet when Jankó calls Rajk before him on the morning of 16 September and asks when he was born, Rajk replies, 'On May 8, 1909, in Székelyudvarhely'.[18]

This was not a translation error; *Majus* and *Marcius* are as distinct in Hungarian as May and March are in English. Nor was it a printing error. The 'Blue Book' contains an 'errata' page in which it could have been amended,[19] yet the contradiction was allowed to stand.

This must have reflected a deal between Rajk and his murderers. Rajk would make the confession they wanted, while indicating to those who knew him well that everything that he said was a lie.[20]

Nor was Rajk the only one to utilise this trade-off. For example, Szőnyi testified that when his group returned to Hungary in March 1945, 'we flew from Marseille to Naples and from Naples directly to Belgrade'. The 'witness' Kálmán testified similarly that 'we did not stop in Bari'. However, the ÁVH's 'true' report on the group's return twice specified that they did travel to Bari.[21]

What is difficult to explain is why such deals were adhered to. Rajk and his 'accomplices' were either dead or immured in ÁVH prisons when the 'Blue Book' was finally published. It would have been easy for Rákosi to renege, had he wished.[22]

'Noel Field, an American spy'

In dealing with how Field was portrayed in the Rajk trial, I have left the sterile Stalinist stanzas virtually untouched.

In the indictment Noel was described as 'one of the chiefs in Switzerland of the American espionage organisation known as the "Office of Strategic Services"'. It was alleged that Field 'specialised in recruiting spies from among so-called "left-wing" elements and the various *émigré* espionage groups of different nationalities in Switzerland were subordinate to him'. Szőnyi stated that

The chief helpmate and closest collaborator of Allan (*sic*) Dulles in his work of organising spies among the political émigrés was Noel H. Field, who was officially the head of […] the Unitarian Service Committee […] His duty […] was to extend financial help and assistance to the political émigrés, and through this to establish connections and friendship with them and do organisation work for the American spy ring.

The 'witness' Kálmán told the court that Noel was 'a member' of the OSS, 'who covered this activity with his function as general manager of […] the Unitarian Service Committee'. Kálmán added that Field 'made financial aid available to refugees of my acquaintance, thus attaching them closely to himself'.[23]

Any communist who had spent the war years in Switzerland would rightly be concerned at the damning juxtaposition of the words 'émigré' and 'espionage'. Any *émigré* who had received financial or other aid from the USC had probably been recruited as a spy by American intelligence.

Regarding the group's return to Hungary, Szőnyi testified that 'in connection with our journey home, I and the other members of my group received 4,000 Swiss francs from Field on Allan Dulles' instructions for our travelling expenses'.

Kálmán specified that they 'crossed the Swiss-French frontier illegally at the beginning of 1945. This was made possible by the help of Noel Field who gave our group 4,000 Swiss francs before our departure'.

'Witness' Földi 'knew of the American and Yugoslav intelligence services' co-operation in transporting this spy group back to Hungary:

Thus I am aware that Noel Field, an American spy, was the one who organised the Szőnyi group's illegal crossing of the Swiss-French frontier as well as their further journey to Marseille, and that he had aided this move with the sum of four thousand Swiss francs.[24]

So according to the trial's 'script' the journey back to Hungary was organised by Dulles and Lompar and financed by Field. There is no mention of the role played by the OSE. Noel organised the crossing into France too, although in fact he had nothing to do with it. Moreover, Field apparently handed over 4,000 Swiss francs to the group, on Dulles' instructions, before their departure.[25] There is nothing on the Marseille meeting, where Noel had actually given the group 4,000 far less valuable French francs.

Once the absent Noel was labelled 'guilty of espionage' in the Rajk trial, all who had been in contact with him were 'infected', and guilty by association. This was underlined through a number of warnings which were put into the mouths of the accused.

Szőnyi spoke of a meeting in November 1944 with Dulles when the American, 'as a means of terrorising me', showed Szőnyi 'the receipt I had signed on a previous occasion for Noel H. Field'.[26] So not only those who had known and worked with Field were 'infected', but so was anyone–either at liberty or in the camps–who had simply signed a receipt for food, medicine, clothes or money provided by the USC.

Later in his 'evidence' Szőnyi added that

in all countries where, with Noel Field as intermediary, such aid organisations of the Unitarian Service Committee were set up, these organisations were in reality the cover organisations of the American secret service.[27]

Szőnyi further testified that he 'definitely knew' that in Switzerland Field was in 'contact with the Czechoslovak group, notably with Pavlík' and 'the Polish political émigré groups'. Later he maintained that he had 'certain knowledge that the American intelligence centre built up such a secret organisation' in Czechoslovakia.[28] Brankov added that Yugoslav 'espionage and wrecking activities [...] worked much better in Czechoslovakia than in Hungary'.[29]

Falling into another 'category' of communists who were now officially under threat were former members of the International Brigades. Rajk testified about the 'very strong Trotskyist political activities in the French internment camps', whose 'chief organisers' were 'those in the Yugoslav group'. Naturally, these Yugoslav 'Trotskyists' organised like-minded factions in the other national groups, while in their spare time, as typical 'Trotskyists', they worked for the Vichy secret police and the Gestapo.[30]

Less overt was the warning that the Rajk trial sounded for Jews. Szőnyi, Szalai, Pálffy and Korondy were specifically asked their original names (Hoffman, Ländler, Österreicher, Dergán) at the outset of the trial.[31] There was also an odd scene at the very end of Rajk's testimony where he was challenged about the legality of his using the name Rajk, as his grandfather's name was Reich and László was born with the surname Rájk. László, who was 'irritated' (according to the Blue Book's 'stage directions'), retorted that 'I am of Aryan descent, and genuinely too, because on one side I am Saxon'.[32]

Presumably the concentration upon changed names by five of the accused was an attempt to suggest that they were all Jewish. Add Justus, who was Jewish, and perhaps the sub-text is that the whole business was not only a 'Titoist plot', but a 'Zionist conspiracy' too.

Asked if he was a Zionist, Szőnyi's odd answer was that as far as he knew Vági and Demeter 'were members of the Zionist movement'. Then, more ominously, he added 'that in general the Zionist movement maintained very close cooperation with the American secret service'.[33]

'Death, as full sentence'

The accused had all pled guilty to the charges and offered no defence. Their counsels had not once posed a germane question during the proceedings, nor produced more than legal quibbles in their speeches for the defence.[34] Since there was no question of the accused being innocent, their counsels resorted to 'mitigating circumstances' and appeals for leniency and mercy.

Leniency and mercy were all that the wretched prisoners could ask for as they parroted their last pleas, which were written for them by their jailers. Rajk alone seems to have 'negotiated' his last words.[35]

At 9.45 a.m. on Saturday 24 September 1949 Jankó pronounced the sentences agreed between Rákosi and Stalin. 'In the name of the Hungarian People's Republic', Rajk, Szőnyi and Szalai were condemned 'to death, as full sentence'. Brankov and Justus received life sentences and Ognjenovich was jailed for nine years. Having heard the cases of Pálffy and Korondy, Jankó now decided that his court was 'not competent to hear the charge' against them. So their cases were passed to 'the competent military court'.[36]

The executions of Rajk, Szőnyi and Szalai took place in the courtyard of the Conti utca prison at dawn on Saturday 15 October. The date was deliberately chosen by Rákosi, or perhaps Stalin. It was the fifth anniversary of Horthy's overthrow and his replacement by the fascist regime of Szálasi.

Farkas was determined to see Rajk hung and he brought Kádár along, contending that he 'should see it—it won't do any harm'.[37] The state prosecutor Alapi was there too, as were the senior ÁVH torturers.[38] Rajk, it would seem, welcomed death. Shortly before being led out into the execution yard, he embraced Szűcs and asked him to 'Remember me to the comrades'.[39]

Kádár watched the hanging of the three men. He later recalled that

Rajk went to his death crying, "Long live Stalin! Long live Rákosi!", Szőnyi without a word, Szalai crying out, "I am innocent. I was tortured." I was shocked by this unbelievable behaviour by men I thought of as convicted spies.[40]

One myth that we can dispose of is that Júlia Rajk heard, let alone watched, the execution of her husband from her cell above the courtyard.[41] She didn't, if only because she couldn't. At that time Júlia was imprisoned in 60 Andrássy út.[42] Three days after László's execution she was handed a copy of the 'Blue Book' and from it learned that her husband had been sentenced to death.[43]

However, there was an uninvited witness. Cardinal Mindszenty was then in Conti utca prison. That morning he had heard 'considerable hammering as the carpenters set up the gallows'. With a nail he broke some of the wires from the grating over the window, drew himself up by the windowsill and peered out.

Beneath the gallows stood a middle-aged man clad only in underwear.[44] The hangman knotted the noose on the rope; the party of spectators seemed to let that in no way diminish their good humour. But suddenly the babble of conversation stopped as the condemned man screamed: 'I die an innocent man!'[45]

Following the executions the audience indulged in breakfast and booze and then decided that they wanted to 'see Mindszenty'. So the cardinal was brought to them, routinely humiliated, and then taken back to his cell.[46]

On 10 October a military court sentenced Pálffy, Korondy, and two lieutenant colonels of the border guard to death. They were shot eleven days later. The executions of Rajk, Szőnyi and Szalai were mentioned briefly in the Hungarian press of 16 October, and those of Palffy and Korondy on 25 October.[47]

The circus had already moved on, headed for other lands and fresh victims. Stalin, along with his Hungarian helpmate, had got the show trial on the road. In the next three years the underlying process would seemingly judder in various directions before the Boss steered it along the required route.

TIME OF TRIALS 1949–1953

24

THE URGE TO PURGE

TRIAL AND TERROR, 1948–53

An overview

As soon as the CPY was expelled from the Cominform on 28 June 1948, and in some cases even before that event occurred, a mandatory hunt for 'Titoists' commenced. Once they realised in which direction Stalin's intentions were pointing, satellite leaders began the process of identifying human sacrifices. First off the mark was the Romanian party, soon followed by those of Poland, Albania and Bulgaria.

The Romanian justice minister, Lucreţiu Pătrăşcanu, was attacked as a 'nationalist' as early as February 1948, for reasons that had more to do with a power struggle within the Romanian Communist Party than the influence of Tito. Arrested in April 1948, he was mentioned by Brankov in the Rajk trial.[1] At the third Cominform conference in November 1949 the Romanian party leader, Gheorghe Gheorghiu-Dej, named Pătrăşcanu as an agent of the Western powers.

Pătrăşcanu was not tried until after Stalin's death when the Soviets had lost all interest in his 'case'. But Gheorghiu-Dej continued to pursue it to the end. Pătrăşcanu appeared at his secret trial in April 1954 with one leg amputated. He was sentenced to death and shot in the back of his head through the spy hole in his cell on the night of 16–17 April.[2]

As we shall see in the next chapter, Władysław Gomułka, the secretary-general of the Polish Communist Party, was under attack from June 1948 for his 'rightist nationalist deviation'. He lost his chief party posts in early September.

Another to fall was the Albanian interior minister, Koçi Xoxe. Born in 1917, a former tinsmith, Xoxe was pilloried as 'short, fat, smug, uneducated and vindictive; a coward and a sadist'.[3] His nemesis, Enver Hoxha, the prime minister and secretary-general of the Albanian Communist Party, also suffered the snooty esteem of the Foreign Office. 'Hoxha himself', sneered the Belgrade embassy, 'with his wasp-waisted lounge suits and scent is not an edifying character'.[4]

The CPY was instrumental in creating the Albanian party, and both Hoxha and Xoxe had demonstrated total fealty to Tito.[5] However, handsome Hoxha, educated and radicalised in France, proved to be more adept at reading the runes of Stalin's policy; he got his denunciation in first.

On 2 October 1948 Xoxe was downgraded from interior minister to minister of industry, of which backward Albania had virtually none. At the end of that month he was relieved of all party and governmental duties. Arrested with others on 22 November, Xoxe was brought to trial on 12 May 1949. Charged with being a 'Titoist', which of course he was, and a spy for the Western powers, which he was not, Xoxe was sentenced to death and shot on 11 June.[6]

Nine days later the Bulgarian leader Traicho Kostov was arrested. As we shall see, he had the pride, stubbornness and sheer courage to deny certain of the charges against him, but he did confess to what was effectively 'economic Titoism'. Brought to trial after Rajk was disposed of, Kostov was executed in December 1949.

In none of these Balkan show trials was Noel Field mentioned, since there had been no communist groupings from these three countries for the USC to aid in Switzerland.

Yet even before the Rajk trial the 'Field factor' was in evidence elsewhere, as Rákosi sent his lists of 'Fieldists' to Warsaw and Prague. In Poland, despite the purge of Gomułka, those who suffered most were the small fry, minor Jewish communists who had known Noel or Hermann Field. In Prague it was initially the same story as the CzCP floundered in its search for a 'Czech Rajk'.

After the Rajk trial in September 1949 the 'Field factor' came fully in play. Since Stalin had 'spoken' through the indictment and trial record a further Pavlovian response from the satellite leaders was in order. They were alerted to the fact that not only did they have 'Titoist-Trotskyist spies' within their ranks, but that 'Westerners', 'Spaniards' and Jews were all suspect categories, as was anyone who had worked with Field in the USC, or had simply signed a receipt for him.

As a result, in Czechoslovakia and the GDR the initial arrests and interrogations concentrated upon CzCP members who had assisted Noel during his visits there in 1947 and 1948, and those KPD *émigrés* aided by Noel and the USC in France and Switzerland. Other issues were to shape the ultimate fate of these particular victims, but the starting-point in both cases was the 'Field factor'.

Quite independently of these purges in Eastern Europe, in 1949–52 Stalin indulged in what was, by his standards, a minor bloodletting in the USSR. The so-called 'Leningrad affair' had nothing to do with Field or Tito. Only one of those executed was a Jew, and there appeared to be no anti-Semitic motive. The two chief victims, CPSU Central Committee secretary, Alexei Kuznetsov, and Politburo member and chairman of state planning, Nikolai Voznesensky, were Russians.

A CPSU Politburo resolution of 15 February 1949 dismissed Kuznetsov and others from their chief state and party roles and reprimanded Voznesensky. The latter was removed from his government and party posts between 5–7 March. Kuznetsov was arrested on 13 August and Voznesensky on 27 October 1949.

The two men and the other chief accused were tried in Leningrad on 29 September 1950 and executed on 1 October. Others followed, including Voznesensky's brother and sister. In all, over one hundred people, both defendants and relatives, were executed. About two thousand were imprisoned or exiled to the camps. Arrests and trials continued until 1952.[7]

The whole business may have originated in a faction-fight for the 'succession' to Stalin, with the Malenkov-Beria axis removing the chief acolytes of the dead Zhdanov. It may have been a low-key replay of Stalin's distrust of the Leningrad party, with its shades of Zinoviev and Kamenev. Possibly Stalin was simply reminding the CPSU that he required total obedience from them too.

Then there was the other Soviet affair, which concerned the JAC. In March 1950 Abakumov closed the case. The tortured prisoners had made their 'confessions'. All was ready for the trial, but nothing further happened for two years. Either because Stalin gave the 'Leningrad affair' priority, or because there was a shortage of torturers, the MGB thugs concentrated their attentions upon the 'Leningraders'. Even after the leading 'Leningraders' were executed, the JAC prisoners were simply left in their cells.

However, on 12 July 1951 the MGB boss Abakumov was arrested. Later that month Stalin withdrew the chief MGB 'adviser' from Czechoslovakia and demanded the removal of Slánský as secretary-general of the CzCP. On 31 July the Polish communists finally arrested Gomułka. As we shall see, this sequence of events suggested renewed activism by Stalin.

From this juncture the anti-Semitic element in Stalin's policy predominated: he steered the investigations in Czechoslovakia towards Slánský and other Jewish communists; he was merciless in the case of the JAC trial; he ensured that Paul Merker was punished for his deviant views on Jewish victimhood; and he was instrumental in constructing the 'Doctors plot'.

'The duty of my conscience'

Traicho Kostov was born in Sofia in June 1897. In his younger days he was a law student and a stenographer in the Bulgarian parliament. In 1919 he was a foundation member of the Bulgarian Communist Party (BCP), which was made illegal in 1923.

Arrested in 1924, Kostov was brutally tortured by the royalist Bulgarian police. Fearing he would betray his comrades, he jumped from the fourth floor of police headquarters. His fall was cushioned by telegraph wires, but he still broke both legs and damaged his spine, and thereafter he was a hunchback.[8]

Released in 1929, Kostov left Bulgaria for the first of three stays in Moscow. He became a Central Committee member in early 1932 and in spring 1935 he was co-opted onto the BCP Politburo. From 1940 he was political secretary of the underground party.

On 29 April 1942 Kostov was arrested. He was sentenced to death, but King Boris instructed the military court to commute the sentence to life imprisonment.[9] Transferred to Pleven prison in March 1943, Kostov was freed from its confines when the Red Army invaded Bulgaria in early September 1944. Thereafter he was instrumental in destroying the old order and constructing a communist state.[10]

At the end of 1948 Kostov appeared to be the most powerful man in Bulgaria, given the precarious health of Premier Dimitrov and the other veteran leader Vassil Kolarov.[11] The general assumption was that he would inherit the mantle of Dimitrov, once the older man stepped down or died.

Kostov was first secretary of the BCP and a member of its Politburo. Although only a deputy premier, the Foreign Office claimed that Kostov acted as premier for the last six months of 1948 and, when Kolarov was absent ill, as foreign minister too. He was the overlord of economic affairs in his capacity as chairman of the Committee for Economic and Financial Matters. He was also director of the Central Cooperative Union with its influence upon agriculture.[12]

But was this portrait of potency accurate? Meeting with Dimitrov in Moscow on 6 December 1948, Stalin severely criticised Kostov for refusing to allow Soviet representatives in Sofia to obtain information about the Bulgarian economy from the relevant bodies. 'This is exactly how our conflict with Tito began', snarled the Boss.[13]

This was true enough, as was the reason behind it, the USSR's colonial exploitation of the people's democracies. In this case Moscow had bought up the bulk of Bulgaria's principal exports, tobacco and rose of attar, at prices well below the cost of production. When Bulgaria tried to market the remainder, she found herself competing with the USSR, which was selling its haul at below world prices. It was to prevent a recurrence of this situation that Kostov applied Bulgaria's November 1948 law on state secrets against the Soviet exploiters.[14]

On 9 December, with Dimitrov and Kostov back in Sofia, the BCP Politburo condemned Kostov's 'error' and took 'measures to clear up the mistrust regarding our relations with the USSR'.[15] One of these measures was for Dimitrov to assume the new post of BCP Secretary-General in January 1949. Kostov remained in the Politburo and kept his government posts, but he was excluded from the secretariat.

On 19 January Dimitrov accused Kostov of nationalism and 'intellectual individualism'.[16] At the end of the month, the British legation in Sofia noted press reports that Kostov had been granted six months leave for health reasons. His political health was certainly suffering, and by the end of February 1949 there were persistent rumours that he was under house-arrest.[17]

On 26–27 March 1949 Kolarov delivered a report to the Third Central Committee plenum upon 'The Crude Political and Anti-Party errors of Traicho Kostov'. Kostov was removed from the Politburo and his government posts on grounds of his 'lack of friendship and sincerity towards the Soviet Union'. He remained a Central Committee member.[18] To add to his degradation, on 14 April Kostov was appointed director of the National Library. This was 'an astonishing and almost ludicrous' post 'for a man of Kostov's antecedents', the Sofia legation reported to Whitehall.[19]

It is not at all clear whether Kostov was in Moscow or Bulgaria during these events,[20] but he was certainly in Sofia on May Day. The British legation reported that Kostov was 'at the head of the contingent of representatives of the National Library'. Some published photographs 'clearly show Kostov walking with his library colleagues as if on a day's outing, and smiling up at the tribune, albeit with a grimly closed mouth'.[21] Perhaps he was on an outing–from house-arrest.

On 11–12 June Kolarov, as acting premier, introduced a new report to the Fourth Central Committee Plenum. It went much further than his effort in March, although it stopped short of labelling Kostov a spy. The plenum expelled Kostov from both the BCP Central Committee and the Party itself.

Kostov was under house-arrest before this plenum opened. He was formally handed over for interrogation by state security on 20 June, although this was not made public until 20 July.[22] Nor could he expect any further support from Dimitrov, who had died in the Borovikhov sanatorium near Moscow on the morning of 2 July.[23]

By all accounts Kostov suffered horrendous torture at the hands of both the Bulgarian secret police and the Soviet 'advisers'.[24] Yet not until 27 October did he sign his 'confession'. On 30 November the Indictment against 'Traicho Kostov and his group' was published. The 'group' consisted of another ten individuals, most of whom were involved with the Bulgarian economy.[25]

On the afternoon of 7 December 1949 Kostov entered the dock. He bowed to the court, and the president granted his request 'to make use of certain notes' while giving evidence. Kostov then spoke again.

'Citizens Judges! I plead guilty of having had an incorrect attitude toward the Soviet Union, expressed in the method of bargaining, adopted in our trade with the Soviet Union, in withholding certain prices in transactions with the capitalist countries, and also in my order concerning the application of the Law for the Safeguarding of State

Secrets and in my liberal attitude regarding anti-Soviet statements, made in my presence [...] I plead guilty of nationalist deviation in relation to the Soviet Union, which deserves a most severe punishment'.[26]

But that was as far as he was prepared to go.

'I do not plead guilty to having capitulated before the fascist police, nor to having been recruited for service in the British Intelligence, nor to conspirative (sic) activities with Tito and his clique'. He refused to confirm the deposition which he had provided prior to the trial; in other words he renounced the confession that he had made and signed under torture.[27]

The court questioned him a little further, before removing Kostov from the courtroom and reading his original deposition into the record.[28] His co-defendants thereupon confessed their 'crimes', and the 'witnesses' bore witness to such dastardly deeds.

In his last plea Kostov considered 'it the duty of my conscience' to reaffirm his innocence regarding certain of the charges.[29] On the evening of 14 December 1949 Kostov was sentenced to death.[30]

Later that evening Kostov allegedly petitioned the Presidium of the Grand National Assembly for mercy. He reaffirmed 'the depositions written in my own hand during the inquiry', and regretted sincerely 'this conduct of mine which was the result of extremely excited nerves and the morbid self-love of an intellectual'.[31]

That the Presidium met and rejected the petition on 16 December is unlikely. Such matters were decided in conformity with Stalin's will by the local leadership, which was currently dominated by Vulko Chervenkov, the late Dimitrov's brother-in-law and a contender for his crown. A 'Press Department Announcement' recorded that the 'the traitor Traicho Kostov' was executed on Friday, December 16, 1949.[32]

Although various sources suggest that Kostov's trial was a carbon copy of Rajk's, there are important differences: there was no anti-Semitic element in Kostov's trial and there was no 'Field factor'.

The idea that Kostov worked with Tito is blatantly ridiculous. Kostov opposed the Yugoslav plans for a merger with Bulgaria, and he was a BCP representative at the Cominform meeting which expelled the CPY in June 1948. Tito reciprocated this hostility by denouncing Kostov as a Western 'spy' even before the Soviets got around to doing so.[33]

Kostov died because Stalin wanted it that way. The BCP gave the game away in their greetings to Stalin on his seventieth birthday on

21 December 1949. 'Only thanks to your wise and timely instructions, highly esteemed comrade Stalin [...] Only your deeply penetrating eye could see in time the criminal spy gang of Kostov'. At the celebrations in Moscow, Chervenkov proudly announced in Stalin's presence that the BCP had 'learned to beat and annihilate their enemies in the Stalinist way'.[34]

25

THE EVADED SHOW TRIAL

SACRIFICING THE POLISH 'FIELDISTS'

Big fish and small fry

The Kostov affair is blotched with grey areas, but it remains a model of clarity compared to events in Poland. Here such evidence as exists is often contradictory and of dubious veracity.

Who was meant to be 'the Polish Rajk' or 'the Polish Slánský'? Was it to be the Polish heretic, Władysław Gomułka, or the manipulative Jew, Jakub Berman? Were both under threat, or were neither ever genuinely in danger? Neither Gomułka nor Berman came to trial, and the latter remained free throughout the period when he alleged that Beria was gunning for him.[1]

Gomułka did lose his liberty. In July 1951 he and his Jewish wife, Zofia, were arrested. Later they were confined to the comfortable upper storeys of the same villa in Miedzeszyn where Hermann Field was incarcerated in a basement dungeon.

Gomułka was not interrogated until February 1952 and even then in a half-hearted fashion. During three and a half years of detention he was questioned in all for about fifteen days. Most importantly, he was never tortured. Following day-release in September 1954, he was quietly freed in December. In October 1956 events restored him to the post of secretary-general of the Polish Communist Party (PCP).

Gomułka did not come to trial because Bolesław Bierut, the 'Muscovite' who had replaced him as secretary-general in 1948, protected him. Bierut protected Berman too. At least this is the picture painted by Berman. As to why Bierut behaved in such manner with regard to both men, the chief reason offered is probably the correct one; Bierut did not want a replay of the bloodletting of 1938, when the PCP was dissolved by Stalin and most of its leading cadres were murdered in NKVD execution cellars.

So both Gomułka and Berman survived Stalin. However, someone had to be brought to book to implement the 'lessons' of the Rajk trial. Those who suffered in their stead, besides some of Gomułka's allies, were certain minor members of the PCP who had had some form of contact with Noel Field.

On Rákosi's orders, ÁVH Colonel Szűcs travelled to Warsaw in mid-July 1949 with the names of twelve people, most of whom had spent the war years in Switzerland. These names had emerged from the ÁVH interrogations of Noel Field and members of the Szőnyi group.

These twelve persons, most of whom were PCP members, and all of whom were Jewish, were arrested by Poland's Ministry of Public Security in connection with the Field affair.[2] Most underwent brutal torture. Some would not be released until many months after Stalin's death. At least two attempted suicide, another lost his mind, and one died in prison from the ordeal.

Gomułka and Berman

Władysław Gomułka was born into a working-class and socialist family in February 1905 in the Western Galician town of Krosno. Leaving school at fourteen, he trained as a locksmith, and joined the PCP in 1926. In 1934–35 he spent a year in Moscow. In 1936 he was arrested in Polish Silesia and sentenced to seven years imprisonment. He was in jail when Stalin dissolved the PCP and liquidated its leadership.

He was still imprisoned when the Germans attacked Poland on 1 September 1939. Escaping from jail, he crossed to that part of Poland now occupied by the USSR. Following Hitler's attack on his ally in June 1941, Gomułka moved to his home area. Only in summer 1942 did he journey to the capital to lead the Warsaw section of the reconstituted PCP.[3] That December he became a member of its Central Committee.

Following the deaths of two incumbents Gomułka was appointed to the post of PCP secretary-general in November 1943, without Moscow's knowledge. He retained this position after the war, even though senior Polish communists returned to Poland from the USSR. Gomułka was also a deputy premier and minister for the 'Recovered Territories' in the communist-dominated, post-war government.

Gomułka came under attack even before Tito was expelled from the Cominform, but the main assault occurred in August–September 1948. His views on the Cominform, collectivisation, and the merger of the PCP with the Polish Socialist Party were the root issues. Ultimately Gomułka made a full self-criticism, admitting that his 'positions on fundamental political questions were false and anti-Marxist, and resulted in the danger of a rightist, nationalist deviation within the party'.[4]

Stripped of his post as secretary-general on 3 September 1948, Gomułka also lost his seat on the Politburo. In January 1949 he was removed from his ministerial offices and given a modest economic post. He remained a Central Committee member until November 1949 when he was expelled from the PCP. By then he had been cited in the Rajk trial,[5] so it was in his interest to emphasise that he was not a 'Titoist'.[6]

On 31 July 1951 Gomułka was arrested by the Tenth Department of the Ministry of Public Security, the MBP (also known as the UB).[7] The Polish security agencies were supervised by Jakub Berman, and during his tenure at least 200,000 Poles were imprisoned and some six thousand executed.

Berman was born in 1901 into a middle-class Jewish family in Tsarist-ruled Warsaw. He gained a law degree from Warsaw University in 1925 and three years later he joined the PCP. When Hitler and Stalin invaded Poland, Berman made his way to the Soviet-occupied east. When Hitler launched his war on the USSR Berman escaped to Moscow. He acted as a Comintern instructor, and in 1944 he became a member of the PCP Politburo. Along with Bierut, a Pole, and another Jew, Hilary Minc, Berman made up the 'troika' which misruled Poland until 1956.

When in 1956 Berman's record was under attack by fellow-communists, part of his defence was that he could not act decisively in Polish interests, because he was under pressure from Beria. After all, in September 1948 he had accepted a letter from the 'American spy', Noel Field, which was brought to him by one of his secretaries, the twenty-five-year-old Anna Duracz (p. 130).

Berman and Anna

Although Berman showed Field's letter to Bierut,[8] his accounts imply that he didn't inform Stalin about it. One has to be sceptical about this. Not only would it have been inadvisable to withhold such information, but it would have been simple for him to tell Stalin about the letter. As Anna later recalled, 'Berman had regular phone contacts with Moscow; I myself connected him several times to Stalin himself'.[9]

In October 1956 Berman offered his version of events to a plenum of the PCP Central Committee.[10] He referred to his own 'situation' in the years 1949–53 'when Beria accused me of espionage and connections with Noel Field'.

In 1948 Field 'tried to have a talk with me. I refused at the time, as I did not know him'. Field then handed me a letter 'through comrade Anna Duracz, who was working in my secretariat'. Anna regarded Field 'as an idealistic and honest man' and 'this is why I accepted his letter'. This 'asked for the clarification and the amendment of the accusations made against him, and for the recognition of his meritorious work for the anti-fascist movement'.

In 1949 Field 'gave evidence in Budapest mentioning this letter to me and his acquaintance' with Anna Duracz. 'These matters came to the ears of Beria and Stalin, and from that time there began a great campaign against me, and accusations began to pour [in] charging me with espionage and treason'.

In the case of Anna Duracz 'there was direct intervention on Stalin's part. I was against the arrest until the very end. I was deeply convinced of her innocence, not knowing at the time how much truth there was' in the charges made against Field. 'We know very well' the fate of those who 'were under the charge of having been in contact with Field'. If Bierut had not 'defended my case so well, I would, at the most, be exhumed today'.[11]

Let us allow for now that Stalin insisted upon the arrest of Anna Duracz. This would have occurred when Bierut and Berman travelled to Moscow in early October 1949. They were there to discuss the 'attitude towards Gomułka [...] in the light of experience coming from the Budapest trial'.[12] Whether the Poles had been summoned or were voluntarily seeking instruction is not clear. Nor do we know what 'attitude towards Gomułka' they were told to adopt.

However, we do know a little more about Anna's arrest. In the fiery and fascinating interview which Teresa Torańska conducted with Berman shortly before his death in April 1984, he gave more details about what he claimed was his last conversation with the Boss.

During this October 1949 meeting in Moscow, Stalin 'suddenly asked me about Anna Duracz'. Berman informed Stalin about her 'but he was not convinced by my explanation [...] and Anna was arrested shortly afterwards [...] A directive came from Stalin, and there was nothing I could do, because it was a move directed against me personally, and indeed that was how everyone regarded it'.[13]

But was this the case, at least at this juncture? Anna Duracz was arrested on 15 October 1949,[14] which was much later than the others on Rákosi's list, and suggests that Berman may have protected her. But initially at least Anna's role as a prisoner was not directed against Berman. Rather, she was used to finger Gomułka, as she later explained when living in Israel.[15]

At the outset there were no charges of a 'Jewish' or 'Zionist' character. 'I knew Field and was friendly with him', Anna recalled. And since 'Gomułka was chosen to be the scapegoat [...] I could play the role of liaison' between the wartime PCP leadership and 'the European resident agent of the American secret service (Field), the main link on which the indictment could be based'.[16]

One wonders who was responsible for this implausible script. Was it Berman? 'All the time I opposed the arrest of comrade Gomułka', he claimed in 1956.[17] But one Central Committee member recalled matters differently, telling Berman that 'I remember how you spoke after the Rajk trial, how you told us you were going to seek out "Rajks" here in Poland. This was at a Central Committee meeting where everyone expressed full solidarity with the murderers of Rajk'.[18]

So, quite possibly, in this first flush of enthusiasm Berman had reacted to Stalin's interest in Anna (for which we only have Berman's word), by sacrificing her in order to turn Gomułka into the 'Polish Rajk'. But if this was the plan then it soon rebounded on Berman.

As Anna Duracz later recalled, once no satisfactory proof against Gomułka emerged, her interrogator duly recorded 'everything connected with Berman [...] They were interested in everything I was able to tell them about Berman'.[19]

It is impossible to say with any accuracy when the spotlight switched from Gomułka to Berman. There is evidence of a switch as early as

1950. Perhaps in Anna's case the change to an anti-Semitic context came later. Tortured in mind and body, she slit her wrists on 31 January 1951.[20] However, she survived her suicide attempt and was released and 'rehabilitated' late in 1954.[21]

Who instituted this change of focus? Obviously it was not in Berman's interest, nor Bierut's. Presumably the new focus was directed from Moscow and implemented by the numerous MGB 'advisers' attached to the MBP/UB. Nor should it come as any great surprise that many of the Polish security officers promoting the new 'anti-Zionist' line were themselves Jewish.

Światło and co

In October 1948 a special unit was set up in the MBP, which was the direct antecedent of what was formally to become the MBP's notorious Department Ten in November 1951. Ten's function was surveillance of high-ranking PCP members and their associates. The department had its own investigators, archives and prisons.[22]

The head of Department Ten was Colonel Anatol Fejgin who reported to the deputy-chief of the MBP, General Roman Romkowski.[23] One of Fejgin's three deputies was Lieutenant Colonel Józef Światło.

Światło was another Jewish communist from Eastern Galicia. He was born on 1 January 1915 in the *shtetl* of Medyn, which lay some 40 km east of Tarnopol. He came into the world as Izaak Fleischfarb, but took the name Światło from his wife Justyna whom he married in 1943.

Like Aleksandar Ranković and Gábor Péter, Światło had also been a tailor at some point in his life, before joining the MBP in 1945. Among his arrests Światło counted Hermann Field and Gomułka. A small, 'heavyset figure',[24] he was known for good reason as 'the Butcher'.[25] However, in the MBP's highly-competitive torturing stakes, the odds-on favourite amongst these sadists appears to be the head of its Investigations Section, Colonel Józef Różański.[26]

Shortly before the Rajk trial Światło and Romkowski spent twelve days in Budapest. They interrogated Noel and Herta and members of the Szőnyi group.[27] On 27 August 1949 Noel provided them with written answers to their questionnaire;[28] there were no questions about Gomułka or Berman.

In November 1952 Światło and Romkowski attended the Slánský trial.[29] A year later Światło was in East Berlin with Fejgin. He gave his colleague the slip and defected to the American authorities in West Berlin. The CIA flew him to West Germany and then to the USA.

Recycled as an anti-communist and granted political asylum by the USA, Światło was presented to the world in Washington on 28 September 1954. It was on this occasion that he first revealed the fate and location of the Fields.

In March 1954 he had begun his Radio Free Europe broadcasts to Poland, exposing in detail the abhorrent system of repression in which he had but recently been a major player. His attacks led to the closure of the Tenth Department and the reorganisation of the MBP. His revelations also led to the release of those PCP members who had been unfortunate enough to be named on Rákosi's list.

The list

The twelve listed 'Fieldists' were Anna Duracz, Tonia Lechtman, Dr Leon Gecow, Dr Anna Gecow, Dr Jan Lis, his wife Lisa, Janusz Sokolowski, and five others.[30]

Noel claimed to have hardly known Sokolowski in wartime Switzerland, yet he admitted paying him via Tonia Lechtman a monthly stipend. He knew Jan Lis pre-war through Hermann and Jean. It was also through Hermann that he met Leon and Anna Gecow in Zurich in the 1930s. Noel emphasised that the Gecows were Hermann's friends rather than his,[31] and that he had only met them a few times.[32]

Both Leon Gecow and Anna Zylberszac were born in January 1911, she in the textile town of Łódź and he in nearby Zduńska Wola. Both came from well-off, assimilated Jewish families. They met in their schooldays and both decided to study medicine, although Leon's greater loves were politics and journalism. Given the 'quotas' applied against Jews in certain professions in pre-war Poland, they studied abroad, in Vienna, Prague–where they married–and finally Zurich. Anna qualified in 1935 and Leon the following year.

In September 1936 Anna joined a medical team serving with the Republicans in Spain. She operated with anarchist militia units on the Aragon front, but she left in spring 1937 because of her father's serious illness. Now reunited with Leon, who had returned to Poland to perform military service, both found poorly-paid medical posts, since there was a 'delay' in recognising foreign diplomas.[33]

When Germany invaded Poland Leon went to besieged Warsaw, before returning to Łódź to treat Polish casualties. Later he and Anna fled to the Soviet-occupied east. From April 1940 until June 1941 the Gecows worked in a primitive hospital in the small but beautiful Volhynian town of Poczajów (now Pochayev in western Ukraine). A 'wonderland' (*Märchenwelt*) Anna dubbed it,[34] yet all around, in both parts of divided Poland, the occupiers were busy creating their respective versions of hell-on-earth.

On 22 June 1941 the fires grew hotter still when Hitler invaded the USSR. Leon was drafted into the Red Army and retreated with it. Anna stayed at her administrative post until captured by the Germans. Only by luck did she survive internment in the Radom ghetto and work in a forced labour camp. She was freed by communist partisans in June 1944 and, after two months with them, she met up with the advancing Red Army, which initially treated her as a spy.

On 26 October 1944 she was reunited with Leon, by then a Soviet major in the advancing Polish Second Army.[35] He had been at the front as a medical administrator throughout the Soviet-German war, and he was to be highly-decorated for several outstanding acts of courage by the Soviets, and the post-war Polish and Czechoslovak governments.

Anna joined a Polish army medical unit for the final months of the war, which ended for the Gecows near to fire-gutted Dresden. By July 1945 they were both back in an equally gutted Warsaw. Both stayed in the Polish army. Remaining an administrator, Leon rose to the rank of colonel. Captain Anna worked as a paediatrician in the defence ministry hospital.

Leon had lost his entire family in the Holocaust. One of Anna's three sisters survived in Belgium, as did her two brothers who were in Palestine. Leon began writing his independent articles again under the *nom de plume* Pawel Konrad until the PCP warned him to stop. He appears only to have joined the PCP in 1947, with Anna being even tardier in taking up membership.[36] In summer 1947 Hermann Field, who was travelling at the time, stayed briefly with the Gecows in Warsaw.

Leon was arrested by Department Ten in Warsaw on Monday 25 July 1949, Anna was picked up the following day in Wrocław (formerly Breslau), where she was inspecting some children's facilities. She was taken to Światło's Warsaw office where he questioned her about Noel and ordered her to write her 'autobiography'. The next day she was taken to the capital's Tsarist-era Mokotów prison.

Jan Lis was born Simon Rosenbluth in Tarnów in Western Galicia in September 1913, and Janusz Sokolowski too appears to hail from this town.[37] Originally a Zionist, Lis later joined the PCP. In 1932 he left for Switzerland where he graduated as a doctor in 1938.

In wartime Switzerland he and Sokolowski obtained about 1,000 Swiss francs per month from Noel to fund a legal pro-communist newspaper, plus further finance to support some sick Polish communists who had been brought from France to Davos. According to Lis, on one occasion Noel managed to free him after he was arrested in Switzerland.

On his return to Poland Lis was appointed deputy chief doctor with the Warsaw police. Sokolowski worked in the foreign ministry, primarily as a consul in Italy, before returning to Poland in early 1949.

Both were arrested in July 1949, as was Lis's wife. Even though she was not a party member and knew nothing about Field, she was still imprisoned for two years. Sokolowski was held at the Miedzeszyn villa for two months and interrogated by Światło and Różański, and then transferred to Mokotów. Lis recalled that his first interrogation was conducted by a Soviet general who was accompanied by Światło.

Because of their relationship with Field both men were accused of espionage. This charge appears to have hung over them throughout, whereas in the case of Anna Gecow the 'Field factor' was dropped in favour of the great catch-all of 'Trotskyism'.[38]

After Stalin's death Anna was tried on some spurious charge in Mokotów prison in July 1953 and sentenced to six years imprisonment. This was halved to three years because of her behaviour during and after the war. The result of this judicial hocus-pocus was that she was released on 27 July 1953, having served a year longer than her reduced sentence.[39]

Her husband was less fortunate.[40] Leon was brutally beaten and tortured. A fellow-prisoner of Leon's told Lis that 'once the cell's door was opened, Różański told the jailers: "You can pound this son of a bitch (Gecow), this Yid, to death…"'[41]

Leon was tried secretly in Mokotów prison on 16 April 1952. Lis, summoned as a 'witness', saw him briefly. He was just 'skin and bone' (*Haut und Knocken*), Lis recalled. Gecow was sentenced to fifteen years. Fourteen days later he died in the prison hospital as a result of his treatment, either from internal bleeding or a blood-clot on the brain. As another humane idealist with no illusions left about the system he had served, he probably welcomed death.

Lis was never tried. Twice he made half-hearted attempts at suicide, and he provided a 'confession' to stop the torture, although this was not as intense after Stalin's death. Released in November 1954, Lis was 'rehabilitated' in 1956 and received 55,000 złoty in 'compensation'. In 1958 he didn't renew his party card. Later he left for Israel, where he died in 2000.

Lis briefly saw Tonia Lechtman too. Another who was just 'skin and bone', her torturers had hung her by her hair, and she bore the marks of her treatment until her death in Tel Aviv in 1996. Released from Mokotów on 19 October 1954, her so-called 'rehabilitation' could only be political.[42]

Janusz Sokolowski's 'trial' probably took place in late 1952. He was brought to a cellar in Mokotów prison. It contained a gallows and a long candlelit table at which his accusers sat. He was ordered to confess his 'political sin' of being an American spy because he had known Field. When he protested that it was all a 'provocation', they sentenced him to death, and put the noose around his neck. He next remembered coming to his senses when lying on the floor. The rope had been cut.

Six months later his torturers repeated the whole process. This time he lost his mind. He was interned in various hospitals until the summer of 1955. He believed that his heart had been cut out, that he was Jesus, that he was Napoleon. Drugs and psychiatric help eventually brought him back to a semblance of normality.

Yet what he and others had experienced was the other 'normality', the insane world of fear and suspicion that marked Stalin's last years. In the GDR matters appeared more orderly, but beneath the surface calm the same controlled lunacy was at work.

26

'FORMER GERMAN POLITICAL *ÉMIGRÉS*'

WITCH-HUNT IN THE GDR

The 'Field Decision'

In 1949 Germany was formally divided. In May the US, British and French occupation zones were fused into the Federal Republic of Germany. On 7 October the Soviet Occupation Zone (SOZ) became the German Democratic Republic (GDR). Its foundation occurred eight days before the execution of Rajk, whose trial had 'proved' that Noel Field was an 'American spy'.

This event would have a devastating impact upon those KPD members who had known and worked with Field during the war. As happened to so many communists of the Stalin era, their problems lay in being unable to predict the past. Their deeds during the antifascist war against Hitler, when Britain, America and the USSR were 'allies', would now be re-evaluated in the context of the Cold War, in which the USA was Stalin's 'main enemy'.

In April 1946 the KPD and SPD in the SOZ had merged into the *Sozialistische Einheitspartei Deutschlands* (Socialist Unity Party of Germany). The merger was proscribed in the western zones, where the SPD and KPD continued to function as separate and antagonistic parties. The SED was allowed to operate in all four occupation sectors of Berlin, but by the time of the 1948–49 Berlin Blockade it was a force only in the Soviet sector (East Berlin). The SPD dominated politics in Berlin's three Western sectors.[1]

With the intensification of the Cold War, the influence of former SPD members in the SED waned ever more. In January 1949 the First Party Conference of the SED began its transformation into a so-called 'Party of the New Type', which effectively meant its complete Stalinisation.

Prior to this, on 16 September 1948, the SED set up its *Zentral Parteikontrollkommission* (Central Party Control Commission) 'to ensure the purity (*Sauberkeit*) of the Party' and 'to lead the struggle against the activities of enemy agents'. In other words the ZPKK was to enforce ideological conformity and expose and punish deviations from the Party line. The commission's hierarchy of sanctions were first a warning, followed by a reprimand, then a strict reprimand, and ultimately expulsion from the Party.[2]

In reality further sanctions against 'offenders' were available, such as being handed over to the tender mercies of the secret police. Those security bodies already existing in the SOZ were institutionalised in the GDR, when on 8 February 1950 the *Ministerium für Staatssicherheit* (Ministry for State Security) was established. Commonly known as the Stasi, the MfS was closely controlled by the MGB.

The fate of the German 'Fieldists' would be largely determined by these bodies. On 18 October 1949, three days after Rajk's execution, the SED Politburo decided to mount a check on all important functionaries who had been *émigrés* or POWs in the West. On 14 November the SED set up a special commission (*Sonderkommission*) of the ZPKK to execute this task.[3] All KPD *émigrés* in wartime France and Switzerland were automatically suspected of being in contact with Field, and by association operating as 'American spies'. This was made clear to the SED membership at large in the protocol of the Third Party Conference in early July 1950.[4]

The initial sanctions against these *émigrés* were applied in what came to be known as the 'Field Decision' (*Field Beschluß*) of 24 August 1950. This was a joint statement (*Erklärung*) of the SED Central Committee and the ZPKK on 'the relations (*Verbindungen*) of former German political *émigrés* with the leader of the USC Noel H. Field'.[5]

The upshot was that Paul Merker, Leo Bauer, Bruno Goldhammer, Willi Kreikemeyer, Lex Ende and Maria Weiterer, who were 'the most closely linked' to Field and had 'provided help to the class enemy in countless ways', lost their official positions and were expelled from the Party.[6] Paul Bertz, who would doubtless have suffered the same fate, was already dead. Four other officials lost their posts but were not expelled.[7]

The futures of the expellees would vary considerably, and only Mia Weiterer would emerge relatively unscathed. Following consideration of the fates of Bertz, Goldhammer, Mia, Ende and Rudolf Feistmann, the cases of Kreikemeyer and Bauer are treated separately, for reasons which should become clear from the narrative. Merker's downfall is discussed later.

Back in the GDR

Between May and July 1945 Paul Bertz illegally left Switzerland and journeyed to the SOZ. There he was made deputy-head of the Central Administration (*Zentralverwaltung*) for Justice. Inevitably he fell out with his superiors. He opposed the merger of the KPD with the SPD as well. Over time he was demoted to less important administrative posts.

In October 1949 he was summoned before the ZPKK to report upon his relationship with Field. The hearings took place in room 118 of the 'House of Unity' (*Haus der Einheit*), the seven-storey SED headquarters in Lothringerstraße in East Berlin.

Later, Bertz was charged with espionage for the USA. On learning of these accusations, and already suffering coronary problems, he died of heart-failure at his home in Chemnitz on 19 April 1950.[8] This did not save him from opprobrium in the subsequent 'Field Decision'. In it he was accused of acting on the orders of the American 'imperialists', and sabotaging the development of an antifascist resistance movement in wartime France. Bertz was not rehabilitated.

On the instructions of the KPD leadership Bruno Goldhammer left Switzerland illegally in June 1945 and entered the US occupation zone. Although the Americans did not then permit German political parties, he became secretary of the illegal Munich KPD. Following its legalisation, from November 1945 Bruno was second secretary of the Bavarian KPD organisation and chief editor of the Party's local newspaper.

In June 1946 an American military court sentenced him to four months imprisonment for illegally crossing into the SOZ to attend a national KPD conference in East Berlin. In January 1947 the Party ordered him to Berlin where he performed a variety of tasks, primarily for Berlin radio and the government's information office, where he worked under Gerhart Eisler.[9]

The ZPKK accused Bruno of bearing the greatest guilt for Field's infiltration of the KPD *émigrés* in Switzerland, since he was the first to link up with Noel. Such behaviour, it was alleged, induced other German communists to adopt the same casual attitude towards this 'American agent'. Moreover, in wartime Switzerland Goldhammer was also in contact with Szőnyi, a 'self-confessed' American spy.[10]

Called before the ZPKK on 23 August and expelled, Bruno was arrested by the Stasi as he left the 'House of Unity'. From April 1951 to mid-1953 he was in Soviet custody on GDR territory. On 28 April 1954 the GDR's Supreme Court sentenced him at a secret trial to a ten-year stretch for alleged espionage. Released in April 1956, he was 'rehabilitated' in October. Thereafter Goldhammer held some minor journalistic posts. He died in Dresden in 1971.

Maria Weiterer left France for Heidelberg in August 1945. There, and later in Berlin, she was primarily engaged in work for the KPD/SED-controlled Democratic League of German Women (*Demokratischer Frauenbund Deutschlands*).

On 23 October 1949 she wrote about the Fields to the ZPKK: 'I knew them as honest and upright people, and I don't believe that their enthusiasm for the Soviet Union was sham (*geheuchelt*) [...] Personally, I always had feelings of gratitude and respect towards them both'.[11]

This courageous act of loyalty from a decent woman was derided and harshly criticised in the 'Field Decision'. Maria Weiterer had virtually deified (*vergötterte*) Field because he had helped her escape from Marseille to Geneva in autumn 1942. In her 'undisciplined attitude' towards him she exhibited 'neither class-consciousness nor the slightest trace of revolutionary vigilance'.[12]

Following her expulsion, from October 1950 Mia worked as a book-keeper and then as a section-leader in a factory in Thuringia. Her attempts to regain admission to the Party were rebuffed until after the Fields were released. In May 1956 Mia was fully 'rehabilitated'. She died in East Berlin in December 1976.

Lex Ende only met Noel once,[13] but, as with infidelity, once can be enough. From August 1940 to October 1945 Lex lived illegally in Marseille under a false French identity, initially helping to arrange the emigration of other KPD members.

In November 1941, in the wake of Hitler's attack upon the USSR, the underground PCF permitted the KPD *émigrés* to form a leadership body (*Westleitung*) in Paris and ordered leading KPD members in unoccupied Vichy France to join it. Ende's response was to the effect that he took his orders from the KPD Central Committee, not the French party.[14] He tried even harder to send his comrades overseas. In April 1942 the PCF forbade further KPD emigration, but this order was ignored by both Ende and Merker. The latter left Marseille for Mexico the next month.

Lex was relieved of his functions in August 1942. After the war he was 'tried' in Paris before a form of party court (*Parteiverfahren*) by his comrades and expelled from the KPD in July 1945.

Ende travelled to Berlin in October and was allowed back into the Party the following April. From July 1946 he was deputy editor, then chief editor, of the SED daily, *Neues Deutschland*. In June 1949 he was demoted to chief editor of *Friedenspost*, the weekly organ of the Society for Soviet-German Friendship.[15] He was hauled in front of the ZPKK several times. In July 1950 this body decided that he could not be trusted with confidential party work.

Following his expulsion Lex was transferred to a factory in Freiburg in Saxony, where he worked as a book-keeper. He was banned from visiting Berlin where his family lived. His new circumstances presumably took their toll upon this gregarious man, who was something of a 'champagne communist'. On 15 January 1951 Lex died of a heart-attack. In November 1989 the SED, by then on its last legs, rehabilitated Ende.

Another victim of the attack upon the German 'Fieldists' was Rudolf Feistmann. Born in Bavaria in 1908 into a religious Jewish family, Feistmann was a law student when he joined the KPD in 1929. He worked for the Party as a journalist, emigrated to France in March 1933, and operated there for some of the time with Münzenberg. In 1939 he was interned in Le Vernet, but he made it to Mexico in 1941.

Feistmann returned to Berlin in spring 1947 and in July was made foreign policy editor of *Neues Deutschland*. He was caught up in matters mainly because he had been a prominent member of Merker's circle in Mexico. But the 'Field factor' was also introduced.

At an interrogation by the ZPKK special commission on 1 June 1950, he was asked about Noel. 'I never had anything to do with Field and his wife', contended Rudi. 'In Marseille someone told me about him. I don't know who. I was told he looked after children. In Mexico I had nothing to do with Field'.[16]

He was then asked if he had brought a letter of Field's from Prague when Rudi was there in April 1948.[17] 'That was completely out of the question', retorted Feistmann. But it was known, countered his interrogator, that both Bertz and Mia had received unsealed letters from Field, and Feistmann had brought these from Prague. Now the doubts arose. 'I don't even know Field', protested Rudi. 'Perhaps Gisela [Kisch] gave the letters to me as I was leaving'.[18]

Then he was forced to admit that it was possible that he had delivered letters from Noel to both Mia and Bertz, although insisting that he had never 'consciously' (*mit Bewußtsein*) taken possession of a letter from Field. Yet Feistmann knew that such 'subjective' errors were no excuse in Stalin's world. Since he had carried letters from the 'American spy' Noel Field, 'objectively' he was Field's 'courier' and involved in espionage himself.[19]

Feistmann was ordered to produce his entire foreign correspondence and to return to the ZPKK with a detailed report in about a week. He never made it. Rudi committed suicide on 7 June 1950.[20] His death was attributed to blood-poisoning.

The man who disappeared

From October 1941 Willi Kreikemeyer was both the KPD contact man with Noel and in charge of distributing his funds. After the war he continued to play a role in France, repatriating antifascist Germans. Following his return to the SOZ in February 1946 Kreikemeyer held several posts with German railways (*Deutsche Reichsbahn*). In January 1949 he was made director-general of the railways in East Germany.

Then the 'Field factor' kicked in. In the wake of the Rajk trial and the charges against Field, the ZPKK demanded a report from the German communist who had disbursed Noel's largesse. They received one and discussed it on 5 October 1949.[21]

They then ordered Willi to provide them with a list of those who, through him, had received packages and money from Field. Kreikemeyer dredged his memory and provided a typed list of over two hundred names, comprising both genuine identities and pseudonyms (*Decknamen*).

On 5 June 1950 the ZPKK interrogated Kreikemeyer about this list of names.[22] As they were going through them one by one, Kreikemeyer uttered the fateful words '*Leistner ist Mielke*'. His startled interrogator observed that they would have to make further inquiries regarding this matter.[23] However, with this candid explanation that 'Leistner is Mielke' Willi had signed his death-warrant.

Why should this be? Why should Erich Fritz Emil Mielke, then deputy-chief of the MfS and from 1957 to 1989 head of the Stasi, be concerned about Kreikemeyer's identification of him by the pseudonym Leistner? The brief answer is that Willi knew too much about Mielke's sublimely airbrushed past.

Mielke was a thug and a murderer. Born in Wedding, Berlin's 'reddest' borough, in 1907, his working-class parents were founder-members of the KPD. Following in parental footsteps, Mielke joined the communist youth in 1921 and the KPD in 1927.

A small man, although burly and fit, Mielke joined the KPD's self-defence unit (*Parteiselbstschutz*), whose paramilitary 'heavies' bounced hecklers at meetings and provoked clashes with their Nazi and SPD rivals. In August 1931, under KPD orders, Mielke and another man went a step further and shot dead two SPD police officers in Berlin.

Both murderers were spirited to the USSR. There, Mielke received military and political training and was later recruited into the NKVD. He had little chance to use such talents in the Soviet purges, but he blossomed in Spain where he played his part in the Stalinist repressions. Kreikemeyer met him in Albacete, the headquarters of the International Brigades, when Mielke was operating under the name Captain Fritz Leistner.

With the end of the Spanish Civil War, Mielke/Leistner fled to France, where he was interned from May 1940 to April 1941. Having escaped, Mielke adopted another identity, that of a Latvian named Richard Hebel, while he worked as a lumberjack in southern France.

The irony was that he was also receiving via Kreikemeyer aid from Noel Field, later defined by Mielke and company as an American spy. So 'objectively' what did that make Mielke? At another point Mielke sought emigration to Mexico, and when confronted with the choice of joining the resistance in France or conscription for forced labour in the Nazi *Organisation Todt* (OT), he chose the latter.

Having retreated with the OT across the Rhine, Mielke eventually got back to Berlin in July 1945. He was immediately invested by the KPD and the Soviets with police and security functions. He was made deputy-minister of the MfS when that body was set up in February 1950. By then his biography looked somewhat different. In later years he was lauded for his mythical wartime resistance activities in Germany and on the eastern front! The full fraudulent story of Mielke's sanitised career only emerged with the collapse of the GDR.[24]

Willi Kreikemeyer was on holiday when he was expelled in his absence from the SED on 23 August 1950. Ordered back to Berlin, he came before the ZPKK on Friday 25 August. He was read a statement, dated 18 July, outlining his dark deeds with 'the American agent Field' and then informed of the decision to expel him from the Party.[25]

Willi was arrested by the Stasi, probably as he left SED headquarters, and taken to the MfS gaol in Schumannstraße. Until 1945 it had been a Gestapo prison and it came seamlessly under MGB jurisdiction until early 1950, when it was transferred to the Stasi. Willi was put in cell number 2.

On the night of 25–26 August he was visited by Mielke. The secret policeman banned any use of the comradely *Du* and demanded to be addressed by his formal title. Mielke claimed to have spoken with an unnamed senior SED functionary, and together they had found a way for Kreikemeyer to redeem himself. He was to provide Mielke personally with a written confession of his 'guilt' and thereafter make no further statements. This was the only way he could be 'saved'.[26]

Desperately clutching at this straw of salvation that might see him readmitted to the Party which had been his life for thirty years, Willi rewrote his relationship with Field.[27] The Party had told him that Noel was an 'American spy', and 'the Party is always right!' No communist who had kept his faith throughout the 'dialectical' contortions of the previous thirty years could have held firm without that belief; '*Die Partei hat immer Recht!*'

Willi admitted his errors, but could not disguise his turmoil. Expulsion was 'the worst thing that can happen to a person who loved his Party. It meant a death sentence. How can one live without the Party'. If only he could undo his mistakes. Inside he was completely torn apart.[28] When he finished his anguished screed, he signed and dated it Sunday 27 August 1950.

Then he wrote an undated note begging *Herr Staatssekretär Leistner* to pass on a letter to the unnamed senior official who might help him back into the Party.[29] To this 'esteemed comrade' Kreikemeyer repeated that he had made mistakes in his relationship with Noel, 'who led us all around by the nose in such masterful fashion'.[30]

This letter, written on 29 or 30 August 1950 according to Wolfgang Kießling,[31] constituted the last known record of the existence of this loyal party wheel-horse. As we have seen, in Spain and France Kreikemeyer had risked his life and liberty for the cause in which he so fervently believed. He had executed without complaint and to the best of his ability every task that his party had ordered him to perform. Now he was at the mercy of a killer and a coward, who could only benefit from the death of the man who knew too much about Mielke's guilty secrets.

It took nearly seven years for the GDR authorities to finally give any information about Kreikemeyer's fate to his suffering wife.[32] Even then it was worse than useless. According to the death certificate which was finally issued to Marthe Kreikemeyer on 9 July 1957, Willi died in Berlin on 31 August 1950. However, there was no entry in the register of deaths, because this was somehow neglected (*verabsäumt*) at the time.[33] Other matters were 'neglected' too: there was no doctor's report; the cause of death was not specified; there was no grave.

Eight days later the SED was slightly more forthcoming in a letter to the PCF. They told their French comrades that Kreikemeyer had killed himself in prison six days after his arrest.[34] At least they didn't try and put over the original tale prepared by the Stasi in October 1954, that Willi had hung himself with three handkerchiefs knotted together.[35]

Kreikemeyer may indeed have killed himself. How could one live without the Party? However, it seems far more likely that he was murdered by Mielke or Stasi goons acting under Mielke's orders. It even looks like the perfect murder; we can suggest the 'why', but the 'how', 'where' and 'when' of the deed remain total mysteries to this day.[36]

Darkness and light

Leo Bauer's career as a major player in the KPD in West Germany had come to an end in October 1947, when he was involved in a serious car crash near Eisenach. He was in hospital in the GDR until 1948 and then convalesced in Czechoslovakia, where he met Noel and Herta, and was involved in trying to help Noel relocate to the SOZ.

In June 1949 Bauer was appointed chief editor of East Berlin radio. In summer 1950 he was called before the ZPKK several times. On the afternoon of 23 August he was informed of his expulsion from the SED. The Stasi arrested Bauer as he left the 'House of Unity' and took him to the Schumannstraße prison.

There, at 10 p.m. on 25 August, shortly before he visited Kreikemeyer, Mielke entered Bauer's cell. He told Bauer that it was the Party's intention to stage a show trial of the five men expelled under the 'Field Decision' by February 1951 at the latest.[37]

This may be true, except that it was most unlikely that Mielke would ever allow Kreikemeyer to appear in an open court. Moreover, Bauer, Ende, Goldhammer and Kreikemeyer were all second-rank party officials. Only Merker had the status to act as a 'German Rajk', and although humiliated, he was not arrested until December 1952, in part because he was protected by GDR President Wilhelm Pieck. Then there is the question of how Erica Wallach fitted into this 'plan'.[38]

Erica and Robert Wallach's second child, Robert, was born in Geneva in early 1950. Yet in June of that year Erica suddenly decided that she wanted to 'find' the Fields. She telephoned Bauer in his office, and without identifying herself, save by her voice, proposed that they meet in Frankfurt.

Already under suspicion, Bauer told Erica that he would write her a letter. He informed the Party of this and the Soviet authorities forced him to lure Erica to East Berlin. On 9 June 1950 he wrote to Erica. He informed her that he couldn't travel to the West because of the pressure of work, and suggested that she come to Berlin instead.[39]

This is what Erica did. Arriving at Tempelhof airport in the US sector of Berlin on Friday 25 August, two days after Bauer's arrest, Erica called him at his office. When told that he was away, she rang Goldhammer's number. His wife Esther answered. With her own husband arrested, she was in no position to warn the other woman. Instead she told Erica that the only place she could discover Bauer's address was at the 'House of Unity' in East Berlin.

The following day Erica went there and to some other locations. Late in the afternoon she was arrested by the Stasi and found herself in cell number 7 in the Schumannstraße prison, where Bauer and Kreikemeyer (and possibly Goldhammer) were already confined. Naturally, her disappearance was not publicised, although her husband presumably reported her non-return. Moreover, her likely arrest could be inferred from the 'Field Decision' printed in *Neues Deutschland* on 1 September.[40]

Erica and Leo were held for various periods in the Stasi prisons in Schumannstrasse and Hohenschönhausen, and the MGB prison in Berlin-Karlshorst. They were tortured by both the Stasi and the MGB. Both signed forced confessions. Eventually, in the deepening anti-Semitic context of Stalin's last days, they were secretly put on trial.

For three days Bauer and Erica were tried as 'American spies' by a Soviet military court sitting in Lichtenberg prison in Berlin. On 24 December 1952 they were sentenced to be shot. In January 1953 both were shipped to Moscow for execution.

In the summer of 1953, following Stalin's death, they were reprieved. Bauer was sentenced instead to twenty-five years in a Siberian forced labour camp. Erica's fifteen years were to be served in Vorkuta, a camp complex above the Arctic Circle.[41] Both were released in October 1955.[42]

27

THE LAGGARDS OF PRAGUE

THE FIELDS AND THE SLÁNSKÝ TRIAL

'It's his problem'[1]

After Field was abducted and handed over to the ÁVH, the CzCP secretary-general Rudolf Slánský adjudged Prague's involvement to be at an end. He assured President Klement Gottwald that the StB was 'scrupulously following your wishes that our authorities don't get involved with the Field case under any circumstances'.[2] However, the two men had reckoned without the Pavlíks.

Dr Gejza Pavlík was born Géza Politzer into a Hungarian Jewish family in 1884 in what is now Slovakia; he changed his name in 1946. A soldier in the Habsburg army, he was captured by the Russians, and later joined the Bolsheviks. On his return to Hungary Pavlík took part in Kun's short-lived revolution in 1919. When that collapsed he returned to Slovakia and acted as a lawyer to the then-legal Slovak Communist Party.

Endangered on both political and racial grounds, in May 1939 he and his Hungarian wife (*née* Sárolta Heller, later Charlotta Pavlík), emigrated to France. Trapped there by the war, in 1942 they quit Marseille and illegally entered Switzerland. In spring 1943 Pavlík linked up with Szőnyi in Zurich and joined both the HCP and the MNFF groups. In 1944 he met Field, and Noel provided support for him and Sárolta.[3]

In September 1945 Pavlík left for Prague, and that autumn Field appointed him provisional head of USC Czechoslovakia. Noel warned him that he could not expect a permanent post, since Boston was determined to have an American director in Prague. Moreover, although he sent four reports to the USC, in general Pavlík proved to be both idle and incompetent and made a poor impression on Charles Joy, who visited Prague in 1946. Pavlík had also joined the CzCP and was secretary to the Slovak Party's parliamentary group. Unsurprisingly, in spring 1946 USC headquarters ordered Noel to sack Pavlík, and Noel sent a courteous letter of dismissal from Boston.

On 28 May 1949 the imprisoned Field produced a written statement about Pavlík. It was hardly damning, but it made a connection between Pavlík, Szőnyi, Field and the OSS.[4] That was enough for the ÁVH.

That same Saturday, Karel Šváb, then head of the CzCP cadres section, noted that 'Comrade Szűcs unexpectedly returned to Prague and recommended that Pavlík be arrested'.[5] According to Szűcs, Szőnyi and others had stated that Pavlík belonged to a Hungarian Trotskyist group and was the link-man between them and Noel Field. The StB reluctantly complied and arrested the Pavlíks. After interrogating them to little avail, they deported the hapless couple to Budapest the following day.

Despite their advanced years, the Pavlíks were brutally tortured and forced to sign statements about Field and numerous Czechoslovak communists. Early on in his ordeal, Pavlík confessed to being an agent of Field and passing 'intelligence material' to this 'American spy'. Some interrogations were witnessed by attendant StB officers. When they reported the savage treatment of the Pavlíks to Gottwald, he merely observed, 'Different country, different customs'.[6]

Following their eventual return to Prague on 30 June, the Pavlíks retracted their 'confessions' six days later. However, they were still imprisoned and, in emulation of Hungarian 'customs', for three months Pavlík was cruelly beaten by the StB and later by Soviet 'advisers', until he 'confessed' again.

By then Noel had provided the ÁVH with a deposition. This detailed the Czechoslovak 'informants' from whom he had obtained material in 1948 for his projected book on the people's democracies. Dated 17 June, it named Pavlík, Dr Alice Kohnová, Dr Dora Kleinová, Vilém Nový, Dr Evžen Loebl, Ludvík Frejka, Rudolf Feigl and Dr Oskar Kosta.[7]

Around this time Rákosi met with Stalin. Before leaving for the USSR, he ordered Gábor Péter to assemble a list of those communists of various nationalities who had been named in the ÁVH interrogations. On his return to Hungary Rákosi referred to the list of some sixty Czechoslovak functionaries. He told Péter that they would have to be careful about whom they handed it to in Czechoslovakia, since they didn't yet know who was the 'enemy' there. 'It's best if I myself hand it to Gottwald', opined Rákosi. 'After that it's his problem!'[8]

And that is what happened when Rákosi and Péter visited Prague from 21–24 June 1949. Submitting the list of names to Gottwald, the disciple told the Czech that some of them 'are even involved in the espionage we unmasked'.[9] Rákosi emphasised that the common denominator amongst those named was either wartime exile in the West or home front resistance in Slovakia.

Although the Prague communists never doubted the 'enemy's' existence, they were uncertain how to proceed. A trio of minor officials were arrested, purely on the strength of the depositions of Field and the Pavlíks.[10]

Stalin and Rákosi were dissatisfied with such pathetic efforts. On 3 September Rákosi wrote a letter to Gottwald, which criticised the dilatory pace of the Czechoslovak investigation and suggested that it should be aimed at higher levels of officialdom.

Rákosi reminded Gottwald that the list of sixty names indicated that the conspiracy in Czechoslovakia was as extensive as in Hungary. Moreover, Prague had 'more returnees from wartime Western exile', and they occupied higher positions too. 'We (read Stalin) are very disturbed' that 'people, who can with good reason be suspected of serving American imperialists', are 'without exception' still 'running around scot-free'.[11]

Gottwald and Slánský were justifiably scared, fearing that if they did not 'unmask' these 'American agents', they might fall under Stalin's suspicion themselves. So they sent Šváb back to Budapest where he held talks with Rákosi and Bielkin on 7–8 September. Šváb reported to Gottwald that Rákosi thought Prague was underestimating the problem, and that some of Czechoslovakia's highest government departments were filled with officials working for the enemy.

So in late September twelve more second-rank officials were arrested. They included Kosta and Dr Evžen Klinger who had invited Noel to Czechoslovakia in 1948, as well as Dr Karel Markus who was with Hermann Field in Krakow and assisted Noel in Prague in 1948.[12]

Deputy Minister for Foreign Trade Evžen Loebl and his wife were picked up on 24 November 1949. Vilém Nový, editor of the CzCP daily

Rudé Právo (Red Right), and his wife were taken two days later.[13] Both men had assisted Hermann Field in 1939 and had given information to Noel in 1948. All were taken to Ruzyně prison near to Prague airport. However, such relative unknowns hardly provided a 'Czech Rajk'.

Searching for a 'Czech Rajk'[14]

Both Bielkin and Rákosi recommended that Prague ask for Soviet advisers. So on 16 September 1949, the day Rajk's trial opened, Gottwald and Slánský asked Moscow for such assistance. A week later Moscow replied that the MGB would send the required specialists to Prague.

We have already met these creatures. MGB Colonels Likhachev and Komarov, who had been involved in preparing the Rajk trial, arrived in Prague early in October 1949, and others followed.[15] The 'teachers', as the MGB men came to be known, rapidly came to the conclusion that the StB 'handled the class enemy with kid gloves'. They advised that 'people speak the truth only on security's turf, not on party turf'.[16] It was necessary to start arresting people of higher rank and on a larger scale.

Even before the arrival of the 'teachers', but on their advice, the CzCP set up a special StB unit to uncover 'enemies' in the Party. Slánský, who had virtually taken over the StB, outlined its charter.

This special investigative unit would be headed by Karel Šváb, who was made a deputy chief of the StB. However, Šváb would 'remain an employee of the Party' and would not 'in any way be answerable to the Ministry of the Interior'. The Party would supply him with staff and the Ministry would provide him with everything else 'he needs for the job'.[17] When the CzCP created a separate Ministry of State Security in May 1950, Šváb was appointed its deputy minister.

Born in 1904 into a Czech working-class family, Šváb was 'slim and small with an energetic, military stride'.[18] A pre-war party member, he had endured the war years in KZ Sachsenhausen. Obedient, of limited intelligence and unscrupulous, he later admitted that 'I did whatever the leadership wanted and never stopped to think whether it was correct'.[19]

Ironically, the man driving the hunt at this juncture was Rudolf Slánský, who was to be its chief victim. Born in July 1901 near Plzeň into a Jewish merchant family, Slánský was a foundation member of the CzCP in 1921.[20] At the Party's Fifth Congress in 1929 he entered its Politburo. Following the 1938 Munich agreement, he and most of the

CzCP hierarchy left for Moscow. In autumn 1944 Slánský participated in the Slovak uprising. In May 1945 he returned to Prague as secretary-general of the CzCP.

Red-headed, handsome and smartly-dressed, it would seem that in his party role Slánský was feared more than respected and often thoroughly disliked. But working in tandem with his long-time friend, Klement Gottwald,[21] Slánský's position appeared unassailable.

On 8 December 1949, in his capacity as witch finder-general he instructed CzCP regional secretaries that: 'We cannot be satisfied with not having found our own Rajk or Kostov, for plenty of them have been planted here.... Examine the past of every (party) member, especially the dark spots in his history'.[22]

A man whose past was peppered with 'dark spots' was Dr Vladimír Clementis. Born in 1902 into a middle-class Slovak family, Clementis joined the CzCP in 1924. As a Bratislava lawyer he defended accused party members. He was also an MP in the years 1935–38. In 1939 he was expelled from the Party for his criticism of the Nazi-Soviet Pact and the Soviet invasion of Finland.

Clementis spent the war years in London and was readmitted into the Party in 1945. He became deputy minister of Foreign Affairs that same year and minister in 1948. Having already marked his file by denouncing Stalin's pact with Hitler, he jeopardised himself further in July 1948 by thanking the Yugoslavs for the recent performance of their athletes in Prague.[23]

Clementis was dismissed from his post on 14 March 1950 and moved to the State Bank. His various self-criticisms were deemed mere excuses and soon his case came to be part of an inquiry into 'Slovak bourgeois nationalism'. Yet this matter was adjudged too parochial by the 'teachers' to constitute the basis for a show trial.[24]

This did not mean that Clementis would escape the net; he had doubted the Boss's infallibility. Rákosi too was out for his blood, since Clementis and other Slovak leaders had obdurately sought to expel Slovakia's Magyar minority to Hungary.[25] Clementis was arrested on 28 January 1951.

Before that the search for a 'Czech Rajk' had switched to Otto Šling. Blond, beefy and dictatorial, Šling was regional secretary in Brno, the capital of Moravia. He was born Otto Schlesinger in a market town in southern Bohemia in 1912. His father, a Jewish businessman, moved the family to the northern spa town of Teplice in the nineteen-twenties and built up a prosperous paper works there.

In 1932 Šling enrolled in the German university in Prague to study medicine. In 1934 he joined the CzCP. His role in Spain is a matter of dispute. Did he organise a medical unit for the Republicans? Was he shot in the lung and twice buried alive at the front?[26] Or was his role more sinister? Was he the political commissar of all Czechoslovak volunteers in Spain? Was he working 'under the direct orders of Russian agents', liquidating 'those suspected of political heresy'?[27]

Recalled from Spain by the Party, Otto was sent to Poland after Munich. He arrived in Britain in March 1939, shortly before Hermann Field's mission in Krakow began. However, Šling did work for the CRTF in Britain. In November 1941 he married Marion Wibraham, a middle-class, Oxford-educated, British communist.

Leaving his then pregnant wife, Šling joined the entourage of the Czechoslovak government-in-exile which arrived in Moscow in March 1945. Together with the CzCP exiles already there, they entered their homeland from the east in the wake of the Red Army. A new government was formed in Košice in eastern Slovakia in April. Otto took up his post in Brno shortly afterwards. Marion and their two sons joined him in May 1946.

Šling and his wife were arrested by the StB on 6 October 1950. The initial charge against Otto was 'espionage'. Later his case developed into an alleged inner-party coup headed by Šling and Marie Švermová against the Gottwald-Slánský leadership. Marie was one of Slánský's deputies. She was also the sister of Karel Šváb, and he too was swept up in the wave of arrests occurring in January and February 1951.

On 24 February the CzCP Central Committee ratified the 'concept' of a grand conspiracy against the existing party leadership. Yet already moves were afoot not to stage a trial based upon a 'conspiracy' against Slánský, but to create the scenario for a 'conspiracy' led by Slánský.

Field placings[28]

The Slánský trial ran from 20–27 November 1952. Fourteen members of the CzCP stood in the dock for that lethal anti-Semitic charade. All had held senior party or government posts. Eleven of the men were tastefully described as 'of Jewish origin'.

The accused 'Londoners', Loebl, Šling and Ludvík Frejka provided the main testimony against Hermann and the BCRC/CRTF. They were aided by the 'witness' Nový, who was let out of prison for the day.[29] Frejka, Loebl, Artur London and Bedřich Geminder were Noel's chief accusers. However, the simple appellation 'Field' was frequently used, so that on occasion it is none too clear which brother was being cited. In some instances such confusion was deliberate and intended to mask blatantly false 'evidence'.[30]

The indictment specified that as early as 1938 the 'imperialists' were well aware of the strength of the CzCP. Therefore they prepared at this early date to infiltrate the Party to serve their post-war objectives, using the BCRC/CRTF. Initially, Hermann Field in Krakow selected 'agents' from the ranks of CzCP refugees. Later Noel took over such activities. Both brothers were described as the closest collaborators of Dulles, although Hermann had never met the latter.

As to the type of cadres the Field brothers chose, the indictment cited a communication sent on 14 May 1939 by the Czechoslovak consul in Krakow to the government-in-exile in London. When the consul inquired about the criteria for selecting refugees to be sent to Britain, Hermann Field replied that they had to be leftists or Jews.[31]

This was probably true, but of course the Jewish focus had now altered. In 1939 Jewish CzCP members were threatened by the Nazis on both political and racial grounds. In 1952 the entire Slánský trial was designed to demonstrate that these Jewish 'communists' were in fact 'Zionist agents', recruited by the Anglo-American intelligence services during their time in Britain.

Ludvík Frejka was born Ludwig Freund in 1904. He was a member of the KPD before joining the CzCP in 1923. He spent the war years in Britain. On his return home, Frejka headed the Party's economics commission.

At his trial Frejka 'testified' that the 'important American spy' Hermann Field was the recruiting-sergeant of these 'Zionist agents'. It was he who decided upon the distribution of British visas for the Czechoslovak refugees, and in this manner recruited agents for American intelligence. The CRTF kept a card-index (*Karthotek*) on all *émigrés* with whom it dealt, which included their past political activities.

Šling echoed this charge and displayed his detailed knowledge of the BCRC/CRTF, for which he had worked. Both bodies recruited agents for the US and British intelligence services, with the aim of realising their imperialistic aims in Central Europe in the post-war period. Amongst the CRTF staff, he noted slyly, was Kate Thornycroft, 'later the wife of the well-known American agent Field'.[32]

Frejka 'confessed' that he had been an agent of 'the Intelligence Service' since 1941.[33] During the war he made contact with Hermann Field and Konni Zilliacus.[34] He renewed contact with them after the war and provided both with important confidential reports, mainly on the Czechoslovak economy.[35]

Frejka told the court that in autumn 1947 he was searching for Zilliacus in the lobby of the Alcron Hotel in Prague, when at that very moment Field entered the foyer. Frejka made to introduce them, but Zilliacus said he already knew Field. Frejka only spoke with Field briefly and Field informed him that he was on his way to Poland. Therefore they agreed that Field would visit Frejka on his return, and several weeks later they had a ninety minute conversation in Frejka's office.[36]

Field wanted information about the Czechoslovak economy, so Frejka gave him a review of its various sectors and their role in fulfilling Czechoslovakia's Two Year Plan. Field showed an interest in the various heavy industry sectors, and Frejka detailed some of the problems they faced. Field made notes.[37]

In his testimony Loebl repeated the charges against Hermann and the CRTF, and 'confessed' that he too had committed 'espionage' with Zilliacus. As to Loebl's relationship with Hermann, the trial account can in part be tested against later evidence.

According to Nový's testimony, Loebl was a delegate to a wartime UNRRA conference in the USA where he met Hermann.[38] At the trial Loebl related that in summer 1947 Hermann wrote to him from the USA, to inform Loebl that he would be leading a delegation of architects to Czechoslovakia.

Shortly after Hermann's arrival, Nový telephoned Loebl and invited him to his home to meet Field and his wife. When they met Field learned from Loebl 'everything he needed to form a full picture of conditions in Czechoslovakia'.[39]

Unsurprisingly, Hermann expressed an interest in the current status of those men whom he had helped to get to Britain in 1939. He also discussed a range of economic issues with the two Czechoslovaks (or was this Noel?). Apart from the 'spy-spin' there is nothing exceptional here. Three men, who had experienced danger together, reminisced and talked.

Loebl then referred to summer 1949 when Karel Markus, then a section chief in the Ministry of Foreign Trade, telephoned Loebl.[40] Markus told Loebl that Hermann was in Prague and wanted to talk about certain 'important matters'. Loebl invited them both to his home that evening and gave Hermann 'the required information'.[41] This meeting, like the one in 1947, certainly took place.[42]

Obviously, any 'required information' that Loebl gave Hermann in 1949 would have been about Noel's disappearance, since that was the only reason that Hermann was in Prague. What Loebl knew and what he told the American is unknown. Markus knew that Noel had been kidnapped. It couldn't have been easy for him to remain silent.

Artur London told the court that he was in contact with Noel in Geneva in 1947. Field was then leader of the USC, although in practice this body was a cover for the American 'espionage service' (*Spionagedienst*). He said that Field was a subordinate of Dulles who had his residency in Switzerland;[43] and that under cover of the USC Noel created a network of American agents, who upon their return to the people's democracies could infiltrate the state and Party apparatus.

From April to September 1947 Noel sought out London several times in both his Swiss sanatorium and his temporary home.[44] Noel also came to the Czechoslovak information office in Paris in 1948. He had recently left Czechoslovakia and he now wanted information as 'payment' for subsidising the treatment of London's tuberculosis.[45]

In March 1949 London was appointed a deputy foreign minister, and Noel sent a congratulatory letter, stating that the next time he was in Prague he would pay a visit.[46] According to London's 'evidence', Field sent him another two letters. One was for the 'Trotskyist' Paul Merker. London claimed that he destroyed this letter in order to prevent the exposure of his collaboration with Field in espionage.[47]

Born in 1901, Bedřich Geminder was a Sudeten German Jew. Described as 'a small and colorless man' with an attractive French wife,[48] he had joined the CzCP in 1921, but had thereafter worked mainly for the Comintern in Moscow. He returned to Prague in 1946 and headed the International Department of the Party secretariat. He was arrested on 24 November 1951, the same day as his close friend Slánský.

Geminder 'linked' Merker and Slánský, although the latter two never met.[49] Geminder told the court that on Slánský's orders he made contact in 1949 with the German 'Trotskyist' Paul Merker, who was later exposed as a collaborator of the American spy Field.

In 1949 Merker sent Geminder a letter, asking him to help settle Field's application to extend his stay in Czechoslovakia. Since Field had already been exposed by this time, on this occasion Geminder did nothing.

It is hard to know what this nonsense was about. Merker's letter was sent in November 1948, not in 1949, and was co-signed by Franz Dahlem. Dahlem's disgrace would come later. But Merker, with his unorthodox views upon the 'Jewish question', would be slotted into Stalin's schemes as his anti-Semitic campaign reached its zenith.

28

'TERRORIST ACTIVITIES'

STALIN'S LAST KILLINGS

'Who needs this?'

In a way Noel Field helped fuel Stalin's anti-Semitism. Most of Noel's close contacts in the East European communist parties were Jewish. Yet the Rajk trial 'proved' that those who associated with the 'American spy' Field were themselves US 'agents'. Therefore, in Stalin's view, his distrust of this suspect race was vindicated.

On 1 December 1952 he asserted at a Politburo meeting that 'every Jew is a nationalist and an agent of American intelligence'.[1] Yet, as in the thirties, Stalin sought to show that he opposed anti-Semitism.

At a Politburo meeting on 26 February 1952 the lists of candidates for Stalin prizes were under consideration. Stalin noted that some names were followed by another name in brackets. 'Why is this being done?' demanded the Boss. 'If a man chose a literary pseudonym–that's his right.... But apparently someone thought to underline the fact that this man had a double name, to underline that he was a Jew.... Why would you do this? For what purpose instil anti-Semitism? Who needs this?'[2] The answer to the last question was obvious.

As usual he was the master puppeteer. The satraps at the end of his strings were privy to but parts of the Boss's overall scheme. Only at certain points did Stalin provide some idea of what he was seeking to achieve, and how he intended to 'solve' the 'Jewish question'. At other times there appeared to be no activity at all on this front. There were reasons for this.

Despite this obsession, the *Vozhd* had to deal with such major foreign policy issues as the Berlin Blockade and the onset of the Korean War. The development of the Soviet atomic and hydrogen bombs was another call on his time. Moreover, as the supreme 'teacher' and ideologist of the world communist movement, Stalin was obliged to pontificate on 'scientific' matters, such as the economic problems of socialism. Yet sometimes inactivity was simply the result of an ageing and ailing vacationer by the Black Sea evading issues, preferring instead to tend his roses and lemon trees.[3]

Such bouts of lassitude were offset by occasions when Stalin intervened forcefully in the 'Jewish question', as he had done in earlier years. At certain junctures from July 1951 to early 1953 he was the driving force behind the major actions taken against Soviet and satellite Jewry. These comprised the JAC and Slánský trials, the concoction of the 'Doctor's plot', and the fate of Paul Merker.

All of these moves occurred against an overall background of the 'Black Years' of Soviet Jewry. Nor was this period painted in brighter hues for the Jews of the people's democracies. The years 1949–53 saw mass dismissals and demotions of Soviet Jews, frequent arrests, and even some executions, while the satellites suppressed Jewish institutions, and limited and then halted emigration to Israel.

Doctors and policemen

In March 1950 the imprisoned JAC members and employees had been informed that the investigation was over and that their trial would soon begin. But with some of the accused retracting their confessions, and documentary evidence completely lacking, it was obvious that no show trial could be staged. The JAC defendants would have to be tried in secret and such a trial, in Stalin's view, would not produce the requisite effect.

Whether this prompted Stalin to pursue a different course in the 'Jewish Question' cannot be stated with certainty, yet it seems probable. He had used the 'killer-doctor' motif in the 1938 show trial of Bukharin and Rykov. He had also filed for future use a letter from Lidia Timashuk, the cardiologist attending Zhdanov in August 1948. She contended that Zhdanov died because of the incorrect medical treatment applied by the doctors tending him.[4]

The initial move in Stalin's new course occurred shortly after the 'Leningrad affair' executions, when the MGB arrested Dr Yakov Etinger. Born in Minsk, of bourgeois background, Etinger was a highly-respected Soviet diagnostician. He was also a pro-Israeli Jew, who made little effort to hide his opinions about Stalin's lack of support for Israel and the anti-Semitic drive in the USSR.[5] He was denounced in April 1949, but Stalin held off arresting him, ordering the MGB to investigate further.

Sixty-four years old and in poor health, Etinger was arrested on 18 November 1950. On 20 November Lieutenant Colonel M. D. Ryumin became his interrogator. One or two days later Ryumin spoke to that bane of Jews, Colonel Likhachev, who was a deputy chief of the IUEIC (the Investigative Unit for Especially Important Cases of the MGB). Ryumin claimed that Etinger had made a confession concerning the murder of Politburo member A. S. Shcherbakov, who died in May 1945.

Likhachev immediately informed Abakumov, who questioned the doctor about Shcherbakov's death. Etinger had only acted as a consultant in the case, and he emphasised that Shcherbakov was very ill with heart disease. Abakumov dismissed any idea that Etinger was a 'killer-doctor', adjudging him guilty solely of harbouring anti-Soviet views. Neither Ryumin's allegation of what Etinger had 'confessed', nor Abakumov's interview with Etinger, were formalised into protocols.

Although Etinger had links with leading members of the JAC, he was never questioned about this organisation. In early January 1951 Abakumov moved his prisoner from the Lubianka to a refrigerated cell in the hell-hole that was Moscow's Lefortovo prison. This was seemingly at Stalin's behest, who told Abakumov 'Let him sit'.[6]

On 28 or 29 January Abakumov ordered Ryumin to shelve the case against Etinger. However, Ryumin ignored this order, as well as warnings from an MGB doctor about Etinger's weak heart. He continued to question Etinger and on 2 March, after returning from interrogation, Etinger collapsed in his cell and died.

Ryumin had interrogated Etinger in Lefortovo thirty-nine times between 5 January and 2 March. How many of these sessions had occurred after Abakumov's stop-order is unknown, since Ryumin produced no written protocols.[7] And it was because of this, not because he helped cause Etinger's death, that Ryumin received a formal reprimand from his party organisation some time in March. However, there appear to be no other sightings of Ryumin during the four months between Etinger's death and the letter which he wrote to Stalin on 2 July 1951.

The usual interpretation of Ryumin's letter is that he got his denunciation in first, before he was himself penalised for his laxity and misconduct. This may well be the case. Yet it is possible that he was used by Stalin, not only to further the idea of a 'plot' by 'killer-doctors', but also to initiate a purge of the MGB's current hierarchy.

Born in 1913 of peasant stock, Ryumin was bald, paunchy and very small. Stalin called him a pygmy (*shibsdik*), which, coming from a man who himself stood under five foot five (164 cm),[8] implied that Ryumin was indeed tiny. This was no novelty for the Boss, who had used the diminutive Yezhov for even dirtier work during 'the Great Terror'.

Ryumin did not write his letter to Stalin unaided. Summoned to the Kremlin, he met with Malenkov's deputy and rewrote the screed eleven times in ten hours.[9] Stalin was clearly involved too. He must have been the cause of the many rewrites, as he edited the letter to meet his needs. It was to be considered by the CPSU Central Committee, and this body met on 2 July, the same day as the letter was allegedly sent.[10]

In 'his' letter Ryumin contended that Etinger 'acknowledged that he was a confirmed Jewish nationalist and in consequence of this bore hatred toward the Party and Soviet government'. Therefore, 'when he was commissioned to cure comrade Shcherbakov in 1945 he acted so as to shorten his life'.

Ryumin complained that when Abakumov questioned Dr Etinger, he 'retracted his confession about the villainous murder' of Shcherbakov. Abakumov then forbade Ryumin from questioning Etinger 'along the lines of unmasking his […] terrorist plans'. The letter glosses over Ryumin's unauthorised interrogations, noting only that Etinger 'suddenly died and his terrorist activity remained uninvestigated'. This was despite his 'wide contacts', particularly with other leading physicians, 'including several who had a relationship to' Etinger's terrorist activity.

The letter denounced Abakumov as 'a dangerous person to the government', who was naturally 'keeping quiet about serious defects in the work of the organs of the MGB'. The IUEIC was particularly infected by this malaise, since it was filled with people who, 'receiving their careers from his (Abakumov's) hand, gradually lose their party spirit […] and obsequiously fulfil everything that comrade Abakumov wants'.[11]

The Central Committee meeting on 2 July set up a commission of four, including Beria and Malenkov, to verify Ryumin's charges. It 'reported' in the latter's favour on 4 July. Abakumov was dismissed that same day.

A week later the CPSU Central Committee issued a decree entitled 'On the Unsatisfactory Situation in the Ministry of State Security of the USSR'. The following day, 12 July 1951, Abakumov was arrested on charges of betraying the motherland. On 13 July a secret letter containing the text of the Central Committee decree was sent to CPSU committees and secret police units throughout the Soviet Union.[12]

These bodies were informed that there was an 'unquestionably real conspiratorial group of doctors', who were serving foreign intelligence agencies, by performing 'terrorist activities against the leadership of the party and government'. Stalin inserted a chilling reminder too,[13] noting that it was 'impossible to forget' the 'crimes' to which Doctors Levin and Pletnev 'confessed' in the 1938 Moscow show trial.[14]

It was certainly impossible for the Party to forget the thirties. Fears of another blood-letting increased.

'Relieve Comrade Slánský'

In that same month Stalin extended his purge of the MGB to Czechoslovakia. On 20 July 1951, eight days after Abakumov's arrest, he informed Gottwald that there had been 'an insufficiently serious approach' to the investigations in Prague. Therefore he had decided to recall the MGB's chief adviser to the StB, Vladimir Boyarski.[15]

Although Gottwald provided a 'positive evaluation' of Boyarski's work and hoped he might continue in his role, Stalin was adamant. In a letter to Gottwald on 24 July, he charged that Boyarski's activities in Prague had 'shown that he is not qualified well enough to discharge responsibly his obligations as an adviser'.

More importantly, Stalin now wanted another dismissal. He thought 'it would be correct to relieve comrade Slánský of the office of general secretary'. It was clear from 'what we have received from our Soviet personnel' that Slánský had committed 'a number of errors in promoting and posting leading personnel'. The result was that 'conspirators and enemies' had harmed the CzCP.[16]

A stunned Gottwald drafted a reply in which he defended Slánský, until his letter stopped in mid-sentence. Instead he caved in, as he always did when faced with Stalin's will. He informed the Boss that he would relieve Slánský of his post during a later government reshuffle. He assumed that Slánský 'should continue in a responsible position', but in a different sphere. Plaintively he asked Stalin, 'Please let us know what you think of this solution'.[17]

The Boss did precisely that. On 31 July, in celebration of Slánský's fiftieth birthday, praise poured into Prague from fraternal parties.[18] Eulogies by the CzCP filled most of the pages of *Rudé Právo*.[19] But from Moscow there came not a word.

On 6 September the CzCP Central Committee formally removed Slánský from his post as general secretary. Party Chairman Gottwald assumed this role. Two days later Slánský was appointed a deputy prime minister.

On 11 November Politburo member Anastas Mikoyan arrived in Prague bearing Stalin's order to arrest Slánský, on the grounds that he was planning to escape to the West. The alcoholic Gottwald, ever ready to lay down a friend for his life, gave the order and Slánský was arrested in the early hours of 24 November 1951. Geminder was held that same day.

With the new scenario settled, certain prisoners were selected to play fresh parts, while the StB rounded up some other characters. All these men would be cast in specific roles in Stalin's latest production. It was to be a full-blown 'anti-Zionist' show trial, bill-boarded under the catchy title, 'The Trial of the Leadership of the Anti-State Conspiratorial Centre led by Rudolf Slánský'.

Of the fourteen men who would ultimately stand trial, ten–Slánský, Geminder, Loebl, Šling, London, Clementis, Šváb, Bedřich Reicin,[20] Vavro Hajdů,[21] Otto Fischl,[22]–were already in Ruzyně with its three thousand cells.[23] In January 1952 Frejka and Rudolf Margolius[24] were arrested to help present the 'economic' aspects of the 'plot'. On 25 May Josef Frank was added to the pot.[25]

The final catch was a man who genuinely knew too much, the philandering propagandist and spy, Otto Katz. Best known for his authorship of the 'Brown Book' on the *Reichstag* fire, and his claim to be the first husband of Marlene Dietrich,[26] Katz was arrested on 9 June 1952 and tried under his final pseudonym, André Simone.[27]

'Fulfil my demands'

While the new MGB chief adviser, General Alexei Beschasnov, was busy in Prague, a sadistic shrimp lorded it in the Lubianka. Appointed acting head of the IUEIC in July 1951, Ryumin was made its head in November, when he was also promoted to deputy minister of the MGB. This was against the wishes of Abakumov's replacement, Semyon D. Ignatiev.

Stalin's response was to tell Ignatiev that 'I am not a supplicant to the MGB. I can demand and give it to you in the face, if you don't fulfil my demands'. If Ignatiev didn't 'expose the terrorists, the American agents among the doctors', he would join Abakumov in jail.[28] Ryumin was 'excellent', Stalin told Ignatiev in August 1952, 'and I demand that you listen to him and take him closer to yourself. Keep in mind–I don't trust the old workers in the MGB very much'.[29]

Not that there were too many 'old workers' left by then. Between July 1951 and September 1952 some 42,000 individuals were purged from the MGB.[30] Among them were Likhachev, Komarov and Bielkin, who were arrested in October 1951, along with virtually all Jewish generals and colonels in the MGB.[31]

The 'excellent' Ryumin was not only involved in torturing doctors and former colleagues, he also directed the case against the imprisoned JAC members. He obtained a questionnaire framed by Stalin for use in his interrogations. It was mainly devoted to discovering the links of the defendants with foreign intelligence.[32]

Despite the absence of such links or any other worthwhile evidence against the hapless prisoners, fifteen defendants, headed by Solomon Lozovsky and Itzik Fefer, were handed over for trial in March 1952.[33] These twelve men and three women were given eight days to read through a mere forty-two volumes of the entire case file.

On 3 April Ignatiev sent Stalin 'the official indictment in the case of the Jewish nationalists and American spies, Lozovsky, Fefer et al.' In accordance with the norms of Stalinist justice, the MGB proposed the sentences before the trial took place. All defendants were to be shot, save Dr Lina Shtern, who was 'to be exiled to a remote area for ten years'.[34] Politburo approval came the next day, although that body recommended that Dr Shtern's sentence be reduced to five years.

A secret 'trial' before three judges of the Military Collegium of the USSR Supreme Court began on 8 May 1952 in the Lubianka. There were no prosecutors or defence attorneys. Only two defendants admitted their guilt, four refused to plead guilty at all, while the others pleaded guilty 'in part'.[35] Despite this, on 18 July all were convicted of anti-Soviet acts in the service of US intelligence. Thirteen were sentenced to death.[36] Appeals for clemency were turned down and on 12 August they were shot in the Lubianka basement.

By then some doctors were under interrogation, while Stalin was dribbling information about Timashuk's 1948 letter and the death of Zhdanov to the MGB. On 2 November 1952 he criticised the investigators for working 'like waiters in white gloves' and ordered them to beat confessions from the doctors.[37]

This order was implemented on 12 November. The next day Ignatiev summoned the 'excellent' Ryumin from a brutal interrogation and showed him a Central Committee decision dismissing him from the MGB, because he was 'unequal to the task'.[38] On 14 November Ignatiev apparently had a heart-attack requiring hospitalisation.

His temporary replacement later reported that almost daily the Boss expressed 'dissatisfaction with the course of the investigation'. He 'demanded that the prisoners be beaten [...] with death blows'.[39] After all, it had worked in Prague.

'Eleven ropes'

In late October 1952 Stalin discussed the upcoming Slánský trial with Gottwald in Moscow. The latter was heading the CzCP delegation to the Nineteenth Congress of the CPSU. Unsurprisingly, Stalin 'showed detailed familiarity with the matter'.[40] The indictment drafted by StB interrogators and Soviet advisers went to Moscow in November. Whether Stalin amended it is unknown, but it clearly satisfied his needs.

Fourteen men faced the court in Pankrác prison when the trial opened on 20 November. Between them they were charged with high treason, espionage, sabotage and military treason. Eleven were described as 'of Jewish origin'.[41] Frank and Šváb were labelled Czechs, although both would be designated 'war criminals'.[42] Clementis, listed as a Slovak, was of course a 'bourgeois nationalist' too.

The defendants were variously described as Trotskyite, Titoist, Zionist and bourgeois nationalist traitors, serving Western, Yugoslav and Israeli espionage agencies. Gathered in an anti-state conspiratorial centre directed by Slánský, they sought to undermine the people's democratic regime, frustrate the building of socialism, wreck the economy, restore capitalism, carry out espionage, weaken national defence, tear Czechoslovakia from its close alliance and friendship with the USSR, and drag the country into the imperialist camp.

In the case of those 'of Jewish origin', the reason for their treasonous behaviour was explained in the scripted exchange between the presiding judge and Otto Fischl. Asked to explain why he 'had such a hostile attitude towards people's democratic Czechoslovakia', Fischl replied, 'Your Honour, I couldn't have any other attitude than a hostile one', because 'I am a Jewish bourgeois nationalist'.[43]

The language used by the defendants was brutal, clichéd, unreal, and ultimately laughable. In his 'testimony' Šváb described the linked activities of twelve of the accused. His single sentence snakes along seventeen lines of text. He manages 'Jewish bourgeois nationalist' and 'spy' on several occasions, along with 'war criminal', 'saboteur', 'agent', 'cosmopolite', 'Trotskyist', and 'profiteer'.[44]

The 'Titoite fascist clique' makes the occasional appearance, but Stalin now seemed little interested in this squabble. Even Katz, who had interviewed Tito, was only required to put the boot in gently.[45]

Sentences were handed down on the morning of 27 November 1952. As usual they were predetermined. One source claims that the Soviets insisted that eleven of the defendants be executed.[46] Another writes that the CzCP leadership met briefly on 26 November. Gottwald proposed 'eleven ropes' and life for Hajdů, Loebl and London, and the others tacitly agreed.[47]

After sentencing the condemned were urged to waive their right of appeal in favour of pleas for clemency. All save Slánský petitioned for mercy. Naturally, Klement Gottwald denied them clemency. The eleven condemned to death were informed that their executions would take place on the morning of 3 December.

The night before, fenced off by wire-mesh which made it impossible even to touch fingertips, most received visits from their wives. Frejka probably regretted it most. Since he never lied, his wife believed his 'confession' and berated him as a traitor in his final hours. His teenage son had already demanded that his father be executed.[48] The condemned were allowed to write both to their families and to Gottwald. Slánský wrote to neither.[49]

The executions in Pankrác prison began at 0306 with Geminder and concluded at 0545 with the death of Slánský.[50] The bodies were cremated and the ashes poured into a sack. The StB vehicle carting these off for disposal got stuck in a snowdrift. The ashes proved useful.

Endgame

In July 1946 Paul Merker returned from Mexico to the SOZ. In his absence he had been elected to the SED's highest bodies. In Berlin Merker dealt with social and agricultural issues, but he was also deeply involved in the 'Jewish question' as he had been in Mexico.[51]

In Mexico Merker had worked with Otto Katz. He had even protected the Czech from accusations that he was a British spy.[52] Merker had known Solomon Lozovsky too. As head of *Profintern*, Lozovsky had sent Merker to New York in 1931. There he worked extensively with Jews, who made up about three-quarters of the CPUSA's small New York membership. In March–April 1934, when Merker was working illegally in Nazi Germany, he was hidden by a Jewish family.[53]

To Merker Jews were 'neither angels nor devils, but just people like everyone else'.[54] Yet it was precisely because of their treatment as 'devils' by the Nazis and their collaborators that Merker, an orthodox Stalinist, challenged Stalinist orthodoxy in Jewish matters.

He argued that the Jews were a nation, which Stalin in his seminal work for communists, *Marxism and the National Question*, emphatically denied.[55] Not only was Merker a supporter of a Jewish state, he also challenged the orthodox hierarchy of victims of fascism, where communist 'fighters against' outranked Jewish 'victims of' fascism. His central argument was that the Nazis persecuted communists because of what they did, while they persecuted Jews because of who they were. This led Merker to help draw up a restitution law for German Jews.[56]

In November 1948 Merker and Dahlem pressed Geminder to grant Noel a residence permit in Czechoslovakia. His relationship with Field was of course held against Merker following the Rajk trial, and he was not re-elected to the SED Politburo and Central Committee at the Third Party Conference in July 1950.[57] Instead, as a German 'Fieldist' Merker was expelled from the SED in August.

Exiled from Berlin, Merker was given his old job of waitering in a guest-house. Unlike Bauer and Kreikemeyer he was not arrested, in part because he was protected by GDR President Wilhelm Pieck. However, when he was accused at the Prague trial by Geminder of being in contact with Slánský, he protested his innocence to Pieck in vain.[58]

'TERRORIST ACTIVITIES': STALIN'S LAST KILLINGS

On 30 November 1952, three days after the verdicts in Prague, the Stasi arrested Merker. On 20 December the SED Central Committee passed a resolution entitled 'Lessons from the trial of the Slánský conspiratorial centre'.[59] It was introduced by Hermann Matern, the head of the ZPKK. Its language and arguments emulated those of the Slánský trial, and it was probably concocted by a Soviet source.[60]

A 'Jewish nationalist' was by now a synonym for a 'Zionist', which in turn was a synonym for 'an agent of American imperialism'. So the resolution argued that Merker's Mexican writings against anti-Semitism were pro-Zionist and therefore served the needs of American imperialism. He and Katz were both described as American agents, reference was made to Merker's deviant view of a nation, his derisive treatment of the 'real' anti-fascists, and his false evaluation of the Nazi-Soviet Pact.

It was probably intended that Merker would be 'the German Slánský' and head some group at a show trial. As the casting for the 'Doctors' Plot' indicated, it was not necessary for Merker to be Jewish, as long as he 'served' Zionist and thereby American interests.[61] He was first interrogated about his relationships with Jews on 16 January 1953.[62] This was three days after 'the Doctors Plot' was publicised in the USSR.

The headline in the CPSU daily *Pravda* on 13 January was 'BASE SPIES AND MURDERERS UNDER THE MASK OF PROFESSOR-DOCTORS'. The accompanying article, which Stalin had annotated extensively, claimed that 'The unmasking of the band of doctor-poisoners dealt a shattering blow to the American-English instigators of war'.[63] It also emphasised the Jewish names among the accused doctors, even though most of those arrested were Russians.

Yet not all of the doctors named had been arrested, nor had they 'confessed'. Most unusually for Stalin, a plotter of infinite patience, he had moved too fast and now had to wait for the necessary confessions to catch up with the allegations. In consequence there was a lull in the anti-Semitic press campaign in mid-February.[64]

This hardly stopped the rumours flying around a fearful Jewish community. Some alleged that the trial of the doctors would conclude with public executions in Red Square, followed by an organised pogrom. Others believed that extra trains had been laid on to transport Jews to camps in Siberia. Yet, while there is plenty of evidence of attacks upon individual Jews, no hard evidence has been produced to substantiate the wilder rumours.

There was a permanent lull in the anti-Semitic campaign from Monday 2 March, when *Pravda* was completely free of such nauseating drivel. Stalin had been felled by a stroke the previous day. Thereafter he suffered a lingering death, expiring finally at 2150 on Thursday 5 March 1953.[65]

Like Lenin, the Boss was mummified. The funeral of his embalmed body took place on 9 March.[66] Even in death Stalin killed, when hundreds of mourners were crushed to death by the uncontrolled crowds.

On 31 March the MGB, under Beria's direction, issued a decree 'on the termination of criminal prosecution and the freeing of the prisoners in the doctors' plot'. It acknowledged that they were 'illegally imprisoned' and that there was no basis for the 'charges against them of anti-Soviet terroristic and espionage activity'.[67] Thirty-seven defendants were released. Two had died in custody.

Immured in his Budapest cell, Noel Field had no knowledge of the deeds of his distant nemesis, nor of his death.

THE GHOSTS RETURN

29

BELATED TEARS FOR STALIN

PRISON, RELEASE AND ASYLUM

The letter[1]

Following his tribulations in the villa at 41 Eötvös utca and his time with the MGB in Gorki fasor, Noel Field was imprisoned in 60 Andrássy út. On 11 October 1949 he was moved to the ÁVH prison situated at 8a Conti utca/41 Tolnai Lajos utca in Pest.[2] Under the name János Földes (John Field) he was detained there until early May 1954. At this point he was transferred to the Fő utca prison in Buda where the inquiry into his 'case' was conducted. Herta too was moved to Fő utca in summer 1954.

The Conti utca prison had been a military prison in Habsburg times, and was about one hundred years old.[3] However, it had held civilians under the Horthy regime, including János Kádár.[4] Following the Soviet occupation of Hungary it became an NKGB/MGB prison from 1945 to 1948, when it was turned over to the ÁVH.[5]

Herta, who had preceded Noel to the Conti utca prison, spent most of the first year of her ordeal below ground in a cramped and damp dungeon. It contained nothing but a bed of wooden planks and a blanket or two. It's likely that Noel was similarly accommodated. Later Herta had a roomy (*geräumig*) cell on the ground floor with a chair,

299

table and mattress. At some point she and Noel received books. Like the Hungarian-born British communist, Edith Bone, who festered in the same prison from October 1949 until May 1954,[6] they were allowed exercise too.[7]

Once Noel was moved to Conti utca he was only interrogated sporadically. There are ÁVH reports from January 1950 and December 1951. In the latter case he told his interrogator that if he had been imprisoned as a communist in the USA, within a week he would be free. He would have an attorney as well as basic rights, which were completely denied to him in Hungary.[8] At some point in 1952 Noel received a visit from 'a Soviet person', but nothing more is known of this intriguing detail.[9]

There were no interrogations in 1953. Noel knew nothing of the turbulent events in both the USSR and Hungary which followed Stalin's death. His health worsened. He contemplated suicide, but he also wanted to leave to posterity his own testimony about the events in his life.

On 1 December 1953 Field began a hunger-strike. He complained to an ÁVH major that he had never been sentenced by a court.[10] He expected to die in prison and therefore he intended to hasten the process. However, he would eat again if he was allowed to write to the Soviet leadership, and correct the many untruths recorded in his 1949 'confessions'.

Since it was clear from ÁVH documents that they had no intention of freeing the Fields, on 17 March 1954 Noel was given permission to write his letter. So for five days, from 18 to 22 March, Noel composed his missive to the CPSU Central Committee.[11] He wrote it in German with a pencil.[12] The entire screed ran to sixty-five pages and comprised a letter proper plus four appendices (*Beilagen*).

Noel felt duty-bound to write the truth and he expected to receive the strictest sanctions for any deliberate falsehoods. He intended to qualify lapses of memory or lack of knowledge with the word 'probably' (*vermutlich*), or some other appropriate expression. He would try not to repeat what he had written in 1949–51, except where it was necessary to correct details which had been twisted into lies by his interrogators. He also emphasised that without being tried or sentenced, he had been imprisoned in solitary confinement since 11 October 1949.

He claimed that the point of his letter was not to gain his liberty, which meant little to one who was now over fifty. It was also clear to him that the full truth about his 'case' couldn't be vented in the current international climate, since such publicity would only serve the interests of the 'imperialist war-mongers'.

Field's aim was threefold. Firstly, he requested the CPSU to order a thoroughgoing review of the case of 'Field and his comrades'. In Noel's opinion, it was in the Party's interest to establish quite unambiguously the truth about this affair, and thereby enable all those unjustly punished comrades who were still living ('my former friends and colleagues') to return to party life. Secondly, he wanted the CPSU to take all possible measures to avoid a repeat of such events. Thirdly, Field asked them to restore his honour as a communist to where it stood prior to summer 1949. As to his behaviour during that summer, he was deeply conscious of his 'guilt', and he was prepared unconditionally to accept the Party's verdict regarding his actions.[13]

In writing the letter Noel believed that he had 'fulfilled his final and most sacred party duty'.[14] On 19 April a translation was handed to Interior Minister Gerő. Soviet authorities in Hungary received a copy too and this was presumably dispatched to Moscow.

On 22 April Noel wrote to the 'authorities' (*Behörden*), asking whether the inquiry (*Untersuchung*) into his case had begun, and whether he could expect hearings (*Verhöre*) to begin in the near future.[15] In answer János Földes was moved to the Fő utca jail in early May.[16] The inquiry began on 15 June 1954 with Noel's first interrogation.[17]

The interrogations were conducted by ÁVH Majors Árpád Kretschmer and Lajos Hullay. The interpreter and translator was ÁVH Captain Erzsébet Kuhari, a lady who was proficient in English and German. Both interrogators proceeded from the premise that Field's case was a genuine espionage affair, although some evidence was rather weak.[18]

Between interrogations Noel wrote statements (*Aussagen*) of varying lengths about issues and personalities relevant to his case.[19] He built up his 'archive' of innocence, but it had no effect upon his interrogators. They wrote grandiose plans to question any number of people about Field, including the dead Bertz and Kreikemeyer, and then did nothing. At other times they planned to plant another stool-pigeon (*Kammeragent*) in Noel's cell. Nothing came of this either.

Yet, even had they wished to, the interrogators could not have acted differently. Following Stalin's death the question of releasing political prisoners became a bone of contention in both the USSR and the satellites. In Hungary in particular their release would challenge Ráko-si's tyrannical authority, since he had turned his country into one vast prison.[20]

'Objects of history'[21]

Following the Rajk trial, other Hungarians arrested during its prepara-tion were sentenced in secret at subordinate trials. Members of the Szőnyi group, plus individuals who had no affiliation to it, like Ilona Kojsza, were sentenced in the first instance on 27 March 1950. They were convicted variously of conspiracy to overthrow the democratic order, espionage for the USA and Yugoslavia, and high treason.

Most sentences were increased on 20 May 1950, save that of Ferenc Vági, who was sentenced to death upon both occasions.[22] Fatalistically he told Hódos, 'We are objects of history'.[23] This may have consoled him when he was hanged in Vác prison six days later, aged thirty-two.[24]

While it was the general population who suffered most, Rákosi did not neglect the 'elite'. There were victims among the former left-wing social democrats and the army leadership. In June 1950 Kádár was replaced as interior minister and arrested the following April.[25]

Gábor Péter's turn came later. In December 1952 Stalin informed Rákosi that the imprisoned Bielkin had 'confessed' that Péter was a Western agent. Acutely aware of the contemporaneous anti-Semitic events in the USSR and Czechoslovakia, Rákosi took the hint.[26] On 3 January 1953 he invited Péter and his wife, Jolán Simon, to dine at his villa. Both were arrested by Rákosi's bodyguard, handcuffed, and locked in the villa's icy cellar.

Péter's arrest was followed by those of forty high-ranking ÁVH officers, all Jewish.[27] Rákosi naturally added some Jewish doctors to the pot. An 'anti-Zionist' show trial was in preparation in Hungary when Stalin died. So Rákosi simply altered the charges against 'Péter and his accomplices', and made the former ÁVH leadership into scapegoats for the crimes of himself and the HCP hierarchy. In this he again emulated Moscow, where Khrushchev, Malenkov and other uneasy 'heirs' offloaded the bloody handiwork of Stalin and themselves onto Beria and Abakumov. On 24 December 1953, the day after Beria and certain minions were shot in Moscow, Péter was sentenced to life imprisonment.[28]

By then the CPSU leadership had made some attempt to curb Rákosi's excesses. An HCP delegation was summoned to Moscow and met with their new Soviet overlords from 13 to 16 June 1953.[29] Rákosi was ordered to surrender his role as prime minister, which he had assumed in August 1952. His replacement was the non-Jewish 'Muscovite', Imre Nagy. However, the disciple retained the post of HCP secretary-general.

The factional struggle between Rákosi's unrepentant Stalinists and the 'reformists' supporting Nagy's 'New Course' was fought over a number of issues, of which the amnesty question for political prisoners was one.[30] Unsurprisingly, the ÁVH supported Rákosi, and initially there was no question of a general amnesty for political prisoners; only a trickle of individuals regained their freedom in late 1953 and early 1954.

The first inquiries into collective cases, such as Kádár's, commenced in March 1954. There followed further high-level consultation in Moscow on 5 May 1954. Khrushchev insisted that Hungary's judicial 'errors' had to be corrected in such a way that nothing should tarnish the reputation of Rákosi and the HCP Central Committee. This was an impossible command.

From August to October 1954 Nagy succeeded in getting most of the HCP prisoners released.[31] It was in October too that Noel and Herta were freed. But this was not Nagy's doing. In fact it seems likely that he had no idea that they were in a Hungarian jail at all.

Free Fields [32]

On 28 September 1954 the former MBP officer Józef Światło, who had defected to the Americans in December 1953, was 'unveiled' to the world's press in Washington. Since he had arrested and interrogated Hermann Field, he was able to report that Hermann was held at the Department Ten villa in Miedzeszyn, near Warsaw. Since he had also interrogated Noel and Herta in Budapest in late August 1949, he was able to report their presence in Hungary, although for various reasons Światło thought that they were no longer alive.

This information prompted the State Department to send fresh notes to both Warsaw and Budapest, demanding consular access to the trio of American prisoners.[33] Kate Field, who had remained in Britain with her sons after Hermann disappeared, and Elsie Field, who was then in Europe, redoubled their efforts to get their relatives freed.

On 30 September the MBP moved Hermann Field from his basement cell in Miedzeszyn to a villa in the Otwock pine forest, fifteen miles southeast of Warsaw. There he was prepared for release, while some delicate internal and international negotiations took place. His main contact was with a lady who called herself Mrs Markowska, but who was in fact a notorious member of the MBP, Julia Bystriger.[34]

In early October 1954 Rákosi left Hungary for a sanatorium near Moscow.[35] On 22 October he was visited there by his PCP counterpart. Bierut told Rákosi that the Americans were pressing for Hermann Field's release, but that Hermann was making it a condition of his post-release behaviour that Noel too was set free and fully 'rehabilitated'.[36]

Rákosi replied that the Hungarians would make no difficulties about freeing Noel. He knew that his prisoner had no desire to return to the USA and face a congressional inquiry or possible arrest. Field had already indicated that following release and 'rehabilitation' he wanted to stay in Hungary and would apply for political asylum. So, having consulted with the Soviet leadership and obtained their agreement, Rákosi telephoned Gerő in Budapest and ordered the Fields' release.[37]

On Monday 25 October Hermann's release was officially announced in Poland. The statement naturally placed all the blame for his arrest upon Światło, 'an agent provocateur of the U.S. Secret Service'. An investigation had shown that 'the charges brought by Światło against Hermann Field were groundless. Consequently Hermann Field has been released and has been given full satisfaction'.[38] From then on he was in contact with the US embassy and with Kate in London.

On 28 October a shaved and showered Noel was given clean underwear and 'furnished with a brand-new suit and shoes'. Led into a large office in the Fő utca prison, he was informed that he was free. Then Herta was brought in. After falling tearfully into each other's arms, Noel tried to catch up with events. Upon learning that Stalin had died more than a year before, the Fields were again 'shaken by sobs'.[39]

Released that evening, although this was not yet made public, the Fields were driven into the Buda hills to a safe-house. Amazingly, it turned out to be the villa at 41 Eötvös utca, and it seems unlikely that this was a coincidence.

At least they were more comfortable this time around. Instead of cubby-holes in the coal-cellar, they had a bedroom and living-room to themselves (if one discounts the concealed microphones). The Fields were under constant watch, as well as constant medical observation on account of their frail physical conditions. They were also provided with a 'political counsellor', the German-speaking ÁVH captain Tibor Meszler.

The following day the Fields requested that the Hungarian government grant them political asylum.[40] Over the next few days Noel worried about the issue of a communiqué announcing their release. He fretted at the prospect of meeting the American envoy and the press. He was concerned about his stomach pains. He tried to retrieve items taken from him on his arrest. He watched Soviet films. He complained about the negative effect of being returned to the villa. On occasion he discussed 'political' matters with Captain Meszler.

On 8 November Meszler informed the Fields that they would probably be able to inspect their new home the following day. More good news followed, when he added that the Hungarian government had decided to pay them a one-off lump-sum of 100,000 forints in compensation for their ordeal. In addition they would receive for as long as was necessary a monthly stipend of 10,000 forints to cover their needs.[41]

On the evening of Tuesday 16 November 1954 Hungarian radio finally announced that the Fields were free.[42] That same day they took up residence in their new home. Situated in the Buda hills at 38 Meredek utca, their detached villa had three rooms. It also contained a separate apartment for the caretaker and his wife, who were both employed by the Interior Ministry. In addition the Fields were provided with a German-speaking female 'secretary', ÁVH Captain Molnár. External ÁVH units watched them constantly. Both their house and telephone were bugged.

On 18 November the Fields reported to their 'secretary' that they had slept badly owing to Noel's stomach pains. This was also the day when US envoy Christian Ravndal was calling upon them, and when it was arranged that they would speak by telephone with Hermann in Otwock.

Ill and nervous, Noel hid the Soviet journals in his living-room from view. He considered hiding the bugged telephone too, in case Ravndal thought it was bugged! However, the meeting with the American diplomats went smoothly. Most of the talk appeared to be in the form of reminiscing about State Department days and personnel.[43] The Fields did not ask for new passports, but the news-hungry Noel requested some American newspapers and magazines.

That afternoon Noel and Hermann spoke on the telephone. Their first conversation, tapped by the ÁVH, lasted from 1505 to 1545 local time.[44] However, Hermann's version of events implies a far briefer duration, and is a dishonest record in other respects.[45]

In Hermann's account their conversation begins: 'Hermann, it's Noel, your brother. I was afraid you'd already left. I've been trying for hours'.[46] The only accurate part of this record is the word 'Hermann', since Noel had no idea that his brother was flying to Zurich the following day. He only learned of this after they had spoken for several minutes about their respective health conditions and Noel's 'perfectly wonderful villa'.

After that Noel certainly endeavoured to get Hermann to come and stay with him in Budapest, but he accepted without rancour that Hermann had to leave for the West for various reasons.[47] Nor does Hermann record the fact that the brothers had a second telephone conversation which commenced at 2220 local time.[48] This probably lasted longer than the first call and this time Hermann spoke with Herta too.

Hermann told Noel and Herta that rather than speaking too openly on the phone about his reasons for leaving, he would have them conveyed by Dr Monica Felton,[49] one of his and Kate's 'best friends',[50] who was then in Poland.

Monica flew into Budapest on 20 November, the day after Hermann departed for Zurich. That evening Monica met with Deputy Interior Minister Major General István Dékán. The following day she visited the Fields at their villa. Noel had left hospital for the occasion. Monica and the Fields spoke together for about nine hours. Naturally, the ÁVH eavesdropped on their somewhat rambling conversation, but failed to record or understand some of it. At the request of the three foreigners, Dékán joined their talks on 22 November.[51]

Monica told the Fields that Hermann asked them to avoid any irreversible steps, like applying for asylum, if they wanted Hermann to convince Kate to return with him to Poland. She contended that Elsie, Kate and Kate's father had 'drifted to the right' under the pressure of events, which she seemed to find surprising.[52]

Monica was also very enthusiastic about writing a 'feel-good' book about the Fields' experiences, which somehow neglected to dwell upon the fact that they had festered in prison without trial for over five years. Dékán was less keen, and Noel too later cooled towards both the project and Monica.

From early December Noel and Herta were back in hospital until 15 January 1955. They were there when on Christmas Eve it was announced that the Hungarian government had granted their earlier request for political asylum.[53] Noel never publicly explained the reason behind his action; his attempts to do so remained unpublished.[54]

Ravndal wrote to the Fields on 31 December 1954, asking 'to hear from you direct whether the announcement was valid and, if valid, what the reasons were for your decision'. He required this information 'in order to clarify your status under the applicable provisions of United States law'.[55] One month later he met with the Fields for the second and last time, and Noel informed him that their application for asylum was both voluntary and irrevocable.

On 15 February Ravndal wrote to them again. He told the Fields that 'while your request for asylum in Hungary is not of itself a hostile act, the coupling of this request with your indicated desire and intention to render service to a foreign state and to work against the interests of the United States is wholly inconsistent with American citizenship'. He warned them that if they ventured 'into United States jurisdiction', they would be held accountable for 'all treasonable acts which you have committed while you remain American citizens'.[56]

Noel replied next day that neither he nor Herta would voluntarily renounce their US citizenship. Even if they were legally deprived of it they would not recognise this unilateral act, and would continue to consider themselves as Americans. Washington dropped the matter, but ended any further contact with the Fields.

In the meantime Hermann had landed in Zurich in the early afternoon of 19 November 1954. To avoid the scrum of pressmen, the US consul's car containing Kate and Elsie picked him up and took him to a hotel. Later the Fields decamped to Pension Quardalej in Champfer, a small hamlet near St Moritz. There they remained incognito, thanks to an arrangement with the Swiss government. Their sons visited them there during the Christmas holidays.

The Swiss police authorities didn't make contact with Hermann until late December. Having established that his health would permit it, they took a long statement from Hermann on 4–5 January 1955.[57] In this Hermann noticeably failed to mention either the visit made by him and his first wife to the USSR in 1934, or his secret mission to Prague in 1939. This was hardly surprising; all of the Fields still had much to hide.

30

FADE-OUT

BYSTANDER, APOLOGIST, NOBODY

Making amends[1]

Noel's secret was not much of one. It was that he remained a convinced communist. He told Hermann on the telephone, 'And I believe you'll understand that I haven't changed [...] And I must emphasise this, nor has Herta'.[2] However, his minder, ÁVH Captain Meszler, instructed him not to flaunt his red credentials, but rather to present himself as a 'progressive' person and a supporter of the 'peace camp'.

In any case, there was the Fields' old problem of proving that they had been accepted as covert members of the CPUSA in 1938. Eventually, in November 1956 they were granted membership of the latest incarnation of the HCP. In the aftermath of the Hungarian Revolution, which had seen the Party's disintegration, it certainly needed reinforcements.

Noel still felt guilty that former friends and comrades had lost their freedom and possibly their lives upon the basis of his forced confessions in 1949. To his credit, particularly given his uncertain status after his release, Field sought to make amends.

He began with his foster-daughter, Erica Glaser. From reading the Western press and from telephone conversations with Hermann and Elsie, Noel knew that she was now in a labour camp in Vorkuta. On

7 December 1954 he wrote to the 'competent (*zuständig*) authorities'. He was convinced that Erica had never been a 'traitor', and he asked for a fresh inquiry into her 'case'. If the Hungarians agreed, the Fields were prepared to provide a home for her in Budapest until she could stand on her own two feet.[3]

Noel knew nothing of the Slánský trial and the role that he and Hermann had played in it until January 1955. As for the 'Field Decision' of August 1950 in the GDR, he only learned of its details by accident on 31 July 1956. But by then he had got the gist of things when Marthe Kreikemeyer wrote to him from Alsace on 7 May about her missing husband.

She explained that Willi was expelled from the SED on account of his links with 'the American spy Noel Field'. But since Noel was free this charge was now untenable. She asked if Field could do anything, or at least tell her where she might obtain some worthwhile information.

Noel replied on the day he received her letter, 14 May 1956. In a sympathetic response he promised to do what he could. But first he wrote in English to ÁVH Captain Erzsébet (Erzsi) Kuhári, who was now his link with the HCP.

Field told Erzsi that both he and Herta were deeply moved by Marthe's letter and had to do what they could for her. They wanted Erzsi to pass on a request to the Hungarian authorities. The Fields asked the latter to take some action at party or governmental level on behalf of Kreikemeyer, and other German comrades who might have suffered in the affair.

If the SED claimed that this was a purely German matter, then the Hungarians should refer to the phrase about Kreikemeyer's connection with 'the American spy Noel Field'. Kreikemeyer's fate was a direct consequence of his own case, Noel contended, and therefore it was automatically a concern of the HCP. Moreover, the Fields could not view themselves as genuinely 'rehabilitated' if their closest friends were still under suspicion because of them.

Marthe wrote again on 28 June. Noel didn't answer this letter. Marthe wrote again three months later, wondering whether the Fields had received it, or whether they no longer wanted her to correspond with them. In the interim the desperate Marthe had understandably allowed extracts of her letter to the GDR prime minister to be broadcast by West Berlin radio.[4] This led finally to the callous response that Willi Kreikemeyer had died seven years ago in prison.

Noel too had contacted the GDR authorities, but without publicity. On 10 September 1956 the HCP Central Committee forwarded to the SED two protest letters from Field, dated 31 July and 4 August. He denounced the charges made against himself and the others in the 'Field decision' as total inventions (*von A bis Z erfundenen*). He proposed a rapid and fundamental review of the whole affair and the public 'rehabilitation' of himself and the other accused.

The SED gave him no satisfaction, and in April 1957 Noel was complaining to the HCP of a degree of confusion regarding his status. In the absence of an unambiguous and widely-publicised statement about Noel's 'rehabilitation', many of his former comrades still avoided him, while some Western communist papers still referred to him as a spy.

The best deal that the Fields appear to have got was a sort of 'certificate of innocence', issued to them by the Hungarian solicitor-general's office on 12 June 1957. This informed them of what they already knew: their imprisonment from 1949 to 1954 had been illegal since there wasn't a shred of evidence against them.

Burying an epoch[5]

In early July 1955 Herta's mother, Katharina Vieser, visited the Fields from West Germany. They made it quite clear to the old lady that they had no intention of returning to the West.

Later that month Noel went to work at the Corvina publishing house which was located at 12 Váci utca, one of Budapest's swankiest streets. At first he was engaged in proof-reading translations from Hungarian into English. Later he was employed as a translator himself, since by early 1956 Field could read Hungarian without much difficulty.[6]

In mid-September Noel spent a fortnight at a spa in Héviz near Lake Balaton. However, his poor state of health didn't prevent him from asking his minders whether he might be allowed to go skiing in the Polish resort of Zakopane in the winter.[7]

Winter had already struck Hungary's politics. In April 1955, with Soviet support, Rákosi finally ousted Imre Nagy from the premiership and replaced him with one of his satraps. Removed from the HCP Politburo too, Nagy was expelled from the Party in December.

The return of Rákosi to power was a challenge not only to the HCP 'reformists', but also to Tito, who had never forgiven Rákosi for his role in helping defame the CPY leader in the East European show trials. At the same time the Soviet leadership was attempting to woo Tito back into the 'socialist' fold.

Khrushchev and Bulganin made a Canossa-like journey to Belgrade in May 1955. Expressing his deep regret for the anti-Tito campaign begun by Stalin in 1948, Khrushchev naturally heaped all the blame onto the executed Beria and Abakumov. Emboldened, Tito launched a stinging attack on the Hungarian and Czechoslovak Stalinists. He demanded that they too should recognise their errors regarding Yugoslavia and revise the content of their show trials.

In November 1955 Rákosi permitted the Hungarian Supreme Court to 'rehabilitate' Rajk and the other victims of his trial, although this judgement wasn't publicised. On 25 February 1956 Khrushchev gave his 'secret speech' at the Twentieth Congress of the CPSU. This detailed in selective fashion the crimes of Stalin, while glossing over those of Khrushchev and the Boss's other lackeys.

Only in the wake of this denunciation did Rákosi publicise Rajk's 'rehabilitation'. Speaking in Eger on 27 March, he acknowledged that the Rajk trial was based upon a 'provocation' by Gábor Péter and was conducted unlawfully. On 29 May at a Budapest party meeting he admitted his own responsibility, as Hungary's leader, for Rajk's judicial murder and other breaches of legality. Naturally, this had only happened because poor Rákosi was duped by Péter and the 'Beria gang'.

Rákosi's days were numbered. The drip-drip effect of his crimes and his disastrous economic policies was destabilising Hungary. Those returning from his jails provided the HCP's 'reform' wing with 'quiet, calm, objective reports from hell'.[8] Many writers found their critical voices. As one put it, they were no longer content to produce 'books as hollow as an empty nest'.[9] Workers condemned to shortages and peasants suffering harsh requisitions were increasingly restless.

Tito visited Moscow in June 1956 and there were serious riots in the Polish city of Poznań that same month. Both events augmented the pressure upon the CPSU leadership to deal with the volatile situation in Hungary. On 18 July, prompted by the attendant CPSU leader Anastas Mikoyan, Rákosi 'resigned' his post at an HCP Central Committee meeting, citing 'health reasons'. He and his wife were flown out of Hungary some days later to their new home in the Kirghiz SSR.[10] Rákosi's replacement as head of the HCP was the equally loathed Ernő Gerő. It was hardly a solution.

FADE-OUT

On 6 October 1956 the 'show-burial' of Rajk, Szőnyi, Pálffy and Szalai took place in the Kerepesi cemetery in Pest.[11] The date was a deliberately chosen anniversary. In Arad on 6 October 1849 the Habsburgs had executed thirteen generals who had led the defeated Hungarian forces in the 1848–49 war of independence. Each of these was viewed as a martyr of the nation, a *vértanu* or blood-witness.[12] For the 'reformists' the time had come to re-inter their new martyrs.

Júlia Rajk was the driving force behind the reburial of one particular *vértanu*; her husband.[13] On 7 September the HCP Politburo had given permission for the reburial. Kádár forced the issue through, probably in part to assuage his guilty conscience. He even proposed that the Party should mobilise two or three thousand members to attend.

Júlia wanted more. The HCP had exploited Rajk's 'guilt' in its propaganda; now they should propagandise his innocence. She wanted and got a lying-in-state of the dead men's coffins. She wanted and got the opening of the cemetery's main gates to allow mass attendance. The military, not the ÁVH, should ensure order. Besides the official speakers, one of Rajk's fellow-accused should speak.

On the day of Rajk's reburial *Szabad Nép* ran the headline 'Never Again' (*Soha Többé*). A crowd of between two and three hundred thousand attended the event. Ignoring the wind and driving rain, they passed the black-draped catafalques raised high on a dais.

As plain-clothes ÁVH men mingled amongst them, they listened to the speeches of the official HCP delegates; a 'procession of stiff-faced criminals and their henchmen, pretending to mourn the victims'.[14] They also heard Béla Szász speak on behalf of those victims.

Rajk's death 'looms like a warning symbol before the Hungarian people and the world', declared Szász. When thousands passed before these coffins, it was 'not only to pay the victims the last honours'. It also showed 'their irrevocable resolution to bury an epoch; to bury, for ever, lawlessness, tyranny, the Hungarian disciples of iron-fisted rule: the moral dead of the shameful years'.[15]

Amongst the mourners was the vacillating Imre Nagy, flawed martyr of the Hungarian Revolution.[16] Also present, by invitation, was Noel Field, who would prove to be an abject apologist for its suppression.

Bedridden bystander

On 15 October 1956 Noel, his stomach again bleeding, returned to the HCP hospital in Kútvölgyi út, where he would remain until 4 December.[17] When the Hungarian Revolution broke out on Tuesday 23 October, Noel was ill and bed-ridden. He was also in Buda which, despite the fighting in Széna Tér, was not the scene of the main events. These took place primarily in the 8th and 9th districts of the capital on the Pest side of the Danube.

As he related later Noel received 'reports' from Herta, who was presumably staying in Meredek utca, and had to negotiate several steep streets to visit Noel in hospital. But Herta was hardly informed of the big picture, or unbiased in what she saw.

She observed the initial student-organised march to the Bem statue on 23 October,[18] its ranks soon swollen by hundreds of young workers. Later she glowered disapprovingly as red flags were torn down, Marxist-Leninist literature was burnt in the streets, and the hated Rákosi emblem was ripped from Hungarian tricolours. All these happenings are well-documented in both books and photographs.

Other than this, Herta, whose knowledge of Hungarian was then far inferior to Noel's, simply discussed events with a few equally-ignorant acquaintances. Her 'reports' consisted of little more than tittle-tattle from uncomprehending fellow-Stalinists.

The Revolution was an atavistic explosion of wrath by the Hungarian people against a detested regime and its Soviet backers. It was unplanned, it had no central leadership, and most revolutionaries were hardly seeking to 'restore capitalism'. They were primarily young workers, who were mostly members of the HCP or its youth wing.

There were no CIA agents operating in Hungary at that time. If there were former 'Horthyite' officers amongst the fighters, they were there solely as uninfluential individuals, not leaders. The Americans had no intention of intervening militarily. The 'rollback' doctrine of Secretary of State John Foster Dulles, as applied to Eastern Europe, was not a policy but purely hot air, with no military dimension save nuclear war. The Eisenhower administration was too busy with the presidential election to seriously involve itself in Hungary. Its main foreign policy activity at the time was designed to halt and roll back the ill-conceived Anglo-French Suez adventure.[19]

The second and decisive Soviet military intervention in Hungary peaked on Sunday 4 November, and from this date armed resistance by the 'freedom fighters' crumbled. For Noel though, the 4 November was the day that 'socialism' was 'saved' in Hungary. It was the occasion when 'the days of counter-revolutionary terror are coming to an end'.[20]

In his articles Noel repeated most of what was to be the standard propaganda fare of the pariah Kádár regime in the following years.[21] He wrote of 'Horthyites' leading the 'counter-revolution' and summoned out of thin air some emblematic 'White Guards'. He contended that the 'counter-revolution' was prepared in advance, without ever being able to name one individual who was involved in such detailed planning.

Then there was the 'White Terror', which allegedly involved a pre-planned indiscriminate murder of communists.[22] Here Noel, like the Kádár regime and the Soviet leadership, could make reference to reports and pictures of the bloodiest action taken against the ÁVH.

On 30 October a fire-fight between 'freedom fighters' and ÁVH defenders erupted at the headquarters of the Greater Budapest branch of the HCP at 26 Köztársaság Tér (Republic Square). After killing numerous attackers, as well as civilians in food queues, the ÁVH surrendered. Those emerging from the building were gunned down and some bodies were disgustingly mutilated. These events were captured on film by Western photographers and published.

The pictures are ugly, as lynchings always are, but equally repellent are massacres of unarmed civilians, such as occurred in front of Parliament on 25 October and in the small West Hungarian town of Mosonmagyaróvár the following day. Dead women and children predominate in these photographs.[23]

Possibly Noel knew nothing of the slaughter of unarmed civilians, despite Herta's 'reports'. However, there is no doubt where his sympathies lay.[24] He had none for the revolutionaries, nor for the elected workers' councils which tried to preserve some of the gains of the revolution once the fighting ceased. How he reacted to Kádár's murderous revenge on those who had taken up arms is unknown.[25]

Yet he still abhorred the use of force. This was made clear when Endre Márton and his wife, Ilona, became the only journalists ever to talk to the Fields at length.[26]

'A true believer'[27]

Attractive, intelligent, sophisticated and courageous, the Mártons were non-religious Jews who raised their daughters as Catholics, concealing from them their Jewish ancestry. Both Endre and Ilona had earned doctorates. They had survived the Arrow Cross killings in Budapest in 1944–45. Later, both worked for American press agencies, and Endre attended both the Mindszenty and Rajk trials. There was no doubting their pro-Western sympathies, and it remains a mystery why Rákosi left them at liberty until 1955.

Arrested on 25 February Endre was taken to the Fő utca prison. At one point he was in Noel's old cell, and he too was interrogated by Major Kretschmer.[28] Ilona was arrested on 23 June. In November the Mártons were tried for treason and espionage. Endre was sentenced to thirteen years and Ilona to six. Seemingly to ease Hungarian-American relations, Ilona was freed in April 1956 and Endre in August. Both operated as reporters not only throughout the Revolution, but after the Soviet crackdown too.[29]

It was on 28 December 1956 on a cold snowy night that the Mártons drove up to the Fields' house, since learning their address was then no problem. The Fields' Hungarian maid led them into 'a comfortably heated living room on the ground floor'.

Both Noel and Herta wore dark-blue overalls. Endre viewed Noel as ageing and tired, a 'gaunt intellectual with thin white hair over the dome of his delicately shaped head'. As for Herta, Márton was one of those who thought that she was 'by far the stronger character of the two, a domineering personality and a clever woman whom neither the years nor prison could break'.[30]

'Speaking in low tones for about an hour, always calm and self-composed, Noel did not conceal his real sentiments'. He repeated his view that Kádár had 'saved this country from white terror'. Despite his imprisonment 'he was and remained a Communist'. He 'accepted the Marxist doctrine but not the necessity of violence'.

Field impressed Márton as 'a cultured, refined man, and an inveterate daydreamer'. However, his interlocutor 'did not want to play an active role in life any more'. He was content with 'his relatively carefree life, his modest job with no politics involved, and with his comfortable house'.[31]

This was probably an accurate assessment. However, Field's life did still involve some politics, and Noel the apologist would be wheeled out on two further occasions.

In June 1957 Radio Budapest broadcast a brief statement written by Field. In it he denounced the UN report on Hungary as 'slanderous falsehoods interspersed at best with misleading half-truths'. Having covered all bases, he defended Hungary's right to refuse to admit a UN investigating commission.

'Neither four hundred nor four thousand pages of dubious testimony by a hundred or ten times that number of defectors'[32] could 'hamper the forward march' of Hungary and other 'socialist' states along 'the high-road toward Communism, which all other nations will ultimately follow in their own manner and in their own good time'.[33]

Noel probably penned this quasi-mystical bunkum unaided. Only 'an inveterate daydreamer' could believe that in the wake of the brutal crackdown in Hungary, other nations would follow 'the highroad toward Communism'. Rather, most recoiled yet further from treading the downhill path towards scarcity and repression, which the Hungarian Revolution had so starkly exposed as the system's dominant features.

Field's second venture into propagandising his dream-world was the article he wrote in summer 1960, which was published in the CPUSA monthly *Mainstream* in January 1961. Noel entitled it 'Hitching our Wagon to a Star', and he made it clear that the star was red.

There were perhaps two reasons for Field to break his tradition of privacy. First, in September 1959 he was invited to do so by the journal's editor. He informed Noel that if he couldn't present his life 'in narrative fashion', he might 'write it as a kind of intellectual biography'. This could show 'what it is that might make a man of principle remain stead-fast despite the most severe strains brought to bear on his belief and his mental resources'.[34]

The second reason for writing the article was to present his own por-trayal of his life before the American journalist Flora Lewis published her biography of him. He had learned from both Elsie and Jean Liebermann that Flora had begun collecting material about him from his relatives, acquaintances and friends. Of course, the person whom Flora most wanted to interview was Noel himself.

On 10 July 1960, 'a brilliant summer day', she took a taxi across the Danube to the Fields' villa in Meredek utca. She sent no word that she was coming, although she knew that Noel was at home. He had little option, having fractured his leg in twelve places while skiing in the Polish mountains in spring.

'The villa was on a steep hillside, with a long flight of steps leading up through a modest flower garden from the street. An iron fence with a locked gate guarded the approach to the steps'. Flora rang the bell and eventually a Hungarian maid appeared. Reaching through the gate the journalist handed over a card on which was printed solely her name.

When the maid reappeared it was to return the card. On its reverse Noel had written, 'Mrs. Gruson,[35] Sorry, it is my consistent practice, not to receive foreign journalists. N. H. Field. July 10, 1960'.

Flora then penned a note explaining that she hadn't come for a journalistic interview, but 'because of the obvious obligation to hear what he might wish to say', and because 'people once close to him' had told her to 'ask Noel about that point. It is up to him to say'.

When the maid returned again she bore a longer message from Field. 'If any friend or relative of mine wished me to talk to you, they would have informed me in writing. I have had previous experience with persons from the West making unsubstantiated claims, and I am afraid you will have to take "no" for an answer. Sincerely, Noel H. Field'. Defeated, Flora climbed back into the taxi 'and went away without ever talking to Noel or Herta Field'.[36]

Having seen off his putative biographer, Noel turned to writing his own version of his life. Seemingly he took up the invitation to present it 'as a kind of intellectual biography'.

The result was a highly stylised portrait of how 'a typical middle-class intellectual [...] could become the militant communist of later years'.[37] Most of the events in his hardly dull life are covered, some but fleetingly. Of course there are no references to his espionage activities. The Massings, Reiss and Krivitsky aren't mentioned, nor is his visit to Moscow in 1938. Instead there are some rather convoluted lines about the Fields' decision not to return to the USA.

Since Noel was comfortable with his relatively privileged world, and he knew which side his bread was buttered on, he made not the slightest effort to examine forensically the forces which consigned him to torture and imprisonment. Instead he pontificates about 'the regenerative power of essential health within the socialist body'.[38]

Then he once more promotes the idea of the 'wind of socialism realized and the wind of communism in the making' triumphing over 'the wind of capitalism, monopoly, imperialism'. Having stretched the credulity of his readers, he adds that to 'some perhaps this may sound like the idle fantasy of the denizens of an ivory tower'.[39]

Indeed it does. He wrote these pages during a period of naked power-politics, which comprised the most dangerous years of the Cold War. Field's dreamy article appeared in the midst of the 1958–63 Berlin Crisis. The Wall would be built through that city a few months later in August 1961. The Cuban Missile Crisis of October 1962 would follow.

By then the Fields had moved into a new house, taking up residence at 13 Péthenyi út in autumn 1961.[40] According to his brother, Noel had bought it with his 'American money'. Hermann and Kate visited them in 1964.[41] Noel was then working for the *New Hungarian Quarterly*.

Hermann did not learn much from Noel during this and other visits in 1966 and 1969. 'After his release, he would never talk to me about his years in prison', Hermann observed later. 'He dismissed the episode as a Stalinist aberration. He was a true believer'.[42]

The 'true believer' returned to fleeting prominence when Flora Lewis's biography of him was published in January 1965.[43] Field was one of the first to read it. He was not overly impressed.

Noel described it as 'a largely well-written, often exciting and sometimes moving book'. But after reading it 'in the capacity of its apparent hero', he was 'amazed to discover in it such a hodgepodge of truths, half-truths and untruths that it would be a well-nigh hopeless task to try to sift out fact from fiction'. He was convinced that the meaning of his life was 'expressed in the heading [...] Hitching our Wagon to a Star'.[44]

Noel died from cancer in Budapest on 12 September 1970, aged sixty-six. Herta lived for another decade, dying on 13 November 1980.[45] They are buried side-by-side in Buda's Farkasréti cemetery, sharing the ground with the composers Bartók and Kodály, who are among the Hungarian luminaries interred there. Present too are Rákosi's polluting ashes.

NOTES

1. 'AN OUTSIDER FROM THE BEGINNING': SWISS CHILDHOOD, 1904–22

1. Peter Bull generously supplied me with information from *Ancestry* records, both in answer to my specific questions and from his independent researches. This information, which is used here and in subsequent chapters, relates primarily to: US and UK censuses; US passport applications; disembarkations in the USA; and UK births, marriages and deaths. I have also used data from copies of birth, marriage and death certificates supplied by the General Registry Office. Other than these sources and those specified in the notes this chapter is based upon information to be found in: B-R. Barth and W. Schweizer, eds, *Der Fall Noel Field, Band I: Gefängnisjahre 1949–1954*, Berlin, 2005, pp. 114, 158–60, 160 n48, 220, 260, 266–68, 272, 276–79, 284, 289, 664–65, 665 n3, 826, 837–38, 896; B-R. Barth and W. Schweizer, eds, *Der Fall Noel Field, Band II: Asyl in Ungarn 1954–1957*, Berlin, 2007, pp. 190–91; H. Field and K. Field, *Trapped in the Cold War: The Ordeal of an American Family*, Stanford, 1999, pp. 185, 298, 329; F. Lewis, *The Man who Disappeared: The Strange History of Noel Field*, London, 1965, pp. 21–27. All translations from German and French are by the author.
2. 'Sunnyside' is given as Hermann Eschwege's residence in the 1881, 1891 and 1901 British censuses. In 1871 he was living at 27 Wood Vale, a somewhat smaller house situated a few streets to the west of Mayow Road. 'Sunnyside' has since been replaced by modern housing.
3. Barth and Schweizer, eds, *Der Fall Noel Field, Band I*, p. 158. Whilst imprisoned in Hungary Noel wrote an extensive report upon his family in February or March 1950. Unfortunately this is not to be found in the twelve volume investigative dossier on Noel and Herta Field. Ibid., p. 159 n43. Dr Barth's work frequently notes that most material relating to the 'production' of the Rajk trial was destroyed on the orders of the HCP leadership in 1959 and 1962. See also I. Rév's account, *Indicting Rajk*, http://ccat.sas.upenn.edu/slavic/events/slavic_symposium/Comrades_Please_Shoot_Me/Rev_Rajk.pdf, last accessed 26 May 2013.
4. Elizabeth Foot's Irish parents were James Foot born in 1795 and Letitia Foot born in 1806. Elizabeth was born in London on 28 November 1843 and died on 24 November 1916, leaving an estate worth just over £690, which represents perhaps £50,000 in current values.
5. Flora Lewis writes that when the British exhibited 'outbursts of hysterical hatred for all things German during World War I, Nina's family exchanged its German name for that of her grandmother, and she became Nina Foote Field'. Lewis, *The Man who Disappeared*, p. 22. This is wrong on several counts. The name is spelt Foot, never Foote. In 1914 Nina had been Nina Sefton Field for ten years and was living in Zurich, a German-speaking city in a neutral country. Moreover,

she applied for her passport in 1919 simply as Nina Field. However, her younger brother Fritz Salo Eschwege (1882–1930) did change his name to Thomas James Foot, presumably in order to serve as a doctor with the Royal Army Medical Corps on the Salonika front in 1918. Information from Peter Bull. This explains why Hermann's will lists him as his son under that name. In the will Thomas (Fritz) and his three married sisters, specified as Kathleen Round, Ida Marcial and Nina Sefton Field, each receive the interest on a fourth share of Hermann's residuary estate, which was held in trust. The trustees and executors were the Public Trustee and Noel's father Herbert. Copy of Hermann Eschwege's will supplied by Leeds Probate Registry.

6. On the marriage certificate Herbert specified his residence as Great Neck, Nassau County, New York State, despite the fact that he was running a scientific institute in Switzerland. Presumably as an American citizen he was expected to have an address in the USA. According to Great Neck library's local history blog, Herbert's parents had a large waterfront estate named 'Ardsley' in Great Neck. This source also states that the founder of the American Field family was one Robert Field, who left York for Massachusetts in 1630.

7. In 1918 an American diplomat in Switzerland recalled Herbert as 'a Quaker, a burly man, with bushy gray hair and beard, heavy gray eyebrows, behind which lay the gentlest, bluest, most candid pair of eyes that I ever saw on an adult man. They were the eyes of an unsophisticated and lovable child'. Cited in R. Smith, *OSS: The Secret History of America's First Central Intelligence Agency*, New York, 1973, p. 205.

8. The sixth report of the secretary of Harvard's 'Class of 1888', April 1909. (www.archive.org/.../ n6secretarysreport1888harvuoft/n6secretarysreport1888harvuoft_djvu) Reports by the ÁVH, the Hungarian secret police, mention that Herbert was also a lecturer at the University of Zurich. Barth and Schweizer, eds, *Der Fall Noel Field, Band I*, p. 114, p. 220. Presumably this detail came from Noel's initial interrogations in 1949, the records of which are long-destroyed.

9. Noel mentions occasional summer holidays with the Eschweges.

10. Ibid., p. 158.

11. Noel's sister Elsie became a doctor and had to will herself for years before she could carry out operations. Ibid., p. 266.

12. Ibid., p. 160.

13. Ibid., 267.

14. Hermann Field claimed that the family spent the years 1915–1917 in Lugano, but seems to be a year out. He is not good with dates. He also asserts incorrectly that Herta came to the USA in 1923. Ibid., p. 114 n7. She arrived in 1922.

15. Hermann writes that after Lugano they moved to the village of Oberengstringen, north-west of Zurich. Herta says that the Fields moved to Höngg, which is also north-west of that city.

16. Ibid., p. 279.

17. Field and Field, *Trapped in the Cold War*, pp. 80–81; A. Schlesinger, *A Life in the Twentieth Century: Innocent Beginnings, 1917–1950*. Boston/New York 2000, p. 502.

18. A brief account, utilising Herbert's papers in the Hoover Institute, is in R. Service, *Comrades. Communism: a World History*, London, 2008, pp. 90–92.

19. In his passport application of 5 November 1919, Herbert wrote that he was 'obliged to go to England on repeated occasions to confer in the execution of this Trust'.

20. There is a short obituary of Herbert in the New York Times of 7 April 1921. Several details are incorrect. The possibility of an earlier heart-attack is in Lewis, *The Man who Disappeared*, pp. 25–26.

21. Barth and Schweizer, eds, *Der Fall Noel Field, Band I*, p. 267.

22. 'They had an uncle in Cambridge, Massachusetts, who had always been like a second father to the children, although they had not seen him often'. Lewis, *The Man who Disappeared*, p. 26. I have chosen Herbert's step-brother, Henry C. Field, as the uncle through a process of elimi-

nation. Herbert's natural bother, Hamilton Easter Field, died of pneumonia some time in 1922. Herbert's other step-brother Edward S. Field seemed to have little reason to be in Cambridge. In 1920 he and his wife were living in the old Field home at 104 Columbia Heights. The census described him as a wholesale merchant of cotton goods, while his wife kept a boarding-house.

2. NEW WORLD: HARVARD, SOCIAL WORK AND PACIFISM, 1922–26

1. This chapter is based upon information in: B-R. Barth and W. Schweizer, eds, *Der Fall Noel Field, Band I: Gefängnisjahre 1949–1954*, Berlin, 2005, pp. 114 n7, 116, 260, 269–73, 280–86, 292–93, 665, 665 n3, 896; F. Lewis, *The Man who Disappeared: The Strange History of Noel Field*, London, 1965, pp. 27–32.
2. F. Lewis, *The Man who Disappeared*, p. 27.
3. B-R. Barth and W. Schweizer, eds, *Der Fall Noel Field, Band I*, p. 277.
4. At some time in 1924, between leaving Harvard, travelling to Europe and pursuing his social work course, Noel served as secretary to a wealthy businessman, who indulged in peace propaganda as a sideline. For some reason their relationship did not pan out and after a month Noel was dismissed, albeit with his salary of $100 for the period paid in full. Ibid., p. 270.
5. Noel has Herta working as a schoolmistress (*Erzieherin*) rather than a nursemaid. This seems most unlikely, given her qualifications, age and status.
6. Like Nina, Herta called Noel 'Laddie'. E. Anderson, *Love in Exile: An American Writer's Memoir of Life in Divided Berlin*, South Royalton (Vt.), 1999, p. 194.
7. The reference to advice by Noel's uncle is in Barth and Schweizer, eds, *Der Fall Noel Field, Band I*, p. 665. In note 6 on this page, Barth incorrectly identifies this uncle as the painter Hamilton Easter Field, whom he refers to as Herbert's step-brother. Not only was Hamilton the natural brother of Herbert, but he was dead by this time. The uncle involved was indeed a step-brother and most probably Henry C. Field. See Chapter 1, footnote 22. Herta too thought that Hamilton Easter Field was Herbert's step-brother. Ibid., p. 826.
8. Lewis, *The Man who Disappeared*, p. 32.
9. Barth and Schweizer, eds, *Der Fall Noel Field, Band I*, pp. 285–86. 'The oral interview before a panel of Foreign Service officers was really all that mattered. Style, grace, poise, and, above all, birth were the key to success. The standards were similar to those of a fashionable Washington club: "Is he our kind of person?"' Anyone who obviously was not would not pass. But if 'a black slipped through the net, he was sent to Liberia until he resigned. Women were sent to the jungles of South America. Jews could not be handled as crassly, but they were made to feel unwelcome and shut out of the better assignments'. M. Weil, *A Pretty Good Club: The Founding Fathers of the U.S. Foreign Service*, New York, 1978, p. 47.
10. All quotations in Lewis, *The Man who Disappeared*, p. 31. Since Ms Lewis rarely cited anybody's words directly and provided no footnotes in her biography of Field, I have assumed that these quotations were genuine and were given to her by sources in the State Department.

3. 'PERFECT BUREAUCRAT': STATE DEPARTMENT YEARS, 1926–34

1. This chapter is based upon information in: B-R. Barth and W. Schweizer, eds, *Der Fall Noel Field, Band I: Gefängnisjahre 1949–1954*, Berlin, 2005, pp. 161–62, 260, 271–73, 286–89, 292 n3, 293 n4, 298 n13, 292–302, 665–72, 896–99; F. Lewis, *The Man who Disappeared: The Strange History of Noel Field*, London, 1965, pp. 33–50.
2. M. Weil, *A Pretty Good Club: The Founding Fathers of the U.S. Foreign Service*, New York, 1978, p. 47.

3. According to Noel the other successful entrants were almost all from wealthy backgrounds. Among their number was George Kennan. B-R. Barth and W. Schweizer, eds, *Der Fall Noel Field, Band I*, p. 286 n16. For Kennan's own experiences as an entrant, see J. Gaddis, *George F. Kennan: An American Life*, New York 2011, pp. 39–41.

4. Lewis, *The Man who Disappeared*, London, 1965, p. 35.

5. Flora Lewis stated incorrectly that Noel was not part of the American delegation. Ibid., p. 40.

6. For Noel's meeting with President Roosevelt in 1935, see Ibid., p. 76.

7. Cited in Barth and Schweizer, eds, *Der Fall Noel Field, Band I*, p. 303 n39 (Original English text).

8. Ibid., p. 304.

9. Lewis, *The Man who Disappeared*, p. 35.

10. I don't know when this pre-conference took place. Field gives it but a passing mention. Barth and Schweizer, eds, *Der Fall Noel Field, Band I*, p. 298. The records show Noel sailing from Le Havre on the *Leviathan* and arriving back in New York on 6 August 1934.

11. Following a brief and unhappy marriage Traudi had recently divorced her husband, Andrew Bakonyi. She had custody of their daughter Ancy, who was born in Washington DC on 2 January 1932.

12. Barth and Schweizer, eds, *Der Fall Noel Field, Band I*, p. 300.

13. Lewis, *The Man who Disappeared*, p. 33.

14. N. Field, 'Hitching our Wagon to a Star', *Mainstream*, Vol. 14, January 1961, p. 6.

15. The CPUSA and the Comintern were involved in the orchestrated campaign to save the anarchists' lives through the International Labour Defense organisation. Not that acquittal was the objective. 'What earthly good would they do us alive?' asked one ILD leader. The function of the campaign was education and recruitment. S. Koch, *Double Lives: Stalin, Willi Münzenberg and the Seduction of Intellectuals*, London, 1995, p. 35.

16. Field, 'Hitching our Wagon to a Star', p. 6.

17. In March 1954 Noel described himself as a communist sympathiser since around 1925, an active non-party communist since about 1931–32, and a member of the CPUSA since 1936. He noted that his formal entry into the CPUSA was in fact into the American section of the ECCI. Effected in Moscow in 1938, it was made retrospective by two years, and confirmed early in 1943, Barth and Schweizer, eds, *Der Fall Noel Field, Band I*, pp. 146–47. The idea that he was a CPUSA member proved to be wishful thinking on Noel's part, as we shall see.

18. Field, 'Hitching our Wagon to a Star', p. 4.

19. Lewis, *The Man who Disappeared*, p. 67.

20. In one of his prison statements in 1954 Noel refers to his diaries of that time. Barth and Schweizer, eds, *Der Fall Noel Field, Band I*, p. 162. His use of the present tense implies that they were still in existence at the time of his kidnap in May 1949. There is no indication as to what might have happened to them.

4. I SPY: THE MASSINGS AND THE FIELDS, 1934–36

1. For Hede Massing's life from 1900 to early 1934, see H. Massing, *This Deception*, New York, 1951, pp. 3–160 *passim*. The later German version (see H. Massing, *Die grosse Täuschung: Geschichte einer Sowjetagentin*, Freiburg, 1967) is largely an exact translation of her original work. However, there are certain minor excisions and additions in it to which I shall make reference when appropriate. Dr Barth's short biographies of Hede and Paul Massing are in B-R. Barth and W. Schweizer, eds, *Der Fall Noel Field, Band II: Asyl in Ungarn 1954–1957*, Berlin, 2007, pp. 426–27. J. Kisselhoff, 'Hede Massing's Story', on his website 'The Alger Hiss Story'. https://files.nyu.edu/th15/public/hedemassingstory.html, last accessed 26 May 2013, is an important source. Under a Freedom of Information Act request he obtained the FBI and INS files on both Hede

and Paul and blended extracts into his article. It is not paginated, so I can only refer to it as a whole. On Gerhart Eisler, see R. Friedmann, *Ulbrichts Rundfunkmann: eine Gerhart-Eisler-Biographie*, Berlin, 2007; C. Epstein, *The Last Revolutionaries: German Communists and their Century*, London, 2003.

2. R. Lamphere and T. Shachtman, *The FBI-KGB War*, London, 1987, pp. 50–51. After reading Hede's autobiography, Lamphere had 'the uneasy feeling that I had actually written it'. A colleague explained that he was not far off the mark, because Hede had obtained from the FBI a copy of Lamphere's interviews with her, and used 'that as a basis of her autobiography'. Ibid., p. 302 n. This document, 'Personal History of Hede Massing', was supplied by the FBI to Hede, with some source data redacted, in 1950. A second document, 'Reiss, Ignace. French and Swiss Police Documents Regarding the Investigation of his Murder', was given to her by the CIA, for whom she later worked as a researcher. See W. Duff, *A Time for Spies: Theodore Stephanovich Mally and the Era of the Great Illegals*, London, 1999, p. 197 n10. Together they constitute the Hede Massing Papers in the Hoover Institution Archives in California. They are cited in the works of Barth and Duff.

3. Hede's date of birth, 6 January 1900, is one of the few indisputable facts about her life, Massing, *This Deception*, p. 3. The German version simply states that she was now 'over fifty', whereas she was then sixty-seven. Massing, *Die grosse Täuschung*, p. 9.

4. Hede does write elsewhere 'although I come from Vienna'. Massing, *This Deception*, p. 59.

5. When they arrived in the USA in November 1904 Rosa's age was registered as twenty-nine and that of Hedwig/Hede as about four. Both were described as 'Austrian-Hebrew' and their last place of residence was given as Jezierna. Hede spells it Jescerna. Ibid., p. 7. These immigration records give us the names of Hede's parents. Her autobiography betrays her loathing of them both, and she never mentions their names. She describes them as 'undoubtedly an extremely ill-assembled pair, and it was as unhappy as a marriage can be'. Ibid., p. 19. I have been unable to determine Rosa's maiden name.

6. Jezierna (now Ozerna in Western Ukraine) lies northwest of Ternopil' (Tarnopol in Polish) and is situated on the main railway line from L'viv (Lwów) to Ternopil'. In 1900 it had a Jewish population of about 1100, most of whom were murdered in the Holocaust. A train deported 200 of them to the Bełżec extermination camp on 29 August 1942. See Y. Arad, *Belzec, Sobibor, Treblinka: The Operation Reinhard Death Camps*, Bloomington/Indianapolis, 1999, p. 386. According to Hede, Rosa Tune was another victim, transported from Vienna to Auschwitz. Massing, *This Deception*, p. 9. However, we can't be sure of either of these details. Rosa may have been taken from Jezierna, while Viennese Jews were transported to and murdered in other places than Auschwitz.

7. The surname Tune was supposedly French. Philip (perhaps Filip in Polish) was the son of a peasant woman, who allegedly had some sixteen children by four different partners. Ibid., p. 19. Whether he too was Jewish is unclear. A tall, red-haired and attractive philanderer, Philip left Rosa and his three children shortly before the end of The First World War. His subsequent fate is unknown. Hede's siblings were Walter, born in 1907, and Elli who was born in Vienna on 15 November 1908.

8. Ibid., p. 14. I have yet to see a photo of Hede aged under fifty.

9. Ibid. pp. 26, 30. Hede was an aficionado of eyes.

10. Eisler's biographer has finally settled the matter of whether Hede and Eisler were ever actually married, citing as his definitive source *Magistrat Wien, Heiratsurkunde* 10068/1921. See Friedmann, *Ulbrichts Rundfunkmann*, p. 54, p. 55 n14.

11. Kisselhoff, 'Hede Massing's Story'. The possibility exists that they never formally divorced and that both later contracted bigamous marriages.

12. Friedmann, *Ulbrichts Rundfunkmann* p. 54. Gerhart certainly kept things in the family. In

Vienna on 15 July 1931 he wed Hede's sister, Elli. He'd been living with her, with Hede's blessing, since she was a teenager. Their daughter Anna was born in Moscow on 2 November 1931. Ibid., pp. 106, 160.

13. According to Barth, Hede and Julian were married in the USA in summer 1927, and Hede thereby obtained American citizenship. Barth and Schweizer, eds, *Der Fall Noel Field, Band II*, p. 426. However, on arrival in New York in August 1926, although on the aliens' list, Hede gave her surname as Gumperz, described herself as married and gave her occupation as housewife. Her passports show that her naturalisation was granted by the Supreme Court of White Plains, New York, on 10 January 1927.

14. Massing, *This Deception*, pp. 34–35.

15. On Willi Münzenberg and his activities, see S. McMeekin, *The Red Millionaire: A Political Biography of Willy Münzenberg, Moscow's Secret Propaganda Tsar in the West*, New Haven, CT, 2003; S. Koch, *Double Lives: Stalin, Willi Münzenberg and the Seduction of Intellectuals*. London 1995; J. Palmier, *Weimar in Exile: The Antifascist Emigration in Europe and America*, London, 2006.

16. Oranienberg was the location of and precursor to the KZ (concentration camp) Sachsenhausen complex.

17. Massing, *This Deception*, p. 128.

18. Did Hede, a striking woman, a Jewish communist who was quite possibly on a Gestapo list, and a Soviet agent to boot, really travel to Nazi Germany just to stand mutely outside the barbed wire of Oranienberg? And why, just to pick up Paul's passport?

19. On Mally, whose real name was Tivadar Mály, see Duff, *A Time for Spies*; N. West and O. Tsarev, *The Crown Jewels: The British Secrets Exposed by the KGB Archives*, London, 1998.

20. Massing, *This Deception*, p. 141.

21. On arrival in New York Hede gave the address where she would be staying as c/o Mrs Brucker, 121 Madison Ave/W 30th Street. The actual name of the lady was Becki Drucker, and she had a different function. 'She was my mail drop–it was important that my mail come in care of an inconspicuous person'. Ibid., pp. 146–47.

22. Ibid., p. 149. For her vitriolic pen-portrait of Markin, see Ibid., pp. 154–59. Against this, see Dr Chervonnaya's biography of him on her website Documentstalk.com.

23. Hede says that she usually delivered the microfilm to a stranger who announced himself from her hotel lobby. Massing, *This Deception*, p. 160.

24. Barth and Schweizer, eds, *Der Fall Noel Field, Band I: Gefängnisjahre 1949–1954*, Berlin, 2005, pp. 162 n52, 162–64, 261, 386–92, 396, 749–51; H. Massing, *This Deception*, pp. 165–72.

25. Ibid., p. 165. Marguerite Young contested this version, telling the FBI in February 1949 that it was not Noel who asked to meet Hede. Rather, Hede approached Marguerite about getting a visa for her husband, and asked if she knew anyone in the State Department who could help. Ms Young recommended Field and Larry Duggan and subsequently introduced Hede to both men. See Kisselhoff, 'Hede Massing's Story'. Noel writes that he met the Massings through Marguerite and her husband, although elsewhere he states that he met Hede through two other journalists. See B-R. Barth and W. Schweizer, eds, *Der Fall Noel Field, Band I*, p. 388, p. 749. The Young connection seems more convincing.

26. Massing, *This Deception*, pp. 165–66.

27. This was a retrospective view of their past friendship. In 1954 Noel's belief was that the Massings had betrayed him when he was USC director, and that this had led to his dismissal, and indirectly to his incarceration. As 'traitors' they were now his mortal enemies. In fact the Massings were in no way to blame for Field's dismissal from the USC. See Barth and Schweizer, eds, *Der Fall Noel Field, Band I*, pp. 3–5.

28. Massing, *This Deception*, p. 167.

29. Ibid.

30. Ibid., p. 153; Barth and Schweizer, eds, *Der Fall Noel Field, Band I*, p. 388 n24. Paul's book

was written under the pseudonym Karl Billinger, and published under various titles in 1935 in the USA, Britain and France. Later translations were produced in Denmark, Norway and Poland. Ibid., p. 389 n31. There was also a Russian edition. Hede and Paul spent the 'enormous amount of money' he received for his book in the USSR, when financing their stay in Moscow in 1937–38. Massing, *This Deception*, p. 261.

31. Ibid., p. 167.
32. Ibid., pp. 168, 171.
33. Ibid., p. 168.
34. Noel claims that his 'development' was also retarded by the Massings' foolish endeavour to make him more amenable through the 'gift' of a car, which he simply saw as a bribe. Barth and Schweizer, eds, *Der Fall Noel Field, Band I*, p. 163, p. 392. Hede implies that this offer was the fault of her new boss Izkhak Akhmerov. Massing, *This Deception*, p. 166.
35. For the differing times in 1935 when Noel claims to have begun to 'work' for the Soviets, see Barth and Schweizer, eds, *Der Fall Noel Field, Band I*, p. 164, p. 392, p. 750.
36. Ibid., p. 751.
37. Noel certainly had an elastic attitude to patriotism. He would claim that his talent for languages laid the basis for his 'internationalism' (positive), as well as inducing a certain 'cosmopolitanism' (negative). He contended too that his time spent living in a foreign land (Switzerland), together with his father's pacifism, not only hindered any nationalist development in him, but also promoted a certain lack of patriotism (*Vaterlandlosigkeit*). Ibid., p. 277. However, this did not mean that he had no love for his country, only that such was weakly ingrained in him. Ibid., p. 290.
38. Ibid., pp. 163–64, p. 392.
39. According to Hede, the FBI later tallied her trips to the USA as 'about twenty'. Massing, *This Deception*, p. 57. This may mean ten round-trips. My own tally is nine round-trips, including certain voyages that are not recorded in Hede's autobiography.
40. Barth states that Hede and Paul married in New York in 1936. Barth and Schweizer, eds, *Der Fall Noel Field, Band II*, p. 426. However, Paul was not in the USA between March 1935 and January 1937. Hede registered herself as divorced (from Gumperz) on arrival in New York in October 1933, and married when disembarking in January and September 1934, although still using the name Gumperz. Thereafter Hede always registered herself as married. In January 1934 Paul described himself as single, but as married when he returned to the USA in January 1937. In short, I don't know when or where they married, although 1934 or early 1935 in the USA appears to be the likeliest time.
41. For the various options, see G. Kern, *A Death in Washington: Walter G. Krivitsky and the Stalin Terror*, New York, 2004, pp. 30–33.
42. Hede's portrait of Akhmerov can be found in Massing, *This Deception*, pp. 163–64, p. 185, p. 224. Much of this is belied by his looks in photographs and by his career in espionage, which is outlined in Weinstein and Vassiliev, *The Haunted Wood*. See also Dr Chervonnaya's biography of him on her website.
43. Barth and Schweizer, eds, *Der Fall Noel Field, Band I*, pp. 162, 261, 290, 292–93, 298, 303–04, 394–95, 669, 751–53, 873, 900–01.
44. Massing, *This Deception*, p. 172; Barth and Schweizer, eds, *Der Fall Noel Field, Band I*, p. 395.
45. Anyone wondering why such nocturnal habits were tolerated by the State Department, should recall that the Foreign Office and the British intelligence services indulged equally 'eccentric' behaviour by the 'Cambridge five'.
46. Barth and Schweizer, eds, *Der Fall Noel Field, Band I*, p. 901. Herta expresses no surprise about Alger's alleged espionage, nor seeks to defend him from such charges. For the so-called 'pumpkin papers', see A. Weinstein, *Perjury: The Hiss-Chambers Case*. New York 1997; S. Tanenhaus, *Whittaker Chambers: A Biography*, New York, 1997.

47. Massing, *This Deception*, p. 166.

48. It seems that Noel thought at one time in terms of a temporary transfer to Geneva. But he was told that in order to go to the League he would have to resign from the State Department. F. Lewis, *The Man who Disappeared: The Strange History of Noel Field*, London, 1965, p. 83.

49. The offer of the German 'desk' is outlined in Ibid. pp. 83–85. However, the fact that the matter was never touched upon in the nearly thirty interrogations that Noel underwent in 1954 suggests to me that no such offer was made.

50. The 'atomic spy' Klaus Fuchs used his 'Marxist philosophy to establish in my mind two separate compartments'. One was for personal relations and the other was for his life as a spy. In his confession Fuchs described it aptly as 'controlled schizophrenia'. R. Williams, *Klaus Fuchs: Atom Spy*, London, 1987, p. 184.

51. See Barth and Schweizer, eds, *Der Fall Noel Field, Band I*, p. 394, 753; Massing, *This Deception*, p. 176.

5. 'WORKING FOR THE SAME BOSS': HISS, HEDE AND NOEL, 1935–36

1. For the organisation of Soviet state security and foreign intelligence, see C. Andrew and O. Gordievsky, *KGB: The Inside Story of its Foreign Operations from Lenin to Gorbachev*, London, 1990; J. Costello and O. Tsarev, *Deadly Illusions*, London, 1993; W. Duff, *A Time for Spies: Theodore Stephanovich Mally and the Era of the Great Illegals*, London, 1999; J. Dziak, *Chekisty: A History of the KGB*, Lexington (Mass.), 1988; G. Kern, *A Death in Washington: Walter, G. Krivitsky and the Stalin Terror*, New York, 2004; D. Rayfield, *Stalin and his Hangmen*, London, 2005. The Russian-language titles of the organisations referred to in this section can be found in these works.

2. Cheka = All-Russian Extraordinary Commission to Combat Counter-Revolution, Sabotage and Speculation; GPU/OGPU = State Political Directorate/Unified State Political Directorate. The term 'Chekist' to describe an official of the secret police remained in use long after the Cheka itself was superseded.

3. In 1941 INO (the Foreign Department) was upgraded to INU (the Foreign Directorate) and retained this title until 1954.

4. There were many names and acronyms for Soviet military intelligence prior to 1942 when GRU came into circulation. See the entry for GRU in the glossary in Documentstalk.com. For convenience I have used GRU throughout.

5. My main sources for the early career of Alger Hiss are A. Weinstein, *Perjury: The Hiss-Chambers Case*, New York, 1997; G. White, *Alger Hiss's Looking-Glass Wars: The Covert Life of a Soviet Spy*, New York, 2004; A. Hiss, *Recollections of a Life*, New York 1988. On Whittaker Chambers, see additionally W. Chambers, *Witness*, London, 1953; S. Tanenhaus, *Whittaker Chambers: A Biography*, New York, 1997. The websites of Dr Chervonnaya, Documentstalk.com, and Kisselhoff, 'The Alger Hiss Story' are replete with information on various aspects of the Hiss-Chambers affair.

6. Cited in Weinstein, *Perjury*, p. 65n.

7. Cited in White, *Alger Hiss's Looking-Glass Wars*, p. 7. Like Noel, Hiss travelled to Europe in summer 1924. Unlike Noel, he travelled third-class.

8. Cited in Weinstein, *Perjury*, p. 67.

9. Ibid., p. 68.

10. Cited in White, *Alger Hiss's Looking-Glass Wars*, p. 13. Tony was born in 1941.

11. Hiss, *Recollections of a Life*, p. 54.

12. This section is based primarily on: B-R. Barth and W. Schweizer, eds, *Der Fall Noel Field, Band I: Gefängnisjahre 1949–1954*, Berlin, 2005, pp. 392–93, 753, 774–76; H. Massing, *This Decep-*

tion, New York, 1951, pp. 172–79; A. Vassiliev, *Yellow Notebook 2*, Wilson Center Cold War International History Project Digital Archive, http://www.wilsoncenter.org/sites/default/files/Yellow_Notebook_No. 2_Original.pdf, last accessed 26 May 2013, pp. 4–6.

13. Barth and Schweizer, eds, *Der Fall Noel Field, Band I*, p. 395, p. 753.

14. See J. Kisselhoff, 'Hede Massing's Story', on his website 'The Alger Hiss Story'. https://files.nyu.edu/th15/public/hedemassingstory.html; Chambers, *Witness*, p. 273.

15. This 'solution' still requires me to enter a number of caveats. See footnote 24. Readers must make up their own minds on how convincing they find the arguments overall.

16. Massing, *This Deception*, p. 166, p. 195.

17. Ibid., pp. 183–84. Born in 1893 in the Tsarist empire (in today's Belarus), Boris Yakovlevich Bazarov grew up in Vilnius (capital of today's Lithuania). His real name was Shpak. See Dr Chervonnaya's interesting and sympathetic biography of him in Documentstalk.com. Hede knew him as 'Fred', although she soon learned his first name. She describes him as 'a small man, shy, and soft-spoken, partly bald and crowding fifty, unassuming and of good education'. Massing, *This Deception*, p. 183.

18. Ibid., p. 173.

19. My account is based on those in A. Cooke, *A Generation on Trial: U.S.A. v. Alger Hiss*, London, 1951 pp. 291–92 and Massing, *This Deception*, pp. 174–75. The former is presumably what Hede said in the trial record. Her autobiographical account is more flowery and slightly expanded, but does not differ significantly. In fact, Hede used very similar phraseology to the FBI and Grand Jury in December 1948. Kisselhoff, 'Hede Massing's Story'. A cynic might say that the actress had learned her lines well.

20. Massing, *This Deception*, p. 178. The phrase 'that same day' (*noch am selben Tage*) is an addition to be found in H. Massing, *Die grosse Täuschung: Geschichte einer Sowjetagentin*, Freiburg, 1967, p. 172.

21. Vassiliev, *Yellow Notebook 2*, p. 5. This quotation comes from Moscow Centre to New York, 3 May 1936, and is a reminder about an earlier directive. Neither Bazarov's report on the Hede-Hiss meeting nor the original directive from Moscow appear in the Vassiliev notes.

22. Massing, *This Deception*, p. 179.

23. Ibid. Hiss received similar orders from his own superiors, but could have been left in little doubt about Hede's identity. See Akhmerov to Moscow 18 May 1936, in Vassiliev, *Yellow Notebook 2*, pp. 5–6.

24. Ibid., p. 5. Akhmerov's exact phrase regarding Noel's flat is: 'After meeting with "Redhead" and speaking with her in our 17's apartment, "J" no doubt informed his superiors about the meeting'. I have tried to avoid code-names and overmuch 'spook-speak' in the main text, but 'Redhead' (*Ryzhaya* in Russian) is Hede, Noel was then '17', and 'J' for 'Jurist' is the code-name that INO gave to Hiss; it is not his GRU code-name. At the time Hiss was employed in the Solicitor General's office in the Justice Department. For the record, Bazarov was 'Nord' and Akhmerov was 'Jung'. I promised caveats. Firstly, Akhmerov says that the meeting took place in 'winter'; but November is wintry in New York. Secondly, Bazarov informed Moscow on 26 April 1936 that 'more than a couple of months ago, Redhead and Hiss also got exposed to each other'. Ibid., p. 5. Obviously, this could imply that the Hede-Hiss confrontation in Noel's flat took place in early 1936. Then one can show that this was impossible because Noel was at the London naval conference or on the high seas from late November 1935 to 19 March 1936. In my opinion, Bazarov's woolly phrase 'more than a couple of months ago' is elastic enough to reach back to November 1935.

25. Text in Ibid., p. 4. Hede alludes to the 1935 meeting with the line, 'When A. (Alger), whom, as you probably recall, I met through E. (Field)'. E. stood for 'Ernst' which was Noel's new code-name.

26. He had given a full report to Paul Massing in Arosa.

27. When he was interrogated in Budapest prior to his release, Noel was forced to admit shame-facedly the number of times he had revealed his identity as a Soviet agent, and to name the persons involved. See Barth and Schweizer, eds, *Der Fall Noel Field, Band I*, pp. 774–76. His list did not include Duggan. I have used the word 'reveal' to translate the ugly German verb *dekonspieren*, which derives as a negative from the Russian word *konspiratsiya*. 'The word in Russian did not mean "conspiracy" or plotting as we know it, but, rather, the utmost secrecy or stealth in the avoidance of detection'. H. Rappaport, *Conspirator: Lenin in Exile*, London, 2010, p. 38.

28. Barth and Schweizer, eds, *Der Fall Noel Field, Band I*, p. 393. The meeting in Noel's apartment had already revealed Hede's status.

29. Ibid. Although he uses the word *sofort* (immediately, at once), Noel hardly reported to Hede immediately. Hede's note says that Hiss made his approach 'roughly a week before he (Field) left Washington', while Noel only told Hede about it on 'the day before he left for Europe'. Vassiliev, *Yellow Notebook 2*, p. 4. This suggests a guilt-ridden last minute admission.

30. Barth and Schweizer, eds, *Der Fall Noel Field, Band I*, p. 393, p. 753.

31. See Ibid., pp. 301, 390–91.

32. Vassiliev, *Yellow Notebook 2*, p. 18. 'Steady work' was an overstatement. See Dr Chervonnaya's biography of Duggan in Documentstalk.com.

33. Vassiliev, *Yellow Notebook 2*, p. 4.

34. Weinstein, *Perjury*, pp. 187–89.

35. Vassiliev, *Yellow Notebook 2*, p. 5.

6. MURDER AND DEFECTION: THE FIELDS, REISS AND KRIVITSKY, 1936–37

1. For the careers of Krivitsky and Reiss, see W. Duff, *A Time for Spies: Theodore Stephanovich Mally and the Era of the Great Illegals*, London, 1999; G. Kern, *A Death in Washington: Walter G. Krivitsky and the Stalin Terror*, New York, 2004; W. Krivitsky, *In Stalin's Secret Service*, New York, 2000; E. Poretsky, *Our Own People: A Memoir of 'Ignace Reiss' and his Friends*, London, 1969; their biographies on Documentstalk.com.

2. Before the First Partition of Poland in 1772 Jews had been excluded from the Russian Empire altogether. Once the former Polish territories were incorporated into the Tsarist realm, Jews were restricted to the so-called 'Pale of Settlement', consisting of twenty-five western and southern provinces of the empire. In today's terms this area covered the territories of Lithuania, Belarus, central Poland and eastern Ukraine, plus the province of Bessarabia (today divided between Moldova and Ukraine) and the Crimea. The status of Jews in Imperial Russia was defined solely by religion. Conversion to Christianity was sufficient to 'free' them from the restraints imposed upon Jews by the Tsarist regime, which became ever more onerous in the late nineteenth century. Restricted to the towns of the Pale, needing permits merely to travel in this vast area, suffering 'quotas' in education, limitations upon occupation, and ultimately the pogrom, hundreds of thousands of Jews left Russia for Western Europe and particularly the United States. P. Johnson, *A History of the Jews*, New York, 1988, pp. 358–65 gives an informative summary of conditions in the Pale.

3. 'Galician Jewry was basically of the East European type, lower middle class and proletarian, extremely conspicuous in local commerce [...] and in the cities, but still retaining a strong *shtetl* (small town) component. Jewish Orthodoxy was traditionally very strong [...] and Hasidism possessed in this region one of its greatest strongholds [...] Indeed it was from Galicia that adherents to Hasidism, with their black coats, white stockings, and long side curls (*peyes*), symbols of Jewish foreignness and peculiarity in the eyes of gentiles, spread to such neighboring regions as Bukovina, Moldavia, northern Transylvania, and Subcarpathian Rus'. E. Mendelsohn, *The Jews of East Central Europe between the World Wars*, Bloomington, Indiana, 1983, p. 18. The Habsburg

province of Bukovina is now divided between Romania and Ukraine. Hungarian-ruled northern Transylvania and Subcarpathian Rus are now respectively parts of Romania and Ukraine. Moldavia (not Moldova) is a province of Romania.

4. Johnson, *A History of the Jews*, pp. 365, 370.
5. Krivitsky, *In Stalin's Secret Service*, p. xvi.
6. For confirmation from Soviet files that Krivitsky and Reiss were born on exactly the same day, see Duff, *A Time for Spies*, p. 198 n4. Reiss's surname in Polish was Porecki; Poretsky is the Russian transliteration.
7. The town, now Pidvolochysk in western Ukraine, was situated about 20 kilometres east of Tarnopol. On the Russian side of the Zbruch was the town of Volochisk. Following the Polish-Russian war of 1919–20, the Zbruch frontier was re-established by the 1921 Treaty of Riga. It marked the southern line of the Soviet-Polish border until the twin invasions of Poland by Germany and the USSR in September 1939.
8. Reiss graduated from the University of Vienna Law School in 1919. Besides Polish, German and Russian, he spoke French. Whether he knew English is unclear. Krivitsky spoke Polish, Russian and German, some Ukrainian, and read Yiddish. Kern, *A Death in Washington*, pp. 6, 175. Later he learned both French and English. According to Reiss's son, when together the two men spoke Polish. Ibid., p. 438 n225.
9. Reiss's older brother was killed fighting on the Polish side, a factor that was to be used against him when his recall to Moscow was under consideration in 1937. Poretsky, *Our Own People*, pp. 25–26.
10. Kern, *A Death in Washington*, pp. 28, 50; Poretsky, *Our Own People*, pp. 22–23; Massing, *This Deception*, New York, 1951, p. 77.
11. See Chapter 16, footnote 24.
12. Poretsky, *Our Own People*, pp. 137, 150.
13. Ibid., p. 150.
14. B-R. Barth and W. Schweizer, eds, *Der Fall Noel Field, Band I: Gefängnisjahre 1949–1954*, Berlin, 2005, pp. 164–65, 165 n63, 304–09, 395–96, 484, 752–53, 752 n7, 826–29, 827 n9, 834, 834 n40, 898; B-R. Barth and W. Schweizer, eds, *Der Fall Noel Field, Band II: Asyl in Ungarn 1954–1957*, Berlin, 2007, p. 191; H. Field and K. Field, *Trapped in the Cold War: The Ordeal of an American Family*, Stanford, 1999, pp. 86–87, 298–99; Massing, *This Deception*, pp. 170–71, 177–78, 199–201, 291.
15. Barth and Schweizer, eds, *Der Fall Noel Field, Band I*, p. 304.
16. F. Lewis, *The Man Who Disappeared: The Strange History of Noel Field*, London, 1965, p. 87.
17. Field and Field, *Trapped in the Cold War*, p. 298.
18. See Ibid., p. 299; Barth and Schweizer, eds, *Der Fall Noel Field, Band I*, pp. 664, 826 n2; Barth and Schweizer, eds, *Der Fall Noel Field, Band II*, p. 191.
19. Massing, *This Deception*, p. 170. See also Poretsky, *Our Own People*, p. 144; Barth and Schweizer, eds, *Der Fall Noel Field, Band I*, pp. 395–96.
20. Nina had made at least one visit to Europe before this. In June 1928 she and her three younger children sailed from Boston to Liverpool. She took the children to the Continent as well. They sailed back to the USA from Naples in September.
21. 'The Fields, Noel's mother, Paul and I took a trip in Noel's car through Switzerland into France and back. I remember the time we spent together as one of the best I have ever had. *Noel had a list of the best restaurants on our route, we laughed and sang, it was so wonderfully carefree'*. Massing, *This Deception*, p. 177; H. Massing, *Die grosse Täuschung: Geschichte einer Sowjetagentin*, Freiburg, 1967, p. 172. The italicised section was added by Hede nearly twenty years later in the German version of her autobiography.
22. Hede left for Europe for a three month break in summer 1936. Massing, *This Deception*, p. 199.

She probably departed at the end of June. There is the following entry in the NKVD records, dated 13 July 1936: 'Redhead (Hede) left for Paris and no longer works in Nord's (Bazarov's) division'. A. Vassiliev, *Yellow Notebook 2*, Wilson Center Cold War International History Project Digital Archive, http://www.wilsoncenter.org/sites/default/files/Yellow_Notebook_No. 2_ Original.pdf, last accessed 26 May 2013, p. 7.

23. Barth and Schweizer, eds, *Der Fall Noel Field, Band I*, pp. 395–96.
24. In August 1937 Akhmerov informed Moscow that recently Nina had stayed at the Massings' apartment. She told Paul that she'd been to the USSR 'and was well-pleased with her trip'. Vassiliev, *Yellow Notebook 2*, p. 18.
25. Barth and Schweizer, eds, *Der Fall Noel Field, Band I*, p. 396.
26. Ibid., pp. 164–65, 263, 304–09, 398–99, 752–55, 787–88, 790, 800, 809, 874–75; H. Massing, *This Deception*, pp. 176–78.
27. Ibid., p. 177. Akhmerov informed Moscow on 2 August 1938 that 'Redhead (Hede) has been in Raymond's (Reiss's) *apparat* in Switzerland'. Vassiliev, *Yellow Notebook 2*, p. 24.
28. Barth and Schweizer, eds, *Der Fall Noel Field, Band I*, p. 397.
29. Akhmerov informed Moscow on 15 August 1937 that when Paul was in Switzerland, he introduced the Fields to Reiss and his wife Elsa. They went to 'the movies and Noel's apartment'. Vassiliev, *Yellow Notebook 2*, pp. 17–18.
30. Massing, *This Deception*, p. 178; Vassiliev, *Yellow Notebook 2*, p. 18.
31. Hede had first met Krivitsky in Berlin in 1932. Massing, *This Deception*, pp. 108–09.
32. Barth and Schweizer, eds, *Der Fall Noel Field, Band I*, p. 755, p. 790. At another point Noel suggests that he may have met Krivitsky through Reiss, which seems unlikely. Ibid., p. 809. Again he gives the date of their first meeting as spring 1937, which would have been impossible if it was the Massings who introduced him to Krivitsky. Moreover, Walter was in the USSR from 16 March 1937 and did not return to The Hague until 27 May. Krivitsky, *In Stalin's Secret Service*, pp. 212–18. Krivitsky was not a general, even though Noel thought this to be an honorary rank. Like Reiss, Walter was a captain of state security, equivalent to a Red Army colonel. He operated as an illegal *rezident*, who ran various networks in Western Europe. His current base was in The Hague, where he posed as an Austrian art dealer.
33. Barth and Schweizer, eds, *Der Fall Noel Field, Band I*, pp. 399–401, 756–58, 788–89, 796, 809–10, 909–10; Massing, *This Deception*, pp. 220–23. For detailed studies of the defection and assassination of Reiss, see H. Dewar, *Assassins at Large*, London, 1951; Duff, *A Time for Spies*; Kern, *A Death in Washington*.
34. Poretsky, *Our Own People*, p. 229.
35. Unlike the steady survivor Akhmerov, who was of Tartar origin, Bazarov was Jewish. He was recalled to Moscow around July 1937, interrogated from August to the following March, and arrested on 3 July 1938, a few days after the Massings had returned to America. He was sentenced to death for 'espionage and treason' on 21 February 1939 and executed that same day. See Dr Chervonnaya's biography on Documentstalk.com.
36. The Massings told Akhmerov that Reiss knew about Larry and Helen Duggan. On 15 August Akhmerov informed the Centre that when he was last in Moscow Reiss had read all the personal files of the New York illegal network, and that on returning to Paris in 1936 he questioned Hede about Helen Duggan. Vassiliev, *Yellow Notebook 2*, p. 17. Reiss's interest in the New York network was probably quite professional, since there had been talk of sending him to the USA to replace Bazarov. Poretsky, *Our Own People*, p. 151.
37. Vassiliev, *Yellow Notebook 2*, p. 18.
38. A *Treff* was a meeting, deriving from the German verb *treffen*, to meet. German was the original *lingua franca* of the Comintern, until superseded by Russian when Stalin rose to power. I am speculating that Akhmerov's letter of 15 August brought Noel into play. But it remains

impossible to date this event precisely. Using the timelines offered in Noel's woolly account simply provides contradictory and incredible information, while Krivitsky doesn't mention this encounter at all. However, a less than watertight case can be made that Krivitsky went to Geneva some time between 22 and 25 August 1937. At 1950 hours on 21 August Krivitsky was seated on the train which would be leaving for Le Havre, from where he was to sail to the USSR. He left the train upon being ordered to stay in Paris, whose streets he walked that entire night. On the evening of 26 August he was at the theatre. From 27 August he lived 'quietly' for a week with his wife and sick child in Breteuil, two hours from Paris. Krivitsky, *In Stalin's Secret Service*, pp. 225–26.

39. On Shpigelglas see Dr Chervonnaya's biography in Documentstalk.com. Kern, *A Death in Washington*, pp. 118, 123; and Chapter 7.
40. Barth and Schweizer, eds, *Der Fall Noel Field, Band I*, p. 401.
41. Vassiliev, *Yellow Notebook 2*, p. 18. Elsa Poretsky escaped liquidation and eventually found refuge in the USA. She arrived there on Tuesday 11 February 1941, to be met with banner headlines recording Krivitsky's death. He had committed suicide in a Washington hotel the previous morning.
42. Kern, *A Death in Washington*, p. 135ff.
43. Vassiliev, *Yellow Notebook 2*, p. 21.

7. PROMISED LANDS: PILGRIMAGE TO MOSCOW; MISSION IN SPAIN, 1937–39

1. For the careers of Lisa and Vassili Zarubin I have used information contained in: Dr Chervonnaya's biographies in Documentstalk.com; a link to the Wikipedia entry for Elisabeth Zarubina, *Tanistvennaya Erna* ['Mysterious Erna'—Erna was one of her cover-names]; the books by I. Damaskin with G. Elliot, *Kitty Harris: The Spy with Seventeen Names*, London, 2001; H. Romerstein and E. Breindel, *The Venona Secrets: Exposing Soviet Espionage and America's Traitors*, Washington, 2001; P. Sudoplatov, *Special Tasks: The Memoirs of an Unwanted Witness—a Soviet Spymaster*, London, 1994; and M. Wilmers, *The Eitingons: A Twentieth Century Story*, London, 2009. For the interrogations of Hede and Paul in New York and Moscow, see H. Massing, *This Deception*, New York, 1951, pp. 224–73; H. Massing, *Die grosse Täuschung: Geschichte einer Sowjetagentin*, Freiburg, 1967, pp. 217–261. There are a number of minor differences between the two accounts, none of which alter the overall picture presented by Hede.
2. Under Habsburg rule Czernowitz, the capital of Bukovina, was often referred to as 'little Vienna'. It is now called Chernivtsi and along with L'viv is one of the architectural and cultural jewels of Western Ukraine. In 1920 both Bukovina and Bessarabia were part of Romania. In June 1940 Bessarabia and Northern Bukovina were 'incorporated' into the Ukrainian SSR. They were reoccupied by Romania in 1941–44, but reverted to Soviet rule thereafter.
3. When he was recalled to Moscow from Harbin in Manchuria in 1925, Zarubin left behind his first wife Olga and his daughter Zoya. Olga later married another Chekist, Leonid Alexandrovich Eitingon. Born Naum Isakovich Eitingon in Mogilev (in today's Belarus) in 1899, he would oversee the assassination of Trotsky in Mexico in August 1940.
4. E. Poretsky, *Our Own People: A Memoir of 'Ignace Reiss' and his Friends*, London, 1969, pp. 145–46.
5. Sudoplatov, *Special Tasks*, p. 188. She must have changed her appearance as effectively as she displayed courage, when one learns that Lisa's last mission in Nazi Germany was as late as April 1941. Like Zarubin, and indeed several senior Soviet figures, Sudoplatov was a non-Jew married to a Jewish wife.
6. Massing, *This Deception*, pp. 224–25. Apparently she was known to American intelligence as 'Lisa Big Hands and Big Feet'. Wilmers, *The Eitingons*, p. 159.
7. Massing, *This Deception*, p. 157.

8. See B-R. Barth and W. Schweizer, eds, *Der Fall Noel Field, Band I: Gefängnisjahre 1949–1954*, Berlin, 2005, pp. 398, 755, 809. In none of these references does Noel suggest that the purpose of the Massing's visit to Moscow was to resign from the NKVD.

9. Massing, *This Deception*, p. 280.

10. Ibid., p. 251. Presumably Zarubin took his son's name Peter as cover. He kept things in the family when he served as the legal *rezident* in the USA from 1941–44. Then he adopted the cover-name 'Betty' as tribute to his wife. Damaskin with Elliot, *Kitty Harris*, p. 110.

11. This description of Shpigelglas is by Reiss's widow. Poretsky, *Our Own People*, p. 188.

12. Massing, *This Deception*, p. 257. Shpigelglas also spoke fluent Polish and French.

13. See M. Jansen and N. Petrov, *Stalin's Loyal Executioner: People's Commissar Nikolai Ezhov 1895–1940*, Stanford, 2002, pp. 68–69; and the biography of Slutski on Documentstalk.com. Zarubin had been deputy director of INO in 1937, presumably while Shpigelglas was in Paris, hunting Reiss. It would seem that Shpigelglas resumed this post on his return and became acting director on Slutski's death. On 28 March 1938 Zalman Isaevich Passov was appointed head of INO. Passov was arrested on 22 October 1938 and shot on 15 February 1940. See his biography on Documentstalk.com and a disparaging assessment of his abilities in Sudoplatov, *Special Tasks*, pp, 41–42, 56–57. Shpigelglas was arrested on 2 November 1938. After torture he began confessing at the end of May 1939. He was convicted of treason on 28 November 1940 and executed on 29 January 1941. J. Costello and O. Tsarev, *Deadly Illusions*, London, 1993, p. 469 n46. Both Dr Chervonnaya and Dr Barth write that Shpigelglas was executed on 29 January 1940. See Documentstalk.com and Barth and Schweizer, eds, *Der Fall Noel Field, Band I*, p. 396 n59. It is hardly surprising to learn that INO almost collapsed in 1938, and that for some four months not a single intelligence report was forwarded to Stalin. C. Andrew and V. Mitrokhin, *The Mitrokhin Archive: The KGB in Europe and the West*, London, 2000, p. 106.

14. Barth and Schweizer, eds, *Der Fall Noel Field, Band I*, pp. 165, 263, 396–97, 396 n58, 401–6, 403 n83, n85 and n86, 405 n93, 513–14, 758–71, 769 n30, 875–76, 910; Massing, *This Deception*, pp. 273–88; Massing, *Die grosse Täuschung*, pp. 261–76. Again Hede's alterations are not significant.

15. Barth and Schweizer, eds, *Der Fall Noel Field, Band I*, p. 401. Later Shpigelglas told Noel that his entry visa had been temporarily deferred, in order not to alert the Swiss authorities.

16. Nina had both breasts removed. F. Lewis, *The Man who Disappeared: The Strange History of Noel Field*, London, 1965, p. 48. Despite the diagnosis she lived for another ten years.

17. The uncertainty is Noel's, who stated in interrogation, 'Doubtless I also met with Hiss, but my memory regarding this is no longer certain'. Barth and Schweizer, eds, *Der Fall Noel Field, Band I*, p. 759. By then Noel had learned that Krivitsky, after hiding out for over a month in the south of France, had emerged in Paris. In November 1937 he asked the French authorities for political asylum.

18. There was one strange incident in March or April 1938. The Massings' close friend, the American journalist Louis Fischer, who was then still a communist, arrived in Geneva. He told the Fields that the Massings wanted them to speed up their plans to get to Moscow, since they expected to be sent to the USA any day. Ibid., p. 402. This raises the question of whether the couples were in contact while the Massings were in Moscow. On Noel's relationship with Fischer, see Ibid., pp. 395–96.

19. Presumably this roundabout route was determined by train schedules. Noel did not inform his office that he was travelling to the USSR. He simply took his 1938 leave, added on some 'sick-leave', and got away with a seven week vacation. His Hungarian interrogator was noticeably bemused, and perhaps impressed, by the frequency and duration of holidays in the capitalist world. Ibid., p. 760.

20. Ibid., p. 403.

21. Massing, *This Deception*, p. 276. Hede ascribes Noel's reaction to his naive, pro-Soviet views. One must assume that he did not enlighten the Massings about his role in the Reiss murder, and that the NKVD did not inform them of it either. Apparently Noel boasted about it to Paul later. Lewis, *The Man who Disappeared*, p. 97.

22. Barth and Schweizer, eds, *Der Fall Noel Field, Band I*, p. 404, p. 761, p. 910.

23. Hede's account is in Massing, *This Deception*, pp. 268–70. It may well be that in this instance Hede was seeking to protect the imprisoned Noel, by omitting such 'anti-Soviet' actions from her book. Noel's version emerges from an interrogation, and is in Barth and Schweizer, eds, *Der Fall Noel Field, Band I*, pp. 762–69. During this long, acerbic and nauseating session Noel was forced to admit that the humanitarian motives from which he acted were politically unsound. Nor did he report his charitable actions to the NKVD, being too frightened to do so. A vivid portrait of the conditions endured by German communist women in Moscow's grim Butyrka prison can be found in M. Buber-Neumann, *Under two Dictators: Prisoner of Stalin and Hitler*, London, 2009.

24. Compare the accounts in Massing, *This Deception*, pp. 276–78 and Barth and Schweizer, eds, *Der Fall Noel Field, Band I*, pp. 404–05. Noel merely records her threat. Otherwise, all one can say about the location and sequence of events in Hede's account is that things may have occurred in this way. She certainly goes into great detail about the meal they ate.

25. Massing, *This Deception*, p. 278. However, she met Noel in the summer of 1939.

26. Hede writes that they were diverted to Wilmington, Delaware. Ibid., pp. 286–87.

27. Barth and Schweizer, eds, *Der Fall Noel Field, Band I*, p. 405.

28. Ibid., p. 406; B-R. Barth and W. Schweizer, eds, *Der Fall Noel Field, Band II: Asyl in Ungarn 1954–1957*. Berlin 2007, p. 206 n17 (Original English text).

29. A later Soviet memo on Field states that after he left Moscow for Switzerland 'he was conserved as an agent'. Barth and Schweizer, eds, *Der Fall Noel Field, Band I*, p. 782, p. 782 n2.

30. Ibid., pp. 103–4, 117, 165 n65, 271–72, 307–08, 419–23; Lewis, *The Man who Disappeared*, pp. 104–10.

31. H. Thomas, *The Spanish Civil War*, London, 1990, pp. 980–85.

32. Lord Thomas makes Noel the secretary of an entirely different commission. Ibid., pp. 853–54. Herta was in Spain too, acting unofficially as the commission's provisioning officer.

33. Ibid., pp. 852–53.

34. The New York World Fair ran from 30 April to 31 October 1939 and from 11 May to 27 October 1940. Barth and Schweizer, eds, *Der Fall Noel Field, Band I*, p. 421 n182.

35. Massing, *This Deception*, p. 306.

36. A. Vassiliev, *Black Notebook*, Wilson Center Cold War International History Project Digital Archive, http://www.wilsoncenter.org/sites/default/files/Black%20Notebook%20Original.pdf, last accessed 26 May 2013, p. 159. I assume that 'works' here refers simply to Noel's professional activity. As far as I am aware, none of the major studies on Soviet espionage in the USA have noted the reference to the Massings by the codename 'Peter and his wife'. The same source provides two further references. See Ibid., pp. 23, 161. On Krivitsky's activities in America, see G. Kern, *A Death in Washington: Walter G. Krivitsky and the Stalin Terror*, New York, 2004, p. 169ff.

37. Barth and Schweizer, eds, *Der Fall Noel Field, Band I*, p. 422. This reference to Hiss is one more piece of evidence of his links with Soviet intelligence. Krivitsky didn't inform the American authorities about Field, although he told his ghost-writer and Whittaker Chambers that Noel had been his agent. Kern, *A Death in Washington*, p. 312; Barth and Schweizer, eds, *Der Fall Noel Field, Band I*, p. 422 n187.

38. Ibid., p. 383 n4 and n6.

39. 'I am not and never have been a communist. I am not and never have been a member of the

communist party nor of any other radical organization. I have never engaged in any radical activities. By no stretch of the imagination can my brief membership in the Fellowship of Youth for Peace during my student days be considered as a "radical" activity'. Ibid., p. 272 n14 (Original English text).

40. G. Perrett, *Days of Sadness, Years of Triumph: The American People 1939–1945*, New York, 1973, p. 17.

8. 'AT THE RISK OF DEATH': HERMANN FIELD 1939–40

1. B-R. Barth and W. Schweizer, eds, *Der Fall Noel Field, Band I: Gefängnisjahre 1949–1954*, Berlin, 2005, pp. xix, 416–17, 829, 835–36; B-R. Barth and W. Schweizer, eds, *Der Fall Noel Field, Band II: Asyl in Ungarn 1954–1957*, Berlin, 2007, pp. 41–42, 41 n3, 42 n4 and n8, 191; H. Field and K. Field, *Trapped in the Cold War: The Ordeal of an American Family*, Stanford, 1999, pp. 2–3, 13, 127–30.

2. Sali was the eldest child of Chaim Liebermann, who as both Jew and Bolshevik had fled Russia in 1908, and then worked as a tailor in Zurich. Barth and Schweizer, eds, *Der Fall Noel Field, Band I*, p. 417 n.155.

3. Kate writes that she met Hermann in summer 1938. Field and Field, *Trapped in the Cold War*, p. 122. Hermann thought that they met that autumn. Barth and Schweizer, eds, *Der Fall Noel Field, Band I*, p. 829 n19. Women are usually correct in such matters.

4. Field and Field, *Trapped in the Cold War*, p. 129.

5. Ibid., p. 122.

6. On the Sieberts, who left Britain in 1947 to live in East Germany, see Barth and Schweizer, eds, *Der Fall Noel Field, Band II*, p. 43 n9; Field and Field, *Trapped in the Cold War*, p. 130. On Christopher Thorneycroft, see Barth and Schweizer, eds, *Der Fall Noel Field, Band II*, p. 138 n9.

7. Field and Field, *Trapped in the Cold War*, pp. 3, 70. In September 1950 Hermann's brother-in-law Hans Siebert was questioned by the ZPKK, which was investigating the activities of German communists who had contact with the Field brothers. Siebert said that Hermann 'never told me that he was a member of the Party; but he always acted as though he was one'. Barth and Schweizer, eds, *Der Fall Noel Field, Band II*, p. 41 n3. Herta was emphatic that Hermann was never in the Party. Barth and Schweizer, eds, *Der Fall Noel Field, Band I*, p. 828.

8. Ibid., pp. 431–32, 601–02, 829–30; Barth and Schweizer, eds, *Der Fall Noel Field, Band II*, pp. 42, 192; Field and Field, *Trapped in the Cold War*, pp. 3, 69–72, 122–24, 157–58, 166–69; Y. Kapp and M. Mynatt, *British Policy and the Refugees, 1933–1941*. London 1997, pp. 18–23. For the activities of BCRC/CRTF personnel in Czechoslovakia, see W. Chadwick, *The Rescue of the Prague Refugees 1938–39*, Leicester, 2010. On Leo Bauer, see P. Brandt, et al., *Karrieren eines Außenseiters: Leo Bauer zwischen Kommunismus und Sozialdemokratie 1912 bis 1972*, Berlin/Bonn, 1983, pp. 13–77 *passim*; Barth and Schweizer, eds, *Der Fall Noel Field, Band II*, p. 400.

9. Field and Field, *Trapped in the Cold War*, p. 69. Given the nature of this task, it is hard to disagree with Dr Barth's contention that Hermann was acting on the instructions of the KPD, CPGB and the Czechoslovak Communist Party (CzCP). Barth and Schweizer, eds, *Der Fall Noel Field, Band I*, p. 432 n225. See also Noel's view, Ibid., p. 312. According to one of Hermann's CzCP assistants in Krakow, 'the Party had issued instructions that we should collaborate with Field'. E. Loebl, *Sentenced and Tried: The Stalinist Purges in Czechoslovakia*, London, 1969, p. 35.

10. See Chapter 10.

11. In July 1950 Bauer claimed to have rescued virtually the entire CzCP Central Committee, including the leading comrades, Gottwald and Slánský. Barth and Schweizer, eds, *Der Fall Noel Field, Band I*, p. 432 n224.
12. Bauer was among a handful of foreigners given asylum in the British legation on 15 March. R. J. Stopford, the British Liaison Officer for Refugees in Prague, made specific reference to 'a communist called Katz (i.e. Bauer)' and appended a lengthy footnote to explain his presence. W. Chadwick, *The Rescue of the Prague Refugees 1938–39*, p. 24, p. 102. Unfortunately, Chadwick provides no details from this footnote.
13. According to Herta Field, Hermann returned to Britain before being sent by the CRTF to Krakow. She also says that Kate visited Poland in summer 1939. Barth and Schweizer, eds, *Der Fall Noel Field, Band I*, pp. 829–30.
14. Field and Field, *Trapped in the Cold War*, p. 167.
15. See Chadwick, *The Rescue of the Prague Refugees, 1938–39*, pp. 102–03.
16. Hermann adjudged Bauer to be 'domineering (*heerisch*) and arrogant'. Brandt, et al., *Karrieren eines Außenseiters*, p. 77. Later Noel took a similar view of him. See Barth and Schweizer, eds, *Der Fall Noel Field, Band I*, p. 663. The precise form and nature of the clash between Hermann and Bauer, and the internal party conflict behind it, are very difficult to assess from the published sources. My account is based upon Ibid., pp. 432, 432 n224 and n225; Brandt et al., *Karrieren eines Außenseiters*, pp. 68–77.
17. Field and Field, *Trapped in the Cold War*, p. 169.
18. Loebl, *Sentenced and Tried*, p. 32.
19. Holič lies about 100 km north of Bratislava and is very close to today's frontier with the Czech Republic.
20. E. Loebl, *My Mind on Trial*, London, 1976, pp. 15, 57
21. Ibid., pp. 52, 137–38; Slánský Trial, *Prozess gegen die Leitung des staatsfeindlichen Verschwörungszentrums mit Rudolf Slánský an der Spitze*, Prague, 1953, pp. 372–74.
22. Barth and Schweizer, eds, *Der Fall Noel Field, Band I*, pp. 505 n20, 601; Slánský Trial, p. 384.
23. V. Nový, *Zeiten and Zeugen: Erinnerungen eines tschechischen Kommunisten*, (East) Berlin, 1979, pp. 195–227.
24. On the Nazi-Soviet Pact, the German and Soviet invasions of Poland and the consequent atrocities, see: N. Bethell, *The War Hitler Won*, London, 1976; A. Cienciala et al., eds, *Katyń: A Crime without Punishment*, London, 2007; R. Evans, *The Third Reich at War: How the Nazis led Germany from Conquest to Disaster*, London, 2008; J. Gross, *Revolution from Abroad: The Soviet Conquest of Poland's Western Ukraine and Western Belorussia*, Princeton/Oxford, 2002; A. Read and D. Fisher, *The Deadly Embrace: Hitler, Stalin and the Nazi-Soviet Pact 1939–1941*, London, 1988; A. Rossino, *Hitler strikes Poland: Blitzkrieg, Ideology and Atrocity*, Lawrence (Kansas), 2003; R. Sontag and J. Beddie, *Nazi-Soviet Relations 1939–1941: Documents from the Archives of the German Foreign Office*, Washington, 1948; S. Zaloga, *Poland 1939: The Birth of Blitzkrieg*, London, 2004. I have used the accounts of Clare Hollingworth, Maria Kuncewiczowa and Zoe Zajdlerowa in an attempt to evoke the chaotic situation on the ground that Hermann would have experienced.
25. C. Hollingworth, *The Three Weeks' War in Poland*, London, 1940, p. 16.
26. M. Kuncewiczowa, *The Keys: A Journey through Europe at War*, London, 1946, p. 26.
27. Z. Zajdlerowa, *My Name is Million*, 1940, p. 50. Although *My Name is Million* was written anonymously, some of its content and language is identical to parts of Ms Zajdlerowa's better-known work *The Dark Side of the Moon*. Originally this too was published anonymously in 1946.
28. Kuncewiczowa, *The Keys*, p. 11.
29. Ibid., pp. 42, 46.
30. Hollingworth, *The Three Weeks' War*, p. 56.

31. The secret additional protocol to the Nazi-Soviet Pact of 23 August 1939 allocated Finland, Estonia and Latvia to the Soviet 'sphere of influence' and Lithuania to the German. In Poland the boundary between the two predators was 'approximately…the rivers Narew, Vistula, and San'. The secret supplementary protocol to the German-Soviet Boundary and Friendship Treaty, signed by Ribbentrop and Molotov on 28 September, allocated Lithuania to the Soviet sphere. Germany received territory in central Poland in return. See texts in R. Sontag and J. Beddie, *Nazi-Soviet Relations 1939–1941*, pp. 78, 107.

32. Barth and Schweizer, eds, *Der Fall Noel Field, Band I*, pp. 417, 417 n159, 830–32; Barth and Schweizer, eds, *Der Fall Noel Field, Band II*, pp. 191–92; Field and Field, *Trapped in the Cold War*, pp. 3, 13, 71; Nový, *Zeiten und Zeugen*, pp. 227–46. A map showing Hermann's trek across Poland is in Field and Field, *Trapped in the Cold War*, and generally tallies with Nowý's account.

33. Kapp and Mynatt, *British Policy and the Refugees*, p. 23.

34. Barth and Schweizer, eds, *Der Fall Noel Field, Band I*, p. 829.

35. Kapp and Mynatt, *British Policy and the Refugees*, p. 22.

36. Field and Field, *Trapped in the Cold War*, p. 70. However, Hermann's role in saving communist cadres had its downside too. The last BCRC representative in Prague, the feisty Canadian Beatrice Wellington, complained to London about his activities. The Gestapo had made it clear to her that she would be expelled if she attempted 'to aid the women and children of men who have got to Poland illegally, and are now in England or en route to England, as a result of the activities of the Committee representative in Poland, which are now well known in Berlin'. Chadwick, *The Rescue of the Prague Refugees, 1938–39*, p. 125.

37. Field and Field, *Trapped in the Cold War*, p. 124; Barth and Schweizer, eds, *Der Fall Noel Field, Band I*, p. 828 n21. Stopford (see footnote 12 above) gives the figure as over 15,000. However, there had been possibly as many as 200,000 refugees in the post-Munich Czech lands. Chadwick, *The Rescue of the Prague Refugees, 1938–39*, pp. xv, 36.

38. Slánský Trial, p. 488. Otto Šling, a senior CzCP functionary and one of the accused, provided this 'evidence'. Šling had been admitted to Britain as early as April 1939, and worked for the CRTF.

39. Herta Field stated that Hermann 'returned to London via Italy and Geneva'. Barth and Schweizer, eds, *Der Fall Noel Field, Band I*, p. 830. She does not mention Zurich, Paris or Calais. It seems that Hermann did not visit Noel and Herta while in Geneva.

40. W. Kießling, *Partner im 'Narrenparadies': der Freundeskreis um Noel Field und Paul Merker*, Berlin, 1994, p. 35.

41. In November 1954, shortly after his release from prison in Budapest, Noel expressed the opinion that Hermann's marriage to Kate was not really happy, since Hermann was deeply in love with Jean, and remained so even after their divorce. Barth and Schweizer, eds, *Der Fall Noel Field, Band II*, p. 43. It is impossible to offer an opinion upon this matter. What is indisputable is that Kate and Hermann remained married from 1940 until Hermann's death in 2001. Noel made similar pronouncements about Erica's marriage to Robert Wallach.

9. FAMILY BREAKDOWN: NOEL, HERTA AND ERICA, 1939–41

1. B-R. Barth and W. Schweizer, eds, *Der Fall Noel Field, Band I: Gefängnisjahre 1949–1954*, Berlin, 2005, pp. 417, 417 n159, 627–28; B-R. Barth and W. Schweizer, eds, *Der Fall Noel Field, Band II: Asyl in Ungarn 1954–1957*, Berlin, 2007, pp. 192, 192n 10, 417–18, 641; E. Wallach, *Light at Midnight*. New York 1967, pp. 27–32, 140–51, 248–55, 267–74; F. Lewis, *The Man who Disappeared: The Strange History of Noel Field*, London, 1965, pp. 110–15; H. Field and K. Field, *Trapped in the Cold War: The Ordeal of an American Family*, Stanford, 1999, p. 143; W.

Kießling, *Partner im 'Narrenparadies': der Freundeskreis um Noel Field und Paul Merker*, Berlin, 1994, pp. 34–36.

2. The age given on Willy Glaser's death certificate, registered on 21 June 1948, is sixty-two. Most sources concur that Willy was Jewish, although Flora Lewis writes that he was half-Jewish. From various accounts it is clear that Frau Glaser was addressed as Therese. Born on 4 September 1888, she was still living in Epsom in 1971, but I do not know where or when she died.

3. Details are provided in internet sources: Martin Sugarman, 'No 3 (Jewish) Troop, No 10 Commando'; the entry for VI Commando, which also contains a photo of Kurt. See also Chapter 14, footnote 10.

4. Erica's autobiography makes no mention of Kurt's presence in Spain.

5. Barth and Schweizer, eds, *Der Fall Noel Field, Band I*, p. 123 n43. Dr Barth dates this agreement as 26 January 1939, but this does not seem possible. The frontier was not opened until 28 January, while Erica and Therese were still in Le Boulou in mid-February. Perhaps the agreement was made on 26 February.

6. Later Willy opened a medical practice in Surrey.

7. Barth and Schweizer, eds, *Der Fall Noel Field, Band I*, pp. 291, 308–12,. 627–28; Lewis, *The Man who Disappeared*, pp. 48–50, 89–91, 121–22.

8. E. Anderson, *Love in Exile: An American Writer's Memoir of Life in Divided Berlin*, South Royalton (Vt.), 1999, p. 195.

9. Lewis, *The Man who Disappeared*, pp. 49, 91.

10. Ibid., p. 90.

11. Barth and Schweizer, eds, *Der Fall Noel Field, Band I*, p. 171.

12. Ibid., p. 627.

13. '...*dass sie bei den Fields nicht mehr leben könne, da beide Teile der Familie zu ihr sexuelle Beziehungen aufgenommen hätten*'. Barth and Schweizer, eds, *Der Fall Noel Field, Band I*, p. 627 n2. Goldhammer's statement was made in East Berlin in November 1949 to the ZPKK. See Chapter 26. This version of events was confirmed by a dying Erica in December 1993. She wrote of the 'inexcusable abuse' committed against her by Noel and Herta when she was seventeen. Barth and Schweizer, eds, *Der Fall Noel'Field, Band II*, p. 349.

14. A. Weinstein, *Perjury: The Hiss-Chambers Case*, New York, 1997, p. 310.

15. Barth and Schweizer, eds, *Der Fall Noel Field, Band I*, p. 312. There is no indication of what was planned for Erica's future, in the event of the Fields returning to the USA.

10. CADRES AND CAMPS: THE USC AND THE KPD FOREIGN SECRETARIAT

1. B-R. Barth and W. Schweizer, eds, *Der Fall Noel Field, Band I: Gefängnisjahre 1949–1954*, Berlin, 2005, pp. 65, 170–76, 312, 314, 318–21, 515–16, 872; F. Lewis, *The Man who Disappeared: The Strange History of Noel Field*, London, 1965, pp. 126–27.

2. He was a minister of the Unitarian Church and Vice-President of the Unitarian Association. Noel viewed him as a 'liberal airhead (*Wirrkopf*)' and 'naive idealist', who was easily influenced, particularly by beautiful women. Barth and Schweizer, eds, *Der Fall Noel Field, Band I*, pp. 173, 319. Some might say that this description fitted Noel too. On Joy's career, see B-R. Barth and W. Schweizer, eds, *Der Fall Noel Field, Band II: Asyl in Ungarn 1954–1957*, Berlin, 2007, pp. 420–21; S. Subak, *Rescue and Flight: American Relief Workers who defied the Nazis*, London, 2010, *passim*. The title Unitarian Service Committee deliberately aped that of the Quakers' Friends Service Committee.

3. According to Noel the Unitarian Church in America formed the 'extreme left' of the American churches, and had among its membership several CPUSA members. The remit that it gave the USC was that its principal aim should be to aid antifascists. Barth and Schweizer, eds, *Der Fall Noel Field, Band I*, pp. 172–73, 318–19. As to the political leanings of the five extravagantly

named individuals–Dr Charles Rhind Joy (1885–1978), Robert Cloutman Dexter (1887–1955), Elisabeth Williams Anthony Dexter (1887–1972), Waitstill Hastings Sharp (1902–84) and Martha Dickie Sharp (1905–99)—there is little to suggest that they were more than decent and committed humanitarians, although the events they were involved in doubtless made them into antifascists too. Beyond that we can note that Joy had been a pacifist in the First World War, and that MI5 kept tabs on Dexter when he was in Britain. In the mid-1940s Noel thought Martha Sharp to be a dyed-in-the-wool anti-communist (see Ibid., pp. 191, 486), while about the same time the FBI vainly investigated her for communist 'tendencies'. Israel's Yad Vashem Institute honours as 'Righteous among the Nations', those gentiles who put their lives at risk to save those of Jews during the Holocaust. Varian Fry (1907–67) in 1995 and the Sharps in 2006 were rightly honoured, and are the only Americans among the 'righteous'. Playing devil's advocate, I wonder why Hermann Field has not joined them, unless it is because he saved the 'wrong sort' of Jews.

4. Subak, *Rescue and Flight*, p. 84. Ms Subak's work is a welcome study of the overall role of the USC in the Second World War. It is particularly good on the differences between the 'big five' of the USC, and shows too that there was often a close working relationship between the USC and the ERC. But since she has not used the German sources which discuss the role of the Fields in the USC, I diverge from her findings upon certain issues.

5. Barth and Schweizer, eds, *Der Fall Noel Field, Band I*, p. 172. Joy sent a *résumé* about Noel to Boston, which included the fact that Noel smoked. 'He has also written speeches for Roosevelt', added Joy, 'but don't let that prejudice you'. Most important was the fact that the Fields were trilingual in English, German and French. Subak, *Rescue and Flight*, pp. 85–86.

6. Barth and Schweizer, eds, *Der Fall Noel Field, Band I*, p. 170.

7. It is not clear whether Noel had in mind the Moscow-based International Red Aid, known by its Russian-language initials as *MOPR*, or Münzenberg's International Workers' Relief (*Internationale Arbeiterhilfe*). He would not be the only one to be confused. For more on the turf wars between these bodies, see S. McMeekin, *The Red Millionaire: A Political Biography of Willy Münzenberg, Moscow's Secret Propaganda Tsar in the West*, New Haven, CT, 2003.

8. Barth and Schweizer, eds, *Der Fall Noel Field, Band I*, p. 171.

9. Noel began working in Marseille at the end of March 1941. Herta, who became associate director of USC France, joined him there in June.

10. Barth and Schweizer, eds, *Der Fall Noel Field, Band I*, p. 174.

11. For the KPD, the French internment camps, the problems of emigration, and the activities of the aid organisations, see sources cited in the notes. For individual German communists see: P. Brandt, et al., *Karrieren eines Außenseiters: Leo Bauer zwischen Kommunismus und Sozialdemokratie 1912 bis 1972*, Berlin/Bonn, 1983; R. Friedmann, *Ulbrichts Rundfunkmann: eine Gerhart-Eisler-Biographie*, Berlin, 2007; J. Herf, *Divided Memory: The Nazi Past in the Two Germanys*, London 1997; W. Kießling, '*Leistner ist Mielke': Schatten einer gefälschten Biographie*, Berlin, 1998; H. Müller-Enbergs, *Erste Chefredakteur, dann 'Unperson': Lex Ende und Rudolf Herrnstadt. Jahrbuch für Historische Kommunismusforschung 1996*, Berlin, 1995; W. Kießling, *Partner im 'Narrenparadies': der Freundeskreis um Noel Field und Paul Merker*, Berlin, 1994; H. Priess, *Spaniens Himmel und keine Sterne. Ein deutsches Geschichtsbuch. Erinnerungen an ein Leben und ein Jahrhundert*, Berlin, 1996. See also the relevant short biographies in B-R. Barth and W. Schweizer, eds, *Der Fall Noel Field, Band II*, pp. 400–41 *passim* and H. Müller-Enbergs et al. eds, *Wer war wer in der DDR?: ein Lexicon ostdeutscher Biographien*. Berlin 2010. Brief German-language biographies of most KPD/SED members mentioned in this book can be found on the website Bundesstiftung zur Aufarbeitung der SED-Diktatur, http://www.bundesstiftung-aufarbeitung.de/, last accessed 2 June 2013.

12. F. Borkenau, *European Communism*, London, 1953, p. 51.

13. Some 60–100,000 KPD members had been interned by the end of 1933, although many, like

Paul Massing, had also been released. By 1945 at least half of the 1932 KPD membership of 300,000 had endured Nazi jails or KZs. About 20,000 had been murdered or executed. E. Weitz, *Creating German Communism, 1890–1990: From Popular Protests to Socialist State*, Princeton/ Chichester, 1997, p. 280.

14. Ibid., pp. 280, 298–99, During the Nazi-Soviet Pact some four thousand German exiles were turned over to Hitler by the Soviet authorities; between five and twelve hundred of them were on the Gestapo's 'wanted' lists. Ibid., p. 299 n93.

15. Its full title was *Das Sekretariat des Zentralkomitees der KPD-Auslandsleitung in Paris*. It was sited in the French capital because of the victory of the *Front Populaire* in the May 1936 general election. Paris was also the main centre of emigration for Germans who wished or needed to escape Hitler's regime.

16. C. Epstein, *The Last Revolutionaries: German Communists and their Century*, London, 2003, p. 69.

17. G. Regler, *The Owl of Minerva*. London 1959, p. 333. The KPD member and author Gustav Regler was commissar of the Twelfth International Brigade until he was seriously wounded. His experiences in Spain led him to finally break with the Party.

18. A. Koestler, *Scum of the Earth*, London, 2006, p. 95. Arthur Koestler too had broken with the KPD. In Le Vernet both he and Regler were treated by their former comrades as 'BIM People' (*BIM-Leute*). BIM stood variously for *Bureau internationale de mouchardage* (spies or informers)/*de marlous* (pimps). On a good day they were simply referred to as 'renegades' or 'rats'. See S. Hintze, *Antifaschisten im Camp Le Vernet*. (East) Berlin 1988, pp. 46–47. This work, published shortly before the demise of the GDR, does at least provide a positive assessment of the Fields' relief work.

19. Koestler, *Scum of the Earth*, p. 105

20. J. Palmier, *Weimar in Exile: The Antifascist Emigration in Europe and America*, London, 2006, p. 443.

21. Kießling, *Partner im 'Narrenparadies'*, p. 222.

22. Barth and Schweizer, eds, *Der Fall Noel Field, Band I*, p. 324, n93; Kießling, *Partner im 'Narrenparadies'*, pp. 66–73. Noel only visited the American embassy in Vichy on this one occasion. His report to Boston of 6 March 1942 appears to make no mention of his intercessions for the Castres prisoners. He told Boston that he 'was received with open arms and royally treated' at the embassy, where he 'had a long and most cordial interview' with the ambassador, mainly about supply difficulties. Subak, *Rescue and Flight*, p. 126.

23. Some sources claim incorrectly that Rädel was executed in Plötzensee prison. Noel partially financed a more successful breakout in September 1943, when a multinational group of thirty-six prisoners escaped from Castres. See Priess, *Spaniens Himmel und keine Sterne*, p. 181ff; Hintze, *Antifaschisten im Camp Le Vernet*, pp. 280–83; Barth and Schweizer, eds, *Der Fall Noel Field, Band I*, p. 456 n312.

24. From the sources I have read, it remains unclear why Ende was moved from Le Vernet to Marolle, the internment camp from which he escaped.

25. Max Fischer is the pseudonym given by both Kießling and Barth. Another author states that Merker's alias was Paul Franke, although he wrote as Max Fischer for the CPUSA's theoretical journal. Herf, *Divided Memory*, p. 44.

26. Ibid., 45. For the German original and further detail, see Kießling, *Partner im 'Narrenparadies'*, pp. 14–20

27. Les Milles camp was an abandoned tile and brick factory. Initially conditions there paralleled those in Le Vernet. R. Sullivan, *Villa Air-Bel: The Second World War, Escape and a House in France*, London, 2007, pp. 117–19.

28. Kießling, *Partner im 'Narrenparadies'*, p. 89.

29. A number of *Abschnittsleitungen* were set up by the exiled KPD in countries bordering Nazi

Germany. Their function was to receive information brought out of the *Reich*, and to convey personnel, instructions and literature into Germany. Despite the courage and dedication of those involved their efforts were largely irrelevant, at least in the period before the German attack upon the USSR in June 1941.

11. 'SAVING OUR CADRES': MARSEILLE AND GENEVA 1941–44

1. B-R. Barth and W. Schweizer, eds, *Der Fall Noel Field, Band I: Gefängnisjahre 1949–1954*, Berlin, 2005, pp. 175, 181–82, 184 n119, 320–21, 320 n85, 412, 425 n197 and n198, 430–31, 448, 449 n289, p. 454 n304, 511–12, 516–518, 773, 867, 872, 879 n4.

2. Hotel Bompard was previously a holding centre for victims of the 'White Slave trade', prior to deportation from Marseille. Under Vichy it had become an extension of the Marseille prison system. W. Kießling, *Partner im 'Narrenparadies': der Freundeskreis um Noel Field und Paul Merker*, Berlin, 1994, p. 39.

3. Madame Esmiol, a middle-aged Gaullist who worked in the Marseille prefecture, played a vital role in warning and assisting Merker, Maria Weiterer and other threatened refugees. Later this humane and patriotic woman was slandered by the Stasi as an agent of French intelligence. Ibid., pp. 74–76.

4. Ibid., pp. 30, 56.

5. See S. Subak, *Rescue and Flight: American Relief Workers who defied the Nazis*, London, 2010, pp. 86–88, 109–11, 119–25, for details and photographs.

6. Between 1940 and 1946 the United Spanish Aid Committee, later the Joint Antifascist Refugee Committee (sometimes known as the Barsky Committee, after one of its leading figures) distributed through the USC between four and five million dollars. USC Boston was seemingly unaware of this. In its 1946 report it could only account for that which went through the books. 'Of the millions of dollars received by the Unitarian Service Committee since its founding, $269,280 has come from the J.A.F.R.C'. This original English text as well as the other information in German is in Barth and Schweizer, eds, *Der Fall Noel Field, Band I*, p. 320 n85.

7. W. Kießling, *'Leistner ist Mielke': Schatten einer gefälschten Biographie*, Berlin, 1998, p. 103.

8. Barth and Schweizer, eds, *Der Fall Noel Field, Band I*, p. 512.

9. This is suggested by the courteous and grateful letter that Bertz wrote to Noel on 7 July 1944, although it is by no means certain that he sent it. The Stasi found a copy among Bertz's papers following his death in April 1950. For the text see Kießling, *Partner im 'Narrenparadies'*, pp. 110–11. Another KPD cadre also recalled the Fields positively. 'Field was an extremely sympathetic person, very discreet', while Herta was 'an extremely nice woman both in her manners and demeanour, very simple, with no airs'. Ibid., p. 53.

10. Barth and Schweizer, eds, *Der Fall Noel Field, Band I*, pp. 170, 183–84, 314, 317–18, 453–54, 517, 658 n4, 662 n4, 725, 851; Lewis, *The Man who Disappeared, The Strange History of Noel Field*, London, 1965, pp. 135–36.

11. Subak, *Rescue and Flight*, p. 153.

12. Cited in Lewis, *The Man who Disappeared*, p. 129.

13. Barth and Schweizer, eds, *Der Fall Noel Field, Band I*, p. 332. Elsewhere Noel wrote that he spent four months in hospital from the beginning of 1944. On another occasion he specified 'winter 1943–44'. See Ibid., pp. 178, 459.

14. H. Massing, *This Deception*, New York, 1951, p. 308.

15. Barth and Schweizer, eds, *Der Fall Noel Field, Band I*, pp. 165–67, 166 n71, n72 and n73, 263–64, 263 n7, 406–08, 449–52, 449 n287, 452 n298, 771–74, 782–83; Lewis, *The Man who Disappeared*, pp. 152–56.

16. Possibly such ineptitude was a result of the liquidation of skilled INO operatives in the 1937–

38 bloodbath, and their replacement by poor quality recruits from backgrounds more conge-
nial to Stalin and his aims.

17. Noel held onto the letter, keeping it hidden until the spring of 1949, when he destroyed it at
Herta's urging. In her view it was extremely compromising.

18. The Soviet report is printed in Barth and Schweizer, eds, *Der Fall Noel Field, Band I*, pp. 782–
83. It is undated. Barth suggests that it was composed in the early 1960s. There is another
account that gives some credence to 'Brook's' record. This was a statement made by Bertz to
the ZPKK in October 1949. Bertz had used Noel's stay in the Basel eye hospital to quiz him
about his past. The reason for this was that some time before Noel had given Bertz the following information: 'A man had appeared at his Geneva home and invited him to collaborate with
our friends over there (i.e. Soviet intelligence). However, since this fellow couldn't prove his
identity and Field didn't know him from former times, Field sent him on his way without his
having achieved his purpose'. Ibid., p. 451 n295.

12. DANGEROUS LIAISONS: NOEL, DULLES AND THE OSS, 1942–45

1. For Dulles and the OSS, see P. Grose, *Allen Dulles: Spymaster: The Life and Times of the First
Civilian Director of the CIA*. London 2006; C. Mauch, *The Shadow War against Hitler: The Covert
Operations of America's Wartime Secret Intelligence Service*. New York/Chichester 2003; L. Mos-
ley, *Dulles: A Biography of Eleanor, Allen, and John Foster Dulles and their Family Network*, New
York, 1978; N. Petersen ed., *From Hitler's Doorstep: The Wartime Intelligence Reports of Allen
Dulles, 1942–1945*, University Park (Pa.), 1996; R. Smith, *OSS: The Secret History of America's
First Central Intelligence Agency*, New York, 1973. For Dulles and the Fields in Switzerland in
1917–18, see Mosley, *Dulles*, pp. 47–49; Grose (who rechristens Herbert Field 'Henry'), *Allen
Dulles: Spymaster*, pp. 32, 68. For Noel's recollection of contact with Dulles before 1942, see
B-R. Barth and W. Schweizer, eds, *Der Fall Noel Field, Band I: Gefängnisjahre 1949–1954*, Ber-
lin, 2005, pp. 199, 302, 523.

2. This section is based upon information in Ibid., pp. 195–96, 211, 436, 686. Dulles gave Field
the code identification number 394. See Petersen ed., *From Hitler's Doorstep*, p. 594. This meant
nothing more than that Noel's number and not his name was used in communications.

3. Barth and Schweizer, eds, *Der Fall Noel Field, Band I*, p. 202. Noel wrote an unknown number
of letters to Dulles (p. 198).

4. Ibid., p. 211.

5. Mosley, *Dulles*, pp. 48–49.

6. It is impossible to say whether this alleged meeting in 1918 did or did not take place. However,
in my view the alleged later meetings between Fields and Dulles (see Ibid., pp. 129–30, 147–
48, 171–72, 275–77) derive from the same fantasy portrait of super-spy Dulles that permeates
the risible assessment of the Field-Dulles relationship in *Operation Splinter Factor* by Stewart
Stevens.

7. The fullest published account of Dulles's journey to Switzerland and arrival there on 9 November
is in Grose, *Allen Dulles: Spymaster*, pp. 148–51. Some sources date his arrival as 8 November.

8. For the meetings with Dexter, the OSS official, and the December 1942 meeting with Dulles,
see Barth and Schweizer, eds, *Der Fall Noel Field, Band I*, pp. 197–99, 433–39, 521–23, 679–
82. For the Bauer affair, see Ibid., pp. 192–93, 192 n147 and n150, 193 n153, 198–200, 438–
39, 441–45, 445 n271, 519 n7, 526, 662–63; P. Brandt, et al., *Karrieren eines Außenseiters: Leo
Bauer zwischen Kommunismus und Sozialdemokratie 1912 bis 1972*, Berlin/Bonn, 1983,
pp. 88–108, *passim*; W. Kießling, *Partner im 'Narrenparadies': der Freundeskreis um Noel Field
und Paul Merker*, Berlin, 1994, pp. 61–63, 82–86; F. Lewis, *The Man who Disappeared: The
Strange History of Noel Field*, London, 1965, pp. 143–44; E. Wallach, *Light at Midnight*, New
York, 1967, pp. 32–33; W. Schweizer, email to T. Sharp, 12 June 2013. For the two meetings
concerning an exchange of CALPO material for funds from Dulles, see Barth and Schweizer,

eds, *Der Fall Noel Field, Band I*, pp. 204–06, 445–49, 542–44, 555, 684. On Noel's wish to use OSS as a bank and a communications centre, see Ibid., pp. 209–10, 441, 544–45, 554. On the OSE bombing request, see Ibid., p. 613.

9. Dexter and his wife Elisabeth were recruited into the OSS by Dulles in New York in June or July 1942, and given the code names 'Corn' and 'Cornette'. They flew to Lisbon in August. Robert alone travelled on to Marseille. There Dexter made an identical recruitment approach to a representative of the ERC. See S. Subak, *Rescue and Flight: American Relief Workers who defied the Nazis*, London, 2010, pp. 137–41, 147–48; R. Sullivan, *Villa Air-Bel: The Second World War, Escape and a House in France*, London, 2007, pp. 410–11. 'The Fields are both fine people', wrote Dexter to Boston in September 1942, 'but I am worried about them both. They are overworking and undereating'. Subak, *Rescue and Flight*, p. 149. Noel didn't return the compliment. He described Dexter as 'an unhealthy, fat and extremely lazy person' who sat around for hours in Field's office, disturbing his work. Barth and Schweizer, eds, *Der Fall Noel Field, Band I*, p. 197.

10. Subak repeats Flora Lewis's error that while he was in Switzerland Dexter took Field to meet Dulles in Bern. Subak, p. 148; Lewis, *The Man who Disappeared*, pp. 141–42. As observed in note 7 above Dulles did not reach Switzerland until 9 November 1942, while as she herself shows Dexter was back in Marseille in October. Subak, *Rescue and Flight*, p. 149.

11. Bauer's German-Jewish wife was interned in the women's camp in Rieucros and deported by Vichy to Germany in August 1942. She died in KZ Ravensbrück. Brandt, et al., *Karrieren eines Außenseiters*, pp. 66–67.

12. In the only two published telegrams sent by Dulles which refer to his relationship with Field, he acknowledged that he 'furnished part of [the] funds for financing this group's [CALPO's] activities'. See Petersen ed., *From Hitler's Doorstep*, pp. 404, 431.

13. The cooperation of USC Boston with the OSS earned them the dubious privilege of using the OSS pouch to speed up their communications with Lisbon. New York's OSS office read most of the messages passing between the two USC centres. Subak, *Rescue and Flight*, pp. 164, 209.

14. Barth and Schweizer, eds, *Der Fall Noel Field, Band I*, pp. 206–08, 210–11, 474, 478–81, 549–53, 560–76, 689–95, 705–12.

15. In August 1944 Noel illegally undertook a short trip to the Alpine area of France liberated by the Resistance. He witnessed the US army's entry into Grenoble and the public execution of French collaborators. Slipping into the German-occupied area, he received his baptism of fire from a German aeroplane, followed by a head wound when his car overturned and propelled Noel through the windscreen. Ibid., p. 178, p. 473; B-R. Barth and W. Schweizer, eds, *Der Fall Noel Field, Band II: Asyl in Ungarn 1954–1957*, Berlin, 2007, pp. 207–08; Subak, *Rescue and Flight*, pp. 197–98.

16. Petersen, ed., *From Hitler's Doorstep*, p. 404.

17. Ibid., p. 431. OSS and CALPO were already working together in January 1945. See Mauch, *The Shadow War against Hitler*, pp. 176–78.

18. Noel claimed to have forgotten the major's name.

19. None of this detail emerges from the account in A. Schlesinger, *A Life in the Twentieth Century: Innocent Beginnings, 1917–1950*, Boston/New York, 2000, pp. 334–35, and his record is totally at variance with Field's. Schlesinger writes that he had 'several conversations' with Noel. Schlesinger is also the source of the contention that Noel somehow sought to subvert American policy in Germany by promoting CALPO, which nobody appeared to realise was under communist control. See the various 'Cold War' accounts in Grose, *Allen Dulles: Spymaster*; Lewis, *The Man who Disappeared*; Mosley, *Dulles*; and S. Steven, *Operation Splinter Factor*, London, 1974. In fact the OSS was perfectly aware that CALPO's membership was about 90 per cent communist. Mauch, *The Shadow War against Hitler*, p. 177.

20. The nebulous timeline in Noel's account suggests that the meeting probably took place on 30 January 1945.

13. TEETERING EDIFICE: USC EUROPE 1945–47

1. B-R. Barth and W. Schweizer, eds, *Der Fall Noel Field, Band I: Gefängnisjahre 1949–1954*, Berlin, 2005, pp. 176, 189, 193–94, 211, 314–17, 323, 350–58, 410–13, 446, 474–78, 517, 550, 561–62, 735–45, 738 n13, 847–62, 847 n3 and n4, 848 n5, 850 n14; B-R. Barth and W. Schweizer, eds, *Der Fall Noel Field, Band II: Asyl in Ungarn 1954–1957*, Berlin, 2007, pp. 423–24 (Kojsza biography), p. 438 (Tempi biography); F. Lewis, *The Man who Disappeared: The Strange History of Noel Field*, London, 1965, pp. 131–33, 166; W. Kießling, *Partner im 'Narrenparadies': der Freundeskreis um Noel Field und Paul Merker*, Berlin, 1994, pp. 116–23.

2. Barth and Schweizer, eds, *Der Fall Noel Field, Band I*, p. 176. 'Saving the cadres' was no empty phrase. Gustav Regler recorded the following incident in Le Vernet in 1940. The Quakers had just provided the prisoners with bundles of blankets, clothing and footwear. Paul Merker drew Regler to one side and handed him a list of those who were first in line to receive blankets. '[T]hey were all Party officials. Only after them were all the other "ordinary prisoners" to be considered. Thus had the professional revolutionaries decided. The words "preservation of the cadre" were used'. Regler noted that the cadres already had two blankets each. G. Regler, *The Owl of Minerva*, London, 1959, pp. 342–43.

3. Lewis, *The Man Who Disappeared*, p. 133. Elsewhere Field admitted that his shyness with women made it particularly difficult for him to criticise his female employees or to give them orders, let alone to sack them. Barth and Schweizer, eds, *Der Fall Noel Field, Band I*, pp. 176–77.

4. Ibid., p. 193. Charles Joy, who had an affair with Jo, described her as having 'certain definite masculine traits' as well as being 'essentially and charmingly feminine'. S. Subak, *Rescue and Flight: American Relief Workers who defied the Nazis*, London, 2010, p. 202. There is a posed profile of Jo in Ms Subak's book in which she looks distinctly masculine. This contrasts sharply with the very feminine full-face portraits of her in Dr Barth's work. In fact the photos seem to be of two different women. Jo was an abbreviation of 'Johanna', one of her party names.

5. Jurr's early death in December 1947 was a consequence of his harsh treatment in prison and KZ Sachsenhausen. See Barth and Schweizer, eds, *Der Fall Noel Field, Band I*, pp. 189 n137, 413 n133.

6. An enthusiastic skier, Noel taught himself from a book. Ibid., pp. 289–90.

7. Joy had replaced Robert Dexter as executive director in September 1944. The Dexters resigned from the USC in October. See Subak, *Rescue and Flight*, pp. 207–08.

8. Since 1939 Jo had lived with the Russian-born PCF member and resistance fighter, Cyrille Znosko-Borowski. Barth and Schweizer, eds, *Der Fall Noel Field, Band I*, p. 413 n131. She married him (perhaps again bigamously) following the death of Werner Jurr.

9. Joy had already met Jo in Marseille in 1941. Subak, *Rescue and Flight* p. 202.

10. On Ilona's internment in France, see Barth and Schweizer, eds, *Der Fall Noel Field, Band I*, pp. 350 n2, 735 n10, 849 n9, 850 n14.

11. Heinz Priess, the head of CALPO's military commission, used Ilona's facilities before crossing into Switzerland in early 1945. Priess also met Noel, whom he found very sympathetic. This brief meeting would later lead to a ZPKK investigation of Priess. H. Priess, *Spaniens Himmel und keine Sterne. Ein deutsches Geschichtsbuch. Erinnerungen an ein Leben und ein Jahrhundert*, Berlin, 1996, pp. 276–77.

12. Barth and Schweizer, eds, *Der Fall Noel Field, Band I*, pp. 184, 191, 314, 317, 326–28, 326 n95, 485–95, 487 n434, 778 n40, 854; Barth and Schweizer, eds, *Der Fall Noel Field, Band II*, pp. 192–93, 425 (Lechtman biography); Lewis, *The Man who Disappeared*, pp. 174–75; H.

Field and K. Field, *Trapped in the Cold War: The Ordeal of an American Family*, Stanford, 1999, pp. 1, 3, 13–14, 39, 47, 298; Kießling, *Partner im 'Narrenparadies'*, pp. 133–35; internet sources on Tonia Lechtmann.

13. As an example of the stories about Noel's activities, see Varian Fry's letter of 26 March 1945 in Subak, *Rescue and Flight*, p. 209.

14. Barth and Schweizer, eds, *Der Fall Noel Field, Band I*, p. 317. Flora Lewis contended that the Fields were originally hired in 1941 at a joint annual salary of $5,750. Lewis, *The Man who Disappeared*, p. 127.

15. From early 1941 to the summer of 1947 Hermann worked in New York as an architect in an office near Grand Central Station. Thanks to the contract that his firm had with the US Army Corps of Engineers, he was never conscripted. During the war Kate worked for the British Press Service and then for *Time* magazine.

16. Anna Seghers (1900–83) had fled to France in 1933. She, her husband and children left Marseille in March 1941 for Mexico. They ended up in New York and were detained on Ellis Island, before reaching Mexico in June. There Anna wrote her novel *Transit*, based upon her experiences.

17. In February 1946 CRALOG was set up to coordinate the work of the twenty-two aid agencies then operating in the US occupation zone of Germany. Barth and Schweizer, eds, *Der Fall Noel Field, Band I*, p. 314 n66. Noel volunteered to work for CRALOG in the mistaken belief that it would be politically advantageous. However, as he admitted, control of the aid agencies through the welfare department of OMGUS was too great for him to have any impact upon policy.

18. Hermann Field later noted that she was at least spared watching the family's disintegration.

19. The issue of whom Noel may have met in Czechoslovakia in 1947 arises in the Slánský trial. The problem is compounded by the fact that Hermann Field was also in Czechoslovakia in summer 1947. See Chapter 27.

20. Field and Field, *Trapped in the Cold War*, p. 39. They had more than a brief conversation at an air terminal. As revealed by the second telephone conversation between the Field brothers following their release in autumn 1954, they had an evening meal in Paris. See Barth and Schweizer, eds, *Der Fall Noel Field, Band II*, p. 101. Monica Felton (Chapter 29 footnote 49) was also present. This is not the only example of Hermann ignoring or suppressing inconvenient facts.

21. Barth and Schweizer, eds, *Der Fall Noel Field, Band I*, pp. 170–71, 176, 194–95, 314, 495–99; Lewis, *The Man who Disappeared*, London, 1965, pp. 175–80.

22. Ms Subak provides a different account to that written by Field, on which I have relied. In her version Joy denied any wrongdoing and was sacked, while Jo resigned. However, her resignation was rejected because she was considered indispensible, and she was asked to return to France. Subak, *Rescue and Flight*, pp. 224–25.

23. Noel weighed in for the flight at eighty kilos, about twelve stone eight pounds or 176 pounds.

24. Barth and Schweizer, eds, *Der Fall Noel Field, Band I*, pp. 170–71, 176.

14. THE SEARCHERS: NOEL AND HERTA 1947–49

1. B-R. Barth and W. Schweizer, eds, *Der Fall Noel Field, Band I: Gefängnisjahre 1949–1954*, Berlin, 2005, pp. 4–7, 148, 213–14, 219, 289, 329–31, 713–14, 714 n9.

2. Ibid., p. 193.

3. Ibid., p. 331.

4. K. Kaplan, *Report on the Murder of the General Secretary*, London, 1990, p. 21. This is the only source that mentions the April 1948 invitation. Noel met Kosta in Geneva several months before

his 1948 trip, but makes no mention of any invitation. See Barth and Schweizer, eds, *Der Fall Noel Field, Band I*, p. 600.

5. The earliest record of overt Soviet/Eastern bloc interest in Field is dated February 1948. This was in a report by an agent of Hungarian military intelligence see Chapter 20.

6. Barth and Schweizer, eds, *Der Fall Noel Field, Band I*, pp. 152, 152 n22, 208, 501–02, 585 n6, 605 n63, 611–12, 616–26, 629–30, 659–61, 660 n8, 662 n4; B-R. Barth and W. Schweizer, eds, *Der Fall Noel Field, Band II: Asyl in Ungarn 1954–1957*, Berlin, 2007, pp. 400, 417; F. Lewis, *The Man who Disappeared: The Strange History of Noel Field*, London, 1965, pp. 184–90.

7. Barth and Schweizer, eds, *Der Fall Noel Field, Band I*, p. 208.

8. L. Mosley, *Dulles: A Biography of Eleanor, Allen, and John Foster Dulles and their Family Network*, New York, 1978, p. 172.

9. This may have reflected specific distrust of the Glaser family, rather than an overall policy line. A report by the Spanish Republican security service SIM cited all four Glasers as untrustworthy, on account of their activities in Spain. Kreikemeyer had warned Noel of concerns about Erica.

10. Kurt Joachim Glaser had fought his former countrymen as Captain Keith James Griffith, a member of No 3 (Jewish) Troop of No 10 Commando, which was attached to the Royal West Kent Regiment. He became his unit's first Jewish commander, but was killed by a sniper's bullet at the River Aller crossing on 11 April 1945, less than a month before VE Day. He was buried at Becklingen in Lower Saxony. The members of the commando were urged to take English names using the initials of their original names.

11. Robert and Erica were still married when Robert died in 1990.

12. Barth and Schweizer, eds, *Der Fall Noel Field, Band I*, pp. 7–8, 15–26, 212–15, 320, 330–31, 502–03, 715–16, 721; Barth and Schweizer, eds, *Der Fall Noel Field, Band II*, p. 411 (Duracz biography); Lewis, *The Man who Disappeared*, pp. 12, 195, 256; T. Toranska, *'Them': Stalin's Polish Puppets*, London, 1987, pp. 313–14.

13. On Poland's post-war frontiers, see T. Sharp, 'The Origins of the "Teheran Formula" on Polish Frontiers'. *Journal of Contemporary History*, Vol. 12 (1977), pp. 381–93; T. Sharp, 'The Russian Annexation of the Königsberg Area 1941–45'. *Survey*, Vol. 23, No. 4 (105) (1977–78), pp. 156–62.

14. Barth and Schweizer, eds, *Der Fall Noel Field, Band I*, p. 502.

15. Ibid., p. 721.

16. For the letter to Berman, see Ibid., pp. 15–17. The 'short party history' is in Ibid., pp. 18–26. The quotations are from Ibid., p. 16.

17. Ibid., pp. 8–12, 27 n7, 27–35, 33 n3, 34 n5, 35 n13, 148, 214–16, 289, 331, 503–09, 503 n10, 505 n17, 597, 601–02, 620, 625, 804–05; Kaplan, *Report on the Murder*, pp. 21–23; W. Kießling, *Partner im 'Narrenparadies': der Freundeskreis um Noel Field und Paul Merker*, Berlin, 1994, pp. 152–58.

18. Barth and Schweizer, eds, *Der Fall Noel Field, Band I*, p. 28.

19. Text in Kießling, *Partner im 'Narrenparadies'*, pp. 156–57.

20. Kaplan, *Report on the Murder*, p. 23. In his report of 7 February 1949 (see Barth and Schweizer, eds, *Der Fall Noel Field, Band I*, pp. 33–37) ÁVH Colonel Szűcs stated that the StB interrogated Noel on 15 October. It is probable that this was a factual error, since this report is riddled with them, as are most ÁVH reports. Such errors are in addition to the deliberate lies and distortions the reports contain. It is also noteworthy that this meeting with the StB was never mentioned in Field's statements or interrogations in 1954. See Ibid., p. 34 n5. It is possible that certain matters were then designated as 'off-limits', owing to developments in Czechoslovakia.

21. Ibid., p. 11. Szűcs wrongly dates his departure as 27 November. Ibid., p. 33.

22. When the French refused to accept London as counsellor at the Czechoslovak embassy, he was

appointed a deputy foreign minister. London took up the Prague post in March 1949, and headed the cadres department as well as the courier service with its links to intelligence. Ibid., pp. 36 n20, 598 n39.

23. Kaplan, *Report on the Murder*, p. 23. It is unclear whether this meeting was arranged or simply took place on the off-chance. In 1954 Noel made no reference to this particular meeting with London. But see footnote 20 above and Chapter 27, footnote 45.

24. On 11 January 1949 Noel wrote (in German) to Tonia Lechtman: 'So we're now simply short-term tourists in Switzerland, after living in Geneva for more than twelve years'. Barth and Schweizer, eds, *Der Fall Noel Field, Band I*, p. 11.

15. PAST BECOMES PRESENT: HEDE'S FRIENDS, OLD AND NEW

1. H. Massing, *This Deception*, New York, 1951, pp. 287–306. On the Zarubins and Soviet wartime espionage in the USA, see: their biographies on Documentstalk.com; J. Haynes, H. Klehr and A. Vassiliev, *Spies: The Rise and Fall of the KGB in America*, London, 2009; T. Morgan, *Reds: McCarthyism in Twentieth-Century America*, New York, 2003; H. Romerstein and E. Breindel, *The Venona Secrets: Exposing Soviet Espionage and America's Traitors*, Washington, 2001; K. Sibley, *Red Spies in America: Stolen Secrets and the Dawn of the Cold War*, Lawrence (Kansas), 2004; P. Sudoplatov, *Special Tasks: The Memoirs of an Unwanted Witness–a Soviet Spymaster*, London, 1994; A. Weinstein and A. Vassiliev, *The Haunted Wood: Soviet Espionage in America–the Stalin Era*, New York, 1999. On Browder, the CPUSA, HUAC, and the various high profile cases (other than Hiss-Chambers), see in addition A. Knight, *How the Cold War began: The Gouzenko Affair and the Hunt for Soviet Spies*, Toronto, 2005; K. Olmsted, *Red Spy Queen: A Biography of Elizabeth Bentley*, Chapel Hill, University of North Carolina Press, 2002; J. Ryan, *Earl Browder, The Failure of American Communism*, Tuscaloosa, 1997; E. Schrecker, *Many are the Crimes: McCarthyism in America*, Princeton/Chichester, 1998; R. Williams, *Klaus Fuchs: Atom Spy*, London, 1987.

2. A. Vassiliev, *Black Notebook*, Wilson Center Cold War International History Project Digital Archive, http://www.wilsoncenter.org/sites/default/files/Black%20Notebook%20Original.pdf, last accessed 26 May 2013, p. 161.

3. In a communication to New York in April 1941 Moscow referred to its valuable deactivated agents. 'We are singling out the agents "Vatsek" and "Redhead", who were deactivated in 1939 [1938?], as the most gifted agents, who could be used not only in the press line, but also in econ[omic] intelligence'. Ibid., p. 173. In a report written on 23 December 1949, which listed Soviet 'failures' in the USA in the years 1938–48, the writer notes: 'Redhead, Hedwiga Gumperz, Vatsek's [Paul's] wife. Sent to USA in 1938 to carry out our assignments. Traitor since 1948'. Paul is also listed as a 'traitor'. Ibid., p. 77.

4. Massing, *This Deception*, p. 291.

5. In 1937 Dr Elsie Field married a mathematics lecturer, Dr Joseph Doob. They lived in Urbana, Illinois. B-R. Barth and W. Schweizer, eds, *Der Fall Noel Field, Band I: Gefängnisjahre 1949–1954*, Berlin, 2005, p. 664.

6. Massing, *This Deception*, p. 291.

7. Ibid., p. 294. The Massings kept on an apartment in Manhattan throughout the period when they had farms in Bucks County.

8. Barth and Schweizer, eds, *Der Fall Noel Field, Band I*, p. 396. Herta mentions that Hede felt particularly bitter towards Hermann. Ibid., p. 884.

9. Massing, *This Deception*, p. 305.

10. From October 1939 to January 1940 Zarubin played a role in the preliminaries to Katyń. See Romerstein and Breindel, *The Venona Secrets*, pp. 4–7. In April–May 1940 the NKVD cold-bloodedly murdered some 22,000 Polish POWs at three sites in western Russia and Ukraine.

This heinous crime, subsumed under the name Katyń (the burial site uncovered by the Germans in 1943), was ordered by Stalin and Beria. On Katyń, see A. Cienciala et al., eds, *Katyń: A Crime without Punishment*, London, 2007.

11. INO (the Foreign Department) was upgraded to INU (the Foreign Directorate) in 1941.

12. In Budapest Herta told her interrogators that Hermann Field knew 'Natasha' (Lisa Zarubina), although she didn't know how this came about. See Barth and Schweizer, eds, *Der Fall Noel Field, Band I*, p. 831, p. 833.

13. The Marxist-oriented Institute of Social Research was founded in 1924 at the University of Frankfurt. The Nazis closed it down in 1933, and it eventually relocated to Columbia University in New York. Both Julian Gumperz and Paul Massing had studied in Frankfurt. Franz Neumann had emigrated to the USA in 1936. A left-wing member of the SPD, Neumann was the author of *Behemoth: The Structure and Practice of National Socialism*. Details of Paul Massing's contact with Neumann and Lisa are in A. Vassiliev, *White Notebook 3*, Wilson Center Cold War International History Project Digital Archive, http://www.wilsoncenter.org/sites/default/files/White_Notebook_No. 3_Transcribed.pdf, last accessed 26 May 2013, pp. 133–36. Lisa Zarubina definitely 'handled' Paul, and possibly Hede too, over some period in 1942–44. Lisa also met Neumann directly.

14. After her recall to Moscow in July or August 1944, Lisa is described as working at the Centre until her dismissal from INU in September 1946. See her biography in Documentstalk.com. Therefore one must wonder what Lisa had been up to in the USA, shortly after her 'dismissal'. She is recorded as arriving—under her own name Elizabeth Zarubin—in Gothenburg on 1 November 1946, having sailed from New York aboard the *Gripssholm*. This information was unearthed by Peter Bull. Unfortunately, he was unable to discover Lisa's date of entry into the USA. However, it leaves open the possibility, amongst many others of course, that Lisa was in contact with the Massings again in 1946.

15. Barth and Schweizer, eds, *Der Fall Noel Field, Band I*, pp. 261–62, 391, 488–89, 488 n438, 778–81, 802, 883–85; Massing, *This Deception*, pp. 168, 307–10. Minor details are altered in H. Massing, *Die grosse Täuschung: Geschichte einer Sowjetagentin*, Freiburg, 1967, pp. 163, 295–98.

16. Massing, *This Deception*, p. 307. This would seem to be another example of Hede's studied vagueness about facts when it served her purposes.

17. Duggan told Noel that Paul was in contact with Raymond Murphy, the security officer in the State Department. Barth and Schweizer, eds, *Der Fall Noel Field, Band I*, p. 780.

18. Jean and Sali Liebermann, along with their children Stephen and Margot, had arrived in New York from Marseille on 17 December 1945. They moved to California in 1946.

19. Massing, *This Deception*, pp. 168, 310.

20. Ibid., p. 312.

21. Herta also pointed out that it was very unlikely that there was any documentary proof about Noel's espionage activities in the USA, because the working relationship between the two couples had ended when the Massings were still loyal to the USSR. Barth and Schweizer, eds, *Der Fall Noel Field, Band I*, p. 884.

22. On the Massings and the INS, see J. Kisselhoff, 'Hede Massing's Story', on his website 'The Alger Hiss Story'. https://files.nyu.edu/th15/public/hedemassingstory.html, last accessed 26 May 2013. On Eisler, see E. Bentley, ed., *Thirty Years of Treason: Excerpts from Hearings before the House Committee on Un-American Activities, 1938–1968*, New York, 1971; C. Epstein, *The Last Revolutionaries: German Communists and their Century*, London, 2003; R. Friedmann, *Ulbrichts Rundfunkmann: eine Gerhart-Eisler-Biographie*, Berlin, 2007; Schrecker, *Many are the Crimes*.

23. Massing, *This Deception*, p. 296. Herta was under the false impression that Paul too was a naturalised US citizen. Barth and Schweizer, eds, *Der Fall Noel Field, Band I*, p. 884.

24. Paul actually told the INS that he didn't know about Hede's marriage to Eisler. J. Kisselhoff, 'Hede Massing's Story'.

25. He wasn't exactly truthful with his own people either. When questioned about Hede in East Germany in July 1951, Eisler replied that after splitting with her in 1922, they 'met once more in Moscow in 1935'. Friedmann, *Ulbrichts Rundfunkmann*, p. 54. This is highly unlikely. There is no evidence that Hede was in Moscow in 1935, and she claims to have been in Europe that summer. However, she was in Moscow with Paul in January 1931 when Gerhart and Elli returned from China, and the two couples saw each other then. Hede also claims to have seen him 'quite often' in the USA. On one occasion he advised her about obtaining false passports. She also wired Eisler before leaving for Moscow in 1937. Massing, *This Deception*, pp. 95–97, 182, 187, 241.

26. Brunhilde Rothstein was another communist who originated amongst the Jews of Galicia. Born in Tarnopol in 1912, she grew up in Frankfurt am Main. Hilde joined the KPD in 1931 and operated as a courier. Arrested in Germany in 1935, only her Polish citizenship saved her from a severe sentence. She was expelled to Poland. In spring 1937 the KPD ordered her to Paris, where she met Eisler. Gerhart divorced Elli, who was in Sweden, in early 1942 by an exchange of letters under Mexican law. He married Hilde in Connecticut in August 1942. Friedmann, *Ulbrichts Rundfunkmann*, pp. 129–31, 159–61.

27. Detained with them was Anna Seghers, the novelist, who like Eisler was German, Jewish and a KPD member. Yet she was allowed to leave for Mexico. See Chapter 13, footnote 16.

28. R. Lamphere and T. Shachtman, *The FBI-KGB War*, London, 1987, p. 42.

29. The brief verbal duel between Eisler and HUAC is printed in Bentley, ed., *Thirty Years of Treason*, pp. 57–59. This volume also contains the vituperative evidence of Ruth Fischer against her brother Gerhart, as well as HUAC's later hearing of Eisler's younger brother, the composer Hanns Eisler. Ibid., pp. 59–109. Hanns composed several film scores as well as the GDR national anthem.

30. Hilde was arrested after Gerhart's flight and deported on 22 June. She was flown to Europe where she joined Eisler in East Berlin later that month.

31. See Barth and Schweizer, eds, *Der Fall Noel Field, Band I*, p. 486.

32. Massing, *This Deception*, pp. 313–35. On the FBI and the Massings, see J. Kisselhoff, 'Hede Massing's Story'; Lamphere and Shachtman, *The FBI-KGB War*. On Hiss-Chambers, see S. Tanenhaus, *Whittaker Chambers: A Biography*, New York, 1997; A. Weinstein, *Perjury: The Hiss-Chambers Case*, New York, 1997; G. White, *Alger Hiss's Looking-Glass Wars: The Covert Life of a Soviet Spy*, New York, 2004.

33. Massing, *This Deception*, p. 314. According to one account Hede testified at Eisler's second trial. Lamphere and Shachtman, *The FBI-KGB War*, p. 59. Hede makes no mention of this.

34. Kisselhoff, 'Hede Massing's Story'.

35. The Court of Appeals confirmed this conviction on 7 December 1950. The Supreme Court denied a further appeal on 12 March 1951, and Hiss was jailed ten days later. He was released on 27 November 1954 and died in November 1996.

36. Kisselhoff, 'Hede Massing's Story'. Hede's plaudits for the FBI are in Massing, *This Deception*, pp. 314–16. After her divorce from Paul she converted to Catholicism in 1953. 'I am one of those people who need to believe in something', she wrote later. Massing, *Die grosse Täuschung*, p. 320. Hede died of emphysema in Greenwich Village on 8 March 1981, aged eighty. Paul remarried in 1954. After retiring from university teaching he returned to Germany and died in Tübingen in April 1979.

16. 'DECISIVE MEASURES ON OUR PART': STALIN'S ROLE

1. Dr Chervonnaya offers plausible grounds for destruction in her biography of Field on Documentstalk.com.
2. Cited in R. Conquest, *The Great Terror: A Reassessment*, London, 1990, p. 56.
3. Although Stalin's official date of birth was 21 December 1879, he was born Iosif Vissarionovich Djugashvili in Gori in Georgia on 18 December 1878. The above are New Style dates conforming to the Gregorian calendar introduced by the Bolsheviks. Under the Old Style Julian calendar, which was in force in the Russian empire when Stalin was born, he would have come into the world twelve days earlier on 6 December 1878.
4. S. Montefiore, *Stalin: the Court of the Red Tsar*. London 2003, p. 473. This informative book is also the source of the dates of Stalin's vacations.
5. Yezhov was arrested on 10 April 1939, tried in secret on 2 February 1940, and shot that night. For more on his bloody career, see M. Jansen and N. Petrov, *Stalin's Loyal Executioner: People's Commissar Nikolai Ezhov 1895–1940*, Stanford, 2002.
6. Abakumov claimed to have been born in 1908, although he was probably a good bit older. From 14 April 1943 until 16 March 1946 he headed GUKR-NKO (the chief directorate of Counter-Intelligence of the People's Commissariat of Defence), more popularly known as SMERSH (an acronym of *Smert Shpionam*: 'Death to Spies'). In this capacity Abakumov reported directly to Stalin, as he did when head of the MGB. SMERSH was staffed not by the military but by state security (NKGB) officers. On Abakumov and SMERSH, see M. Parrish, *The Lesser Terror: Soviet State Security*. London 1996; D. Rayfield, *Stalin and his Hangmen*, London, 2005; J. Dziak, *Chekisty: A History of the KGB*, Lexington, Mass., 1988.
7. Despite his numerous crimes, Beria had little, if anything, to do with these events. Khrushchev and the dominant post-Stalin faction made Beria the scapegoat later, following his arrest and execution in 1953. Beria was in any case too busy to involve himself closely in such matters. From 1945 to 1953 he supervised the development of first the Soviet atomic bomb and then the hydrogen bomb. Indeed, his life depended upon his success in the initial venture. See his letter from prison to Malenkov of 1 July 1953 in V. Zubok and C. Pleshakov, *Inside the Kremlin's Cold War: From Stalin to Khrushchev*, 1996, p. 151. The Soviet atomic bomb was tested successfully on 29 August 1949, and the hydrogen bomb on 12 August 1953 when Beria was in prison.
8. See Chapter 20.
9. V. Rogovin, *Stalin's Terror of 1937–1938: Political Genocide in the USSR*, Oak Park (MI), 2007, p. 134. At the time of the Red Army purge in summer 1937, Stalin argued that 'if there is even five per cent of the truth then that is already something'. V. Rogovin, *1937: Stalin's Year of Terror*, Oak Park (MI), 1998, p. 433. 'As is well-known' (*kak izvestno*) was a favourite phrase of Stalin and was adopted by his satraps. No evidence was required to substantiate these well-known 'facts', while disputing them was risky and often lethal. 'It is not accidental' (*ne sluchayno*) was another gem, used to assert a non-existent connection between two events. See Conquest, *The Great Terror*, p. 56.
10. There is sufficient relevant information in the Vassiliev notebooks, which I have used in earlier chapters, to justify this assertion.
11. B-R. Barth and W. Schweizer, eds, *Der Fall Noel Field, Band I: Gefängnisjahre 1949–1954*, Berlin, 2005, p. 153.
12. See Chapter 19.
13. The SOZ was proclaimed the GDR (German Democratic Republic) on 7 October 1949.
14. S. Alliluyeva, *Twenty Letters to a Friend*, London, 1967, p. 171.
15. In 1907 in an underground newspaper in Baku Stalin wrote: 'Somebody among the Bolsheviks remarked jokingly that since the Mensheviks were the faction of the Jews and the Bolshe-

viks that of the native Russians, it would be a good thing to have a pogrom in the Party'. Cited in Conquest, *The Great Terror*, p. 65.

16. Cited in A. Vaksberg, *Stalin Against the Jews*, New York, 1994, p. 16.

17. See Chapter 6, footnote 1.

18. O. Figes, *A People's Tragedy: The Russian Revolution, 1891–1924*, London, 1997, p. 678.

19. In 1918 65.5 per cent of all Jewish Cheka officials were described as 'responsible officials'. In 1923 15.5 per cent of leading officials in the OGPU were Jewish. Y. Slezkine, *The Jewish Century*, Princeton/Oxford 2004, p. 177. Jews were in charge of eleven of the twelve major slave-labour camp complexes. Vaksberg, *Stalin Against the Jews*, p. 98.

20. N. Cohn, *Warrant for Genocide: The Myth of the Jewish World Conspiracy and the Protocols of the Elders of Zion*, London, 1996, p. 132. However, Trotsky (born Lev Davidovich Bronshtein in Ukraine in November 1879) rejected Lenin's offer of the posts of Commissar for Internal Affairs and Deputy Premier precisely because of his Jewish origins. Figes, *A People's Tragedy*, p. 804.

21. Ibid., pp. 676–79.

22. Cited in G. Kern, *A Death in Washington: Walter G. Krivitsky and the Stalin Terror*, New York, 2004, p. 36.

23. Presumably Lenin's caveat about the 'sanctity' of Bolshevik lives also applied to Trotsky's nauseating contention: 'We must put an end once and for all to the papist-Quaker babble about the sanctity of human life'. Cited in Figes, *A People's Tragedy*, p. 641.

24. Jews made up 38.5 per cent of the top leadership of the NKVD under Yagoda in 1934, 32 per cent under Yezhov in 1937, but only 3.5 per cent under Beria in 1940. Members of the 'suspect nations' (Poles, Germans, Balts) held 14 per cent of these posts in 1934, 12 per cent in 1937, and absolutely none in 1940. The big winners were Russians, rising from one third under Yagoda to two-thirds under Beria, and Ukrainians who tripled their representation. Unsurprisingly, Georgians more than doubled their proportion under Beria. P. Gregory, *Terror by Quota: State Security from Lenin to Stalin (an Archival Study)*, London, 2009, pp. 62–64. The repression of members of the 'suspect nations' in the NKVD leadership took place during 'the Great Terror', which Yezhov and Stalin unleashed in July 1937. Yet this was only a minor aspect of the broader 'national terror' launched against both communist and non-communist members of these minorities. Professor Snyder's superb work details the horrific toll. About 85,000 Poles living in the USSR were executed in 1937–38. More thousands were shot as 'spies' for Estonia, Latvia, and Finland. Taken together, 'national terror' operations directed against groups amounting to 1.4 per cent of the Soviet population resulted in the murder of nearly a quarter of a million people, or 36 per cent of the fatalities of 'the Great Terror'. See T. Snyder, *Bloodlands: Europe between Hitler and Stalin*, London, 2010, pp. 89–109.

25. Vaksberg, *Stalin Against the Jews*, pp. 73–77. Quotations are on p. 76.

26. The fullest account of the proceedings of the trials is in Conquest.

27. J. Rubenstein and V. Naumov, *Stalin's Secret Pogrom: The Post-War Inquisition of the Jewish Anti-Fascist Committee*, London, 2005, p. 33, p. 421 n77. The original statement included the line that 'Active anti-Semites are punished with death by the laws of the USSR'. Vaksberg, *Stalin Against the Jews*, p. 59. This author adds that there 'had never been trials for anti-Semitism ending in a death sentence'.

28. G. Kostyrchenko, *Out of the Red Shadows: Anti-Semitism in Stalin's Russia*, New York, 1995, p. 36.

29. Text in Ibid., pp. 45–47.

30. Rubenstein and Naumov, *Stalin's Secret Pogrom*, p. 20.

31. Even while the Red Army was retreating towards Stalingrad in 1942, the priority of some officials was to submit a report to the Central Committee secretariat, complaining that many Russian artistic institutions were 'filled by non-Russian people (mainly by Jews)'. Kostyrchenko, *Out of the Red Shadows*, p. 15. The Jewish editorial staff of the Red Army paper *Krasnaya Zvezda*

(Red Star) was purged in 1943. There was also a deliberate and mendacious understatement of the medal tally awarded Jewish soldiers fighting against the Germans.

32. Rubenstein and Naumov, *Stalin's Secret Pogrom*, p. 23.
33. Ibid., p. 31; Vaksberg, *Stalin Against the Jews*, p. 195.
34. Kostyrchenko, *Out of the Red Shadows*, p. 83. She received a ten-year sentence in May 1948, and her sister-in-law Anna Redens one of five years, which was arbitrarily doubled in December 1952. Vaksberg, *Stalin Against the Jews*, p. 217n.
35. Alliluyeva, *Twenty Letters to a Friend*, p. 207.
36. Vaksberg, *Stalin Against the Jews*, p. 182. After Stalin's death the imprisoned Abakumov stated: 'As far as I recall, in 1948 […] Stalin gave me an urgent assignment—to quickly organize the liquidation of Mikhoels […] Mikhoels had arrived in Minsk […] When this was reported to Stalin, he immediately gave orders that the liquidation be done in Minsk'. Ibid., p. 180.
37. See A. Krammer, *The Forgotten Friendship: Israel and the Soviet Bloc, 1947–53*, London, 1974.
38. See Chapter 28.
39. Rubenstein and Naumov, *Stalin's Secret Pogrom*, p. 41.
40. In fact the purge extended beyond the JAC. In January 1949 one hundred and forty-four Jewish writers were arrested, not only in Moscow, but in Kiev, Odessa and Minsk. Vaksberg, *Stalin Against the Jews*, p. 201.
41. Lozovsky's interrogation took place on 13 January, the anniversary of Mikhoels's murder. S. Montefiore, *Stalin: The Court of the Red Tsar*. London 2003, p. 521; Vaksberg, *Stalin Against the Jews*, p. 202. Stalin loved to use anniversaries for driving home a message. The death penalty, which was abolished somewhat amazingly by Stalin on 26 May 1947, was reintroduced on 13 January 1950. The article which would publicise the so-called 'Doctor's Plot' appeared in *Pravda* on 13 January 1953.
42. Kostyrchenko, *Out of the Red Shadows*, pp. 153, 165.
43. See Chapter 24.

17. HERESY: TITO VERSUS STALIN

1. L. Adamic, *The Eagle and the Roots*, New York, 1952, p. 27.
2. Stalin was made a marshal in February 1943, and Tito the following November. Stalin was 'promoted' to generalissimo in June 1945.
3. Cited in H. Smith, *The State of Europe*, London, 1950, p. 368.
4. J. Gunther, *Behind Europe's Curtain*, London 1949, p. 95. As the Yugoslav deputy foreign minister put it in November 1948, the Soviet Union 'invented all sorts of objections of an ideological nature to make the break appear plausible when they found that we were not ready simply to obey their orders'. J. Korbel, *Tito's Communism*, Denver, 1951, p. 301.
5. For an exception, see C. Sulzberger, *A Long Row of Candles: Memoirs and Diaries 1934–1954*, Toronto, 1969, p. 412.
6. Tito's birthplace was the north Croatian village of Kumrovec, near to the border with Slovenia. Like Stalin Tito later created an official birthday, celebrated on 25 May.
7. While Tito was the acting and then official head of the CPY its membership rose from 1,500 in autumn 1937 to 8,000 in spring 1941. The Party's youth organisation SKOJ, which had at most 3,000 members in 1935, had nearly 18,000 in September 1939. There was a higher proportion of women in SKOJ than in the CPY. P. Auty, *Tito: A Biography*, Harmondsworth, 1974, pp. 162, 167.
8. Ibid., p. 213.
9. Tito speech of 8 August 1945, cited in S. Pavlowitch, *Hitler's New Disorder: The Second World War in Yugoslavia*, London, 2008, p. 234.

10. J. Tito, 'Political Report of the Central Committee of the Communist Party of Yugoslavia', Report Delivered at the V Congress of the CPY. Belgrade 1948, p. 163.

11. Overall wartime deaths in Yugoslavia were initially estimated by Tito's government as 1.7 million. Later calculations give a lesser but still dreadful toll of between 900,000 and 1,150,000. See Pavlowitch, *Hitler's New Disorder*, p. xi; M. Tanner, *Croatia: A Nation Forged in War*, London, 1997, p. 152; N. Malcolm, *Bosnia: A Short History*, London, 1994, p. 286 n1. It seems probable that the majority of Yugoslav deaths were inflicted by other Yugoslavs. Malcolm, *Bosnia*, p. 174. Perhaps half a million others were wounded or disabled. F. Maclean, *Disputed Barricades: The Life and Times of Josip Broz-Tito Marshal of Jugoslavia*, London, 1957, p. 341.

12. Malcolm, *Bosnia*, p. 193. There is no dispute that Tito's forces massacred some thirty thousand anti-communist Yugoslavs repatriated by the British in May–June 1945. They also slaughtered numerous Germans and Italians during the YPA's forty-day occupation of Trieste. R. West, *Tito and the Rise and Fall of Yugoslavia*, London, 1994, pp. 192–93, pp. 201–04.

13. Maclean, *Disputed Barricades*, p. 132. Once in power Tito would not sign death warrants. M. Djilas, *Tito: The Story from Inside*, London, 1980, p. 132. This only meant that somebody else signed them.

14. M. Radulovic, *Tito's Republic*, London, 1948, p. 118. OZNA's central headquarters in Belgrade were in the pre-war Ministry of Health. OZNA combined the roles of Internal Affairs and State Security, although its conventional police duties were conducted by the People's Militia. OZNA was also responsible for espionage and counter-espionage both at home and abroad.

15. Malcolm, *Bosnia*, p. 193.

16. In June 1945 the American journalist Hal Lehrman passed 'dozens of little scaffolds cartooned on the sidewalk, with a little figure labelled "speculator" dangling from a white-washed rope'. H. Lehrman, *Russia's Europe*, London, 1947, p. 62. Lehrman was in Yugoslavia from June to early September 1945 and again from March 1946. He is the author of the concept 'Titolitarianism'. Ibid., p. 122.

17. Ibid., p. 93.

18. Tito, 'Political Report of the Central Committee', p. 120.

19. K. Zilliacus, *Tito of Yugoslavia*, London, 1952, p. 140.

20. Radulovic, *Tito's Republic*, p. 111. Addressing the People's Front in September 1947, Tito stressed that its programme was that of the CPY. Zilliacus, *Tito*, pp. 188–89. On the CPY's registration and legality, see the interesting interview given by Tito on 14 October 1946 in Sulzberger, *A Long Row of Candles*, pp. 319–20.

21. Radulovic, *Tito's Republic*, p. 87.

22. Ibid., 86.

23. Sometimes written UDBa to facilitate pronunciation as an acronym.

24. Maclean, *Disputed Barricades*, p. 347.

25. Ibid., p. 349.

26. Zilliacus, *Tito*, p. 180.

27. In what he called his 'naughty document' Churchill proposed a 'percentages agreement' of: 90–10 predominance in favour of the Western allies in Greece; the obverse in favour of the USSR in Romania; 50–50 in Yugoslavia and Hungary; and 75–25 in Moscow's favour in Bulgaria. It is often overlooked that in the wake of the destruction of the Polish Home Army [*Armija Krajowa*] during the heroic Warsaw Uprising, Churchill was desperately trying to negotiate 50–50 in Poland as well. A clear account of these talks is in M. Gilbert, *Road to Victory: Winston S. Churchill 1941–1945*, London, 1989.

28. Molotov: 'What did 60/40 for Yugoslavia mean? It meant the coast where Russia would have less interest and would not interfere, but they were to have greater influence in the centre'. At the conclusion of their talks, Churchill suggested that it was 'a pity that when God created the

354

world he had not consulted them'. Stalin riposted that 'it was God's first mistake'. Prime Minister's Files 3/434/2, p. 13, p. 41. Public Record Office Kew.

29. Royal Institute of International Affairs, *The Soviet-Yugoslav Dispute: Text of the Published Correspondence*, London, 1948, p. 36.

30. Zilliacus, *Tito*, p. 198.

31. The 'two camps' concept was probably introduced into Zhdanov's speech by Stalin. V. Zubok and C. Pleshakov, *Inside the Kremlin's Cold War: From Stalin to Khrushchev*, London, 1996, p. 133.

32. Zilliacus, *Tito*, p. 195. Dimitrov noted an 'enormous rally'. I. Banac, ed., *The Diary of Georgi Dimitrov 1933–1949*, London, 2003, p. 433. How accurate the crowd numbers given for Tito's various visits were, let alone how spontaneous the turnout was, is impossible to say.

33. Maclean, *Disputed Barricades*, pp. 359–60.

34. M. Djilas, *Rise and Fall*. London,1985, pp. 152–53.

35. V. Dedijer, *Tito Speaks: His Self-portrait and Struggle with Stalin*, London, 1954, p. 321.

36. Maclean, *Disputed Barricades*, p. 360.

37. Ibid., p. 360.

38. Records of this meeting on Tuesday 10 February 1948 can be found in two similar Yugoslav accounts, Dedijer, *Tito Speaks*, pp. 325–32 and Djilas, *Rise and Fall*, pp. 163–70. The Bulgarian record is in Banac, pp. 436–44. Based upon shorthand notes by Traicho Kostov (see Chapter 24), who was once a stenographer in the Bulgarian parliament, it is far more detailed and covers topics neglected by the Yugoslav accounts.

39. Dedijer, *Tito Speaks*, p. 327.

40. Ibid., p. 330. The issue that prompted this was Stalin's blatant refusal to acknowledge that the 'ne' in 'Benelux' represented the presence of the Netherlands in that federation!

41. Ibid., p. 330.

42. Ibid., p. 337.

43. All quotations from the letters are from Royal Institute of International Affairs, *The Soviet-Yugoslav Dispute*.

44. Although the 1948 correspondence suggested that Stalin and Molotov were penning missives on behalf of the CPSU Central Committee, it is quite likely that Stalin simply wrote all the letters himself. On the Yugoslav side Tito certainly drafted the replies. He accepted some amendments from his colleagues, but the Yugoslav responses bore the stamp of Tito's personality and objectives.

45. These caused the Yugoslavs later to claim that they had new proof that the earth was round. 'For five years we hurled mud at the West, now it comes flying back at us from the East'. Adamic, *The Eagle and the Roots*, p. 32. 'Mud' was probably a polite translation.

46. The exiled Trotsky was murdered in Mexico by an NKVD agent in August 1940. B. Patenaude, *Stalin's Nemesis: The Exile and Murder of Leon Trotsky*, London, 2010 provides a pacy account.

47. Stalin goaded Tito with this lack of democracy in the CPY. His hypocrisy was breathtaking, given the manner in which the CPSU operated at this time. See Y. Gorlizki and O. Khlevniuk, *Cold Peace: Stalin and the Soviet Ruling Circle, 1945–1953*, New York, 2005, a fine study based upon Soviet archives.

48. Djilas's 'insult' related to the rape and murder of Yugoslav citizens by men of the Red Army as it traversed north-east Yugoslavia in 1944. The shocked Partisans collected detailed figures of such acts. See M. Djilas, *Conversations with Stalin*, London, 1962.

49. Tito made this decision on 25 May, his official birthday. Naturally he received no fraternal greetings from Stalin, although Dimitrov sent his. Tito reciprocated on Dimitrov's birthday on 17 June.

50. On St Vitus's Day in 1389 the Ottoman Turks destroyed the Serbian army at 'the Field of Blackbirds' (*Kosovo Polje*). A centuries-long Turkish occupation of Serbia ensued.

51. Texts in Royal Institute of International Affairs, *The Soviet-Yugoslav Dispute*, pp. 61–79.

52. K. Kaplan, *Report on the Murder of the General Secretary*, London, 1990, p. 4.

53. Tito, 'Political Report of the Central Committee', pp. 128–36. The first personal attack upon Stalin appears to be an article by Djilas in *Borba* in early October 1948. 'We've spared Stalin long enough', conceded Tito. Djilas, *Rise and Fall*, pp. 248–49.

18. LESS THAN RHAPSODIC: RÁKOSI'S HUNGARY

1. E. Bone, *Seven Years Solitary*, London, 1960, p. 44.

2. J. Hay, *Born 1900: Memoirs*, London, 1974, pp. 238–39. He noted too Rákosi's 'deep, sonorous voice' and 'the kind of gentle, velvety grey eyes that are generally taken to be sure signs of goodness and humanity'.

3. Ada lies just west of the River Tisza. Until 1918 it was in the Hungarian Bácska. It is now in the Serbian province of Vojvodina.

4. Rákosi's mother died in 1926. His father was murdered in Dachau in 1945. B-R. Barth and W. Schweizer, eds, *Der Fall Noel Field, Band II: Asyl in Ungarn 1954–1957*, Berlin, 2007, pp. 431–32 (Rákosi biography).

5. Estimates of those killed in the 'White Terror' range from 2,000–6,000. B. Cartledge, *The Will to Survive: A History of Hungary*, London, 2011, pp. 314–15. One source says that there were 27,000 legal processes during the 'White Terror', with 329 executions after trial, 1,200 simply murdered, and 70,000 interned. N. Nagy-Talavera, *The Green Shirts and Others: A History of Fascism in Hungary and Romania*, Stanford, 1970, p. 54. Kun's wife spent nine years in a camp. P. Lendvai, *The Hungarians: A Thousand Years of Victory in Defeat*, London, 2006, p. 525 n29.

6. Ibid., pp. 373–75; D. Cornelius, *Hungary in World War II: Caught in the Cauldron*, New York, 2011, pp. 7–8. Only 10.4 per cent of the population did not speak Hungarian as their mother tongue. 552,000 Germans (7 per cent) and 142,000 Slovaks were the chief minorities.

7. He was apparently jailed in Italy and Denmark. 'Were there a chair of Comparative Prisons', he boasted to a press conference during his 1946 visit to the USA, 'I could qualify for the professorship'. G. Shuster, *In Silence I Speak: The Story of Cardinal Mindszenty*, London, 1956, p. 104.

8. The issue still remained live when he returned to Moscow in 1940. On the other hand, he was praised for the robust defence of the communist position which he made in all three of his trials. See A. Dallin and F. Firsov, *Dimitrov and Stalin 1934–1943: Letters from the Soviet Archives*, London, 2000, pp. 181–83.

9. János Kádár, Hungary's later communist dictator, was jailed in Szeged prison in early 1937. He was amused by the sight of convict Rákosi operating a foot-pumped spinning-wheel. R. Gough, *A Good Comrade: János Kádár, Communism and Hungary*, London, 2006, p. 14.

10. 'I have listened to you patiently for the last two hours', moaned one weary judge to Rákosi, 'but so far you have hardly spoken of the points of the indictment'. M. Rákosi, *The Imprisonment and Defence of Mátyás Rákosi*, London, 1952, p. 151. This work, which I have cited as Rákosi, was written by an HCP body in Budapest in 1950. The translation, with no named author, was produced by the CPGB's publishing house Lawrence and Wishart in 1954.

11. Béla Kun had recommended exchanging the flags for Rákosi as early as 1926. G. Borsányi, *Béla Kun: The Life of a Communist Revolutionary*, Boulder (Col.), 1993, p. 311. Altogether Rákosi spent fifteen years and thirty-seven days in jail.

12. I. Banac, ed., *The Diary of Georgi Dimitrov 1933–1949*, London, 2003, p. 207. Rákosi was formally leader of the HCP at this time. Kun had been shot in the USSR on 29 August 1938. Rákosi eventually made it to America in 1946. Being the only member of the Hungarian delegation who could speak English, he was in great demand with the press. Besides English and Russian, Rákosi was fluent in French and German. He also spoke Italian and Turkish.

13. The total territory regained was 78,567 square kilometres, 53 per cent of that which had been lost at Trianon. About 5.3 million inhabitants were 'returned' to Hungarian rule, although only 42 per cent were Magyars. Cartledge, *The Will to Survive*, p. 382.

14. The figure for 'Trianon Hungary' was nearly 268,000. R. Braham, *The Politics of Genocide: The Holocaust in Hungary*, Detroit, 2000, p. 252.

15. Horthy appointed Szálasi as head of state on 16 October and was then interned. 'Horthy committed political suicide when he named Szálasi', opined Stalin in December 1944. 'We would have accepted Horthy, but the Germans took him away. Horthy is morally a corpse'. W. McCagg, *Stalin Embattled 1943–1948*, Detroit, 1978, pp. 314–15.

16. K. Ungváry, *The Siege of Budapest: One Hundred Days in World War II*, London, 2005, p. 350. An estimated 50–200,000 rapes took place throughout the country. Later the Hungarian authorities introduced free abortion to deal with the unwanted consequences. L. Borhi, *Hungary in the Cold War 1945–1956: Between the United States and the Soviet Union*, Budapest/New York, 2004, p. 56. Did the men of the Red Army know whom they were violating? Not that it should have mattered. Did they know where they were? Soviet military maps didn't show national frontiers. C. Eby, *Hungary at War: Civilians and Soldiers in World War II*, University Park (Pa.), 1998, p. 253. Nor can one censure the Red Army alone for such behaviour. It is not a moral equivalent that can comfortably be made, but after Stalingrad many Red Army men marched westwards through their own destroyed homes and past the graveyards of their loved ones. The Soviet 'case' was made to some protesting Hungarian communists as follows: 'And what did you do in the Soviet Union? You not only raped our wives before our eyes, but for good measure you killed them together with their children, set fire to our villages, and razed our cities to the ground'. Ungváry, *The Siege of Budapest*, p. 351. See also the accounts in C. Merridale, *Ivan's War: The Red Army 1939–45*, London, 2006.

17. Rákosi informed Dimitrov on 19 February 1945 that 'mass rape and looting are repeated after the liberation of every district'. P. Kenez, *Hungary from the Nazis to the Soviets: The Establishment of the Communist Regime in Hungary, 1944–1948*, Cambridge, 2006, pp. 44–45. He was aware too of the arbitrary deportation of Hungarian soldiers and civilians to the USSR to work on 'reconstruction'. Of 550–600,000 deportees perhaps 200,000 didn't return. L. Borhi, *Hungary in the Cold War*, p. 56.

18. H. Lehrman, *Russia's Europe*, London, 1947, p. 295. Lehrman arrived in Budapest in early September 1945, the first correspondent there 'with Soviet authorization'. In that 'single month of September, 1,998 murders were counted in Budapest'. He left in December 1945 and returned to Hungary the following June. Lehrman, *Russia's Europe*, pp. 172, 176, 206.

19. In Prague cinemas, when the documentary of the Yalta Conference showed a scene of President Roosevelt, seated next to Stalin, glancing at his watch, the whole audience would erupt into '*Davai chasi!*' Eventually the communist minister of information ordered the scene cut. Even one year after liberation a watch was a rarity in industrialised Czechoslovakia. J. Stransky, *East Wind over Prague*, London, 1950, pp. 28–29.

20. Lehrman, *Russia's Europe*, p. 295. 'Sent to Moscow for repairs' was another common phrase to describe the widespread looting throughout the Soviet sphere.

21. V. Bartlett, *East of the Iron Curtain*, London, 1949, pp. 76–77.

22. Borhi, *Hungary in the Cold War*, p. 184. Soviet economic exploitation was applied throughout its sphere. 'Our trade treaty with Moscow provides that Russia gets our coal, and in return we give them our textiles', observed a cynical Polish socialist in 1947. S. Welles, *Profile of Europe*, New York, 1948, pp. 222–23.

23. Lehrman, *Russia's Europe*, p. 227.

24. Kenez, *Hungary from the Nazis to the Soviets*, p. 125. Twenty-four zeroes constitute a quadrillion.

25. Hungary certainly needed land reform, both for economic reasons and to democratise her semi-

feudal social structure. In the 1930s 6 per cent of all landowners owned two-thirds of the land. At the apex of the system, less than 1 per cent of landowners, the gentry and aristocracy to whom the largest estates belonged, held 41–46 per cent. The land reform of March 1945 expropriated about eight million acres, some 35 per cent of all land. Of this total 4.7 million acres was divided among 650,000 landless labourers and 'dwarf' peasants. Given the small size of these holdings, the numbers receiving no land, and the lack of machinery, tools and draft animals, the problems of rural over-population remained. Figures from D. Warriner, *Revolution in Eastern Europe*, London, 1950, pp. 131–35; Y. Gluckstein, *Stalin's Satellites in Europe*. London 1952, pp. 21–22.

26. As one 'Muscovite' HCP leader put it on 7 November 1944, 'It is not a correct viewpoint to urge the construction of socialism upon the rubble of defeat'. B. Kovrig, *Communism in Hungary: From Kun to Kádár*, Stanford, 1979, p. 157.

27. Figures from Ibid., p. 168; C. Gati, *Hungary and the Soviet Bloc*, Durham (N.C.), 1986, p. 82; Kenez, *Hungary from the Nazis to the Soviets*, p. 45.

28. In 1945, when Jews comprised between 1 and 2 per cent of the population, an estimated one-seventh of HCP members were Jewish. Ibid., p. 156. Reporting to the HCP Central Committee on 17 February 1953, Rákosi recalled how in 1945–46 'when petty-bourgeois Jews were applying to join the Party', it was enough for a person to 'say he had been in Auschwitz or three of his relatives had been killed' to be accepted. I. Rév, *Indicting Rajk*, pp. 1–31, http://ccat.sas.upenn.edu/slavic/events/slavic_symposium/Comrades_Please_Shoot_Me/Rev_Rajk.pdf, last accessed 26 May 2013, p. 13 n15.

29. Kenez, *Hungary from the Nazis to the Soviets*, p. 47. 'Look, these little fascists aren't bad fellows, really', Rákosi told Lehrman. 'All they have to do is sign a pledge, and we take them in [...] After all, you can't jail six hundred thousand people'. As Lehrman sardonically observed, 'it was quite clear that Comrade Rákosi's doubts about the capacity of Hungarian prisons were elastic'. Lehrman, *Russia's Europe*, p. 187. The 'pledge' is printed here too. See also Borhi, *Hungary in the Cold War*, p. 70.

30. Nor was the NPP, which betrayed marked anti-Semitic tendencies. See Gati, *Hungary and the Soviet Bloc*, p. 103 n5. Yet this party was also perceived as the 'peasant arm' of the HCP.

31. N. Nyaradi, *My Ringside Seat in Moscow*, New York, 1952, p. 249. Miklós Nyárádi was SHP finance minister until fleeing Hungary in October 1948.

32. Borhi, *Hungary in the Cold War*, p. 65.

33. Lehrman, *Russia's Europe*, p. 203.

34. The HCP held 'most of the leadership positions in the police', Rákosi reported to Dimitrov on 17 March 1945. 'We will of course take care that the key positions remain in our hands.... In this question we will not yield'. E. Roman, *Hungary and the Victor Powers 1945–50*. New York 1996, p. 43. On Nagy's brief tenure, see J. Rainer, *Imre Nagy vom Parteisoldaten zum Märtyrer des ungarischen Volksaufstands: eine politische Biographie 1896–1958*. Paderborn 2006; C. Gati, *Failed Illusions: Moscow, Washington, Budapest and the 1956 Hungarian Revolt*, Stanford, 2006.

35. Lehrman, *Russia's Europe*, p. 209.

36. Rákosi, *The Imprisonment and Defence of Mátyás Rákosi*, p. 55.

37. Kovrig, *Communism in Hungary*, p. 191.

38. On this complex matter, see Kenez, *Hungary from the Nazis to the Soviets*; I. Szent-Miklósy, *With the Hungarian Independence Movement: An Eye-witness Account*, London, 1988; H. Seton-Watson, *The East European Revolution*, London, 1956.

39. Lehrman, *Russia's Europe*, p. 210.

40. Kenez, *Hungary From the Nazis to the Soviets*, pp. 260–61.

41. Hay, *Born 1900*, p. 332.

42. Gluckstein, *Stalin's Satellites in Europe*, p. 235.

43. H. Dewar, *The Modern Inquisition*, London, 1953, p. 166.

44. Roman, *Hungary and the Victor Powers 1945–50*, p. 221.
45. V. Zubok and C. Pleshakov, *Inside the Kremlin's Cold War: From Stalin to Khrushchev*, London, 1996, p. 99.
46. V. Dedijer, *Tito Speaks: His Self-portrait and Struggle with Stalin*, London, 1954, p. 358; M. Djilas, *Rise and Fall*, London, 1985, pp. 127–28.
47. Rajk Trial. *László Rajk and his Accomplices before the People's Court*, Budapest, 1949, pp. 58–59.
48. Gati, *Hungary and the Soviet Bloc*, p. 18. If he did say this, it seems highly likely that Tito's words were reported to the Boss. 'We know that there are anti-Soviet rumours circulating among the leading comrades in Yugoslavia', Stalin noted in his letter of 27 March 1948. 'These anti-Soviet allegations are usually camouflaged by left phrases, such as "socialism in the Soviet Union has ceased to be revolutionary" and that Yugoslavia alone is the exponent of "revolutionary socialism"'. Royal Institute of International Affairs, *The Soviet-Yugoslav Dispute: Text of the Published Correspondence*, London, 1948, p. 14.
49. Dedijer, *Tito Speaks*, pp. 358, 375–76; V. Dedijer, *The Battle Stalin Lost: Memories of Yugoslavia 1948–53*, Nottingham, 1978, p. 138.

19. FATEFUL CONTACT: NOEL AND THE 'SZŐNYI GROUP'

1. Detailed short biographies by Dr Barth of the eight men mentioned can be found in B-R. Barth and W. Schweizer, eds, *Der Fall Noel Field, Band II: Asyl in Ungarn 1954–1957*, Berlin, 2007, pp. 407–40 *passim*. See also G. Hodos, *Show Trials: Stalinist Purges in Eastern Europe*, London, 1987, pp. 51–55. For Anna Abonyi, see B-R. Barth and W. Schweizer, eds, *Der Fall Noel Field, Band I: Gefängnisjahre 1949–1954*, Berlin, 2005, pp. 344 n15, 470 n367. On the MNFF, see Ibid., p. 201 n168.
2. Szőnyi was born Tibor Hoffman. Following his return to Hungary he legally adopted the surname of his mother Ilona Szőnyi.
3. Rajk Trial, *László Rajk and his Accomplices before the People's Court*, Budapest, 1949, pp. 147. 244. On the CPUSA leader Earl Browder and 'Browderism', see J. Ryan, *Earl Browder: The Failure of American Communism*, Tuscaloosa, 1997.
4. Like Hoffmann/Szőnyi, most of the group legally 'Magyarised' their names upon returning to Hungary, probably on HCP orders. György Demeter was originally Henrik Georg Deutsch. Kuti's surname was Katzander and Dobó's was Guttmann. Ferenc Vági was born Franz Karl Weisz. Földi's original surname was Bauer and that of Hódos was Hermann. Since Hódos was imprisoned as a member of the group, and because he wrote an important book about the show trials, I have included him here. To avoid confusion I have used only their 'Hungarian' names in the main text.
5. For this section and the next I have based my account upon three sources:
    1. An ÁVH report of February 1955 in Barth and Schweizer, eds, *Der Fall Noel Field, Band II*, pp. 225–31. This was part of the inquiry leading to the release of the surviving members of the Szőnyi group (see Chapter 29), and is the nearest we have to a 'true' account of events.
    2. Parts of the self-incriminating 'testimony' which Szőnyi, Földi and Kálmán were compelled to give at the Rajk trial. If one strips away the 'conspiratorial' context, certain facts emerge which would seem to be plausible elements of another 'conspiracy'; namely, how to get the Szőnyi group back to Hungary. See Rajk Trial, pp. 148, 151–2, 241–43, 245–46.
    3. Details from statements about Field's relationship with Szőnyi's group, which seem to confirm or flesh out events. See Barth and Schweizer, eds, *Der Fall Noel Field, Band I*, pp. 121–22, 200–04, 341–46, 343 n9, 362–65, 556–58, 725–35, 745–748.
6. This is confirmed by Vági's interrogation protocol of 31 May 1949. See Ibid., p. 547 n2. In this Vági also 'confesses' that the MNFF group knew that Noel was in contact with Dulles, although Noel made no secret of the fact.

7. Compare Barth and Schweizer, eds, *Der Fall Noel Field, Band II*, p. 225 n5 and Barth and Schweizer, eds, *Der Fall Noel Field, Band I*, p. 579 n5.

8. Rajk Trial, pp. 148–49, 151. Testifying as a 'witness', Kálmán stated that in 'the autumn of 1944 Szőnyi met Dulles in Berne a number of times'. Ibid., p. 245. Despite all these meetings with Dulles, at the trial Szőnyi was unable to recognise a photograph of Dulles because 'at that time he did not wear spectacles'. Ibid., p. 159. Photos from this period show Dulles wearing glasses.

9. In several accounts Field related that Szőnyi's group was being repatriated with the help of the OSS and US military authorities. He emphasised that he had had nothing to do with it. He was not asked to help, and in any case he did not have the resources. However, the fact that they were receiving OSS help again suggested to him that there had been contact with Dulles.

10. Although Field had heard Szőnyi's then name Hoffman mentioned in Switzerland, this was the only occasion when they actually met.

11. See Barth and Schweizer, eds, *Der Fall Noel Field, Band I*, p. 44 n20. Szőnyi titled his record as 'Brief report on the activities of the Hungarian party group in Switzerland from autumn 1942 to January 1945'. Barth and Schweizer, eds, *Der Fall Noel Field, Band II*, p. 231 n21.

12. Rajk Trial, p. 152.

13. In addition to Dr Barth's detailed brief biographies of Gábor Péter and Ernő Szűcs in Barth and Schweizer, eds, *Der Fall Noel Field, Band II*, pp. 429, 437–38, my account is based upon sources cited in the notes to this section.

14. H. Lehrman, *Russia's Europe*, London, 1947, p. 189. The word *út* in Hungarian usually translates as 'road'. However, it seems that translators consider this classy thoroughfare in Budapest to be too grand to be called a mere road and I have seen Andrássy út rendered as Andrássy Street/Avenue/Boulevard. For the record *utca* can be translated as street, *fasor* as avenue, *körút* as boulevard, and *tér* as square. My solution is to leave these names in Hungarian. In December 1949, as a 'gift' to the Boss on his seventieth birthday, Andrássy út was renamed Sztálin út. 60 Andrássy út is now the site of the *Terrorház* (House of Terror).

15. The original political police formation was the PRO (*Politikai Rendészeti Osztály* or Political Police Department). In 1946 it was renamed the ÁVO (*Államvédelmi Osztály*, the State Security Department). ÁVO was upgraded to ÁVH in September 1948. Yet even after it was renamed as ÁVH, the acronym ÁVO remained widely in use because it was easy to say. I have used ÁVH throughout for the sake of convenience.

16. Another advantage to the address was that 'Soviet headquarters and the homes of senior officers concentrated in a wide and heavily-guarded area on both sides of Andrassy-út, one of the city's main boulevards'. Lehrman, *Russia's Europe*, p. 173. This area included MGB headquarters, one of the places where Noel and others were interrogated.

17. B. Kovrig, *Communism in Hungary: From Kun to Kádár*, Stanford, 1979, p. 171.

18. P. Kenez, *Hungary from the Nazis to the Soviets: The Establishment of the Communist Regime in Hungary, 1944–1948*, Cambridge, 2006, p. 55.

19. Péter told a prisoner that he 'once spent nine years in prison'. R. Vogeler, *I was Stalin's Prisoner*, London, 1952, p. 225. This seems unlikely if it refers to a single stretch.

20. Péter visited Moscow in 1932.

21. P. Ignotus, *Political Prisoner*, London, 1959, p. 65. Photos of Péter show a quite ordinary moustache.

22. J. Hay, *Born 1900: Memoirs*, London, 1974, p. 128. 'Péter walked with a limp'. Vogeler, *I Was Stalin's Prisoner*, p. 187.

23. Nyaradi, *My Ringside Seat in Moscow*, p. 276.

24. Mikes, *A Study in Infamy: The Hungarian Secret Police*, London, 1959, p. 42, and E. Marton, *The Forbidden Sky*, Boston, 1971, p. 50, relate this story in similar terms.

25. N. Nyaradi, *My Ringside Seat in Moscow*, p. 276.

26. B. Szász, *Volunteers for the Gallows*. London 1971, p. 20.
27. See Barth and Schweizer, eds, *Der Fall Noel Field, Band I*, pp. 45–46; Barth and Schweizer, eds, *Der Fall Noel Field, Band II*, pp. 46–47. It is unclear whether the Szőnyi group was under continual observation from 1945. I get the impression from these reports that the ÁVH was simply covering its back.
28. Barth and Schweizer, eds, *Der Fall Noel Field, Band I*, p. 46; Barth and Schweizer, eds, Der *Fall Noel Field, Band II*, p. 46 n8.

20. THE SPIDER AND THE SPY: NETTING THE FIELDS

1. B-R. Barth and W. Schweizer, eds, *Der Fall Noel Field, Band I: Gefängnisjahre 1949–1954*, Berlin, 2005, pp. 194 n156, 498 n492, 597–98, 598 n39, 638–39, 642–43; B-R. Barth and W. Schweizer, eds, *Der Fall Noel Field, Band II: Asyl in Ungarn 1954–1957*, Berlin, 2007, pp. 420 (Horngacher biography), 425–26 (London biography); K. Bartosek, *Les aveux des archives: Prague-Paris-Prague, 1948–1968*, Paris, 1996, pp. 267–326 *passim*, 433, 436; A. London, *On Trial*, London, 1970, pp. 15, 23, 33; K. Kaplan, *Report on the Murder of the General Secretary*, London, 1990, p. 22.
2. Text of letters in Barth and Schweizer, eds, *Der Fall Noel Field, Band I*, pp. 651–53. The letter to Dulles is printed in both English and German.
3. In his letter to the CPSU Central Committee in March 1954 Noel wrote, 'Doubtless my correspondence with Dulles has also been found in my Geneva archive'. Ibid., p. 211. Where this correspondence is now, if it still exists, is unknown.
4. Immediately after London's arrest in January 1951 his French wife wrote to the Czechoslovak party and security authorities. She contended that when London was in Switzerland for health reasons in 1948, he learned 'from a Swiss comrade (his first name was Max, and although I can't properly recall his surname, it was something like Hollenauscher) about the existence of a letter, from which it emerged that Field was in contact with Dulles, the head of American espionage in Europe'. London 'sent the Interior Ministry a photocopy of a document, which at the very least established that a dubious relationship existed' (*établissant les relations pour le moins douteuses*) between Field and Dulles. Bartosek, *Les aveux des archives*, p. 436. In the course of his 'rehabilitation' in the mid-1950s, it was noted that London was 'the first to warn the Czechoslovak security services of suspicions about Field, and he did this even before the alarm was raised by the Hungarians'. Ibid., pp. 295–96.
5. Barth and Schweizer, eds, *Der Fall Noel Field, Band I*, p. 598; London, *On Trial*, p. 21.
6. Bartosek, *Les aveux des archives*, p. 273. In Hromadko's view, London's acclaimed book *L'Aveu* (the original French edition of *On Trial*) was 'a mixture of schizophrenia and the professional distortions of an experienced agent'. Ibid., p. 273. On the activities of SIM, see P. Preston, *The Spanish Holocaust: Inquisition and Extermination in Twentieth-Century Spain*, London, 2012.
7. Barth and Schweizer, eds, *Der Fall Noel Field, Band I*, pp. 696–704 (Gát interrogation protocol, August 1954), 699 n15 and n18, 703 n27; Barth and Schweizer, eds, *Der Fall Noel Field, Band II*, pp. 45 n1, 371–72, 413–14 (Ferenczi biography); Kaplan, *Report on the Murder*, p. 23.
8. In March–April 1948 Horngacher gave Ferenczi handwritten reports about Noel, Erica, Leo Bauer, and others whom he suspected of espionage. Ferenczi thought them a mixture of fact and fantasy. Barth and Schweizer, eds, *Der Fall Noel Field, Band I*, p. 702 n23.
9. Perhaps it was simply his nature. One of those arrested in the preliminaries to the Rajk trial described Szőnyi as a 'cold, rigid party functionary'. B. Szász, *Volunteers for the Gallows*, London, 1971, p. 10.
10. Where did Horngacher's reports originate? Obviously the photocopies of Noel's April 1945 letter to Dulles, which Max provided to both London and Ferenczi, came from Horngacher himself, since he was the recipient of the original letter. Knowledge of Noel helping the Szőnyi

group, and his travelling to Czechoslovakia, could have come from conversation with Field. But any other Field-Dulles letters must have come from Noel's own archive. Were they stolen or just photocopied? Was the MGB involved? If so, were they trying to alert in roundabout fashion the ÁVH and the StB, and through them the Party chiefs in Budapest and Prague? I have no answers to these questions; the evidence is too fragmentary.

11. Kaplan, *Report on the Murder*, p. 23. This gives an account based on Czechoslovak records. Whether Noel needed to be 'lured', or whether the ÁVH expected him to return to Prague in any case, is perhaps not of the greatest importance. Kaplan adds that 'Suddenly several of Field's letters to Dulles appeared, all from the same source. The Soviet intelligence had known about them'. I don't really understand this last sentence. Possibly it means that the MGB was supplying Horngacher with Noel's letters to Dulles, who supplied them to London, who sent them on to the StB.

12. Barth and Schweizer, eds, *Der Fall Noel Field, Band I*, p. 37.

13. Ibid., pp. 11–14, 13 n44, 14 n45, 39–41, 147–49, 214–17, 410, 498 n492, 507–08, 598, 626, 715–17, 720, 779–80, 780 n43, 819; Barth and Schweizer, eds, *Der Fall Noel Field, Band II*, pp. 46–47; Kaplan, *Report on the Murder*, pp. 23–24; F. Lewis, *The Man who Disappeared: The Strange History of Noel Field*, pp. 1–4, 196–97; E. Anderson, *Love in Exile: An American Writer's Memoir of Life in Divided Berlin*, South Royalton (Vt.), 1999, pp. 133–34.

14. Barth and Schweizer, eds, *Der Fall Noel Field, Band I*, p. 780 n44. (Original English text).

15. The only sources for this March instruction by Bielkin are G. Hodos, *Show Trials: Stalinist Purges in Eastern Europe*, London, 1987, p. 40 and W. Kießling, *Partner im 'Narrenparadies': der Freundeskreis um Noel Field und Paul Merker*, Berlin, 1994, p. 151. Neither gives a further reference. Biographical details on Bielkin (sometimes spelt Belkin) come from Barth's excellent short biography. See Barth and Schweizer, eds, *Der Fall Noel Field, Band II*, p. 403. Some early Hungarian accounts give his first name incorrectly as Feodor. It is impossible to say whether this was Bielkin's first move in the Field affair, but I would assume that he was involved in events at an earlier stage.

16. Barth and Schweizer, eds, *Der Fall Noel Field, Band I*, p. 498 n492.

17. Ibid., p. 626 n25.

18. Kaplan, *Report on the Murder*, p. 24.

19. Barth and Schweizer, eds, *Der Fall Noel Field, Band I*, pp. 819–22, 823 n14, 832; Barth and Schweizer, eds, *Der Fall Noel Field, Band II*, pp. 49–50, 193–95, 194 n13; H. Field and K. Field, *Trapped in the Cold War: The Ordeal of an American Family*, Stanford, 1999, pp. 1, 12–14, 18–19, 32, 41–48, 72–73, 365–66, 390; Kaplan, *Report on the Murder*, pp. 24–25; London, *On Trial*, pp. 35–36.

20. Barth and Schweizer, eds, *Der Fall Noel Field, Band I*, p. 819. (Original English text).

21. Herta had followed the first Hiss perjury trial in the press. Her worries increased, when on 25 July a Swiss attorney representing Hiss questioned her about the dinner party at the Fields' Washington flat, at which Hede Massing claimed to have met Hiss. Another interview took place in early August just before Herta flew to Prague. Herta denied that Hede and Hiss had ever visited their Washington flat at the same time. Even 'if her recollection should be wrong in this point', recorded the attorney, 'she was definitely sure that no such conversation as I had mentioned [p. 47] had ever taken place in her apartment'. A. Weinstein, *Perjury: The Hiss-Chambers Case*, New York, 1997, pp. 178–79, 179n.

22. Kaplan, *Report on the Murder*, p. 24.

23. In January 1948 Arthur Schlesinger met Hermann and Kate at a dinner party in Cleveland and became 'embroiled in an increasingly angry argument' with them. Hermann 'was glowingly and naively enthusiastic' about the people's democracies, equating 'communism with city planning and land reform', while appearing 'cheerfully oblivious of any machinery of repres-

sion and terror'. A. Schlesinger, *A Life in the Twentieth Century: Innocent Beginnings, 1917–1950*, Boston/New York, 2000, p. 499.

24. Field and Field, *Trapped in the Cold War*, p. 47.

25. Barth and Schweizer, eds, *Der Fall Noel Field, Band I*, p. 820; Barth and Schweizer, eds, *Der Fall Noel Field, Band II*, p. 49 n26. Either in Bern or Prague Herta was told that two telegrams from Noel had arrived at the Palace Hotel. The first, sent from Bratislava, said that Noel was travelling for a few days and asked them to keep his room. The second was sent from Vienna and stated that one René Kimmel would arrive from Bratislava, collect Noel's belongings, and pay the mounting bill. Later the hotel manager said that Kimmel had turned up and taken away Noel's belongings. Naturally, nobody else saw Mr Kimmel. For the different accounts see Barth and Schweizer, eds, *Der Fall Noel Field, Band II*, p. 194; Lewis, *The Man who Disappeared*, p. 4; Field and Field, *Trapped in the Cold War*, p. 73.

26. Noel claimed that Szymon Syrkus was known to Hermann from his time in Krakow in 1939. Barth and Schweizer, eds, *Der Fall Noel Field, Band I*, p. 593. How complicit the Polish couple were in the plot to arrest Hermann is not clear.

27. See Chapter 25.

28. London, *On Trial*, p. 35. London was already anxious about his links with Field. To add to his worries, Herta had brought letters to Prague, including one from Noel congratulating London on his appointment as deputy foreign minister. Ibid., p. 38.

21. 'WHATEVER YOU WANT ME TO SAY': TORTURE AND TRUTH

1. On the torture of the Rajk trial prisoners, see B-R. Barth and W. Schweizer, eds, *Der Fall Noel Field, Band II: Asyl in Ungarn 1954–1957*, Berlin, 2007, p. 221 n10; G. Hodos, *Show Trials: Stalinist Purges in Eastern Europe*, London, 1987; P. Ignotus, *Political Prisoner*, London, 1959; G. Paloczi-Horvath, *The Undefeated*, London, 1959; B. Szász, *Volunteers for the Gallows*, London, 1971; R. Vogeler, *I was Stalin's Prisoner*, London, 1952. For the torture of Noel, besides accounts in the text, see B-R. Barth and W. Schweizer, eds, *Der Fall Noel Field, Band I: Gefängnisjahre 1949–1954*, Berlin, 2005, p. 150; Barth and Schweizer, eds, *Der Fall Noel Field, Band II*, pp. 47–48; E. Anderson, *Love in Exile: An American Writer's Memoir of Life in Divided Berlin*, South Royalton (Vt.), 1999, p. 195.

2. '*Soling*, an expression borrowed from the shoemaking industry, was already used in the vocabulary of the pre-war Hungarian police'. Szász, *Volunteers for the Gallows*, p. 11.

3. Barth and Schweizer, eds, *Der Fall Noel Field, Band I*, p. 345.

4. Ibid., pp. 577–78. Emphasis in the original.

5. Quotations from I. Rév, *Indicting Rajk*, pp. 1–31, http://ccat.sas.upenn.edu/slavic/events/slavic_symposium/Comrades_Please_Shoot_Me/Rev_Rajk.pdf, last accessed 26 May 2013, pp. 26–28. Szűcs was testifying following his arrest by the ÁVH in September 1950.

6. Barth and Schweizer, eds, *Der Fall Noel Field, Band I*, pp. 41–48, 76–79, 77 n11 and n14; Barth and Schweizer, eds, *Der Fall Noel Field, Band II*, pp. 47–48, 220–22; G. Hodos, *Show Trials*, pp. 42–44.

7. Szász, *Volunteers for the Gallows*, pp. 8–9, 14–15. Szász, a friend of Rajk's since their university days, returned to Hungary from Argentina in 1946, and worked as deputy head of the press and information department of the Foreign Ministry. From late 1948 he headed the press department of the Ministry of Agriculture. Ibid., p. 29.

8. Regarding the monolingual Péter, see Barth and Schweizer, eds., *Der Fall Noel Field, Band II*, p. 48 n18. That Field was sometimes interrogated in Russian, see Barth and Schweizer, eds., *Der Fall Noel Field, Band I*, p. 539.

9. Ibid., p. 43. The date of November 1944 is too late. Of course, his interrogators may have suggested this month to Field. What Noel told Vági about providing information to Dulles was

confirmed by Vági, almost word for word, in his interrogation protocol of 31 May. Ibid., p. 547 n2.

10. Barth and Schweizer, eds, *Der Fall Noel Field, Band II*, p. 221.

11. The dates of arrest of Szőnyi and Szalai are given as 18 May in the trial proceedings. Rajk Trial, *László Rajk and his Accomplices before the People's Court*, Budapest, 1949, p. 304. The earlier date was confirmed by Rákosi in a speech delivered on 30 September. 'The arrests of the conspirators', he said, 'began on May 16'. G. Mikes, *A Study in Infamy: The Hungarian Secret Police*, London, 1959, p. 35.

12. Barth and Schweizer, eds., *Der Fall Noel Field, Band I*, p. 76 n8 and n9.

13. At this juncture every arrest, interrogation, and use of torture by Péter had to be authorised by Rákosi by telephone. Barth and Schweizer, eds, *Der Fall Noel Field, Band II*, p. 221 n9.

14. Barth and Schweizer, eds, *Der Fall Noel Field, Band I*, pp. 48, 52–53, 150, 155–56, 341–46, 577–80; Barth and Schweizer, eds, *Der Fall Noel Field, Band II*, pp. 48–49.

15. Barth and Schweizer, eds, *Der Fall Noel Field, Band I*, p. 150.

16. Ibid., pp. 48, 341 n5. This confrontation may have taken place as early as 16 May. See Hodos, *Show Trials*, p. 43.

17. Barth and Schweizer, eds, *Der Fall Noel Field, Band I*, p. 341.

18. Unsurprisingly, the ÁVH refused to accept that Noel's meeting with Szőnyi in Marseille was a coincidence. Ibid., p. 122.

19. Ibid., p. 559.

20. Presumably this was a different photograph from that reproduced in D. Shiels, *Les Frères Rajk*, Paris, 2006, which shows about fifty members of the Rákosi battalion, with Rajk circled. Rajk's head is in profile and his face is identifiable, but without the marker it would take time finding him.

21. Barth and Schweizer, eds, *Der Fall Noel Field, Band I*, pp. 369–70, pp. 534–41; Barth and Schweizer, eds, *Der Fall Noel Field, Band II*, p. 48. In the trial the 'relationship' between the two men was transformed into virtual gibberish. Rajk referred to an attempt to organise him 'as a member of the American intelligence agency' while he was interned in Le Vernet. An 'American citizen called Field, who was as far as I know the head of the American intelligence agency for Central and Eastern Europe', visited the camp. He was instructed by Washington to 'speak with me' and assist Rajk's return to Hungary. Rajk's role there would be to 'disorganise and dissolve the Party and possibly even get the [dissolved!] Party leadership into my hands'. But Noel came too late, since Rajk had already agreed with a Gestapo major to return home through Germany. Rajk remembered 'that Field even expressed his disapproval'. Rajk Trial, pp. 46–47.

Later the president of the court asked Rajk if he recognised a photo of Field. The following rather surreal exchange ensued, when Rajk replied:

I do not know him. I do not remember whether I ever spoke to him. I can definitely remember that he came to the camp and they asked for me at the same time. That is why, as I say, in all probability it is Field, but that was eight years ago and I cannot recall his face.

President: But they definitely told you then that it was Field?

Rajk: It was Field.

President: So you saw him once but because it was so long ago you cannot be sure you remember his face.

Rajk: When I spoke to him they told me afterwards that it was Field, and I did not pay any attention then.

The President ordered a short recess.

Ibid., pp. 159–60.

22. K. Kaplan, *Report on the Murder of the General Secretary*, London, 1990, p. 53, specifies that

fifteen Soviet advisers were sent to Hungary. Another source details forty. P. Lendvai, *Blacklisted: A Journalist's Life in Central Europe*, London, 1998, p. 69.

23. Barth and Schweizer, eds, *Der Fall Noel Field, Band I*, p. 559 n18; I. Fehérváry, The *Long Road to Revolution: The Hungarian Gulag 1945–1956*, Santa Fé, 1989, pp. 186–87.

24. Barth and Schweizer, eds, *Der Fall Noel Field, Band I*, p. 579 n5.

25. I have translated the word *Kammeragent* as 'stool-pigeon' even though *Kammeragent* does not appear in my dated dictionary. The usual German slang word for a 'stool-pigeon' is *Lockspitzel*.

26. Barth and Schweizer, eds, *Der Fall Noel Field, Band I*, pp. 53–55, 93–94; Barth and Schweizer, eds, *Der Fall Noel Field, Band II*, pp. 48–49, 49 n25.

27. There are at least three versions of the life of Cseresnyés and they differ substantially on certain points. Vogeler, arrested on 18 November 1949, was sentenced to fifteen years in February 1950, but released in April 1951. His conversations with Cseresnyés were conducted in both German and English. See R. Vogeler, *I was Stalin's Prisoner*, London, 1952, pp. 160–74. Barth's detailed biography is doubtless based upon the HCP file of Cseresnyés. See Barth and Schweizer, eds, *Der Fall Noel Field, Band II*, pp. 404–05. Schwartz's study of Sephardic Jewry in the Balkans features Sándor's son, Ivica Čerešnješ, and what he knew of his father. See S. Schwarz, *Sarajevo Rose: A Balkan Jewish Notebook*, London, 2005.

28. Vogeler, *I was Stalin's Prisoner*, pp. 160–61.

29. Barth and Schweizer, eds, *Der Fall Noel Field, Band I*, p. 156 n32.

30. Even six months after such torture 'his feet and ankles were still covered with the ugly haemorrhagic patches left by the rubber truncheons'. Vogeler, *I was Stalin's Prisoner*, p. 169.

31. His testimony is in Rajk Trial, pp. 216–20.

32. Barth and Schweizer, eds, *Der Fall Noel Field, Band I*, pp. 155–56. Cseresnyés claimed that Noel introduced the idea of writing to the legation. Sándor informed his interrogator of this, and Gábor Péter gave the go-ahead. See Barth and Schweizer, eds, *Der Fall Noel Field, Band II*, p. 48–49. On an earlier occasion Péter had encouraged the imprisoned Cardinal Mindszenty to contact the American legation. The cardinal's requests for a car and a plane to facilitate his escape were rather more ambitious than Noel's. For this letter, see J. Mindszenty, *Memoirs*. London 1974, p. 133.

33. Barth and Schweizer, eds, *Der Fall Noel Field, Band I*, p. 61. Noel also mentioned ÁVH hints that they had arrested his wife, although at this time Herta was still in Geneva. On Péter's orders Cseresnyés insisted on the inclusion of Dulles as a referee, on the alleged grounds that the letter would not otherwise reach the hands of the minister. Ibid., p. 61 n1.

34. The CzCP security 'specialist', Karel Šváb, was in Budapest in July. He reported to Gottwald on 5 August that he attended several of Noel's interrogations, but Field 'doesn't admit anything'. Kaplan, *Report on the Murder*, p. 46.

35. Barth and Schweizer, eds, *Der Fall Noel Field, Band I*, pp. 62–74.

36. See Chapter 25.

37. F. Lewis, *The Man who Disappeared: The Strange History of Noel Field*, London, 1965, p. 204.

22. 'THE ENEMY'S MAN': LÁSZLÓ RAJK

1. In this and the next chapter I have used as main sources upon Rajk's life, trial and death: Dr. Barth's biography in *B-R. Barth and W. Schweizer, eds, Der Fall Noel Field, Band II: Asyl in Ungarn 1954–1957*, Berlin, 2007, pp. 430–31; R. Gough, *A Good Comrade: János Kádár, Communism and Hungary*, London, 2006; A. Pető, *Geschlecht, Politik und Stalinismus in Ungarn: eine Biographie von Júlia Rajk*, Herne, 2007; I. Rév, *Indicting Rajk*, pp. 1–31, http://ccat.sas.upenn.edu/slavic/events/slavic_symposium/Comrades_Please_Shoot_Me/Rev_Rajk.pdf, last accessed 26

May 2013; D. Shiels, *Les Frères Rajk*, Paris, 2006 and Rajk's 'confession' at his show trial, Rajk Trial, *László Rajk and his Accomplices before the People's Court*, Budapest, 1949, pp. 33–81.

2. In some publications the number of Rajk siblings is given as twelve or thirteen. However, the late Duncan Shiels, who has written the most thorough study of the family, makes clear that there were only eleven. Rajk had seven brothers and three sisters. See the family tree in Shiels, *Les Frères Rajk*. pp. 16–17. Only three siblings concern us here, namely, Lajos (1892–1948), Gyula (1893–1976), and Endre (1899–1960).
The German families of Transylvania were referred to generically as Saxons and those of western Hungary as Swabians.

3. Shiels, *Les Frères Rajk*, pp. 23–25; Rév, *Indicting Rajk*, p. 4, who writes that the Rajks were Sabbatists, a religious minority in Transylvania. Szeklers (*Székely*) were Hungarian-speaking freemen who originally guarded the eastern frontiers of Transylvania. For a fuller portrait, see B. Cartledge, *The Will to Survive: A History of Hungary*, London, 2011; P. Lendvai, *The Hungarians: A Thousand Years of Victory in Defeat*, London, 2006.

4. Rajk Trial, p. 33.

5. B. Szász, *Volunteers for the Gallows*, London, 1971, p. 35.

6. Shiels, *Les Frères Rajk*, p. 53. Barth gives 1930 as the date Rajk joined KIMSZ.

7. Bokor was a Szekler who came from a village near Székelyudvarhely. Although Bokor is referred to as László's brother-in-law, both at Rajk's trial and elsewhere, in strict terms he was only the brother-in-law of Lajos Rajk, who was married to Bokor's sister Véra.

8. For Rajk's arrests see Rajk Trial, pp. 34, 203–04; Barth and Schweizer, eds, *Der Fall Noel Field, Band II*, p. 430. Barth dates the 1933 arrest as June, which may well be correct. Different sources specify that Rajk spent three, four or six months in custody.

9. Shiels, *Les Frères Rajk*, p. 77. Rajk had difficulty using one hand thereafter. Pető, *Geschlecht, Politik und Stalinismus in Ungarn*, p. 40.

10. Born on 19 February 1914 Júlia was the third and youngest daughter of a railwayman who had fought voluntarily in Kun's Red Army, and was interned by the Horthy regime. In early 1940 she joined the SDP, and while remaining in that party she became a member of the HCP in 1941. One of her party duties was assisting interned communists and their families, and it was in the Kistarcsa camp on the outskirts of Budapest that she first met László.

11. Pető, *Geschlecht, Politik und Stalinismus in Ungarn*, p. 36.

12. Endre had fallen under the spell of Ferenc Szálasi in 1934. Lajos Rajk was also an Arrow Cross sympathiser. See Shiels, *Les Frères Rajk*, pp. 103–04, 146–47.

13. G. Paizs, *Rajk Per*. Nyíregyháza 1989, pp. 7–9.

14. In February 1951 Kádár whined that 'when on Rajk's return, I was removed by the Party from the post of Budapest Secretary, I felt neglected and injured'. Kádár got the post back in November 1945. See Gough, *A Good Comrade*, pp. 28, 31, 35.

15. E. Roman, *Hungary and the Victor Powers 1945–50*, New York, 1996, p. 57.

16. Pető, *Geschlecht, Politik und Stalinismus in Ungarn*, pp. 30, 43–44.

17. Shiels, *Les Frères Rajk*, pp. 144–55 passim.

18. P. Ignotus, *Political Prisoner*, London, 1959, p. 47. Júlia was 1.75 metres tall. Pető, *Geschlecht, Politik und Stalinismus in Ungarn*, p. 28.

19. D. Kartun, *Tito's Plot against Europe*, London, 1949, p. 31.

20. Gerő was born Ernő Singer in 1898 in what is now Slovakia. He joined the HCP in 1918, participated in the Kun revolution and fought in the Hungarian 'Red Army'. He was the Comintern's chief operative in Spain in 1936–38, and was heavily involved in the purges in Barcelona. After Spain he was in the USSR until returning to Hungary in November 1944. Adjudged the regime's 'Grey Eminence', his main responsibilities were in the economic sphere. Barth and Schweizer, eds, *Der Fall Noel Field, Band II*, pp. 416–17. 'Well-read, intelligent, untiring and

forceful, Gerő's impact is sombre, humourless and narrow-minded', was the British legation's verdict. R6508/1012/21, FO371/477/3, Public Records Office, Kew.

21. Mihály Farkas was born Herman Loewy in 1904 in the north-east of contemporary Hungary, but moved to Kassa (now Košice in eastern Slovakia). Trained as a printer, he joined the CzCP in 1921. He was in Spain in 1936–37. In 1941 he was transferred from the CzCP to the HCP. As chairman of the HCP's military commission he was responsible for military policy as well as the ÁVH and KATPOL. In August 1948 he was made Minister of Defence. Barth and Schweizer, eds, *Der Fall Noel Field, Band II*, pp. 411–12.

22. József Révai was born József Lederer in Budapest in 1898. The son of a banking family, he was able to indulge his desire to be a poet. Mercifully only one line survived: 'Die, my father! Die, mother! And you my first love–croak!' J. Hay, *Born 1900: Memoirs*, London, 1974, p. 274. Révai was one of the founders of the HCP. In 1934–44 he was in the USSR. In 1945–50 he was chief editor of *Szabad Nép* and had an oversight of cultural affairs.

23. J. Gunther, *Behind Europe's Curtain*. London 1949, p. 176.

24. See for example, F. Nagy, *The Struggle behind the Iron Curtain*, New York, 1948, p. 305; R6559/10116/21, FO370/78521, Public Records Office, Kew.

25. Pető, *Geschlecht, Politik und Stalinismus in Ungarn*, p. 45.

26. See the quotation in Nagy, *The Struggle Behind the Iron Curtain*, p. 287.

27. Ignotus, *Political Prisoner*, p. 47.

28. Paizs, *Rajk Per.* pp. 10–11.

29. B. Kovrig, *Communism in Hungary: From Kun to Kádár*, Stanford, 1979, p. 195; P. Kenez, *Hungary from the Nazis to the Soviets: The Establishment of the Communist Regime in Hungary, 1944–1948*, Cambridge, 2006, p. 130.

30. Cited in H. Dewar, *The Modern Inquisition*, London, 1953, pp. 136–37.

31. R12998/11/21, FO371/67185, Public Records Office, Kew. The rather dim Prime Minister Dinnyés told a member of the British legation that he never had any problems with the 'feared' Rajk. Whenever he enquired about arrests 'he always got a polite and truthful explanation', and in 'more than one case' (two?) obtained a release. R13243/11/21, FO371/67185, Public Records Office, Kew.

32. C. Gati, *Hungary and the Soviet Bloc*, Durham (N.C.), 1986, pp. 122–23.

33. Gough, *A Good Comrade*, p. 40. Kádár had made the effort to learn some Russian. Ibid., p. 32. As far as I know Rajk did not speak that language. Later that year the Rajks spent a month in Romania and László visited his Transylvanian home. Pető, *Geschlecht, Politik und Stalinismus in Ungarn*, pp. 46–47.

34. G. Hodos, *Show Trials: Stalinist Purges in Eastern Europe*, London, 1987, p. 37.

35. Cited in K. Kaplan, *Report on the Murder of the General Secretary*, London, 1990, p. 26.

36. R9673/10116/21, FO371/78523, Public Records Office, Kew. Several sources ignore this transition and make Rajk, not Kádár, responsible for the trial of Cardinal Mindszenty in February 1949.

37. Kaplan, *Report on the Murder*, p. 26.

38. R789/1015/21, FO371/78514, Public Records Office, Kew.

39. Pető, *Geschlecht, Politik und Stalinismus in Ungarn*, pp. 58–59, 63, 75. Rajk was opposed to the 'feudal' practice of naming a son after his father. So his parents drew a name from a hat and out came that of László!

40. Kaplan, *Report on the Murder*, p. 25.

41. R4547/1052/21, FO371//78534, Public Records Office, Kew.

42. R4775/1015/21, FO371/78514, Public Records Office, Kew.

43. R9414/10116/21, FO371/78523, Public Records Office, Kew.

44. G. Hodos, *Show Trials*, pp. 41–42; P. Lendvai, *Blacklisted: A Journalist's Life in Central Europe*, London, 1998, p. 68. The Front won a trifling 96 per cent of the vote.

45. Barth and Schweizer, eds, *Der Fall Noel Field, Band II*, pp. 222–23. See also B-R. Barth and W. Schweizer, eds, *Der Fall Noel Field, Band I: Gefängnisjahre 1949–1954*, Berlin, 2005, p. 77.

46. T. Hajdu, 'The Party did Everything for You'. *The Hungarian Quarterly*, Vol. 37, No. 141 (1996), p. 83; Barth and Schweizer, eds, *Der Fall Noel Field, Band I*, p. 79.

47. For example Cseresnyés was arrested on the night of 23 May and Szász the following day. In May the Czechoslovak ambassador observed deludedly that in the last three months Rajk had 'clearly taken a front seat again', and the problem of his 'alleged nationalist deviations' had been overcome. He expected Rajk now to have 'a future in Hungary's political life'. Kaplan, *Report on the Murder*, p. 26.

48. Ibid., p. 38.

49. Hajdu, 'The Party did Everything for You', p. 84. Bielkin's consent must have been based upon Stalin's agreement that Rajk be arrested.

50. R5584/10321/92, FO371/78702, Public Records Office, Kew.

51. Barth and Schweizer, eds, *Der Fall Noel Field, Band II*, pp. 223–24.

52. Hajdu, 'The Party did Everything for You', p. 84; Gough, *A Good Comrade*, p. 41; Szász, *Volunteers for the Gallows*, pp. 37–38. Held under house-arrest for a fortnight, Júlia was then taken to 60 Andrássy út, while baby László was placed in a state orphanage under a new name. Pető, *Geschlecht, Politik und Stalinismus in Ungarn*, pp. 66–70.

53. The dates of arrest of Rajk and five of his co-defendants were first made known in *Szabad Nép* on 25 September 1949, the day after the trial ended. They are also given in the 'official' record of the trial, the 'Blue Book' (*Kékkönyv*). See Rajk Trial, pp. 303–04. See also Chapter 21, footnote 11.

54. G. Paloczi-Horvath, *The Undefeated*, London, 1959, p. 127.

55. Szász, *Volunteers for the Gallows*, pp. 37–38. I have dated this meeting as occurring on 2 June, because years later Szász concluded that 'the day of our confrontation must have been Rajk's third day in the hands of the ÁVH'. Ibid., p. 37.

56. Hajdu, 'The Party did Everything for You', p. 82.

57. Farkas and Kádár were directly involved in several interrogations. See Barth and Schweizer, eds, *Der Fall Noel Field, Band I*, p. 78. On Kádár's close relationship with Farkas and Péter, see Gough, *A Good Comrade*, pp. 35–36. Rajk had further antagonised this trio with his proposal to bring all Hungarian intelligence services under the aegis of the Foreign Ministry, headed by himself. Hajdu, 'The Party did Everything for You', p. 94.

58. Quotations from Ibid., pp. 87–90, 98–99.

59. R5721/10116/21, FO371/78521, Public Records Office, Kew.

60. Kaplan, *Report on the Murder*, p. 27.

61. Szász, *Volunteers for the Gallows*, pp. 63–64.

62. R5946/10116/21, FO371/78521, Public Records Office, Kew. Tito later told an American editor that after his arrest Rajk was 'sent to Moscow for "overhaul", together with Brankov. And there, according to some method they have there they were prepared for trial'. H. Armstrong, *Tito and Goliath*, London, 1951, p. 260.

63. Hodos, *Show Trials*, p. 51.

64. Y. Gluckstein, *Stalin's Satellites in Europe*, London, 1952, p. 301.

65. Barth and Schweizer, eds, *Der Fall Noel Field, Band I*, p. 78.

66. Gough, *A Good Comrade*, p. 45.

67. Rév, *Indicting Rajk*, p. 15.

68. See Barth and Schweizer, eds, *Der Fall Noel Field, Band II*, pp. 431.

69. Szász, *Volunteers for the Gallows*, pp. 111, 172.

70. E. Loebl, *My Mind on Trial*, London, 1976, pp. 60, 62, 77. It was Likhachev who made anti-Semitic remarks to the imprisoned Loebl in Prague but Komarov's virulence is evident from the letter he wrote to Stalin from Lefortovo prison on 18 February 1953. He bragged that

'Defendants literally trembled before me… Even the minister [Abakumov] did not evoke the terror that they showed when I personally interrogated them…. I especially hated and was pitiless toward Jewish nationalists, whom I saw as the most dangerous and evil enemies…. I was considered an anti-Semite not only by the defendants but by former employees of the MGB who were of Jewish nationality'. J. Rubenstein and V. Naumov, *Stalin's Secret Pogrom: the Post-War Inquisition of the Jewish Anti-Fascist Committee*, London, 2005, pp. xii–xiii. In the chief Czechoslovak works on the Slánský trial the name Komarov is rendered as the near-anagram Makarov. See J. Pelikán, *The Czechoslovak Political Trials, 1950–1954*, London, 1971, p. 80; Kaplan, *Report on the Murder*, p. 28.

71. Bokor's 'testimony' is in Rajk Trial, pp. 203–06, in which he says: 'The content of the declaration was roughly the following: I, the undersigned László Rajk, bind myself immediately and confidentially to denounce to the political police every case I become acquainted with in connection with the preparation […] of the communist revolution in Hungary'.

72. Paloczi-Horvath, *The Undefeated*, pp. 161–62. This author shared a cell with Bokor in December 1949 in the Markó utca prison, which was the ordinary prison attached to the central criminal court. The ÁVH took over its two upper stories to revivify, heal and fatten-up prisoners prior to their public appearance as defendants or 'witnesses'. All of the latter were already in the hands of the ÁVH or the MGB. Similar facilities existed in 60 Andrássy út. Béla Szász shared a cell there with Bokor prior to him being called as a witness on 20 September 1949. See Szász, *Volunteers for the Gallows*, pp. 167–74. For the fate of some other 'witnesses', see Lendvai, *Blacklisted*, pp. 75–77.

73. Szász, *Volunteers for the Gallows*, pp. 121–22.

74. For a selection of such demands, see Ibid., pp. 64–66. Such calls as 'A rope for traitors like Rajk' pointed up the intended outcome. The mass meetings before Mindszenty's trial in February 1949 never demanded that the cardinal be hanged. Gluckstein, *Stalin's Satellites in Europe*, p. 225.

75. Barth and Schweizer, eds, *Der Fall Noel Field, Band II*, p. 369.

76. Rév, *Indicting Rajk*, p. 26.

77. Barth and Schweizer, eds, *Der Fall Noel Field, Band II*, p. 369.

78. Rajk Trial, pp. 26–27. For the indictment as a whole see Rajk Trial, pp. 5–27. I have no intention of analysing the nonsense of the trial proceedings in any detail. Sixty years ago the British Marxist writer and poet, Hugo Dewar (1908–80), performed a splendid hatchet job on all the Stalinist show trials. See Dewar, *The Modern Inquisition*, See also Hodos, *Show Trials*.

79. Barth and Schweizer, eds, *Der Fall Noel Field, Band II*, p. 370. Farkas testified in 1959 that Stalin was so satisfied with Rákosi's handling of the entire Rajk affair, that he presented 'Arsehead' with an autographed copy of his collected works. Rév, *Indicting Rajk*, p. 16.

23. JIGSAW JUSTICE: ASPECTS OF THE RAJK TRIAL

1. Some personal details about the defendants are provided in Rajk Trial, *László Rajk and his Accomplices before the People's Court*, Budapest, 1949, pp. 5–7, 31–33, 303–04. However, the dates of arrest for Szőnyi and Szalai are given as 18 May, not 16 May. See Chapter 21, footnote 11. The date given for Brankov's arrest is in fact the date of his transfer from the Soviet Union to Hungary. The dates of arrest for Pálffy and Korondy are not given in Rajk Trial, but see T. Hajdu, 'The Party did Everything for You'. *The Hungarian Quarterly*, Vol. 37, No. 141 (1996), p. 85; B-R. Barth and W. Schweizer, eds, *Der Fall Noel Field, Band I: Gefängnisjahre 1949–1954*, Berlin, 2005, pp. 83 n38, 225 n7.

2. Had he changed his name because it was too German/Austrian or too Jewish? The British legation noted that Pálffy was believed to be half-Jewish. R6508/1012/21, FO371/477/3, Public Records Office, Kew. The Rajk trial began on his fortieth birthday.

3. This account is based on Barth's fascinating biography of Brankov in B-R. Barth and W. Schweizer, eds, *Der Fall Noel Field, Band II: Asyl in Ungarn 1954–1957*, Berlin, 2007, pp. 403–04.
4. G. Hodos, *Show Trials: Stalinist Purges in Eastern Europe*, London, 1987, p. 47.
5. I have no idea why Dergán changed his name to Korondy. I can't imagine that it was because he was Jewish. He came from a military family and served in the gendarmerie under Horthy.
6. Rajk Trial, pp. 181–82; Szász, *Volunteers for the Gallows*, pp. 128–31.
7. A young Paul Lendvai was an acolyte of Justus until they fell out politically. He provides a portrait of his former mentor in P. Lendvai, *Blacklisted: A Journalist's Life in Central Europe*, London, 1998, pp. 45–79 *passim*.
8. 'We must use simple categories', one interrogator told his prisoner. 'Spy. Traitor. Agent'. G. Paloczi-Horvath, *The Undefeated*, London, 1959, 158.
9. The presence of Red Army units in Hungary, which obviously would have deterred any such coup attempt, is absent from the 'script'. In order to 'explain' why the 'plotters' should persist with the lunatic idea of a coup, the 'script' suggests that planning took place while the USSR was 'distracted' by international events. From June 1948 to May 1949 the USSR was involved in the Berlin blockade, but was hardly 'distracted'.
10. Although Brankov was a spy, much of the so-called espionage material which he received would have been handed to him as a matter of course, given initial HCP deference to Tito. Moreover, such items would hardly be in the 'state secret' category at the time.
11. Many names were thrown up in the trial 'testimony'. Most would mean nothing to non-communist Hungarians, let alone to foreigners. Like the 'witnesses' these people were either in ÁVH prisons or soon would be.
12. For those communists who might somehow have forgotten such matters, Rajk was made to say that 'in general the Trotskyists always, and everywhere, internationally, worked in close contact with the police'. Rajk Trial, p. 40.
13. Certain of Stalin's sallies against Tito were dotted about the proceedings. For example, 'Tito does not fight against the kulaks'. Ibid., p. 16. The former Partisan officer Brankov was forced to recite that the 'Soviet Army, in fact, liberated Serbia and Belgrade'. Ibid., p. 119.
14. Those attending are listed in Ibid., pp. 313–14. It is unlikely that any reporting for newspapers, as opposed to news agencies, spoke Hungarian, and there are photographs of the attendant journalists wearing headphones. What were they hearing? I would assume that they were being fed the already prepared translations of the 'official' version of the trial, which would later be published as the 'Blue Book' (*Kékkönyv*).
15. Lendvai, *Blacklisted*, p. 68. The Foreign Office records include a verbatim BBC monitoring report of the Rajk trial. Appended notes state that the broadcast did not emanate directly from the courtroom. Rather, it had been previously recorded and then broadcast, and showed some signs of editing. R10303/10116/24, FO371/78524, Public Records Office, Kew.
16. The names, occupations and photos of the lay judges are in I. Soltész, *Rajk-Dosszié*, Budapest, 1989. See also Rajk Trial, p. 309. Although Barcs is identified as a journalist (*újságíró*), another source states that he was the head of Hungarian radio, and the boss of the indicted Justus. Summoned to Gábor Péter's office and told of his appointment, Barcs asked what he was supposed to do. 'Absolutely nothing', was the reply. Lendvai, *Blacklisted*, p. 72.
17. R8981/R9414/10116/21, FO371/78522, Public Records Office, Kew.
18. Rajk Trial, pp. 5, 31, 81. This clash of dates was not picked up at the time by the perceptive Hugo Dewar, or other commentators. It was probably accepted as a misprint or viewed as unimportant. In any case it was unlikely that anybody in the West knew Rajk's correct date of birth.
19. Ibid., p. 319. This mainly covers misprints, but upon three occasions it invites the reader to alter 'Vukmanovich' to the fictional 'Vuk-o-manovich'. This is because the 'scriptwriters' had boobed. When speaking about the Yugoslav 'Trotskyist' groups in the French internment camps,

Rajk mentions as one of 'the more important persons…Vukmanovich, who I think at that time was called Tempo'. Ibid., p. 39. The trouble was that Svetozar Vukmanović-Tempo, a leading CPY member and Partisan, was never in Spain or France, had never met Rajk, and did not take the name 'Tempo' until 1940. There were other errors of like nature. See H. Dewar, *The Modern Inquisition*, London, 1953. Tempo's refutation of Rajk's 'evidence' was initially published in the CPY daily *Borba* on 18 September. This was only two days after Rajk had parroted his scripted 'evidence', and strongly suggests that the 'Blue Book' was already printed before the trial began. Adding an 'errata' page was cheaper than pulping all copies and producing a new and 'error-free' version.

20. In a 1969 report the Interior Ministry concluded that 'it is highly probable that on the question of the President of the Court, Comrade Rajk did not give the truthful answer, as if signalling that what was happening with him in the court, did not match reality'. I. Rév, *Indicting Rajk*, pp. 1–31, http://ccat.sas.upenn.edu/slavic/events/slavic_symposium/Comrades_Please_Shoot_Me/Rev_Rajk.pdf, last accessed 26 May 2013, p. 4.

21. Compare Rajk Trial, pp. 150, 246 and Barth and Schweizer, eds, *Der Fall Noel Field, Band II*, pp. 226, 229.

22. On this point I can only speculate. In notes 14 and 19 above I suggest that the 'Blue Book' was printed before the trial began. Once again pulping all copies to remove such little-known or barely-noticeable details was probably deemed worth neither the cost nor the effort.

23. Rajk Trial, pp. 8, 20, 146–47, 244.

24. Ibid., pp. 160, 240–41, 245.

25. In Geneva Noel had provided the group with 4,000 or 5,000 Swiss Francs for propaganda purposes, although not on the instructions of Dulles. Barth and Schweizer, eds, *Der Fall Noel Field, Band I*, p. 730.

26. Rajk Trial, p. 148.

27. Ibid., p. 163. In addition Szőnyi's 'evidence' includes the blatant lie that 'in November 1944, in Berne, Dulles […] told me that he had met Firtos-Rajk in France at the time of the Spanish Civil War'. Rajk Trial, p. 153. Szőnyi also made a statement that refers back to the trial of Cardinal Mindszenty in February 1949, and the widespread belief that his confession was induced by drugs. 'I am a physician and a neurologist, and I have known for a long time that such things are impossible. And now I have learnt from my own experience that such things are out of the question'. Ibid., p. 161. Who needs drugs when the 'conveyor' and repeated 'solings' are at hand?

28. Ibid., pp. 147–48, 162–63.

29. Ibid., p. 141. Brankov also waffled about 'Titoist' activity in Romania, Poland, Bulgaria, Albania and Slovakia. Ibid., pp. 125–26, p. 142. Where relevant this woolly 'evidence' will be discussed later.

30. Ibid., pp. 39–42, p. 144. See also A. London, *On Trial*, London, 1970, p. 36.

31. Rajk Trial, pp. 31–32.

32. Ibid., p. 81. According to Gábor Péter, then under arrest, when Rákosi was considering the list of defence lawyers for the trial, he suggested that 'Rajk's lawyer should be an ugly Jew'. Rév, *Indicting Rajk*, p. 13. In fact Rajk's counsel, Dr Elek Kaszó, was a good-looking man who may have been Jewish. His photo is in Soltész, *Rajk-Dosszié*.

33. Rajk Trial, p. 162.

34. They did manage to add to the political 'lessons' of the trial. 'I think we can all agree', contended Pálffy's counsel, 'that the main accused in this trial are the western imperialists and the Tito agents dangling on their strings'. Ibid., p. 277.

35. 'I fully agree with most of the statements of the Prosecutor; of course, I am not here thinking of the secondary and in any case unimportant details, but of the substance. Now, precisely

because of this, I declare in advance that whatever the sentence of the People's Court may be in my case, I shall consider this sentence just'. Ibid., p. 290.

36. Ibid., pp. 303–06. All the prisoners, including those condemned to death, somewhat redundantly lost their 'political rights' for ten years. In addition 'their entire available property' was confiscated. Despite this, and the fact that all of the condemned men were described as being 'without means', they were 'ordered to pay to the State Treasury the costs in their entirety which have arisen up to now'.

37. R. Gough, *A Good Comrade: János Kádár, Communism and Hungary*, London, 2006, p. 46.

38. Barth and Schweizer, eds, *Der Fall Noel Field, Band I*, p. 94.

39. Gough, *A Good Comrade*, p. 46.

40. Ibid. Szalai's words are also cited as, 'I perish innocently, how can Rákosi tolerate this?' P. Ignotus, *Political Prisoner*, London, 1959, p. 83. Szőnyi regretted that he'd been unable to kiss his new-born son farewell. Barth and Schweizer, eds, *Der Fall Noel Field, Band I*, p. 95.

41. In late summer 1995 the younger László Rajk was kind enough to let me interview him in Budapest. He insisted that his mother had never seen her husband after his arrest and had not witnessed his execution. The source of this story goes back to at least July 1956, when the disillusioned *Daily Worker* journalist Peter Fryer was told in Hungary that 'Julia was made to witness' Rajk's execution. See A. Macleod, *The Death of Uncle Joe*, Woodbridge (Suffolk), 1997, p. 100. However, the prime source for the tale is apparently Júlia herself, in an interview that she gave to the Zagreb paper *Vjesnik* (Courier) at the end of September 1956. 'In a cell directly above the place where the execution has been carried out, Mrs. Rajk was imprisoned–the wife of the man who is being executed! In this very cell she experienced another 51 executions in those months filled with furious terror'. See Open Society Archives (RFE), 'Croat-Yugo Paper Interview with Mrs Rajk', 6 October 1956, HU OSA 398–0–1, Records of Radio Free Europe/Radio Liberty Research Institute: Publications Department: Background Reports; Open Society Archives at Central European University, Budapest, http://www.osaarchivum.org/greenfield/repository/osa:122663e9-ed30–4e6e-afa5–5c6ba962438f, last accessed 26 May 2013, p. 5. The interview was originally conducted in French, so something may have been lost in translation. Possibly Júlia was referring to executions at Sopronkőhida. The article was published on 5 October 1956, the day before Rajk's 'show-burial' and this may well be relevant.

42. See Chapter 22, note 52.

43. A. Pető, *Geschlecht, Politik und Stalinismus in Ungarn: eine Biographie von Júlia Rajk*, Herne, 2007, p. 73.

44. That this was normal procedure in Hungarian executions at that time, see I. Fehérváry, *The Long Road to Revolution: The Hungarian Gulag 1945–1956*, Santa Fé, 1989, pp. 166–67.

45. The account and all quotations are in J. Mindszenty, *Memoirs*, London, 1974, p. 150. Presumably the victim was Szalai.

46. Mindszenty, *Memoirs*, p. 151. The cardinal's account of being mocked is confirmed by a letter written by Kádár in April 1956. See Gough, *A Good Comrade*, p. 46.

47. R10062, R10539/1013/21, FO371/78513, Public Records Office, Kew.

24. THE URGE TO PURGE: TRIAL AND TERROR 1948–53

1. 'He (Ranković) mentioned Patrascanu, then Minister of Justice, who was also following the Tito line and wanted to carry out Tito's plans in Rumania, but the Central Committee of the Rumanian Party removed him in time and isolated him from the Party'. Rajk Trial, *László Rajk and his Accomplices before the People's Court*, Budapest, 1949, p. 125.

2. See R. Levy, *Ana Pauker: The Rise and Fall of a Jewish Communist*, London, 2001, pp. 135–152.

3. R62/1015/90, FO371/78211, Public Records Office, Kew.

4. N12455/11494/38, FO371/66476, Public Records Office, Kew.
5. As late as 1 January 1948 Hoxha told the Albanian people that: 'We are joined in unbreakable brotherhood with the heroic people of the new Yugoslavia of Marshal Tito'. K. Kaplan, *Report on the Murder of the General Secretary*, London, 1990, p. 12.
6. Other accounts say that Xoxe was hanged, or even strangled in the manner of an unsuccessful Ottoman Grand Vizier.
7. On the 'Leningrad affair' see Y. Gorlizki and O. Khlevniuk, *Cold Peace: Stalin and the Soviet Ruling Circle, 1945–1953*, New York, 2005; S. Montefiore, *Stalin: The Court of the Red Tsar*, London, 2003; M. Parrish, *The Lesser Terror: Soviet State Security*, London, 1996; D. Volkogonov, *Stalin: Triumph and Tragedy*, London, 1995.
8. At his trial, as was the way with the wolf-pack mores of Stalin's era, Kostov's deformity was derided in both print and cartoons.
9. Apparently Kostov's sister approached a school-fellow of Kostov who worked in King Boris's private cabinet. This young man pleaded for the life of 'a gifted Bulgarian'. The next day the king told him that Kostov's sister could 'relax and sleep well now'. S. Groueff, *Crown of Thorns: The Reign of King Boris III of Bulgaria 1918–43*, London, 1987, pp. 332–36.
10. The BCP more than matched the brutality of the former regime. According to an official statement, by March 1945 2,138 Bulgarians had been executed and over 3,600 sentenced to jail terms of from fifteen to twenty years. H. Seton-Watson, *The East European Revolution*, London, 1956, p. 212. Whether these victims were all representatives of the old order is impossible to say. From June to September 1947 Kostov was involved in the judicial murder of the Agrarian leader, Nikolai Petkov, although mainly at the behest of the ailing Dimitrov who was then being treated in the USSR. See I. Banac, ed., *The Diary of Georgi Dimitrov 1933–1949*, London, 2003, pp. 419–28. On the Petkov affair see M. Padev, *Dimitrov Wastes no Bullets. Nikola Petkov: The Test Case*, London, 1948.
11. See the panegyric of the BCP Central Committee in celebration of Kostov's fiftieth birthday on 17 June 1947, in M. Padev, 'Deviationism in Bulgaria: The Indictment of Kostov', *The World Today*, 1950, Vol. 6, pp. 159–60.
12. R153, R635, R916/1015/7, FO371/78239, Public Records Office, Kew. Two of Kostov's brothers-in-law oversaw the press and the churches.
13. Banac, *The Diary of Georgi Dimitrov*, p. 452. Kostov was present, taking shorthand notes. Ibid., p. 450. I considered the possibility that Stalin's animus towards Kostov might have been exacerbated by the fact that he was Jewish. However, the legation in Sofia, reporting in November 1948 on the exodus of most Bulgarian Jews to Israel, asserted that 'no Jew stands in the front rank of Bulgarian communism'. R14350/85/7, FO371/72139A, Public Records Office, Kew.
14. Regarding the wide-ranging Bulgarian law on state secrets, see Padev, *Deviationism*, p. 162n.
15. Banac, *The Diary of Georgi Dimitrov*, p. 453.
16. J. Bell, *The Bulgarian Communist Party from Blagoev to Zhivkov*, Stanford, 1986, p. 104.
17. R1235/1015/7, FO371/78239; R3421, R3576/1015/7, FO371/78240; R11833/10116/7, FO371/78251, Public Records Office, Kew.
18. R3680/1015/7, FO371/78240; R5747/1015/7, FO371/78241, Public Records Office, Kew. Technically it was illegal for the BCP, rather than parliament, to remove Kostov from his government posts. The illegality of this act was rectified by a Grand National Assembly decree of 7 April. It was all rather suggestive of a rush-job.
19. R4055/1015/7, FO371/78240, Public Records Office, Kew.
20. In late April Kostov was reportedly in a sanatorium in Moscow. R4688, R5667/1015/7, FO371/78241, Public Records Office, Kew.
21. R4854/1015/7, FO371/78241, Public Records Office, Kew.
22. On 20 July 1949 the Grand National Assembly announced that its Presidium, meeting on 20 June, had agreed to the Chief Prosecutor's request that Kostov lose his parliamentary immu-

nity and be arrested and charged under Article 102 of the Bulgarian penal code. Unsurprisingly, the assembly approved the decisions of its Presidium. R7077/1015/7, FO371/78241, Public Records Office, Kew. The 20 June date of arrest is confirmed in Kostov Trial, *The Trial of Traicho Kostov and his Group*, Sofia, 1949, p. 125.

23. Regarding Dimitrov's death a British Foreign Office official minuted, 'We would not wish, I imagine, to stress our grief unduly'. Having been mummified by the man who embalmed Lenin, Dimitrov's body was displayed in a temporary mausoleum in Sofia on 10 July. Various communist bigwigs attended in the manner of 'crowned heads', including Gerő, Slánský, Pieck and the CPGB leader Harry Pollitt. Stalin sent a wreath. Even though it was Dimitrov's funeral, it naturally ended with 'Long live our leader and teacher, the leader and teacher of all progressive mankind, Joseph Vissarionovich Stalin'. The British minister complained that Western heads of missions stood 'in alternatively rain and scorching sun without support or sustenance for over six hours'. R6471, 6672, 6720, 6851/10113/7, FO371/78247, Public Records Office, Kew.

24. G. Hodos, *Show Trials: Stalinist Purges in Eastern Europe*, London, 1987, p. 19. The interrogation and trial preparations were supervised by Abakumov. Bell, *The Bulgarian Communist Party*, p. 106. The Agrarian Party deputy, Peter Koev, composed a vivid description of his appalling treatment at the hands of the communist militia. His testimony, written during a brief spell of freedom, was read to the Grand National Assembly by Nikola Petkov on 3 December 1946. See Padev, *Dimitrov Wastes no Bullets*, pp. 93–94.

25. The indictment, printed in Kostov Trial, pp. 5–57, charged Kostov and his 'group' with treason, espionage, sabotage and wrecking. The defendants were 'to be tried, found guilty, and punished according to the laws of the country'. It is noteworthy that unlike the pretence that 'witnesses' in the Rajk trial were at liberty, nineteen of the fifty-one listed 'witnesses' at the Kostov trial had as their address 'Sofia Central Prison'. Kostov Trial, pp. 55–56.

26. Ibid., pp. 66–67.

27. Ibid., p. 68.

28. It is reproduced in Ibid., pp. 74–126.

29. Ibid., pp. 608–09.

30. Ibid., p. 611. He was also divested of his civil rights 'for ever' and ordered 'to pay a fine of 1,000,000 leva, replaceable in case of insolvency by one year's imprisonment, and confiscation of all his property'!

31. Ibid., pp. 623–24. A facsimile of this 'petition' is included in the trial record. Whether Kostov wrote it is impossible to say.

32. Ibid., p. 624. One account, given by a Western minister to Sofia, says that 'Kostov was hanged with a rope of tobacco leaves'. G. Shepherd, *Russia's Danubian Empire*, London, 1954, p. 50.

33. See A. Ulam, *Titoism and the Cominform*, Cambridge (Mass.), 1952, pp. 207–08.

34. Padev, *Deviationism*, p. 162.

25. THE EVADED SHOW TRIAL: SACRIFICING THE POLISH 'FIELDISTS'

1. As noted in Chapter 16 Beria had little, if anything, to do with Field and the East European show trials. Here Berman was simply parroting the 'blame it all on Beria' line of the post-Stalin (and post-Beria) Soviet leadership.

2. G. Hodos, *Show Trials: Stalinist Purges in Eastern Europe*, London, 1987, pp. 141–42; B-R. Barth and W. Schweizer, eds, *Der Fall Noel Field, Band I: Gefängnisjahre 1949–1954*, Berlin, 2005, pp. 54–55. All twelve are usually identified as communists, but Dr Lis later specified that his wife was not in the PCP. C. Hoff, *Anna und Leon: Ihre Lebensgeschichte*, Potsdam, 2005, p. 314. It is possible that some others too were not party members.

3. It was in fact entitled the Polish Workers' Party, but in the text I have continued to call it the

Polish Communist Party (PCP), both to prevent confusion, and because it was the party of Poland's communists.

4. K. Kaplan, *Report on the Murder of the General Secretary*, London, 1990, p. 9.

5. Brankov 'testified' as follows: 'I can recall the case of Gomułka in Poland. They were attaching great hopes to it; they hoped Gomułka would carry out Tito's plans in Poland, and they were awaiting developments.... But, as is known, Gomułka did not carry it out, and admitted that this was the wrong line'. Rajk Trial, *László Rajk and his Accomplices before the People's Court*, pp. 125–26. See also T. Toranska, *'Them': Stalin's Polish Puppets*, London, 1987, p. 326.

6. See N. Bethell, *Gomułka: His Poland and his Communism*, London, 1972, pp. 167–68.

7. MBP = *Ministerstwo Bezpieczeństwa Publicznego*. Due to its ubiquitous existence in Poland's towns and regions the MBP was generally known as the UB (*Urząd Bezpieczeństwa* = security office).

8. Toranska, *'Them'*, p. 313.

9. M. Checinski, *Poland: Communism, Nationalism, Anti-Semitism*, New York, 1982, pp. 74–75.

10. 'Speech by Władysław Gomułka', 20 October 1956. HU OSA 300–8–3–4129; Records of Radio Free Europe/Radio Liberty Research Institute: Publications Department: Background Reports; Open Society Archives at Central European University, Budapest, http://www.osaarchivum.org/greenfield/repository/osa:6410fa2c-d85d-4634-9655-220f2d31b46b, last accessed 26 May 2013. This text also includes contributions by other Central Committee members, including Berman. I shall refer to it in the notes as 'Gomułka speech'.

11. Gomułka speech, p. 55. Berman outlined his position in similar terms in a statement of 30 September 1956. See Ibid., p. 63.

12. L. Kamiński, 'Why did Gomułka not become a Polish Slánský?' http://ece.columbia.edu/files/ece/images/kaminski-1.pdf, last accessed 26 May 2013, pp. 1–6, p. 2.

13. Toranska, *'Them'*, p. 313.

14. G. Kaiser, 'Kurzen Prozess machen! Hermann Field in den Fangen der polnischen Geheimpolizei'. *UTOPIEkreativ*, H.84 (Oktober 1997), http://www.rosalux.de/fileadmin/rls_uploads/pdfs/84_Kaiser.pdf, last accessed 26 May 2013, p. 64.

15. In 1968, during the anti-Semitic campaign in Poland, Anna left her homeland first for Sweden and then for Israel, where she died in 1976. B-R. Barth and W. Schweizer, eds, *Der Fall Noel Field, Band II: Asyl in Ungarn 1954–1957*. Berlin 2007, p. 411.

16. Checinski, *Poland*, p. 79.

17. Gomułka speech, p. 54.

18. Bethell, *Gomułka*, p. 174.

19. Checinski, *Poland*, p. 80.

20. Kaiser, 'Kurzen Prozess machen!', p. 64.

21. Berman recalled that Gomułka 'came out at the end of 1954 [...] Other people also started to come out [...] My Anna Duracz and all the people tacked on to the Field affair. We were helped by the fact that the Field affair had gone bankrupt in Hungary'. Toranska, *'Them'*, pp. 343–44. On events in Hungary, see Chapter 29.

22. L. Gluchowski, 'The Defection of Józef Światło and the Search for Jewish Scapegoats in the Polish United Workers' Party, 1953–1954', http://ece.columbia.edu/files/ece/images/gluchowski-1.pdf, last accessed 26 May 2013, p. 10. Most of the major documentation regarding Department Ten was destroyed after it was closed down in December 1954. Kaiser, 'Kurzen Prozess machen!', p. 62.

23. Fejgin (1909–2002) and Romkowski (1907–65), who was born Natan Grunspan-Kikiel, were Jewish. The head of the MBP from 1944–54 was General Stanisław Radkiewicz (1903–87), a Pole.

24. H. Field and K. Field, *Trapped in the Cold War: The Ordeal of an American Family*, Stanford, 1999, p. 67; Hoff, *Anna und Leon*, p. 152.

25. F. Lewis, *The Man who Disappeared: The Strange History of Noel Field*, London, 1965, pp. 238–39.

26. Różański (1907–81) was born Josek Goldberg. In pre-war Warsaw he was a lawyer. Along with Romkowski and Fejgin he would carry the can for the MBP's violations of 'socialist legality'. They were rightly imprisoned for their crimes, while the head of the whole vile organisation, the Pole Radkiewicz, merely lost office.

27. Barth and Schweizer, eds, *Der Fall Noel Field, Band I*, pp. 54–55; Hodos, *Show Trials*, p. 143.

28. Text in Barth and Schweizer, eds, *Der Fall Noel Field, Band I*, pp. 62–74.

29. Kaiser, 'Kurzen Prozess machen!', p. 65.

30. The full list is given in Checinski, *Poland*, p. 84 n23. The other five were: Szymon Jakubowicz who worked in the PCP secretariat; an engineer named Jerzy Nowicki; Paulina Born; Henryk Held; and Dr Jerzy Kawa. The first four were in Switzerland during the war. There is no information on Kawa save his name. Noel mentions some of them in his prison writings. See Barth and Schweizer, eds, *Der Fall Noel Field, Band I*, pp. 18, 18 n3, 64, 70–71, 590–91. See also Hoff, *Anna und Leon*, p. 304.

31. They were indeed two of Hermann's closest friends. He and Jean met them first as students in Zurich in autumn 1934. Field and Field, *Trapped in the Cold War*, p. 87.

32. Barth and Schweizer, eds, *Der Fall Noel Field, Band I*, pp. 62–64, 70–71. It seems that Noel made no contact with the Gecows during his visits to Poland in 1947 and 1948. Yet Anna, who was in Paris in May 1949, was certain that Noel would be attending the Partisans for Peace conference there and looked out for him. Hoff, *Anna und Leon*, p. 145.

33. In 1937 Anna was promised a post in Poznań–in 1943. Ibid., p. 37.

34. Ibid., p. 47.

35. Leon was a Red Army officer until 1944. Apparently he also became a Soviet citizen. Barth and Schweizer, eds, *Der Fall Noel Field, Band I*, p. 63 n5.

36. Hoff, *Anna und Leon*, p. 126.

37. The accounts by Lis and Sokolowski are in Ibid., pp. 286–324. A senior Polish communist in Paris advised Lis to drop his euphemistically-termed 'German' name of Rosenbluth before returning to his homeland. Ibid., p. 301.

38. Anna refuted the idea of Noel as an American spy by telling her interrogator 'if he really was a spy, he'd be a Russian spy'. Ibid., p. 166.

39. Ibid., p. 198.

40. Anna Gecow wrote later that she was shown a copy of the Rajk trial transcript in December 1949, and informed that her husband was to be 'the Polish Rajk'. Ibid., p. 215.

41. Checinski, *Poland*, p. 80. In the version Lis gave to Ms Hoff, Różański says, 'You can do what you like with him [Gecow]. He's a spy and he won't leave here alive'. Hoff, *Anna und Leon*, p. 177.

42. Barth and Schweizer, eds, *Der Fall Noel Field, Band II*, p. 425; Hodos, *Show Trials*, p. 143; Hoff, *Anna und Leon*, p. 317. At her rehabilitation hearing Tonia was pressured to give evidence against her torturers, but only those of Jewish descent. Checinski, *Poland*, p. 98.

26. 'FORMER GERMAN POLITICAL *ÉMIGRÉS*': WITCH-HUNT IN THE GDR

1. On events in the Soviet occupation zone in 1945–49, see N. Naimark, *Russians in Germany: A History of the Soviet Occupation Zone*, London, 1997. For occupation zones and sectors in Germany and Berlin, see T. Sharp, *The Wartime Alliance and the Zonal Division of Germany*, Oxford, 1975.

2. W. Kießling, *'Leistner ist Mielke': Schatten einer gefälschten Biographie*, Berlin, 1998, p. 102.

3. R. Friedmann, *Ulbrichts Rundfunkmann: eine Gerhart-Eisler-Biographie*, Berlin, 2007, p. 219; Kießling, *'Leistner ist Mielke'*, p. 106.

4. See Ibid., pp. 138–39.

5. The statement of 24 August 1950 is printed in 'Erklärung des Zentralkomitees und der Zentralen Parteikontrollkommission zu den Verbindungen ehemaliger deutscher politischer Emigranten zu dem Leiter des Unitarian Service Committee Noel H. Field', Dokumente der Sozialistischen Einheitspartei: Beschlüsse und Erklärungen des Parteivorstandes, des Zentralkomitees, sowie seines Politbüros und seines Sekretariats, Band III. (East) Berlin 1952, 197–213. It was published in the SED daily Neues Deutschland on 1 September 1950. There is no point in detailing either its errors of fact or its falsifications of motives and actions. It was a document of its time and deliberately constructed to serve a particular purpose.

   The records of all ZPKK interrogations of the German 'Fieldists' went to both the Stasi and the MGB, and doubtless from the latter to Stalin. The original draft of the statement, which was considered by the SED Politburo on 22 August, was apparently written in rushed fashion by the MGB with German collaboration. Although the statement bears the date 24 August, all of the expellees, except the holidaying Kreikemeyer, were called before the ZPKK on 23 August and informed of their expulsion. Kießling, 'Leistner ist Mielke', pp. 116, 126, 140–44. Was this another anniversary celebrated by the Boss? On 23 August 1939 the Nazi-Soviet Pact was signed. Merker, Bertz and Ende are known to have opposed it. The others may have done so. Such 'Trotskyist' views were noted in the statement. See 'Erklärung des Zentralkomitees', pp. 202–03. On this interpretation, Stalin was as closely involved in the 'Field affair' in Germany, as he was in Hungary, Poland and Czechoslovakia.

6. 'Erklärung des Zentralkomitees', p. 212.

7. Bruno Fuhrmann, Hans Teubner, Walter Beling and Wolfgang Langhoff were removed from their posts. Although their relations with Field were adjudged to be equally close, the activities of this quartet were deemed to lead only to 'indirect (mittelbar) support of the class enemy'. Unlike the expelled sextet, they were still addressed as 'Comrade' (Genosse). Ibid., p. 212. Jo Tempi, labelled a 'Trotskyist', was included too. Ibid., p. 209. She and her husband were expelled by the PCF.

8. This is Barth's account of his death. Other sources contend that Bertz committed suicide.

9. Eisler had met Field only once, during Noel's stay in the USA in 1945–46. B-R. Barth and W. Schweizer, eds, Der Fall Noel Field, Band I: Gefängnisjahre 1949–1954, Berlin, 2005, p. 486. Although he was not arrested, between July 1950 and January 1956 he lost his party and government positions. See Friedmann, Ulbrichts Rundfunkmann, pp. 213–37; C. Epstein, The Last Revolutionaries: German Communists and their Century, London, 2003, p. 140.

10. 'Erklärung des Zentralkomitees', p. 206. For Goldhammer's innocent relationship with Szőnyi, see W. Kießling, Partner im 'Narrenparadies': der Freundeskreis um Noel Field und Paul Merker, Berlin, 1994, pp. 90–92.

11. 'Erklärung des Zentralkomitees', p. 201.

12. Ibid., p. 201, p. 209. Mia's illegal entry into Switzerland appears to have taken place in June 1942, not autumn, although the date of December 1941 is also given. She remained hidden in Geneva until November 1944 when she left for Paris. See Barth and Schweizer, eds, Der Fall Noel Field, Band I, p. 425 n197; B-R. Barth and W. Schweizer, eds, Der Fall Noel Field, Band II: Asyl in Ungarn 1954–1957, Berlin, 2007, p. 441; Kießling, Partner im 'Narrenparadies', pp. 79–80.

13. F. Lewis, The Man who Disappeared: The Strange History of Noel Field, London, 1965, p. 225.

14. 'Die französische Partei hat mir nichts zu sagen, nur das deutsche ZK'. K. Becker and A. Roser, 'Das Parteiverfahren gegen Lex Ende im Sommer 1945 in Paris: Dokumente aus dem Nachlaß Herbert Müller', http://www.klaus-j-becker.de/docs/veroeffentlichungen/ENDE.pdf, last accessed 26 May 2013, p. 13.

15. A Hamburg weekly wrote mockingly of 'End(e)'s new beginning: peace post-master'. 'Endes neuer Anfang: Friedenspostmeister', in Der Spiegel, 41/49, 6 October 1949, http://www.spiegel.

de/spiegel/print/d-44438502.html, last accessed 26 May 2013. Was it someone's mordant or vengeful sense of humour that made an opponent of the Nazi-Soviet pact of 1939 into editor of a journal 'celebrating' German-Soviet friendship? On Ende and the pact, see H. Müller-Enbergs, 'Erste Chefredakteur, dann 'Unperson': Lex Ende und Rudolf Herrnstadt'. *Jahrbuch für Historische Kommunismusforschung 1996*, Berlin, 1995, p. 298.

16. Kießling, *Partner im 'Narrenparadies'*, p. 273.

17. Feistmann was in Prague 4–9 April 1948 attending the funeral of Egon Erwin Kisch, who died on 31 March. He was frequently with Gisela Kisch and on the night before his departure Feistmann collected letters from the widow. These acknowledged the many messages of condolence sent to her from Berlin. Among these were letters to Bertz and Mia Weiterer. Noel, then in Geneva, had also sent his condolences and Gisela showed them to Rudi. Ibid., pp. 272–73.

18. Ibid., p. 273.

19. It is impossible to say whether Feistmann had in fact carried letters from Noel to Bertz and Mia. They were never mentioned again. Ibid., p. 274.

20. Possibly adding to Feistmann's despair was the fact that his second wife had recently returned to Mexico with their child.

21. The text of the report is in Kießling, *'Leistner ist Mielke'*, pp. 103–05.

22. See Ibid., pp. 120–31.

23. Ibid., p. 123.

24. This brief biography of Mielke is based upon details in Kießling, *'Leistner ist Mielke'*, plus Mielke's German Wikipedia entry. The latter shows a police photo of the young Mielke with a hairstyle that any British 'Teddy-boy' would have died for. Presumably it helped make him 'taller' than his actual height of 1.62m. In 1993 Mielke was sentenced to six years imprisonment for his role in the 1931 murders, but was released in 1995. He died, aged ninety-two, in an old people's home in former East Berlin in 2000.

25. Text in Ibid., p. 145.

26. Ibid., pp. 157–58.

27. Ibid., pp. 158–68.

28. Ibid., p. 167.

29. Text in Ibid., pp. 168–71.

30. Ibid., p. 169

31. Ibid., p. 173. This may well be correct, but I can't see from his evidence why it should be one of these two days.

32. Marthe Kreikemeyer courageously bombarded both GDR and Soviet authorities with thirty-seven demands to be informed of her husband's whereabouts and fate. Ill herself, with little money, and in an alien country, her moving letters form a large part of Kießling's book. She reminded government and party officials of the country's constitution and laws, but was either ignored or fobbed off with platitudes about the 'continuing investigation', etc. Gradually losing her 'socialist faith', Marthe fled to West Berlin in December 1954 and then back to France. She died in 1986 without ever learning the truth about Willi's fate.

33. Ibid., pp. 280–81

34. Ibid., pp. 281–82. In this letter the SED lifted part of the judgement of the 'Field Decision' against Kreikemeyer. He was 'rehabilitated' to the extent that his party membership up until his death was now unbroken! But their judgement that Kreikemeyer had allegedly encouraged German comrades to remain in the French camps and not to join the resistance remained in force. The 'rehabilitated' Kreikemeyer remained a 'capitulationist'.

35. Ibid., pp. 230–34; W. Otto, 'Das Verschwinden des Willi Kreikemeyers'. *UTOPIEkreativ*, H. 100 (Februar) 1999, pp. 47–53 http://www.rosalux.de/fileadmin/rls_uploads/pdfs/100_Otto. pdf, last accessed 26 May 2013, p. 51. The claim was that Kreikemeyer had a cold and was sup-

plied with two extra handkerchiefs. One must wonder how large these were. In his Czechoslovak prison Evžen Loebl had a pocket handkerchief 'only two inches square, because in one prison a man had succeeded in strangling himself with an ordinary-sized handkerchief'. E. Loebl, *Sentenced and Tried: The Stalinist Purges in Czechoslovakia*, London, 1969, p. 15. Yet in the same Schumannstraße prison Erica Glaser received a sanitary towel with the gauze removed, in case she unpicked it and hung herself with it, E. Wallach, *Light at Midnight*, New York, 1967, p. 59.

36. Kreikemeyer may have been murdered in the Schumannstraße prison and it may have been on Thursday 31 August 1950. However, Leo Bauer, then under interrogation by the MGB, claimed that in October 1951 he was shown a protocol signed by Willi in April or May 1951. Kießling, '*Leistner ist Mielke*', p. 285.

37. P. Brandt, et al., *Karrieren eines Außenseiters: Leo Bauer zwischen Kommunismus und Sozialdemokratie 1912 bis 1972*, Berlin/Bonn, 1983, pp. 196–97.

38. The following section is based upon Barth and Schweizer, eds, *Der Fall Noel Field, Band II*, pp. 152 n7 and n8, 417–18; and the unsatisfactory accounts in Brandt et al., *Karrieren eines Außenseiters*; Lewis, *The Man who Disappeared*; Wallach, *Light at Midnight*. Bauer was an inordinately secretive person, while Erica's accounts have to be weighed against the fact that, as a former communist, she was only admitted to the USA with great difficulty, and that she probably kept a few secrets of her own. Her accounts of why she suddenly decided to 'find' the Fields one year after they disappeared leave me sceptical, but I can offer no other explanation of why she travelled to Berlin.

39. Text of letter in Barth and Schweizer, eds, *Der Fall Noel Field, Band II*, p. 152 n7.

40. It referred to Erica being 'in the pay of the Americans' and also specified that she was the 'lover' of both Noel and Herta Field. 'Erklärung des Zentralkomitees', p. 199. The latter was what Goldhammer had told the ZPKK in November 1949. (See Chapter 9, footnote 13) The statement also described Bauer as being 'now revealed as a longstanding (*langjähriger*) American agent'. 'Erklärung des Zentralkomitees', p. 204.

41. Her book's title, *Light at Midnight*, refers to these years, but it is also a clever play on Arthur Koestler's novel, *Darkness at Noon*, which was a fictionalised study of the trial of Bukharin. Erica had read this book shortly before she was arrested. Wallach, *Light at Midnight*, p. 4.

42. Following the visit of West German Chancellor Konrad Adenauer to Moscow, Bauer was released along with those German POWs who were still alive in the USSR. Leo rejoined the SPD, became an adviser to Chancellor Willy Brandt, and died in Bonn in September 1972. For over two years Erica lived with her mother in Surrey, and was interrogated by the CIA in Germany. She eventually rejoined her husband and children in Virginia in early 1958. That March she appeared before HUAC. Thereafter she taught French and Latin in a school in Warrenton. She died of lung cancer, like her father, in December 1993.

27. THE LAGGARDS OF PRAGUE: THE FIELDS AND THE SLÁNSKÝ TRIAL

1. B-R. Barth and W. Schweizer, eds, *Der Fall Noel Field, Band I: Gefängnisjahre 1949–1954*, Berlin, 2005, pp. 57 n3, 464–66, 519 n14, 596–97, 637, 637 n25; *B-R. Barth and W. Schweizer, eds, Der Fall Noel Field, Band II: Asyl in Ungarn 1954–1957*, Berlin, 2007, pp. 368, 428–29 (Pavlík biography); K. Kaplan, *Report on the Murder of the General Secretary*, London, 1990, pp. 38–60 *passim*; J. Pelikán, *The Czechoslovak Political Trials, 1950–1954*, London, 1971, pp. 72–77.

2. Kaplan, *Report on the Murder*, p. 38.

3. Noel contended that he was always reserved with Pavlík on personal grounds, finding him vain, easily offended and ambitious. Both he and Herta always used the formal *Sie* form of address when speaking German with him and his wife and were never on first-name terms.

4. Text in Barth and Schweizer, eds, *Der Fall Noel Field, Band I*, pp. 57–60.
5. Pelikán, *The Czechoslovak Political Trials*, p. 73.
6. Kaplan, *Report on the Murder*, p. 42.
7. Ibid. Noel wrote short studies of all these people (except Frejka and Feigl) for the ÁVH in 1954. See Barth and Schweizer, eds, *Der Fall Noel Field, Band I*, pp. 594–602.
8. Barth and Schweizer, eds, *Der Fall Noel Field, Band II*, p. 368.
9. Kaplan, *Report on the Murder*, p. 43.
10. On 24 June the StB arrested Feigl, who had spent the war in Switzerland before joining the Ministry of Information in Prague. They also imprisoned his common-law wife, Dr Vlasta Veselá. Both had worked for USC Czechoslovakia. On 7 July they seized Alice Kohnová. She and Veselá had served in Spain as doctors.
11. Kaplan, *Report on the Murder*, p. 47.
12. Kate Field was told that a distraught Sonia Markus, left alone with two small children and her old and ailing mother, had killed the children and then herself. H. Field and K. Field, *Trapped in the Cold War: The Ordeal of an American Family*, Stanford, 1999, p. 137. In June 1950 Markus, Feigl and the Pavlíks were secretly tried for espionage. Markus was sentenced to three years imprisonment, Feigl to thirteen, Pavlík to fifteen and his wife to ten. The Pavlíks were not released until 1956. Dr Veselá committed suicide in prison on 14 June 1950.
13. The British embassy noted that Loebl had been 'in regular and easy contact with British and American officials regarding economic questions', while Nový, despite the tone of his press articles, always showed in conversation 'a reasonable disposition to understand our position'. N10427/10113/12, FO371/77262, Public Records Office, Kew.
14. Kaplan, *Report on the Murder*, pp. 53–115, *passim*; Pelikán, *The Czechoslovak Political Trials*, pp. 78–112, *passim*; M. Šlingová, *Truth will prevail*, London, 1968, *passim*.
15. Displaying typical charm and integrity, Likhachev bawled at one StB officer, 'Stalin sent me here to prepare a trial… I didn't come here for discussions. I came to Czechoslovakia to see heads roll…. I don't care where you get (the information) and I don't care how true it is. I'll believe it, and you leave the rest to me. What do you care about some Jewish shit, anyway?' Kaplan, *Report on the Murder*, pp. 54–55. 'You are not a Communist, and you are not a Czechoslovak', he berated Loebl. 'You are a dirty Jew. Israel is your only real fatherland, and you have sold out Socialism to your bosses, the Zionist, imperialist leaders of world Jewry…. [T]he time is approaching fast when we'll have to exterminate all your kind'. E. Loebl, *My Mind on Trial*, London, 1976, p. 62.
16. Kaplan, *Report on the Murder*, p. 54.
17. Pelikán, *The Czechoslovak Political Trials*, p. 82. Slánský acted without informing the 'Londoner' Interior Minister, Václav Nosek, whom he distrusted.
18. Loebl, *My Mind on Trial*, p. 87.
19. Kaplan, *Report on the Murder*, p. 58.
20. It was frequently alleged that Slánský's real name was Salzman, but Slánský was an old Bohemian-Jewish name. D. Schmidt, *Anatomy of a Satellite*, Boston, 1952, p. 464. Virtually all of Slánský's family were murdered in the Holocaust. A memorial plaque upon the wall of his parents' home was removed after Slánský's arrest.
21. Gottwald was CzCP Secretary-General from 1929 to 1945 when he became Party chairman. From May 1948 he was also President of Czechoslovakia.
22. Kaplan, *Report on the Murder*, p. 62. The previous day the British ambassador wrote that if he had to select a 'Czech Rajk', 'I think that I would pick out Zapotocky'. N10547/10113/12, FO371/77262, Public Records Office, Kew. Antonín Zápotocký, then Czechoslovak Prime Minister, later succeeded Gottwald as President. He was entirely untouched by the purges.
23. V. Dedijer, *The Battle Stalin Lost: Memories of Yugoslavia 1948–53*, Nottingham, 1978, p. 136. This gesture took place after the expulsion of the CPY from the Cominform. As late as autumn

1949 Clementis played mid-Atlantic deck tennis on the *Queen Elizabeth* with Dedijer and the British MP Barbara Castle. Ibid., pp. 227–28.

24. A separate trial of the 'Slovak bourgeois-nationalist' leaders occurred in April 1954, thirteen months after Stalin's death.

25. In the Rajk trial Brankov was made to say that the 'Titoist' spies and wreckers were 'most successful in Slovakia', where they could 'rely on the Slovak nationalists'. Rajk Trial, *László Rajk and his Accomplices before the People's Court*, Budapest, 1949, pp. 141–42.

26. Šlingová, *Truth will prevail*, p. 17.

27. H. Dewar, *The Modern Inquisition*, London, 1953, p. 232.

28. E. Loebl, *Sentenced and Tried: The Stalinist Purges in Czechoslovakia*, London, 1969, pp. 84, 89, 143, 158–59, 163–65, 186–87, 192–3; Slánský Trial, *Prozess gegen die Leitung des staatsfeindlichen Verschwörungszentrums mit Rudolf Slánský an der Spitze*, Prague, 1953, pp. 9–10, 137, 164–65, 210, 219–21, 281, 293–302, 372, 374, 383–84, 471, 479–84, 587–90.

29. It seems that Nový was imprisoned from 1950 to 1954. Whether he was actually tried and sentenced is not clear from either English or Czech-language accounts.

30. Artur London 'testified' that he provided 'the American agent Noel Hermann [sic] Field' with intelligence. Slánský Trial, p. 210. This was probably genuine ignorance, since London never met Hermann Field.

31. Ibid., p. 10.

32. Ibid., p. 480.

33. The bland 'Intelligence Service' or simply 'I.S.' was used to designate unspecified British and American intelligence organisations.

34. On Zilliacus (1894–1967), see A. Potts, *Zilliacus: A Life for Peace and Socialism*, London, 2002. Zilliacus served in Russia in 1918–19, and then worked for the League of Nations until October 1938. There he and Noel met, but little is known of their relationship. Elected a Labour MP in July 1945, Zilliacus stood very much on Labour's left wing, and was expelled from the Party in May 1949. Until June 1948 Zilliacus was decidedly *persona grata* in Eastern Europe. His support for Tito, an act of *lèse Staline*, caused the Boss to cast him as a 'Titoist' in the Rajk trial. Zilliacus was upgraded to 'Titoist-Zionist agent' in the Slánský trial. He was re-admitted to the Labour Party in February 1952. His biography of Tito was published seven months later. The original manuscript was shredded by persons unknown, when Zilliacus was travelling by express from Paris to Belgrade in September 1951.

35. Zilliacus certainly knew Frejka. 'During my (September) 1946 visit I met several of the leading men concerned in framing that plan (for economic reconstruction), notably Frejka, who, in grey flannel trousers, soft shirt, Norfolk jacket and cardigan, smoking a big pipe, looked and spoke like a Cambridge don'. K. Zilliacus, *A New Birth of Freedom? World Communism since Stalin*, London, 1957, p. 141.

36. This Field is supposed to be Hermann, who visited Czechoslovakia in summer 1947 as head of a team of architects. Hermann may have visited the Alcron hotel. He may even have met Zilliacus. However, unlike Noel, Hermann did not know Zilliacus and would have required an introduction. Moreover, the scenario of Field travelling from Czechoslovakia to Poland and then back to Prague several weeks later would fit Noel's movements in 1948, (See Chapter 14) not those of Hermann in 1947.

37. This too would seem to be consistent with Noel's activities in 1948.

38. Loebl attended UNRRA conferences in 1943 and 1944. Loebl, *My Mind on Trial*, p. 11. Neither he nor Hermann say that they met then.

39. E. Loebl, *Sentenced and Tried*, pp. 192–93.

40. Loebl testified that Karel Markus corresponded with Hermann and was also friendly with Noel. During his visit to Prague in 1947 Hermann stayed with Markus. Field and Field, *Trapped in the Cold War*, p. 137.

41. Slánský Trial, p. 384.
42. In his book Hermann mentions neither meeting with Loebl. However, in December 1969 he informed Anna Gecow that he'd met Loebl both in 1947 and 1949. C. Hoff, *Anna und Leon: Ihre Lebensgeschichte*, Potsdam, 2005, p. 243.
43. Dulles left Switzerland for Germany in July 1945.
44. Noel records only two meetings with London in Switzerland.
45. Slánský Trial, p. 220. The reference to Noel having recently left Czechoslovakia for Paris is further confirmation that a meeting between Field and London took place in November 1948 (p. 132). Apparently, Noel was accompanied by 'a certain American woman' whom London did not know. Ibid. Nor can I identify her.
46. Herta delivered this personally in August 1949. See Chapter 20, footnote 28.
47. Ibid., p. 221. It is impossible to say whether such a letter existed. It seems like an invention to smear Merker, whose arrest was pending.
48. Schmidt, *Anatomy of a Satellite*, p. 478.
49. See Chapter 28, footnote 58.

28. 'TERRORIST ACTIVITIES': STALIN'S LAST KILLINGS

1. J. Rubenstein and V. Naumov, *Stalin's Secret Pogrom: The Post-War Inquisition of the Jewish Anti-Fascist Committee*, London, 2005, p. 62. This was in fact a meeting of the Presidium of the CPSU Central Committee. Organisational changes in the Party's leadership bodies were introduced at the Nineteenth Congress of the CPSU in October 1952. For details see Y. Gorlizki and O. Khlevniuk, *Cold Peace: Stalin and the Soviet Ruling Circle, 1945–1953*, New York, 2005, pp. 148–53, 214 n29. For our purposes these changes are irrelevant. Only one man was determining the outcome of the issues discussed in this chapter.
2. J. Brent and V. Naumov, *Stalin's last Crime: The Doctor's Plot*, London, 2003, pp. 201–2. In fact it was Stalin who in the 1930s had instructed Jewish journalists to use Russian pen-names. G. Kostyrchenko, *Out of the Red Shadows: Anti-Semitism in Stalin's Russia*, New York, 1995, p. 58. As in the thirties he again acted as the sole arbiter of truth. Stalin ordered Abakumov's successor to send all material relating to the 'Doctors' Plot' directly to him, bypassing the Politburo. Nothing was to be altered in these documents, since 'we ourselves will be able to determine what is true and what is not true, what is important and what is not important'. Brent and Naumov, *Stalin's last Crime*, p. 130.
3. On the 'vacationing gardener' see S. Montefiore, *Stalin: The Court of the Red Tsar*, London, 2003.
4. None of these doctors were Jewish. The medical treatment of Zhdanov is covered exhaustively in Brent and Naumov, *Stalin's last Crime*. Excellently researched and very detailed, this work utilises material from the Soviet-era archives and is the most substantial study of the 'Doctor's Plot'.
5. 'Yakov Etinger was a talkative man who loved to discuss politics—with anybody and in any company. And he was far from careful in airing his views'. Y. Rapoport, *The Doctors' Plot: Stalin's Last Crime*, London, 1991, p. 131.
6. Brent and Naumov, *Stalin's last Crime*, p. 101. No date is given for this order.
7. Ibid., pp. 101, 119. I have no evidence for the following speculation. Perhaps Ryumin ignored Abakumov's stop-order, because he was encouraged to do so by Stalin working through one of his minions. Although Ryumin produced no protocols of these interrogations of Etinger for the MGB, possibly he produced some for the Kremlin.
8. D. Rayfield, *Stalin and his Hangmen*, London, 2005, p. 26. Stalin's height was a state secret. A. Vaksberg, *Stalin Against the Jews*, New York, 1994, p. 120.
9. Brent and Naumov, *Stalin's last Crime*, pp. 114–15; P. Sudoplatov, *Special Tasks: The Memoirs of an Unwanted Witness—a Soviet Spymaster*, London, 1994, p. 299.
10. If this was a full Central Committee meeting, rather than a get-together of Stalin and his clos-

est cronies, then its rapid convocation suggests that the Boss certainly had 'advance notice' of the contents of Ryumin's letter.

11. Ryumin's letter is printed in Brent and Naumov, *Stalin's last Crime*, pp. 115–18.

12. The secret letter had to be returned to the Central Committee's 'Special Sector' within fifteen days. For a summary of the letter and the full text of the Central Committee decree of 11 July, see Ibid., pp. 137–39.

13. Stalin's name appears nowhere in the secret letter or decree, but there can be little doubt that he wrote both. One can speculate whether the Central Committee even met to authorise his decree.

14. This was an example of Stalin's 'cold revenge'. Apparently both doctors had refused to sign a death certificate testifying that Stalin's second wife had died of appendicitis in November 1932. In fact she had shot herself. Rapoport, *The Doctors' Plot*, p. 32. Dr Levin was Jewish, but Dr Pletnev was not.

15. K. Kaplan, *Report on the Murder of the General Secretary*, London, 1990, p. 125. Stalin received all the interrogation protocols, which were translated on the spot into Russian. It is probable that he also conveyed instructions to Prague on how the questioning should proceed. What Boyarski's particular faults were is unclear. Perhaps he was one of the old guard in the MGB, and destined to join the clear-out.

16. Ibid., p. 128.

17. Ibid., p. 129.

18. The PCP daily *Trybuna Ludu* (People's Tribune) wished Slánský 'many more years of life for the good of the great ideal of socialism'. That same day other idealists in the MBP, led by Światło, arrested Gomułka. N. Bethell, *Gomułka: his Poland and his Communism*, London, 1972, pp. 177, 180–82. It is possible that this represented the result of strong pressure by Stalin, given his activism in July 1951.

19. See J. Slánská, *Report on my Husband*, London, 1969, pp. 3–10.

20. Born Bedřich Reisinger in Plzeň in September 1911, Reicin was the son of a poor Jewish cantor and a boyhood friend of Šling. He joined the CzCP in 1929. From 1940 to 1945 he was in the USSR. Initially involved in propaganda, later he was political commissar of the Red Army's Czechoslovak brigade. On his return to Prague he became Deputy Minister of Defence and Chief of Military Intelligence. He was heavily involved in Czechoslovak military aid to Israel in 1948. He was arrested on 8 February 1951. D. Schmidt, *Anatomy of a Satellite*, Boston, 1952, p. 477; A. Krammer, *The Forgotten Friendship: Israel and the Soviet Bloc, 1947–53*, London, 1974, pp. 68, 84; J. Pelikán, *The Czechoslovak Political Trials, 1950–1954*, London, 1971, p. 350.

21. Hajdů (1913–1977) studied law in Prague and Paris. He served in the Czechoslovak army in France and Britain in the Second World War. He joined the CzCP in 1940. Appointed a Deputy Foreign Minister in 1950, he was arrested on 2 April 1951. Pelikán, *The Czechoslovak Political Trials*, p. 333; I. Margolius, *Reflections of Prague: Journeys through the Twentieth Century*, Chichester, 2006, p. 306.

22. Fischl was born in August 1902. A member of the CzCP since 1928, he became a Deputy Minister of Finance in 1949. From December 1949 he served as ambassador to the GDR until he was recalled in June 1951. H. Dewar, The *Modern Inquisition*, 1953, p. 257; Pelikán, *The Czechoslovak Political Trials*, p. 330; Slánský Trial, *Prozess gegen die Leitung des staatsfeindlichen Verschwörungszentrums mit Rudolf Slánský an der Spitze*, Prague, 1953, p. 446. He was arrested on 30 June 1951, according to Margolius, *Reflections of Prague*, p. 306. I have relied on this source where there are conflicting or previously unknown dates of arrest.

23. M. Cotic, *The Prague Trial: The First Anti-Zionist Show Trial in the Communist Bloc*, London, 1987, p. 58.

24. Born into a merchant family in Prague in August 1913, Dr Margolius was, like Loebl, a Dep-

uty Minister of Foreign Trade when he was arrested on 10 January 1952. In October 1941 he and his wife Heda were deported by the Germans to the ghetto in Łódź. In August 1944 they were briefly interned in Auschwitz. Separated thereafter, Heda escaped from a death march to Belsen, while Rudolf was liberated by the Americans from Dachau. Both lost most of their families in the Holocaust. Both joined the CzCP in December 1945. Margolius's widow and son have provided portraits of this incorrigibly idealistic man.

25. Born February 1909, Frank joined the CzCP in 1930. He was interned in KZ Buchenwald in the war. Appointed Deputy Secretary-General of the CzCP in May 1948, he was arrested on 25 May 1952. Pelikán, *The Czechoslovak Political Trials*, p. 330. .

26. Katz, 'a small pale man', was described by one American pressman as 'the Jew with a duelling scar'. G. Cox, *Countdown to War: A Personal Memoir of Europe 1938–1940*, London, 1988, p. 123. Diana McLellan made heroic efforts to ascertain whether Katz married Marlene in Teplice in the early 1920s, but he appears to be merely one of the bisexual Dietrich's numerous conquests. See D. McLellan, *The Girls: Sappho goes to Hollywood*, London, 2001. Otto's own tally was of rock-star proportions too. Ms McLellan suggests that Marlene funded Otto and the exiled KPD over many years.

27. The son of a well-to-do businessman, Katz was born into a German-speaking Jewish family in Jistebnice in southern Bohemia on 27 May 1895 (although McLellan, *The Girls*, p. 102n makes a good case for the year 1893). Katz grew up in Prague and Plzeň. In 1921 he left Czechoslovakia for Berlin with his first wife and daughter. He joined the KPD in 1922. In April 1931 Otto travelled to Moscow where he received Comintern and OGPU training. Following the *Reichstag* fire Katz rejoined his original patron, Willi Münzenberg, in Paris. Thereafter he alternated between Paris and the USA, helping to organise the 'Hollywood Anti-Nazi League'. He was in Mexico with Paul Merker. On his return to Europe in 1946 he joined the CzCP and was chief foreign editor for *Rudé Právo*. He was under StB surveillance from October 1949. For a detailed biography, see J. Miles, *The Nine Lives of Otto Katz: The Remarkable Story of a Communist Super-Spy*, London, 2010.

28. Brent and Naumov, *Stalin's last Crime*, pp. 186–87.

29. Ibid. pp. 206–07.

30. Ibid. p. 153.

31. Sudoplatov, *Special Tasks*, p. 301. Komarov and Likhachev were shot with Abakumov on 19 December 1954, nearly two years after Stalin's death. M. Parrish, *The Lesser Terror: Soviet State Security*, London, 1996, pp. 274–75. Bielkin was spared and freed in June 1953. Dismissed from the MGB in October, he worked as a motor mechanic from 1955 to 1980. He died in 1996. B-R. Barth and W. Schweizer, eds, *Der Fall Noel Field, Band II: Asyl in Ungarn 1954–1957*, Berlin, 2007, p. 403.

32. Rubenstein and Naumov, *Stalin's Secret Pogrom*, p. xvi.

33. The other defendants were: the Yiddish poets Peretz Markish, Leyb Kvitko and David Hofshteyn; the novelist David Bergelson; the medical director Dr Boris Shimeliovich; the scientist and sole female member of the Soviet Academy of Sciences, Dr Lina Shtern; the leading actor of the State Jewish Theatre, Benjamin Zuskin; and six functionaries who had little or nothing to do with the work of the JAC–Joseph Yuzefovich, Leon Talmy, Emilia Teumin, Solomon Bregman, Ilya Vatenberg and his wife Khayke.

34. Ibid., p. xviii.

35. The details of the trial, including elegantly-translated extracts of the defendants' own evidence of their innocence, can be found in the excellent work by Rubenstein and Naumov. There was not even a hint that the JAC trial was taking place, despite the fame of some defendants. The victims were secretly 'rehabilitated' in 1955. Not until 1988 was the JAC case referred to openly in the USSR.

36. Bregman collapsed in a coma during the trial and died in prison in January 1953.

37. Brent and Naumov, *Stalin's last Crime*, pp. 218–19.
38. Ibid., p. 222. Whether the Central Committee was involved in dismissing Ryumin, or whether Stalin acted alone, is impossible to say. Ryumin was arrested on 17 March 1953 and tried and executed in June 1954.
39. Ibid., p. 217.
40. Kaplan, *Report on the Murder*, p. 232.
41. The Soviets had wanted the phrase 'Jewish nationality', but this was changed by Gottwald in a meeting on 13 November 1952. Ibid., pp. 222–23.
42. Frank and Šváb were presumably *Kapos* in KZ Buchenwald and KZ Sachsenhausen respectively. I have no idea whether they actually acted in these camps in the manner described in the trial record.
43. Slánský Trial, p. 445.
44. Ibid., p. 524.
45. For the argument that elsewhere Katz, in cleverly 'coded' fashion, condemned Stalin in his 'evidence' and indicated that his 'confession' had a completely opposite meaning, see Dewar, *The Modern Inquisition*, pp. 235–37.
46. Margolius, *Reflections of Prague*, p. 220.
47. Kaplan, *Report on the Murder*, p. 232. For the 'legal' reasons for 'sparing' Hajdů, Loebl and London from the gallows, see E. Loebl, *Sentenced and Tried: The Stalinist Purges in Czechoslovakia*, London, 1969, pp. 247–48.

Although I have no evidence for this view, I believe that Stalin would have required Gottwald to make his 'own' decision on sentencing, as he had done with Rákosi. The Boss may have alluded to the fact that the MGB had recently executed thirteen JAC 'Jewish nationalists'. He may have recalled that only three of the eight accused in the Rajk trial were spared the death penalty, thereby implying that this was the 'going rate' for mercy. He then let Gottwald 'do the maths' and endorsed—perhaps tacitly—the Czech's 'eleven ropes' decision.
48. H. Kovály, *Under a Cruel Star: A Life in Prague 1941–1968*, New York, pp. 139, 145. When the truth about the trial was eventually revealed, Frejka's son committed suicide.
49. These letters are printed in Kaplan, *Report on the Murder*, pp. 249–84. Most are very moving. The families received their letters ten years later.
50. Margolius, *Reflections of Prague*, pp. 239–40. The executions were not conducted in public as contended in Brent and Naumov, *Stalin's last Crime*, p. 191.
51. On Merker's activities and writings from 1942 to 1955, see: J. Herf, *Divided Memory: The Nazi Past in the Two Germanys*, London, 1997, pp. 40–161 *passim*; W. Kießling, *Partner im 'Narrenparadies': der Freundeskreis um Noel Field und Paul Merker*, Berlin, 1994, pp. 9–20, 159–206, *passim*.
52. Herf, *Divided Memory*, p. 63.
53. Kießling, *Partner im 'Narrenparadies'*, pp. 167–68, 196–97.
54. Ibid., p. 166.
55. This was despite Stalin's temporary support for Israel in 1947–48, not to mention his attack upon 'Jewish bourgeois nationalists' which is the main theme of this chapter. Stalin's work was written in 1913. For an analysis of its content regarding Jews, see Vaksberg, *Stalin Against the Jews*, pp. 1–5.
56. Such a law was never implemented in the GDR. Following Merker's arrest a number of Jews in East Germany, both communist and non-communist, fled to the West. Herf, *Divided Memory*, pp. 120–26; J. Geller, *Jews in Post-Holocaust Germany, 1945–53*, Cambridge, 2005, pp. 169–76.
57. Dahlem's fall came later in 1953. However, on 18 October 1949 he was relieved of his 'responsibility for SED cadre matters'. Kießling, *Partner im 'Narrenparadies'*, p. 267. This was three days after his former Hungarian counterpart, Szőnyi, was hung.

58. Merker told Pieck that 'on a personal level Slánský is completely unknown to me. I've had no contact with him, I've never had anything to do with him, I've never visited him, and I've never spoken to him'. Ibid., p. 162.

59. See 'Lehren aus dem Prozess gegen das Verschwörerzentrum Slansky', Dokumente der Sozialistischen Einheitspartei Deutschlands: Beschlüsse und Erklärungen des Parteivorstandes, des Zentralkomitees, sowie seines Politbüros und seines Sekretariats, Band 1V. (East) Berlin 1954, pp. 199–219.

60. Kießling, *Partner im 'Narrenparadies'*, pp. 163–65.

61. Four days after the SED Central Committee resolution Leo Bauer and Erica Glaser were sentenced to death by a Soviet military court in Berlin. Yet Bauer's 'confession' had been made in autumn 1951. P. Brandt, et al., *Karrieren eines Außenseiters: Leo Bauer zwischen Kommunismus und Sozialdemokratie 1912 bis 1972*, Berlin/Bonn, 1983, p. 201. Since Bauer and Erica were transported to Moscow for execution, it is unlikely that they were to be linked to Merker's probable show trial. Was Stalin removing them from the scene as 'Fieldists' or simply because they were Jews?

62. Herf, *Divided Memory*, pp. 142–43. Although Stalin's death removed the threat of a show trial, Merker was still tried in secret before the GDR's Supreme Court, which on 8 March 1955 sentenced him to eight years in prison. Freed on health grounds in February 1956, he was declared innocent and partially 'rehabilitated' in July. Readmitted to the SED, Merker never held high office again. He died a broken man in May 1969. Ibid., pp. 151–57; Barth and Schweizer, eds, *Der Fall Noel Field, Band II*, p. 428.

63. Brent and Naumov, *Stalin's last Crime*, p. 288.

64. Ibid., p. 308. At some point after 17 February Stalin received from Ignatiev the draft indictment of Abakumov and his group. At that time it consisted of seven other MGB officers, including Likhachev and Komarov. The trial was to be held in secret. All eight were sentenced in advance to be shot. Stalin heavily annotated the indictment. See Ibid., pp. 308–11. This was hardly the behaviour of a man bored with the whole purge process, as some sources claim.

65. The composer Sergei Prokofiev died on the same day, aged sixty-two. Nine days after Stalin's demise, Klement Gottwald died in Prague of a burst artery in his heart. Booze and syphilis are offered as alternative causes. He was fifty-six. Perhaps life imitated 'art'. At his trial Slánský 'confessed' that he arranged for a Dr Haškovec, 'a Freemason, and therefore an enemy' to attend Gottwald. The doctor, 'being an enemy' did not provide proper medical care for Gottwald 'and thus caused the shortening of the President's life'. Loebl, *Sentenced and Tried*, p. 123.

66. It was Molotov's sixty-third birthday. He got his present the next day when Beria, who had taken over the MVD and reincorporated the MGB within it, released Molotov's wife from the Lubianka. She had been brought there from exile in January, presumably to play some role in the affair of the 'killer-doctors'.

67. Brent and Naumov, *Stalin's last Crime*, pp. 324–25.

29. BELATED TEARS FOR STALIN: PRISON, RELEASE AND ASYLUM

1. B-R. Barth and W. Schweizer, eds, *Der Fall Noel Field, Band I: Gefängnisjahre 1949–1954*, Berlin, 2005, pp. 94, 99, 106–12, 129, 136–44, 227–29, 231, 236–38, 241–44, 262 n13, 631, 644–50, 723–24, 784–86, 825, 841.

2. Conti utca is now called József utca. I don't know when or why the name-change occurred. Possibly it was altered because of its distasteful connotations. The building no longer appears to be a prison.

3. E. Bone, *Seven Years Solitary*, London, 1960, p. 66.

4. R. Gough, *A Good Comrade: János Kádár, Communism and Hungary*, London, 2006, pp. 23–24.

5. There is a plaque outside of the prison which reads: 'Between 1945 and 1948 this building

housed the secret service and temporary court-martial of Soviet state security, which sentenced many innocent Hungarian young people to lengthy terms of imprisonment or to death'. The plaque was placed there in 1998 by the Organisation of Political Prisoners and Forced Labourers in the Soviet Union. I am indebted to Judit Forrai for the translation from Hungarian.

6. Edith Bone (1889–1975) went to Hungary as a free-lance journalist associated with the *Daily Worker*. She was arrested by the ÁVH in October 1949. In December 1950 she was sentenced to fifteen years as a British spy, although in January 1954 the ÁVH noted that she'd been sentenced to life imprisonment. Bone, *Seven Years Solitary*, pp. 76–77; Barth and Schweizer, eds, *Der Fall Noel Field, Band I*, p. 144. She was freed during the Hungarian Revolution.

7. Noel wrote of 'the five or ten minute walk in the courtyard with its high walls that admit only the sun's rays and the twittering sparrows enjoying priceless freedom'. N. Field, 'Hitching our Wagon to a Star', *Mainstream*, Vol. 14, January 1961, p. 3. Dr Bone was taken through an iron-barred double gate into a small yard, surrounded by high walls and guarded by an armed policeman. From there she passed through sheet-steel double doors into another yard, twenty feet wide and one hundred feet long, and bounded on each side by walls fifty feet high. The gates were locked behind her and two more armed guards supervised her walk. Bone, 106. Presumably Rajk, Szőnyi and Szalai were hung in the larger yard.

8. Barth and Schweizer, eds, *Der Fall Noel Field, Band I*, p. 112. This was a somewhat rosy view of what was happening to American communists at the time. See T. Morgan, *Reds: McCarthyism in Twentieth-Century America*, New York, 2003, pp. 312–24.

9. Barth and Schweizer, eds, *Der Fall Noel Field, Band I*, p. 99.

10. Formally the ÁVH, the State Security Authority, no longer existed. Following the Soviet example, on 7 July 1953 it was incorporated into the Interior Ministry by the new minister, Ernő Gerő. See Barth and Schweizer, eds, *Der Fall Noel Field, Band I*, p. 696 n2. Hungarians continued to refer to the secret police by the name ÁVH (and even more commonly ÁVO).

11. The letter is reprinted in Ibid., pp. 145–219. Since I have used most of its content in earlier chapters, I have concentrated here upon the purpose of the letter. See Ibid., pp. 145–47.

12. Field apologised for his poor handwriting. Not having held pen or pencil for over three years he'd almost lost the art. He suggested that it would be worthwhile to supply him with a typewriter, since he was an expert stenographer. He was left with the pencil.

13. Noel viewed his 'guilt' as cracking under torture and bearing false witness against others. He frequently refers to himself as a physical coward (*Feigling*). In these matters he is too harsh to himself.

14. Barth and Schweizer, eds, *Der Fall Noel Field, Band I*, p. 229.

15. *Verhör* can also be translated as 'interrogation'. Noel underwent twenty-seven sessions with his interrogators between 15 June and 5 October 1954. They varied greatly in intensity. Some were mere question and answer sessions, while others were long and brutal interrogations.

16. Barth dates the transfer as both 5 and 10 May. Barth and Schweizer, eds, *Der Fall Noel Field, Band I*, pp. 236, 240 n8.

17. Herta's hearings began at the end of June or the beginning of July. Even though they were often imprisoned in adjacent or nearby cells, Noel didn't know whether Herta was alive or dead. His touching written request of 20 June 1954 to be told of her fate went unanswered. See Ibid., p. 291. However, Herta knew that Noel was alive. See Ibid., pp. 841–46.

18. On 4 August Field protested about the continued assumption that he was a spy. Ibid., pp. 640–41. Nothing changed.

19. To these statements Dr Barth adds extensive footnotes, many of which impart additional information.

20. For estimates of the numbers suffering internment, imprisonment and death under Rákosi, see Ibid., pp. 99, 131; B. Cartledge, *The Will to Survive: A History of Hungary*, London, 2011, p. 425.

21. Barth and Schweizer, eds, *Der Fall Noel Field, Band I*, pp. 132–36, 142 n3, 221 n9, 231–36, 246 n12. On the post-Stalin leadership conflicts in the USSR and Hungary see also the relevant sections in: C. Gati, *Failed Illusions: Moscow, Washington, Budapest and the 1956 Hungarian Revolt*, Stanford, 2006; W. Leonhard, *The Kremlin since Stalin*, London, 1962; A. Knight, *Beria: Stalin's First Lieutenant*, Princeton/Chichester, 1993; B. Kovrig, *Communism in Hungary: From Kun to Kádár*, Stanford, 1979; D. Rayfield, *Stalin and his Hangmen*, London, 2005, and sources cited in the notes.

22. The sentences are detailed in Barth and Schweizer, eds, *Der Fall Noel Field, Band I*, p. 248 n4.

23. G. Hodos, *Show Trials: Stalinist Purges in Eastern Europe*, London, 1987, p. 91.

24. András Kálmán, who was sentenced to fifteen years, committed suicide on 27 October 1952 when it was planned to cast him as a 'Zionist agent' in another show trial. Barth and Schweizer, eds, *Der Fall Noel Field, Band II*, p. 422. Ilona Kojsza was sentenced to fifteen years and Iván Földi to thirteen years.

25. Kádár was sentenced to life imprisonment on 18 December 1951 and found himself back in the Conti utca prison. See Gough, *A Good Comrade*, pp. 48–61. This excellent biography details the behaviour of this cowardly and dishonest man at the time.

26. That Rákosi was acting consciously against Jews, in emulation of Stalin's 'Zionist equals imperialist spy' policy, is made crystal-clear in his report to the HCP Central Committee on 17 February 1953. See I. Rév, *Indicting Rajk*, pp. 1–31, http://ccat.sas.upenn.edu/slavic/events/slavic_symposium/Comrades_Please_Shoot_Me/Rev_Rajk.pdf, last accessed 26 May 2013, p. 13n.

27. Barth and Schweizer, eds, *Der Fall Noel Field, Band I*, p. 132. These did not include Colonel Szűcs who was arrested as a 'spy' in September 1950. Along with his brother, he was beaten to death during interrogation by former colleagues on 21 November. Barth and Schweizer, eds, *Der Fall Noel Field, Band II*, pp. 437–38. There are gorier, but inaccurate, accounts of their murder.

28. This sentence was confirmed on 15 January 1954. In June 1957 Péter's sentence was reduced to fourteen years. In January 1959 Kádár pardoned him. Thereafter Péter worked as a bookkeeper until retiring in 1971. Ibid., p. 429. Just one of many blood-stained pensioners in Stalin's former empire, Péter died in Budapest in 1993, aged eighty-six.

29. The mind reels upon reading and picturing the following lecture by the small, fat, balding Beria to the smaller, fatter, balder Rákosi: 'A person who's beaten will make any kind of confession that interrogation agents want, will admit that he is an English or American spy or whatever we want. But we will never learn the truth this way. This way, innocent people may be sentenced. There is law, and everyone must respect it'. Cited in W. Taubman, *Khrushchev: The Man and his Era*, London, 2004, p. 247. Beria, a rapist, torturer and murderer, and now head of the MVD, was the source of most of the 'reformist' agenda that constituted the 'Thaw' in the USSR. He was arrested on 26 June 1953. His trial began on 18 December. He was found guilty and shot on 23 December.

30. On the amnesty in autumn 1953 for other categories of prisoners and internees, see J. Rainer, *Imre Nagy vom Parteisoldaten zum Märtyrer des ungarischen Volksaufstands: eine politische Biographie 1896–1958*, Paderborn, 2006, p. 89; Ferenc A. Váli, *Rift and Revolt in Hungary: Nationalism versus Communism*, Cambridge, Mass., 1961, pp. 145–46.

31. Ibid., p. 149. Júlia Rajk was freed on 14 June 1954, Kádár on 22 July. Except for Iván Földi, the surviving members of the Szőnyi group were released on 1 September, as was Béla Szász. György Pálóczi-Horváth was freed twelve days later. Földi was released in January 1955, Sándor Cseresnyés and Ilona Kojsza in September, and Pál Justus in November. The social democrat Pál Ignotus had to wait until 29 March 1956. Brankov was freed on 3 April. Ognjenovich was also released in 1956.

32. On the Światło defection, his RFE broadcasts to Poland, and the freeing of Noel, Herta and

Hermann Field see: Barth and Schweizer, eds, *Der Fall Noel Field, Band II*, pp. 4–12, 19–24, 33–40, 58–65, 71–78, 125–31, 169–75, 435; H. Field and K. Field, *Trapped in the Cold War: The Ordeal of an American Family*, Stanford, 1999, pp. 335–411 *passim*; L. Gluchowski, 'The Defection of Józef Światło and the Search for Jewish Scapegoats in the Polish United Workers' Party, 1953–1954', http://ece.columbia.edu/files/ece/images/gluchowski-1.pdf, last accessed 26 May 2013, pp. 14–28; F. Lewis, *The Man who Disappeared: The Strange History of Noel Field*, London, 1965, pp. 237–47.

33. There had been some earlier diplomatic efforts. See Barth and Schweizer, eds, *Der Fall Noel Field, Band II*, pp. 26–32; Field and Field, *Trapped in the Cold War*, pp. 112–121, 133, 140–41, 269, 285–86.

34. See her Wikipedia entry and Field and Field, *Trapped in the Cold War*, p. 359.

35. Rákosi's role is discussed at length in Barth and Schweizer, eds, *Der Fall Noel Field, Band II*, pp. 8–12.

36. In fact Hermann posed seven other conditions to 'Mrs Markowska'. See Field and Field, *Trapped in the Cold War*, p. 352. Some were fully implemented, others partially. His attempt to 'negotiate' their fulfilment was one reason for Hermann's delayed departure from Poland. Shortly before he left Poland he met with the recently-released Polish 'Fieldists', Jan and Lisa Lis, and later Anna Gecow. See Barth and Schweizer, eds, *Der Fall Noel Field, Band II*, p. 90; Field and Field, *Trapped in the Cold War*, pp. 356–58.

37. On 18 October Major Hullay had recommended the release of Noel and Herta subject to certain conditions. Barth and Schweizer, eds, *Der Fall Noel Field, Band I*, pp. 814–17, 817 n9.

38. Full text in Field and Field, *Trapped in the Cold War*, pp. 387–88. Hermann had certainly not been given 'full satisfaction' at that juncture.

39. N. Field, 'Hitching our Wagon to a Star', pp. 8–9.

40. Text in Barth and Schweizer, eds, *Der Fall Noel Field, Band II*, p. 25.

41. In 1954 the average monthly wage of a Hungarian worker or employee was 1,080 forints. Ibid., p. 60 n2. Hermann Field received the sum of 50,000 American dollars from the Polish government to reimburse him for lost earnings. Field and Field, *Trapped in the Cold War*, p. 391; Barth and Schweizer, eds, *Der Fall Noel Field, Band II*, p. 199. Noel's monthly stipend was reduced at his own request after he got a job in publishing. Ibid., p. 261 n7.

42. For the text of the announcement, see Ibid., p. 66.

43. See the (original English) extract from his letter of 13 March 1955 to Hermann, then in Britain, in Ibid., p. 130 n4.

44. See Ibid., pp. 79–99. The brothers spoke in English. The snoopers' record was translated into Hungarian. Dr Barth has translated this into German. It would surprise me if my resultant translation from the German was anything like the original English used by the Fields.

45. Hermann's version was published in 1999, although I suspect that the book co-authored by him and his wife was written much earlier. In 1993 Hermann was in Budapest and read the German-language records of Noel's experiences. It is unlikely that he knew about the tapped and taped records of their two phone conversations, unearthed by Dr Barth later. The latter makes no reference to these differences.

46. Field and Field, *Trapped in the Cold War*, p. 404.

47. Initially Hermann had endeavoured to get Kate to come to Poland with their sons. Kate, backed by the redoubtable Elsie, stolidly refused for obvious reasons. On the telephone Hermann told Noel that it was possible that they'd meet in six or nine month's time, if he could convince Kate to return with him to Poland. See Barth and Schweizer, eds, *Der Fall Noel Field, Band II*, p. 82.

48. See Ibid., pp. 100–24. Hermann was again in his villa in Otwock, while Noel was now in the HCP hospital in Kútvölgyi út in Buda.

49. Monica Felton (1906–70) was crippled in childhood by a spinal degeneration. She joined the

Labour Party in 1926 and was a member of the London County Council from 1937 to 1946. In 1946 she was appointed vice-chairman, later chairman, of the Stevenage (New Town) Development Corporation. She was dismissed, when in 1951 she left this post without permission to visit North Korea and China during the Korean War. Her subsequent booklet and talks led to her expulsion from the Labour Party, as well as to calls that she be prosecuted for treason. She was awarded a Stalin Peace Prize that year. Clearly she had a range of contacts with Soviet bloc security services. Her ÁVH profile noted that she wore very low-cut dresses and dyed her hair flaming red. See Ibid., pp. 132–33; D. Caute, *The Fellow-Travellers: Intellectual Friends of Communism*, London, 1988, pp. 317–18; Field and Field, *Trapped in the Cold War*, p. 355.

50. Barth and Schweizer, eds, *Der Fall Noel Field, Band II*, p. 84, 101. In his book Hermann writes dismissively of Monica, while in his telephone conversations with Noel he constantly emphasises his close friendship with her.

51. On her talks with the Fields and Dékán, see Ibid., pp. 134–50, 180–86.

52. Noel tried to get Elsie to visit him in Budapest. She told him that her husband had threatened to divorce her if she did. Ibid., p. 182.

53. Ibid., p. 179.

54. He prepared three versions of a statement. In the last, written on 30 January 1955, Field explained his action as siding with the 'peace-loving' socialist bloc in its fight against the 'growing danger' of a Third World War, promoted by 'reactionary forces' in the USA. Noel presented a version of his life to underscore how he'd fought for 'peace' and 'social justice' for more than thirty years. For the text of this unpublished statement, altered in several places by his Hungarian minders, see Ibid., pp. 201–215.

55. Ibid., p. 174 n86. (Original English text).

56. Ibid., p. 233 n6. (Original English text).

57. See Ibid., pp. 187–200. It contained some typical errors with dates.

30. FADE-OUT: BYSTANDER, APOLOGIST, NOBODY

1. B-R. Barth and W. Schweizer, eds, *Der Fall Noel Field, Band II: Asyl in Ungarn 1954–1957*, Berlin, 2007, pp. 34, 61, 174–76, 239, 241–42, 247–49, 249 n11, 256–57, 262–72, 288, 300–02, 325;

2. Ibid., p. 86. In his maudlin Mainstream article Noel records the following unlikely conversation between himself and Herta, immediately upon their release: "'Do they know we are innocent?' she whispers in my arms. "Yes," I say, and then ask, "Have you remained true?" "Yes," she answers, "never for one moment have I doubted." "Nor I."" N. Field, 'Hitching our Wagon to a Star', *Mainstream*, Vol. 14, January 1961, p. 9.

3. Barth and Schweizer, eds, *Der Fall Noel Field, Band II*, pp. 151–53. On 20 October 1955 he informed Dékán that he would offer 'to influence her in a positive fashion'. Ibid., p. 176 n95. Apart from Noel's continued unrealistic expectations about Erica, she was by then in Moscow. On 27 October she finally regained her freedom when she was flown to Berlin. She politely declined Field's invitation to join him in Hungary.

4. For the correspondence between Marthe, the Fields and Captain Kuhári, see Ibid., pp. 293–300; W. Kießling, *'Leistner ist Mielke': Schatten einer gefälschten Biographie*, Berlin, 1998, pp. 261–86 *passim*. Marthe did receive a reply to her third letter from Herta, dated 19 October 1956. Herta apologised for 'our long silence'. She referred to the fact that Marthe had gone public, and while understanding the reasons for this, Herta wondered 'whether it was wise'. She counselled Marthe 'most urgently not to do anything rash'. Extracts in F. Lewis, *The Man who Disappeared: The Strange History of Noel Field*, London, 1965, p. 253.

5. Barth and Schweizer, eds, *Der Fall Noel Field, Band II*, pp. 155–69, 237–40, 241 n4, 273–84, 288–92, 300–09, 316 n139, 431. For developments in Hungary, Yugoslavia and the Soviet bloc,

and certain aspects of the 1956 Hungarian Revolution, see sources referred to in the last chapter and those cited in this.

6. Ibid., p. 289. On the Fields' diligent study of Hungarian, see Ibid., p. 237, p. 289 n64; W. Kießling, 'Leistner ist Mielke', 1998, p. 263. Meeting with him in December 1956, a Hungarian journalist commented on Noel's 'remarkable command' of Hungarian. E. Marton, The Forbidden Sky, Boston, 1971, p. 243.

7. The Fields apparently toured Hungary frequently after their release. Ibid., pp. 243–44.

8. J. Hay, Born 1900: Memoirs, London, 1974, p. 300.

9. C. Gati, Failed Illusions: Moscow, Washington, Budapest and the 1956 Hungarian Revolt, Stanford, 2006, p. 61.

10. Rákosi died in the Russian city of Gorki in February 1971. His ashes, secretly returned to Hungary, ended up in Buda's Farkasréti cemetery.

11. On Rajk's reburial, see A. Pető, Geschlecht, Politik und Stalinismus in Ungarn: eine Biographie von Júlia Rajk, Herne, 2007, pp. 110–26; B. Szász, Volunteers for the Gallows, London, 1971, pp. 233–39; K. Benziger, Imre Nagy: Martyr of the Nation, Lanham (Md)/Plymouth, 2010, pp. 46–47.

On 26 September the remains of the executed men were eventually located in a wood in Gödöllő, north-east of Budapest. The remains of Colonel Korondy, the fifth man executed, were reburied later.

12. Benziger, Imre Nagy, p. 9. Evidence suggests that the HCP leadership simply forgot about the significance of the 6 October date when they agreed to Rajk's reburial. C. Békés, et al. eds., The 1956 Hungarian Revolution: A History in Documents, Budapest/New York, 2002, p. 13 n22.

13. Released in June 1954, Júlia was forced to bear the surname Györk. Only in June 1956 was the name Rajk restored to her and her son László. At the time of his parents' arrest in May–June 1949, the younger László Rajk was only a few months old. He was originally placed in a crèche under the name István Györk. The dogged efforts of Júlia's sister and mother to reclaim him only succeeded in 1953. Once Júlia was released in 1954 the complex process of re-bonding between son and mother commenced. See Pető, Politik und Stalinismus in Ungarn, pp. 68–69, 84.

Later László Rajk, then an architect and political dissident, would help design the setting of another show-burial. On 16 June 1989 the remains of Imre Nagy and two supporters who were executed with him on 16 June 1958, plus two others killed earlier, were brought to Hösök Tér (Heroes Square). A sixth casket represented an unidentified revolutionary. The coffins were re-interred in the Új köztemető cemetery in Budapest. On the Nagy show burial, see Benziger, Imre Nagy. Kádár, Nagy's executioner, was then no longer in power. He died on 6 July 1989, the very day that Nagy was finally 'rehabilitated'. Like the parents of the younger László Rajk, Kádár too is buried in the Kerepesi cemetery.

14. Szász, Volunteers for the Gallows, p. 235.

15. Ibid., p. 238.

16. Nagy, readmitted to the HCP on 13 October 1956, was reappointed Prime Minister on 24 October. An admirer assessed him as 'an unhurried man, shaped by doubts and also by deep-rooted party discipline, who simply needed more time to make decisions than one should or could afford in a revolution. He was always two to three days behind in his decisions'. Cited in P. Lendvai, One Day that Shook the Communist World, Princeton and Oxford, 2008, p. 67.

17. Barth and Schweizer, eds, Der Fall Noel Field, Band II, p. 310 n125. Ilona Kojsza, scarred in mind and body by torture and imprisonment, was also a patient in this hospital for the HCP elite. A tough lady, Ilona lived on until 1996, dying in Budapest at the age of ninety-one. Ibid., pp. 319 n150, 423–24.

18. The Polish General Józef Bem led Hungarian troops in Transylvania against the Habsburg and Tsarist forces in 1848–49. One purpose of the student march was to show solidarity with the

Poles. The turbulent situation there was calmed once Gomułka was appointed PCP Secretary-General on 19 October 1956.

19. These matters are dealt with on the basis of recent research by: Békés, et al. eds., *The 1956 Hungarian Revolution*; Gati, *Failed Illusions*. Lendvai, *One Day that Shook the Communist World*; J. Matthews, *Explosion: The Hungarian Revolution of 1956*, New York, 2007; V. Sebestyen, *Twelve Days: Revolution 1956*, London, 2006.

20. Field, 'Hitching our Wagon to a Star', p. 12. See also his earlier article, 'Der Vierte November in Ungarn', which he sent on 17 January 1957 to the editors of a left-socialist Swiss journal called *Zeitdienst*. Text in Barth and Schweizer, eds, *Der Fall Noel Field, Band II*, pp. 309–24.

21. Kádár replaced Gerő as HCP Secretary-General on 25 October, and initially appeared to support the Nagy government and the objectives of the revolution. On the night of 1 November he left for Moscow and agreed to head a 'government' imposed by Soviet military force. On his activities, see particularly Gough, *A Good Comrade*. His regime later produced a series of 'White Books' to 'justify' its view that the spontaneous uprising of the Hungarian people was from the outset a planned 'Horthyite-fascist counter-revolution' abetted by 'foreign imperialists'. Noel was proof-reader for the English language versions of this propaganda. See Barth and Schweizer, eds, *Der Fall Noel Field, Band II*, pp. 304–05, 304 n110.

22. Noel wrote that it was hardly any wonder that many patients in his hospital refused to allow 'suspect' medical staff to give them injections. Ibid., p. 313. Perhaps there was a hangover element from the 'Doctor's Plot' in such thinking. One must note, however, that a twenty-four-year-old medical student, Ilona Tóth, was convicted in February 1957 of killing an ÁVH patient, by injecting gasoline into his veins. She and her fellow-accused did not deny the charges and they were executed soon after their trial. See Matthews, *Explosion*, p. 536; Barth and Schweizer, eds, *Der Fall Noel Field, Band II*, p. 313 n131.

23. R. Gadney, *Cry Hungary! Uprising 1956*, London, 1986 has graphic photographs of the killings by both sides.

24. 'From the first day [...] we knew that this so-called revolution was essentially a counter-revolution'. 'The Soviet troops have come in defense of socialism, the next stage in Man's evolution towards greater freedom and happiness for all. They–and not those poor misled youngsters throwing away their lives in a hopeless struggle against them–are the real "freedom fighters."' '[W]e went through the black days of the counter-revolution'. Field, 'Hitching our Wagon to a Star', pp. 12, 14–15.

25. In the years 1956 to 1961 about 330 revolutionaries were executed by the Kádár regime, some 22,000 jailed, and about 13,000 interned in camps. The majority of these victims were young industrial or agricultural workers. Amongst those executed were several women. Some teenagers were sentenced to death with the qualification that they would be hung once they reached their eighteenth birthday. It seems that most were executed before they reached eighteen. See Matthews, *Explosion*, p. 561; Sebestyen, *Twelve Days*, p. 287.

26. See E. Marton, *The Forbidden Sky* pp. 234–46. Ilona Márton is sometimes identified by her maiden-name Nyilas. The Mártons' younger daughter has written a vivid and moving portrait of her parents. See K. Marton, *Enemies of the People: My Family's Journey to America*, London, 2009.

27. Barth and Schweizer, eds, *Der Fall Noel Field, Band II*, pp. 325–28, 415, 418; Lewis, *The Man who Disappeared*, pp. 261–66; H. Field and K. Field, *Trapped in the Cold War: The Ordeal of an American Family*, Stanford, 1999, pp. 413–15.

28. Endre wrote that he 'learned much about the Fields' from Kretschmer. E. Marton, *The Forbidden Sky*, p. 235. During the revolution Márton's Buda home in Csaba utca provided brief sanctuary to ÁVH Major Kretschmer. K. Marton, *Enemies of the People*, p. 191.

29. Endre's report alerted the world to the massacre in front of Parliament on 25 October. In early December Ilona passed on to *Reuters* the plans of the Greater Budapest Central Workers' Coun-

cil for a general strike. This allowed Western radios to broadcast the information to Hungarian workers. Ibid., pp. 190–200 *passim*. The Márton family left Hungary for Austria in January 1957 and were in the USA in early April.

30. Noel wrote of how often Herta helped him 'to see things straight'. Field, 'Hitching our Wagon to a Star', p. 8.

31. E. Marton, *The Forbidden Sky*, pp. 238, 242–45.

32. A reference to the evidence given by some of the 200,000 Hungarians who left their country in the aftermath of the failed revolution.

33. Lewis, *The Man who Disappeared*, p. 255.

34. Barth and Schweizer, eds, *Der Fall Noel Field, Band II*, p. 326 (Original English text).

35. Flora Lewis was born into a Jewish professional family in Los Angeles in 1922. As a reporter with *Associated Press* she was sent to London in 1945, where she married *New York Times* foreign correspondent Sidney Gruson. Their marriage lasted until 1972. In 1956–66, which included the years when she was writing her biography of Field, she was foreign correspondent for the *Washington Post*. She died of cancer in Paris in 2002.

36. For the Lewis-Field non-meeting, see Lewis, *The Man who Disappeared*, pp. 261–63; Barth and Schweizer, eds, *Der Fall Noel Field, Band II*, p. 327.

37. Field, 'Hitching our Wagon to a Star', p. 4.

38. Ibid., p. 12.

39. Ibid., p. 15.

40. Their new home was again in the Buda hills, but was situated much closer to the hospital in Kútvölgyi út. That this was a factor in their moving house is merely my surmise.

41. Field and Field, *Trapped in the Cold War*, p. 413. After travelling from Switzerland to London in February 1955, Hermann held an impromptu press conference in the Hampstead garden of his parents-in-law on 18 February. Hermann and his family remained in London for over a year. On 27 March 1956 he and Kate and their sons, Hugh now aged twelve and Alan now ten, arrived in New York aboard the *Queen Mary*. A daughter, Alison, was born to them in 1957. Hermann published two novels which he'd co-written with a Polish prisoner in Miedzeszyn. He also taught at Tufts University for many years. Hermann died on 23 February 2001, aged ninety, at Valley Farm, Shirley, Massachusetts. Kate died in 2005.

42. A. Schlesinger, *A Life in the Twentieth Century: Innocent Beginnings, 1917–1950*, Boston/New York, 2000, p. 502. According to another account by Hermann, Noel's faith was 'somewhat shaken by the Soviet suppression of the Czechs during the Prague Spring of 1968'. However, Noel was still 'unwilling to discuss his past actions' with his brother, and 'remained a believer in communism to the end of his life'. Field and Field, *Trapped in the Cold War*, p. 413.

43. The American title was *Red Pawn: The Story of Noel Field*. In Britain it was published as *The Man who Disappeared: The Strange History of Noel Field*.

44. Barth and Schweizer, eds, *Der Fall Noel Field, Band II*, p. 328 (Original English text).

45. In 1976 Erica travelled to Hungary to see Herta, but the older woman didn't recognise her. Ibid., p. 418.

BIBLIOGRAPHY

Unpublished sources

Foreign Office Papers, Public Records Office, Kew.

Published Sources

L. Adamic, *The Eagle and the Roots*, New York, 1952.

S. Alliluyeva, *Twenty Letters to a Friend*, London, 1967.

E. Anderson, *Love in Exile: An American Writer's Memoir of Life in Divided Berlin*, South Royalton (Vt.), 1999.

C. Andrew and O. Gordievsky, *KGB: The Inside Story of its Foreign Operations from Lenin to Gorbachev*, London, 1990.

C. Andrew and V. Mitrokhin, *The Mitrokhin Archive: The KGB in Europe and the West*, London, 2000.

Y. Arad, *Belzec, Sobibor, Treblinka: The Operation Reinhard Death Camps*, Bloomington/Indianapolis, 1999.

H. Armstrong, *Tito and Goliath*, London, 1951.

P. Auty, *Tito: A Biography*, Harmondsworth, 1974.

I. Banac, ed., *The Diary of Georgi Dimitrov 1933–1949*, London, 2003.

B-R. Barth and W. Schweizer, eds, *Der Fall Noel Field, Band I: Gefängnisjahre 1949–1954*, Berlin, 2005.

——, eds, *Der Fall Noel Field, Band II: Asyl in Ungarn 1954–1957*, Berlin, 2007.

V. Bartlett, *East of the Iron Curtain*, London, 1949.

K. Bartosek, *Les aveux des archives: Prague-Paris-Prague, 1948–1968*, Paris, 1996.

C. Békés, et al., eds, *The 1956 Hungarian Revolution: A History in Documents*, Budapest/New York, 2002.

J. Bell, *The Bulgarian Communist Party from Blagoev to Zhivkov*, Stanford, 1986.

E. Bentley, ed., *Thirty Years of Treason: Excerpts from Hearings before the House Committee on Un-American Activities, 1938–1968*, New York, 1971.

K. Benziger, *Imre Nagy: Martyr of the Nation*, Lanham (Md)/Plymouth, 2010.

N. Bethell, *Gomułka: His Poland and his Communism*, London, 1972.

——, *The War Hitler Won*, London, 1976.

K. Billinger (pseudonym of P. Massing), *Fatherland*, New York, 1935.

E. Bone, *Seven Years Solitary*, London, 1960.

BIBLIOGRAPHY

L. Borhi, *Hungary in the Cold War 1945–1956: Between the United States and the Soviet Union*, Budapest/New York, 2004.

F. Borkenau, *European Communism*, London, 1953.

G. Borsányi, *Béla Kun: The Life of a Communist Revolutionary*, Boulder, (Col), 1993.

K. Boterbloem, *The Life and Times of Andrei Zhdanov 1896–1948*, Montreal, 2004.

R. Braham, *The Politics of Genocide: The Holocaust in Hungary*, Detroit, 2000.

P. Brandt, et al., *Karrieren eines Außenseiters: Leo Bauer zwischen Kommunismus und Sozialdemokratie 1912 bis 1972*, Berlin/Bonn, 1983.

J. Brent and V. Naumov, *Stalin's last Crime: The Doctor's Plot*, London, 2003.

M. Buber-Neumann, *Under two Dictators: Prisoner of Stalin and Hitler*, London, 2009.

B. Cartledge, *The Will to Survive: A History of Hungary*, London, 2011.

D. Caute, *The Fellow-Travellers: Intellectual Friends of Communism*, London, 1988.

W. Chadwick, *The Rescue of the Prague Refugees 1938–39*, Leicester, 2010.

W. Chambers, *Witness*, London, 1953.

M. Checinski, *Poland: Communism, Nationalism, Anti-Semitism*, New York, 1982.

A. Cienciala et al., eds, *Katyń: A Crime without Punishment*, London, 2007.

N. Cohn, *Warrant for Genocide: The Myth of the Jewish World Conspiracy and the Protocols of the Elders of Zion*, London, 1996.

R. Conquest, *The Great Terror: A Reassessment*, London 1990.

A. Cooke, *A Generation on Trial: U.S.A. v. Alger Hiss*, London, 1951.

D. Cornelius, *Hungary in World War II: Caught in the Cauldron*, New York, 2011.

J. Costello and O. Tsarev, *Deadly Illusions*, London, 1993.

M. Cotic, *The Prague Trial: The First Anti-Zionist Show Trial in the Communist Bloc*, London, 1987.

G. Cox, *Countdown to War: A Personal Memoir of Europe 1938–1940*, London, 1988.

A. Dallin and F. Firsov, *Dimitrov and Stalin 1934–1943: Letters from the Soviet Archives*, London, 2000.

I. Damaskin with G. Elliot, *Kitty Harris: The Spy with Seventeen Names*, London, 2001.

V. Dedijer, *Tito Speaks: His Self-portrait and Struggle with Stalin*, London, 1954.

———, *The Battle Stalin Lost: Memories of Yugoslavia 1948–53*, Nottingham, 1978.

H. Dewar, *Assassins at Large*, London, 1951.

———, *The Modern Inquisition*, London, 1953.

M. Djilas, *Conversations with Stalin*, London, 1962.

———, *Tito: The Story from Inside*, London, 1980.

———, *Rise and Fall*, London, 1985.

W. Duff, *A Time for Spies: Theodore Stephanovich Mally and the Era of the Great Illegals*, London, 1999.

J. Dziak, *Chekisty: A History of the KGB*, Lexington (Mass.), 1988.

C. Eby, *Hungary at War: Civilians and Soldiers in World War II*, University Park (Pa.), 1998.

C. Epstein, *The Last Revolutionaries: German Communists and their Century*, London, 2003.

R. Evans, *The Third Reich at War: How the Nazis led Germany from Conquest to Disaster*, London, 2008.

I. Fehérváry, *The Long Road to Revolution: The Hungarian Gulag 1945–1956*, Santa Fé, 1989.

H. Field and K. Field, *Trapped in the Cold War: The Ordeal of an American Family*, Stanford, 1999.

N. Field, 'Hitching our Wagon to a Star', *Mainstream*, Vol. 14, January 1961, pp. 3–17.

O. Figes, *A People's Tragedy: The Russian Revolution, 1891–1924*, London, 1997.

R. Friedmann, *Ulbrichts Rundfunkmann: eine Gerhart-Eisler-Biographie*, Berlin, 2007.

J. Gaddis, *George F. Kennan, An American Life*, New York, 2011.

R. Gadney, *Cry Hungary! Uprising 1956*, London, 1986.

C. Gati, *Hungary and the Soviet Bloc*, Durham (N.C.), 1986.

BIBLIOGRAPHY

————, *Failed Illusions: Moscow, Washington, Budapest and the 1956 Hungarian Revolt*, Stanford, 2006.

J. Geller, *Jews in Post-Holocaust Germany, 1945–53*, Cambridge, 2005.

M. Gilbert, *Road to Victory: Winston S. Churchill 1941–1945*, London, 1989.

Y. Gluckstein, *Stalin's Satellites in Europe*, London, 1952.

Y. Gorlizki and O. Khlevniuk, *Cold Peace: Stalin and the Soviet Ruling Circle, 1945–1953*, New York, 2005.

R. Gough, *A Good Comrade: János Kádár, Communism and Hungary*, London, 2006.

P. Gregory, *Terror by Quota: State Security from Lenin to Stalin (an Archival Study)*, London, 2009.

P. Grose, *Allen Dulles: Spymaster: The Life and Times of the First Civilian Director of the CIA*, London, 2006.

J. Gross, *Revolution from Abroad: The Soviet Conquest of Poland's Western Ukraine and Western Belorussia*, Princeton/Oxford, 2002.

S. Groueff, *Crown of Thorns: The Reign of King Boris III of Bulgaria 1918–43*, London, 1987.

J. Gunther, *Behind Europe's Curtain*, London, 1949.

T. Hajdu, 'The Party did Everything for You'. *The Hungarian Quarterly*, Vol. 37, No. 141 (1996), pp. 83–99.

J. Hay, *Born 1900: Memoirs*, London, 1974.

J. Haynes, H. Klehr and A. Vassiliev, *Spies: The Rise and Fall of the KGB in America*, London, 2009.

J. Herf, *Divided Memory: The Nazi Past in the Two Germanys*, London, 1997.

S. Hintze, *Antifaschisten im Camp Le Vernet*, (East) Berlin, 1988.

A. Hiss, *Recollections of a Life*, New York, 1988.

G. Hodos, *Show Trials: Stalinist Purges in Eastern Europe*, London, 1987.

C. Hoff, *Anna und Leon: Ihre Lebensgeschichte*, Potsdam, 2005.

C. Hollingworth, *The Three Weeks' War in Poland*, London, 1940.

P. Ignotus, *Political Prisoner*, London, 1959.

M. Jansen and N. Petrov, *Stalin's Loyal Executioner: People's Commissar Nikolai Ezhov 1895–1940*, Stanford, 2002.

P. Johnson, *A History of the Jews*, New York, 1988.

K. Kaplan, *Report on the Murder of the General Secretary*, London, 1990.

Y. Kapp and M. Mynatt, *British Policy and the Refugees, 1933–1941*, London, 1997.

D. Kartun, *Tito's Plot against Europe*, London, 1949.

P. Kenez, *Hungary from the Nazis to the Soviets: The Establishment of the Communist Regime in Hungary, 1944–1948*, Cambridge, 2006.

G. Kern, *A Death in Washington: Walter G. Krivitsky and the Stalin Terror*, New York, 2004.

W. Kießling, *Partner im 'Narrenparadies': der Freundeskreis um Noel Field und Paul Merker*, Berlin, 1994.

————, *'Leistner ist Mielke': Schatten einer gefälschten Biographie*, Berlin, 1998.

A. Knight, *Beria: Stalin's First Lieutenant*, Princeton/Chichester, 1993.

————, *How the Cold War began: The Gouzenko Affair and the Hunt for Soviet Spies*, Toronto, 2005.

S. Koch, *Double Lives: Stalin, Willi Münzenberg and the Seduction of Intellectuals*, London, 1995.

A. Koestler, *Scum of the Earth*, London, 2006.

J. Korbel, *Tito's Communism*, Denver, 1951.

Kostov Trial. *The Trial of Traicho Kostov and his Group*, Sofia, 1949.

G. Kostyrchenko, *Out of the Red Shadows: Anti-Semitism in Stalin's Russia*, New York, 1995.

H. Kovály, *Under a Cruel Star: A Life in Prague 1941–1968*, New York, 1997.

B. Kovrig, *Communism in Hungary: From Kun to Kádár*, Stanford, 1979.

A. Krammer, *The Forgotten Friendship: Israel and the Soviet Bloc, 1947–53*, London, 1974.

W. Krivitsky, *In Stalin's Secret Service*, New York, 2000.

M. Kuncewiczowa, *The Keys: A Journey through Europe at War*, London, 1946.

BIBLIOGRAPHY

R. Lamphere and T. Shachtman, *The FBI-KGB War*, London, 1987.

H. Lehrman, *Russia's Europe*, London, 1947.

P. Lendvai, *Blacklisted: A Journalist's Life in Central Europe*, London, 1998.

———, *The Hungarians: A Thousand Years of Victory in Defeat*, London, 2006.

———, *One Day that Shook the Communist World*, Princeton/Oxford, 2008.

W. Leonhard, *The Kremlin since Stalin*, London, 1962.

R. Levy, *Ana Pauker: The Rise and Fall of a Jewish Communist*, London, 2001.

F. Lewis, *The Man who Disappeared: The Strange History of Noel Field*, London, 1965.

E. Loebl, *Sentenced and Tried: The Stalinist Purges in Czechoslovakia*, London, 1969.

———, *My Mind on Trial*, London, 1976.

A. London, *On Trial*, London, 1970.

F. Maclean, *Disputed Barricades: The Life and Times of Josip Broz-Tito Marshal of Jugoslavia*, London, 1957.

A. Macleod, *The Death of Uncle Joe*, Woodbridge (Suffolk), 1997.

W. McCagg, *Stalin Embattled 1943–1948*, Detroit, 1978.

D. McLellan, *The Girls: Sappho goes to Hollywood*, London, 2001.

S. McMeekin, *The Red Millionaire: A Political Biography of Willy Münzenberg, Moscow's Secret Propaganda Tsar in the West*, New Haven, (CT), 2003.

N. Malcolm, *Bosnia: A Short History*, London, 1994.

I. Margolius, *Reflections of Prague: Journeys through the Twentieth Century*, Chichester, 2006.

E. Marton, *The Forbidden Sky*, Boston, 1971.

K. Marton, *Enemies of the People: My Family's Journey to America*, London, 2009.

V. Mastny, *The Cold War and Soviet Insecurity: The Stalin Years*, Oxford, 1996.

H. Massing, *This Deception*, New York, 1951.

———, *Die grosse Täuschung: Geschichte einer Sowjetagentin*, Freiburg, 1967.

J. Matthews, *Explosion: The Hungarian Revolution of 1956*, New York, 2007.

C. Mauch, *The Shadow War against Hitler: The Covert Operations of America's Wartime Secret Intelligence Service*, New York/Chichester, 2003.

E. Mendelsohn, *The Jews of East Central Europe between the World Wars*, Bloomington (Ind.), 1983.

C. Merridale, *Ivan's War: The Red Army 1939–45*, London, 2006.

G. Mikes, *A Study in Infamy: The Hungarian Secret Police*, London, 1959.

J. Miles, *The Nine Lives of Otto Katz: The Remarkable Story of a Communist Super-Spy*, London, 2010.

J. Mindszenty, *Memoirs*, London, 1974.

S. Montefiore, *Stalin: The Court of the Red Tsar*, London, 2003.

T. Morgan, *Reds: McCarthyism in Twentieth-Century America*, New York, 2003.

L. Mosley, *Dulles: A Biography of Eleanor, Allen, and John Foster Dulles and their Family Network*, New York, 1978.

H. Müller-Enbergs, 'Erste Chefredakteur, dann 'Unperson': Lex Ende und Rudolf Herrnstadt'. *Jahrbuch für Historische Kommunismusforschung 1996*, Berlin, 1995.

H. Müller-Enbergs et al., eds, *Wer war wer in der DDR?: ein Lexicon ostdeutscher Biographien*, Berlin, 2010.

F. Nagy, *The Struggle behind the Iron Curtain*, New York, 1948.

N. Nagy-Talavera, *The Green Shirts and Others: A History of Fascism in Hungary and Romania*, Stanford, 1970.

N. Naimark, *Russians in Germany: A History of the Soviet Occupation Zone*, London, 1997.

V. Nový, *Zeiten and Zeugen: Erinnerungen eines tschechischen Kommunisten*, (East) Berlin, 1979.

N. Nyaradi, *My Ringside Seat in Moscow*, New York, 1952.

K. Olmsted, *Red Spy Queen: A Biography of Elizabeth Bentley*, Chapel Hill, (NC), 2002.

M. Padev, *Dimitrov Wastes no Bullets. Nikola Petkov: The Test Case*, London, 1948

BIBLIOGRAPHY

————, 'Deviationism in Bulgaria: The Indictment of Kostov', *The World Today* 1950, Vol. 6, pp. 157–64.

G. Paizs, *Rajk Per*, Nyíregyháza, 1989.

J. Palmier, *Weimar in Exile: The Antifascist Emigration in Europe and America*, London, 2006.

G. Paloczi-Horvath, *The Undefeated*, London, 1959.

M. Parrish, *The Lesser Terror: Soviet State Security*, London, 1996.

B. Patenaude, *Stalin's Nemesis: The Exile and Murder of Leon Trotsky*, London, 2010.

S. Pavlowitch, *Hitler's New Disorder: The Second World War in Yugoslavia*, London, 2008.

J. Pelikán, *The Czechoslovak Political Trials, 1950–1954*, London, 1971.

G. Perrett, *Days of Sadness, Years of Triumph: The American People 1939–1945*, New York, 1973.

N. Petersen ed., *From Hitler's Doorstep: The Wartime Intelligence Reports of Allen Dulles, 1942–1945*, University Park (Pa.), 1996.

A. Pető, *Geschlecht, Politik und Stalinismus in Ungarn: eine Biographie von Júlia Rajk*, Herne, 2007.

E. Poretsky, *Our Own People: A Memoir of 'Ignace Reiss' and his Friends*, London, 1969.

A. Potts, *Zilliacus: A Life for Peace and Socialism*, London, 2002.

P. Preston, *The Spanish Holocaust: Inquisition and Extermination in Twentieth-Century Spain*, London, 2012.

H. Priess, *Spaniens Himmel und keine Sterne. Ein deutsches Geschichtsbuch. Erinnerungen an ein Leben und ein Jahrhundert*, Berlin, 1996.

M. Radulovic, *Tito's Republic*, London, 1948.

J. Rainer, *Imre Nagy vom Parteisoldaten zum Märtyrer des ungarischen Volksaufstands: eine politische Biographie 1896–1958*, Paderborn, 2006.

Rajk Trial. *László Rajk and his Accomplices before the People's Court*, Budapest, 1949.

M. Rákosi, *The Imprisonment and Defence of Mátyás Rákosi*, London, 1952.

Y. Rapoport. *The Doctors' Plot: Stalin's Last Crime*, London, 1991.

H. Rappaport, *Conspirator: Lenin in Exile*, London, 2010.

D. Rayfield, *Stalin and his Hangmen*, London, 2005.

A. Read and D. Fisher, *The Deadly Embrace: Hitler, Stalin and the Nazi-Soviet Pact 1939–1941*, London, 1988.

G. Regler, *The Owl of Minerva*, London, 1959.

V. Rogovin, *1937: Stalin's Year of Terror*, Oak Park (MI), 1998.

————, *Stalin's Terror of 1937–1938: Political Genocide in the USSR*, Oak Park (MI), 2007.

E. Roman, *Hungary and the Victor Powers 1945–50*, New York, 1996.

H. Romerstein, *The Venona Secrets: Exposing Soviet Espionage and America's Traitors*, Washington, 2001.

A. Rossino, *Hitler strikes Poland: Blitzkrieg, Ideology and Atrocity*, Lawrence (Kansas), 2003.

Royal Institute of International Affairs, 'The Soviet-Yugoslav Dispute: Text of the Published Correspondence', London, 1948.

J. Rubenstein and V. Naumov, *Stalin's Secret Pogrom: The Post-War Inquisition of the Jewish Anti-Fascist Committee*, London, 2005.

J. Ryan, *Earl Browder: The Failure of American Communism*, Tuscaloosa, 1997.

A. Schlesinger, *A Life in the Twentieth Century: Innocent Beginnings, 1917–1950*, Boston/New York, 2000.

D. Schmidt, *Anatomy of a Satellite*, Boston, 1952.

E. Schrecker, *Many are the Crimes: McCarthyism in America*, Princeton/Chichester, 1998.

S. Schwarz, *Sarajevo Rose: A Balkan Jewish Notebook*, London, 2005.

V. Sebestyen, *Twelve Days: Revolution 1956*, London, 2006.

SED Documents. 'Erklärung des Zentralkomitees und der Zentralen Parteikontrollkommission zu den Verbindungen ehemaliger deutscher politischer Emigranten zu dem Leiter des Unitarian

BIBLIOGRAPHY

Service Committee Noel H. Field', Dokumente der Sozialistischen Einheitspartei: Beschlüsse und Erklärungen des Parteivorstandes, des Zentralkomitees, sowie seines Politbüros und seines Sekretariats, Band III, (East) Berlin, 1952, pp. 197–213.

————, 'Lehren aus dem Prozess gegen das Verschwörerzentrum Slansky', Dokumente der Sozialistischen Einheitspartei Deutschlands: Beschlüsse und Erklärungen des Parteivorstandes, des Zentralkomitees, sowie seines Politbüros und seines Sekretariats, Band 1V, (East) Berlin, 1954, pp. 199–219.

R. Service, Comrades. Communism: A World History, London, 2008.

H. Seton-Watson, The East European Revolution, London, 1956.

T. Sharp, The Wartime Alliance and the Zonal Division of Germany, Oxford, 1975.

————, 'The Origins of the "Teheran Formula" on Polish Frontiers', Journal of Contemporary History, Vol. 12 (1977), pp. 381–93.

————, 'The Russian Annexation of the Königsberg Area 1941–45', Survey, Vol. 23, No. 4 (105) (1977–78), pp. 156–62.

G. Shepherd, Russia's Danubian Empire, London, 1954.

D. Shiels, Les Frères Rajk, Paris, 2006.

G. Shuster, In Silence I Speak: The Story of Cardinal Mindszenty, London, 1956.

K. Sibley, Red Spies in America: Stolen Secrets and the Dawn of the Cold War, Lawrence (Kansas), 2004.

J. Slánská, Report on my Husband, London, 1969.

Slánský Trial. Prozess gegen die Leitung des staatsfeindlichen Verschworungszentrums mit Rudolf Slansky an der Spitze, Prague, 1953.

Y. Slezkine, The Jewish Century, Princeton/Oxford, 2004.

M. Šlingová, Truth will prevail, London, 1968.

H. Smith, The State of Europe, London, 1950.

R. Smith, OSS: The Secret History of America's First Central Intelligence Agency, New York, 1973.

T. Snyder, Bloodlands: Europe between Hitler and Stalin, London, 2010.

I. Soltész, Rajk-Dosszié, Budapest, 1989.

R. Sontag and J. Beddie, Nazi-Soviet Relations 1939–1941: Documents from the Archives of the German Foreign Office, Washington, 1948.

S. Steven, Operation Splinter Factor, London, 1974.

J. Stransky, East Wind over Prague, London, 1950.

S. Subak, Rescue and Flight: American Relief Workers who defied the Nazis, London, 2010.

P. Sudoplatov, Special Tasks: The Memoirs of an Unwanted Witness–a Soviet Spymaster, London, 1994.

C. Sulzberger, A Long Row of Candles: Memoirs and Diaries 1934–1954, Toronto, 1969.

R. Sullivan, Villa Air-Bel: The Second World War, Escape and a House in France, London, 2007.

B. Szász, Volunteers for the Gallows, London, 1971.

I. Szent-Miklósy, With the Hungarian Independence Movement: An Eye-witness Account, London, 1988.

S. Tanenhaus, Whittaker Chambers: A Biography, New York, 1997.

M. Tanner, Croatia: A Nation Forged in War, London, 1997.

W. Taubman, Khrushchev: The Man and his Era, London, 2004.

H. Thomas, The Spanish Civil War, London, 1990.

J. Tito, 'Political Report of the Central Committee of the Communist Party of Yugoslavia', Report Delivered at the V Congress of the CPY, Belgrade, 1948.

T. Toranska, 'Them': Stalin's Polish Puppets, London, 1987.

A. Ulam, Titoism and the Cominform, Cambridge (Mass.), 1952.

K. Ungváry, The Siege of Budapest: One Hundred Days in World War II, London, 2005.

A. Vaksberg, Stalin Against the Jews, New York, 1994.

BIBLIOGRAPHY

Ferenc A. Váli, *Rift and Revolt in Hungary: Nationalism versus Communism*, Cambridge, (Mass.), 1961

R. Vogeler, *I was Stalin's Prisoner*, London, 1952.

D. Volkogonov, *Stalin: Triumph and Tragedy*, London, 1995.

E. Wallach, *Light at Midnight*, New York, 1967.

D. Warriner, *Revolution in Eastern Europe*, London, 1950.

M. Weil, *A Pretty Good Club: The Founding Fathers of the U.S. Foreign Service*, New York, 1978.

A. Weinstein, *Perjury: The Hiss-Chambers Case*, New York, 1997.

———and A. Vassiliev, *The Haunted Wood: Soviet Espionage in America–the Stalin Era*, New York, 1999.

E. Weitz, *Creating German Communism, 1890–1990: From Popular Protests to Socialist State*, Princeton/Chichester, 1997.

S. Welles, *Profile of Europe*, New York, 1948.

N. West and O. Tsarev, *The Crown Jewels: The British Secrets Exposed by the KGB Archives*, London, 1998.

R. West, *Tito and the Rise and Fall of Yugoslavia*, London, 1994.

G. White, *Alger Hiss's Looking-Glass Wars: The Covert Life of a Soviet Spy*, New York, 2004.

R. Williams, *Klaus Fuchs: Atom Spy*, London, 1987.

M. Wilmers, *The Eitingons: A Twentieth Century Story*, London, 2009.

Z. Zajdlerowa, *My Name is Million*, London, 1940.

S. Zaloga, *Poland 1939: The Birth of Blitzkrieg*, London, 2004.

K. Zilliacus, *Tito of Yugoslavia*, London, 1952.

———, *A New Birth of Freedom? World Communism since Stalin*, London, 1957.

V. Zubok and C. Pleshakov, *Inside the Kremlin's Cold War: From Stalin to Khrushchev*, London, 1996.

Internet Sources

K. Becker and A. Roser, 'Das Parteiverfahren gegen Lex Ende im Sommer 1945 in Paris: Dokumente aus dem Nachlaß Herbert Müller', http://www.klaus-j-becker.de/docs/veroeffentlichungen/ENDE.pdf, last accessed 26 May 2013, pp. 1–43.

'Endes neuer Anfang: *Friedenspostmeister*', in *Der Spiegel*, 41/49, 6 October 1949, http://www.spiegel.de/spiegel/print/d-44438502.html, last accessed 26 May 2013.

Documentstalk.com. Website of Dr Svetlana Chervonnaya.

L. Gluchowski, 'The Defection of Józef Światło and the Search for Jewish Scapegoats in the Polish United Workers' Party, 1953–1954', http://ece.columbia.edu/files/ece/images/gluchowski-1.pdf, last accessed 26 May 2013.

G. Kaiser, 'Kurzen Prozess machen! Hermann Field in den Fangen der polnischen Geheimpolizei'. UTOPIEkreativ, H.84 (October 1997), http://www.rosalux.de/fileadmin/rls_uploads/pdfs/84_Kaiser.pdf, last accessed 26 May 2013.

L. Kamiński, 'Why did Gomułka not become a Polish Slánský?', http://ece.columbia.edu/files/ece/images/kaminski-1.pdf, paper presented at the international conference 'Political Trials of the 50's and the Slanský case', in Prague, 14–16 IV 2003, last accessed 26 May 2013.

J. Kisseloff, 'Hede Massing's Story', on his website 'The Alger Hiss Story'. https://files.nyu.edu/th15/public/hedemassingstory.html, last accessed 26 May 2013.

Open Society Archives (RFE), 'Croat-Yugo Paper Interview with Mrs Rajk', 6 October 1956, HU OSA 398-0-1, Records of Radio Free Europe/Radio Liberty Research Institute: Publications Department: Background Reports; Open Society Archives at Central European University, Budapest, http://www.osaarchivum.org/greenfield/repository/osa:122663e9-ed30-4e6e-afa5-5c6ba962438f, last accessed 26 May 2013.

W. Otto, 'Das Verschwinden des Willi Kreikemeyers'. UTOPIEkreativ, H. 100 (February) 1999,

BIBLIOGRAPHY

pp. 47–53 http://www.rosalux.de/fileadmin/rls_uploads/pdfs/100_Otto.pdf, last accessed 26 May 2013.

'Speech by Władysław Gomułka', 20 October 1956. HU OSA 300–8–3–4129; Records of Radio Free Europe/Radio Liberty Research Institute: Publications Department: Background Reports; Open Society Archives at Central European University, Budapest, http://www.osaarchivum.org/greenfield/repository/osa:6410fa2c-d85d-4634–9655–220f2d31b46b, last accessed 26 May 2013.

I. Rév, *Indicting Rajk*, pp. 1–31, http://ccat.sas.upenn.edu/slavic/events/slavic_symposium/Comrades_Please_Shoot_Me/Rev_Rajk.pdf, last accessed 26 May 2013.

A. Vassiliev, *Black Notebook*, Wilson Center Cold War International History Project Digital Archive, http://www.wilsoncenter.org/sites/default/files/Black%20Notebook%20Original.pdf, last accessed 26 May 2013.

A. Vassiliev, *White Notebook 3*, Wilson Center Cold War International History Project Digital Archive, http://www.wilsoncenter.org/sites/default/files/White_Notebook_No. 3_Transcribed.pdf, last accessed 26 May 2013.

A. Vassiliev, *Yellow Notebook 2*, Wilson Center Cold War International History Project Digital Archive, http://www.wilsoncenter.org/sites/default/files/Yellow_Notebook_No. 2_Original.pdf, last accessed 26 May 2013.

INDEX

* defendants in September 1949 Rajk trial.
** defendants in November 1952 Slánský trial

*** those imprisoned as Polish 'Fieldists'
**** defendants in May-July 1952 JAC trial

For explanation of acronyms see pp. xi-xii

Abakumov, Viktor 148–9, 155–7, 202, 230, 247, 248, 287–89, 291, 302, 312, 351, 353, 369, 374 382, 384, 386
Abonyi, Anna 187
Ackermann, Anton 94–6
Adamic, Louis, 159
Agricultural Adjustment Administration 46
Akhmerov, Iskhak 40, 43, 47, 48, 58, 60, 140, 327, 329, 332
Alapi, Gyula 230, 231, 240
Allied Control Commission (Hungary) 181
Alliluyeva, Svetlana 151, 156
Alliluyeva, Yevgenia 156, 353 n34
Anderson, Edith 83
anti-Semitism 4–5, 151–8, 177, 179, 247, 248, 251, 257–8, 280–81, chapter 28, 352–53, 373
Arrow Cross Party 112, 179, 193, 221–2, 316
ÁVO/ÁVH 193–5, 201, 203, 206, 207, 209, 211–13, 217–18, 224, 226, 228–30, 236–7, 240, 254, 275–77, 299–306, 309, 310, 313, 315, 322, 347, 359, 360, 361, 362, 363, 364, 365, 367, 368, 369, 370, 380, 387, 390, 392

Bakonyi, Traudy née Vieser (Herta Field's sister) 19, 26, 65, 324

Barcs, Sándor 236, 370
Bauer, Leo 73–5, 94, 97, 110–11, 127, 128, 131, 203, 204, 264–5, 271–3, 294, 332, 337, 344, 361, 379, 386
Bazarov, Boris 47, 58, 66, 329, 332
BCRC 73–4, 78, 82, 89, 281, 336, 338
Beling, Walter 377
Bentley, Elizabeth 138
Bergelson, David**** 384
Beria, Lavrenti 148, 247, 253, 255–6, 289, 296, 302, 312, 349, 351, 352, 386, 388
Berman, Jakub 130, 150, 253–8, 374, 375
Bertz, Paul 93, 94, 96–97, 101, 102, 104, 105, 110, 111, 121, 122, 265, 268, 301, 342, 343, 377, 378
Beschasnov, Alexei 291
Bielkin, Mikhail 202–3, 211, 215, 226, 229–30, 277, 278, 291, 302, 362, 368, 384
Bierut, Bolesław 254–56, 258, 304
Black, Helen 38
Blumkin, Yakov 62–63
Bokor, Lajos 220, 230, 366, 369
Bone, Edith 300, 387
Boris, King 248, 373
Bosques, Gilberto 94, 96
Boyarski, Vladimir 289, 383

Brankov, Lazar* 233–4, 235, 239, 240, 245, 368, 369, 370, 371, 375, 381, 389
Bregman, Solomon**** 384
Browder, Earl 29, 38, 100, 138, 188
Bukharin, Nikolai 64, 286 379
Bulganin, Nikolai 312
Bulgarian Communist Party 166, 248–52, 373
Bystriger, Julia 304

CALPO 111–15, 119, 343, 344
Cárdenas, President 94
Centrale Sanitaire Suisse 99
Chambers, Whittaker 4, 41, 46, 49, 129, 131, 138, 145–6, 150, 328, 335
Chervenkov, Vulko 251, 252
Churchill, Winston 166, 354
CIA 108, 259, 314, 325, 379
Clementis, Vladimír** 279, 290, 292, 381
Cominform 158, 166, 169–71, 186, 224, 225, 234, 245, 251, 255, 380
Comintern 52, 67, 91, 92, 95, 104, 105, 118, 143, 160, 178, 220, 255, 283, 324, 332, 384
Concilium Bibliographicum 12–13, 15
CPGB 72, 336, 374
CPSU 58, 150, 152, 155, 157–60, 166, 170, 247, 288–9, 292, 295, 300–2, 312, 355, 361, 382
CPUSA 2, 29, 38, 40, 46, 56, 67, 101, 126, 138, 140, 144, 309, 317, 324, 339, 359
CPY 158–60, 162–4, 166, 169–71, 185, 234, 245, 246, 251, 312, 353, 354, 355, 370, 380
CRALOG (Council of Relief Agencies Licensed for Operation in Germany) 121–2
CRTF 74–5, 78, 80, 82, 89, 336, 337, 338
Cseresnyés, Sándor 216–17, 227, 365, 368, 388
CzCP 75–9, 131, 166, 198, 226, 246–8, 275–83, 289–90, 292, 293, 336, 337, 338, 365, 367, 380, 385

Dahlem, Franz 93–6, 121, 127–8, 131, 284, 294, 385
Davis, Norman 26, 42, 86
Dékán, István 306, 390
Demeter, György, 188, 189, 191, 213, 239, 359

Democratic Federation of the South Slavs of Hungary 234
Dewar, Hugo, 369, 371
Dexter, Elizabeth and Robert 89, 109–10, 339, 344, 345
Dies Committee 28, 69–70, 86
Dietrich, Marlene 290, 384
Dimitrov, Georgi 156, 160, 167–68, 178, 249–51, 355, 357, 358, 373, 374
Dinnyés, Lajos 184–5, 367
disarmament negotiations 25–7, 54, 109
Djilas, Milovan 163, 166–70, 355, 356
Dobi, István 185
Dobó, János 188, 213, 359
'Doctors' Plot' 5, 248, 286–9, 295–6, 353, 382, 392
Duggan, Laurence 27, 48–50, 65, 69, 137, 326, 330, 332, 349
Dulles, Allen 3, 106–15, 127, 130, 150, 186, 189–90, 192, 197–99, 201, 213–15, 217, 235, 237, 238, 281, 283, 343, 344, 360, 361, 362, 364, 365, 371, 382
Dulles, John Foster 108, 314
Duracz, Anna *** 130, 255–57, 259, 375

ECCI 155, 177
Eden, Anthony 166
Eichmann, Adolf 179
Eisenhower, President 314
Eisler, Elli née Tune, 325, 350
Eisler, Gerhart 33, 35–6, 94–6, 138, 143–5, 205, 256, 325, 350, 377
Eisler, Hanns 350
Eisler, Hilde née Rothstein 143–4, 350
Eisler, Ida and Rudolf 35
Eitingon, Leonid 333
Ende, Lex 94, 95, 96, 98, 264–5, 266–7, 272, 377–78
Epshteyn, Shakhno 155
ERC (Emergency Rescue Committee) 90
Eschwege, Elizabeth and Hermann (Noel Field's maternal grandparents) 11–12, 16, 321, 322
Eschwege, Fritz (Noel Field's uncle) 12, 321
Esmiol, Mme 342
Etinger, Yakov 287–88, 382

Farkas, Mihály 200, 201, 212, 223, 224, 226, 227, 228, 240, 367, 368, 369
FBI 33, 34, 49, 123, 138–9, 143–6, 350

INDEX

Fefer, Itzik**** 155, 291
Feigl, Rudolf 276, 380
Feistmann, Rudolf 265, 267–8, 378
Fejgin, Anatol 258, 375, 376
Felton, Monica 306, 346, 389–390
Ferenczi, Edmond 199–201, 361
Field, Aaron and Lydia (Noel's paternal grandparents) 12
Field, Edward and Henry (Herbert Field's step-brothers) 12, 16, 322, 323
Field, Elsie (Noel's sister) 13, 15, 56, 64–6, 139, 204, 303, 306, 307, 309, 317, 322, 348, 389, 390
Field, Hamilton (Herbert's brother) 12, 322, 323
Field, Herbert (Noel's father) 2, 11–14, 16, 108, 321, 322, 323, 343
Field, Hermann (Noel's brother) 5, 6, 13, 54–6, 71–5, 78–80, 110, 120, 121, 122, 130, 139, 202, 205–7, 246, 253, 259, 277–8, 281–3, 322, 336–39, 346, 362, 376, 381, 382; release 303–7, 309–10, 319, 389, 393
Field, Herta née Vieser (Noel's wife) 14, 15, 19–20, 25–8, 33, 39–42, 54–7, 59, 64–7, 73, 82–5, 90, 102–5, 120, 121, 125, 131–2, 141–2, 149, 203–7, 218, 322, 323, 340, 342, 349, 362, 363, 379, 382, 387, 390, 393; release 303–7, 314–19
Field, Jean née Clark (Hermann Field's first wife, later Jean Liebermann) 6, 54–6, 71, 79, 82–4, 105, 142, 202, 259, 317, 338, 349, 376
Field, Kate née Thornycroft (Hermann Field's second wife) 71–3, 80, 82, 121, 122, 204–5, 207, 282, 303, 304, 306–7, 319, 336, 337, 338, 346, 362, 380, 389, 393
Field, Letitia (Noel's sister), 13–15, 54–55
Field, Nina née Eschwege (Noel's mother) 12–13, 15, 16, 18, 19, 54–6, 64–5, 85, 102, 121, 139, 321, 323, 331, 332, 334
Field, Noel Haviland, *passim*: childhood and education 11–16; Harvard University 15, 16, 17–18, 21; prisons research in US 18–19, 20; marriage 19–20, 83–4; Fellowship of Reconciliation 20; Fellowship of Youth for Peace 20, 24; International Friendship Club 27–8, 69; 'Banishing War Through Arbitration' 20; move towards communism and espionage 27–9, 38–9, 54–60, 64–7, 104, 324, 327, 330, 335, 336, 340, 343; State Department work 20–21, 23, 150, 305, 324, 328; work for League of Nations 42–3, 48, 53–4, 68–70, 82, 85; meeting with Alger Hiss 46–50, 334, 335; work with Soviet agents in Switzerland pre-war 53–60, 64–70; wartime work in France and Switzerland 89–120, 150, 340–42; contact with OSS chapter 12, 150, 186, 190, 237, 343–44; in US and Europe in late 1940s 121–33, 141–4, 188–9, 197–201, 345–48, 376–79; arrest 133, 147, 158, 202–7, 362, 387; involvement in Rajk case 144, 147, 211–18, 235, 237–8, 359, 364, 371; contact with Artur London 132, 198–9, 361, 363, 382; links to Communist regime purges 246, 251, chapter 25, chapter 26, chapter 27, 379, 381; release in Hungary 299–307, 389–93; autobiography 318–19
Fischer, Hans von 99
Fischer, Louis 334
Fischer, Ruth 350
Fischl, Otto** 290, 293, 383
Földi, Ivan 188, 190, 192, 214, 235, 238, 359, 388
Frank, Josef** 290, 292, 384, 385
Frejka, Ludvík** 276, 281–2, 290, 293, 380, 381, 385
Fry, Varian 90, 339, 346
Fryer, Peter 372
Fuchs, Klaus 138, 328
Fuhrman, Bruno 377

Gát, Zoltán 200–1
Gecow, Anna and Leon*** 259–61, 376, 382, 389
Geminder, Bedřich** 131, 281, 283–4, 290, 293, 294
Gerő, Ernő 200, 223, 224, 226, 227, 301, 304, 312, 366, 374, 387, 392
Gheorghiu-Dej, Gheorghe 245
Glaser, Erica, see Wallach, Erica
Glaser, Kurt Joachim 81, 127–8, 339, 347
Glaser, Wilhelm and Therese 81–2, 127, 129, 339, 379
Goldhammer, Bruno 79–80, 83, 84, 264–6, 272, 339, 377, 379
Gomułka, Władysław 246, 248, 253–5, 257, 258, 375, 383, 392

INDEX

Gottwald, Klement 79, 171, 203, 207, 275–80, 289–90, 292, 294, 337, 365, 380, 385, 386
Gouzenko, Igor 138
Granowska, Mela 206
GRU 43, 47, 52, 69, 166, 200, 328, 329
GUGB 43, 148
Gumperz, Julian 36, 326, 327, 349

Hajdů, Vavro** 290, 293, 383, 385
Haus, Elsie 121
Háy, Gyula 175, 356, 367
HCP 120, 176, 177, 179, 181–5, 187–8, 190–95, 217, 220–28, 302–3, 309–15, 356–59
Hiss, Alger 4, 6, 33, 41, 44–50, 65, 69, 85, 129, 131, 132–3, 135, 138, 145–6, 149, 150, 204, 328, 329, 330, 334, 335, 350, 362
Hiss, Priscilla 45–6
Hodos, György 188, 302, 359
Hofshteyn, David**** 384
Hollingworth, Clare 76
Holmes, Oliver Wendell 45
Hoover, Herbert 16, 26
Hoover, J. Edgar 146
Horngacher, Max 197–201, 361, 362
Horthy, Miklós 176–9, 183, 200, 201, 221, 224, 229, 240, 357
Hoxha, Enver 246, 37
Hromadko, Otto 198, 361
HUAC 4, 69, 70, 129, 131, 132, 138, 144, 145, 150, 350, 379
Hullay, Lajos 301, 389
Humbert-Droz, Jules 104
'Hungarian Community' case 183, 224
Hungarian People's Independence Front 225
Hungarian revolution of 1956 314–17

Ignatiev, Semyon 291–2
Ignotus, Pál 388
ILO 85, 132, 199
INO/INU 2–3, 6, 43, 52–3, 62, 64, 140, 142, 149, 328
INS 139, 142–3
International Agrarian Institute 36, 143
International Brigades 3, 68, 82, 93, 97, 120, 122, 217, 220–21, 239, 269
International Friendship Club 27–8, 69
IUEIC 287–8

JAC 5, 151, 154–8, 229, 247–8, 286–9, 384
Jankó, Péter 230, 231, 236, 240
JARC 144, 215, 342
Jews 51–2, 93, 112, 151–8, 176–7, 181, 247, 254, chapter 28, 330, 339, 352–53, 358, 373, 382, 385
Joy, Charles 89, 90, 119, 123, 276, 339, 345
Jurr, Werner 118, 121–2, 345
Justus, Pál* 229, 233, 235–6, 239, 240, 370, 388

Kádár, János 222, 224–5, 227–8, 240, 302, 313, 315–16, 356, 367, 368, 388, 391, 392
Kaganovich, Lazar 155
Kálmán, András 188, 190–92, 235, 237, 238, 360, 388
Kamenev, Lev 152–3, 247
Kardelj, Eduard 163, 165, 168–70
Kaszó, Elek 371
KATPOL 199–200, 233
Katz, Otto** 290, 293, 294, 384, 385
Kennan, George 324
Khrushchev, Nikita 149, 302, 312
Kirov, Sergei 152
Kisch, Egon and Gisela (Gisl) 121, 131, 204, 378
Kleinová, Dora 276
Klinger, Evžen 126, 277
Koestler, Arthur 341, 379
Kohnová, Alice 276, 380
Kojsza, Ilona 120, 214, 302, 345, 388, 391
Kolarov, Vassil 249, 250
Komarov, Vladimir 229, 278, 291, 368–69, 384, 386
Korondy, Béla* 233, 234–5, 239, 240, 241, 369, 370, 391
Kosta, Dr Oskar 126, 276–7, 346
Kostov, Traicho 246, 248–52, 373–74
Kovács, Béla 182, 183
KPD 3, 36–7, 74–5, 83, 85, 91–7, 99–102, 104, 110, 111, 118–21, 127–9, 143, 221, 263, 265–71, 340–42
Kreikemeyer, Marthe née Fels 97–8, 271, 310, 378, 390
Kreikemeyer, Willi 97–8, 101, 102, 103, 109, 111, 113, 121, 122, 264–5, 268–73, 301, 310, 377–79
Kretschmer, Árpád 301, 316, 392
Krivitsky, Walter 52–3, 56–60, 64, 69, 149, 318, 331–33

INDEX

Kruglov, Sergei 148
Kuhári, Erzsébet 301, 310, 390
Kun, Béla 176, 177, 275, 356, 366
Kuti, Gyula 188, 189, 359
Kuznetsov, Alexei 247
Kvitko, Leyb**** 384

Langhoff, Wolfgang 377
Latinović, Lazar 189, 190, 191
League of Nations 2, 24–5, 42, 68, 74, 82
Lechtman, Sioma 122
Lechtman, Tonia*** 122, 129, 202, 259, 262, 376
Lehrman, Hal 179, 182, 354, 357–58
Lendvai, Paul 370
Lenin, Vladimir 152, 209, 296, 352
'Leningrad affair' 229, 247–8, 287
Lewis, Flora 317–18, 393
Liebermann, Jean, see Field, Jean
Liebermann, Sali 70, 83, 84, 104
Likhachev, Mikhail 229, 278, 287, 291, 368, 380, 384, 386
Lis, Jan and Lisa*** 259, 261–2, 374, 376, 389
Loebl, Evžen** 75, 130, 276, 277–8, 281–3, 290, 293, 379–82, 384–85
Lompar, Miša 189–92, 238
London, Artur** 128, 132, 149, 198–9, 202–4, 206, 281, 283, 290, 293, 347–48, 361, 363, 381, 385
Lozovsky, Solomon**** 154–5, 157–8, 291, 294, 353

Maddalena, Hilda and Max 99–100
Malenkov, Georgi 158, 247, 289, 302
Mally, Teodor 37, 40, 43
Margolius, Rudolf** and Heda, 290, 383–84
Markin, Valentin 38, 40, 43, 63
Markish, Peretz**** 384
Markus, Karel 75, 130, 277, 283, 380, 381
Márton, Endre and Ilona 315–16, 392
Massing, Hede and Paul 33–41, 43, 46–50, 53, 55, 63–6, 103, 121, 131, 137–43, 145–46, 149, 318, 325–27, 329, 331–32, 334–35, 348–50
Matern, Hermann 295
Matthews, Joseph B. 69
Matthey, Hélène 125
MBP/UB 206–7, 255, 258, 304, 375, 376
McCarthy, Joseph 138

Meir, Golda 157
Merker, Paul 5, 93, 94–6, 100, 104, 122, 130, 131, 141, 204, 248, 264–5, 267, 272, 283–4, 294–5, 377, 384, 385, 386
Merkulov, Vsevolod 148
Meszler, Tibor 304–5
MfS/Stasi 264, 269–70, 295
MGB 148, 156, 157, 166, 198, 202, 209, 211, 215–17, 229, 248, 258, 264, 273, 278, 287–9, 291–2, 299, 360, 377, 379
Mielke, Erich 269–71, 378
Mikhoels, Solomon 154–6, 353
Mikoyan, Anastas 290, 312
Miller, Persis 121
Minc, Hilary 255
Mindszenty, József 240–41, 367, 369, 371, 372
MNFF 188, 199
Molnár, Captain 305
Molotov, Vyacheslav 152, 155, 158, 166, 168–9, 185, 354, 355, 386
Münzenberg, Willi 37, 118, 267, 384
MVD 148

Nagy, Ferenc 182–3
Nagy, Imre 182, 223, 303, 311, 313, 358, 391
National Committee for Free Germany (NKFD) 111
National Guardian 129, 132
naval conferences 24–5, 26–7, 41–2, 49
Nazi regime 5–6, 37, 55, 72–4, 92
Nazi-Soviet Pact 92, 95–6, 235, 279, 338, 377
Neues Deutschland 267, 272
Neumann, Franz 140–41, 349
New Statesman 126
Niebergall, Otto 113–15
NKGB 148, 166
NKVD 2, 40, 43, 58–60, 63, 64, 66, 69, 92, 105. 137, 140, 148, 149, 155, 198, 202, 254, 269, 299, 352
Nosek, Václav 205, 380
Nový, Vilém 75–6, 78–80, 130, 276–8, 282, 380, 381
Nye Committee 46

Ognjenovic, Milan* 233–4, 235–6, 240, 388
OGPU 62, 202, 352
OSE 189, 190, 216, 238

INDEX

OSS 106, chapter 12, 119, 127, 150, 186, 190, 192, 237, 276

OZNA/UDB 162, 163, 164, 171, 186, 190, 191–2, 194, 217, 234, 235, 354

pacifism 13–14, 20–21, 27, 29
Palestine/Israel 156–7, 287, 385
Palffy, György* 233–4, 239, 240, 241, 313, 369, 371
Pálóczi-Horváth, György 388
Partisans (Yugoslavia) 161–2, 189, 234
Passov, Isaevich 334
Pătrășcanu, Lucrețiu 245, 372
Pavlík, Gejza and Charlotta 214, 275–7, 379–80
PCE 91, 119
PCF 118, 271
PCP 253–62, 304, 375
People's Front (Yugoslavia) 163, 164
Péter, Gábor 193–4, 217, 223, 224, 226, 227–8, 276–7, 302, 312, 360, 363, 364, 365, 368, 370, 371, 388
Pieck, Wilhelm 127, 272, 294, 374, 386
Polish Socialist Party 255
Poretsky, Elsa 332, 333
Pravda 158, 295, 296
Priess, Heinz 345
Profintern 155, 294
Progressive Party 126
purges in Soviet Union in 1930s 53, 58, 64, 66, 92, 152–4, 209, 254, 286, 288, 289

Quakers 2, 11, 20, 54, 82, 98, 339

Radek, Karl 154
Rädel, Siegfried 94–5, 100
Radio Free Europe 259
Radkiewicz, Stanisław 375, 376
Rajk trial 1, 3, 5, 144, 147, 158, 185, 187, 190, 192, 207, chapter 21, chapter 22, chapter 23, 245, 257, 294, 312, 359, 364, 369–72, 385
Rajk, Béla 223
Rajk, Endre 219, 222, 223, 365
Rajk, Gyula 220, 365
Rajk, Júlia née Földi 194, 221–2, 225, 227, 240, 313, 366, 368, 372, 388, 391
Rajk, Lajos 220, 223, 365, 366
Rajk, László* 1, 182, 184, 194, chapter 21, chapter 22, chapter 23, 312–13, 364–70;

execution 240–41, 387; reburial 313, 372, 391
Rajk, László [Jr] 225, 367, 368, 372, 391
Rákosi, Mátyás 1, 3, 172, 175–8, 194–5, 200, 203, 211, 215, 222, 223–7, 230–31, 234, 240, 254, 259, 276–9, 302–4, 311–12, 356–58, 364, 369, 371, 385, 387–89, 391
Ranković, Aleksandar 162, 163, 166, 171, 234, 372
Rau, Heinrich 94–5
Ravndal, Christian 305, 307
refugee relief and rescue 72–80, 82, chapter 10, chapter 11, chapter 12, 188–92, 215
Regler, Gustav 341, 345
Reich, József 219
Reicin, Bedřich** 290, 383
Reiss, Ignace 37, 40, 43, 50, 52–3, 56–60, 62, 64, 67, 149, 318, 331–32
Révai, József 223, 226, 367
Révész, Géza 201
Ricol, Lise 198–99, 361
Romkowski, Roman 218, 258, 375, 376
Roosevelt, President 25, 46, 126
Różański, Józef 258, 261, 376
Rudé Pravo 278, 290
Rykov, Alexei 64, 286
Ryumin, Mikhail 287–9, 382–83, 385

Sacco and Vanzetti case 28, 54, 198
Sayre, Francis B. 50, 85–6
Schillinger, Ilona 220, 223
Schlesinger, Arthur 113, 344, 362
SDP 176, 177, 181–2, 193, 221, 224, 235
SED 195, 263–8, 294–5, 310–11, 377–78
Seghers, Anna 204, 346, 350
Sharp, Waitstill and Martha 89–90, 340
Shcherbakov, A.S. 287–8
Shimeliovich, Boris**** 384
Shpigelglas, Sergei 59, 64, 149, 334
Shtern, Lina**** 291
Siebert, Hans 72, 336
SIM 198, 347, 361
Simon, Jolán 194, 302
SKOJ 162, 163, 353
Slánský, Rudolf**; Slánský trial 79, 126, 131, 151, 248, 258, 275, 277–80, 289–94, 374, 380, 383
Šling, Otto** 279–81, 290, 338 n38, 383 n20

INDEX

Šlingová, Marion née Wibraham, 280
Slutski, Abram 64, 334
Smallholders Party (SHP) (Hungary) 181–4
SMERSH 202, 351
Sokolnikov, Grigori 154
Sokolowski, Janusz*** 259, 261–2, 376
Sorge, Richard 37, 43
Spanish Civil War 3, 67–8, 72, 97, 99, 122, 198, 216–17, 220–21, 235, 259, 269, 280
SPD 73, 91, 263, 269
Stalin, Joseph 1, 3, 5, 6, 29, 53, 58–9, 62, 67–8, 78, 91–3, 133, 147–54, chapter 17, 185–6, 201, 202–3, 209, 211, 230–31, 240, 241, 245, 252, 254, 256–7, 261–2, 263, 273, 276, 284, chapter 28, 300, 351–53, 355–56, 357, 360, 368, 369, 373, 374, 377, 380–83, 385, 386
Stasi/MfS 264, 269–70, 295
StB 130, 132, 150, 198, 199, 201, 202–4, 207, 275–6, 278, 280, 289, 347
Stibi, Henny 101
Suslov, Mikhail 155–6
Šváb, Karel** 276, 277–8, 280, 290, 292, 365, 385
Švermová, Marie 280
SwCP 71, 99, 104, 149, 198
Świ.atło, Józef 206, 218, 258–9, 303, 383, 388
Syrkus, Szymon and Helena 206–7, 363
Szabad Nép 185, 222, 227, 228, 229, 230
Szakasits, Árpád 183, 226
Szalai, András* 240, 213, 233, 239, 313, 364, 369, 372, 387
Szálasi, Ferenc 179, 222, 240, 357
Szász, Béla 212, 220, 227, 230, 313, 363, 368, 369, 388
Szőnyi, Tibor*; Szőnyi Group 3, 112, 119, 150, 158, 186, chapter 19, 240–41, 258, 266, 275–6, 302, 313, 359–62, 364, 369, 371, 377, 385, 387
Szűcs, Ernő 194, 201, 203, 254, 276, 347, 363, 388

Talmy, Leon**** 384
Tempi, Jo 118–19, 128, 132, 191, 199, 345, 377
Teubner, Hans 377
Teumin, Emilia**** 384
Tildy, Zoltán 182, 185
Timashuk, Lidia 286–7, 292

Tito, Josip Broz 4, 151, 157, chapter 17, 185–6, 217, 225, 227, 230, 234, 235–7, 245–7, 251, 255, 293, 311–12, 353–56, 359, 368, 370, 373, 381
Torańska, Teresa 257
torture chapter 21, 227–9, 248, 250–51, 258, 261–2, 273, 276
Trotsky, Leon 62, 152, 169, 352
Truman, President 127
Tsanava, Lavrenti 156
Tune, Rosa and Philip 35, 325

UB/MBP 206–7, 255, 258, 304, 375, 376
UDB/OZNA 162, 163, 164, 186, 190, 191–2, 194, 217, 354
Ulbricht, Walter 127
UNESCO 199
United Nations 156, 317
UNRRA 282
USC 2, 84, 85, 89–90, 101–5, 109–14, chapter 13, 129–30, 132, 149, 191, 197, 199, 237, 246–7, 276, 283, 339
USPD [Independent Social Democratic Party, Germany] 95

Vági, Ferenc 120, 188–9, 192, 194, 213, 239, 359, 363
Vatenberg, Ilya and Khayke**** 384
Veselá, Vlasta 380
Veselý, Jindřich 202
Vieser, Katherina and Karl (Herta Field's parents) 19, 26, 311
Vogeler, Robert 216, 365
Vojvodina 190, 234
Voroshilov, Kliment 152, 181, 182
Voznesensky, Nikolai 160, 247
Vukmanović-Tempo, Svetozar 370–71
Vyshinsky, Andrei 153

Waldman, Seymour 38
Wallace, Henry 126
Wallach, Erica née Glaser 6, 81–2, 84–5, 102–3, 110, 115, 122, 126–8, 132, 203, 272–3, 309–10, 338, 339, 379, 386, 390, 393
Wallach, Robert 128–9, 132, 379
Weill, Joseph 189–90
Weiterer, Maria 99–100, 104, 113, 115, 119, 120, 121, 122, 264, 266, 268, 377, 378

INDEX

Wilson, President 16
Winant, John 85
World Congress of the 'Partisans for Peace'
    203, 376
World War, First 15, 16
World War, Second 76, 92–8, chapter 11,
    chapter 12, 117–20, 152, 156, 161–2,
    169, 178–9, 198–9, 221–2, 260, 267,
    269, 275
World Youth Peace League 16

Xoxe, Koçi 246, 373

Yagoda, Genrikh 64, 152, 154, 352
Yezhov, Nikolai 148, 288, 352
YMCA 86

Young, Marguerite 38, 40, 100, 326
Yuzefovich, Joseph**** 384

Zapotocký, Antonín 380
Zarubin, Vassili 62–3, 67, 333, 348
Zarubina, Elizaveta (Lisa) 61, 62–3, 66, 67,
    333, 349
Zhdanov, Andrei 157, 166, 170, 247, 287,
    292, 355, 382
Zhemchuzhina, Polina 158
Zilliacus, Konni 126, 281, 381
Zinoviev, Grigori 152–3, 247
Zionism 189, 239, 281, 295
ZPKK 264–71, 295, 377
Žujović, Sreten 168
Zuskin, Benjamin**** 384 n33